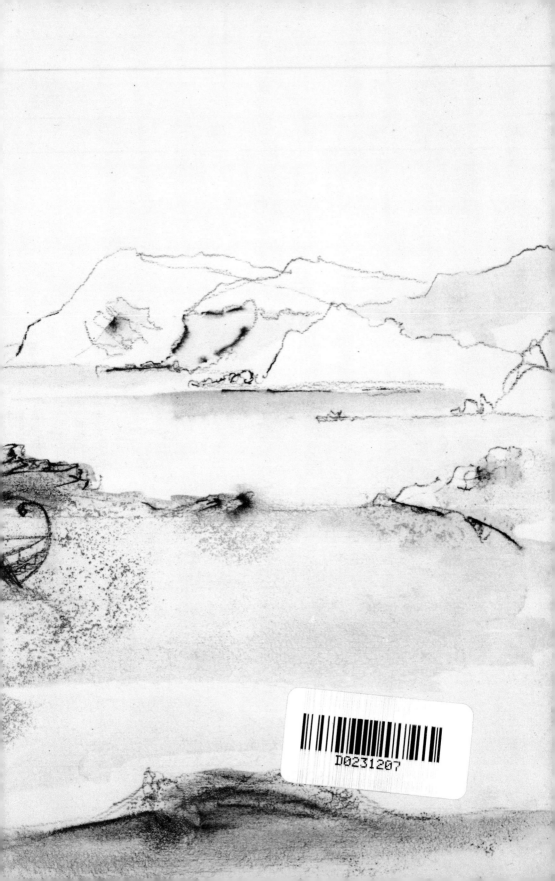

THE JASON VOYAGE

THE JASON VOYAGE

The Quest for the Golden Fleece

Tim Severin

DRAWINGS BY TRONDUR PATURSSON

PHOTOGRAPHS BY JOHN EGAN,
SETH MORTIMER AND TOM SKUDRA

HUTCHINSON

By the same author

Tracking Marco Polo
Explorers of the Mississippi
The Golden Antilles
The African Adventure
Vanishing Primitive Man
The Oriental Adventure
The Brendan Voyage
The Sindbad Voyage

Hutchinson & Co. (Publishers) Ltd
An imprint of Century Hutchinson Ltd
17–21 Conway Street, London W1P 6JD

Hutchinson Publishing Group (Australia) Pty Ltd
16–22 Church Street, Hawthorn, Melbourne, Victoria 3122

Hutchinson Group (NZ) Ltd
32–34 View Road, PO Box 40–086, Glenfield 10, Auckland

Hutchinson Group (SA) Pty Ltd
PO Box 337, Bergvlei, 2012 South Africa

First published 1985

Set in CRTronic Bembo
by The Castlefield Press, Northampton

Printed in Great Britain by
Butler & Tanner Ltd, Frome and London

ISBN 0 09 161880 8

Contents

Illustrations

Commemorating *Argo*'s arrival at Colchis*
'Princess Medea'*
Solid gold bangles of the 4th century BC†
A Svan gold-gatherer of the Caucasus Mountains†
Sheepskins trap the gold of the mountain streams†

*Photographs by John Egan
†Photographs by Seth Mortimer
‡Photographs by Tom Skudra

Introduction

To row and sail a twenty-oared galley from Greece to Soviet Georgia, a distance of some 1500 sea miles, was a team achievement *par excellence.* As skipper of *Argo* I feel that there is no more appropriate way to introduce my account of the Jason Voyage than to list the men and women who made up the twentieth-century crew – whether for all 1500 miles plus trials and delivery, or just a single day's rowing. They were the New Argonauts:

Main Voyage

Dave Brinicombe: Volos to Georgia – *sound recordist*
Miles Clark: Volos to Istanbul
Jonathan Cloke: Armutlu to Georgia
Peter Dobbs: Volos to Canakkale
John Egan: Volos to Georgia (also trials and delivery) – *photographer*
Richard Hill: Volos to Georgia – *film cameraman*
Nick Hollis: Volos to Georgia – *doctor*
Adam Mackie: Zonguldak to Georgia – *doctor*
Peter Moran: Volos to Georgia (also delivery) – *cook*
Seth Mortimer: Paleo Trikeri to Georgia – *photographer*
Cormac O'Connor: Istanbul to Georgia
Trondur Patursson: Volos to Abana (also delivery) – *artist*
Tim Readman: Volos to Georgia (also delivery) – *purser*
Mark Richards: Volos to Georgia (also trials and delivery) – *rowing master*
Tim Severin: Volos to Georgia (also trials and delivery) – *skipper/helmsman*

Peter Warren: Canakkale to Georgia (also trials and delivery)
Peter Wheeler: Volos to Georgia (also trials and delivery) – *ship's carpenter*

Greek Volunteers

Costas Ficardos (also delivery)
Elias Psareas
Theodore
Antonis Karagiannis

Turkish Volunteers

Ali Uygun
Deniz Demirel
Umur Erozlu
Erzin Yirmibesoglu
Kaan Akca
Mustafa Pikdoken
Husnu Konuk
Ziya Derlen
Yigit Koseoglu
Bulent Doveci
Nurettin Kumru
Ertunc Goksen
Cevdat Tosyali
Mehmet
Yuksel

Bosphorus Volunteers

Ferruh Manau
Taner Tokay
Emir Turgan
Mehmet Yavas
Elfi Cetinkaya
Nejat Akdogan
Yunus Yilmaz
Berattin Kokcay
Mehmet Burckin
Ozgen Korkmazlar
Bulent Tanagan
Engin Cezzar

Georgian Volunteers

Vladimir Beraija
Jumber Tsomaya
George Topagze
Anatoly Akaev
Leonti Negeftidi
Paata Natsvlishvili
Vladimir Petruk
Givi Tskhomarya
Aivar Strengis
Zurab Tsitskishvili

Trials Crew

James Neeves
Jason Hicks
Chris Murphy
Chris Bedford
Andy Stirrup
Paul Owers
Chris Burton
Robin Gwynn
Mac Mackenzie
John Woffinden
Robert Hamlin
Jane Townson
Jannet Tjook

Delivery Crew

Martin Anketill (also trials)
Stematis Chrisphatis
David Gilmour (also trials)
Mike Kerr (also trials)
Mike Kostopoulos
Clive Raymond (also trials)
Tom Skudra (also trials)
Philip Varveris
Tom Vosmer (also trials)
Ian Whitehead

also:

Lou Lyddon
Doreen
Ron

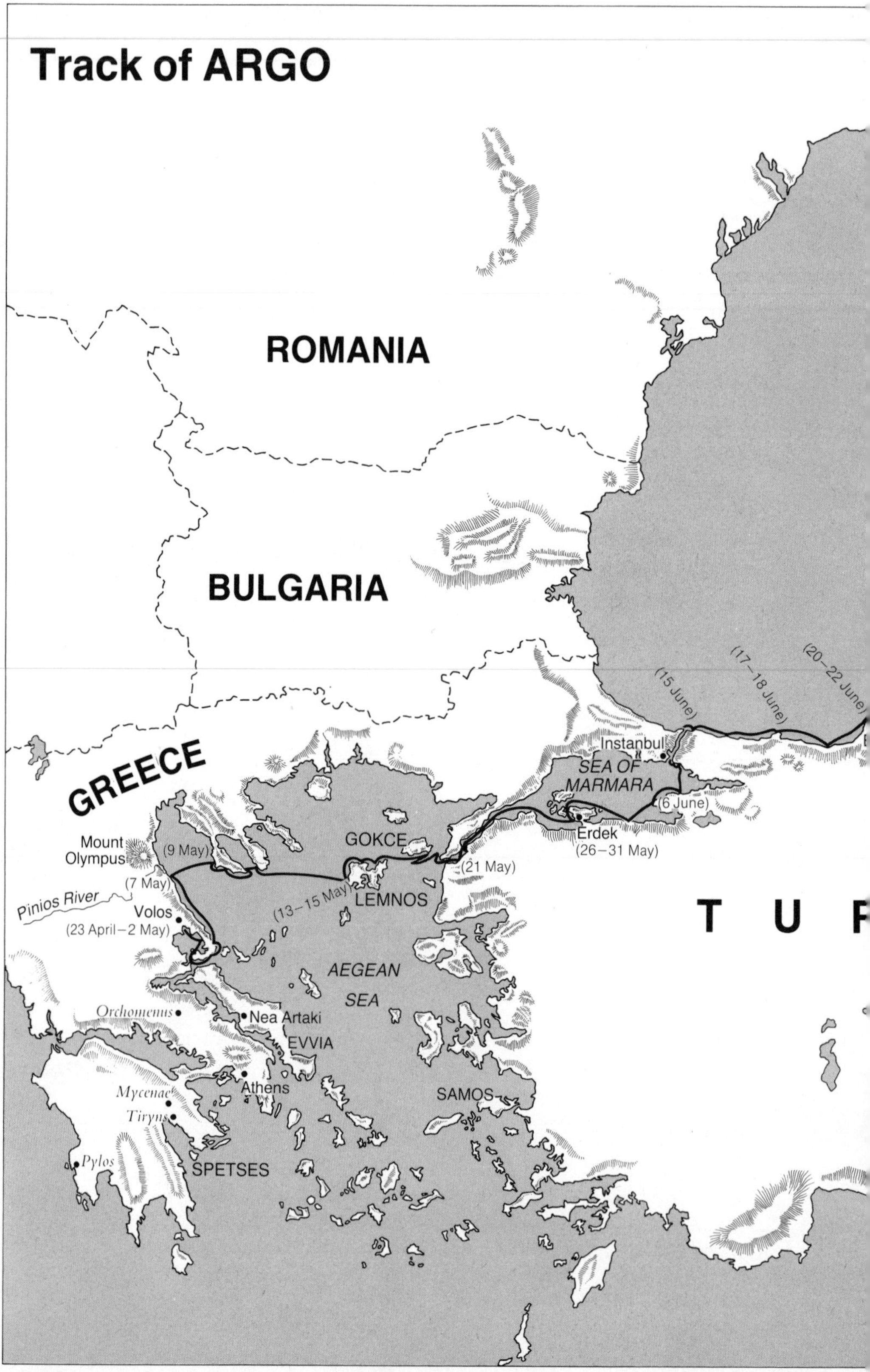
Track of ARGO
ROMANIA
BULGARIA
GREECE
T U R
Instanbul
SEA OF MARMARA
(6 June)
Erdek
(26–31 May)
(15 June)
(17–18 June)
(20–22 June)
GOKCE
(21 May)
LEMNOS
(13–15 May)
Mount Olympus
(9 May)
(7 May)
Pinios River
Volos
(23 April–2 May)
AEGEAN SEA
Orchomenus
Nea Artaki
EVVIA
Athens
Mycenae
Tiryns
Pylos
SPETSES
SAMOS

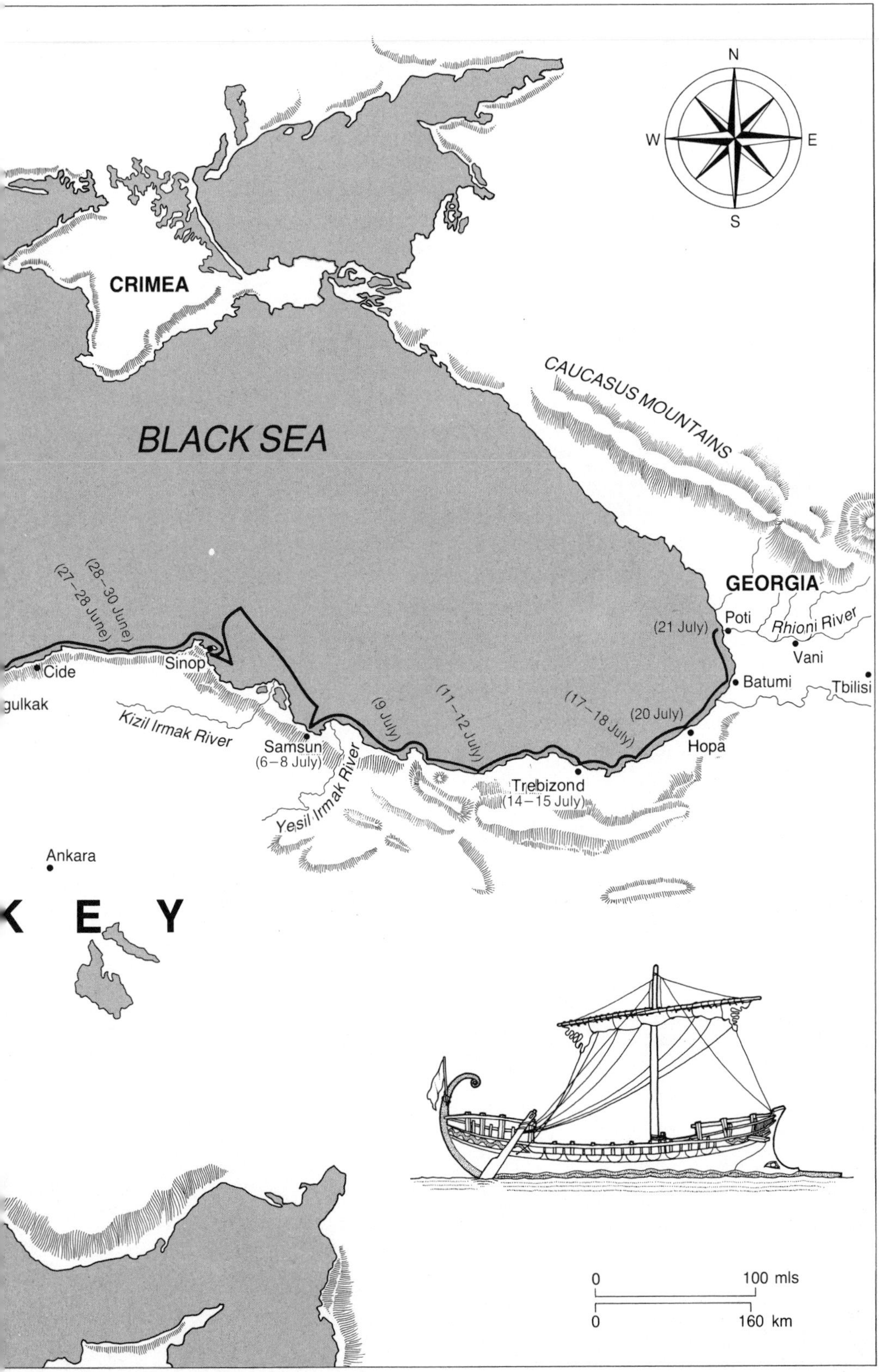

N
W
E
S
CRIMEA
BLACK SEA
CAUCASUS MOUNTAINS
GEORGIA
(21 July)
Poti
Rhioni River
Vani
Batumi
Tbilisi
(28–30 June)
(27–28 June)
Cide
Sinop
gulkak
Kizil Irmak River
Samsun
(6–8 July)
(9 July)
(11–12 July)
(17–18 July)
(20 July)
Hopa
Trebizond
(14–15 July)
Yesil Irmak River
Ankara
K E Y
0
100 mls
0
160 km

1
The Quest

> It was King Pelias who sent them out. He had heard an oracle which warned him of a dreadful tale – death through the machinations of the man whom he should see coming from the town with one foot bare. . . . The prophecy was soon confirmed. Jason, fording the Anaurus in a winter spate, lost one of his sandals, which stuck in the bed of the flooding river, but saved the other from the mud and shortly appeared before the king. And no sooner did the king see him than he thought of the oracle and decided to send him on a perilous adventure overseas. He hoped that things might so fall out, either at sea or in outlandish parts, that Jason would never see his home again.

So begins the first voyage saga in western literature: the tale of Jason and the Argonauts in search of the Golden Fleece. It tells of a great galley manned by heroes from ancient Greece which sets out to reach a land far in the east. There, in the branches of an oak tree on the banks of a great river, hangs a sacred fleece of gold, guarded by an immense serpent. If the heroes can bring home the fleece, Prince Jason, the one-sandalled man, will win back his rightful throne from his half-uncle, the usurper King Pelias. On their voyage, so the story recounts, the heroes meet all manner of adventures: they land on an island populated only by women who are eager to make husbands of the Argonauts; a barbaric tribal chieftain challenges them to a boxing match, the loser of which will be battered to death; the dreadful Clashing Rocks bar their path and only by a whisker do they save their vessel from being smashed to shards. A blind prophet, who is being tormented by winged female demons, gives them guidance; and when the heroes finally reach the far land, the king's daughter, Princess Medea, falls so madly in love with Jason that she betrays her family, helps Jason steal the fleece, and flees back with him to Greece.

Small wonder that such a romantic tale has echoed down through the centuries. Homer said it was already a 'tale on all men's lips' when he came to write the *Odyssey*. Greek poets of the stature of Euripides, Aeschylus and Sophocles based plays upon it. In the third century BC Apollonius Rhodius, head of the great library at Alexandria, wrote the most complete surviving version of the tale in the Greek classical style. 'Moved by the god of song,' he wrote, 'I set out to commemorate the heroes of old who sailed the good ship *Argo* up the Straits and into the Black Sea and between the Clashing Rocks in quest of the Golden Fleece.'

Twenty-two centuries later, my companions and I also set out to commemorate those heroes of old, but in a different manner. Whereas Apollonius had accompanied the Argonauts in verse, we hoped to track them in reality. So we rowed out aboard the replica of a galley of Jason's day, a twenty-oared vessel of 3000-year-old design, in order to seek our own Golden Fleece – the facts behind the story of Jason and the Argonauts. Our travel guide was a copy of the *Argonautica*, the book of Apollonius, wrapped in layers of plastic to guard it from the rain and sea spray aboard an open boat. Pessimists calculated that unless favourable winds helped us on our way, we would have to row more than a million oar strokes per man to reach our goal.

Our galley, the new *Argo*, was a delight to the eye. Three years of effort had been devoted to her research, design and construction, and now her elegant lines repaid every minute of that care. Fifty-four feet long, from the tip of her curious snout-like ram to the graceful sweep of her tail, she looked more like a sea animal than a ship. On each side the oars rose and fell like the legs of some great beast creeping forward across the quiet surface of the dark blue Grecian sea. Two painted eyes stared malevolently forward over the distinctive nose of her ram, and at the very tip of that ram a hollow handhold breathed like a nostril, as it burbled and snorted with the water washing through the cavity.

'What's that over there?' someone shouted suddenly, pointing slightly to one side of the boat's path. 'Look's like the fin of something big, maybe a basking shark.'

'I didn't know there were any sharks in the Mediterranean,' a voice replied.

'What about it, Trondur?' I called forward, from where I stood at the helm. 'Is it worth a try?'

A muscular, bushy-bearded figure seated among the rowers on the oar benches gave a slight nod. Trondur Patursson, seaman and artist-extraordinary, and I had sailed together on two previous expeditions and knew one another so well that it wasn't necessary to waste words. '*Ja!*' he grunted, and leaned down to dig a harpoon head out of the kitbag beneath his oar bench. Then he scrambled forward to the bow of the ship, and a minute later the harpoon head was firmly lashed to its wooden shaft. Trondur took up position, poised on the prow, weapon in hand. He looked like Poseidon himself.

'Everyone pay attention,' I said softly. 'We'll see if we can get that shark for the pot.' The crew began a steady, slow stroke, dipping their oar blades into the water as quietly as possible to avoid alerting the quarry. Now more than ever, the galley was like a sea beast as it manoeuvred into position. It was a predatory animal stalking its prey.

Gently I pushed across the tiller bar so that the nose of the galley swung round and pointed at the black triangle of the great fin dipping slowly up and down in the sea. The shark did not seem to have sensed our presence. Anxiously, I tried to remember the old whaling techniques that I had read about. Was it better to get the crew to take a few hard pulls on the oars and then drift up to the shark with the impetus? Or should we row down on it all the way, pulling stealthily like footpads approaching their victim? The former course seemed more logical.

'Easy, port side oars . . . carry on rowing, starboard side.'

The port side rowers stopped, and held their oars clear, the water dripping from the tips of the blades on to the oily, calm surface of the sea. The starboard rowers took five firm strokes, and then rested their oars as well. The galley slid forward, silently curving towards its mark. We were almost on top of the shark now. I could see its underwater shape, a large blotchy mass, maybe 3 metres long, flickering in the half-light. The shark was becoming vaguely suspicious of the boat's presence, and began to turn away. As the shadow of the galley passed over it the shark began to dive for safety, and at that moment Trondur threw, tossing the harpoon in a short curve.

A hit! The harpoon struck the water with a splash, and stopped abruptly, two-thirds of its shaft sticking out of the water straight up, the harpoon head embedded in the shark's hide. It was as if the harpoon had hit a solid lump of driftwood. Then there was a flurry of spray as the shark twisted, trying to escape. Trondur seized the harpoon line to stop it running out, and there was a moment's pressure. Then the harpoon, which had sunk out of view, bobbed back to the surface and lay flat on the water. The barb had not held firm. Phlegmatically Trondur pulled in the line, and held up the harpoon to show us. The impact had bent the sharp point of the harpoon at right-angles to the steel shank, so that it looked like a gaff hook.

'No good,' said Trondur, shaking his shaggy head in self-reproach. 'Harpoon must be more down,' gesturing that his throw had been too flat. To pierce sufficiently deeply through the shark's tough skin the harpoon should have struck more squarely to its target.

'For anyone a bit wet behind the ears,' announced Peter Dobbs 'there went our breakfast. Shark meat tastes very good, if you cook it right, with fried onions.'

Peter, Trondur and two other men in the galley crew – our doctor Nick Hollis and ship's purser Tim Readman – were old hands at this sort of voyage. They had all sailed with me when we had taken the replica of an eighth-century Arab trading ship 8000 miles under sail from Muscat in the Arabian Sea to Canton in China. On that seven-month trip, investigating the background to the stories of Sindbad the Sailor, our Omani Arab shipmates had shown us the best recipes for cooking shark flesh to supplement and vary our shipboard diet. Naturally, when it came to selecting a crew for an ancient galley to track Jason and the Argonauts, I had first contacted my former shipmates. The response was immediate. Tim and Peter had taken leave of absence from their jobs; Nick had arranged to be between hospital appointments so he could have the summer free; and Trondur, who lived in the Faeroe Islands where he made his living as an artist and a sculptor, only had to pack his rucksack full of artist's materials – as well as fishing hooks and harpoon heads – and make his way to Greece.

There they joined two men who had helped to build the galley: Peter Wheeler, a twenty-six-year-old English engineer, now serving as ship's carpenter, and John Egan, from County Mayo in Ireland, who had been a general handyman at the boatyard and was acting as one of the two expedition photographers. The other photographer, Seth Mortimer, joined at the last minute, and had looked distinctly startled when he first set eyes on the ship's rowing master, who had the job of teaching the newcomers how to handle an oar. Rowing master Mark Richards had shaved his head completely bare, and years of competition rowing had developed his muscles so that he had the torso of a prizefighter. The combination of his gleaming skull and bulging biceps made him look like the slave master in a Hollywood epic. A stranger would have been surprised to learn that Mark had studied classics at Oxford University and could read Latin and Greek with ease, so making him a most suitable companion to help untangle the Greek text of the *Argonautica*.

Alongside Mark on the same rowing bench was a former rowing rival, Miles Clark, who had competed in the Boat Race for Cambridge University, while up in the bows was the most important man of all, Peter Moran, our cook. Having just completed a five-year training course in hotel management, he had

Miles

decided to take a complete break before donning the dark-suited uniform of his profession. Certainly he had his hands full. Grimy and stripped to the waist, with grease smudges on his cheerful face, he ruled a tiny kitchen a few feet square in the very forepeak of the boat where, on a paraffin stove, he was expected to feed up to twenty ravenously hungry galley slaves. He was utterly unperturbed at the prospect.

'If they help me prepare the vegetables and clean up afterwards, the crew and I will get along just fine,' he told me. 'Mind you, I won't let anyone else near the food stores. Otherwise they'd pinch the lot, and we'd have nothing left.'

As I watched this high-spirited crew, it was tempting to compare them with the men who were supposed to have manned the legendary *Argo* on her voyage in quest of the Golden Fleece. The original crew lists differ from text to text, because nearly every city in classical Greece wanted the honour of claiming to have provided a member of Jason's crew, and so the final roster reads like a roll call of all the great provinces and cities of Greece. But certain figures stand out.

For his helmsman Jason had Tiphys, 'an expert mariner who could sense the coming of a swell across the open sea, and learn from sun and star when storms were brewing or a ship might sail'. The lookout was keen-sighted Lynceus who, it was alleged, could see farther and more clearly than any man alive. The ship's carpenter was Argus, who had also been the master craftsman in charge of building the first *Argo*, 'finest of all ships that braved the sea with oars'. The fastest runner in the world, Euphemus of Taenarum, was also aboard. It was said that he could run across the rolling waters of the grey sea without getting his feet wet. Then there were the twins, Castor and Pollux, the one a genius at horse-racing, and the other the boxing champion of Greece, a useful talent which was to save the crew from death on their travels. Two members of the team, Mopsus and Idmon, were seers. They could read auguries, foretell the future and translate the twitterings of birds. Calais and Zetes were sons of the North Wind, from whom they had inherited the ability to fly through the air. Burly Ancaeus, clad in a bearskin, was such a phenomenally strong oarsman that he could balance the rowing power of the strongest man who ever walked the earth – Hercules himself.

Just when and how Hercules joined the Argonauts depends on

which early author tells the legend; and exactly how long he stayed with the expedition is also not clear, as we shall see. But the ancients considered it inconceivable that the great hero Hercules had not taken some part in the quest for the Golden Fleece, and so they wrote him into the tale. Similarly, in the heyday of his popularity as a cult figure the master musician Orpheus was given a major role in the project. Playing his lyre, Orpheus kept time for the oarsmen. His music calmed the storms and soothed the rowers when they quarrelled among themselves; and the charmed sounds of his singing brought fish to the surface of the sea to gambol in the galley's wake.

To me, the tale of Jason and the quest for the Golden Fleece had long held a special fascination. Like most people I first read about Jason in school, in an anthology of Greek legends, among the stories of Theseus and the Minotaur, the Labours of Hercules, and all the spellbinding narratives of the gods on Olympus and their interventions in the lives of men and women in the ancient Greek world. But as a historian of exploration, studying the great voyage epics of literature, I began to realize just how important the Jason story is. It holds a unique position in western literature as the earliest epic story of a voyage that has survived. It predates even Homer's *Odyssey* and – for reasons which I was to learn later – the Argonaut saga describes events that were supposed to have taken place in the late Bronze Age, in the thirteenth century BC. The actual ship that carried the heroes, the immortal *Argo*, is the first vessel in recorded history to bear a name. To a seaman this has powerful appeal: for the first time a boat is something more than an inanimate floating object, an anonymous vehicle. *Argo* is a named, identifiable boat which has a character of her own. In the ancient telling of the story *Argo* could speak with a human voice, and at crucial moments state her own opinions. Even the description of her crew as the 'Argonauts' or 'sailors of *Argo*', comes from the boat herself. In a modern world accustomed to hearing of astronaut, cosmonauts and even aquanauts, it was worth remembering that the Argonauts were the first distant adventurers of an epic.

Yet the study of ancient Greek history and literature has attracted the finest scholars for generations. Could it be possible, I had to ask myself, that they had left anything to be learned about so important a voyage? I felt it was almost impudent to re-examine texts that so many great scholars had studied with such encyclopedic knowledge for so many years. Then, too, there was the problem of the sheer age of the Argonaut tale. In theory the voyage had taken place so long ago that surely there was not enough surviving evidence to enable anyone to retrace their route. And yet, when I reread the *Argonautica* I was struck by the fact that there was virtually no disagreement about the geography of the legend. All the learned scholars agreed that the alleged voyage started in northern Greece and had gone to the far eastern end of the Black Sea, to what was once called the kingdom of Colchis and is now Soviet Georgia.

At that point scholarly accord ended. Some authorities saw the tale as pure fabrication, an engaging myth invented to amuse its audience. Other scholars preferred the theory that the legend had perhaps a minor tap root in the late Bronze Age, but had been altered beyond recognition in the intervening centuries. Some critics pointed out that, although there are passing references to Jason and his voyage as early as Homer, the first full-length version of the story was not written until the middle of the third century BC, nearly a thousand years after the events it describes.

Another school of thought said that the voyage was physically impossible. These critics considered that a boat of late Bronze Age structure could not have survived the 1500-mile coasting voyage from Greece to Colchis. The primitive vessel would have been wrecked or fallen to pieces. Above all, it was beyond credence that such a boat had succeeded in passing through the Straits of the Bosphorus to enter the Black Sea. According to these objectors, the adverse currents in the Bosphorus are far too strong to have been surmounted by Jason's galley. It would require a vessel of at least fifty oars, stacked in two levels one above the other, to row up against the Bosphorus, and maritime historians have no evidence that a boat of this type and power existed before the end of the eighth century BC. As proof, these critics pointed out that, after these boats were invented, there followed a dramatic expansion of Greek interest in the Black Sea and the foundation of many Greek colonies along its coasts. The Argonaut story, they argued, was premature. Jason and his men never got to Colchis or any farther than the present site of Istanbul on the Bosphorus. Not everyone, however, was totally dismissive of at least a kernel of truth in the legend. 'Argonauts,' pronounced the sober and authoritative *Oxford Classical Dictionary*, 'one of the oldest Greek sagas, based originally on a perhaps real exploit. . . .

But was Jason's voyage a 'real exploit'? The only way to settle the matter, at least for practical doubters, was to build a ship of the time, to try rowing her up the Bosphorus against the current, and then to get to Soviet Georgia in her. But long before even considering such an experiment, I had to check the value of the basic Jason text, Apollonius' *Argonautica*. And here I was immediately reassured. Its author was no lightweight. Rather, Apollonius Rhodius was one of the outstanding scholars of his day. He had studied under the great teacher Callimachus, been selected as royal tutor to the Ptolemies, and appointed to the prestigious post of Head of the Library of Alexandria. There he had access to the greatest single repository of learning in the ancient world, its major collection of scrolls and archives, when he came to compose the *Argonautica*. Equally, we know that his fellow scholars scrutinized the *Argonautica*, and were quick to correct its errors and lapses. Indeed, it is recorded that Apollonius first wrote a much longer version of the *Argonautica* which was so severely mauled by the critics that he withdrew the work, left Alexandria and spent several years recasting and shortening his text. This revised version was accepted by the contemporary scholarly community, and even if its critical values were different from those of the modern age, there was no doubt at all that the surviving *Argonautica* of Apollonius was a text of major scholarship, written by an extremely learned man who set out to tell the tale of Jason and the Argonauts in the form in which he had researched it, using the best resources of his day.

So if the written text provided a sound basis for a new Argonaut expedition, what was known about the ships of the time? More particularly, was it possible to assemble enough data to reconstruct a thirteenth-century BC vessel of the right type? Obviously all manner of different vessels had been in use in the eastern Mediterranean in the late Bronze Age – cargo boats, coasting boats, boats operating out of Cyprus and the Levant as well as out of Crete and mainland Greece, rowing boats, sailing boats, warships. And presumably every type of boat had its regional and local variation, depending upon where it was built and what it was used for. Jason's ship, according to every text, was a galley, and this was surely the logical choice for a ship that was going on an expedition that could well have to fight its way through hostile territory. Only a galley could carry enough warriors to undertake what might prove to be a plundering raid if the guardian of the Golden Fleece, the king of

Colchis, did not wish to hand it over.

Painstaking research by maritime historians over the last twenty years has amassed a vast body of knowledge about the early Greek ships, and all the indications are that the Greek galleys were not abrupt new inventions. Like the longships of the Vikings, the Greek galleys evolved gradually over the centuries. Today we are able to trace the line of descent of Viking ships, which in some ways resemble the Greek galleys, over a period of 1300 years, and the alterations in design and construction were very gradual indeed. There is every reason to suppose that the Greek galleys underwent the same conservative process. By assembling and collating all the evidence, I hoped that it might be possible to arrive at a representative ship of Jason's era, a galley of the late Bronze Age.

According to the *Argonautica*, the galley was specially built on a beach close to the city of Iolcos, now called Volos, which was the capital of Jason's royal family. And here I had an excellent stroke of luck. I found that the earliest surviving picture of a Greek galley, painted on some sherds of early pottery, had been excavated from Volos itself. The sherds were small and badly broken, but the Greek archaeologist who found them had been able to piece them together like a jigsaw puzzle and fill in the gaps to form the picture of a boat. It was a modest little sketch, but it was all important because it revealed that as early as the sixteenth century BC, the date of the sherds and several centuries before Jason's time, Greek boats already bore the characteristic ram beak, the upward sweeping stern,

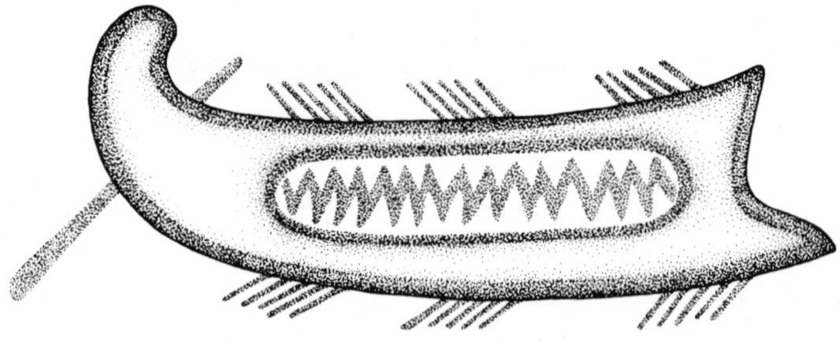

The 'Volos' ship, c. 1600BC

and a side steering oar. Later boat pictures, dating from the seventh to fourth centuries BC, provided a great many more technical details, such as the way the sails were rigged and controlled.

But how big should the galley be? Jason's *Argo* was reputed to be the largest and most splendid ship of its time, her exact size is never stated. On board, according to the different accounts, were anything between thirty and fifty men, or maybe even more, though not necessarily all of them were oarsmen. Early Greek oared ships were not measured by length, but by the number of oars they rowed. In Homer's poems they came in three sizes – the twenty-, thirty- and fifty-oared galleys. I realized at once that building a fifty-oared galley was impossible. I simply could not afford such a large vessel, and where would I find fifty men to row her? On the other hand, if an expedition to the kingdom of the Golden Fleece could succeed in the smallest size of boat – including the task of rowing up the Bosphorus – then my experiment would be all the more convincing. If one could row to Soviet Georgia in a twenty-oared galley, then it would have been even easier for Jason in a bigger ship. So the obvious choice for my vessel was the humble twenty-oared galley. This size of vessel shows up again and again in the early texts; it was the maid-of-all-work of the early Greek fleets, serving as scout, escort and courier ship. It was in a twenty-oared galley, for example, that Telemachus, son of Ulysses, went to seek news of his missing father from the king of Pylos; and this was only a generation after Jason's expedition. If I could build a twenty-oared galley, I would have a representative ship of the age. Aboard her, perhaps, a determined crew of oarsmen could follow in the wake of Jason and his Argonauts.

I knew whom to ask to design the vessel. Colin Mudie, naval architect, had already designed two ancient boats for me. From his drawing board had come the technical specifications for *Sohar*, the eighth-century Arab merchant ship, her planks sewn together with 400 miles of coconut cord, aboard which we had made the Sindbad Voyage. Before that, in 1976–77, Colin's skills had produced the specifications for the skinboat *Brendan*, covered with oxhides, in which three companions and I had made the hazardous crossing of the North Atlantic by way of Iceland, to investigate whether Irish monks could have reached the New World nearly a thousand years before Columbus.

When I telephoned Colin and told him that I was thinking of reconstructing an ancient Greek galley, he seemed not the least surprised. 'Come down and see me,' he said, 'and we'll discuss what can be done.' A week later I was sitting in his office, outlining my idea for an Argonaut expedition, and beginning to realize that once again I was setting him a fiendishly complicated task. To turn my jumble of data into a practical boat shape, Colin cross-examined me about how many men would be aboard, and for how long at a time. Would they spend their nights at sea, or would we always come ashore at dusk? If so, what were the beaches like where we would be landing? What was their angle of slope? In what season of the year would we travel? What was the timber the ancients used for their own boatbuilding, and was it still available? If so, in what lengths and quality? How much of the voyage did I expect to be spent rowing, and how much under sail?

I answered the barrage of questions as best I could, while Colin's pen skipped across the page making notes. I knew from the rapid fire of his questions that this was just the sort of project which he and his wife Rosemary enjoyed tackling as a break from their more normal design work. Whatever I had overlooked during my research, Colin and Rosemary would dig out of their files, applying that genial mixture of scholarship and tradecraft which is the hallmark of all their work. Colin's pen, which was now jotting notes, would soon be making little design sketches, then preliminary drawings, and finally the technical plans of a twenty-oared galley, closing a gap of three millennia. By the time I left their house, we had already touched on such arcane matters as why the early Greeks divided an Olympic cubit into twenty-four finger widths, how many foot pounds of energy a man could exert while rowing steadily for eight hours at a stretch, and whether perhaps ancient Greek shipwrights preshaped their timber by bending over living trees and tethering them to the ground with ropes, so that they grew into the required curves. Design conferences with Colin and Rosemary were always refreshing occasions, and the speed with which Colin came up with a preliminary design study betrayed just how intrigued he was with the problems.

'It's coming together very nicely indeed,' he told me with his next telephone call. 'Everything seems to fit. One solution leads logically to the next.'

'What about the actual construction?' I asked nervously. 'Will the boat be difficult to build?'

'Ah, that will depend on the shipwright you manage to find. This is going to be the most sophisticated of your three historic boats. But then,' he added with a chuckle, 'the harder a boat is to build, the better she usually goes once she's afloat.'

Two weeks later he sent me a drawing of my new ship. '20 Oar galley for Tim Severin, Esq.,' announced the rubric at the top. 'Preliminary Design Study. Drawing No. 365.1.' Sitting on a gently sloping beach was a 54-foot galley with a 9-foot 4-inch beam, benches for twenty rowers, and a distinctly jaunty expression in the roundel that Colin had drawn above her ram nose.

'Show that drawing to your boatbuilder, and see what he says,' Colin told me when I congratulated him. 'Then we'll consider what alterations he feels should be made.'

The trouble was that I hadn't yet found a suitable boatbuilder, nor did I have the slightest idea of where to look for one. Naturally I wanted to build the boat in Greece. But it's not every day that a shipwright is suddenly asked to build a galley from the late Bronze Age, and I knew that I would have to find a very special man. What I needed urgently, I realized, was someone who could point me in the right direction in Greece, someone who could advise me where to search for a traditional shipwright with the skill and imagination to tackle the job, someone to help me with the negotiations, someone to explain to me the proper system of arranging for a boat to be built; someone who possessed a full nautical vocabulary in both Greek and English.

But where could I find such a paragon? In a burst of optimism I decided that the obvious place to start looking was at the annual London International Boat Show just after Christmas, which always includes stands run by charter firms which rent out yachts to summer visitors to Greek waters. Perhaps by asking around I could pick up the name of someone, a charter boat skipper or perhaps a Greek yachtsman, who knew the Greek boatbuilding scene well enough to advise me.

Certainly I had not expected to find the paragon himself at the Boat Show. But at the first charter firm's stand, when I explained my quest, the girl assistant brightened visibly and said, 'Oh, why don't you talk to John Vas?'

'John who?' I asked.

'I'm afraid I don't know his last name properly. It's rather difficult to pronounce, so everyone just calls him John Vas for short. He lives in Athens, and helps us out with any problems in chartering our boats there. He always comes to England for the Boat Show, and he's here now. I saw him only a few minutes ago near the stand. If you'll wait, I'll try and find him.'

Five minutes later I was being introduced to a large, extremely grave-looking man in his sixties, who spoke impeccable English in a deep, deliberate voice. In fact, with his dark blue blazer, grey flannel trousers, yachting shoes and neck scarf, John Vasmadjides could have been mistaken for an Englishman. For more than thirty-two years he had worked for British Airways and its predecessors at Athens Airport, and finished up as their station manager. Recently he had retired to devote himself to his real passion, which was sailing and having as much as possible to do with boats. I surmised that in his long professional career he must have been faced with every conceivable sort of crisis – irate and upset travellers who had missed their planes, or been separated from their baggage, or lost their tickets, or had their flights diverted. In any such calamity John would have been magnificent. Never had I met anyone who had a more calming influence on the people around him. It was partly his bulk, for John was a big and imposing figure, but it was also his careful, deliberate manner. To John no problem was insoluble, no story too long to listen to, no crisis too awkward to handle. His slow-moving appearance was completely deceptive. He got things done very quickly by calling on the help of a vast circle of friends and a huge fund of experience.

From my very first chat with him, I had the impression that John either knew every traditional shipwright, sailmaker, chandler and harbour master in Greece, or at least knew how to contact them. He offered at once to give me all the help he could. I was to get in touch with him as soon as I came out to Greece to search for boatyards, and he would advise me where to look. During the next year and a half of frenzied activity, building and testing the replica of a 3000-year-old galley in a race against time, John was to prove essential. With his knack of untangling difficulties, his avuncular friendliness and his patience, he earned himself the project nickname of 'Uncle John'. If any member of the team ever had a problem in Greece, or needed advice, the natural reaction was to say, 'Why don't you contact Uncle John and ask whether he can help?'

Later that same month, armed with a road map of Greece and a copy of Colin's drawing of the galley, I set out in a rented car to visit the traditional boatyards of Greece that Uncle John had suggested. It was bitterly cold, with deep snow on the central mountain range, and the search very soon made me despondent. Uncle John's list of possible yards was dismayingly short, and the locations seemed to be scattered as widely as was geographically possible around the Greek peninsula. For hour after hour I drove down small side roads which degenerated into potholed tracks, and then ended up on some chilly foreshore, littered with decaying hulks and boats forlornly drawn up for their winter overhaul. I quickly learned that only the owner of the boatyard was qualified to answer my questions, and the shipwrights themselves would shy away from a stranger. Either the owner was absent, or he was half-buried inside the guts of a boat under repair. In the latter case he certainly did not relish being interrupted by a foreigner, talking absurdly about making a ship of the late Bronze Age. Even if I did entice the owner to crawl out from the bilges and listen to my proposal, the conversation usually seemed to be conducted within 6 feet of a bandsaw, whose scream made any sensible discussion well-nigh impossible, particularly when conducted in a broken jumble of Greek and English with confusing interjections from bystanders.

I must have searched out a dozen such country boatyards, driving from one side of the Greek mainland to the other, travelling to the nearer islands, and constantly being disappointed. Uncle John even took me to the vast shipyards of Piraeus where, improbably, a couple of builders of wooden boats still survived. Their workshops were sandwiched between towering hulks of condemned ships that were being torn apart for scrap in a cacophony of fierce hammering and clanking and the hiss of cutting torches. Everything I saw indicated that traditional boatbuilding in Greece was perilously close to extinction. Small fishing boats were being built, but usually they were the work of individual fishermen or part-time carpenters and enthusiasts. Of full-time, professional shipwrights working in timber there was just a handful. At yard after yard only repairs were being made, no new boats. Always I heard the same reasons – lack of suitable timber, no demand for traditional boats, craftsmen retired or moved to better jobs. Sometimes I unfolded Colin's drawing of the jaunty-looking galley and asked if such a boat could be built. The reaction was astonished disbelief or total bewilderment. Why on earth would I want such an odd-looking vessel? Was it something to do with the tourist trade asked the astute ones. When I mentioned the possibility of taking her to the Black Sea, without an engine, people shook their heads at such a crazy idea. What was the sense of it? What a fortune I would have to pay the rowers!

Only near Volos itself, where Jason's *Argo* had been built with timber from Mount Pelion overlooking the town, was there a flash of understanding. A shipwright there glanced at the drawing and remarked casually, 'Oh! You want to build *Argo*!' just as if I was asking him to build an everyday rowing dinghy. Luckily he spoke some German, and I was able to explain haltingly the details of the galley's construction and size. But when I inquired if he felt that the shipyard could do the job, he explained regretfully that it would be very difficult to obtain the right timber, and that he could not guarantee recruiting enough experienced shipwrights to finish the task on time as it was impossible to calculate the man hours required for such an unusual commission. Like most other traditional Greek shipyards, the bulk of his work consisted of repairing old wooden boats, not building new ones.

Feeling rather downcast, I returned to Athens to see Uncle John. Next day was my last in Greece. I planned to fly to another island where, perhaps, there might be a good shipwright. A gale was blowing next morning, and the flight was cancelled.

'Why don't you try visiting the island of Spetses to see if you can find a suitable man there?' suggested John. 'It's rather a long drive, because all the ferries have been cancelled due to the bad weather. But if you drive to a point on the mainland near Spetses, you should be able to get a water taxi to take you across to the island. It's only a mile offshore. I'll ring up a friend of mine there, and see if he can advise a good man for you to meet.'

Spetses seemed to me the most unlikely spot in all Greece in which to find a traditional boatbuilder. I knew it only by reputation as an island which had been popular since the turn of the century with wealthy Athenians who had built summer homes there. Then came the Greek tourist boom. Spetses had been one of the first islands to receive the deluge of package tours. Judging by other towns I had seen, this could mean an ugly fungus of quick-built concrete hotels and apartment blocks along the beaches, the old harbours pillaged by ferry boats disgorging hordes of trippers, and fishermen who abandoned their nets and made a far more lucrative living by taking tourists for day excursions.

My first impression of Spetses confirmed these fears. As I disembarked from the water taxi onto the jetty of Spetses New Harbour, the ravages of tourism were very evident in bleak late January. The inevitable line of cafés around the harbour was tightly

Watched over by his protective goddess, Athena, Jason reaches up to take the Golden Fleece from the sacred oak, while an Argonaut stands by the stern of *Argo*. Detail from a 5th century BC vase in the Metropolitan Museum of Art in New York

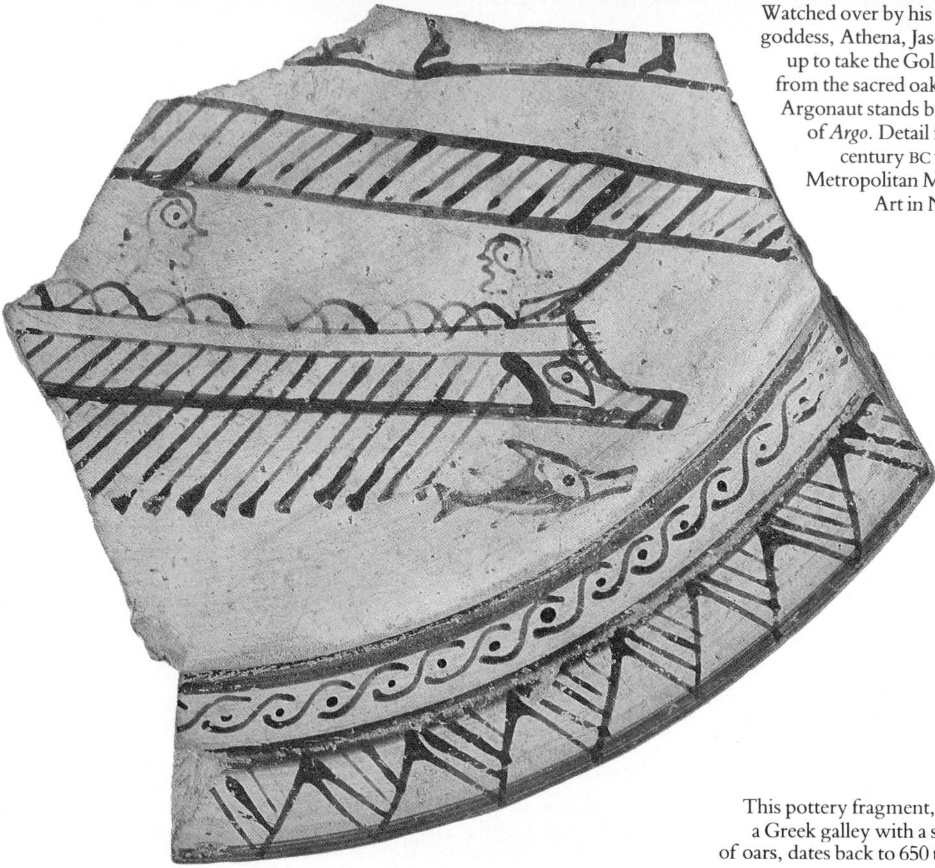

This pottery fragment, showing a Greek galley with a single line of oars, dates back to 650 to 600 BC.

(*Right*) 'Tom Vosper was a genius at making models.' His construction model of *Argo* is held by Tim Severin while Vosper explains the details

(*Top*) 'On his head was stuck a curious hat, a grubby grey cone of felt . . . I was irresistibly reminded of Rumpelstiltskin.' Vasilis Delimitros, the master shipwright of Spetses, who built *Argo*. (*Above*) Vasilis 'turned the roaring tongue of flame on the hull . . . his drastic method of drying out the timber'

(*Left*) 'The launch took place on the first sunny day of spring . . . The Greek Orthodox priest of the village had come to bless her.' (*Top*) The square sail was painted with the expedition symbol – three Mycenaean warriors with twin spears, boars' tusk helmets, and the ram's head device on their shields. (*Above*) 'It is the tool that built the boat, and will bring her good luck.' The *skipani* (adze) nailed by Vasilis to the stern together with a bouquet of flowers on the day *Argo* sailed from Spetses

The newly excavated Mycenaean town of Dimini where Jason may have spent his childhood (*above*). 'You could see where the main street ran, and how the Mycenaean town houses had lined the main thoroughfare . . . Cut into the side of the hill was a passageway (*right*) lined with dressed stone . . . it was the entrance to a Mycenaean burial chamber. Through the arch was the tomb itself (*below*), a beehive-shaped hollow scooped out of the heart of the hill, and lined with beautifully engineered blocks of stone' – possibly the royal tomb of Jason's father

OME MEMBERS
F THE CREW

Top row (left to right): Mark Richards, rowing master; Peter Wheeler, ship's carpenter; Tim Readman, purser

Centre: Dave Brinicombe, sound recordist; Peter Moran, ship's cook. *Foot:* Nick Hollis, ship's doctor; Peter Warren, oarsman

(*Left*) 'It was a good day to start an expedition – no wind and a light veil of high cloud to block the worst of the sun.' The expedition sets out from Volos

(*Below*) Oarsmen at work. In the foreground is Costas Ficardos: 'I wish my company could see me now. Until last year I was Chief Pilot for Olympic Airways, and I had to retire at sixty.' (*Foot*) 'The first blisters appeared within an hour, blisters which were not to heal until the voyage ended'

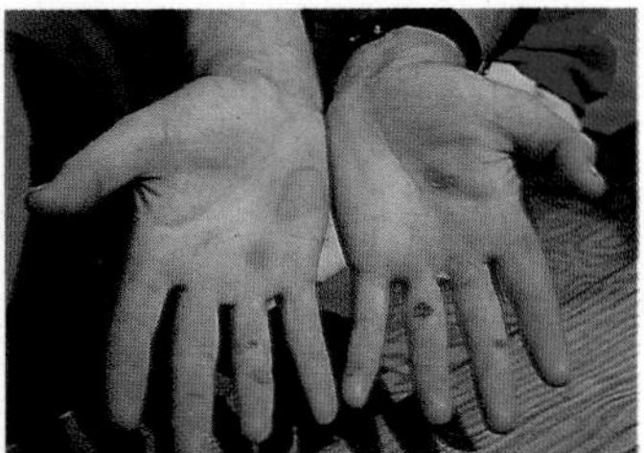

(*Left*) 'It seemed physically impossible for everyone to find enough room to lie down and sleep . . . Yet the new Argonauts somehow managed the impossible' – each man on his own oar bench measuring 8.5 inches by 4 feet

(*Overleaf*) 'We found an idyllic mooring on a small island tucked just inside the mouth of the Bay of Volos.' Trondur Patursson, ship's artist, on his third voyage with the author, sketches the view

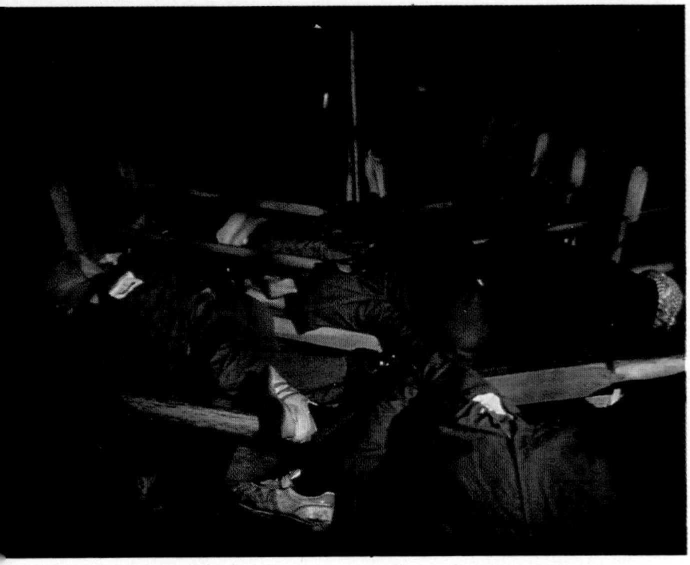

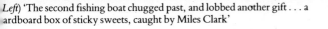

Left) 'The second fishing boat chugged past, and lobbed another gift . . . a ardboard box of sticky sweets, caught by Miles Clark'

shuttered up for the winter. Through the grimy glass hundreds upon hundreds of tatty metal chairs and tables were seen stacked in sad heaps, their legs sticking up like dead insects. Signs advertising the summer's hamburgers, icecreams, rooms to rent, cocktail bars and boat rides were drab and peeling. Ripped awnings flapped wanly in the gale. Spetses had at least been spared the major blight of concrete hotels, and the town's centre was relatively untouched, though that morning its narrow, twisting streets were devoid of life. There was not a living creature to be seen, apart from a couple of half-starved cats crouching under the battered wooden tables in the tiny fish market. Judging by the thin flanks of the cats, there was precious little fish being gutted that winter on Spetses. The driver of the water taxi had tied up his boat and promptly made off, disappearing to his home in the back streets where the population, apparently exhausted from the trauma of dealing with thousands of tourists in a Babel of languages, eighteen hours a day for seven days a week over the entire summer season, had collapsed in their homes to hibernate. The place felt as if it had been evacuated in advance of a tidal wave.

Turning left, I trudged along the coast road which John had told me would bring me to the Old Harbour where the shipwrights still worked. I was to ask for a man called Vasilis Delimitros who, he had been told, was reputed to be the best shipwright on Spetses. Sure enough, as I approached the Old Harbour I began to hear all the usual sounds of boatbuilding – the distinctive whine of electric planers, intermittent hammering, the buzz of drills and the noise of bandsaws. After the complete emptiness and silence of the New Harbour, it was a shock to turn the corner and find the Old Harbour bustling with activity. The place was full of sound and movement. Shipwrights were energetically at work, muffled up against the cold wind, and small motor scooters rattled along the quayside. Electric cables snaked out of the houses across the road to reach at least fifteen boats in various stages of building. These boats were scattered higgledy-piggledy around the harbour, perhaps on a convenient stretch of road as if it were a casually parked car, or in a front garden, or on a gravel path leading to the rocky beach. One boat carcass was even sticking out of a ground-floor garage under someone's house, with the washing on the balcony above and the other half of the garage advertised as a discotheque. This was by far the largest, most active centre of traditional boatbuilding that I had proceeding with extraordinary speed and clearly he was doing his dying elsewhere, continued to flourish in the very shadow of a major tourist centre.

I got curious looks from the shipwrights as I picked my way over the piles of planks and the electric cables, and asked for directions. One advantage about a tourist island was that plenty of people spoke English. Where, please, would I find Vasilis Delimitros? The curious looks became even more pronounced. Keep walking around the harbour, they said. Vasilis has the last boatshed. I couldn't miss it.

Later I was to learn the reason for those odd looks. Vasilis had a ferocious reputation and was generally considered to be a Tartar. Fiercely independent, he worked alone and hated to be disturbed. One story had it that a summer tourist, watching Vasilis at work on a boat, had asked him three times to explain exactly was he was doing. The first two times he got only a grunt for answer; at the third repetition Vasilis whirled on him, scowled menacingly and dumped his tools in the astonished tourist's hands. 'Here! If you're so interested, do the work yourself!' Vasilis is supposed to have growled as he stalked off without a backward glance. The other shipwrights of the Old Harbour must have wondered what sort of reception I would get from Vasilis in the dead of winter, when he could reasonably have expected to be left undisturbed by pestering strangers.

On the far side of the Old Harbour, by a ledge of rocks, I found a lean-to shed attached to the side of yet another discotheque. There were a couple of half-built small fishing boats, a pile of timber and a short, very busy man dressed in working trousers and a heavy jersey. He was scowling, not at me, but at one of the half-built boats. He was attacking it with an adze, a tool like a hammer crossed with a small axe, as though he hated the vessel. Chips of wood were spinning out in all directions as he chopped viciously at his target. Every so often he would stop, take a step back, cock his head on one side and survey his handiwork. Then he would spring back into the attack, grimacing with concentration. On his head was stuck a curious hat, a grubby grey cone of felt with several oil smudges on it, and for a moment I was irresistibly reminded of Rumpelstiltskin in Grimm's fairy tale. He shot one brisk glance in my direction and then ignored me totally. As I stood there watching him, he continued with his work as if I did not exist. He was yet seen in Greece, and it struck me as remarkable that this industry, work entirely by eye. Even as I looked, I could see the curves of several ribs alter into harmony with one another as he chopped pieces away to the precise shape he wanted. He never hesitated, even for a second, but trimmed the excess timber with a staccato series of blows. Then he would abruptly flip the adze onto his shoulder as he stood off to take another look at the lines of the boat.

After watching this virtuoso performance, I went off to find myself an interpreter, for Uncle John had warned me that it was unlikely that Vasilis, as a shipwright building wooden boats almost exclusively for Greek fishermen, would speak any English. Luckily the discotheque owner was inside his building, and he agreed to translate for me. Together we went back to the shipwright.

'Excuse me, *mestri*,' said my interpreter hesitantly. 'This man would like to talk with you for a few minutes about building a boat.'

With an exaggerated air of politeness Vasilis put down his adze and jerked his head to indicate that we should follow him into his workshed. There he fished a cigarette out of the pocket of his jacket, hanging on the back of the door, offered me a smoke, which was declined, and lit up for himself. '*Libon* – well?' he said. It was the first word that he had uttered.

There followed an extremely brief and to-the-point discussion. My interpreter explained that I was looking for someone to construct a wooden boat.

A very special boat, I interrupted, a historic vessel like nothing that had been built for hundreds of years, a copy of an ancient Greek galley.

Vasilis' expression did not change, nor did he utter a syllable.

'Here's a drawing of the boat,' I offered, 'prepared by a naval architect.' I spread out Colin's elegant design study on Vasilis' workbench among the clutter of whetstones, jars of nails and tools. 'Do you think it is possible to build such a boat nowadays?'

With the patient air of someone who would rather be getting on with his job, Vasilis bent over the drawing and studied it. 'How long is it?'

'About 16 metres.'

No reaction.

'The planks,' I added, 'will have to be joined together in the original ancient way, with hundreds of little tongues of wood fitting them together. This is how the old shipwrights did the work. Is that a problem?'

'No.' A single flat statement.

'How long will it take to build?'

'Is there to be a cabin?'

'No, no. It's just an open boat.'

'An engine?'

'No. It will be driven by oars and a sail, just like the original galleys.'

'Four or maybe five months to build,' said Vasilis flatly.

'It won't be just for show,' I cautioned him. 'I want to make a long voyage with this boat, to sail and row her to the Black Sea, to investigate the story of Jason and the Argonauts.'

Vasilis said nothing. The conversation seemed to have no room for hesitation, rather like his work with an adze. So I put the vital question.

'Can you build it for me?'

'Yes.'

'When can you start work? The boat must be ready for a voyage in the early summer of 1984.'

Vasilis considered this for a moment. 'I will start next October.'

He stubbed out his cigarette, strode out of his shed, picked up his adze, and a moment later the chips were flying. The conversation was at an end.

Later, much later, when the completed galley was on the slipway ready to be launched, a newspaper man came down from Athens to interview Vasilis about the building of the boat. Why had he undertaken to build such an unusual and difficult boat, full of unknown problems and not at all the sort of boat that Vasilis normally constructed? Even to agree to undertake the job must have put at risk his reputation as a master craftsman. Why, then, did he do it?

Vasilis looked at the journalist in his usual direct fashion. 'I did it,' he replied, 'for Greece.'

2
Vasilis

Construction drawings arrived at Spetses from Colin. They showed details of how the galley should be made: the width, thickness and length of every plank and beam; the place and shape of those delightfully named items of wooden boatbuilding – stringers, shelves, keelson, knee and futtock. There was a drawing for the precise curve and cross-section of the scorpion-tail keel, and a little sketch showed how the planks might best be joined together with innumerable little tongues of wood. Colin had also worked out how large the sail should be, and what shape. He calculated that a parallelogram of about 300 square feet, a very modest size, should be enough to drive such a slight vessel at a respectable speed. Colin also attached a thought-provoking calculation for my attention – a diagram which warned me, if I pressed the boat too hard, at what angle she would capsize.

Argo's design was made above all to help the oarsmen as they toiled to propel her through the calms. Another of Colin's neat little illustrations depicted three robot-like men, 'standard men', sitting faithfully in their rowing positions to demonstrate how much room they would have to swing their oar handles without knocking one another off the oar bench. But 'standard men', we had agreed, would be hard to come by. Whoever signed up for such a gruelling trip – and I still couldn't guess who would volunteer for hours of sweating at the oar benches – they were not likely to be 'standard men' in any way.

Colin's meticulous attention to detail was vital to the successful building of the galley, but how was I going to coax Vasilis into following such alien ideas? Sheets of paper from a naval architect's office in England meant nothing to him. Vasilis worked from years of experience, from what he had learned as a time-served apprentice, and from turning out so many of his traditional Greek fishing boats that he knew by heart the size and shape of every piece of timber, and just how it should be placed. Vasilis called no man his master, and he certainly did not work from drawings. Clearly I had to find a way of translating Colin's technical drawings into some sort of guidance that Vasilis would accept and follow, but without compromising his fierce pride as a master shipwright. I hoped that I had the answer – I would get a model made of the galley, a superb, millimetre-precise model, so beautifully built that Vasilis would admire it for its craftsmanship, and then use it as his inspiration. I was gambling on the fact that if Vasilis was as good a shipwright as I had been told, he should be able to look at the small model and, by eye, turn it into a full-size ship.

Tom Vosmer, from the Sindbad Voyage, was a genius at making ship models. When I first met Tom he had been working as a professional modeller, restoring damaged antique ship models. Indeed I had never forgotten his wife, Wendy, joking one day that whenever she tried to clean the living room carpet, the vacuum cleaner choked on bits of tiny brass cannon that had fallen into it. At the end of the Sindbad Voyage Tom and Wendy had gone to live in Australia, where he had started a wooden boatbuilding business. Although he was on the other side of the world, I felt that Tom was just the man to take up the challenge of building a Bronze Age ship in miniature.

The result was all that I had hoped for. Three months later a large, drum-like package arrived from Australia at London Airport for me to collect. Opening the package was like solving a Chinese puzzle. After the lid of the drum came off, a series of written instructions told me to unscrew this clamp, twist that latch, remove another layer of wooden baffle, undo this screw, pull on this handle, until finally out of its nest of padding emerged an exquisite model of the galley, perfect in every detail. Even the small tongues of wood which would one day hold the planks of the main ship together were repeated in the model's structure. Each tongue was buried inside the 3mm thickness of the model's planks, and so could not be seen. Yet, with meticulous care, Tom had put them in. All you could detect from the outside were row upon row of neat little dots, each dot no bigger than the tip of a fine needle, yet each was the head of a tiny wooden pin that locked a hidden tongue in place. As always, Tom had been a perfectionist.

I carried the model with me on my next trip to Greece. When I put the model down on his workbench, Vasilis carefully maintained his normal unconcerned expression. 'That's the way the boat should finally look,' I said, also trying to be offhand. For a moment I thought I saw a flicker of approval as Vasilis glanced at the model. 'I've also done some practical experiments since we last met,' I went on. 'I tried bending a large piece of timber to see if I could get the right curve for the keel of the ship, following Colin Mudie's plans.'

Uncle John's nephew, Andy, was acting as my interpreter. Andy was a keen sailor so was able to translate precisely my description of how, back home in Ireland, I had searched the woods for a 16-metre-long tree of the right diameter, felled it, towed it to the village where I lived, cut off the branches with a hand axe, and laboriously trimmed it to the right cross-section. Then I had soaked the timber in seawater to soften it, rigged up a windlass and heaved it up to the correct curve like bending a giant bow. It had all been rather a time-consuming operation, and I hoped that Vasilis would be suitably impressed by the experiment. But at the end of my long dissertation, Vasilis simply replied with one, short phrase.

'What did he say?' I asked.

Andy looked embarrassed.

'Go on, tell me,' I insisted.

'Vasilis just said "So what?"'

Another reason for my trip to Spetses was to learn from Vasilis where he proposed to find the timber for the galley. Broken fragments of early Mediterranean shipwrecks brought up by divers, as well as land excavations by archaeologists, showed that a popular timber for building both boats and houses had been a type of Mediterranean pine, *Pinus brutia*, commonly known as Aleppo pine. I had asked Vasilis to use exactly the same wood in building the galley, and made the happy discovery that Aleppo pine was still the timber that Vasilis and the other Spetses shipwrights preferred for most of their work. This wood came, I was told, from the island of Samos close to the Turkish coast on the far side of the Aegean. So I went to Samos to track down the timber merchant who sent Vasilis his wood. My idea was to ask if he could take special care in selecting the wood for the galley.

High up in the mountains of Samos, in the sort of isolated and unspoilt village beloved of tourist brochures, with a breathtaking view over the Aegean, I found the timber man at his grocery shop in a street so narrow that only mules and pedestrians could pass. Here Vardikos, the timber dealer, explained that the forest had been exploited for hundreds of years, so now the timber cutters were strictly controlled in the amount of timber they could take. Each man had an annual limit. It was fortunate, he said, that I had come to him early enough so that he could set aside Vasilis' special requirements from his quota. He and his son would search the woods, mark the right trees, fell them during the summer months, drag them down to the road with mules, and from there they would be collected by lorries and ferried to mainland Greece.

As I descended the mountain from the village, I left the main road to walk through the straggling forest where Vardikos cut his wood. I could see what he meant by the scarcity of good timber. Most of the pine trees were pitiful specimens, stunted and twisted. Some of the bent trees might suit the curves for the ribs of the boat, but there was scarcely a tree trunk straight enough to provide a decent length of plank. I wondered just how Vasilis could manage with such poor stuff. He was going to have a very difficult task indeed, but there was no choice. I had already seen the bald slopes of Mount Pelion near Volos where Jason's shipwright, Argus, had cut his timber. Now there was not a full-size tree left. The Greek historian Thucydides had complained as early as the fifth century BC that the forests of Greece had been so stripped to build battle fleets that the shipwrights were obliged to travel to Italy and Asia Minor for their timber. A few last stands of Aleppo pine still grew on Samos and the neighbouring island of Mytilene for traditional Greek boat-building. But I was not at all confident that Vardikos would be able to supply Vasilis with what he wanted.

Two months later, Uncle John telephoned me from Athens with shocking news. Even he sounded distressed. 'Tim, I'm afraid we have some trouble. I've just been watching the evening news programme on television, and they report a huge forest fire on Samos. There are pictures of the forest in flames. Fire fighters are being sent there from all over Greece, even special planes are fighting the fire by dropping water and chemicals. It looks very bad. They say that most of the pine forest has been destroyed and I'm afraid that includes the timber for your boat.' Sick at heart, I hung up. There was nowhere else I could obtain the right sort of timber in the time available. It seemed inevitable that the building of the galley would be delayed by at least a year.

A week afterwards Uncle John rang again. He had been trying repeatedly to speak to Vardikos, but without success. The telephone lines on Samos had either been commandeered by the emergency services or had melted. But with characteristic persistence, John had finally managed to get through. 'Tim,' he told me, 'It's almost incredible. Vardikos was not supposed to send your timber to Vasilis until next month. But for some reason he decided to send it early. The wood for Vasilis left Samos by ferry on the day before the fire started. It was the last shipment of timber to get off the island. Everything else, including the cut timber waiting at the roadsides to be picked up and most of the standing trees, is in ashes. But Vasilis will be able to get started on time.'

Samos was not alone in presenting planning worries. I had written a letter to the President of the Turkish Yachting Federation. Could he, I asked, possibly advise me on the correct way to apply for permission to conduct a seaborne expedition around the coast of his country, often coming ashore at night on remote beaches? Would the authorities have any objection? I explained that I was hoping to take a small boat all the distance from the Aegean, through the Dardanelles, the Sea of Marmara and the Bosphorus, and then into the Black Sea as far as the Turkish-Soviet border. Could the Yachting Federation tell me anything about the conditions we could encounter.

Alpay Cin, the Federation President, was courtesy itself. When I arrived in Istanbul to reconnoitre part of the expedition route, he had already been in touch with the Turkish Navy. The commanding officer of the Naval Academy had lent a motor yacht so that I could see for myself the difficulties of rowing up the Bosphorus.

It was a sobering experience. The admiral's motor yacht needed full power to chug up against the swirling water of the Bosphorus, and a pilot of the Bosphorus pilotage service assured me that cargo ships were often the playthings of the currents. Every year at least one luckless vessel was flung ashore, sometimes with its bows crashing through the first-floor windows of houses built on the bank. The broken-backed hulk of a very large tanker lay stranded at the south entrance to the straits; she had come to grief in the currents. Losing control to the eddies, she had collided with another vessel, caught fire, and then blown up in a huge fireball that people living nearby had mistaken for a nuclear explosion.

On the Black Sea coast of Turkey, Alpay's friends in the Yachting Federation had arranged for me to meet the admiral in command of Turkey's Black Sea ships. I was ushered past crisp sentries in white uniforms, white gloves and red-banded helmets to the admiral's office, which was furnished with over-stuffed chairs in almost Ottoman style. He himself was a genial and splendid figure, the very image of the Grand Turk, his ample chest embellished with rows of decorations and ribbons. He offered me tea in fine porcelain cups, and when I explained my schedule for the expedition he gave a throaty chuckle.

'Well, if you manage to get here next summer, at least you'll be visiting us at the right season,' he said. 'The Black Sea has a bad reputation. The locals say that it has only four safe harbours – Samsun, Trebizond, July and August . . . .' And he threw back his head and gave a massive bellowing laugh that made the teacups rattle.

When I got back home, I encountered another of those happy coincidences that seemed to be part of this voyage. I had not intended to start recruiting a crew until the building of the galley was well advanced. But a letter of application from the first, unwitting, crew member was waiting for me. The writer had recently graduated from my old Oxford college, Keble, and was now taking a course in business administration. But he was bored and wanted a change and wondered if, by any chance, I was organizing another expedition. If so, would I consider including him on the team? He apologized that he had virtually no experience of sailing. His main interest was rowing. He had rowed for the Oxford lightweight crew, had been the Captain of Boats at Keble, and was currently coaching the college crew. Then I noticed what he had studied at Oxford: classical languages. My first volunteer was both a classicist and an oarsman. I wondered if Mark Richards, for that was his name, could even guess what he was letting himself in for. He could have had no inkling that I was planning to go in pursuit of Jason and the Argonauts in a twenty-oared galley.

Colin Mudie had by now almost completed his work. Only one element in the galley's design was still undecided – the precise size and shape of the ram. There are no early references to the ram being used as a battle weapon for puncturing the hulls of enemy ships by ramming them at full speed. Colin suspected that it was originally a device to help a galley move better through the water, like the underwater bulge found on the bows of many modern ships. He had arranged for students at the Southampton College of Higher Education to conduct tank tests of a model galley as part of their studies. I was asked to make up a simple tank test model and to provide a selection of three differently shaped noses that could be stuck on the bows and compared during the tests.

One morning I went down to Southampton to see how the students were getting on. I found them hanging upside down from a moving gantry over the testing tank as they took their class notes on the performance of the canary yellow model, which was being towed up and down the tank with much hissing and whirring of the machinery. To my alarm the instructor started up the mechanism that created artificial waves, and on its next run the little boat bounced up and down in demented fashion. Water splashed aboard in such dollops that it was clear that, in real life, it would certainly founder.

'Don't worry,' said the instructor reassuringly. 'The computer that creates the wave mechanism is programmed to make the sort of waves that would be encountered in the North Sea in a gale. I don't suppose your galley will have to face that sort of challenge.'

The tests confirmed what Colin had suspected: the ram made a marked improvement in the galley's behaviour. She slipped through the water more easily, and the ram flattened the bow wave so that the oarsmen would be rowing in smoother water. Obviously the ancient boatbuilders had a very good grasp of boat design, and Colin decided to increase the final length of the ram by 2 feet. The tank tests also underlined a piece of data I thought best not to reveal prematurely to the oarsmen who would eventually have to row the boat from Greece to the Soviet Union: twenty men of average fitness, rowing away at the sort of pace that they could sustain for several hours at a time, would exert, taken all together, only 2 horsepower. Their combined effort, all the muscle-cracking strain, would produce no more power than the size of the tiny outboard motor that propels the very smallest rubber dinghy. How could my crew be expected to move 8 tons of galley, kit and crew up the Bosphorus against the currents that I had recently witnessed? This was a question I preferred not to contemplate.

True to his promise, Vasilis was ready to start work on the galley in early October. He took me to the small sawmill where Vardikos' logs had been delivered from Samos and were to be cut to approximate size. There, for the first time, I saw Vasilis in action with his fellow craftsmen. When we arrived at the sawmill, the place was not ready for us, despite our appointment. There was no one to be seen, and the big bandsaw blade was broken. Vasilis stormed into the mill and let fly: the saw blade must be replaced forthwith and his logs cut immediately. The mill workers took the tirade like lambs. Vasilis stood there muttering under his breath and glaring until the big bandsaw was whirling round and slicing up the wood. Even then he did not relax. From time to time he scowled at the bandsaw operator, picked over the logs, grumbled that Vardikos had not sent precisely what he wanted. But yes, the timber would do. Then the mill owner was bullied into a promise to deliver the cut planks and beams to Spetses in no more than two days' time. Just after dawn on the second day an ancient truck, piled high with our timber, ground its way along the rough track of Spetses Old Harbour. Beside the lorry, bumping along on his scooter and wearing his cone-shaped felt hat, was Vasilis, like a sheepdog snapping at his flock.

Tom and Wendy Vosmer now arrived fromn Australia; they had agreed to spend the winter on Spetses, helping with the boat. Tom's job was to act as technical adviser, maintaining historical authenticity in the boatbuilding and performing whatever work the fiercely independent Vasilis would let him do. It was a mission which Tom had to handle with the greatest diplomacy. Vasilis, I had been warned time and again, never liked any other shipwright to touch a single splinter of wood on any of the boats he built. He worked alone, or with a single hand-picked assistant whose main job was to fetch and carry, hold the other end of the plank, tidy up the workshop and generally serve in support of the maestro. This assistant, a friendly young man named Mimas, skippered a charter yacht in the summer and only helped Vasilis in the quiet winter months. Five months' work at a stretch with Vasilis was enough for Mimas. He told us, incidentally, why Vasilis never spoke directly to Dino, a shipwright working on a boat on the roadway just above Vasilis' workshop. Dino was also an excellent craftsman, and he even shared the same bandsaw as Vasilis. The two men worked within 10 yards of each other for eight hours a day, six days a week, all the year round. Yet they never spoke. According to Mimas, Dino and Vasilis had trained together as apprentices, and when they started work as fully fledged shipwrights it seemed natural that they should form a partnership. But one day, for a reason never explained, there was such a blazing row that one of them finished up in hospital and the other in the police station. From that day they had not spoken a word to one another.

Tom was very understanding. Traditional boatbuilders, he assured me, were notoriously independent. They liked to work on their own and follow their idiosyncrasies. He had no wish to interfere with Vasilis' way of working. That was all very well, I thought, but the entire project depended utterly on one man – Vasilis. If he lost interest, or went off at a tangent, or – heaven forbid – fell sick, there was not the slightest chance that the galley would be built on time. It was an alarming prospect, but if anyone could get on with Vasilis it was Tom. He too was a perfectionist, supremely patient, and now he was conscientiously learning Greek in order to be able to converse with the maestro.

We rented an out-of-season apartment in a house on the hillside overlooking Vasilis' workshop in the Old Harbour. Every morning from the balcony of the apartment we could see the unmistakable figure of Vasilis wheeling down the steep road on the other side of the harbour on his way to the boatyard. Behind his scooter scurried an extremely tatty bundle of grey-brown fur which was his mongrel dog, and which we had nicknamed Rags. The figure would bump along the track around the back of the harbour, disappear from view, and then re-emerge almost underneath our balcony. The putt-putt of the scooter would stop, and Vasilis, followed by Rags, would march down the path to his workshop while from under planks, scraps of cloth, old upturned boats and empty paint tins appeared a band of half-wild cats, all heading for the plastic bag that dangled from Vasilis' fingers. That bag was a tell-tale. Vasilis, the fierce, scowling Tartar, had a soft spot. Every day he brought food to the waifs and strays who clustered round his workplace. Even on Sunday, his rest day, he would come down from his home at the back of the town to feed them.

Vasilis decided to build the galley on a stretch of foreshore just behind his workshed. Mimas was set to cleaning up the site, and blocks of wood were installed on which to elevate the galley's slender keel. Now came the first head-on collision between Vasilis' traditional habits and the requirements of the new boat. I asked Vasilis to build the keel with a slight upward bow in the middle of it. The theory was that, when the galley was afloat, the weight of men and stores loaded in the centre would press down amidships and flatten out the curve so that the keel lay straight in the water.

As I feared, Vasilis was appalled. No one ever put a curve in the middle of a keel of a new ship, he told me. That was the sign of an old, weary, badly built ship that was coming to the end of its days. He was so vehement that he marched me round to the other side of the harbour to show me just such an ageing vessel on the slipway. 'There!' he said, pointing at the offending curve, 'Look! That ship is on its last legs. You can see she has only a few years left. How can you possibly want a new boat to look like that, sagging at the ends? Never in my life have I heard of a ship being built with a curved keel. It's a crazy idea!'

For the fourth or fifth time Tom and I patiently explained the theory behind the bent keel, and fortunately Vasilis was in a sunny mood. After two hours of argument he suddenly threw up his hands. 'All right. I'll do it. But it's your idea. Not mine.' For comic relief, he pantomimed despair. Putting his head in his arms, he pretended to burst into tears.

A couple of weeks later, when the bowed keel of the future galley was in position on its blocks, with its hump glaringly obvious for all to see, two old men were gazing down on the boat from the roadway and remarked on its bizarre, crooked shape. But by now Vasilis had decided to make a virtue out of the unorthodox structure. 'Can't you tell how excellent it is?' he announced to them with a grand sweep of his arm. 'It's just the way it should be.'

Vardikos had failed to find a piece of wood long enough to make the keel in a single piece, so we had to assemble it from several lengths. The massive centre body of the ram was also made up from smaller pieces pegged to a well-curved section of tree root that gave the basic shape. When all was ready, we gathered round to heave the keel and ram beak onto the building blocks. As soon as the long keel was in place, Vasilis scurried up and down each side, hammering in place a phenomenal number of struts and crossbraces, all intended to stop the timber from warping out of true. This precaution was essential, he explained gruffly, because fresh-cut Aleppo pine twists and bends as it seasons. Unless the keel was trussed up immobile, it would lose its shape, and then it would be impossible to build the boat.

Why didn't he use seasoned timber? I asked. Because seasoned timber was not available at short notice, and fresh-cut pine was better for most jobs because it was more supple. There, I realized, was the practical solution to one of the problems that had bothered historians. They had puzzled over how the Greeks in classical times had managed to replace their damaged fleets so quickly after major battle losses. Some authorities supposed that vast stocks of spare timber were kept in the ancient shipyards, ready to build new ships. If so, how had the ancient shipmasters been able to calculate their future needs? The answer to the problem had been provided by our Spetsiot shipwright: the ancient boatbuilders almost certainly did not use seasoned wood. Like Vasilis, they used fresh green timber, cut as needed and preferred because of its suppleness. The shipwright's skill, whether ancient or modern, was in knowing exactly how each piece of wood was likely to behave as it dried out, how much it would shrink and twist and bend; and then to take this into account as he built his vessel.

Our next step departed from the custom of the ancient shipwrights. They built the hulls of their vessels by attaching planks upward from the keel, like an eggshell, and then dropping in the ribs afterwards. Tom, however, now prepared curved pieces of timber to act as guidelines for Vasilis in shaping the hull. Later, when the hull was at a satisfactory stage, some of these moulds would be thrown away, while others would become ribs for the galley. Tom and I had agreed that this method was sensible. Vasilis was having to cope with producing a shape of boat that was entirely new to him. It was too much to expect him also to learn an entirely fresh work sequence, particularly with planks that warped and twisted so erratically. What mattered was to get the finished hull to the shape that Colin had specified.

In the late afternoon of the day on which we finally put the keel and the first few moulds in position, I stayed behind at the boatyard after the others had left. I wanted to get some feel of the character of the new vessel. For the first time there was enough of the structure in position for me to appreciate what a 3000-year-old galley was going to be like. Standing on the foreshore, looking along the bare bones of the skeleton of the boat, I was struck by how fragile she seemed. The pieces of timber had felt solid enough when we were manhandling them into position. But now, seen in proportion, the backbone of the ship seemed so delicate as to be incapable of supporting its length without snapping in half. I was reminded of the skeleton of a crocodile seen in a natural history museum. The head and massive jaw, like the boat's prow and jutting ram, had seemed too heavy to be sustained by the long, slender backbone.

Vasilis did not seem at all worried, at least not to outward appearances. Every morning he would arrive at work, feed the cats, brew up a tiny cup of coffee on woodshavings, and go to work in his inimitable fashion. Neither Mimas nor Tom nor I nor John Egan, who had arrived to take photographs and serve as a general handyman, had the least inkling of what was included in any day's

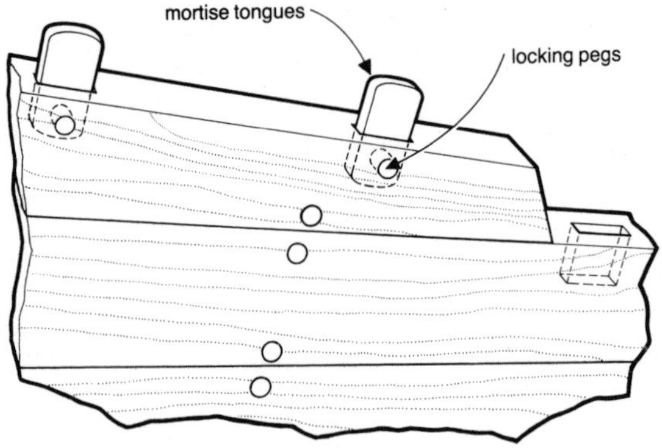

Mortise and tenon joints for hull planks

schedule. There was absolutely no way of knowing what Vasilis would do next; he was totally unpredictable. One moment he would be chopping away with his adze on the shape of the ram; the next moment he would be altering the position or selecting the curve of a plank; or he would suddenly announce that he was going off to the far side of the island to scour the hillside for live oak bushes whose branches he used to make trenails, the wooden pegs for pinning together the structure. Vasilis never gave advance notice of his plans, and he never explained the point of what he was doing. He simply got on with the job to his own rhythm and with his own techniques. Thus Tom and I were utterly baffled when, instead of starting with the first plank near the keel, Vasilis began by putting in what is normally the last plank, right at the top of the hull near the deckline. Then, equally abruptly, he went back down to the keel, and put that plank in place. Tom and I naturally expected that he would next install the matching plank on the opposite side of the boat – not a bit of it. Vasilis put another plank above the first one, on the same side.

'I don't believe it,' Tom said wonderingly. 'I think he's going to plank up one full side of the boat before he even begins the opposite side. He must have terrific confidence that he can get both sides to match. It's the damnedest way I ever saw a boat being made.'

Vasilis promptly turned another theory on its head. Scholars had written at great length about the difficulty of rediscovering the ancient method of joining ships' planks together by the technique known as the mortise-and-tenon method. It was a lost art among boatbuilders, and therefore the experts said it would be exceedingly awkward to recreate. The edge of each plank had to be cut with a series of small pocket-like slots, the mortises. Flat tongues of wood – the tenons – were set in these slots, so that each tongue protruded. When the next plank was put in place, it also had matching slots along its edge, and the projecting tenons fitted into them. Wooden pins then had to be driven at right-angles into the ends of each tongue, locking them in place. It was a very laborious, but extremely strong, way of joining the planks of a ship together to form a single interlocked hull. According to the scholars, hours of experiment would be needed to relearn the technique, calculating the spot where each slot would have to be precut in the edge of each plank, and judging the correct angle and size for the tenon. We were told that it would be such a time-consuming method that it would take two years to build the boat. Vasilis simply scoffed at the idea that it was difficult. Tom made a full-size mock-up of a mortise-and-tenon joint and showed it to him. The shipwright gave his characteristic dismissive shrug. 'That's no problem,' he said. 'I'll prepare the two planks as usual, make the slots and tongues of wood, put the planks together and – tock! tock! tock! –' he gestured like a man swinging a mallet, 'I'll fit them together.'

He was absolutely right. The first plank was joined to the keel with mortises and tenons as quickly and smoothly as if Vasilis had been doing the work all his life. Thereafter each plank was slid into place with equal ease. The only concession was a purely mechanical one. The early shipwrights had worked with large gangs of assistants, often serfs, to cut out the hundreds and hundreds of mortise slots with chisels. But Vasilis was building the hull virtually single-handed, so we found a simple machine to do the same job, and a young English carpentry teacher, Tim Richards, took a break from school to come out to Spetses to help. Tim operated the machine and prepared the tongues of beechwood for Vasilis. Of course the maestro refused to accept any help with the hull. That work, as Vasilis always insisted, was his responsibility alone. He would do it his way and according to his firmly held convictions.

Some of his methods were truly dramatic. He had just finished one side of the hull and it looked splendid – a beautiful, glowing expanse of pale yellow wood dotted with the heads of the wooden pins locking the tenons, a real piece of art. Passers-by would stop to admire the smooth sweep of the timber, the delicate lines of the plank seams, and the sheen of the wood. Then, without warning, Vasilis appeared, dragging behind him a large gas bottle and a blowtorch. With a flourish he lit the torch and turned the roaring tongue of flame on the hull. For a moment it seemed that he had gone mad and was about to burn the boat to cinders. But no – just as the planks began to char and smoulder under the belching flame, Vasilis began waving the blowtorch like a paintbrush. Suddenly it became apparent what he was doing: he was using the flame to dry out a series of holes into which he wanted to drive more wooden pegs. If the wood was dry, the pegs would hold better. This was his drastic method of drying out the timber, and when he was finished the beautiful hull looked as if it had been used for fire-fighting practice.

Then one day Tom and I were in the apartment during our lunch break when we heard shouts and yells from the boatyard. Running to the balcony, we looked down and saw what seemed to have been an accident. The boat was no longer sitting on its keel blocks, but had fallen over on its side and was lying canted on the ground. I imagined all sorts of mishaps – someone crushed beneath the falling hull, the planks cracking on impact. Tom dashed off frantically to the boatyard, then reappeared and ran up the path to the house.

'I've come to collect my camera,' he panted. 'You'd better come and see what Vasilis has done.'

'What's happened?' I asked him. 'Why's the boat lying on its side?'

'That's what I want to take a photo of,' Tom replied. 'Vasilis obviously decided that he's done enough work on the starboard side and it was time to begin planking the port side. Without warning anyone, he removed the props from one side of the boat, called Mimas and Tim, gave a shove and rolled the half-built hull over, leaving them to catch it! He shook his head. 'I just hope nothing's broken!'

I never got used to Vasilis' blithe habit of rolling the galley from side to side like a mahout getting his elephant to turn over while washing it in a river, but this was not my only anxiety. I was very concerned whether the expedition would be given permission to travel all the way to its legendary goal – the ancient land of Colchis where Jason had sought the Golden Fleece, and which is now the Soviet Socialist Republic of Georgia at the far eastern end of the Black Sea. For advice I had gone to Lord Killanin, former President of the International Olympic Committee, in which capacity he had excellent contacts with all manner of world leaders. He immediately put me in touch with the Russian Minister of Sport, who made an intriguing suggestion: the man in the Soviet Union most likely to be interested in my proposed expedition was a well-known medical doctor and television personality, Yuri Senkevich.

The name was familiar to me. Senkevich had sailed as ship's doctor with the Norwegian explorer and anthropologist Thor Heyerdahl aboard his raft replicas *Ra* and *Tigris*. Besides his medical work, Yuri was now the compere of a very popular travel programme on Soviet television. Through the Cultural Department of the Soviet Embassy in London I wrote to him, asking if he could help with my application for the Argonaut expedition to come to Georgia. My letter vanished into the official channels, and for month after month I heard nothing. Time and again I visited the Embassy. The Soviet cultural attaché was charming and polite, but no, he had no reply. I must wait. There was no way in which I could delay the project; I simply had to go ahead, build the boat, select the crew and hope that all would be well. Then I was unexpectedly telephoned by the London correspondent of a leading Soviet newspaper.

'Mr Severin? May I come to interview you?' he asked. 'I want to ask you about your new expedition.' I was puzzled, as I had not yet announced it.

'Yes, of course,' I replied. 'But tell me, how is it that you are interested?'

'My editor in Moscow has been in touch with me to interview you about the voyage in search of the Golden Fleece. Yuri Senkevich spoke about your expedition on his television programme, and said that Soviet TV will be covering your arrival in Georgia.'

Two days later, official confirmation came from the Embassy.

My expedition would be welcome in Soviet Georgia. The Soviet authorities would do all they could to assist, including the provision of extra crew members when we got there. It seemed that the quest for the Golden Fleece had international approval.

By late March Vasilis had almost finished planking up the second, port, side of the galley. Tom was pushing ahead with all the fittings for the boat. He was a first-grade craftsman, and while Vasilis plunged on with the hull – muttering imprecations under his breath which I suspected were directed in equal parts at Colin and at Vardikos – Tom worked on the inside of the boat. He set in thwarts and mast step, shaped the mast and yard from trunks of cypress trees, and carved the blades of the two 12-foot-high steering oars that would guide the boat. He was also an accomplished rigger, and in Athens we had located a supply of hemp rope which Tom spliced, seized and stitched to make the stays, sheets and halyards which now lay ready in tarry-smelling bundles. Whenever fine work was needed, Tom was always on hand to chisel and saw, plane and sand. To top off the sweep of the stern piece he hand-carved a curling tail ornament.

Everything seemed to be perfect. There was only one doubting voice. Up the hill on the roadside, Vasilis' old rival Dino watched the galley take shape and grow. 'That boat's not going to be any good,' he was heard to say. 'It's far too long and too narrow. No wonder the history books are full of stories of the old ships that were wrecked and fell apart. This will be another of them.'

Tim Richards had to return home to take up schoolteaching again, leaving us a legacy of a dozen pulleys for the ship's ropes. He had made them by hand – each pulley a copy of the classical blocks found on Mediterranean shipwrecks, with wooden wheels running on wooden pins. His replacement was a man I had met only once before, and then just for half an hour's conversation. Peter Wheeler had also written to volunteer as a sailor on the expedition, but when he came to see me he was most diffident about his qualifications. Yes, he could sail a bit. What about carpentry or metalwork? His letter had mentioned that he was an engineer. Oh well, he replied cautiously, he could do a few odd jobs around the house – nothing professional, only at handyman's level, mind you. This modesty, I was to learn, was one of Peter's trademarks. He was in fact a very adept carpenter, engineer and designer, the ideal man for looking after the galley's fixtures and fittings while at sea. He could repair a smashed rudder using bits of scrap plank, redesign the tip of the ram, coax any piece of machinery into operating, and always with the minimum of fuss.

Soon after he arrived in Spetses we were all having breakfast in the apartment when someone mentioned that Peter had been out earlier in the morning, at dawn.

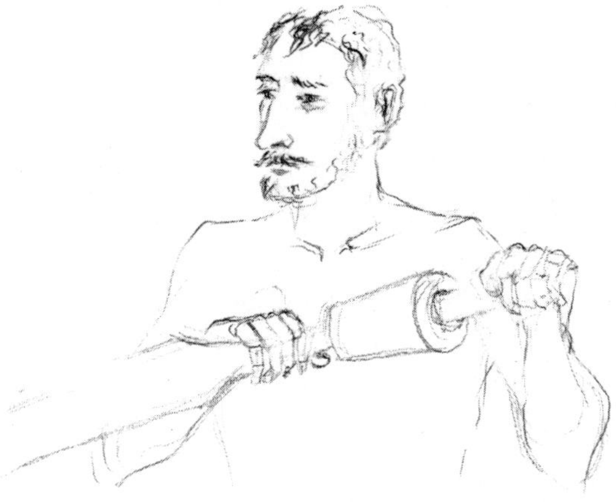

Peter Wheeler

'Do you go jogging?' I asked.

'Er, yes,' answered Peter quietly.

'How far did you go?'

'To the other side of the island, I suppose.'

There was a pause, while the rest of us tried to work out how far it was to the opposite side of Spetses. It was perhaps 10 kilometres.

'Do you ever go in for long-distance running, marathons and that sort of thing?'

'Umm . . . yes.'

'When was the last time you ran a marathon?'

'The day before I came to Spetses.'

Silence around the breakfast table.

With the galley nearly completed, the moment had come to register her official existence with the Greek authorities. There was never any doubt what we should name her. From the very first sketch on the drawing board, we had simply referred to her as *Argo*. It seemed obvious to name her in honour of her predecessor, which Apollonius had said was 'the finest vessel to have braved the sea with oars'. Unfortunately, as I soon discovered, it is easier to name a boat in Greece than actually to get permission to sail her in Greek waters. There were a host of government regulations to observe – official measurements, marine surveys, safety requirements and inspections, documents and so forth. In fact I was soon of the opinion that Greek bureaucracy believed in imposing as many and as tortuous regulations as could be devised, just for the sheer pleasure of then inventing even more ingenious ways of getting round the problems they had created. It was like a very clever man playing chess against himself.

The authorities began by treating *Argo* as if she were a small Greek-built cargo ship being launched. She would not be allowed to sail unless she complied with certain government regulations. For example she had to be surveyed by a marine surveyor and declared to meet established construction standards for vessels of her class. In vain I pointed out that there were no established building standards, as far as I was aware, for late Bronze Age galleys. How many watertight bulkheads were there? None – she was an open boat. Then she could not proceed to sea. Did the vessel have reserves of buoyancy, and were the deck and wheelhouse sufficiently strong to withstand a boarding sea? It made no impression to point out that a deck was not historically authentic, and that the helmsman would stand exposed to the elements. Poor *Argo* failed the test on nearly every count – no buoyancy, no structural survey, no crew accommodation, no radio installation, etc. etc. It was even demanded that *Argo* should have a built-in fire-fighting system for suppressing a fire in the engine room. Unfortunately there was not even an engine.

Clearly this was a case for Uncle John to solve, and he contacted his circle of friends. Advice came in from the Hellenic Registry of Shipping, from naval architects, from senior officers in the Port Police, from lawyers and finally from the office of the Minister of Mercantile Marine itself. To general satisfaction a sharp-eyed advocate spotted a special sub-clause in a minor paragraph in the international treaty drawn up by the International Maritime Convention for the safety of ships at sea. The sub-clause made a special exemption from the jungle of rules and regulations for any boat that was an 'experimental vessel'. Obviously *Argo* had to be classified as an 'experimental vessel'. John arranged a meeting with the Minister himself; the Minister scribbled his signature, the magic wand had been waved. *Argo* was now, with official approval, a special case, and we had a unique embossed and hand-written certificate to prove it. She was, according to the parchment, 'an experimental ship of primitive build'. And instead of fire-fighting apparatus, radios, deck officers with sea-going certificates, union-approved crew berths and kitchen space, I was allowed to proceed to sea provided only that I promised to have on board enough lifejackets and liferafts for all my crew, a bosun, a doctor and a rowing master.

A week before the launch of the new *Argo*, an event so odd happened that I was forcibly reminded of something that Apollonius Rhodius had written about Jason's boat. He had said that the first *Argo* carried a very special piece of timber in her prow – a bough cut from a sacred oak at the holy shrine of Dodona. This timber was some sort of lucky talisman, a charm, and according to Apollonius it gave the boat the power of speech. At special moments, for example on the day she set out from Iolcos on her epic voyage to Colchis, the first *Argo* had cried out in a human voice.

On 21 March the new *Argo* lay slantwise on the slope where she had been built. Apart from a few details, she was ready to be launched. Her underbody had been painted with a coat of black pitch mixed with evil-smelling gobbets of rancid mutton fat to make her slip easily down the skids. Vasilis and Mimas had constructed a stout wooden cradle underneath the boat so that she could be manoeuvred into the correct position for launch down the slipway. They had already turned her from her original position lying parallel to the sea, so that she was poised almost at right-angles to the water. It had been a tricky operation, and halfway through it Vasilis called a halt. The four or five people hauling the various lines that controlled the boat moved back and sat down to rest. *Argo* lay on her cradle on the slipway, quite alone. There was no one within 5 yards of her. All was still. And at that moment *Argo* 'spoke'. Quite clearly and distinctly she gave a deep, slow, human-sounding groan. It was utterly eerie.

For a moment I thought I was imagining it. The sound was a long drawn-out mutter, the sort of noise a man might make sighing in his sleep, but in this case it went on far longer, for maybe as much as fifteen seconds. Then it stopped. There was a brief pause, then the long, slow cry began again. I was so startled that I glanced around to see if someone was playing a joke. But the others apparently had heard nothing. Perhaps the sound could only be heard from where I was, about 10 yards away and to one side of the boat. But someone else had heard *Argo* groan – Vasilis. He stiffened bolt upright and cocked his head on one side to listen. Then he walked over to the hull and stalked along it, like a gundog searching out a hidden woodcock. The noise was softly repeated, as if the boat was grumbling to itself. Vasilis whipped out a carpenter's pencil from his pocket and held the tip of it very lightly against *Argo*'s hull. He stepped swiftly to another position and repeated the touch. Then he located the point. *Argo* was shifting ever so slightly in her cradle, and the greased planks were drawing across the supporting timber to produce the human groan. With the palm of his hand Vasilis gently nudged home a wedge. The groan stopped. *Argo* fell silent, but a shiver had run down my spine.

When the first *Argo* was launched, according to Apollonius the Argonauts dug a trench in the beach wide enough to carry the boat down to the sea. They laid wooden rollers in the trench; the oars were swung inboard and fastened so that their handles projected outwards as grips; and the Argonauts stood on each side ready to heave. Typhis, the helmsman,

> leaped on board to tell the young men when to push. He gave the order with a mighty shout, and they put their backs into it at once. At the first heave they shifted her from where she lay; then strained forward with their feet to keep her on the move. And move she did. Between the two files of hustling, shouting men, Pelion Argo ran swiftly down. The rollers, chafed by the sturdy keel, groaned and reacted to the weight by putting up a pall of smoke Thus she slid into the sea, and would have run still farther, had they not stood by and checked her with hawsers.

The new *Argo*'s launch was scarcely less spectacular. By some special favour the launch took place on the first sunny day of spring. Across on the mainland, just a mile away, lowering thunderclouds were releasing torrential rain, but the Old Harbour of Spetses sparkled in crisp, bright sunshine. Hoists of signal flags fluttered; on *Argo* flew the flags of all the countries she would visit and the nationalities of her crew; a large crowd had gathered, islanders, visitors down for the day from Athens, friends of the project.

Vasilis was in his cleanest, best-pressed jeans, trying to look nonchalant, but he radiated satisfaction. He had said he could build the boat; he had staked his reputation on it. Now *Argo* lay on the slipway, glowing in her new livery – red, blue and white paint copied from the colours found on Mycenaean wall frescoes.

The Greek Orthodox priest of the village had come to bless her. He was a tall, theatrical, handsome figure in his long-skirted black robe, embroidered neckband, luxuriant beard and high black hat. He conducted the blessing with great panache. A table had been erected in front of *Argo*'s ram, for she was being launched stern-first. A cloth was draped over the table to turn it into an altar on which stood a bowl of holy water, an olivewood cross, a censer and a sprig of olive leaves. After the priest had intoned the prayers, he dipped the sprig of olive leaves in the water and advanced majestically on *Argo*. He flicked holy water on the staring 'eyes' above the ram, and then marched firmly up the gangplank to step along the boat from thwart to thwart with his robe hitched up, and spraying holy water over ship and spectators.

When the priest had descended from the boat, Vasilis stepped out from the front rank of the crowd. In his hand he had his *skipani*, the little adze he had used day after day in the building of *Argo*. He walked over to the galley, and with six quick strokes he cut three crosses in a line on the tip of the ram. Then he bent and kissed the marks. It was his personal benediction for the boat. Then he waved to the crowd to stand back, warning them that it was dangerous to should now offer to work directly under Vasilis' orders; it was a tremendous compliment to his achievement. Each shipwright carried a stout wooden stave to help lever the boat along her path in case she faltered. They ranged themselves in two lines, on each side of the slipway. Then they turned towards Vasilis as he stood proudly near the bow of the galley, and awaited his instructions. He crouched down to sight along the line of the keel, waved one man forward and gestured to him to make a minute adjustment with his stave, to inch *Argo* straighter on the slipway by a hairsbreadth.

Then Vasilis gave an order. Four shipwrights swung sledge-hammers and knocked clear the main retaining chocks. When only remain on the slipway when *Argo* began to move. At that instant, in a remarkable gesture, there suddenly appeared from the crowd the dozen leading shipwrights of Spetses. I found it very touching that these men, who normally worked with such proud independence, one chock was left to hold *Argo* back, Vasilis strode forward with a mallet and swung it three times. On the third stroke the chock spun clear and *Argo* began to slide. The two lines of shipwrights encouraged the movement with their staves, and with increasing speed the galley rushed down the slope. The onlookers burst into applause as she plunged into the harbour with a splash, and floated clear of her cradle, pirouetting and bobbing.

Argo looked fabulous, swimming exactly on her painted waterline, the first galley of her type to be launched for perhaps 1500 years. The crowd was cheering. Vasilis stood there, arms akimbo, gazing proudly at his handiwork. Beside me Tom, who had worked so hard to perfect the ship, had tears in his eyes. 'My God,' he said, 'she's beautiful. She's so beautiful she makes me want to cry.'

3
Jason's Kingdom

On the day of *Argo*'s jubilant launch Mark Richards, the rowing master, arrived on Spetses with the first contingent of the volunteer oarsmen he had brought along to test the brand-new galley. Just after the daily ferry from Piraeus docked, a dozen young men appeared, striding purposefully along the quay of the Old Harbour. In the lead was Mark, his shaven head concealed beneath the sort of straw hat worn by English vicars at summer fêtes. He was dressed in a faded tee-shirt, dark blue rowing shorts whose seat was mended with a towelling mat bearing the name of a well-known beer, and broken-down tennis shoes. In each hand he hefted an enormous package. To avoid air freight charges I had asked the trials crew to bring out large quantities of ship's gear, and Mark was bounding forward with great, muscular strides as if on some athletic training mission that involved carrying heavy objects over long distances at top speed. Behind came his rowers, all looking extremely fit, all with packages, and all wearing rowing shorts. A dozen pairs of white, untanned legs betrayed their recent arrival. They loooked like a small platoon of soldier ants on the march.

They were all members, or former members, of the Boat Club from Keble College, Oxford, and had offered to come to Greece for their Easter vacation to put *Argo* through her paces. Next day they were joined by a second batch of college rowers, including two girls, and such was the enthusiasm of the Keble Boat Club that the college cox – whose name was Jason – limped in on crutches. He had recently broken his leg in a motorcycle accident, but was determined not to miss the fun. They were wonderful company, full of good humour and energy, and by the time they left Spetses

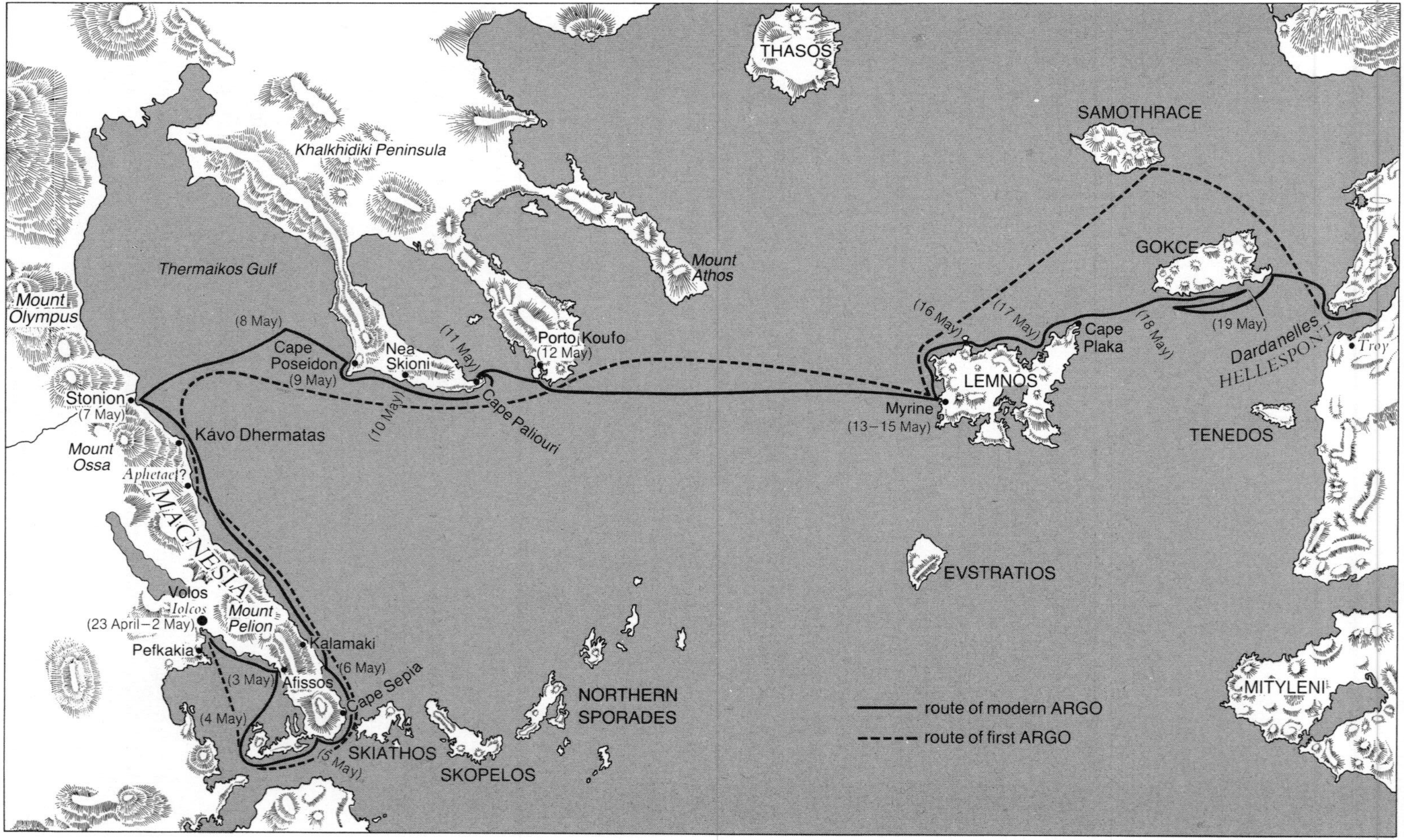
THASOS
SAMOTHRACE
Khalkhidiki Peninsula
Thermaikos Gulf
Mount Athos
GOKCE
Mount Olympus
(8 May)
(16 May)
(17 May)
(18 May)
(19 May)
(11 May)
Porto Koufo
(12 May)
Cape Poseidon
(9 May)
Nea Skioni
Cape Plaka
Dardanelles
HELLESPONT
Troy
LEMNOS
Stonion
(7 May)
(10 May)
Cape Paliouri
Myrine
(13–15 May)
TENEDOS
Kávo Dhermatas
Mount Ossa
Aphetae?
MAGNESIA
EVSTRATIOS
Volos
Iolcos
(23 April–2 May)
Mount Pelion
Kalamaki
Pefkakia
(6 May)
(3 May)
Afissos
Cape Sepia
(4 May)
NORTHERN SPORADES
route of modern ARGO
route of first ARGO
MITYLENI
SKIATHOS
(5 May)
SKOPELOS

two weeks later they had worked out the best way of rowing the boat, and succeeded in getting *Argo* up to the very respectable speed of 6 knots. On their penultimate day they rowed the galley right around the island before lunch. After they left, I found a tiny copy of the college coat of arms, embroidered by one of the girls, stitched in the corner of *Argo*'s new sail.

During the last few days of rowing trials, a delivery crew had been forming. These were the men who would take *Argo* from Spetses north to the port of Volos, the starting point for her main voyage in the wake of Jason and the Argonauts. Again, the delivery crew was composed of volunteers. Some, like Tim Readman and Peter Moran, would be members of the regular crew; but others were men who had only a couple of weeks' holiday to spare from their regular jobs, and so came to help on *Argo*'s delivery trip. They were to have a gruelling, uncomfortable fortnight because the spring weather was still cold and blustery, but *Argo* had to arrive in Volos right at the opening of the sailing season proper, with time in hand in case we needed to make last-minute adjustments before setting out on the 1500-mile voyage to the Soviet Union.

The Spetsiots gave *Argo* a farewell party. It was held in the main square near the New Harbour, the same place that had looked so bleak and deserted when I first arrived there two years before. Now the square was thronged with islanders. Young men and women from the high school dressed in antique Greek costume took part in traditional dances. The mayor made a speech, and everyone cheered Vasilis, who was looking very uncomfortable in a blue suit, collar and tie, though Evgenia, his young daughter, was clearly delighted that her father was such a hero. As the evening light faded, the young men lined the stone steps of the harbour and held aloft burning red flares while *Argo*, with the flag of Spetses at her bow, rowed out. A dove of peace was released from the crowd. The bird flew out over the heads of the oarsmen, ducked through the smoke from the flares, turned in the air and was gone.

Next morning was our last on the island, and Vasilis made his poignant and personal farewell. He came putt-putting on his scooter down to his boatyard where *Argo* was taking on the last of her stores. As always, the cats of his boatyard ran out to greet him, but this time Vasilis ignored them. He walked straight down to the little wooden jetty where *Argo* lay moored. He was carrying a small bouquet of island flowers that he had gathered that morning, and in his other hand he held his *skipani*, his adze. Clambering aboard *Argo* without a word, he hammered two nails into the curling stern piece, and on them hung his *skipani* and the bouquet of flowers.

'Keep the *skipani* with *Argo*,' he told me. 'It is the tool that built the boat, and will bring her good luck. Remember that she is a boat built in Spetses, and if you ever need help with her, please call on me. She's the best I've built.' With Evgenia holding his hand, Vasilis stood on the jetty waving farewell as we rowed out from the Old Harbour to take *Argo* to Volos, and the start of her quest for the Golden Fleece.

The ruins of Mycenae lie four hours' drive to the northwest of Spetses. The site has given its name to the most spectacular civilization of mainland Greece during the Bronze Age, and its citadel still merits its choice as the symbol of Mycenaean culture. It crowns its hill with an imposing array of massive walls; flights of steps lead up to the great palace; and a ring of standing stones fences the shaft graves where half a dozen of the kings of Mycenae were buried with so much bullion among their grave goods that archaeologists are prepared to accept Homer's epithet of 'Mycenae rich in gold'. Mycenae's glowing reputation is unlikely to fade. The famous Lion Gate, claimed as the first piece of monumental sculpture in Europe, must be one of the most photographed subjects in Greece. Homer's verse has spun a web of immortality around King Agamemnon. The gold mask of an earlier Mycenaean lord, whom the archaeologist Schliemann thought was Agamemnon himself when he retrieved it from a shaft grave, stares through empty eye sockets at every turn – from wall posters, from postcards, from the cover of the National Museum catalogue. Less well known is the tale that Hercules was standing in the market square of Mycenae when he first heard the news that Jason was recruiting men to go on the quest for the Golden Fleece. According to the story, Hercules promptly broke off his series of Labours to volunteer. He had just completed his fourth Labour, the capture of the Erymanthian boar, and was standing with the live animal, foaming at the tusks, draped across his shoulders. As soon as he heard the news, he dumped the enraged beast on the flagstones before the astonished citizenry, and set off for Volos where the Argonauts were assembling.

The Greeks, from Homer onwards, looked back on the

Mycenaean Age as a time for such deeds of high endeavour, and this Camelot quality of the Mycenaean civilization is still its most endearing feature. Indeed life must have been very dashing and agreeable for the kinglets and their ladies who ruled the palaces and citadels that were then scattered across Greece. Wall paintings by their court artists show them hunting for wild game, parading in their chariots with hunting dogs, looking like sleek borzois. Occasionally they are shown going off to the more deadly business of war, while the ladies (or perhaps their priestesses) wave farewell and good fortune. In our museums are Mycenaean gold signet rings by the dozen, exquisite bronze daggers inlaid with scenes of boar hunting, tall-stemmed and elegant drinking goblets, and body jewellery. Of course, somewhere at the base of all this luxury and formality toiled the imponderable mass of slaves or serfs or bondsmen who gave the structure its foundation. But between them and the lordly rulers spread a whole trellis of craftsmen and artisans, who supported the more gorgeous aristocratic blooms. There were excellent potters, gem cutters, tailors and skilled armourers, not counting the whole host of more prosaic occupations that gave employment – stewards, huntsmen, chefs, gardeners, house servants and so forth. And also – we have the Linear B tablets to prove it – each palace had its staff of scribes and clerks, counting in this, checking out that, keeping the ledgers, paying the staff their wages of corn and oil. It was a society on a smaller and less imperial scale than that of Egypt or of the great kings of the Hittites in Anatolia, but it was without doubt cultivated, vibrant and possessed a great sense of style.

In this world Prince Jason grew up. He was, so it is said in every version of the legend, a member of the ruling family of Iolcos, a rich city – now called Volos – to the northeast. Iolcos was not quite as grand as Mycenae, nor as martial as gloomy Tiryns with its immense granite castle brooding over the coastal plain like a suspicious pugilist awaiting a slight. Iolcos seems to have been more mercantile-minded, more prosperous and more subtle. Its closest equivalent would have been Pylos, where King Nestor held his court. Neither city saw the need to build a colossal defensive wall, though both were very rich prizes for any invader.

We know now that the thirteenth century BC, the time of the Argonaut epic, was to end with the swift decline of Mycenaean glory. But it was not a twilight era – quite the opposite. Mycenaean society seems to have been more active, more luxurious, than ever before – even a touch frenetic. Recent discoveries have revealed that Mycenaeans had launched themselves overseas and settled pockets of the Aegean coast of Anatolia, on the western marches of the great Hittite empire. The clay tablets of the Hittite official archives report a strange people who must have been the overseas Mycenaeans. They appear as a flamboyant race given to martial display, driving up and down in chariots and issuing challenges to single combat. Enterprising Mycenaeans with less soldierly tendencies were sending their trade goods to Egypt, Italy and far up the Danube. And finally, of course, the ambitious war leaders of all those petty kingdoms and scattered fiefs were sufficiently imaginative to launch the first major amphibious assault in history – a thousand ships, it was claimed, to fall on Troy.

The tumbled ruins and the artefacts turned up by the archaeologists flesh out the tale – the typical Mycenaean palace had its central courtyard with an audience throne for the lord, and side apartments with baths and plumbing, store rooms and guest chambers. The court ladies enjoyed their trinket boxes, fashionable hairstyles, ivory combs from Africa, cosmetics and perfumes. But what they thought, what they believed in, is much less clear. Their religious notions, so important to the Jason story, have been smothered under the later Greek pantheon. Apollonius writes of

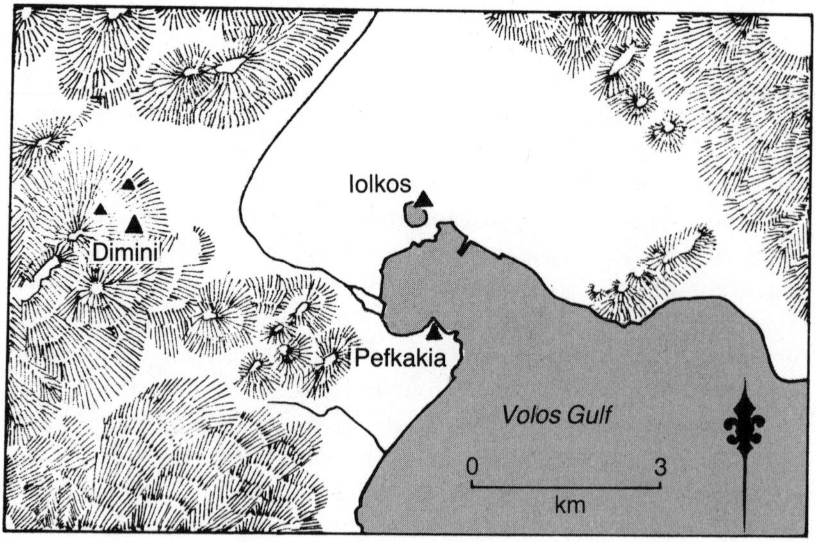

Hera, Poseidon, Apollo, Cupid and the other Olympians who take a hand in Jason's affairs. But, as far as we can tell, these gods did not exist in the thirteenth century BC, or at least not in that form. We can guess that the Mycenaeans believed in an afterlife, for they buried many of their leaders in magnificent beehive tombs. Lords, chiefs and clans probably also had their totems, for we see men grotesquely masked, and women dancing in some holy rite, apparently worshipping the old, mostly animistic, gods. They held sacred the spirits of certain holy places – springs of water and groves of trees in particular – and they seem to have achieved a special reverence for the Great Earth Goddess. Her female shape appears in a number of clay ritual figurines, all-present, all-supreme. Later Greeks were to identify her with Rhea, the mother of Zeus, and she was to reappear in a number of other guises as Dindymene, Demeter and Cybele, all goddesses associated with the earth, with the natural cycle of life, the seasons and nature. She was to have a role, too, in the Jason story.

When we arrived at Volos at the start of our voyage, Vasiliki Adrimi, the curator of the Volos Museum, had something very important to show me. Vasiliki was an archaeologist, and she took me 4 kilometres west of Volos to the top of a low hill surrounded by a crown of cypress trees. The summit of the hill was criss-crossed by low stone walls dating back to the late Stone Age when Dimini, the name of the site, had been one of the first planned towns in European history. But this was not what Vasiliki wanted to show me. Cut into the side of the hill was a passageway, lined with dressed stone, which led straight to a massive stone arch, its lintel a single block of stone 6 feet broad and 4 feet wide. Anyone who had ever seen the Lion Gate of Mycenae would recognize that arch at once: it was the entrance to a Mycenaean burial chamber. Through the arch was the tomb itself, a beehive-shaped hollow scooped out of the heart of the hill, and lined with beautifully engineered blocks of stone. Vasiliki explained that the tomb had been discovered when the roof fell in and a cow had dropped through the hole. Archaeologists had at once recognized it as a Mycenaean tomb, and although the grave inside had been robbed of all but a few meagre pieces of pottery they had no hesitation in pronouncing it to be the burial place of a Mycenaean king who died in the late Bronze Age.

'This was odd,' Vasiliki went on. 'If this was the grave of a king, why wasn't he buried inside the royal city of Iolcos, where we have found other royal graves? Why was he buried out here, at a distance, and inside this hill? Then three years ago a local farmer applied to the archaeological authorities to plough up a field at the foot of this hill. He had to have our permission, because the area surrounding this hill had been declared an archaeologically protected site. So, just to make sure, we excavated the field first, to check that there was nothing important buried there. We had thought that perhaps we might find some more Stone Age remains, connected with the settlement on top of the hill. Imagine our astonishment when we found a small and well-planned Mycenaean town site! No one had expected it. Why should another Mycenaean town have been built so close to the big city of Iolcos? There was no precedent for such a thing. Again, it was difficult to explain.'

Vasiliki walked with me through groves of almond trees to see the walls of this Mycenaean town that she and her colleagues had discovered. They still had not completed their investigations, but one thing was clear: this was a very well thought-out township. You could see where the main street ran, and how the Mycenaean town houses had lined the main thoroughfare. Each house was of typical Mycenaean plan, with three rooms, used for living, sleeping and storage. In the floor of one house the owner had dug a hole to sink a large earthen jar which had been his larder. Vasiliki explained that the town showed all the signs of having been a deliberate foundation, a sort of satellite town to Iolcos, and apparently related to the main city. However it had clearly been a much less prosperous settlement than the metropolis. Everything the archaeologists had found by way of household goods, and that was very little, had been modest and utilitarian.

'And then we noticed two things which were equally strange,' Vasiliki told me. 'First, the town had only been inhabited for a very short period, a century or less. It was built, lived in and then abandoned. And this led to the second puzzle – why did the people leave? They were not driven out by attack or earthquake or fire. We found no trace of these catastrophes. Instead, the people just seem to have cleaned out their homes tidily, and left in an orderly fashion. What made them move out? Where did they go?'

Vasiliki looked at me, and I could sense the fascination of the archaeologist for the detective work of history, seeking to explain past events from a handful of clues.

'You've probably guessed the most obvious explanation. This

site could be connected with the story of Jason and the search for the Golden Fleece. The time when this town was built, occupied and left is the time when the voyage of the Argonauts is said to have taken place. In the legend we are told that Jason's father was dispossessed of the throne of Iolcos by his half-brother King Pelias. Perhaps Aeson, Jason's father, came here with those people still loyal to him, and founded this town outside the city walls. This may be where Jason spent his childhood. The legend says that when Jason returned from the quest for the Fleece, having fulfilled the ordeal, he took back the throne of Iolcos from King Pelias. And that might be when the people of this place evacuated their town, packed up all their belongings, and moved back into Iolcos, following the new king. That is why these Mycenaean houses have been so neatly tidied up by their original owners. And if this is the case, then there is a very good chance that the tomb we visited on the hill was the burial place of King Aeson, Jason's father.'

This was a wonderful boost to the quest for the truth behind the Jason legend. Here, on a hill in his own country, the archaeological data seemed to suggest that the beginning and the end of the ancient legend was true.

According to the legend, Jason had gone on the voyage to win the Fleece, in order to win back the throne of Iolcos, which was his by right, but had been usurped by his step-uncle King Pelias. The latter must have been a terrifying figure. It was said he had been abandoned soon after birth by his mother, a Mycenaean princess who was being victimized by a jealous stepmother. She left the baby in a field, and the infant was found by a group of horse herders after one of their horses stumbled on the baby. Its hoof injured the child's face so that Pelias, who was raised by the horse herders, grew up with a vivid facial scar. After he learned his true parentage, Pelias tracked down the unpleasant stepmother, chased her into the temple of Hera and killed her as she clung to the altar. This crime grossly violated the sanctuary of the temple, and according to Greek notions of divine retribution was to be the reason for his own violent death, which was to be engineered by Jason's wife at the instigation of the vengeful Hera.

Pelias' mother had eventually married the king of Iolcos, and Pelias succeeded in dispossessing Aeson, the rightful heir. He let Aeson live, but as a private citizen. When Jason was born, his parents feared that Pelias would consider the royal child a threat and have him put to death. They announced that the baby had been born dead, and smuggled him out to the countryside where he was brought up, like several of the other ancient heroes, by the wise centaur Cheiron on the slopes of Mount Pelion.

On the day that he was old enough to claim his inheritance, the young man set out to walk to the city of Iolcos. On the way there he came to a ford across the stream called Anavros. There he found an old woman waiting to cross the stream, which was in spate. Though he was in a hurry, Jason stopped to help her. He picked up the old woman, who was the goddess Hera in disguise, and carried her across to the other bank. In doing so, Jason lost one of his sandals, which he left stuck in the mud of the stream bed. Thus, when he appeared in the marketplace of Iolcos he was wearing only one sandal, and this immediately reminded King Pelias, when he first set eyes upon the strange young man, that an oracle had warned him that he would be destroyed by a man who came to him 'with one foot bare'.

Seeking to escape his fate, runs the legend, King Pelias put to Jason the ambushed question: What would he do if he came face to face with the man who, according to a prophecy, would destroy him?

'I would send him to seek the Golden Fleece,' replied the naïve youth.

'So be it,' replied King Pelias.

An alternative version of the tale merely says that Jason revealed his identity to the king and demanded the throne of Iolcos by right, and that, without demur, King Pelias agreed to relinquish the crown provided that Jason proved his worth to Iolcos by bringing back the Golden Fleece. In both versions the task was considered to be suicidal.

The Fleece was of particular significance to Jason's family, the Aeolids, whose clan badge was a ram. Indeed one is left with the strong impression that the Fleece was some sort of sacred cult object which they held in veneration. Its history stemmed back two generations, when there had been a succession of bad harvests in the Boeotian city of Orchomenus, ruled by King Athamas, another Aeolid. Athamas believed that the gods were angry with the city and had to be appeased. The real reason was that Athamas' new wife, Ino, had devised a plot to rid herself of her stepchildren, Prince Phrixus and Princess Helle. Queen Ino had secretly persuaded the woman of Orchomenus to roast the grain seeds before planting them, thereby killing the grain and destroying any prospect of a harvest. Then she arranged that the Delphic Oracle, when consulted for a solution to the famine, should advise King Athamas to sacrifice his two oldest children to allay the curse. Prince Phrixus and Princess Helle had been led to the sacrificial altar when a ram with a golden fleece appeared and told the children to climb on its back. Then the ram flew away eastward. As it passed over the strait dividing Asia and Europe, Princess Helle lost her grip on the wool, slipped off, fell into the strait and was drowned. The strait was thenceforth named the Hellespont in her memory. Phrixus, after a halt on the Black Sea coast of Anatolia, was eventually carried to the far end of the Black Sea, to the kingdom of Colchis, where he was well received by its king, Aeetes. He settled there, married one of the king's daughters, and eventually died in Colchis. At its own request, the ram was sacrificed and its fleece hung in a sacred oak tree.

Possibly the story of the flying ram was a vivid retelling of the escape of the royal children by some other means, perhaps aboard a Mycenaean ship trading eastward, but that is conjecture. As far as the Argonaut legend is concerned, the important point is that the people of Iolcos knew at once what the Golden Fleece was, and where Jason would have to go to fetch it back. All the onlookers, and especially King Pelias, did not expect to see Jason alive again.

Vasiliki, the archaeologist, had another clue to give me. 'When we began to consider the implications of this Mycenaean town,' she told me, 'it was recalled that at the end of the last century, when the first excavations were made on the top of the Dimini hill, the archaeologists – who were interested really in the Stone Age levels – noted in their field books that they cut through some ancient walls resting on top of the Stone Age town. These walls, we now believe, were the remains of a small Mycenaean palace or manor house which stood on top of the hill. That could have been Jason's home. Indeed, now there is this evidence to support the theory, the town council of Volos has been asked to change the name of the stream which runs between Dimini and the town of Volos. This would have been the stream which Jason crossed on his way to meet King Pelias for the first time, the place where he lost his sandal in the mud. It has been suggested that the stream should again be called Anavros.'

From the top of the low hill I could see south to the great sweep of the Bay of Volos, steel-blue in the spring sunshine. To the right a line of hills fell away to a small headland. On the headland a clump of green pine trees gave the place its name – Pefkakia, the place of the pines. Here *Argo* now waited, hauled out on the beach to undergo last-minute adjustments before the start of the voyage to Colchis. Pefkakia, I believed, was the most likely spot for Argos to have built the original *Argo* and it would have been the galley port for Iolcos in Jason's day. The conditions were exactly right: a

sheltered anchorage, a spring of good drinking water nearby, and a smooth and gentle shelving beach for hauling out the galleys. Just the previous day I had watched a northerly squall rush down on the bay like a dervish off the slopes of Mount Pelion. The squall had struck the shipping in the modern harbour, whipped spray off the surface of the sea, rocked the big ships and sent the smaller fishing

Slipway at Pefkakia

boats scurrying for shelter. The place they all ran for was Pefkakia, with its calm lee and good holding for the anchor. What was suitable for a small boat today would have been equally suitable 3000 years ago. And sure enough, not 50 metres from the modern *Argo* on the beach of Pefkakia rose another mound. Here German archaeologists, digging ten years earlier, had cut away the sandy loam and exposed the walls and foundations of a third Mycenaean settlement.

Peter Wheeler was busy on Pefkakia's beach, adapting the tip of *Argo*'s ram. During her delivery voyage from Spetses we had learned that the ram was an ideal platform for all sorts of functions. If one went for a swim, it was the easiest place to climb back on board. For washing or relieving oneself, it formed a platform with running seawater on both sides. This also explained the strange-looking line of pegs which stuck out of the bow timber on several early Greek boat illustrations. The purpose of these pegs, like tiny horns, had puzzled commentators, but I asked Tom to hammer them in place anyhow, supposing that we would find out their function sooner or later. In fact Vasilis knew what they were the moment he saw them. He called them the *scalita*, the little ladder, and that is just how we used them: as a series of hand- and footholds for someone clambering back aboard the boat from the tip of the ram. However, scrambling from the water onto the tip of the ram itself was still a clumsy business, so Peter had decided to install a convenient handhold which a swimmer could grab at the very tip of the ram and then use to swing himself up. When Peter finished, what he had achieved was immediately obvious. His new handhold had turned up the tip of *Argo*'s nose like a boar's snout, and this was exactly how many of the early Greek artists drew their ships.

Trondur, who had joined during the delivery trip, decided that it was time to improve the 'eyes' of *Argo*. At the moment they looked altogether too innocent and naïve, as well as being slightly crossed. He redesigned them, adding a touch of menace, and gave them the sort of aggressive glare more fitting to a warship about to set out on a voyage to bring back the Golden Fleece from a hostile kingdom.

The new Argonauts were now arriving in Volos. Nick, our doctor, showed up, as imperturbable as ever, and big Peter Dobbs – the two Sindbad veterans. Matching Peter in size was Miles Clark, on leave from the British Army, who soon revealed a well-honed talent as a mimic and humorist, with a vast fund of stories that kept everyone laughing. Peter Moran, the cook, explained to Tom why he needed a set of removable deck planks to provide extra storage room for his baskets and boxes of food. A generous supply of *Argo*-brand wine had been supplied by the city fathers of Volos, and there was scarcely any space to stow the gift.

Modern Volos has honoured the memory of the Argonaut epic. The main street of the town is called the Street of the Argonauts; a fine bronze model of Jason's *Argo* stands near the modern quayside; and several tavernas are named after Iolcos' most famous vessel. Now Volos provided a volunteer for the crew – Elias, a local architect who was very eager to join us, even though it was the first time that he had ever been in a small boat. My idea was that, while *Argo* was in Greek waters, I wanted as many Greeks as possible to join the crew, just as I would try to have Turks aboard when we got to Turkey, and hopefully we would find Soviet crewmen when we got to Georgia. It was, I felt, an important part of the project that each country should have its representatives on board, and participate directly in the adventure.

With Elias were two more of his countrymen – big Theodore, who was an electrical engineer by trade, and stocky, white-haired Costas. In April Costas had telephoned me to ask if I would consider him for the trip. He was, he said, a very experienced sailor and owned his own yacht. He lived in Athens and had done much cruising in the Aegean. He sounded ideal, and his English was superb. I was just about to invite him outright to join the crew, when he paused and tactfully said: 'There's only one thing which may be a problem – that's my age. I'm sixty years old.' I gulped. A sixty-year-old galley oarsman? I didn't want anyone having a heart attack from rowing for hour after hour in the heat, so I suggested to Costas that he should join the crew while we were delivering the boat to Volos from Spetses. If he found the going too tough, he could gracefully retire. As matters turned out, Costas was a gem. He was absolutely determined not to give up. For the first few days he suffered agonies of exhaustion, and in the evenings could be seen trembling with fatigue. But his spirit was indomitable. He was such a cheerful, plucky individual that he was tremendously popular with the rest of the crew.

'I wish my company could see me now,' he told me happily. 'Until last year I was chief pilot for Olympic Airways, and I had to retire because the company has a maximum flying age of sixty!'

Our two film-makers also joined us at Pefkakia. They were to make an onboard documentary film of the voyage, and came half-submerged by the inevitable heap of bright aluminium boxes, film stock, cameras, tripods and all the paraphernalia of their trade. Dick Hill was the cameraman, an urbane figure who had the knack, alone of all the crew, of being able to keep a set of clean clothes even under the thwarts of a cramped Mycenaean galley. Whenever Dick went ashore, he managed to present himself immaculately attired in well-pressed light-coloured trousers without a mark on them, and a silk shirt with the ironing creases still in it. His colleague, Dave Brinicombe, was at the opposite pole. He was the sound recordist, and the space under his thwart was an amazing jumble of electronic gear in which he would rummage like a badger. He never cared how he dressed, and he much preferred to go barefoot. His unkempt, bushy beard adorned a cheerful, snub-nosed face, and as he padded happily up and down the central gangway of the boat, with his feet splayed out and a distinctly prehensile curl to his toes, it was Miles who at once saw the resemblance to Stone Age man and gave him the nickname that was to stick – Dave the Cave, a sobriquet which the sound recordist accepted with a large and cheerful grin.

The day of departure was set as 4 May. By early morning the crowds were beginning to assemble by the boat at Pefkakia. The local schoolchildren had been given a holiday to see the galley set out, and already there was a good throng of them gathered on a viewing point on the hillside above the galley. '*Kalo taxidi! Kalo taxidi!* Good journey!' they chanted in unison, and waved excitedly to the Argonauts who were stuffing kitbags under thwarts, greasing the leather strops that held the oars to their thole pins, and joking about the voyage.

'I've calculated that we may have to do 1.5 million oar strokes per man before the end of the voyage,' announced Mark Richards to the crew, evidently relishing his role as rowing master.

'Oh no, I hope not. Let's pray for a wind,' groaned Tim Readman, the ship's purser. 'I'm so unfit.'

'Don't worry. When we get hungry and run out of food, we'll eat you first,' retorted Peter Dobbs. It was a long-standing tease from the Sindbad Voyage that Tim Readman would be the tastiest meal.

'Ten minutes to go!' I called out, and gave a tap on the brass ship's bell that hung by the tiller bar. Tom and Wendy had come to say goodbye. Tom was looking rather wistful at not being able to stay with *Argo*, but had to get back to work as a boatbuilder. Vasiliki, the archaeologist, was there too; so were Uncle John and his family; Borgne, Trondur's wife, had brought Brandur, their small son, to the jetty to say goodbye, and he was looking distinctly overawed by the press of people.

Then it was time to pour a libation to the gods, a gift of wine to request fair winds and calm seas. I dug out a bottle of Argo wine. Nothing less than an entire bottle would satisfy Poseidon that day. No one seemed to have packed a corkscrew, so I reached for the priest, the wooden club we used for knocking in loose thole pins. Holding the bottle over the stern, I smashed off the neck. The wine shot out in a tremendous spurt and a great cheer of appreciation came back from the crowd. Another double tap on the ship's bell, and someone was casting off the stern line.

'*Kalo taxidi! Kalo taxidi!*' called the children on the bluff. Trondur was in the bows, quickly hauling in the dripping anchor line hand over hand. In a moment the anchor came aboard.

'Anchor clear!'

'Come forward!' I called, and the oarsmen leaned forward to the ready position. 'Medium pressure. Are you ready? Go!' The oar blades dipped in the water and began to move in unison. The oarsmen took up the steady rhythm. *Argo* began to glide across the water.

'One million, four hundred and ninety-nine thousand, nine hundred and ninety-nine strokes to go,' muttered Miles. Gingerly I turned *Argo* on course. The twin steering oars worked in opposite directions. One tiller bar had to be pushed forward, and the other pulled back to make the boat turn. It felt very odd, but *Argo* responded obediently.

It was a good day to start an expedition – no wind and a light veil of high cloud to block the worst of the sun. All around us were dozens of small fishing boats, chugging with their engines at dead slow. Ahead was the Volos pilot boat, ready to clear *Argo*'s path and lead her for the first few hundred yards. Light racing shells of the Volos Rowing Club skimmed around and beside us like water beetles. Dip, pull; recover the blade; swing forward; dip and pull again. The steady repetition of the galley's oar stroke seemed ponderous beside the modern racing shells. Up ahead I could see the end of Volos' modern concrete jetty. Standing there were the local dignitaries – the mayor, the army commander, the senior port officer and the Greek bishop in his robes. As *Argo* passed, the mayor raised high an olive branch and tossed it into the water.

'Go in peace! *Kalo taxidi*, good voyage!'

Now we were rounding the tip of the jetty, steering to pass the main waterfront of the town as close as possible to the land. The quay was packed with people, mostly children brought by the coachload to witness the departure of a boat from their country's distant past. '*Kalo taxidi! Kalo taxidi! Kalo taxidi!*' The children were roaring the chant in a steady rhythm, like a crowd of football supporters. The new Argonauts waved back, rowing with one hand and waving with the other. A racing four came slicing past us. In the bow position was an oarsman as splendidly shining bald as Mark. 'You two must go to the same hairdresser,' Miles remarked.

According to Apollonius Rhodius, the departure of the Argonauts 3000 years earlier had been rather more fraught. There had been rumours that King Pelias had bribed Argos, the boatbuilder, to sabotage the boat by making her with weak fastenings, so that she would break up and sink during the voyage. But presumably Argos had no intention of such treachery, because he himself had decided to be a member of Jason's crew. On the evening before their departure, following tearful farewells with their families, Jason's volunteers gathered on the beach. Jason sent for two oxen to be driven down to the shore from the family herds. Hercules and the mighty Ancaeus killed the beasts, one with a single blow from his legendary club, the other chopping through the animal's neck with a bronze axe. The sacred morsels from the thighs were wrapped in fat and burned ceremonially on the flames of an olivewood fire laid on an altar of shingle. This sacrifice was to Apollo, the God of Departures. Idmon, one of the two seers on the crew, peered at the dancing flames and watched the spiral of smoke rising to the sky. He pronounced the omens good, but added gloomily that he himself did not expect to return alive from the expedition. His destiny had been revealed to him, he said. He would die in some lonely spot on the Asian shore.

The rest of the evening was not much more of a success. Idas, the braggart member of the crew, got drunk on too much undiluted wine and began to mock Jason, who was sitting apart from the rest, having last-minute doubts about the wisdom of the expedition. When rebuked by Idmon, Idas abused him too, and the quarrel would have led to blows but for the tactful intervention of Orpheus the musician, who struck up a tune on his lyre and embarked on a long song about the creation of the gods. That night the crew slept on the beach, and in the morning it was Tiphys, the crack helmsman, who roused them from their sleep and got them started in good time. They already knew their oar bench positions, every man having drawn lots for them the previous day. Only Hercules and Ancaeus were excluded from the lottery. The two biggest and strongest men in the boat, they were automatically allocated the central bench, where their greater strength would be of most effect.

Aboard our modern *Argo* we had made a similar decision: Mark and Miles were our best oarsmen, each man having rowed for his university, and it was natural that they should occupy the stroke position, the sternmost bench, where all the other crew members could watch them and try to copy their style and timing. We did not have a full crew of twenty aboard – there were only fourteen men that day; and what with one man to steer and one to cook it left only twelve oars in action. But it was enough. The trick was to keep the galley moving steadily through the water at all times, nibbling away the miles at about 3–3.5 nots. So sleek was *Argo*'s design that she slid steadily along at this pace even when there were only ten men at the oars. This allowed two of the crew to rest for a five-minute interval, and when their break was over they changed places with two others who could then take their turn to relax. Thus *Argo* did not loose momentum, but kept plodding along, south-southeast across the Bay of Volos towards the little town of Afissos.

Afissos was said, in one tradition, to have been the first stopping point for Jason and his men on their journey. The reason, according to this version of the legend, was that *Argo* herself refused to carry Hercules' massive weight. The ship's magic speaking bough had groaned aloud when the huge Hero first stepped aboard, and she soon insisted that he had to be put ashore as she was not prepared to carry his bulk any farther. As a result, the people of Afissos are still said to be taller than other villagers in the district because they are descended from the mighty Hercules. Certainly there was a Mycenaean settlement at Afissos in the late Bronze Age – pieces of Mycenaean pottery have been picked up near the beach – but the real reason for *Argo*'s halt may be rather more mundane. Bubbling down to the shore at Afissos runs a fine spring of excellent drinking water. Today it has been channelled and captured so that it supplies the taps in the central square, but as we filled two earthen amphorae for the new *Argo* we could hear the water rushing under the paving tones. It was entirely logical that Jason would have put in here to water his ship before going on the first stages of the long voyage. Logically, too, any crew members who might have been rethinking their commitment to the expedition could have taken this chance to jump ship and make for home – including Hercules, though, as we shall see, in most versions of the legend he remained on board until the Argonauts reached the Sea of Marmara.

There were no runaways from modern *Argo*'s crew. The 15 miles from Pefkakia to Afissos was a very convenient first day's run – far enough to stretch the muscles but not too far to exhaust the crew. As we came ashore, we found Uncle John ahead of us. He had driven round the bay to meet us, and naturally he had a friend in the area. This friend had a vineyard, and Uncle John was brandishing a plastic jerry can of home-made wine. Beside him stood the schoolteacher of Afissos with two little girls clutching bouquets of roses – '*Kalo taxidi*,' they intoned solemnly as they handed over the flowers. Our journey had begun.

Mycenaean ram's head ornament

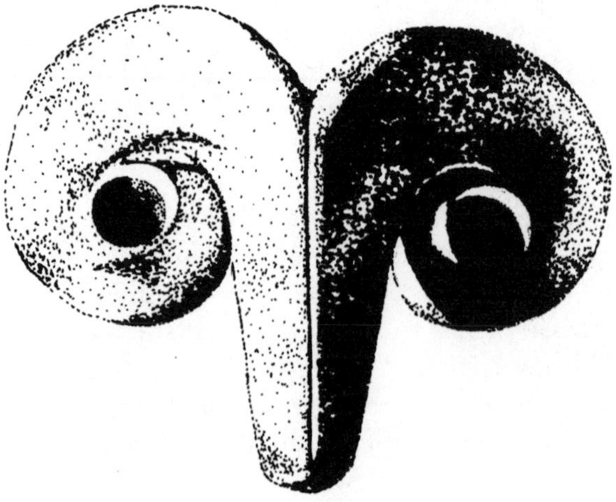

4
Across the Aegean Sea

The Lord of Departures must have heeded the Argonauts' sacrifice, for Jason and his men had the benefit of a heaven-sent wind for the first days of their quest. Scarcely had they left the beach before a fair wind arose and they were able to hoist sail. 'They stepped the tall mast in its box,' wrote Apollonius, 'and fixed it with four stays drawn tight on either bow; then hauled the sail up to the mast head and unfurled it. The shrill wind filled it out; and after making the halyards fast on deck, each round its wooden pin, they sailed on at their ease. . . .'

The twentieth-century Argonauts had no such luck. Our first three days of the voyage were made either in absolute windless calm, or against awkward gusting breezes which scuttled round the headlands and ambushed the labouring galley. Turn and turn about, the crew had to slog on, rowing *Argo* forward across an expanse of unrelenting sea, like men trudging across the desert. The first blisters appeared within an hour, blisters which were not to heal until the voyage ended. The oarsmen had expected the blisters, and each had his own theory about the best remedy or prevention. Some rubbed the palms of their hands with alcohol, others wore cotton gloves or wrapped a protective towel around the oar handle. But it was little use. Nothing cured the problem. Blisters formed, swelled, broke, reformed, broke and hardened. Then, just as the hands seemed toughened, the first exposure to seawater would soften the callouses, and the dead skin peeled away to leave raw patches which were painful to the touch. If, by great care, the blisters were kept dry after they burst, they simply split again under the constant abrasion of rowing, and then another blister swelled beneath the first.

Gradually the crew began to mould together, learning to row as a unit. Mark went up and down the central gangway coaching the novices. He showed them the best way to time their stroke, how to relax the body during the swing forward and how to control the oar blade as it moved through the water. But rowing a twenty-oar galley was very different from rowing a light river-racing shell. The galley's oars were heavier and more unwieldy, and there was no chance to use the leg muscles fully. Rowing *Argo* was largely a question of swinging the weight of the body, pivoting forward and back, forward and back, hour after hour, until repetition dulled the senses. By common agreement, the rowing stroke was kept short. The worst crime of all was to swing too far forward with the oar handle at the beginning of a stroke, and a trifle too late. When that happened, the man in front could be struck in the middle of his back with an oar handle and its 7lb lead counterweight as he leaned into

his next stroke with his full weight. It was like being hit with a sledge hammer, and in those first, less expert, days it was not unusual for oarsmen to come off the benches with telltale black stripes of lead scored between their shoulder blades.

Yet our slow progress had its compensations. On the second evening we found an idyllic mooring on a small island tucked just inside the mouth of the Bay of Volos. The cove where we anchored was enchanting. Rows of olive trees grew on the hillside above us; the ground was covered with wild flowers; a small stone jetty provided easy access to the small beach. A dozen bottles of Argo wine were quickly plunged up to their necks in the water to cool, and Peter Moran prepared a barbecue. As he cooked, a small fishing boat came nosing into the bay, its crew curious to inspect the galley. They presented us with fresh shrimps to add to our supper.

Island mooring at the entrance to the Bay of Volos

It was the time of the spring festival, and down from the hillside above us came a grandfather, a grizzled veteran leading his two grandchildren by the hand. He had retired to a tiny whitewashed cottage above the point, from where he could look across to the mainland. His grandchildren had seen *Argo* arriving, and had been gathering wild flowers for us. Now they brought their offering – an intricately woven wreath of leaves and bright flowers which we hoisted to *Argo*'s masthead as a symbol of May. The old man searched around inside the cuddy of his own small fishing skiff and handed across a great white ball of mutton fat from his own sheep. He had seen us greasing the leather oar strops on *Argo*, and made this simple and practical gesture. It was one of those small deeds, little acts of kindness, which linger. A thousand miles farther on, along the far north coast of Anatolia, we would still be using smears of that mutton fat, and each time I would recall the old man as he sat with us that evening beside the embers of the camp fire, quietly chatting with the Greek crew members.

Next morning we rowed out of the Gulf of Volos and into the Aegean Sea. Our course lay coastwise, hugging the rim of the fishhook shape of the Magnesian peninsula. Again there was scarcely a breath of wind, and by midday the heat was decidedly oppressive. Sweat poured off the men's bodies, forming damp patches on the oar benches and staining the seats of their trousers. It was easy to understand why the classical Greeks often rowed naked, for this must have reduced the risk of boils and skin rashes which came from sitting in sweat-soaked clothes. Peter Dobbs donned an Arab headcloth, a relic of the Sindbad Voyage, and a variegated assortment of hats and headgear came into use to prevent the sweat from pouring into the rowers' eyes, where it was actually painful.

When the wind did come, it was from the wrong direction, a light breeze out of the east which strengthened in the evening so that the crew had to struggle hard to row *Argo* to a safe anchorage by dusk. That headwind was a sobering experience. Ten men pulling steadily could drive *Argo* forward at 3–4 knots, moving her between 20 and 30 miles a day by muscle power. But it had to be in calm conditions. The merest whisper of a headwind, a scarcely perceptible breeze blowing against the prow of the boat, cut down her speed alarmingly. It was not just like walking uphill, but like walking uphill through shifting sand. Every stroke forward was eroded by the boat trying to slither back. Few occupations are more disheartening than trying to row a boat under such conditions, struggling under oars against a contrary wind, losing half a yard for every yard made good. *Argo*'s rowers had every reason to grow discouraged.

Worse still, if the headwind arose when *Argo* was between anchorages, the helmsman found himself left with only two choices, both of them bad. Either he turned back at once and sought shelter downwind, so losing all the precious ground that the crew had accomplished with such sweat-stained effort, or he had to ask the crew to battle on, watching them grow increasingly weary and hungry, hoping to claw forward those last few miles to the next safe anchorage ahead. There was always a painful balance between the crew's reserves of strength and enthusiasm, and the counterforce of the wind. One never knew how long the ordeal would endure, whether the wind would stealthily increase in proportion to the ebbing strength of the crew, whether the sea state would deteriorate so that the crew could no long row effectively in the rising waves, or – worst of all – whether finally the wind would prove too much, and after a couple of hours of gallant effort you would have to put the helm over and abandon the struggle, throw it all away and run downwind to port.

The truth of the matter was that moving a twenty-oared galley into a headwind by oars was a futile exercise in nine cases out of ten. Galleys were not designed to operate in adverse weather, and this was a caution that I had to bear in mind for the entire voyage. It affected every decision whether to push on or turn back. In two of the three seas we were to sail, the Aegean and the Marmara, the weather is notorious for the speed in which it can change from calm to gale. In the third, the Black Sea, there is more warning from the sky and swell when bad weather is on its way, but the adverse conditions can last longer. And to a wind-driven galley a lee shore is murder.

Cape Sepia, which our *Argo* passed on the fourth day, was vivid proof of such a danger. In 480 BC almost an entire fleet, sent by Xerxes to invade Greece, had been smashed here in a single storm. The armada, galleys and transports, was caught by an unexpected gale after the captains had rashly anchored on the nearby coast. More than 400 ships were lost when their anchors failed to hold and the vessels were blown down onto Cape Sepia, presumably with their crews trying desperately to get out their oars and dig their blades into the water and heave their ships into the channel running past the cliffs. As the raging waves on the base of the cliffs grew closer, the galley captains must have tried again and again to cast anchor and hold their vessels off the land. But the water was too deep. Their anchor stones failed to hold and the ships were shattered, with appalling loss of life. *Argo* must have passed over the bones of those galleys as she too rowed past those deadly cliffs, not 50 metres from the wall of rock, with the swell growling and booming in the sea caves. It was impossible not to invoke the memory of all those early shipwrecks, and to remind oneself that any rock-bound coast was the finish for an early ship caught in an onshore gale. No small galley was strong enough to row herself out of trouble, and if the water was too deep to anchor then your ship was lost, and probably the crew with her.

We had negotiated the Cape and turned north, still hugging the shore, when we ran into the first strong wind of the voyage. It came out of the north, a headwind straight down the coast, and I immediately sought temporary anchorage in a little bay called Paltsi, where the fishermen pulled their small boats well up the beach and even had sets of wooden rails to drag them clear of the worst storms, since by no stretch of the imagination could Paltsi be considered a safe anchorage for a modern boat. For *Argo* under these conditions, however, it was shelter enough. Her draught was so shallow, less than 3 feet, that we could lay out two anchors to seaward, run a long line ashore to keep her stern square to the beach, and warp her into the shallows in the very back of the bay to find a degree of shelter. A deep-keel yacht would have had to abandon the bay and put out to sea, but *Argo* clung on, pitching and swooping within 10 yards of the shore, the waves breaking just under the upsweep of her stern as a gull would settle on the water and ride close to rocks and backwash.

As for the crew, they were learning that for a galley crew patience was just as important as physical strength and stamina. The only safe way to sail a Bronze Age ship is to wait until the weather turns fair. Sooner or later, we all knew, *Argo* was sure to be caught offshore in bad weather; that was a crisis that would be dealt with at the time, and the last thing I wanted during the first week of the voyage was to risk the morale of the crew with a useless battering. For the remainder of that day and well into the night we stayed where we were in Paltsi Bay, just as hundreds of galleys must surely have done in the millennia before us, all waiting for a change in the weather before dashing out along the rock-bound coast of Magnesia. Jason and his Argonauts had known the same delay, and along the same treacherous coast. For two and a half days they had been forced to lay up at a place called Aphetae, waiting for a break in the weather. Aphetae's exact location is impossible to identify, because Apollonius does not give enough details, but probably it lay father north than Paltsi, perhaps near the mouth of the Pinios River.

When the wind does turn, a galley must seize her chance to move. So just after midnight, when the north wind eased, it was time to rouse the crew. They came aboard half-drenched. Nearly everyone had chosen to sleep on the beach, rather than on the pitching, anchored boat, so there was much scurrying and shouting and shaking to wake the shore party. In the darkness they had to wade out through the breaking waves to come aboard, toss their sleeping bags and rucksacks on the stern deck and climb half-naked and shivering to take up their rowing positions. Typically, Peter Dobbs volunteered to stay ashore and cast off the stern line as the galley rowed out, so he came last of all, towed into the bay by the stern warp like a drogue.

For an hour or so it was heavy going. Although there was no wind, there was still a choppy sea, and in the dark it was difficult to row steadily. The boat went lurching this way and that; oars were tossed about like spillikins; the men cursed; and poor Theodore hung over the side, heaving with seasickness. But dawn rewarded the effort. A breeze moved in from the south, with the sun, and we could set sail at last. It was the first time that *Argo* had spread her canvas since leaving Volos.

Her rig was another thing that had not been seen on a Mediterranean ship for many centuries. *Argo*'s sail plan and rigging had been derived from the details shown on sixth- to fourth-century BC painted vases that showed galleys under sail. The sail itself was a rectangle of cotton, hung from the cypresswood yard. On the forward side of the sail were sewn eighty-one bronze rings. Through these rings passed nine light ropes which led from the foot of the sail, up through a line of nine rings, and then over the crossyard and back down to the helmsman standing in the stern of the ship. By pulling on these lines, the helmsman and his assistant could gather up the sail to the yard like hoisting a window blind. It was a straightforward and effective, if somewhat cumbersome, method of handling *Argo*'s cotton sail. At times one felt rather like a charioteer in the stadium trying to cope with nine recalcitrant horses and a mass of reins that threatened to tangle themselves in knots. However, with Notus the south wind astern, *Argo* spent all that day skimming over the waves in Jason's wake like a ship out of a dream. Under full sail she behaved superbly. The hull cleaved through the blue sea, and with the merest touch on the two steering bars *Argo* responded like a well-schooled thoroughbred. She turned as deftly as one could wish, and a second touch on the tillers to bring them level brought her back on course, running sweetly forward. Sitting wedged against the rail in the very stern of the ship, under the curling tail ornament, one could feel the ship quiver as she sped downwind, her keel and planks thrumming as she rolled to the following seas while her ram threw aside a cresting bow wave.

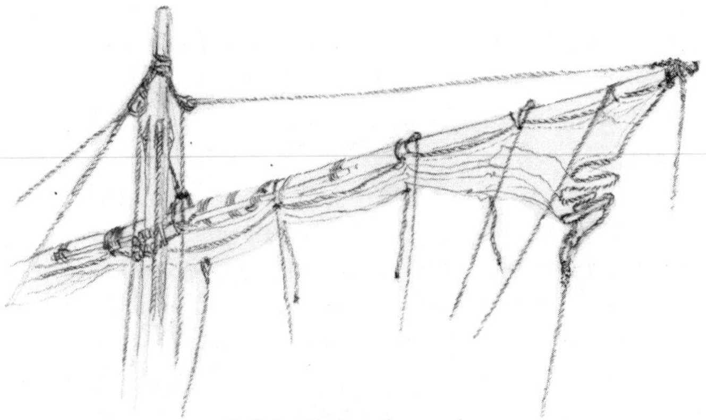

Sail brailed to the yard

That day's run up the wild coast of Magnesia was a delight. For hour after hour *Argo* forged along at 5–6 knots, leaving a clean wake behind her, while the crew relaxed on the benches, their oars hauled inboard out of the way. There was nothing for them to do but sit and relax and enjoy the passing scenery. The mountains marched with the coast, starting with the snow-sprinkled peak of Mount Pelion on whose slopes the centaur Cheiron is said to have educated so many generations of Heroes, including Jason. Then came the massif above Kalamaki with a spectacular waterfall plunging off its flank in a white plume. Finally Mount Ossa rose in view, and behind it the approaches to Mount Olympus, home of the gods.

Along the whole of this rock-bound coast was not a single safe harbour, and in less than eleven hours that blessed wind sped *Argo* 50 miles past all its dangers, while her crew could look up and see high on the mountains the clusters of white-painted houses of the famous Pelion mountain villages, as if a giant had tossed a handful of sugar crystals against the greenery.

On board our spirits soared. The bleary-eyed oarsmen of dawn were now cracking jokes, sunbathing, listening to their portable cassette recorders, relaxing. Tim Readman, puffing on his pipe, judged this the right moment to open his purser's wallet with which he went around the crew, extracting each man's contribution for the week's ration budget which he and Peter Moran would spend ashore buying fresh provisions. Mark, the rowing master, turned out to be a maniac for do-it-yourself handiwork. He was always whittling away on chunks of wood that he had lopped from bushes on the hillsides to make into knife handles or an axe haft, or he would be stitching leather or sewing canvas into bags and holdalls. Now he was embroidering the word 'Argo' in classical Greek script on his sailing smock, below the Union Jack, and he promised he would add the name in Russian script if we ever managed to get to Soviet Georgia. Trondur sat propped against the gunwale, sketching. Dressed in straw hat, baggy trousers and sandals, with a drawing board on his knee and charcoal in hand, he looked, in that brilliant Mediterranean light, like an artist in Provence in the 1920s. Immaculate Dick Hill, true to form, had donned a pair of well-pressed trousers, smart enough to grace the cocktail hour on a millionaire's motor yacht, and had applied suntan lotion to his torso, so that he immediately became known as Sticky Dicky. Miles' trousers, by contrast, already had a seat as baggy and wrinkled as an elephant's backside, a sign of the hard-working stroke oarsman but also good as clown's pantaloons. To round off the general feeling of wellbeing, the day proved to be Costas' birthday. He was sixty-one. From his kitbag he produced a bottle of whisky to celebrate the event, and his health was toasted. He too had collected a nickname. Rowing out of Volos Bay, someone had remarked that the exercise would give everyone tremendous muscles. 'Hey, Costas,' called Peter Dobbs, 'you'll be fit enough to go back to Olympic Airways and kickstart a jumbo jet.' So it was to Kickstart Costas that we raised our glasses.

Jason's route, as described by Apollonius, took the first *Argo* north along the Magnesian coast as far as Mount Olympus. There she turned east and headed out across the open sea towards the headland of Cape Poseidon, the nearest of the remarkable three fingers of the Khalkhidiki peninsula which projects down from the coast of Thrace. Now, as we ourselves approached Mount Olympus along the same route, the reason for the change of course became obvious. Mounts Ossa and Olympus provide excellent landmarks for any ship leaving the coast and striking out to sea. By keeping Mount Ossa directly astern, you can sail across the Thermaikos Gulf and make safe landfall at Cape Poseidon. In the days before compasses good landmarks were vital for early navigators, and they planned their routes accordingly. Their ideal day's run would involve leaving the beach at first light, and being in sight of land and their next anchorage well before dusk. Aboard *Argo* I did not want to use a compass; it was far more interesting to navigate in the old way, by line of sight, by the sun, and by the feel of the waves and wind. There was a compass hidden away for emergencies, but at this stage it proved totally unnecessary. Several crew members were experienced yachtsmen, accustomed to sailing in the tidal waters of the English Channel or the North Sea, where compass, log, echo sounder and radio direction-finder are normal aids. But in the Aegean none of this was required. We could get along very well without any of these modern contrivances. It was enough, most of the time, simply to look where we were going – to the line of the sun, the distant shape of an island as a way marker, and finally to our day's destination itself. Nor did we have a ship's radio – just the two walkie-talkies so that we could communicate between *Argo* and the rubber dinghy when taking photographs, and a waterproof radio beacon that could be switched onto the general distress-and-calling frequency in an emergency. To check our speed we towed a rotor over the side, but this was not accurate enough to help us calculate distances, particularly at low speeds. The only depth-measuring instrument we ever used was an oar counterweight of lead, tied to a long piece of knotted cord.

Only in the matter of charts were we truly anachronistic. It is not known whether in the late Bronze Age anything like a chart existed; perhaps it did, in the form of a stylized diagram. But it is more likely that Jason's expert helmsman, Tiphys, would have worked from a practical experience of the main Aegean routes carried in his head. When he ventured beyond the boundaries of his personal knowledge, he would have inquired of local sailors and fishermen, or even hired the services of a local pilot. However, to take the new *Argo* to the mouth of the Dardanelles, never having sailed those waters before, I had charts to tell me where to go.

Serving breakfast on board, instead of on shore, was the best way to lure modern Argonauts off the beach early enough to make a good start to the day. The prospect of a bowl of porridge or a couple of slices of bread was sufficient to make a hungry oarsman emerge from his sleeping bag on the shingle and come aboard at the first stroke of the ship's bell. So by seven o'clock the next morning, after spending the night in the little harbour of Stonion under Mount Ossa, we were already rowing out to sea, heading away from land and keeping the mountain in direct line with *Argo*'s stern ornament. Our crossing to Cape Poseidon measured 28 nautical miles of open sea, and I hoped to cover the distance in a single long day. But despite a libation to the Sea God – a cup of local wine tossed in the harbour – we failed. First we had a calm, then Boreas the north wind, then calm again, and finally a wind from the southeast which gradually shifted around to *Argo*'s bow and held her back like an unseen hand. When night fell we were still 10 miles offshore, and though we could see the lights of land the oarsmen were too exhaused to row any farther. So we lay down and tried to sleep.

Spending the night aboard *Argo* out at sea was a new experience. Apollonius makes it clear that from time to time Jason and his men also failed to make landfall by dusk, but this was a situation that early Aegean galley sailors mistrusted deeply; they preferred to be ashore on a safe beach by the time the sun went down. Occasionally Jason's helmsman decided to keep travelling at night, usually because he did not wish to waste a fair wind, and once or twice Jason and his oarsmen were obliged to row through the dark because they were becalmed far from land. But there is no mention of them actually sleeping in their open boat at sea, as we did. We had no choice: we were too tired to row on. Each man tried to find enough room to lie down, and this required the greatest personal ingenuity. The entire crew was confined in a space measuring superficially 54 feet by 9 feet at its widest. A third of this was already taken up by the ram, mast, rigging, ship's tackle, cooking area, liferafts and all the other paraphernalia of the ship. The very small spaces under the oar benches were crammed with stores, personal gear and the barrels containing our tools and clothing.

At first calculation it seemed physically impossible for everyone to find enough room to lie down and sleep. Effectively the only area available to each man was his own oar bench, which measured 8½ inches wide by 4 feet long, not a great area to fit a sleeping 6-foot 2-inch oarsman, particularly when shared with several feet of his oar handle which had to be pulled inboard. Yet the new Argonauts somehow managed the impossible. They stretched, crept, wriggled, curled, folded over and draped themselves into whatever gaps they could find. It was like a scene from a yoga class going into its most advanced contortions and postures. Costas lay on his back on his thwart. As his bench was divided by the mast, he had to adopt a right-angle with his legs sticking vertically up the mast. Most of the others took up spoon positions, head to toe on their rowing benches, but Mark achieved a notable first: he excavated a hole in all the dunnage beneath his oar bench and disappeared into the bilge of the boat where, like a corpse in a crowded coffin, he fell

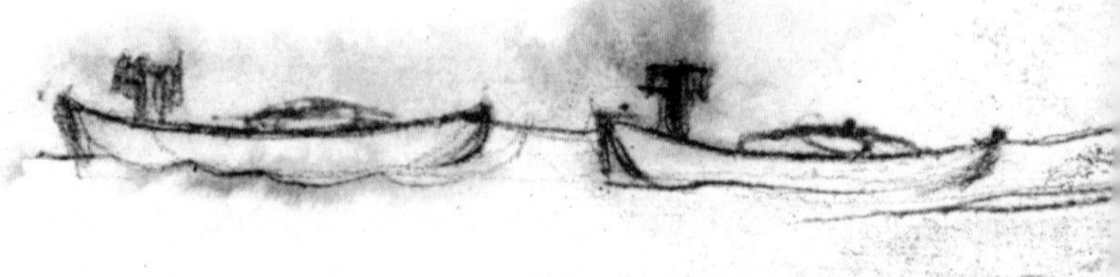

asleep, unable to stretch or move. It showed just how exhausted the crew were, that they slept the night in such cramped conditions, while *Argo* lay motionless on the surface of the sea in such a velvet calm that we might have been tied to a dock.

All around *Argo* moved coloured lights – the navigation lamps of freighters, which steered clear when the night watch flashed a warning torch beam on *Argo*'s limp sail. Occasionally what looked like a whole chain of street lights glided past us as fishing boats set out for their night fishery, towing a string of small rowing boats behind them, each boat equipped with a bright, gas-driven flare to attract the night-feeding fish.

A cloudy sky and a continuing calm brought the dawn, and the cocoons of sleeping bags began to move, disgorging remarkably cheerful men. Mark's bald head emerged from beneath his bench like the body from the mummy's tomb in a horror film. Rolling his eyes in mock frenzy, he leaned over to sink his teeth into Tim

Greek fishing boats

Readman's leg. 'I'm hungry,' the apparition moaned. Thereupon, Pete the Cook, with his inevitable cheroot clenched between his teeth, boiled up eggs and coffee, and the remarkable crew settled down to another three hours of stiff rowing to reach the shore by Cape Poseidon.

The reaction of the Greek fishing communities to *Argo*'s passage of their waters was heart-warming. Some sort of grapevine relayed the message of *Argo*'s presence from one port to the next. After resting on Cape Poseidon's beach, we rowed around its long, sandy spit in strange, unsettled weather. Menacing cloud banks formed; rain dropped from their swollen underbellies; rainbows came, flourished and disappeared. A fickle wind blew now from the land, now from the sea, and *Argo* struggled slowly on, her crew constantly brailing and unbrailing the sail to catch the puffs of wind, or tugging on the oar handles to gain a few more yards. Suddenly a trio of motor fishing boats appeared from the small harbour of Nea Skioni on the mainland. As the boats came closer, we saw that their decks were packed with children gazing at us. With each group of children was a schoolteacher. There were shrieks from the children as the first of the tubby fishing boats cut its engines and turned sharply to pass alongside *Argo*. '*Kalo taxidi! Kalo taxidi!*' Again came the shout we had heard so often.

An unshaven fisherman, villainously scruffy in stained and torn jersey, filthy trousers and sea boots, stepped out from his wheelhouse. Bizarrely, this ruffian figure was holding a delicate bouquet of pink, red and white roses. The flowers were tossed across the gap between the two boats, to be caught in mid-air by the equally piratical figure of Peter Dobbs in his Arab headdress. The second fishing boat chugged past, and lobbed another gift. This time it was a cardboard box of sticky sweets, sent by the ladies of Nea Skioni and caught by Miles. The fishing boats wallowed off, and only one small, battered boat remained. In it stood an old seasoned fisherman. He had stopped his engine and was now rowing in the Greek fishing style, standing upright and facing forward as he pushed on his oar handles. He was a squid and octopus fisherman, for in his worn boat were several tridents, and a large rusty gaslight hung over the stern, wrapped in an old tweed topcoat. At night he would use his lamp to lure his prey to the surface, just as his forbears in Homer's day lit blazing firebrands to attract the fish to the spear. Now he was scrutinizing *Argo* with an air of professional interest, as he shouted across to us in the characteristically laconic style that seamen use as they meet strangers in small craft.

'Welcome,' he called. 'You are at Nea Skioni. How is your voyage?'

'Fine. Just fine,' called back Elias, the architect, leaning over the gunwale.

'There's an old harbour just a little way up the coast – Old Skioni – it's buried beneath the sea, but you can see the columns and blocks of stone if you go there on a calm day and look down into the water. We are descended from the men who returned from Troy!'

It was a curious tale to hear from the mouth of a fisherman, but true. According to the Greek historian Thucydides, Skioni had been founded by Greek troops from the Peloponnese who were returning home from Troy after the fall of the city. One contingent of these soldiers, homeward bound with their boats loaded with booty and captured Trojan women, had come ashore at Skioni to break their journey, and the Trojan women had seized their chance to rebel. They did not wish to become household slaves in Greece, so they burned the boats of the Greeks with the result that the contingent was stranded and the men were obliged to remain on that coast. They married their audacious captives and settled on the spot.

We got a much closer look at Nea Skioni than I had bargained for. Soon afterwards the wind sprang up from the east, a strong breeze from dead ahead. Knowing the futility of trying to row upwind, I turned *Argo* around and we went racing towards Skioni's pier, as if intent on hurtling on to the rocks. At the last minute came the order 'Brail up!' Trondur and Peter Wheeler hauled furiously on the nine bunt lines, whisking the canvas in folds against the yard. 'Oars outboard! Firm pressure! Go!' Ten oars hit the water, and *Argo* shot round the end of the pier with her canvas rattling. She must have looked like a nineteenth-century painting of a fishing boat entering harbour under stress of weather. So Skioni's schoolchildren all got a second holiday, for their afternoon lessons were cancelled in order for them to come down to the little sandy beach at the back of the harbour and stare at the galley.

Argo was giving us invaluable lessons in ancient sailing. Time and again a chance remark or a sudden observation seemed to leap the centuries, and brought us face to face with navigation as it had been practised in a bygone era. At Nea Skioni a local man, Antonis, asked if he could accompany us for the next day's journey. He was an amateur skin diver and knew the local coast well. Soon after we rowed out, I had to duck *Argo* once again into shelter to avoid a headwind. The only possible refuge was a poorly protected open beach with a rocky sea floor on which the anchor slithered and skidded. I was not at all happy about the safety of the anchorage, and remarked on the treacherous combination of rocky coast and sudden shifts in wind in that area.

'Oh yes,' Antonis replied. 'This part of the coast has a very bad reputation. It was a graveyard for ships for centuries. My friends and I in the diving club have found half a dozen ancient Greek and Roman wrecks, lying on the bottom along this short stretch of coast.'

Unwilling to stay longer in that inhospitable spot, I asked the crew to row on. We spent a miserable afternoon thrashing past the jagged rocks of Cape Paliouri, with the sail and yard hauled down to cut the windage, and lashed securely to prevent accidents in the choppy seaway. There were flashes of lightning, peals of thunder, and the sea turned a nasty hostile grey. As soon as we had clawed clear of the rocks of Cape Paliouri I put the helm over, and *Argo* fled for a large and deserted bay, marked on the chart and lying just north of the cape. As we glided into its shelter, Antonis pointed to starboard. 'Just there we found another wreck, a Roman ship. She must have run for the same refuge as *Argo*, but foundered as she came in.'

Roaming the shore that evening, I stumbled across a field of peas, growing wild on the hillside above the anchorage. I called the others, and soon they had gathered enough fresh peas for all of us, while Trondur and Peter Wheeler hunted unsuccessfully for octopus with a trident. After supper we rigged the galley's canvas cover, as the sky was threatening rain, and that night we experienced the most terrific thunderstorm, with strike after strike of lightning spitting from the sky. The wind snatched and rattled at the canvas covers so that we had to cling onto them to prevent them being blown away, and the rain was so heavy that the drops literally smashed onto the sea, spraying the recoil inboard. Yet through it all I heard not a single complaint, only a succession of jokes and laughter as the rain-sodden crew spent a sleepless night.

Jason and his Argonauts had picked up another fair wind off

Mount Olympus. Where the new *Argo* proceeded by fits and starts along the coast, Jason and his men had not had to touch the oars. They sailed straight past Capes Poseidon and Paliouri in a single day and a night; and their second dawn brought them in sight of Mount Athos, the third finger of Khalkhidiki and the next great seamark on their route. Tiphys, the helmsman, decided to push on even farther, to trust to the wind and head direct for the fertile island of Lemnos. It was a good decision. Their weather luck held. 'For the Argonauts, there was a stiff breeze all that day, and through the night,' wrote Apollonius Rhodius. '*Argo*'s sail was stretched. But with the sun's first rays there came a calm and it was by rowing that they reached the rugged island of Lemnos . . . .'

Lemnos was the scene of the first of their adventures during the quest for the Golden Fleece. Unknown to them, the women of Lemnos had recently killed all the men on the island because their husbands had been unfaithful *en masse*. The Lemnian men had been raiding the mainland coast of Thrace, and bringing back Thracian women whom they much preferred to their own wives. Soon the Thracian women had usurped the Lemnian ladies in their own homes, until the moment came when the jealous Lemnian women decided to exact a bloody revenge. They massacred all their men, killed their Thracian concubines, and even slaughtered all the male children on the island. The only male to survive was their aged King Thoas. His daughter, Hypsipyle, smuggled him down to the beach and set him adrift in a wooden chest, in which he was eventually picked up by foreign fishermen, never to return to the island.

For a time after the massacre the Lemnian women managed very well by themselves. They took on all the previous male tasks, the ploughing and the seeding and harvesting, and adapted to their new life. But they also lived in constant fear of a counter-raid from the Thracians. So when they saw *Argo* standing into the harbour of their capital at Myrine, they mistook the newcomers for attacking Thracians, and, dressed in armour, the Lemnian women ran down to the harbour to defend themselves.

Jason reacted cautiously. Seeing the armed host on the beach, he sent ashore his herald, the smooth-tongued Aethalides, a man reputed to have such an all-embracing memory and to be so glib that he could fabricate any apparent truth he wanted without actually telling a lie. Aethalides quickly persuaded the Lemnians that *Argo* should at least be allowed to stay overnight in Myrine's harbour without being molested. This gave the Lemnian women a chance to reflect on their precarious situation. A public meeting was held in the town square, and the royal nurse Polyxo, now a white-haired old woman, pointed out that by killing all their menfolk the Lemnians had condemned themselves to extinction. Either they would be overwhelmed one day by a Thracian war party or, lacking men, they would never bear children and therefore, die out as a race. Accordingly the Lemnian women, led by Hypsipyle who was now their queen, decided next day to invite the Argonauts into their city and encourage them to stay on in Lemnos as their new husbands. The absence of the Lemnian men would be explained away by the fiction that they had been exiled because of their unreasonable liaison with the Thracians.

The stratagem worked very well. Jason, dressed in all his finery, came ashore to be received in the palace by Queen Hypsipyle. There she offered him the throne of Lemnos if he and his men would agree to settle on the island. Jason declined the crown, saying that he and the Argonauts could not abandon the quest for the Golden Fleece. But he did agree that the Argonauts would stay a while as guests.

So pleasant was the visit, with its succession of banquets and

Myrine

(*Previous page*) Tim Readman undergoes the joys of the *hamam* (Turkish bath) at Canakkale at the hands of the masseur, where the author, too, was 'twisted, torn, pummelled, trodden on, and wrenched into every possible contortion'

The Turks entertained the new Argonauts with lavish hospitality (*below*) and with traditional Turkish dancing at Erdek (*far right*). Here Resit Ertuzun, the local historian, showed them the Sacred Harbour (*right*) where Jason's men sought shelter from the gale

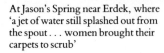

At Jason's Spring near Erdek, where 'a jet of water still splashed out from the spout . . . women brought their carpets to scrub'

(*Right*) *Argo* had 'the best day's sail of the entire voyage' as she sailed up 'the darkly swirling Hellespont', from the Aegean Sea to the Sea of Marmara, with a fresh breeze from the southwest – the same wind that had favoured Jason and his men

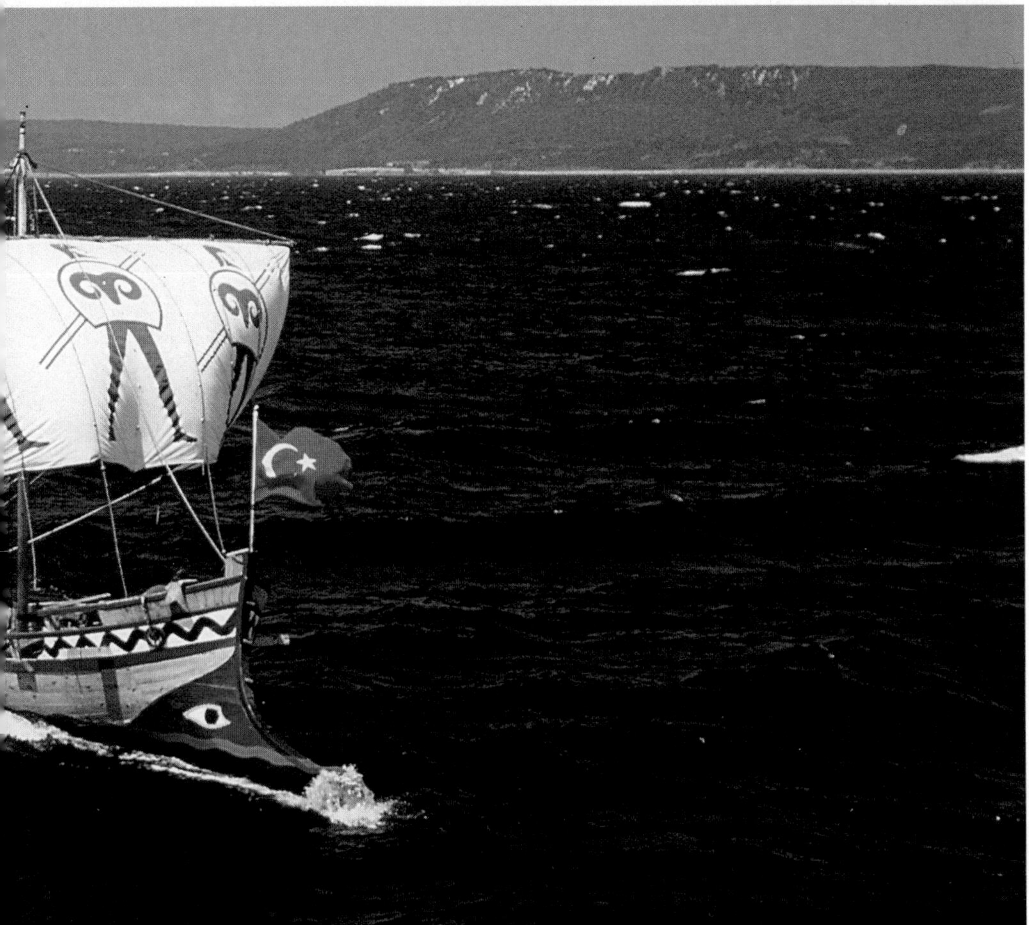

The original Argonauts 'rowed up the Bosphorus by sheer muscle power. Now, three thousand years later, we had to show whether that could have been physically possible. We had to do the same.' *Argo* leaves Istanbul, passing the burnt-out hulk of a wrecked tanker

(*Right*) 'The whole scene was pulsating with activity. Ferries were churning in and out of the Golden Horn . . . Merchant vessels of every description were on the move.' (*Below*) Reinforced by members of Istanbul's rowing clubs (Mustafa, with his sunburnt arm), 'the oar blades chopped into the water in a flurry of quick strokes. The crew grunted with the effort'

As Jonathan Cloke was anointed in readiness for the oil wrestling match at Fenerbache when he was matched against the Turkish heavyweight champion, he 'looked distinctly out of place in a pair of red sailor trousers rolled up to his knees instead of buffalo hide breeches'

At the end of the Straits, near the entrance to the Black Sea, 'are the physical remains of the Clashing Rocks of antiquity' (*above*). On the crest of one of them, the author, with Ali Uygun, one of the Turkish volunteers, examines the remains of a Roman pillar which once served as a landmark for sailors

(*Overleaf*) As they rowed through the most difficult narrows of the Bosphorus at Bebek, 'this was all the muscle power they could produce in a short, concentrated burst'

celebrations, dancing and feasting, and alluring female company, that the whole high-minded expedition for the Golden Fleece almost ended in the arms of the Lemnian ladies. Day followed day on Lemnos, and still *Argo* did not sail. She stayed moored in harbour, while her crew were equally well placed. Jason settled in with Hypsipyle in the palace, and the other Argonauts with their Lemnian ladies. Only Hercules – for in most versions of the story Hercules stayed with *Argo* for a few days yet – abstained from the general sybaritic life. He guarded *Argo* in harbour until eventually he could stand the delay no longer. In a towering rage he stalked through the streets of Myrine, battering on the doors of the houses with his club and calling on the Argonauts to attend a meeting on the shore, without the women being present. There he rebuked his shipmates hotly. They would lose all prestige, he told them, if they gave up the quest for the Golden Fleece, preferring to live at ease with the women of Lemnos. They would become the laughing stock of all Greece.

Shamed, the Argonauts had to agree, and next day they made their farewells. Their parting with the Lemnian women was amiable and sincere. The woman accepted that the Argonauts had to pursue their quest, and they generously offered to take them back if they returned safely. Queen Hypsipyle, suspecting that she would have a child by Jason, asked what she should do. Jason told her that, if it was a boy, he should be sent to Iolcos to live with his grandparents.

This boy, Hypsipyle's son by Jason, was to become King Euneus of Lemnos. According to Homer, Euneus ruled the island of Lemnos at the time of the Trojan War, and during the siege he supported the Greeks, sending them gifts of Lemnian wine and providing the besiegers with supplies. This corresponds to the facts, because Lemnos was famous for its vines and lies on the natural supply route between Greece and Troy. Much more important, however, this reference to King Euneus enables us to give a date to the quest for the Golden Fleece. If Euneus was king when Troy fell, then his father, Jason, must have visited Lemnos a generation earlier. Archaeologists have dated the fall of Troy variously, mostly between 1250 and 1200 BC, with many authorities preferring *c.*1225 BC. Thus Jason's expedition in search of the Golden Fleece would have taken place some twenty to thirty years earlier, in the mid-thirteenth century BC. This date, as we shall see, agrees not just with the occupation of Dimini – the possible home of Jason's exiled family outside Iolcos – but with circumstances which, sailing in the new *Argo*, we ourselves were to find in far-off Colchis, the land of the Golden Fleece.

When Apollonius describes the Argonauts' voyage from Mount Athos to Lemnos, the crossing we too were about to undertake, he makes the interesting observation that the great mountain threw its shadow on the island, even though it was as far from Lemnos as 'a well-found merchantman can travel by evening'. The distance between Athos and the nearest point of Lemnos is, in fact, 34 nautical miles, and this gives the 'well-found merchantman' a twelve-hour run of 2.8 knots average, rather less than the speed we now expected from *Argo* with a fair breeze behind her. Also, our luck finally changed for the better as we too headed from the Khalkhidiki for Lemnos. We had spent the previous evening on the central finger of the Khalkhidiki in the splendid natural harbour of Porto Koufo, where Antonis the diver left us to return to Nea Skioni, and we put out to sea at one o'clock in the morning, hoping to catch a night breeze from the land. As we rowed out, there was a flat calm and a moon so brilliant that we could hear the birds singing on the mountainside as if it were day. Cape Ambelos was a stark black outline against the starry sky, and in the ink-black shadow of the moonlight I found it was possible to steer by sound, judging the distance of the rocks by the roar of the swell reflecting from the cliff face like a sounding board.

An hour later the wind rose softly from the west, and dawn revealed Mount Athos to port, its summit streaked with snow so that it stood all day above the horizon like a massive beacon, an unmistakable signpost for every sailor in the Thracian Sea. For as long as the sun was in the sky the west wind blew fair, and the helmsman needed only to keep Athos receding over his left shoulder, with the sun arching over to his right, and he was steering *Argo* true for Lemnos. We passed two sperm whales – an unexpected encounter in the Aegean – who were travelling stolidly in the opposite direction, puffing out their characteristic forward-slanting spouts. In a twinkling Trondur was swarming up the mast to sit on the cross trees and admire them. He gazed back in our wake, long after they had passed.

By five o'clock in the afternoon Lemnos was faintly in sight, dead ahead. As the sun set in an orange ball behind the shoulder of Mount

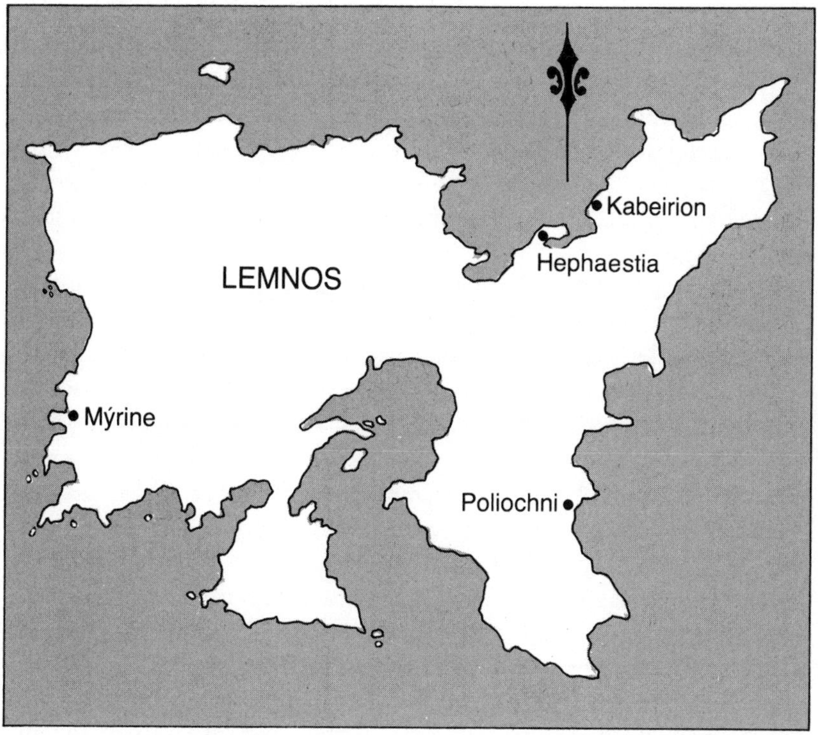

Athos we saw, just as Apollonius had said, how its shadow seemed to fall on the island, and up ahead in the gathering dusk came another armada of welcoming fishing boats to greet us. Watchers on the cliffs of Lemnos had seen *Argo* breast the horizon, and now the fishermen escorted us into the harbour of modern Myrine, their lights bobbing around us and the sound of children's voices singing a welcome. The waterfront itself was jammed with spectators, hundreds upon hundreds of them, craning their necks over the edge of the quay to see *Argo* warp alongside. In the front rank a beaming, robed priest held up a flagon of Lemnian wine.

It was a shock to discover that only a very few Mycenaean remains have been found on Lemnos, although the island figures so strongly in the *Argonautica*. But, as Professor Beschi of the University of Pisa, conducting excavations on Lemnos, explained to me, 'We haven't found any significant Mycenaean remains probably because we haven't been looking for them. There has been so much else to occupy us.' He and his team were busy reassessing the massive archaeological work done on the island in the late 1930s by Italian teams. On the east coast of Lemnos they had uncovered a city, Poliochni, which dates back as early as 3000 BC. Poliochni had been a large and prosperous place, and in the ruins the Italians had discovered exactly the same type and forms of pottery that were in use in Troy on the coast of Asia Minor, clear evidence that trade had flourished between Lemnos and Troy as far back as the middle Bronze Age.

Mysteriously, life in Poliochni seems to have ended about the year 1600 BC. One theory was that, like the fate of the Minoan cities of Crete, that of Poliochni may have been connected with the catastrophic volcanic eruption of the island of Thera. Professor Beschi had little doubt that the story of the Argonauts and the Lemnian women was an echo of some sort of actual historical event. He guessed that Queen Hypsipyle's capital, where Jason and the Argonauts were so enticingly entertained, lay beneath the modern city of Myrine, still waiting to be excavated. For the moment, however, Professor Beschi and his team were far more interested in two sites on the northern rim of Lemnos: the city of Hephaestia, and a cult temple to the mysterious Kabeiri. Both places were linked with the tradition of Jason and the Argonauts.

Hephaestia apparently dated from the seventh century BC and was named in honour of the god Hephaestos. According to Greek mythology Hephaestos was the Smith God, being cunning in all metallurgy and design and serving as the artificer and armourer to the Olympians. It was Hephaestos, by tradition, who had introduced the art of metalworking to the ancient Greeks. He had sided with the goddess Hera when she was quarrelling with her husband Zeus, and the latter had grown so angry that he had picked up Hephaestos and flung him down from Olympus. Hephaestos had fallen on the island of Lemnos, and the impact broke his legs, laming him for life. The original inhabitants of Lemnos, a people known as the Sintians, had been kind to the cripple and given him shelter. In return Hephaestos had taught them the secret of metalworking; and from Lemnos that skill was passed onto the rest of the Greek world.

There is good reason to believe that the transmission of the knowledge of metallurgy was connected with Lemnos' key position astride the sea route to Asia Minor. The archaeological evidence is that one of the earliest centres of metalworking in the

Near East was on the north coast of Anatolia, near the Black Sea. Here have been found some of the earliest smelters and mines in history. If the knowledge of how to work metal was carried by sea from this region towards Greece, it would have come first to the island of Lemnos, and the legend of Hephaestos would have been invented to explain why metallurgy apparently was first taught to the Greeks in this remote island of the northern Aegean. Most scholars are of the opinion that Hephaestos was an imported god of Asian, not Greek, origin, and his significance to the Jason story is that this sea route, between Lemnos and the Black Sea, was exactly the same route that Jason and the Argonauts now proposed to follow, the same track taken by Phrixus, Helle and the flying ram. To emphasize the link, some versions of the Argonaut legend maintain that among Jason's heroes was Palaemon, son of Hephaestos and lame like his father.

Professor Beschi's second site also had a direct connection with the Argonaut tradition and Asia Minor. On the high shoulder of a cliff, looking northwest across the Thracian Sea, the limestone had been cut away to make a platform on which had worshipped a secret cult called the Kabeiri. So secret was this cult that today very little is known about its so-called mysteries, because initiates to the cult swore never to reveal its secrets. However, it is known to have been some sort of fertility cult, and to have been linked with black magic and with the great earth mother in some form. It arrived from Asia Minor and Lemnos and Samothrace became its major cult centres; obviously the position of these islands once again played a role.

What was of special interest to us was that the cult was also connected with seafaring, and specifically with two of the Argonauts – the twins Castor and Pollux. Later pictures of the twins would show them with two stars on their foreheads, the sign used for those initiated into the mysteries of the Kabeiri. It was said that sailors who knew the Kabeiri arts had the power to control the winds and calm storms, and that the twins would appear to them as St Elmo's Fire. Even a glimpse of the two stars, Castor and Pollux, after the twins had been set as a constellation in the sky, meant that the worst of a storm at sea was past. Thus the voyage of the Argonauts entered maritime folklore while, as Isaac Newton observed, other signs of the zodiac were also inextricably mixed with the quest for the Golden Fleece – the water carrier, the fish, the twins and, of course, the ram itself.

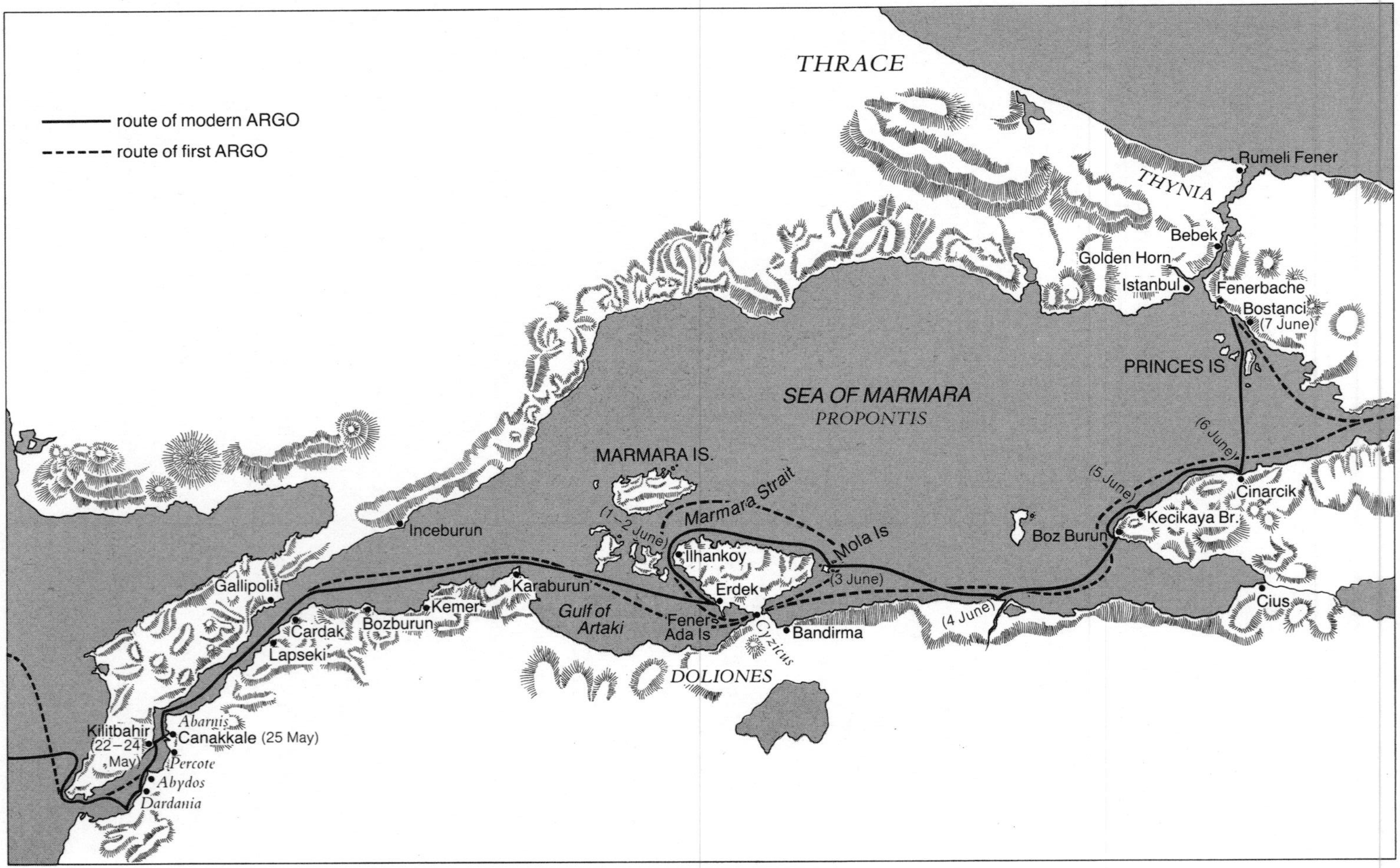

route of modern ARGO
route of first ARGO
THRACE
THYNIA
Rumeli Fener
Bebek
Golden Horn
Istanbul
Fenerbache
Bostanci
(7 June)
PRINCES IS
SEA OF MARMARA
PROPONTIS
(6 June)
(5 June)
Cinarcik
Kecikaya Br.
Boz Burun
MARMARA IS.
Marmara Strait
(1–2 June)
Ilhankoy
Mola Is
(3 June)
Erdek
Inceburun
Gallipoli
Karaburun
Kemer
Bozburun
Cardak
Lapseki
Gulf of Artaki
Feners Ada Is
Cyzicus
Bandirma
(4 June)
Cius
DOLIONES
Kilitbahir
(22–24 May)
Abarnis
Canakkale (25 May)
Percote
Abydos
Dardania

5
The Dardanelles and Marmara Sea

Argo was badly short-handed when we left Lemnos on 18 May. Our three Greek volunteers had said goodbye and returned to their own homes, and so we were only fifteen on board. As he left, I asked Elias, the architect from Volos, how he had enjoyed his trip, since it had been his first experience of a small boat journey.

'Were you frightened at any time during the voyage?'

'Yes, I was,' he answered truthfully, 'but not for long. Everyone else seemed so calm. So I just said to myself that there was nothing to be frightened about.'

'So why did you decide to join *Argo*?' I asked.

'It was for the adventure . . . the idea. . . . I wanted to know what people were like who did such a thing.'

The same question must have crossed the mind of the skipper of the Turkish fishing boat which spotted *Argo* at dusk that evening. We had spent the entire day slogging under oars across the strait which divides Lemnos from Gokce, the first island in Turkish waters. With such a small crew our relief periods from rowing had been cut by half, and we were extremely tired. When the Turkish skipper saw a large rowing boat pulling wearily across the sea he thought we were shipwrecked mariners in a lifeboat, so he hauled in his nets, put on full power, and came racing over, thinking to rescue us. When our true situation was explained, with much pantomime, there were smiles and laughter, and he insisted on presenting us with a large box of freshly caught sprats for our supper.

That night I became aware that I had made a navigational blunder. Apollonius said that Jason and his Argonauts had gone from Lemnos to the island of Samothrace, where the Argonauts had visited another Kabeiri shrine. Then they had sailed for the entrance to the Dardanelles, thereby passing along the north of Gokce Island. But on the chart this route seemed wrong. It was a very roundabout way of going from Lemnos to the Dardanelles, adding 40 miles to the journey. I wondered if Apollonius had made a mistake. Perhaps he had introduced the detour to Samothrace because that island, too, was associated with the Kabeiri. In any event I decided that it was more logical to sail a direct course from Lemnos to the Dardanelles, passing south of Gokce.

But logic is not always the best guide to navigating a Bronze Age rowing boat, and this was one case where the use of a modern chart was a disadvantage, instead of a help. A huge volume of water constantly gushes out of the mouth of the Dardanelles, creating head currents for a galley rowing up from the south. I had anticipated some sort of current, but I had no idea that its effect would be so strong off the south coast of Gokce, where it was to delay us badly. In fact I would have done better if I had taken *Argo* around the north of Gokce, following Jason's original route.

So we spent a curious sort of night after the Turkish fishing boat left us, becalmed off the western tip of Gokce. All around us the upwelling water muttered and grumbled like a living mass. In the moonlight the cloud shadows moved and changed on the water. Lines of froth formed and dispersed. *Argo*, her crew dozing uncomfortably, spun in slow, erratic circles, now clockwise, now counter-clockwise. There was barely a breath of wind, yet patches of water suddenly broke into small white-capped wavelets where currents collided, and then as abruptly fell back into treacherous-looking slicks that disturbed *Argo*'s hull and rocked the boat as if a giant fish was nuzzling her keel.

At dawn I saw that we had been carried off course, and were drifting northward. It was vital to anchor and get some rest before we lost any more ground, and gather our strength so that we could tackle the currents with some hope of progress. But now we faced another problem. The only place we could sensibly reach and where we could find anchoring depth was off the western end of Gokce Island, some 5 miles away and rising sheer from the sea. But on the chart was written a strict warning: 'PROHIBITED AREA'. The pilot book said the same. Gokce was a sealed-off military zone, and the Turkish authorities strictly forbade anyone, especially foreigners, from landing there. If *Argo* even came close to the island, I risked getting us all arrested. But there was no alternative; the crew were so tired that they had to get some relief. I hoped that we might not be spotted or, if we were, there would be no objection if we only anchored in the shallows, and did not actually set foot on the forbidden island. Not very optimistically, I aimed *Argo*'s ram nose at the Prohibited Area.

The western end of Gokce is a forbidding-looking scarp which rises steeply from the water and is utterly barren. On the scrub-covered slope there was not a house, a path, or even an animal to be seen. The place seemed totally deserted. We rowed in closer, and soon came upon a small, attractive cove. Again there was not a living creature in sight – not even a track leading from the back of the cove to show that people came here sometimes. I wondered if the Turkish government had forbidden settlement here for so long that all trace of habitation had been expunged. *Argo* crept into the deserted cove and dropped anchor. Everyone shipped their oars, and we lay down gratefully on the benches to get some rest.

Not twenty minutes later a voice said gloomily, 'Oh! Oh! Here comes the military!' I raised my head and peered over the gunwale. Two men in combat uniform were climbing down the hillside, accompanied by a tracker dog. The soldiers had appeared from nowhere, and were obviously heading down to the cove to intercept *Argo*. One man was carrying a submachine gun, and they both looked very serious. I began to regret bringing *Argo* into the anchorage, and imagined all that might now possibly go wrong: the crew being put under military arrest; the boat impounded; having to explain first to a sergeant, then a lieutenant, then a captain, and so on up the military chain of command exactly what we were doing in a forbidden military zone; and then waiting for the reaction from the military authorities in Ankara, who would inevitably have to be consulted as to what should be done. It would be a disastrous start to our visit to Turkey. To make matters worse, *Argo* didn't have any Turkish entry papers. The nearest customs post lay 60 miles farther on, so we did not have Turkish immigration stamps on our passports. I could foresee days and days of delay while we sorted out the mess.

The army patrol clearly meant business. The two soldiers strode out onto the beach, looking very tough in their battledress and combat boots. The man with the submachine gun swung his weapon to point it at us. His companion shouted sternly, and beckoned. With sinking heart, I gathered up my passport and the ship's documents and Peter Dobbs prepared to take me ashore in the rubber dinghy. I told the crew to be patient, and warned them that I might be away for quite some time. The two soldiers looked distinctly unfriendly as we approached in the rubber dinghy. One was a private and the other a corporal, and from the blue berets I supposed they were troops of the special border guards. I scrambled out onto the rocks, and gingerly approached them. The private moved his gun muzzle, which continued pointing at me. How on earth was I going to explain to a corporal of the Turkish Army what a Bronze Age galley of Greek origin was doing trespassing on the western end of a military zone. I could remember only a few courtesy phrases of Turkish, and I doubted that a Turkish-English phrase book would be adequate to explaining the situation.

Putting on my most cheerful expression, I held out my hand. '*Merhaba* – welcome,' I said breezily. The corporal's brown Anatolian eyes gazed back at me stolidly. He was a block of muscle and bone, the very epitome of the hardened non-commissioned officer, determined to carry out his orders precisely, to do everything by the book. I noticed that his hair was cropped bristle-short underneath his beret, and even in the baking heat every button on his tunic was fastened in the correct fashion, right up to the collar. The corporal refused the handshake. Instead he raised his arm and pointed at my ship.

'*Ar-go*?!' he announced slowly. I was flabbergasted. How on earth did a corporal of the Turkish Army, patrolling this godforsaken spot on a remote island, know about *Argo*? It was incomprehensible. But a wave of relief swept over me. If the soldier knew the name *Argo*, then he was not about to arrest us for trespass.

We never learned the corporal's name, because neither he nor his companion spoke a word of any language other than Turkish. But we did persuade the corporal to come out to *Argo*, and he stiffly accepted a cup of coffee for himself and some biscuits for his dog, who loyally swam out behind the rubber boat. Officially, therefore, the corporal did his duty. There was no landing on Gokce. He stood guard over us until we were ready to leave, and then we put him ashore again with another packet of biscuits for the private, who had stood immobile all this time, his gun unwaveringly aimed at *Argo*.

Two hours later, as we rowed along the Gokce coast, a gunboat of the Turkish Coastguard came racing over the horizon. It headed straight for *Argo*, swerved aside, and then came churning past us, its crew mustered on deck and all standing at attention while whistles blew a formal naval salute.

'Welcome to Turkey!' boomed an amplified voice over the ship's loudhailer. It was the gunboat commander on his bridge. 'Do you need any help?'

'No. No, thank you very much. Everything is fine. But it's very nice to see you.'

The gunboat loomed over us, its engines bellowing. 'I've been sent to escort you, and give you any help you need. . . .'

Lieutenant Asaf Gunegren, commander of Patrol Boat No. 33, spoke excellent English and was a very likeable young naval officer. He came aboard *Argo* to meet the new Argonauts and accept our hospitality. Apparently all those letters I had sent with the help of

Port steering oar

the Turkish Yachting Federation so long ago had been read in government offices in Turkey, considered and acted upon. Alpay Cin of the Federation and his friends had worked wonders. The Ministry of the Interior, the Sports Ministry, the Ministry of Tourism and the civic authorities had made up their minds to assist *Argo* in every possible way and – for a start – had dispatched Patrol Boat No. 33 to look after us. Asaf had been scouring the coast for the last two days, and alerted the Gokce garrison to look out for us. 'That's how the corporal must have known the name of your boat,' he explained with a boyish grin.

We were sitting on *Argo*'s stern deck. The crew had taken a break from rowing, and *Argo* was anchored close off one of Gokce's sandy beaches. While we were chatting, a group of men in tracksuits appeared on the sand dunes and came jogging down onto the beach. They seemed to be on holiday. Some played volleyball, others went for a walk along the beach; and one burly figure plunged into the sea and swam out to within hailing distance of *Argo*.

'Who are those men?' I asked Asaf. 'Are they part of the island garrison or are they on holiday?'

'I don't know who they are,' he replied, 'but I'll find out for you.'

He shouted to the swimmer, who called back and swam closer. There followed a lengthy conversation in Turkish before the swimmer gave a last shout and swam strongly back to his beach.

'Well?' I asked Asaf. 'Who was he?'

Asaf paused. 'As a matter of fact, he's a prisoner,' he replied.

'A what?'

'He says that good prisoners, of the first category, are sent to live on Gokce. They must stay here.'

'What did you talk to him about?'

'He wanted to know who you were, and what you were all doing. So I told him that you had come from Greece and were rowing all the way to the Black Sea.'

'What did he say to that?'

'He said he'd rather stay on Gokce than have to row your boat!'

The gunboat left *Argo* after lunch and went back to the mainland to refuel. Lieutenant Asaf promised to return next afternoon to see how we were getting on. When he did come back, twenty-four hours later, he must have been very perplexed. He had left *Argo* halfway along the south coast of Gokce, rowing doggedly eastward with her under-strength crew. Yet the next day at much the same time he found us still at the oars, still heaving away, but in exactly the same spot. It was as though *Argo* had been stuck in treacle. What had happened was my second miscalculation of the Dardanelles current. Throughout the first afternoon we had rowed eastward, having a gruelling time against a headwind. At nightfall the wind had eased and, totally exhausted, the crew had lain down to spend the night on the oar benches, as we had done the previous night and off Cape Poseidon. There was a flat calm, and the boat lay motionless on the water. The night watches were peaceful; there were a few lights on Gokce Island, which seemed to be the moving lights of vehicles. Then, to my intense chagrin, as the sun rose I recognized the cove nearly abeam of *Argo*. It was the same cove where we had anchored on reaching Gokce twenty-four hours earlier. During the night the current out of the Dardanelles had silently and inexorably carried us backwards. All the previous day's labour, hour after hour of rowing, had been squandered. Tactfully, no one said anything, but I vowed to myself that never again would I let *Argo* drift at night in an unlit area where there was no way of judging what tricks the current might be playing. It took half the next day to recoup the loss, and now – the fifth day since we had last been able to obtain food – our stock of supplies and water was running low. The only replenishment was a case of beer that Asaf dropped off, a kind deed which subsequently gave rise to a rumour on the mainland that *Argo*'s slow progress was due to the fact that all her crew were drunk.

Indeed I was becoming rather worried. With a crew of only fifteen, there was a real doubt in my mind whether *Argo* would be able to row up against the powerful current once we entered the mouth of the Dardanelles. We simply did not have enough oarsmen on board. Every mile we advanced towards the entrance of the straits, the stronger became the current against us. If we succeeded in rounding the tip of the Gallipoli peninsula and entering the main channel, we could expect to meet the full force of a hostile current which might run up to 3 or 4 knots. Against that obstacle *Argo*'s reduced crew could probably exert only a little over one horsepower.

We were saved by the most extraordinary wind, a changing wind that might have been whistled up specially for us. Starting as we rowed across the final gap between Gokce and the Gallipoli peninsula, it came from the east, directly astern of us. Gratefully we spread the sail and made for land, expecting to anchor when we got there. But when we were no more than 50 metres from the peninsula shore the wind abruptly changed to the north, again exactly the best direction for us to sail around the tip of the peninsula. So I turned *Argo* to run the mile or so down the coast to the lighthouse that marked the end of Gallipoli's spit.

Once again, Turkish soldiers watched us – tiny figures standing on the clifftops by the gun emplacements that guard the straits. As *Argo* circled the point, keeping just beyond the barbed wire entanglements that run down into the sea, the wind again swung round, switching to the opposite direction to the one it had been blowing an hour before. It was uncanny. Once again it was the ideal wind. I turned *Argo* to double the point and entered the Dardanelles strait itself, all sail set, and the crew with nothing to do but sit and watch one of the great maritime spectacles of the world.

To our left was the long whaleback ridge of the Gallipoli peninsula itself, with its succession of monuments to the French, British, Australian and Turkish war dead of the bloody campaigns of the First World War. On the opposite bank the ground ran for about a mile, a flat, featureless shore, and then began to climb up to a distant escarpment. On that hill lay the ruins of Troy, the city which had controlled the trade of the Dardanelles in the Bronze Age. Even today that same commercial and strategic importance is just as evident. As far as the eye could see, commercial shipping was arriving and leaving through the straits – tankers, bulk carriers, general cargo boats, fishing vessels, ferries, cruise ships.

As our twenty-oared warship out of history sailed jauntily up the straits, modern warships came down on us in procession. A Soviet submarine was running on the surface, escorted southward by two Turkish naval destroyers; a squadron of Turkish Navy warships was manoeuvring on the horizon, and no fewer than four patrol boats of the Turkish Coastguard were in sight at one time. Three were engaged on routine patrol duties, but the fourth was our own, Gunboat No. 33, standing over us and warning all this shipping to give little *Argo* a wide berth. By general accord, Asaf and his men were given three cheers and we made Asaf an honorary Argonaut.

The massive arch which is the Turkish War Memorial on Gallipoli was the mark I used to steer *Argo* towards the opposite shore, and slant across the main current. Even with the fine southwest breeze pushing her at more than 5 knots through the water, the galley barely crawled forward in relation to the land. We had scarcely come within a quarter of a mile of the shore and entered slack water there, when our heaven-sent wind finally and abruptly died away. It had done its work. A baking stillness enveloped us, and the crew took up their oars to row to the spot where a little cluster of Turkish officials was waiting on shore to greet us. It seemed that nothing was too much trouble for the Turkish authorities. The officials had come specially from Canakkale, the port of entry, in order to give *Argo* her customs, health and immigration clearance. As the rubber dinghy ferried the officials out, the Argonauts could wait no longer. There were fourteen loud splashes as the oarsmen dived overboard and swam ashore to go racing up the beach and set foot in Asia.

For two more days we waited in the Dardanelles, cleaning up ourselves and *Argo*. It was difficult to decide which was the more travel-worn – the boat or her crews. *Argo* was unloaded of every last item, and we scraped foul-smelling black slime from her bilges. Then the crew themselves were similarly overhauled in the public *hamam*, or Turkish bath, of Canakkale. Nothing could have been better suited to getting rid of a week's grime and unknotting the aching muscles of oarsmen than to immerse themselves in steam and hot water on the marble slabs. By the time I eventually got to the *hamam* the rest of the crew had departed. But Turkish hospitality was vigilant. As I collected my bath towel in the lobby a brawny Turk, wearing only a towel and sitting reading a newspaper by the cash desk, looked up and recognized me. 'Aaah! Captain Tim!' He gave a slow grin that revealed a mouthful of broken teeth. He was the bath masseur, and determined to show his skill, so I was obliged to spend the next half hour on a marble slab, being twisted, torn, pummelled, trodden on and wrenched into every possible contortion until finally the masseur flipped over my limp and tortured body, threw a smart salute, and rapped out, 'Finish, captain!' which indeed I was.

Peter Dobbs' holiday had ended, and another Peter came to replace him, Peter Warren, an ex-Marine from Oxfordshire. He had rowed on *Argo*'s delivery voyage, and so enjoyed the camaraderie that he had decided to rejoin the main expedition. We also took on our first Turkish volunteers. Deniz was a twenty-three-year-old archaeology student with all the energy and enthusiasm of a terrier. Umur, by contrast, arrived looking so glum that I couldn't imagine why he was there. It turned out that he had been sent by his father, a mining engineer, who felt that since his eighteen-year-old son was having to retake his examinations, a spell on a twenty-oared galley might give him a new way of looking at life. As a result Umur started out as a very quiet and retiring young member of the crew. But as time went on, his attitude changed. Originally he said he would come with us only as far as Istanbul, but when we got there he volunteered a second time, and finished up by going on the entire Turkish sector of the voyage, a very gallant effort indeed. Erzin was the third of our new volunteers. He was the captain of a 150,000-ton supertanker operating from Turkey to the Arabian Gulf, so it must have been a great change pulling an oar on an 8-ton galley. But Erzin, a former officer in the Turkish Navy, was one of those people whom everyone likes instantly. He was an excellent seaman and a first-class shipmate. The two remaining Turkish volunteers were old friends. Ali was a marine archaeologist and diver; a serious and scholarly person, he was to be my guide and interpreter throughout the Turkish voyage. At sixteen, Kaan was the youngest of any of the Argonauts during the entire expedition. He was the son of an Istanbul family I had known for twenty-three years. His father, Irgun, had befriended me and my companions when, as college students, we had visited Turkey on motorcycles during my first expedition, to follow the route of Marco Polo. I had never lost touch with the family, and when Irgun learned that I was coming to Turkey with *Argo* he immediately sent his son to join us. Kaan, it transpired, had already done some rowing with one of Istanbul's boat clubs, and thought it all a great adventure.

In theory there should have been two more Turkish volunteers to join the crew, as *Argo* needed maximum oar-power if she was to get the rest of the way up the Dardanelles, where the current ran even more strongly. In fact two extra Turkish oarsmen did turn up in Canakkale, and they helped us move *Argo* from one side of the straits to the other where we were to have an official reception by the governor. It was a short, energetic crossing – only a mile and a half of water, but it took nearly two hours of rowing flat out to get across the racing current. When the two volunteers then failed to show up for the evening meal, the other Turks roared with laughter. 'They took one look at the job, and thought about the 190 miles to Istanbul, and decided that the trip's not for them. They've run away!'

The governor of Canakkale's official reception for *Argo* was the first of a whole series of civic welcomes that had been organized by the local authorities all along our route. A team of dancers performed on the quayside to the drone of pipes and the clatter of a Turkish drum. Boy dancers dressed in baggy shorts with half-gaiters in black embroidered with gold, and waistcoats over matching shirts, leaped and pranced and shouted. The girls dipped and swayed and linked arms, their costume an elegant combination of long flowing pantaloons and soft slippers, aprons and full blouses. On their heads were handkerchiefs sewn with jewellery which tinkled and swayed in time with the music.

The ancient Greeks had called the Dardanelles the Hellespont, for this is where Princess Helle had slipped from the back of the flying ram with the Golden Fleece and drowned in the sea. When the first *Argo* came this way, following the course of the flying ram on its way to Colchis, Jason and his companions had slunk through the straits under cover of darkness, probably to avoid attracting the attention of the Trojans who resented intruders who might bypass their commercial monopoly. 'Just as the sun was setting they reached the foreland of the Chersonese [the tip of the Gallipoli peninsula],' wrote Apollonius.

> There they met a strong wind from the south, set their sail to it and entered the swift current of Hellespont, which takes its name from Athamas' daughter. By dawn they had left the northern sea; by nightfall they were coasting the Rhoetean shore, inside the Straits, with the land of Ida [Mount Ida] on their right. Leaving Dardania behind, they set course for Abydos, and after they had passed in turn Percote, Abarnis with its sandy beach, and sacred Pityeia, before dawn *Argo* by dint of sail and oar was through the darkly swirling Hellespont.

I could scarcely believe the modern *Argo*'s weather luck when she too picked up exactly the same wind – a strong southerly – as we cleared Canakkale harbour and breasted the 'darkly swirling Hellespont'. Normally the wind blows from the north in May and June, but here we had a splendid fresh breeze from the southwest, occasionally rising to just short of gale force, and blowing directly up the Straits in our favour. *Argo* responded by giving us the best day's sail of the entire voyage. She ran like a dolphin with the following sea. Rhythmically she first buried her snout deep in the water, pressed down by the weight of sail so that the sea was rushing past her half-submerged eyes. Then like a sea beast coming up for a breath of air, her snout began to rise towards the surface, boring upward through the rushing water, bubbles streaming, until the tip of the ram broke surface in a fine welter of foam, spurting a foot in the air. A second later followed twin jets of water gushing out to port and starboard from the handhold in the snout, just like an animal clearing its nostrils with a whoosh of air. There *Argo* would hang suspended for a moment, her long hull thrusting out of the body of the wave until the crest passed and she began the cycle once again, the nose starting to dip and bury itself in the rushing sea.

For hour after hour she maintained this motion at a steady 6–7 knots as she scoured her way up the Dardanelles until, just like her predecessor, she had swum the entire length of the straits and entered the Sea of Marmara, the sea the Greeks called Propontis, the vestibule to the Black Sea itself. As Apollonius wrote:

> In Propontis there is an island sloping steeply to the sea, close to the rich mainland of Phrygia, and parted from it only by a low isthmus barely raised above the waves. The isthmus, with its two shores, lies east of the river Aesepus; and the place itself is called Bear Mountain by the people round about. . . . *Argo* pressing on with a stiff breeze from Thrace behind her, reached the coast and ran into a harbour called Fair Haven. Here, on the advice of Tiphys, they [the Argonauts] discarded their small anchor stone and left it at the Spring of Artace, replacing it with a heavier and more suitable rock.

Today, the peninsula which Apollonius called Bear Mountain is known as Kapidag or Door Mountain, and the harbour he knew as Fair Haven has adopted the name of the sacred spring itself – Artace – now written in its Turkish version, Erdek. *Argo* dropped anchor there in the early hours of 27 May, and the next morning I walked just half a mile to the spot where, 3000 years earlier, the first Argonauts had left their anchor stone as a thanks-offering.

By an extraordinary piece of luck – a chance meeting six weeks earlier – I knew exactly where to look for the place which had once been called 'Jason's Spring'. A tipsy crew and a bout of bad weather

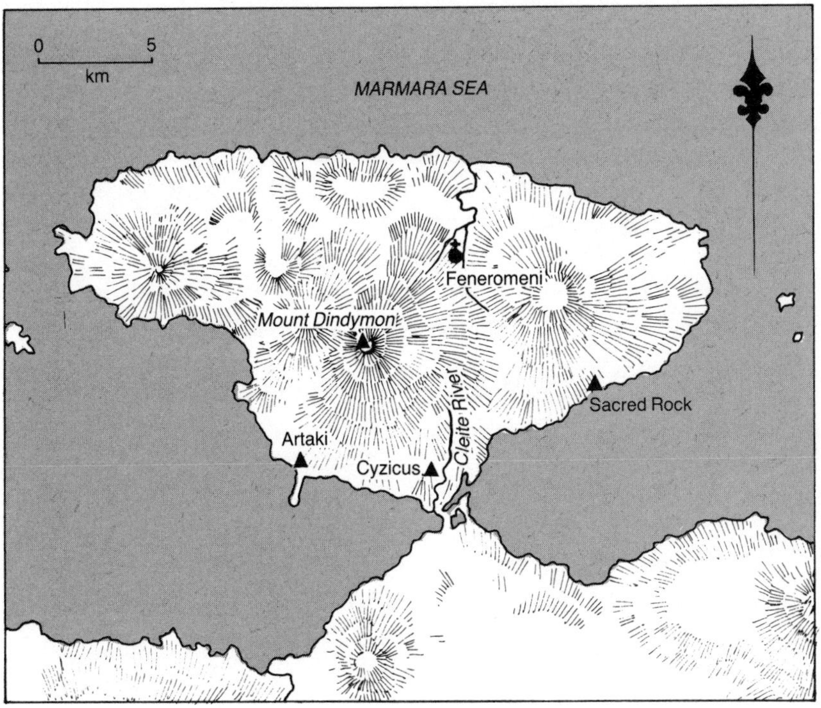

had led me to the discovery. We had been making the delivery voyage of *Argo* from her building place at Spetses northward along the Peloponnese coast to Volos. Our route lay through the channel between the Greek mainland and the large island of Evvia. The weather had been atrocious – cold, rainy and blustery. In fine seagoing tradition several members of the delivery crew had fortified themselves against the elements in a harbourside taverna in the town of Khalkis. They came back aboard in no fit state to row, and shortly after leaving harbour we encountered a gale from the north. For the safety of the vessel and her more incapacitated crew members I ran *Argo* for shelter into the first small harbour in sight. It was certainly not a place I had planned to visit, but with the wind gusting and the rain slashing diagonally across the straits we were glad to moor *Argo* and take refuge in an empty outbuilding, waiting there like wet hens for the weather to improve.

Only then did I notice the name of the little port. It was called Nea Artaki – New Artaki – and I recalled the name of the spring sacred to the goddess Artaki where Jason had left his anchor stone. I went into the town to check whether there was any connection between this modern small port in Evvia and the spring on the peninsula in the Sea of Marmara. At the fishermen's cooperative I was told that New Artaki had been founded by the Greeks who came back from the original Artaki or Erdek during the exchange of population between the Greeks and the Turks in the early 1920s. This information was a complete surprise. Was there, I asked, anyone, by any chance, who still remembered the old life in the days when the Greeks had lived at Erdek, someone who could tell me of the folk tales and traditions of the area? The fishermen, also storm-bound, had plenty of time to consult with one another, and they agreed that there was a sole survivor whom I should talk to – Vasilis Kalatheri.

'Do you think that he would be willing to talk to me about his memories of the old days in Artaki?' I asked. 'Perhaps he is too old now, and does not remember clearly.'

'Oh no, you can judge for yourself,' I was told. 'Vasilis is a remarkable person. Since leaving Artaki he has travelled all over the world. He knows many things, and he remembers his life very clearly.'

Jason's Spring

Mount Dindymun

Later that evening I went to the café where it had been arranged for me to meet Vasilis Kalatheri. He was indeed one of those remarkable people who succeed in living to a great age without losing their faculties. He had been born in 1892, and lived in Erdek until he was in his late twenties, and he remembered every detail of that early life. First I asked him if he knew any place in Erdek that was connected with the story of Jason and the Argonauts. Immediately he knew what I meant. Of course, he replied, there is the spring that everyone had called Artaki Krini or Iason Krini – the spring of Artace or the spring of Jason. It was very well known, though some people had begun to call it Pagatho.

Where was this spring? You had only to follow the main path that led up from the harbour for about a kilometre and a half, and that would bring you directly to Jason's spring. When he was a young man, everybody took it for granted that this was the spring where the Argonauts had left their anchor stone. In fact, said Vasilis, in 1906 a British yacht had visited the port, and in the night sent some men to carry away the stone itself. The stone had been round, and was split open down the middle, and inside there had been some sort of writing that no one was able to read. How would I be able to recognize the spring, I asked. It was quite easy, the old man told me. When I got there, I would find two large fig trees and two chestnut trees growing beside it.

In Erdek, six weeks later and 300 miles away from that conversation with the old man at the café table, I found that only one gnarled fig tree remained of the four trees that Vasilis had last seen sixty years before. The others had been cut down when a local farmer extended his olive grove closer to the fountain. A jet of water still splashed out from the spout and dropped into a trough. Turkish women brought their carpets to scrub, children played in the puddles, and the carters of Erdek stopped here for their horses to drink. Once again it was obvious that favourite watering places had played a vital role in the voyages of the Bronze Age explorers. Knowing where to find good, clean water to replenish a galley with its large and thirsty crew was an essential part of a pilot's job, and, as we had seen at Aphissos, such watering places became the fixed points of a coasting tradition. They became fixed points in folk memory, too. The Mycenaeans had believed in springs of water and groves of trees as sacred places, a common feature of animistic belief. A spring sacred to the goddess Artace was a natural place to leave an anchor stone as a thanks-offering for a voyage safely accomplished so far, and the habit of dedicating the anchor stone of a ship was known in ancient Egypt as well as in Greece. Of course it was not Artace who was the goddess of the spring in Jason's time; she was a more recent invention, part of the classical Greek pantheon. In Jason's day the spring would have been sacred to the Great Goddess herself, the Mother Goddess, whose earth-mother role was inherited by Artace. His offering harked back to a far more primeval spirit world.

Nor had that spirit world entirely vanished from Erdek, even in the twentieth century. Just half a mile farther up the path from Jason's Spring was a sacred grove, a place that felt perhaps rather as Jason's Spring would have done when the Argonauts came there. It was a spinney of enormous, venerable chestnut trees, isolated on the side of a low swell in the ground. Another water source broke out from the side of the hill and ran through a natural channel before being led out through a double spout into a basin, and then sliding away down the slope towards some orchards. All around the land was densely cultivated, but this grove of trees had not been touched. It had been left strictly alone, though not shunned. It was a holy place, and felt like it. A great calm seemed to envelop the spot. There was absolutely no sound except the burble of the water and an occasional burst of birdsong. The leaves of the great trees themselves were totally silent. Even the air was cool to the skin. It seemed as if all time was suspended, and here, in the middle of the grove beside the brook, was a great tree so ancient that its heart had rotted away. A tunnel had opened through its great trunk. The sides of the tunnel gleamed, polished slick by the passage of human bodies, over and over again, crawling through the hole in the heart of the tree. It was a wishing tree. At night, I was told, the country people would come secretly to this sacred spot to invoke its magic. They would circle the ancient tree the prescribed number of times and then crawl through the tunnel, making their wish. If they performed the ceremony correctly, the spirits of the place would grant their desire. The supplicants had left tokens on the wishing tree, and its lower branches were hung with strips of cloth torn from their clothes, and little human effigies. The old beliefs, it seemed, still lingered after 3000 years.

Resit Ertezun, the historian of Erdek, was glad to have the identity of Artaki Krini confirmed. He had first come to Erdek in May 1946 as its governor. One day he had noticed pieces of white stone glittering in the surface of a new road that was being built. On inquiry, he was told that some of the new roadstone had been quarried from the ancient ruins of the city of Cyzicus nearby. He went to inspect the ruins, the remains of a Roman city, and that visit changed his life. Forbidding all further robbing of Cyzicus, he began to study the ancient history of the peninsula called Kapidag. He taught himself Latin and Greek in order to be able to read Apollonius and the other authors in the original, and to research the historical background of the Argonaut legend. Now he was the perfect guide to escort the new Argonauts around the sites which he had identified with the early legend.

Soon after Jason and his companions arrived in Kapidag they were met by King Cyzicus, leader of the Doliones, the tribe inhabiting the lowland at the isthmus joining Kapidag to the mainland. King Cyzicus was a young man of about Jason's age, and recently married. His wife, Cleite, had only just arrived from the mainland. Cyzicus invited the Argonauts to shift their boat to the harbour of his city, and to feast with him. During the festivities, according to Apollonius, a wild tribe of aborigines – said to be men with six arms – descended from the interior highlands and attacked *Argo* in her harbour. They were driven off by Hercules (who according to Apollonius was still with the expedition, and would not leave it until the next stage of their journey) and suffered heavy losses.

After the feasting was over, *Argo* put to sea. She sailed out into the Marmara and began rounding the peninsula, only to be hit by a gale which drove her back to land where the crew managed to get a mooring line around a rock at a place they called the Sacred Harbour. What the storm-tossed mariners did not realize was that they had been driven back on to the Kapidag peninsula, and were again in the territory of the Doliones. In the darkness the latter mistook the Argonauts for a band of sea raiders and attacked them. A bloody skirmish followed. Several leading Doliones were cut down and, worse yet, Jason himself killed King Cyzicus without realizing who he was. Dawn revealed the ghastly mistake, and the two sides promptly broke off battle. The shocked Doliones withdrew into their city wall, bearing the corpse of the dead king with them, and the appalled Argonauts set about expiating the terrible crime of killing the man who had been their host only recently.

> For three whole days they and the Doliones wailed for him [King Cyzicus] and tore their hair. Then they marched three times round the dead king in their bronze equipment, laid him in his tomb, and held the customary games out on the grassy plain, where the barrow they raised for him can still be seen by people of a later age.

Cleite, the king's new bride, so Apollonius continues, was unable to face life alone, with her husband in the grave. Capping the evil she had suffered with a worse one of her own devising, she took a rope and hanged herself by the neck. Her death was bewailed even by the woodland nymphs, who caused the many tears they shed to unite in a spring which the people called Cleite in memory of a peerless but unhappy bride.

Resit suggested that King Cyzicus' burial mould could be the large burial tumulus which lies a few miles south of the isthmus, near the town of Bandirma, and which has yet to be excavated. 'Cleite's Spring' is the stream that meanders through the Roman ruins of the city of Cyzicus, named to commemorate the dead Doliones leader. The spring runs through the exact centre of the huge Roman amphitheatre whose jackdaw-infested ruins now dominate cherry orchards and fields of mulberry bushes. In the great days of the ancient city, the spring could be dammed so that it filled the entire floor of the amphitheatre, and mock sea battles were performed by actors in model ships to amuse the audience.

For twelve days after King Cyzicus' funeral, Jason and his

companions were pinned on the Kapidag coast by bad weather, and Resit was confident that he had identified the Sacred Rock around which *Argo*'s hawser had been tied. There was only one offshore rock that would fit the description, and Resit took us to the place that the present inhabitants call Black Rock. Local fishermen still used it as a port of refuge, for it gave good shelter from the northerly wind and waves. The end of the twelve-day period of storms was announced to the seer Mopsus by the arrival of a halcyon or kingfisher which fluttered over Jason's head as he lay asleep on the beach. Mopsus, who understood the language of birds, could interpret the omen. He told the Argonauts that they should now climb to the holy peak of Mount Dindymun in the centre of the island, and make a sacrifice to Rhea, the Great Mother Goddess.

> Leaving a few of their comrades in the ship, they [the Argonauts] climbed the mountain. From the summit they could see the Macrian Heights, and the whole length of the opposite Thracian Coast – it almost seemed that they could touch it. And far away on the one side they saw the misty entrance to the Bosphorus and the Mysian Hills, and on the other the flowing waters of Aesepus and the Nepeian Plain of Adresteia.

Here Argus the shipwright made a sacred image of the Great Goddess, carving it from the trunk of an ancient vine. This statue the Argonauts set up on a rocky point under the shelter of some tall oaks trees, and made an altar of small stones nearby. Then they crowned themselves with oak leaves and made the ritual sacrifices to the goddess Rhea, beseeching her to send the storms elsewhere. Finally, to the music of Orpheus 'the young men in full armour moved around in a high-stepping dance, beating their shields with their swords' to drown the ill-omened wailing and grief that still came up from the city where the Doliones were mourning their king. As a sign of her favour, Apollonius continues, the Great Goddess made the trees shed abundant fruit, and the wild beasts left their lairs and came forward wagging their tails. Moreover, a spring gushed out of the ground where no running water had been seen before.

Resit accompanied us up into the central hills of Kapidag to try to identify the sacred Mount Dindymun, but what had seemed a fairly easy task turned out to be decidedly baffling. The central upland was dotted with various peaks that were much the same height, and we went from one to the other hoping to identify the spot where simultaneously we could see to the Bosphorus, across to Thrace on the other side of the Sea of Marmara, and back down to the Dardanelles whence we had come. The existence of the miraculous spring of water was of little help. We came across at least five small water sources seeping out in the high glens. The most likely peak, we eventually decided, was the point which the Turks called Grandfather Mountain or Dedebayr, the highest summit in Kapidag.

Kapidag coast village

In a pleasant wooded valley to the northeast of the Grandfather Mountain were the ruins of a Greek monastery – the Cherry Monastery, as the Turks now call it, but which was once the monastery of Feneromani. In the early part of this century a Cambridge professor made the interesting observation that the people of the district performed a curious ceremony that may have been a folk memory of the Argonauts' mystic dance around the altar of the goddess Rhea. According to Professor Hazluck, the priests of the monastery would parade every year a sacred icon of the Virgin in the presence of the people of the peninsula. This icon, which was said to have had magic powers, could heal the sick and the lame, and sometimes it would be seized by a man in a religious ecstasy who would run ahead of the crowd with it, crying out and leaping in a frenzy as he ran up into the mountains, while the people all followed him. The professor suggested that perhaps this echoed the ecstatic dance of the Argonauts around the altar to the Earth Mother.

Today the monastery lies in ruins, and the famous icon has vanished. No one in Erdek knew what had become of it – rumour said it was carried away to Istanbul. I, however, knew its real whereabouts, for old Vasilis Kalatheri had also answered that question for me. He told me that the ceremony used to take place every May when he was a young man. Almost the entire population of Erdek would walk across the peninsula to visit the monastery, and the priests would emerge, holding up the icon, and calling 'Hooo! Hooo!' while the crowd followed them. Vasilis had never seen a fanatic snatch the icon and run into the mountains. But he certainly knew where it was now. When the Greeks left Erdek, he told me, they went secretly to the monastery and carried away the icon, and hid it so that they could take it with them when they left. And that evening he showed it to me: it hangs in the raw, new church of Nea Artaki.

Modern *Argo*'s departure from Kapidag was a subdued version of the departure by Jason and his crew. We had been warned that the sea passage around the peninsula was notorious for rough seas and dangerous gusts of wind. Barely had we gone one-third of the way around Kapidag than we were forced to double back and run for shelter, coming so close inshore as we scuttled for harbour that *Argo*'s port steering oar bumped across the rocks with a horrible grating sound. That impact, as it turned out, was to spell trouble for us later on.

After waiting a full day for the gale to cease, we laboured out, rowing through the swell towards the east until we cleared the peninsula and could pick our route along the southern shore of the Sea of Marmara. On 3 June Mark, who had been calculating the number of oar strokes, announced that each oarsman had now completed 100,000 strokes since leaving Volos. A great cheer went up from the crew. This milestone was reached late in the evening, as we were struggling to get to the uninhabited Fener Ada islands for night anchorage. As we rowed, all around us the phosphorescence was stirred into small whirlpools by the oar blades, and below the boat a plume of phosphorescence curled away underwater from the steering oar like a submarine coxcomb. We crept into the anchorage, a deep bay surrounded by cliffs, and our probing torch beams awoke immense numbers of screaming seabirds roosting on the rocks, until they fluttered back and forward in the torchlight like flakes of snow.

Once again we were sharing the experiences of the first Argonauts. This was where, according to Apollonius, the favourable wind had deserted Jason and his men, and they had been forced to row through the hot, long day until everyone was drooping at the oar handles. In the same area we suffered the very same experience. We laboured on, with blistered hands and aching muscles. *Argo* seemed to creep slug-like across the flat, burnished sea. The rhythm of the oars grew slower and slower, as boredom and fatigue set in. I detected a slight counter-current setting against us, and the hazy outline of the land seemed to unroll with agonizing slowness as we clawed along the Marmara shore.

Each day we followed the same grinding routine. We rose at dawn, had a light breakfast, and then took up the oars to begin rowing until noon. Then there was a half-hour break for lunch, before the rowing began once more, on and on, until the sun began to set. Then we headed for the nearest beach, and tried to find a temporary resting place for the night on sand or shingle or perhaps a disused café floor.

Somewhere on this coast, according to Apollonius, Hercules had finally left Jason's team. It was after their most exhausting day of rowing, when the entire crew was so tired that only Hercules and Jason himself had the strength left to row *Argo* to land. At that moment the mighty Hercules had snapped his oar in anger at the weakness of his shipmates. On coming to land he strode off to tear up a small tree and make himself a replacement blade. While he was gone from the Argonaut camp, his squire, Hylas, set off to fetch water. The young man came to a spring called Pegae, and as he leaned over to fill the bronze pitcher, the water nymph of the pool was so entranced by Hylas' beauty that she fell in love with him and determined to keep him. Reaching up, she put her arms around him and drew him down into the water, never to be seen again. Another Argonaut, Polyphemus from Larissa in Thessaly, happened to hear Hylas cry as he was drowning, and went to look for him. He met Hercules on the path, and the two men began to hunt for the missing boy.

Hercules was distraught, and ran here and there calling Hylas' name. Just then a favourable breeze sprang up and Tiphys, the experienced helmsman, decided that it should not be wasted. He ordered the Argonauts to put to sea. Only after *Argo* had made some distance was it noticed that Hercules, Hylas and Polyphemus were not on board. Some of the Argonauts, led by Telamon, a good friend of Hercules, wanted to put back at once and collect them. Another faction, led by Calais and Zetes, the Sons of the North Wind, said no: the gods had sent the favourable breeze as a sign, and it should not be squandered. *Argo* should proceed without the missing men. A quarrel flared up, and soon it was too late to turn back. *Argo* went on without Hercules.

The exact spot where Hylas drowned while going to fetch water is impossible to define. The details about the pool of Pegae are too scanty, and the low ground along the south Marmara shore between Kapidag and the Gulf of Cius is soggy with marshes, springs and even hot mineral waters. According to Greek tradition, Hercules stayed on for some time in the area, continuing his vain hunt for Hylas. When he finally relinquished the search, because he had to go on with his Labours, he forced the people of the area to continue to look. In later years they would hold an annual festival when the young men would go running through the forest calling out 'Hylas! Hylas!' Polyphemus, it is said, founded the city of Cius; and Calais and Zetes, who had advocated leaving Hercules behind on shore, were to suffer the consequences. When the quest for the Golden Fleece was over, and the Argonauts had returned to their homes, Hercules tracked down the Sons of the North Wind and exacted his revenge.

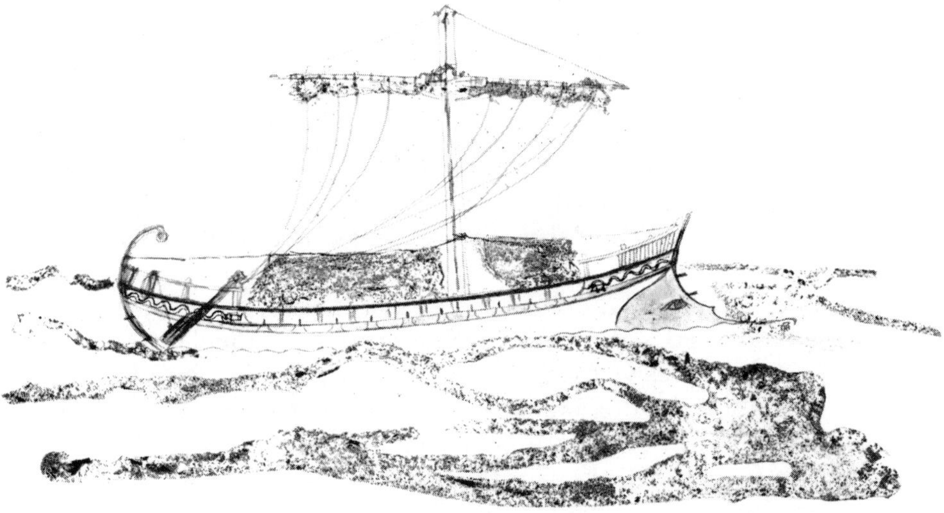

6
Rowing up the Bosphorus

At 6 feet 5 inches Jonathan Cloke was the tallest Argonaut of all. He arrived on 5 June, shortly before *Argo* reached the mouth of the Bosphorus, so he was in time to reinforce the crew for their attempt to row up the straits against the currents and challenge the theory that such a feat was impossible for a late Bronze Age ship. In terms of sheer muscle power, I reckoned that we now stood at least as good a chance of succeeding as anyone. The majority of the new Argonauts were big men, at least 6 feet tall and extremely strong. Of the smaller men, Mark was of course the experienced rowing master and an expert with the oar; Peter Wheeler's stamina as the marathon man was very obvious; and Trondur was a natural sea oarsman, toughened by years of rowing small boats in the rough waters around the Faeroe Islands as well as rock climbing for birds' eggs on the ledges of the Faeroese cliffs.

In addition we were joined at Istanbul by a former curragh-racing champion from Ireland. Curraghs are the small, canvas-covered skiffs peculiar to the west coast of Ireland. They are descended from the original skin-covered native boats which, as early as Roman times, ranged the wild Atlantic coasts, and they are still used by the fishermen as tenders and for netting and lobster fishing. Every summer, at small harbours in the west of Ireland, these fishermen compete in a series of curragh regattas to select the toughest, fastest crew. It is a vividly fought series, conducted with considerable betting and a dash of skullduggery, and the race is started with alarming realism by the umpire firing a shotgun over the heads of the contestants. Two years earlier the winning crew had included Cormac O'Connor, first mate on an Irish trawler. Now he arrived in Istanbul, ready to row for the Argonauts. He was 6 feet 3 inches tall, weighed 216 lb and wore an extra, extra large size in sailing oilskins.

Jonathan's sporting nature was quickly put to the test. He allowed himself to be talked into entering a wrestling match. But this was no ordinary match, nor did he have an ordinary opponent. Jonathan was to compete at Turkish oil wrestling, and he was to wrestle against the Turkish national champion in the heavyweight class.

Jonathan

The reason for this unexpected contest was that a major Turkish newspaper was taking a very keen interest in the progress of *Argo*. Every couple of days an enthusiastic Turkish journalist would show up to check on our condition and interview the crew. Some of his reports were spectacularly wrong. By a mix-up in translations he had understood that our doctor, Nick, who worked as an anaesthetist in hospital life, was a hypnotist. So he informed his readers that Nick's crucial role was to hypnotize the Argonauts into a trance so that they were able to eat the food served aboard. This was a dreadful calumny, both on Nick who was a very conscientious and popular doctor from two expeditions, but above all on Pete the cook, who was having to defend his corner against hungry Argonauts who were highly complimentary of his cooking, and quite undeterred by the regular volley of oaths that greeted them from Pete when meals were ready to be collected from the foredeck.

The Turkish newspaper was determined to make *Argo*'s voyage a success. They had been advertising in their pages for Turkish volunteers to join the crew, acted as our mailbox, and produced a team of traditional dancers on the quayside when we docked at Istanbul's yacht club in the suburb of Fenerbache on 9 June. It was their idea to hold an oil wrestling match, which was meant to be a substitute for the famous boxing match held between the original Argonauts and the ferocious King Amycus of the Bebryces tribe.

According to the legend, Jason and his companions, after marooning Hercules, had taken advantage of a strong favourable wind to push on briskly towards the Bosphorus. A day and a night's sail duly brought them to a wide bay where they beached at dawn. Immediately they were accosted by Amycus, who had a reputation, according to Apollonius, as 'the world's greatest bully'. It was Amycus' habit to challenge any stranger who entered his territory to fight a boxing match with him. Amycus was a great brute of a man, an expert and deadly fighter, and in the vicious boxing style of the time he was capable of killing his opponent. Already he had killed several of his neighbours and the surrounding tribes lived in dread of him. Backed by his followers, he swaggered down to the Argonauts as they were disembarking on the beach, and announced that they would not be allowed to leave unless they put forward their champion to fight him. Pollux, who was the boxing champion of Greece, took this as a personal affront, and immediately accepted the challenge. The two men, according to the story, were complete opposites – Pollux was young, lithe and skilled; Amycus was older, surly, and like a bull in his tactics. The two were to fight wearing toughened gloves of hardened rawhide which, on the hands of an expert, were lethal weapons. A suitable spot was selected; the gloves bound in place; and, watched by the two groups of supporters, Argonauts and Bebryces, the two champions fought it out to the death.

Amycus, relying on his greater strength and experience, charged at once into the attack, confident of overwhelming and crushing the younger man by sheer power. At first Pollux gave way before the heavyweight onslaught, eluding the tribal chief's furious rushes and relying on his own speed and technique to avoid Amycus' massive blows. But as soon as Pollux had gauged the measure of his opponent's skill and strength, he began to stand up to him, and the two men traded blow for blow, until exhaustion forced them to draw apart and rest, each panting for breath with the sweat pouring off them. Then they rushed together again and took up the fight, battering away to settle the outcome.

> Amycus, rising tiptoe like a man felling an ox, stretched up to his full height and brought his heavy fist down on the other. But Pollux dodged the blow by a turn of his head, taking the forearm on the edge of his shoulder. Then, closing warily, he landed a lightning blow above the ear, and smashed the bones inside. Amycus collapsed on his knees in agony; the Minyan lords [the Argonauts] raised a shout of triumph; and in a moment the man was dead.

The Bebryces took the defeat of their leader badly. They jumped up, drew their weapons and rushed at Pollux to cut him down. The Argonauts ran to the rescue and a pitched battle ensued on the beach: Castor, defending his twin, split the skull of the first attacker; and Pollux, still with plenty of fight left in him, took a running jump at Itymoneus, a huge Bebrycian, and kicked him in the wind so that he fell to the ground. A right-handed blow put Mimas, another Bebrycian warrior, out of action, the slashing edge of the rawhide glove tearing away the man's eyelid and leaving the eyeball exposed. One Argonaut, Talaus, was wounded in the side by a spear thrust, but not mortally. And Iphitus, another Argonaut, was badly shaken by a shrewd blow from a Bebrycian warclub. But both of the attackers were killed by other Argonauts, and then the Bebryces broke and ran, leaving the field to the battle-weary sailors.

Again, there are not enough details in the early text to allow a positive identification of the spot where the battle took place. The events read very much as though the Argonauts came up against a hostile tribe who resented the intrusion of strangers into their territory, and attacked them on the beach. It is logical that this battle could have taken place somewhere near the southern entrance to the Bosphorus or on its banks, where a local tribe either stopped strangers from passing through, or demanded some sort of toll. Certainly the Argonauts would have landed near the mouth of the Bosphorus or during their passage up the straits, simply to gather strength for the effort of rowing up against the current. A later tradition places the adventure of the boxing match with King Amycus on the east bank of the Bosphorus, at about its halfway point near modern Hisarlik, but does not explain why. The only clues as to the exact spot are the 'wide bay' where the Argonauts landed on the beach, and a bay tree around which they tied the hawsers of their ship. The bay tree became, by tradition, a tree which drove men into mad rages, possibly a reference to the berserk fighting style of the barbaric King Amycus.

Oil wrestlers

Fortunately for Jonathan Cloke, his contest with the Turkish wrestling champion was conducted in a rather more good-natured spirit. The spot picked for the oil wrestling match was a grassy field on the east bank of the Bosphorus at Fenerbache, near where *Argo* was a guest of the yacht club. Turkish oil wrestling is said to have originated as a sport for Turkish soldiers celebrating a military victory. After battle the troops would assemble around the parade ground and wrestle with one another simultaneously in a knockout competition. The part played by oil will be described in due course. Today the sport has been revived and is divided into several divisions, like boxing, ranging from heavyweight to juniors and flyweights.

The contest at Fenerbache was more of a light-hearted demonstration match than a championship bout, and an amused crowd of sightseers gathered under the trees. At least fifty oil wrestlers turned up to fight each other. Their costume was a special pair of low-cut breeches made of buffalo hide, tied at the knees. Otherwise the torso and feet were bare. As the wrestlers stood there, thumbs hooked into waistbands and muscles rippling, they looked suitably ferocious, and the most impressive of all, of course, was Jonathan's picked opponent, the heavyweight champion. A man of about forty-five, with close-cropped iron-grey hair, he was built like a locomotive. He had not an ounce of surplus weight, his muscles stood out in sculpted mounds, and he looked like a weathered rock on which the sea had beaten for centuries. His fighting name – Pire Cevat, which means Cevat the Flea – was picked out in brass studs on his breeches. At least, as I pointed out to Jonathan, the Turkish champion had a kindly face. 'Can I go home now?' Jonathan asked mournfully.

A master of ceremonies marshalled the wrestlers. Like a barker at a fairground he was expected to entertain and inform the spectators, as well as judge the contest. He was a short, barrel-shaped man, sporting a large flat hat, a loose white shirt, and an enormous pair of baggy grey pantaloons ornamented with black frogging down the side and girdled with a tasselled white scarf. In this outfit he stalked up and down the grassy ring with tremendous panache, calling out the rules of the contest and bellowing out the name of each wrestler, who stepped forward to take his bow. When he called Jonathan's name, the crowd gave a special cheer. Jonathan looked distinctly out of place in a pair of red sailor trousers rolled up to his knees instead of buffalo hide breeches. I asked my neighbour in the crowd what was the object of the contest. 'To pin your opponent's back to the ground, and offer his belly to the sky!' came the reply.

The master of ceremonies blew on a whistle, and the wrestlers advanced across the grass in the opening ceremony. This was pure theatre. They flexed and rippled their muscles, puffed out their chests, took huge, loping strides and tried to look as ferocious as possible. Every few paces each man would drop to one knee, offer up a short prayer, pick a handful of dust and touch it to his forehead in a formal act of obeisance. Then it was time to begin the contest. The wrestlers divided into pairs. A pipe began to wail, and a drummer started pounding a steady rhythm. The contest would go on as long as the music lasted. As one man emerged victorious from each pair of wrestlers, he could go on to find and tackle another opponent still standing on his feet, until finally only a single victor emerged.

Jonathan eyed his opponent nervously, clearly aware that he was doomed. The two men sparred for a moment to try to find handholds, and suddenly Jonathan found himself snatched up and held upside down, as though his 6-foot 5-inch frame was in the featherweight contest. Gently he was lowered, shoulders first, upon the grass. His second bout lasted slightly longer. This time his opponent dropped into a defensive position and crouched on all fours on the grass. Vainly Jonathan tried to find some way of turning him over. 'It was like trying to pick up a huge, slippery stone, weighing a couple of tons,' he confessed later. 'Absolutely impossible. The man was a solid block of bone and muscle.' A couple of minutes later, Pire Cevat darted out a hand, grabbed Jonathan's leg, and tumbled him head over heels to a roar of appreciation from the crowd who applauded the Englishman's good sportsmanship.

Usually the knockout contest in oil wrestling lasts for several hours, but on this occasion it was speeded up for our benefit. The oil was introduced when the number of wrestlers began to dwindle. Assistants rushed out with tins of olive oil which they poured liberally over the wrestling men, making it even more difficult for them to get a firm grip. The master of ceremonies marched up and down, blowing short blasts on his whistle to denote falls, and acting as referee until finally the field which had been a mass of grunting, grappling contestants was reduced to the winners in each weight division. Cevat the Flea, I was glad to see, had gone on to his usual championship victory in the heavyweights.

A very welcome contingent of Turkish muscle power was also on hand to help us tackle the Bosphorus on 12 June. Eleven Turkish volunteer oarsmen showed up at the yacht club that morning. Six were from the Fenerbache Rowing Club, and five from Galataserai Club. They included the trainer of Turkey's national rowing team, and both clubs' senior coaches.

The day began explosively. The manager of the Sheraton Hotel in Istanbul had generously given free accommodation to the

Argonauts. The crew had already climbed into the minibus that was to take them to *Argo* when Mark came down late to the hotel lobby. Seeing the loaded bus out in the forecourt he ran to catch it, not realizing that the hotel front door, of well-cleaned heavy plate glass, was firmly shut. Mark ran full tilt into it and hurtled straight through in a welter of glass fragments with a tremendous crash that left everyone gasping. Our rowing master tottered for a moment on the pavement, sat down dazedly, and then got back to his feet. Nick checked him for shock and picked out bits of glass from his arms and head, but Mark insisted that he was fit enough to row. As we left the hotel, the magnificently uniformed doorman was still standing there, more stunned than Mark, holding all that was left of his portals – two ornamented door handles that he had collected from the roadway.

There was a certain amount of nervous banter, mostly at Mark's escapade, as the Argonauts took up their familiar places on *Argo*'s

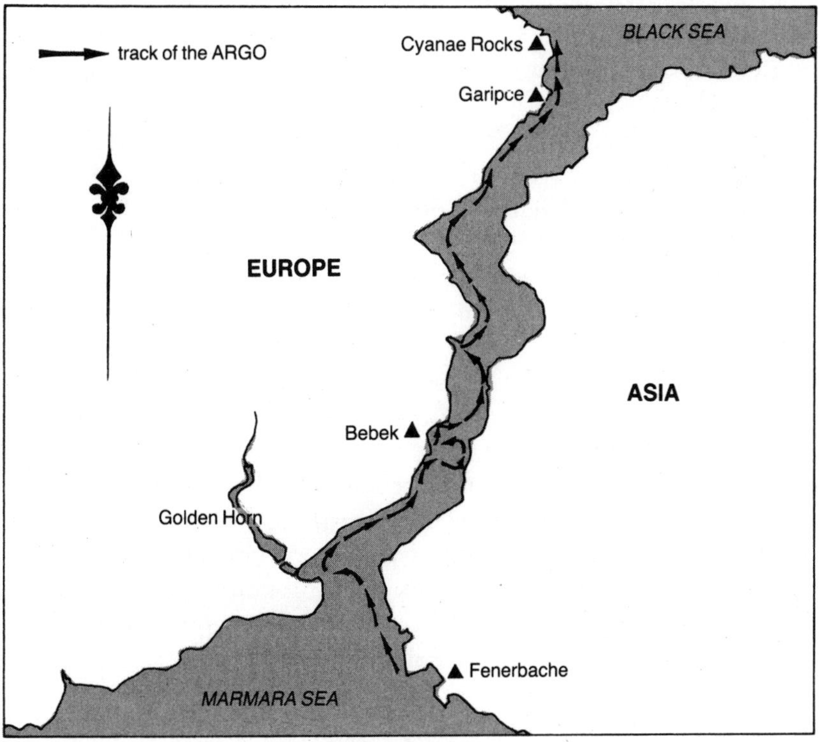

rowing benches and demonstrated the best galley rowing style to our Turkish volunteers. We were well aware that the conditions for rowing up the Bosphorus were far from ideal that day. A breeze was blowing down the channel, a definite headwind. Worse still, a north wind had been blowing strongly all the previous week and this had steadily increased the flow of the current. Before the days of motor power, the normal practice for boats going upstream was to wait until one of the rare southerly winds arose, which at least slowed the current and, if strong enough, could be used under sail; alternatively, the smaller boats were towed up-current by gangs of men on the shore, and a towpath had been provided all along the bank for this purpose. Now, however, the towpath had fallen into disuse. In extreme cases, I was told, the big sailing ships heading for the Crimea had taken more than a month to work their way up the Bosphorus, laboriously heaving themselves up against the current by their windlasses, using cables to the shore as well as patiently dropping anchors in the shallows and kedging forward. But of course none of these options would have been available to Jason and his men. They would have been in potentially hostile territory, with no towpath conveniently at hand, and with the risk of being attacked if they did venture ashore. They would have stayed aboard their galley, which is precisely what Apollonius said they did. They rowed up the Bosphorus, he wrote, by sheer muscle power. Now, 3000 years later, we had to show whether that could have been physically possible: we had to do the same.

We cast off from the yacht club and pulled cautiously out of harbour. Mark and Miles, on the stroke oar position, kept the pace gentle so that the new Turkish oarsmen could get accustomed to the weight and balance of the 14-foot oars. To our starboard side was a low breakwater that gave temporary shelter from the wind and current. Ahead rose one of the world's most evocative and unique skylines – the palaces and minarets of Istanbul, overlooking the Golden Horn. It was a highly emotional moment to be steering a small galley out into this teeming waterway which has been a main artery of trade and seafaring since time immemorial. There is no other place like it on earth. Here is the most important point of contact between Europe and Asia, straddled by a city splendidly worthy of the site.

Ahead of *Argo* sprawled Topkapi Palace with its trees and cupolas, ornate chimneys, steeples, terraces and pavilions dominating the headland which the Ottoman sultans had considered the finest building site in the known world. Behind and alongside Topkapi rose the minarets, domes and semi-domes of truly inspired architecture – the mosques of Suleymanie, Hagia Sophia, Sultan Ahmed and Yeni Cami in a cascade of elegance. Opposite them, across the Golden Horn, Galata Tower stood like a blunt pencil point above the old Genoese quarter of the empress of cities. The whole scene was pulsating with activity. Ferries were churning in and out of the Golden Horn, bustling up-channel towards the northern suburbs or charging recklessly across to Asia, the water foaming around their blunt bows. Downstream we could pick out line upon line of anchored ships in the southern roadstead, where they were waiting to load cargo, receive orders or take on pilots for the straits. Merchant vessels of every description and foreign flag were on the move. A Rumanian bulk carrier was heading north, followed by a Soviet deep sea trawler bound for her home port in the Ukraine. An Israeli freighter was coming south, riding high after discharging cargo in the Black Sea. Behind her a huge oil tanker flying the Liberian flag, deep laden and certainly from a Soviet oil port, glided downstream like a juggernaut with at least 100,000 tons of crude oil aboard. In that treacherous current and shuttling maze of shipping there was no margin for error by anyone. A single false move, and leviathans collided with tremendous force.

Argo rowed past the grim relic of the broken-backed hulk of the crashed tanker that I had seen on my reconnaissance visit to Istanbul eighteen months earlier. The pilot of that doomed ship had headed the blazing vessel out of the main channel and run her aground in the shallows. Teams of men were now cutting up the huge carcass for scrap, like flensing a stranded whale, and *Argo* was utterly dwarfed beneath the huge bow section, looming over us like a rusty cliff. Beyond the tanker wreck was the main current, and I eyed the choppy waves doubtfully.

This part of the Bosphorus, its southern entrance, is some 2½ miles wide, and presented a vast disturbed mass of water spewing south towards the Sea of Marmara at 3–4 knots. That day it was broken into white caps and short maverick waves by the wind and the constant coming and going of ferry boats. *Argo* emerged from the protection of the breakwater, and suddenly we were in the full force of wind and current.

'*Hidi Alla! Hup! Hup! Hup!*' roared the Turkish rowing squad enthusiastically, applying full pressure. The regular Argonauts smiled grimly and heaved on the oar handles in silence. They had already rowed 400 miles, and preferred not to waste a single gasp of breath. There were yells in Turkish of 'Come on! Come on! Pull harder! Pull harder!' as the newcomers realized that rowing 8 tons of galley was not like pulling a featherlight racing craft. *Argo* did not shoot forward like a competition boat; this was going to be a dour, long drawn-out contest against wind and current. 'Hey, is the anchor up?' came a shout, and the Turks laughed.

I set *Argo*'s course at 20 degrees across the current, and tried to slant her towards the opposite bank, just upstream of the Golden Horn. But for every yard we made on that course, we were being swept 2 yards sideways towards the Sea of Marmara. Poor *Argo* was like a floundering beetle fallen into an emptying gutter, in danger of being swallowed down the drain. We were labouring across the surface of the water as fast as we could, but the water itself was washing us away. I began to doubt whether we could actually make it to the opposite shore without being swept helplessly to the southern anchorage. The disturbed surface of the water was our main enemy. Rowing was extremely difficult for the newcomers, unaccustomed to the cumbersome sweeps. *Argo* was bucking and lurching in the waves, and on each forward swing of the oars several blades hit the tops of the waves, breaking up the rhythm of the rowers and reducing our speed. The crew's morale was sky-high, and the oarsmen were laughing and joking. But they could not see – as I could from the helm – that *Argo*'s real progress was barely perceptible.

Then I spotted what I was looking for: the counter-current. The discharge of the Bosphorus is so powerful that, near the banks, the water literally curls round and flows backwards in giant eddies, to fill the vacuum left by the main body of water hurrying south. These counter-currents, which vary in strength and speed and do not form a continuous line along the bank, are the key to a boat getting up the Bosphorus under oars. They exist in patches, particularly in the bays, and there they can assist a boat going upstream. The skill lies in finding the counter-currents and riding them northwards wherever possible. A fisherman had told me that there was an important counter-current just to the north of the Golden Horn on the European side, and now I saw it – a clearly defined line, marked by a grubby streak of foam. On one side the main current was churning and bobbing south; on the other, no more than 5 feet away, the water was virtually flat, moving slowly and calmly in precisely the opposite direction.

'Fifty yards to go and we're out of the worst!' I called out to the crew, and they redoubled their effort, heaving with all their might to gain the last yards of advantage. Suddenly *Argo* slid across the divide. In a single boat's length we passed from chaos to calm, from a hostile environment to a favourable one. It was as if a giant hand had been pulling back on the keel of the boat and shaking it from side to side, and then had abruptly released its grip. In a few seconds the strain was off the oarsmen and they eased their stroke. *Argo* steadied her lurching, and with gentle pressure the crew paddled her northwards. I glanced at my watch. It was 10.30. The crew had been rowing for an hour and a half and all we had yet done was cross from one side of the Bosphorus to the other. Our real northward progress was less than a mile.

Now it was time to keep *Argo* as close as possible to the west bank where the counter-current ran strongest in our favour. It was just like student days when, as cox of a college racing eight, one had to steer the boat as close as possible to the riverbank to gain maximum advantage in a race. But instead of a soft Oxfordshire riverbank of dark loam, the galley's oar blades dipped and rose a yard from the dressed stone river walls of a former Sultan's palace, now a national museum.

I could see that the effort had already taken a lot out of the crew, and they were glad to take the stroke easily for the moment. But the counter-current was fickle. At times we advanced at a brisk walking pace; in the more exposed stretches, where the headwind caught us, we barely crawled along. The palace was followed by another, then by a mosque. Pedestrians using the riverwalk stopped, first to stare and then to wave at us. At 11.40 a shadow passed over us. It was cast by the Bosphorus Bridge, its deck seemingly incredibly high above us as it carried the constant traffic between the two continents while a small Bronze Age galley toiled past below. Guests lunching at a fashionable waterside restaurant, its tablecloths bright yellow, gaped in surprise as we passed, then put down their knives and forks to applaud the labouring oarsmen who grinned and waved back. Next came a line of ships moored against the bank for routine maintenance. Shipyard workers, suspended high above us on bosun's chairs to chip rust from the ships' sides, stopped their hammering and turned to yell encouragement. Their shouts echoed off the towering steel hulls.

Away to our right, out in the main stream, a cluster of small fishing boats rose and fell in the current like a flock of gulls resting on the water. Each fishing boat had its engine running steadily just to hold position in the straits, while they hung their fishing lines into the edge of the deep channel to tempt the shoals of fish which migrate through this single vital artery that joins the Black Sea with the rest of the world's seas and oceans. On the surface the Bosphorus flows steadily north, but deep down another current, which the Turks call the *kanal*, heavier and more salty than the Black Sea's surface water, is seeking to escape in precisely the opposite direction.

At the suburb of Bebek, which was our target for the night, the Bosphorus bends and narrows. This is the choke point of the straits. Here Mehmet II, Ottoman conqueror of Constantinople, built his mighty fortress, Rumeli Hisar, to control the passage. A cannon shot reaches easily to the opposite bank. Through this gap drains all the extra water carried into the Black Sea by the great rivers of eastern Europe and southern Russia, the Danube, the Don, the Dnieper and a host of other rivers and streams rising in an immense arc from the Carpathians in the west to the Caucasus in the east. Some of this water is lost by evaporation, but the bulk of it, 325 cubic kilometres annually, spills out through the Bosphorus. And at Bebek this huge outpouring is constricted to a channel just 800 yards wide.

The result, with a north wind behind it, can be a millrace. The main current ricochets from one bank to the other, from Europe to Asia, twisting and bouncing from one rocky promontory to the next, and in flood times produces tongues of disturbed water that few man-powered vessels could surmount. Certainly *Argo* with her 8 horsepower of human muscle at maximum effort did not have a chance of pulling directly against such an awesome rush of water. Only by using the counter-currents could she proceed. But to reach the counter-currents we had to cross from one shore of the Bosphorus to the next; and in the interval the boat was exposed to the full force of the current.

The little galley crept up the European shore, the crew still rowing easily to save their strength before the next ordeal. I saw the millrace at Bebek point from at least half a mile away. The water was shooting round the corner in a seething mass where a rocky spur thrust out into the current flow. Whirlpools gyrated away from the edges of the race; blobs of foam dipped and spun in the hurrying current. As we drew nearer, I called a warning to the crew: 'Thirty yards to go to the race! . . . Twenty . . . start building up boat speed!' Led by Mark and Miles on the stroke oar bench, the crew increased the rating – the number of strokes per minute – and packed in more effort. *Argo* accelerated. 'Ten metres . . .,' I warned. Just in front of me, Mark began to say, 'Couldn't we stay on this side? Perhaps get round the point, inside the current, and . . .' But before he finished his sentence *Argo*'s bow hit the race, and I heard his startled gasp.

It was like steering failure in a moving car. *Argo* simply went out of control. She skidded sideways as the rushing water flung her off-course, and the current, striking her ram, spun the boat through 90 degrees in an instant. For an awful moment I thought *Argo* was going to be turned right around and projected downstream. She was heeling over from the force of the water, like a small aircraft making a banking turn. The twin steering oars were quite useless, lifeless in my hands as *Argo* lost all forward motion and was swept sideways, her deck at an angle. There was no need to tell the crew what to do. They realized exactly what was happening. At one moment they had been sitting looking down-channel past *Argo*'s stern, and the next instant they were staring at the great curtain wall of Rumeli Hisar with the boat, at right-angles to her previous course, being swept south like a twig.

We had to break out of the millrace. Chunk! Chunk! Chunk! The oar blades chopped into the water in a flurry of quick strokes. The crew grunted with the effort, and rowed at maximum rating. There was no husbanding of effort now. This was all the muscle power they could produce in a short, concentrated burst, twenty men rowing in unison and to the limits of their strength. *Argo* steadied in her crazy swerve; the steering came back to life in my hands, and I could feel the water rushing past the great blades of the steering oars, making the tiller bars quiver. I turned *Argo* to point almost directly up the sweeping current. If only the crew could hold her there, breasting the rushing water, I could inch the galley sideways, across towards the Asian shore. Too much of an angle and *Argo* would be spun once again.

'Come on now! Come on! Maximum pressure! Keep it up! Well done!' *Argo* hung there, poised like a salmon fighting its way upriver. Ever so slowly we began to gain the advantage: it was a barely discernible movement over the ground. I increased the boat's angle of attack to the stream by a hairsbreadth. The gap between us and the European shore began to open up as *Argo* sidled out into the centre of the Bosphorus. On the chart we had just 600 yards to go to reach the area of the counter-current on the opposite bank, but a quarter of a mile against the current meant at least four times that distance through the water. Now, in mid-channel, the wind was much worse. We were exposed to it, and the breeze caught the high prow of the galley and held us back. Even so, I reckoned that *Argo* was making at least 6 knots through the water.

It was a magnificent effort. But was it enough? A quarter of an hour had passed since the first staggering impact of the Bebek current, and the crew were losing their aggressive edge. They were visibly tiring, and a false sense of security was setting in. The shore was too far away for them to judge progress, and we were now out of the most impressive part of the millrace. Only I, as helmsman constantly monitoring the boat's relationship to the shore points, was able to detect that we were no longer advancing. Just perceptibly, *Argo* was being borne downstream. We were no longer in control. The current was now in charge of the galley, dictating her position. If this continued for another five minutes we would become part of the current pattern, swept from one bank to the next, farther and farther south like flotsam as the crew ran out of strength. I realized that the Argonauts had to succeed on this first attempt. If they failed now, the damage to their morale might be irreparable, and the eleven Turkish volunteers might not think it worth coming back for a second attempt. For the first time, as captain of *Argo* I really yelled at the men.

'Come on! Come on!' I bellowed at the top of my lungs, 'You're losing it! We'll be pushed back down to the point we crossed over!' The regular Argonauts looked startled: they had not heard me so vehement before. They went back to full power, and the Turks kept pace with them. Some of the men I could see were at the limit of their stamina. Veins bulged on the forehead of the senior Turkish rowing coach, and he was crimson with effort, gritting his teeth. Chunk! Chunk! Chunk! Thank heaven the rhythm had not been broken. The crew, so many of them new to the boat, were rowing as a real team. The far shore stopped moving in the wrong direction, held still, and then we began to gain ground again.

'They had reached a point', wrote Apollonius of Jason's passage through the Bosphorus,

> where they could see the vast sea opening out on either side, when they were suddenly faced by a tremendous billow arched like an overhanging rock. They bent their heads down at the sight where it seemed about to fall and overwhelm the ship. But Tiphys just in time checked her as she plunged forward, and the great wave slid under her keel . . . . Euphemus ran along, shouting to all his friends to put their backs into their rowing, and with answering shouts they struck the water. Yet for every foot that *Argo* made, they lost two, though the oars bent like curved bows as the men put out their strength . . . .

That is how the first *Argo* struggled through the Bosphorus. And it was exactly how the new Argonauts succeeded. Even as their new burst of energy began to wane, the toiling oarsmen – British, Turkish, Irish and a single Faeroese – heaved *Argo* those last few yards and into the saving counter-current. Gasping with exhaustion, the crew unwound their muscle-cracking stroke, and pulled normally. 'Now that's what I call rowing,' Jonathan grunted.

Once more that day we had to recross the main channel, first creeping up the Asian side to gain a few hundred yards' progress in our friendly counter-current, and then launching out again into the main stream and rowing mightily through the kicking current, back again to an overnight anchorage at Bebek. It was odd, but in those bursts of total effort I noticed that not only were the crew rowing and moving as a single unit, every man swinging in the same motion, but their breathing came in great coordinated gasps as well. It was as if *Argo* in her moment of crisis had acquired a single great set of lungs, pumping with sobs of effort. As we moored *Argo* you could almost taste the feeling of accomplishment. The oarsmen had successfully achieved their day's target: halfway up the Bosphorus against the current and under conditions that were far from favourable. The regular Argonauts burst into a spontaneous round of applause for our Turkish volunteers, who went off proudly comparing their new-won blisters.

'You need forty men today,' Turkey's national rowing coach said next morning as we stood on the quayside at Bebek. A northerly gale was blowing, and the Bosphorus was really showing its teeth. Rowing conditions were totally impossible. Small freighters bound upstream for the Black Sea had their engines at full throttle and the water was piling up around their bows, but they stood almost motionless against the land. In the opposite direction a small rowing boat running downstream was whirling along like a leaf, faster than a man could run, with its canny owner, sitting coolly on the thwart, riding the waves with no need to touch his sculls. I cancelled the day's rowing and went instead to scout the northern entrance to the straits. I got there aboard a sixty-passenger motor launch, and the waves were breaking so steeply that the skipper of the launch refused to venture the last mile; he told me that conditions were too dangerous, and he feared his boat would be swamped.

Twenty-four hours later the gale had eased. The wind was still from the north, and the current was running strongly against us, but with a dozen Turkish volunteers eager to row I decided that *Argo* could still make progress. So we slogged on. This time we had fewer worries. The choke point at Bebek was behind us, and as the straits grew wider so the current speed slackened. To pick up the counter-currents we had to cross to Asia, then back again, but from that point forward we were able to keep along the European side, where the current was weakest and occasionally in our favour. As we approached the Black Sea we began to sense the swell of the open water as the waves came rolling down from the north. Tucking *Argo* as close as I dared to the western shore, we toiled north. The crew had been rowing for more than ten hours when finally we turned into the fishing harbour at Rumeli Fener, the Roman lighthouse. The light marked the end of the Bosphorus. The Black Sea lay before us. The new Argonauts had rowed the entire 18-mile distance from the Marmara to the Black Sea against the current and against the wind. They had shown beyond any doubt that the passage of the Bosphorus could be done in a twenty-oared galley, and the straits had not been an insuperable barrier to Jason and his men in their search for the Golden Fleece.

The experience had also taught me something else: the pattern of currents and counter-currents in the Bosphorus is a clue to the particular shore locations visited by Jason and his companions as described in the *Argonautica*. The currents dictate just where a galley crosses from side to side, either to find helpful eddies or to avoid the worst races. A galley's upstream track is as clearly defined as a footpath that winds through a mountain pass seeking the natural contours of the land. This told me where to look for the home of the blind prophet Phineas who, according to the legend, lived on the banks of the Bosphorus and advised Jason and the Argonauts what would happen to them once they entered the unknown dangers of the Black Sea.

Garipce cliffs

Phineas is the most sympathetic character in the entire Argonaut story. He lived, it was said, within sight of the Black Sea, on the side of the straits. He was a man gifted with the power of seeing into the future, and he had been so accurate in his forecasts and so honest in revealing his predictions to people who came to seek his help that the gods, out of anger at his mortal presumption, had afflicted him with blindness. If he dared see into the future so clearly, then he would not have the power to witness the present. As an additional punishment the Harpies were sent to torment him. These were three winged demons, half-bird, half-woman, and they were reputed to come from a mountain cave in Crete. Whenever blind Phineas was about to eat a meal the Harpies would drop down from the clouds, swoop in with shrieks, snatch away the food from his plate and foul the table with their stench and droppings. As a result, poor Phineas lived in misery and hunger. Local people still came to ask his prophecies and bring gifts of food, but since his blindness Phineas had refused to tell them the entire future, dreading further punishment from the gods.

The figure of Phineas is identical to the same type of wise hermit who, in the Christian era, would choose to live in isolation in a desert cave or on a rocky island at the edge of the ocean. These recluses, too, were credited by local people with special powers, such as healing or prophecy, and were looked after by them. In the same way the people at the north end of the Bosphorus would have left gifts of food for Phineas, who had become their local wise man, and it is hardly surprising that seabirds learned to rob him of food, leaving their droppings on the rocks. Roman commentators reading Apollonius believed they had identified the exact place where Phineas had lived: they called it Gyropolis, the Place of the Vultures, because they believed the Harpies were a local species of vulture that snatched away the blind man's food. The spot they identified, a place on the European shore near the northern end of the Bosphorus, matches Apollonius' description, for he says that Phineas lived near a bay, and from his home he could tell the visiting Argonauts which way they should turn when they emerged from the straits into the Black Sea.

No vultures live today, if they ever did, near Gyropolis; it is now called Garipce, meaning 'strange' or 'weird', because of its curiously shaped rocks and crags which make very suitable sites to be associated with a lonely hermit seer. Moreover the same cliffs are pockmarked and striated with cavities and ledges that make excellent nesting sites for seabirds, and their droppings streak the cliff faces. The seabirds have selected the site not just for its nesting potential, but for the rich fishing grounds nearby. Here the Black Sea forces its way into the narrow funnel of the Bosphorus and the mingling and swirling of the waters produces ideal conditions for fish to feed; and here too pass the huge shoals of fish which migrate annually through the straits. In short, Garipce is the natural location for the species of predatory seabirds that may have preyed on the blind Phineas, and then entered mythology as the Harpies.

But our experience in the new *Argo* offered another reason why Garipce could have been the site of Phineas' home. It is the last sheltered place where one can go ashore in the Bosphorus before embarking on the wide expanse of the Black Sea, and it lies exactly on the galley track dictated by the currents. For the last 6 miles, northward-bound, an oared vessel is obliged by the current to hug the western shore of the Bosphorus. And then, just as the Black Sea opens up before the mariner, he finds the tiny cove of Garipce on his left-hand side, offering a perfect haven. The sailor would go ashore for three reasons: to rest after the exertions of the Bosphorus and before entering the Black Sea; to seek sailing directions in the unknown waters ahead; and, most important of all, to take on his essential need – fresh water.

That, surely, is what Jason would have done. Garipce is still the last natural harbour before the Black Sea. Today both sides of the northern approaches to the Bosphorus are military zones, forbidden to civilians. But tucked away inside this military enclave survives the village of Garipce; where the curious, black, contorted cliffs are pierced by the small gap of the tiny cove a handful of fishing boats are pulled up on the beach, completely safe from the massive swells of the Black Sea which heave down on the entrance to the Bosphorus, driven by gales sweeping out of Russia. Garipce is just a hamlet of traditional wooden Turkish houses with a simple mosque, a charming, traditional place, untouched by modern life because of its military isolation. And above it lie the ruins of a fort.

In days gone by, no boat bound for the Black Sea would have passed by this haven without stopping. At the foot of the cliff at the back of the village I found what I half-knew would be there – a spring of superb fresh water bursting out of the rock. A splendidly worked brass spigot closed off the waterpipe which tapped a water source emerging from the base of the cliffs. Irgun, whose father, when I first met him, made his living as a water seller in Istanbul, tasted the Garipce spring water and pronounced it delicious. It was, he said, as good as any water imported to the city. Even if they had not needed to visit Phineas to ask his advice about navigating the Black Sea, Jason and his men would have stopped here to take on fresh water for the next stage of their long journey.

The legend says that Jason did much more than resupply *Argo*. When they heard of Phineas' troubles with the Harpies, two of the heroes, Zetes and Calais, offered to deal with the three bird-women. For this task they were particularly well qualified: as Sons of the North Wind, they had the power of flight. A banquet was spread as a bait for the Harpies, and Zetes and Calais hid in ambush with drawn swords. Sure enough, they soon heard the rushing sound of the Harpies' approach and the creatures' dreadful screeches as they swooped down and began to tear at the food. At that moment Zetes and Calais leaped out of ambush and chased off the intruders; the Harpies took wing and flew away, and the Sons of the

North Wind followed them. After a long chase Zetes and Calais caught up with their quarry, some say near the rocks called Strophades off the west coast of Greece. There the two heroes would have cut down the Harpies with their swords if the Olympian gods had not intervened. They sent the goddess Iris as their messenger to warn the sons of Boreas that they were not to harm the Harpies, but let them go free, and in future the bird-women would no longer torment the blind seer. So Zetes and Calais gave up the chase, and turned back to bring the good news to Phineas and the Argonauts, waiting at the northern end of the Bosphorus.

In gratitude Phineas now gave the Argonauts all the directions they needed for the next part of their quest. He told them to turn east as they emerged from the Bosphorus and row far along the north coast of Asia Minor, hugging the shoreline. He listed the tribes they would encounter, the harbours they would find and the adventures they would have. But what would happen to them when they finally reached Colchis, the Land of the Golden Fleece, he refused to divulge. That, he said, would be to reveal too much; the Argonauts would have to learn for themselves.

Phineas' greatest service was more immediate. He revealed to the Argonauts the secret by which they could escape the greatest physical danger of their entire voyage, the danger which had destroyed every ship that had previously attempted to pass through the straits. This was the menace notorious throughout the ancient world as the Clashing Rocks.

Garipce village

7
The Black Sea

'When you leave me,' said Phineas,

> the first thing you will see will be the two Cyanean Rocks, at the end of the straits. To the best of my knowledge, no one has ever made his way between them, for not being fixed to the bottom of the sea they frequently collide, flinging up the water in a seething mass which falls on the rocky flanks of the straits with a resounding roar. Now if, as I take it, you are god-fearing travellers and men of sense, you will be advised by me. You will not brashly throw away your lives or rush into danger with the recklessness of youth. Make an experiment first. Send out a dove from *Argo* to explore the way. If she succeeds in flying between the rocks and out across the sea, do not hesitate to follow in her path, but get a firm grip on your oars and cleave the water of the straits.

The stratagem with the dove worked beautifully. As Jason's crew rounded the last corner of the straits they saw the Cyanean or Clashing Rocks ahead of them. The rocks were two great moving masses of stone which floated about the mouth of the straits, colliding repeatedly with tremendous shocks. Whenever a ship tried to pass between them the rocks closed together like a giant trap, pulverizing the intruder. Even now, the Argonauts saw, the rocks had just snapped shut, and were beginning to move apart again. As *Argo* rowed up to the gap Euphemus, the runner, released the dove, which flew low and straight between the rocks.

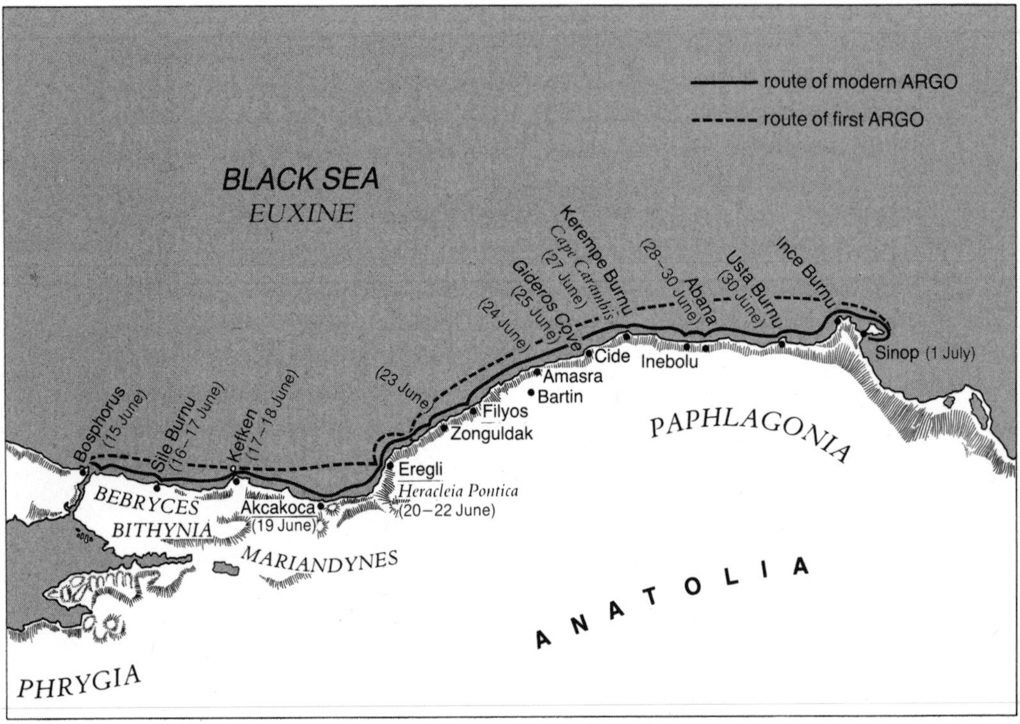

Immediately they collided again, but too late. The Argonauts saw that the dove had dashed through the gap, and the rocks only succeeded in nipping off her tail feathers.

This was the signal for Jason and his men to forge ahead. As the rocks sprang apart, the rowers made a terrific spurt, and *Argo* sped into the gap. For a dreadful moment the boat hung there, caught in the swirling backwash and unable to move either forwards or back. It seemed certain that the rocks would crush her. At that moment, according to the *Argonautica*, the goddess Athena intervened to save them. With one hand she held back the rocks, and with the other she pushed *Argo* through the gap. It was in the nick of time. The Clashing Rocks banged shut, sheering off the galley's stern ornament. From that time forward, wrote Apollonius, 'the Rocks were now rooted for ever in one spot close to one another. It had been decided by the happy Gods that this should be their fate when a human being had seen them and sailed through.'

For hundreds of years attempt after attempt has been made to attribute the phenomenon of the Clashing Rocks to natural causes.

They have been explained as a shallow reef which, it is said, was sometimes exposed and sometimes covered by the tide on the Asian side, where many coast-hugging ships had come to grief. Another idea was that the Clashing Rocks were huge ice floes, brought south from the Crimea in the spring break-up, which damaged ships in the approaches to the straits. But sea ice has very rarely been recorded so far south in the Black Sea; nor are there really dangerous reefs on either side of the Bosphorus' northern entrance, only a few offshore rocks which are easily spotted and just as easily avoided in waters that have very little tidal rise and fall.

Yet much of Apollonius' description does ring true to anyone who navigates the straits in a rowed boat. His description of the swirling back eddies between the rocks, the manner in which *Argo* lay helpless in the current, how it seemed that at the last moment Athena literally seized the boat and pushed her forward at the critical instant when the oarsmen no longer had the strength to drive her on against the current – these are dramatized versions of very real difficulties. Farther down-channel, when struggling up through the Bebek section of the Bosphorus, any galley would encounter the millraces, the uncontrollable behaviour of a small boat whirled suddenly around in the current, the odd sensation when a counter-current picks up the boat and lifts her forward, just as the goddess Athena was supposed to have saved *Argo*. Then, 11 miles farther north at the entrance to the Black Sea, comes the rest of his description: the spray being flung high by the storm-driven swells surging into the constricting funnel of the Bosphorus' northern mouth, and the booming crash of the waves as they strike the headlands on either side and rebound in a tossing backwash.

Here, too, are the physical remains of the Clashing Rocks of antiquity. The ancients did not hesitate to identify them as the two large chunks of rock which lie 80 yards off the northern headland at Rumeli Fener. Their other name was the Cyanean, or Dark Blue, Rocks because as Mark, our classicist aboard the new *Argo*, told me when we had clambered up to the top of them, dark blue was the colour of menace and danger in classical times. In reality the rocks are a charcoal colour with tones of green; they are formed of huge lumps of conglomerate that appear to have broken away from the nearby cliffs. A narrow cleft cuts them in two, so that by a stretch of the imagination one could suppose that they had once been apart and floating like vast lumps of pumice stone on the surface of the sea. Their evil reputation as the Clashing Rocks was pure myth, an invented symbol to explain the real difficulties of passing through the straits of the Bosphorus. Once Jason and his Argonauts had succeeded in making the passage and entered the Black Sea, the rocks symbolically lost their power; never again did they menace any ship passing that way.

Ironically, the dreaded rocks have now been converted into a shelter, not a threat, for shipping. A very recent concrete mole joins the rocks to the mainland, and in its lee nestles a large fleet of fishing craft. The fishermen say that in the winter gales the spray still bursts right over the rocks, some 40 feet high, and the accompanying roar can be heard far inland. And the rocks, they claim, are still the true boundary of the Bosphorus' dangers. In bad weather no ship, however large, can be considered to be in safe water until she has passed north of the rocks, clearing the turbulence of the shallowing mouth to the straits.

On the flat crest of the innermost rock Mark and I found the

Mustafa

remains of a Roman pillar, a fluted block of marble some 4 feet high and about 3½ feet in diameter. It was a segment of a stone column which had once served as a landmark for ships entering and leaving the straits. Before that, the Greeks had built their own altar on the same spot, for here they made sacrifices and sought the favour of the gods before they dared venture upon the northern sea. This was a crucial moment in a voyage, the place when a man embarked upon the sea the ancients feared so much that they called it 'The Inhospitable Sea'.

The Black Sea still keeps its notoriety. Time and again we had been warned – by Turkish fishermen in the Bosphorus and the Sea of Marmara, and by Greeks in the Aegean – that the Black Sea was no place for an open boat. There were sudden gales, they said, which struck without warning. Even the wave pattern, according to some of the Turks, was different from anything else they knew. In some areas off the coast we would encounter a peculiar repetition of three waves, larger than the others, which came one after another close together. No boat was entirely safe or comfortable among the triple waves, they said. She could be swamped or damaged, and would ride the seas unhappily, shaking herself to pieces. So notorious was the triple wave that no fishing boat would operate off certain sections of the coast: the sailors just refused to work there.

So it was with a certain amount of trepidation that on 15 June *Argo* steered out from the harbour behind the Clashing Rocks, and we began the long haul eastward along Turkey's north coast. A fresh batch of Turkish volunteers had replaced the men who had helped us from Canakkale to Istanbul. Mustafa was black-bearded and serious; Ziya normally worked as a translator in an import-export company; his great friend Yigit was a twenty-six- year-old economics student who turned out to be a natural seaman; and Husnu was a friend of Ali's, an architect by training and with a similarly excellent command of English. Young Umur, who had seemed so glum when he first joined, now announced that, far from ending his trip aboard *Argo* in Istanbul as had been the original plan, he would like to stay with the Argonauts as long as possible. Finally there was a twelve-year-old supernumerary aboard – my daughter Ida, who had been promised a few days on *Argo* to make up for the long absences of her father while the expedition was preparing and the galley was being built.

Ida was delivered to *Argo*, while at sea, by Kaan's family, my Istanbul friends of long standing. There was nothing the family would not do to help the expedition. Irgun, the eldest son, was now a businessman on his own account, running an office that arranged driving licences and car registration with the traffic police. His energy and optimism were boundless. 'When other people give up,' he told me with his characteristic confidence, 'that is when I begin. There is no such word as impossible.' Indeed Irgun seemed to be some sort of genie appearing out of the Turkish lamp. At Istanbul the Turkish Coastguard had decided that *Argo* was not going to sink forthwith, and so we no longer needed a constant patrol boat escort. Instead the Coastguard would keep an eye on us from time to time when they had a vessel in the area. Now it was Irgun who kept on popping up in unexpected places. Like Uncle John back in Greece, he seemed to know everyone connected with harbour life – captains of ferry boats, skippers of fishing trawlers, yachtsmen, customs officials, coastguard controllers, Bosphorus pilots. If they glimpsed *Argo* rowing past their stretch of coast, they contacted Irgun and he would suddenly appear on the quay of some obscure port or his voice would surprisingly answer back from the little walkie-talkie radio which I used to contact the rubber dinghy when it went on shopping trips to collect supplies.

But Irgun had a rival. Mukaddes, his youngest sister, was determined to outdo him. I had last seen her as a shy thirteen-year-old with enormous fawn-like eyes, the seventh in her family of eight, all happily clustered round the dining table in their two-room apartment. Since that time, however, Mukaddes had flourished extraordinarily. She was now a highly successful Istanbul businesswoman, just as energetic and enthusiastic as her brother. She struck up an alliance with an older sister, Ikun, who was a supervisor in a telephone exchange, and together, by telephone, they put together a watching system which was the equal of Irgun's. Not a lighthouse keeper or a harbour master was left undisturbed by telephone calls from Ikun and Mukaddes, checking whether *Argo* had been sighted.

Mukaddes picked up Ida at Istanbul's airport, whisking her away under Irgun's nose, for he too had gone to meet her, and the next morning Mukaddes had persuaded a fishing boat skipper to set out in chase of the galley which was by then in the Black Sea. Mukaddes, Ikun and several other members of the family were waving from the bridge of the trawler when it caught up with us and Ida scrambled aboard. At the same time Irgun's voice could be heard calling us faintly on the walkie-talkie, and by the time we got into the next little harbour there he was, having driven four hours to get to us. Searching the sea with binoculars, he had spotted us from a clifftop and was on hand to greet us with the words: 'Is there anything you need? Just let me know.' He had already advised the harbourmaster, the local mayor and the corporal in charge of port security that *Argo* was on her way. Then he left us for another four-hour drive back to Istanbul – in the wake of a major operation, after which he had emerged from hospital only two weeks before.

Such meetings were bright interludes in our long, gruelling haul eastward. It was no holiday. The day's routine normally began at 6 a.m. when the crew roused themselves and left the beach where they had been sleeping on the sand. They climbed back aboard to join the three or four men who had spent the night asleep on the foredeck and central gangway to provide an emergency team in case the wind increased in the night and *Argo* began to shift her moorings. We weighed anchor and rowing began immediately. The men would row for an hour, keeping to the standard rota of ten men at the oars, while their companions rested. Every five minutes one bench of two oarsmen was replaced by a fresh pair of rowers. Then, after an hour's hard work, the system changed. The entire crew divided into two equal groups, and one group rowed for a quarter of an hour while the other group took breakfast. Then the two groups switched places until, breakfast completed, the normal rota was resumed, and *Argo* went grinding forward at 3–3½ knots for another five hours, with just a mug of tea for sustenance.

Newcomers found the regime crippling. Even the fittest of them were sagging with exhaustion after three hours of such toil. The regular Argonauts kept rowing on and on until midday, when there was a break for lunch. We would anchor *Argo* in the shallows, and the crew wolfed down their meal before going for a swim. Then at about 1.30 in the afternoon the cry went up again: 'Oar bench positions! Time to get going! Oars outboard. Are you ready? Row!' and the aching routine would continue until we reached our evening's halting place. On the very worst days the crew rowed for eleven blistering hours before *Argo* put ashore for the night.

Understandably, everyone loathed the actual rowing. It was mindless, repetitive and boring, and almost any diversion was welcome. Some tried reading as they rowed, propping up a book on the bench beside them. Others put on headphones and listened to music on cassette players until the tapes themselves became tedious. Word games were played and joke lists were instituted. Each man in turn had to tell a joke, the longer the better, but if the joke was too awful a time ban was placed on it and it could not be repeated for at least two weeks; truly painful jokes were forbidden for two years. By far the most successful activity was singing, whether solo or in chorus. Songs gave a rhythm to the oars and coordinated the efforts of the rowers. Modern pop songs rarely fitted. The best tunes were either beer-drinking songs or rousing Church of England hymns, whose rhythm was particularly suited to a galley stroke. So the Turks listened in puzzled wonder as the regular Argonauts, led usually by Tim Readman, roared out *Hymns Ancient and Modern*, interspersed at random with bar-room ballads. Our champion singer proved to be Cormac, who had a fine singing voice and a wide repertoire of sea shanties and traditional Irish songs; with the crew taking up the chorus behind him, Cormac sang our way along the Anatolian coast.

Steadily the expedition crept eastwards. On good days the breeze might come to our aid and the crew would take a break, resting their rowing while *Argo* glided forwards under sail. At such times there was no question of halting to pick up food supplies. Even ten minutes of the favourable freeze was far too precious to be wasted. Pete the cook and Tim the purser would set off in the rubber dinghy with its little outboard engine, from which we also took photographs, and make their way ashore to find a town and buy food, while *Argo* continued down the coast. Later the supply party would rejoin us whenever they were ready, and in the meantime *Argo* made use of every whisper of breeze.

Food was becoming increasingly difficult to obtain in the smaller settlements: the demands of a large, very hungry crew of oarsmen were sometimes more than a village grocer or butcher could meet. Peter the cook had to work hard to satisfy everyone's appetites – we ate tubs of yoghurt, sacks of fruit and bread, and whatever meat was available. Fish was virtually unobtainable – the only time we ate fish was when Cormac caught it for us. Peter Warren, Peter Wheeler and Trondur were fanatical fishermen, and the areas around their benches were booby trapped with a repellent-looking selection of lines, rusty hooks, lead weights and rotting pieces of meat and fancy lures. But they only ever caught tiddlers. Cormac, on the other hand, had the magic touch. If there were fish, they came to his hook, and he successfully pulled in several dogfish, 3 feet long, that made good eating.

Trondur, however, harvested the sea in other ways. At the port of Kefken, and again near Zonguldak, he went hunting in the sea caves for nesting seabirds. Over his tennis shoes he pulled thick socks of grey Faeroese wool so that he would not slip on the weed-covered rocks, and he disappeared with the rubber dinghy into the gaping mouths of the caves where cormorants and seagulls could be seen coming and going. At the back of the cave Trondur would jump ashore and begin clambering towards the upper ledges.

'It was a great sight,' Tim Readman told me after returning from one hunt. 'Trondur went straight up the rock face, with the young cormorants peering out from their nests above him, clucking and gobbling with curiosity and alarm. Then, suddenly, Trondur's shaggy head appeared over the edge, and the next thing there was a frantic squawking and squalling, and feathers flying out in all directions and a terrific scuffling. By then all you could see of Trondur were his woolly socks sticking out from the ledge while he grabbed his prey. Then he reappeared and came back down dangling a young cormorant in each hand, by the neck.'

'A cormorant's neck is long enough,' said Cormac, looking at the catch, 'but when Trondur's finished with the creature it looks more like a giraffe.'

Skinned and boiled in sauce, cormorant casserole *à la* Trondur Patursson was a great success. The flesh had the colour and taste of jugged hare, and the best meals started with an appetizer of mussels gathered off the cave walls and baked over a driftwood fire on the shingle.

On 19 June, at 2.30 in the afternoon, the 200,000th oar stroke of the voyage was announced by rowing master Mark, and the crew were still exuberant enough to speed up the rating, churning the water with exaggerated power and roaring out the countdown. It didn't seem to matter that they had been rowing since 7.15 in the morning, without a proper break for either breakfast or lunch. That evening a thunderstorm brewing out to sea gave us a helping breeze, and we sighted the headland of Eregli, behind which, according to Apollonius, lay the Mouth of Hell and the next identifiable point on the track of the original *Argo*.

An armada of fishing boats was waiting to greet us. They came churning out of Eregli and formed up in a jostling phalanx all around, their decks crowded with spectators. To my alarm, one large trawler cut across directly ahead of *Argo* and a burly Turk, stripped to his underpants, climbed on the rail of the flying bridge and flung himself into the sea, a 25-foot drop, landing directly in our path. He disappeared from sight, and I was terrified that he would be chopped to mincement by the propellors of the fishing boats crowding in behind us. By a miracle, he grabbed the handhold which Peter Wheeler had made for *Argo*'s ram – and came climbing up the bow, dripping, moustachioed and as furry as a seal. He was drunk, and determined to give a huge hug of greeting to the first Argonaut he met. That Argonaut happened to be Trondur, in full beard and bushy hairdo, and the tipsy Turk was slightly disconcerted.

'This lofty headland,' wrote Apollonius of Eregli,

> with its sheer cliffs, looks out across the Bithynian Sea. Beneath it at sea level lies a solid platform of smooth rock on which the rollers break and roar, while high up on the landward side it falls away in a hollow glen. Here is the Cave of Hades with its overhanging trees and rocks, from the chill depths of which an icy breath comes up and covers everything with sparkling rime that melts under the midday sun. The frowning sea mingles for ever with the rustling of the leaves as they are shaken by the wind from Hades Cave. Here, too, is the mouth of the River Acheron, which issues from the mountainside and falls by way of a deep ravine, into the eastern sea . . . . The Argonauts brought their ship to the same spot. Shortly after the wind dropped, they beached her in the shelter of the Acherusian Cape.

The Mouth of Hell is the second in a row of three caves which pierce the limestone hillside on the left bank of what is now called Frog River, Der Bagh, by the inhabitants of modern Eregli. The river, as Apollonius said, runs out into the Black Sea just beside the Acherusian Cape, which is now a military zone, for Eregli is a strategic harbour on the north coast of Turkey and the headquarters of the Turkish naval commander. The development of the modern town of Eregli has covered over the classical Greek harbour and altered the shoreline, but it is still possible to follow the road that leads up the winding course of Frog River where, until the beginning of this century, small boats used to moor beside the first of the caves, which contains the remains of a mosaic floor and a very early Christian chapel.

The second cave is far larger. Its entrance is only a narrow cleft in the rock, and it was easy to see why it was considered to be the Mouth of Hell. Apollonius wrote that an 'icy breath' came out of it. In spring and winter, said our guide, who was the local apothecary's son, a dense mist fills the thickly overgrown valley and shrouds the

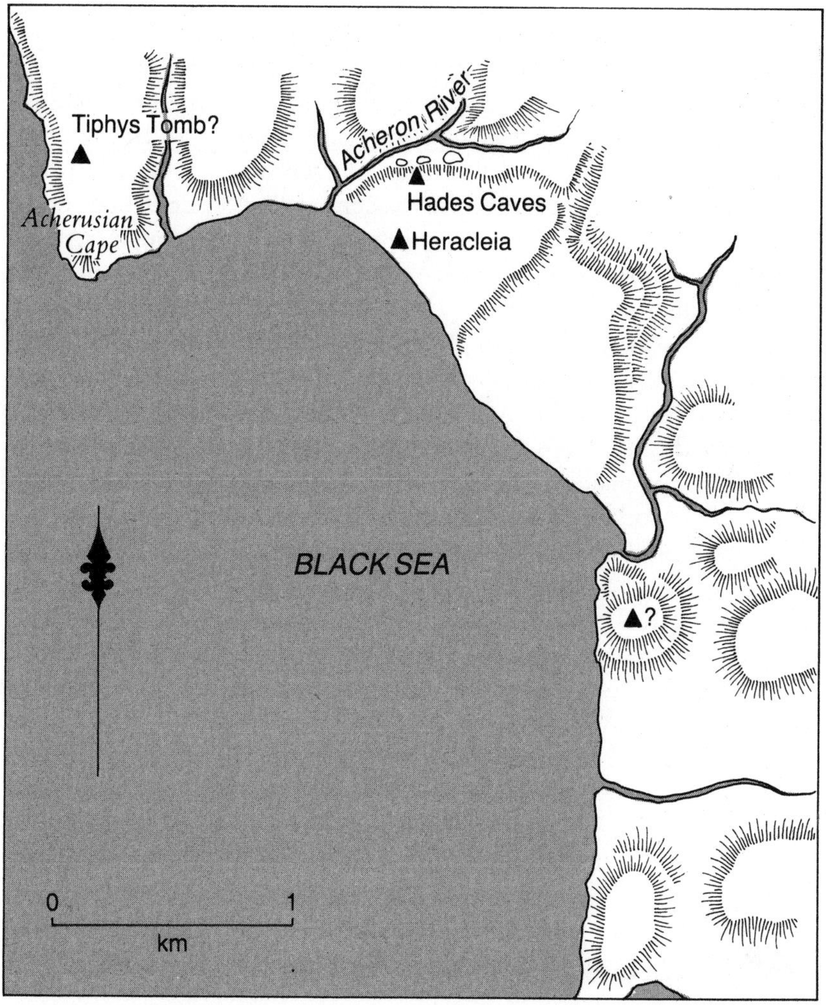

bushes and trees and the surrounding slopes with a clammy white fog that seems to emanate from the cleft. The narrow cave entrance, just big enough to squeeze through, plunges downwards and turns a tight spiral, so the visitor must hold onto the clammy rock, which glistens with condensation and Apollonius' 'sparkling rime', the limestone surface sheen. Inside, the temperature drops still further, and the passageway leads out onto the floor of an underground cavern which once penetrated 1½ kilometres into the heart of the mountain, though in 1960 a massive rock fall closed off the back of the great cave. In the centre of the underground chamber lies a pool of deep, clear water; the sides of the grotto shimmer with runnels and gutters of limestone glaze; and the chill air is filled with the constant sound of water dripping from the ceiling, or trickling down the walls to embalm everything with lime. To a Bronze Age visitor, standing there with only a firebrand or oil lamp for illumination, it must indeed have seemed like an entrance to the Underworld. Scraps of pottery, broken Greek and Roman statuary and the soot marks of lamps have been found where the ancients practised their cult worship.

Hercules was said to have come here on his Labours, to drag out the guardian of the Underworld, the hideous dog Cerberus. The creature slavered at the indignity of his capture, and it is said that where the deadly drops of his spittle flecked the ground, there grew the poisonous plant aconite, which is still gathered around Eregli and used as a folk medicine. Whether this was Hercules' only visit to the place is not known, but legend has it that he also passed this way when he went to capture the jewelled girdle of the Queen of the Amazons, another of the Labours, and assisted the local people in their tribal wars. In any event, the modern town commemorates the Hero, for Eregli is the modern version of ancient Heracleia Pontica, named in his honour.

The Acherusian Cape

When Jason and his Argonauts arrived, they were particularly well received. The local tribe, the Mariandyni, were bitter enemies of the Bebryces, whose bullying King Amycus had recently been killed by Pollux in the boxing match. The Mariandyni and the Bebryces had been fighting a border war, and King Lycus of the Mariandyni was delighted that the Argonauts had inflicted such a punishing defeat on the Bebryces. Pollux, of course, was lionized as the man who had slain the bully himself, and he and the other Argonauts were invited to stay at Lycus' palace and share in a feast of celebration. King Lycus also announced that in honour of the great Castor and Pollux he would build a monument on the headland, where it would serve as a sea mark to all future sailors who passed that way. Moreover he would send his own son, Dascylus, with the Argonauts to serve as their guide and to act as their envoy to friendly tribes living farther along the coast of Asia Minor.

Sadly, though, the visit to Lycus ended in a double tragedy. From the start of the venture Idmon, the soothsayer, had known that he would never return alive from Jason's voyage; he was doomed to die on a foreign shore. At dawn, as the travellers were returning to *Argo* from Lycus' feast, loaded with presents from the king, they disturbed a sour old wild boar lying in the reed beds of the river. The brute charged out and gored Idmon, gashing his leg. Idmon fell, mortally wounded, and though his companions killed the boar with javelins, they could do nothing to save Idmon's life. They carried him back to *Argo* where he died in his friends' arms. His death demanded three days of formal mourning, and on the fourth day the Argonauts buried their shipmate on the slopes of the headland, raising a barrow over the grave and planting it with a wild olive tree as a memorial.

The delay caused by the funeral rites was fatal for another Argonaut, this time their crack helmsman, Tiphys. He sickened and died after a short, unexplained illness which may have been fever contracted in the marshy swamps of the Acheron. Tiphys, too, was buried on the headland, close to his companion, and for a total of twelve days the quest for the Golden Fleece came to a gloomy halt. Jason was downcast by the loss of his two companions and lost all will to continue with the voyage. The other Argonauts were equally despondent, and it was left to Ancaeus to take the initiative. He offered to replace Tiphys as helmsman, pointing out that he also was a very experienced sailor, and he managed to rouse the others from their glum mood and cajole them into continuing with the quest.

By a fortunate chance the most likely site for the graves of Tiphys and Idmon has escaped the expansion of modern Eregli. The 'Acherusian Height', where they were buried, according to the

Argonautica, lies within the present military zone and is still unspoilt countryside covered by turf and small trees. As we rowed out aboard *Argo* we could look up from the sea, as the early sailors had done, and there on the very peak of the hill noted the ruins of an ancient building, almost certainly the base of a former lighthouse or watchtower. The ruins stand on a low mound which appears to be artificial, and could be an ancient barrow grave. When the military zone is open to the archaeologists, this must be the first place to be searched for the last remains of two of the men who sailed with Jason aboard *Argo*.

Beyond Eregli, where my daughter Ida left us, we came to the coal town of Zonguldak, and the mayor sent out two tugs to divert the galley into harbour. Another dance troupe was waiting for us on the jetty, this time to perform a true Black Sea dance. They were clothed in tight tunics of jet black and performed the Fish Dance, quivering and shaking in imitation of a shoal of anchovies taken by the fishermen's nets and spilled flapping on the deck. Flashing silver chains, shimmering tassels and leather straps, all trimmed in silver, glistened and glittered as the dancers mimicked the capture and the death throes of the struggling fish.

Akcakoca, Eregli, Zonguldak – every town we passed on this coast wanted to make us welcome with gifts, flowers, folk dances and food for the new Argonauts. The delay in Zonguldak had put us behind schedule, so dusk found us rowing tiredly off a bleak and exposed beach. A few local fishing boats were moored in the shallows, but the rest of the fleet was drawn far up the beach, well out of harm's way. It did not look a very safe spot to stay for the night, but we were too exhausted to continue. The anchor went down, we ran out a stern line to the shore and had our supper. Then most of the crew bedded down as usual on the sand dunes, while with the members of night watch I remained on board. At about midnight, the stars were blotted out by great black clouds that swept in from the north. Suddenly there was frantic activity on the beach. Lights began to bob up and down as the local boat owners appeared and began to run back and forth. There was much shouting.

'The black wind is coming!' Ali called to me from the beach. 'They say it is dangerous, and we must be careful!'

The local fishermen were wading out into the sea to reach their moored boats and manhandle them to the sand with tow lines.

Argo sails past the Clashing Rocks and into the Black Sea.

'At Eregli an armada of fishing boats was waiting to greet us'

(*Above*) 'Pete the Cook and Tim the Purser would . . . make their way ashore to find a town and buy food'

(*Right*) Dr Adam Mackie, a medical colleague of Nick Hollis, finds himself in cramped conditions

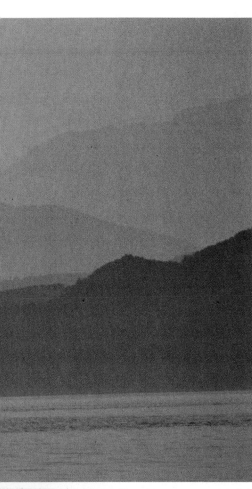

(*Left*) Off the Black Sea coast of Turkey. 'On the very worst days the crew rowed for eleven blistering hours'

(*Below*) Cormac O'Connor 'had the magic touch. If there were fish, they came to his hook'

(*Foot*) Sheltering from bad weather in Gideros Cove on the north coast of Turkey. 'It was a refuge as perfect as nature could devise'

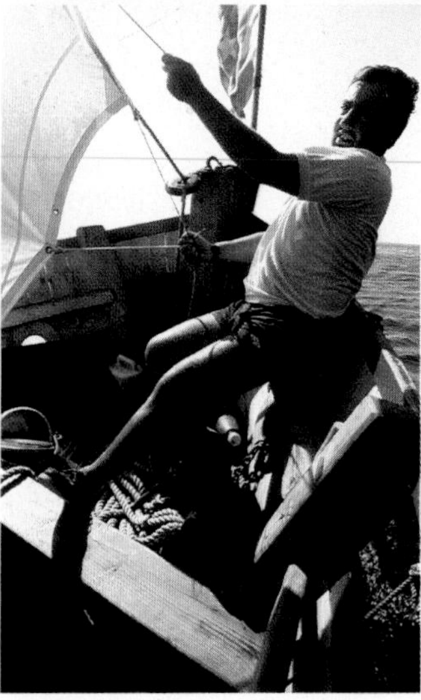

(*Top left*) 'There was a horrendous, rending crack. The port steering oar had snapped . . . It was important to get into shelter as quickly as possible.' (*Top right*) Tim Readman and Peter Wheeler 'grabbed the ropes that hauled the sail up to the spar.' (*Above*) Pete the Cook held on to one corner of a makeshift headsail, made from a rain cover, to help steer *Argo* off the rocks

(*Left*) Peter Wheeler inspects the broken steering oar. The shaft had snapped where it joined the blade. (*Centre*) Jonathan Cloke helps Peter Wheeler (in red) to repair it and (*above*) Cormac O'Connor and Mark Richards put on a temporary lashing under Peter's supervision

'This was the moment of truth for . . . the sea-keeping qualities of a Bronze Age vessel.' (*Below*) Prelude to heavy weather – the sky off Sinop. (*Left*) 'We lowered the mainyard a few feet on the mast, and set the sail loosely so that the wind spilled out most of

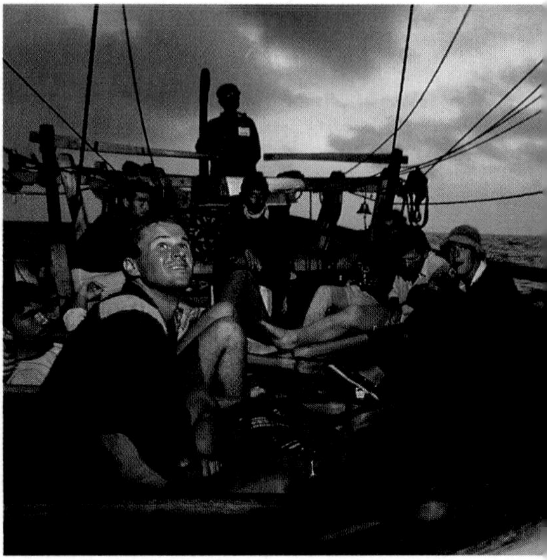

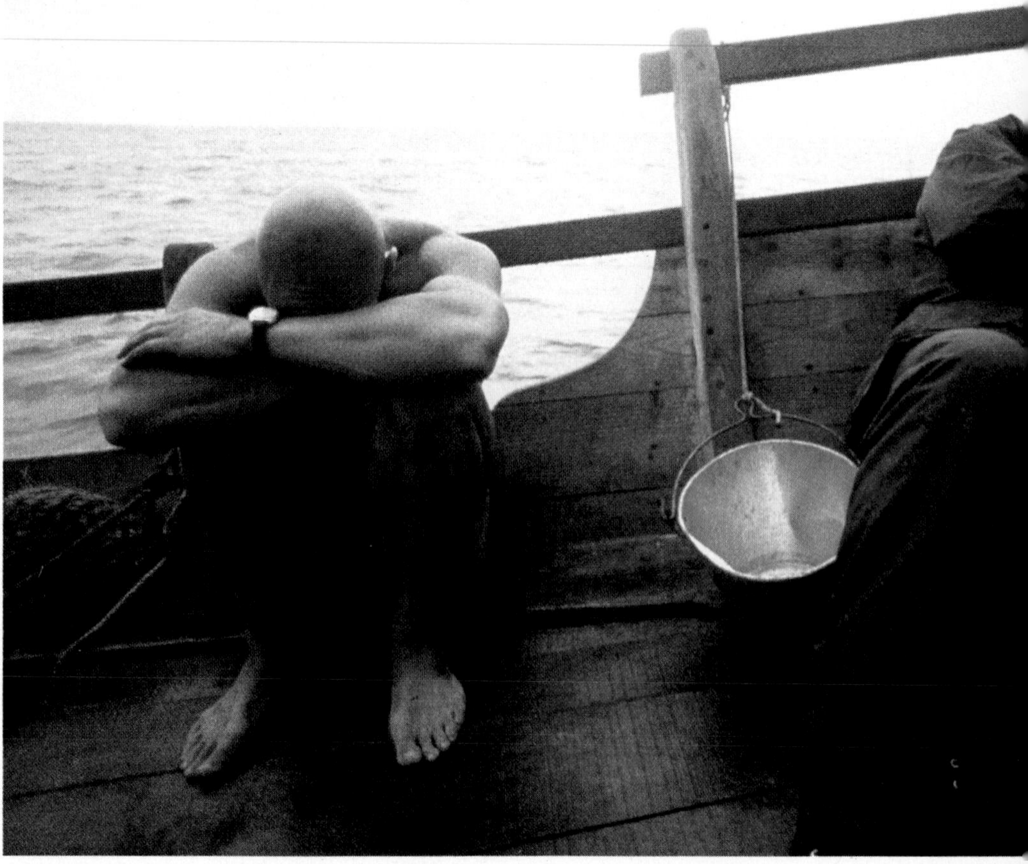

e crew were beginning to show increased signs of physical
ed haggard and drawn.' Mark Richards (*left*) and Peter

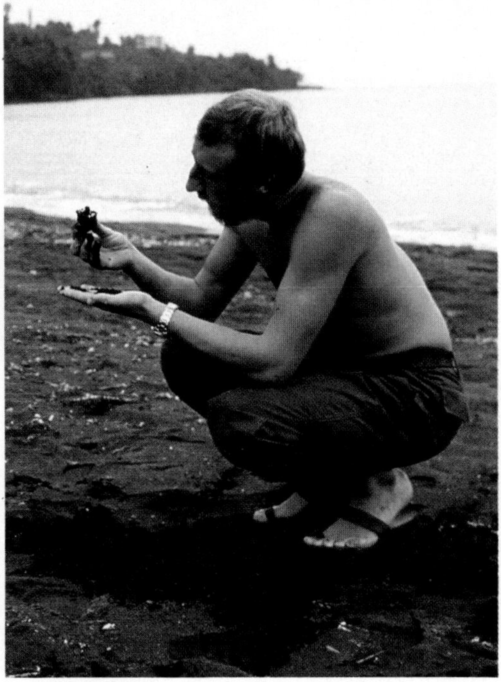

The land of the Chalybes. 'This black sand is so rich in iron that the grains can be picked up with a magnet' (*below*). Peter Wheeler (*left*) on the iron-bearing beach

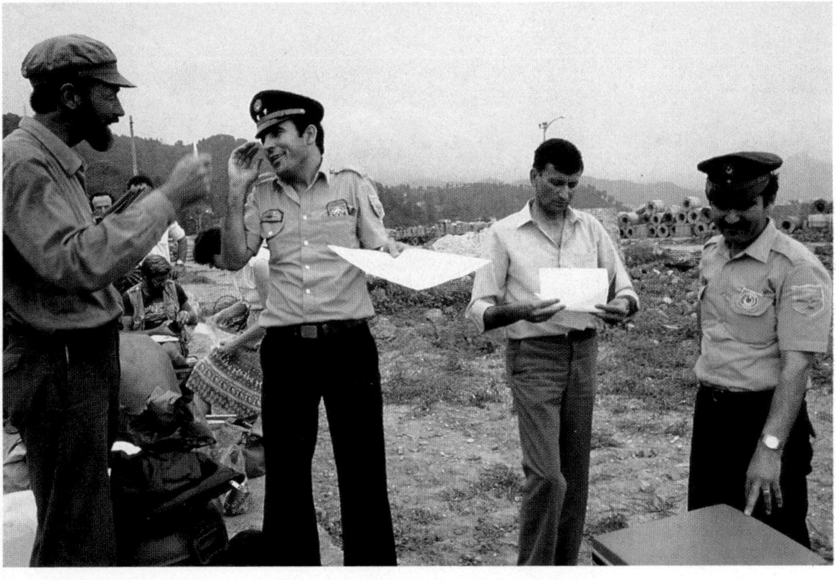

'You have very special clearance,' Turkish customs officers told the author (in red cap) as *Argo* left for Soviet waters. 'No ship has been cleared from Hopa since the Second World War'

(*Overleaf*) *Argo* enters Soviet waters

Others were turning home-made beach windlasses to haul the craft high out of the water.

'They say it will be better if you take *Argo* from the sea,' Ali shouted again. 'They say there is a big windlass to pull her, and they will help.'

I decided that it would be wiser to trust to *Argo*'s anchors, and leave her where she was. Fiddling around on an open shore, in a rising wind and in the dark, was not likely to be effective, and *Argo* ran more risk of being damaged in the manoeuvre if she was caught half-in and half-out of the water when bad weather hit us. The onboard emergency watch was stirring – I could see the three sleeping bags on the foredeck change shape. Their occupants had been awakened by the pandemonium and were obviously peeping out, reluctant to crawl out into the rain which was beginning to spit down in the darkness. They soon realized that there was nothing of it but to pull on oilskins, tend to the anchor warps and start rigging the wet-weather canvas cover.

We were still lashing down the last corners of the canvas when the squall struck. It was not as fierce as the fishermen had feared; nevertheless the onboard crew were kept busy, casting off the rope that held *Argo*'s stern to the beach, pulling in on the main anchor so that the boat floated out into deeper water, and heaving out a storm anchor to hold her from being driven ashore by the rapidly increasing waves. By then the rain was really coming down hard, and the first flashes of lightning illuminated the scurrying black shapes of the shore-based Argonauts running pell-mell for shelter from the downpour. They could crawl under upturned boats to keep dry, while the onboard watch got soaked.

'So they call this the luck of the Irish!' muttered one of the drenched figures beside me on board as we struggled to heave in a soggy mooring warp. It was Cormac, and I realized that, by chance, the onboard night watch was composed entirely of the Irish Argonauts. From that day forth the foredeck where the three of them had decided to sleep that damp night was known to the rest of the crew as the 'Irish Embassy'.

The thunderstorm was a portent of a change in the weather. For another three days, as we rowed and sailed eastwards, the rain showers became more and more frequent. Beyond the ancient and beautiful port of Amasra, where we spent one night moored in the oval of the old galley harbour, the coastline of Turkey began to change. Steep hills now came right down to the sea, and the land had a much wilder and more desolate air. We rowed past magnificent precipices where the seagulls wheeled against the rocks like white specks of foam. The mountains behind them were covered with forests of chestnut and mile upon mile of hazelnut bushes which were harvested by the local farmers. From time to time we passed an isolated cove, joined to the interior only by a narrow earth track. At the back of each cove was often a small flat area of meadow land where we could see a wooden farmhouse, one or two barns, and several small fields divided by wooden rails. There were horses or cows in the fields, and seen from afar the tiny figures of the animals and buildings looked just like a child's model farm taken from a toy box and spread out on the carpet.

On 26 June we reached the nastiest-looking stretch of coast we had encountered so far. Cliffs and rocks, more cliffs and more rocks, were all that we saw as we laboured forwards, a few hundred yards offshore. The weather was foul – that morning the sun had come up behind banks of rain clouds so thick that by 9 a.m. the light was already so poor that it felt like dusk. In the grey gloom the mountains to our right were merely black shapes behind the cloud wrack. Strands of mist dragged against the cliff faces, and patches of cloud oozed in the high valleys. For the previous twenty-four hours the wind had been blowing steadily from the northern quarter, and somewhere out in the Black Sea a storm must have been brewing, because the swell was rolling in heavily and breaking sullenly on the rocks, the spume floating out in the backwash. It began to rain. The first few minutes of heavy downpour made the crew's skin glisten, for the oarsmen were still naked from the waist up. Then the rain settled down to a relentless, pattering insistence and the coast vanished into a grey blur. The hands of the rowers turned white and clammy, and their hard-won blisters looked like dead flesh.

Life on board should have been miserable but – astonishingly – the crew actually revelled in the conditions. The heavy rain made a change, and any break in the monotony of rowing was welcome. They began to sing – song after song, mostly scurrilous, as well as some childhood favourites, ballads and drinking songs. Tim Readman jumped up on the central gangway and performed a cabaret turn on the slippery catwalk. He was joined by Adam, a doctor colleague of Nick's who had joined us near Zonguldak, and then by Mark, who for his act produced a Turkish fez from his kitbag. The crew sang and laughed, and kept on rowing. During the cabaret, the wind freshened and turned more to the east. Now *Argo* was barely making a knot through the water, and ahead, over the crew's cheerful faces, I could see that the little galley was being driven towards the rocks. The prospect was distinctly uncomfortable. The water was much too deep to anchor off this grim iron-bound coast, and our only chance was to find a cove, marked on the Turkish charts, which cut a notch in the forbidding line of cliffs. As *Argo* was pushed closer and closer to the coast, I grew increasingly concerned. We were getting dangerously near the rocks, and the crew were falling quieter as the constant slog began to sap their energy.

Then I saw a white mark at the foot of a cliff, a small dot which turned out to be a short stone pillar. It stood on a shelf of rock to one side of a narrow cut in the cliffs. Without the pillar to mark it, one would not have spotted the entrance to the cove until too late. The cove was a freak of geology. Some time in the distant past, the sea had weakened a fault in the line of cliffs, gnawing a hole about 30 yards wide. Breaking through this gap, the water had rushed in and submerged a small glen behind the cliffs, to form a nearly land-locked basin. Its only entrance was the almost indistinguishable cleft in the cliff wall.

'Watch out! There's a rock in the middle of the entrance,' suddenly called Ziya in alarm as a great, round-shouldered wave rolled into the narrow entrance and erupted in a welter of foam. But the leap of water had been caused by the wash of the sea rebounding from the cliffs on each side, when it met and clashed in the middle of the narrow channel, kicking up as if it had broken on rock. I turned *Argo* at right-angles to the entrance and drove her hard at the gap. She rose on the back of a wave, heaved forward, fell back and was picked up a second time. The crew rowed flat out to keep her moving through the water so that I had enough speed to steer her and to keep the boat from wavering off-course or broaching to the waves. In a spectacular roller-coaster ride the galley went tearing through the gap, her fierce eyes staring straight ahead, and we entered the haven.

The cove was a world apart. In 50 feet, *Argo* passed from the outside waves and swell to a flat calm. All that remained of the angry sea outside was an arc of foam which fanned out into the cove from its entrance, and undulated gently. The water of the cove was scarcely disturbed. It was like being inside a great glass jar. On all sides the ground around the haven rose so steeply that the cove was completely walled in and protected from the elements. Outside the Black Sea grumbled, and overhead the north wind swept a veil of grey scud to swirl about the mountain slope. But inside the drowned glen, the merest breeze ruffled the leaves of the bushes growing on the hillside. It was a refuge as perfect as nature could devise. At one end of the cove stood a hamlet of three or four buildings; at the opposite end a single, one-storey house with a porch, a small boatshed, a tiny strip of beach and a neat jetty that had been cunningly constructed to join together a line of half-submerged rocks. The owner of the little house must have seen *Argo* bursting out of the gloom, for he was already climbing into a small rowing boat to come and meet us.

Entering Gideros Cave

Argo glided across to his corner of the haven, dropped anchor, and the stranger greeted us courteously, taking a mooring line ashore for us and looping it around a boulder. The galley would be completely safe inside Gideros Cove, he assured us. In the worst winter storms no wave or swell ever penetrated the secret haven.

He had lived there for twenty-five years, and had never once been disturbed by bad weather. Gales might rage not 400 yards away, but the vines on his porch scarcely rustled in the wind. In summer, by a quirk of nature, not even mosquitoes disturbed his life. When the weather was right, he made his living by fishing the waters outside the cove. For the rest of the year he tended his garden, grew vegetables, in the tiny fields on the steep slope above his house, and looked after his cherry trees. There was no road to his house, only a steep track gluey with mud. But it was only a short climb to the main road, and there he could catch the bus into town 5 miles away. His life, like the cove, seemed an idyll.

Paphlagonia was the name the Greeks gave to this section of the coast, and the natives had a reputation as tough warriors who resented foreigners and were fully capable of throwing them back into the sea. Even today this remains the most inaccessible and remote region of Turkey's Black Sea coast. The broken terrain, and the high mountains so close to the coast, have isolated the region from the rest of Turkey. The first coast road is still under construction, and the small towns have no natural hinterland. Their people depend on forestry and fishing, and the indifferent farming of the foothills. Cide, the town closest to Gideros Cove, was a run-down, sad place. Most of its young people had left to find work in Ankara or Istanbul or abroad. Only the older generation were left, many of them living on money sent home by their children. Yet even here, in this obvious poverty, the town council of Cide was not going to let the Argonauts pass by without offering hospitality. The mayor sent a bus to collect us from the cove, and we went scrambling up the slippery footpath in the mud and drizzle to be ferried into town where we were given a meal, a bath at the *hamam* and beds for the night.

By dawn we were already back on the sodden oar benches. *Argo*'s sail had not had a chance to dry out in the last damp days and black stains of mildew were spreading across it, giving her a somewhat bedraggled appearance. Her crew were equally mottled. Even debonair Dick Hill's immaculate wardrobe was showing the first signs of decay, while for the rest of us the damp and the lack of space for stowage gave a very sea-stained appearance to our gear. All our clothing was smeared with mutton fat from the oar strops, our shirts were torn and dirty, our grubby trousers misshapen by hour after hour of rowing. Our eating utensils were battered and none too clean, either. The metal army-style canteens, which had looked so trim and neat when we began the voyage, were now dented and scratched. We drank from an assortment of grimy plastic cups or squalid metal mugs. Anything which accidentally slipped down into the bilge had to be condemned and thrown overboard, for it was impossible to wash out the stench from the slimy, black bilge water. Books and magazines were carefully hoarded and passed around, but their pages were swollen with damp. Jonathan had stepped on his reading glasses, and now cut a strange figure: one lens was totally starred and opaque with a fracture right across it, so that he looked like a man with one blind eye.

For another four days we laboured on past a long, dark coast which was periodically slashed with river gorges. Headlands succeeded one another, and moved astern with wearying slowness. At Cape Carambis, according to Apollonius, the north wind split, deflected on one side westward and on the other to the east. The modern Argonauts hoped sincerely that this was true, for at least we would then have a following breeze beyond the Cape. The crew were beginning to show the strain. Peter Wheeler and Peter Warren were unstoppable – apparently they had the stamina to row on for ever. Mark, the rowing master, was so game that he never gave anything less than maximum effort, but although he was growing muscles on his muscles he often finished the day in a state of physical collapse, totally drained by the effort of pulling an oar for six or seven hours with only short breaks. The really big men – Jonathan and Cormac – had the sheer weight and power to help them keep up the pressure. But in varying degrees everyone began to show fatigue – there were drawn faces, sunken eyes, aching backs, sore elbows and buttocks, skin peeling off in strips.

There was not a man aboard who could not lead the team, rowing in the stroke position and adjusting the rowing style to suit the changing conditions. In calm water a long stroke was fine, but when the sea grew choppy a shorter and more exhausting stroke was essential to control *Argo* as she heaved and rolled. Every oar had taken on its individual character. We all knew which oar was stiff, or too heavy, or slightly warped. Others were too light and whippy, while the best had just the right amount of spring in them, so that one found oneself, in the long turn and turnabout of crew reliefs, looking forward to the moment when the crew change brought you to a good blade.

Keeping the boat level became an obsession. After almost two months at the rowing benches the crew were as sensitive as any spirit level to the change in trim. If *Argo* heeled by only half a degree the oarsmen on the upper side found it twice as hard to reach the water with their blades. Then the cry came down the boat: 'Trim ship!', which sent the men on relief watch scrambling from one side of the boat to the other to balance *Argo* with their weight. Occasionally the water-soaked stitching of an oar strop would break in mid-stroke, and the luckless rower would be catapulted backwards off his bench into the bilges. When that happened, no one laughed. The crew were too tired, and it had happened too often. Apollonius had described it all:

> They laboured at the indefatigable oar. They worked like oxen ploughing the moist earth. The sweat pours down from the flank and neck; their rolling eyes glare out askance from under the yoke; hot blasts of air come rumbling from their mouths; and all day long they labour, digging their hooves into the soil. Thus the crew of *Argo* all through the night ploughed the salt water with their oars.

Off Cape Carambis the wind did begin to show signs of shifting in our favour, as Apollonius had said it would, but the weather had a treacherous feel to it. As we sped past the Cape, sails spread to a strong breeze from a lowering, rain-spattering sky, we were swept by a couple of squalls that whipped the spray over the boat and made me decide that discretion was still the better part of valour. The new Argonauts were excellent oarsmen, but their skill as heavy-weather sailors was untried. Until now, perhaps 70 per cent of the voyage's duration had been spent under oars, rowing and not sailing. Half the crew – all the Turks and several of the regular Argonauts – had virtually no experience of handling open boats in heavy weather, and *Argo* was, after all, very vulnerable in bad conditions.

In the hands of an inexperienced or tired crew she could rapidly get into trouble. A breaking sea could swamp her. She had no deck to throw off a boarding wave, and loose water slopping up and down the bilge would make her dangerously unstable. And if she was taken aback, so that her sail filled with wind on the wrong side and pressed against the mast, only quick thinking and smart action would save her from being rolled over if the mast did not snap quickly enough to reduce the leverage. In a stiff breeze a rogue wave could throw her off-balance, and then the crew would have to move their body weight very quickly to bring her back to trim. After ten or twelve hours of rowing, a crew was far too tired to react with the necessary speed. All in all, I felt it better to sail defensively and still try to put ashore each night. The last thing that I wanted was for *Argo* to be hit by a vicious squall or a sudden gale in the dark with an exhausted crew, several of whom were likely to be seasick.

My caution increased when, on 29 June, Trondur, the most experienced sailor on board, had to leave us to go home to the Faeroes. It was sad to see him go, particularly as he would be missing the last and potentially most exciting sector of the voyage. But he had been called home, and filled every last possible hour with preparing his sketches of the voyage, working both on board and from the rubber dinghy. The day of his departure was made even more depressing by the total opposition of the wind. We set out from the little port of Abana at 5 a.m. and rowed and tacked, rowed and tacked, for more than six hours to try to make headway, before I finally had to admit defeat and put back into the little harbour. It all seemed a terrible waste.

Then, as is so often the case on a long voyage, the worst day was followed by one of the best. Again we rose in the half-light and by sunrise were rowing out of Abana harbour. This time the calm held all morning, and in the afternoon came a gentle breeze from the west so that we were able to make sail. Cormac put out a fishing line and caught several meaty dogfish which were enough to make supper for the entire crew. When the sun went down the breeze was still in the west, and the weather looked so settled that I decided to take the risk of sailing on through the night. The crew were well rested and totally relaxed. Two of the Turks, Mustafa and Umur, were playing chess; the cassette player was sending out gentle classical music; and the rest of the crew were reading or chatting among themselves. We had passed the last safe harbour, and it seemed a shame to turn back. To reward us, that heaven-sent wind blew all through the night, with a sky full of stars to steer by, and *Argo* ran forward at 3–4 knots while the watches changed. Each sailing watch consisted of four men: two of them, the watch leader and his deputy, had sailing experience; the other two were novices, but they too had their turn at taking the helm and learning to sail a square-rigged galley. It was not easy, and a mistake usually meant that the wind got on the wrong side of the sail and then the other members of the watch had to pull out the oars and row *Argo*'s head round so that she was pointing in the right direction and could begin sailing again.

By dawn we were passing Ince Burnu, the most northerly cape on Turkey's shore, where the Black Sea narrows to a waist. Here we were only 160 miles from the coast of the Crimea, and had come farther east than Suez. With the waves rolling in from the north, we scudded past cave-riddled limestone cliffs, uninhabited except for the solitary lighthouse on the cape which marked this crucial turning point in our voyage. Pete the cook served up a breakfast of scrambled eggs, water melon and bread, and at last the distant tabletop hill of Sinop, our destination for the day, came in sight. We had made splendid progress: *Argo* was clipping off the miles in fine style. The wind was gusting now, and the waves growing steeper as they heaped up out of the deeps, expending the energy they had gathered on their long fetch from the Ukraine. With considerable caution I set course to avoid Sinop's headland by a wide margin, and aimed well clear of the area where waves were bursting against the rocks. It was a defensive decision and one for which I was to be very thankful over the next few hours.

A large wave picked up *Argo*. She skidded across the crest, slipped down the far side, and there was a horrendous, rending crack. Her port steering oar had snapped. The shaft of the oar, 3 inches by 7 inches of prime, hand-picked timber, had broken where it joined the blade, which flapped uselessly to one side, joined only by a few twisted splinters of wood. Perhaps the steering oar had been weakened when we scraped over the rocks back in the Sea of Marmara; perhaps it was just a freak wave. Whatever the reason for the break, half of *Argo*'s steering capability was now gone.

At first the situation did not seem to be too serious. *Argo* was still running with the wind on her quarter, and the remaining steering oar, on the starboard side, seemed to be holding her on course to clear the wave-lashed headland. There seemed to be a very good chance of slanting the galley's course gently so that she skimmed past the menacing rocks. The horrified looks on the faces of some of the crew members, when they heard the crack of the rudder, were replaced by expressions of interest to see what would happen next. Peter Wheeler, the ship's carpenter, came aft and stoically examined the broken fragments of the steering gear. Calm as always, Peter merely shook his head over the damage, hauled the broken bits aboard, and tied them safely with cord.

'I'll have a go at repairing the damage when we get into Sinop,' he said reassuringly.

Argo sailed on. She cleared the first headland. Then I eased back on the starboard steering oar to turn her right-handed to run past the cliff face, picking a channel between the rocks and a small jagged offshore islet. My plan was to shoot through the gap and then duck round the back of the headland to find shelter from the wind, which was ricocheting off the cliffs. The manoeuvre seemed simple enough. It only needed a steady nerve and good timing, for I knew it was important to get into shelter as quickly as possible. If we were blown past Sinop's headland with only a single steering oar, we would be in trouble. Our Bronze Age galley could not turn back in a strong following wind if we overshot the mark, and if we failed to duck into Sinop we would be blown onwards into the 50-mile-wide bight of Bafra Bay. On the far side of that bay was the Bafra foreland, a low, flat delta pushed seawards by the outflow of the Kizilirmak River. It was a bleak coast, without a single harbour, and constantly changing shoals and banks. The pilot book warned shipping to give it at least 5 miles' clearance for safety, as even the charts were unreliable. The next port beyond that was Samsun, nearly 100 miles by sea from Sinop, and much too far to attempt with a half-crippled ship.

But as I pulled back on the starboard steering oar I had a sharp, frightening lesson in the way a galley steers. For a few seconds everything went well: *Argo* turned smoothly. Then, as she swung past a certain critical angle, the tautly filled square sail suddenly took control of the boat: *Argo* simply went maverick. The sail had more turning power than the single steering oar, and the smooth turn abruptly became a violent right-handed swerve. Instead of pointing at the gap between the cliffs and the islet, *Argo* rushed straight at the cliff wall. The single steering oar flopped weakly in my hand. With a will of her own *Argo* settled on a natural course, tucked down her shoulder and began to accelerate fast, heading fatally for the rocks. I felt exactly like a novice skier who, turning gently on a slope, finds his skis taking control and rushing him towards the lip of a precipice.

'Starboard brace, let go! Hard in, port brace! Ease out starboard sheet! Haul in port mainsheet!' With a rapid-fire sequence of orders I tried to swing the sail round and get *Argo* to straighten up. But it was no use. The ram was now behaving as a forward rudder, biting into the water and steering the galley on a suicidal track. The bulging sail was a menace. Without two steering oars to control her, *Argo* was as wild as a bolting horse.

'Brail up!'

Tim Readman had the knack of always being at hand in a shipboard emergency, and with Peter Wheeler he scrambled to the aft position and grabbed the ropes that hauled the sail up to the spar.

'Hands to oar bench positions! Blades outboard! Starboard side row on! Port side back her down hard!' The oarsmen on the starboard side began to row frantically ahead, while on the port side their companions plunged the blades of their oars into the water and pushed backwards to serve as a brake. The idea was to turn the boat about its axis, but the combined strength of fourteen oarsmen was not enough. *Argo* continued to drive forwards at the rocks, gripped by the wind. Now there was only 50 yards to go before we hit the cliff. Somehow the head of the boat had to be turned downwind, and quickly. On a modern yacht the foresail or jib would do this work. But *Argo* had just a single square sail. A jib, temporary jib. . . .

'Quick! Get the forward rain cover and rig it to the forestay as a sail.'

Tim Readman and Pete the cook hurried to where the rain covers were stowed in a sail bag, wrenched open the draw cord and pulled out the small triangle of canvas that normally sheltered the foredeck from the rain. 'Quick!' Crippled *Argo* was still blundering onwards to the rocks, despite the best efforts of the oarsmen. The men trying to brake the vessel were flattened by the pressure of their oar handles, leaning back and hanging on with one hand to the gunwale to stop themselves being pushed down below the oar benches.

Tim and Pete ran back down the central catwalk with the canvas. Big Cormac flung down his oar and went to join them. He hoisted Tim on his shoulders so that Tim could reach up high enough to attach one corner of canvas well up the forestay. There was no time to rig control ropes, so Pete the cook held another corner of the sail and Peter Warren hung onto the third. The small scrap of canvas clattered in the wind, and then bellied out. Distinctly I felt the tug of the mini-sail in the bow, urging *Argo* to straighten up. Slowly the galley's ram turned to the correct course, and *Argo* was heading in the right direction again.

Five minutes later I decided to try using the mainsail again, but as soon as it filled with wind *Argo* again spun round and streaked off towards the cliffs. This time we were well prepared – up went the makeshift jib-cum-awning, and *Argo* curtsied out of the danger sector. In this lopsided fashion the stricken galley zigzagged crazily along the foot of the cliffs. Now the port-side rowers dug in and held their blades rigid to act as rudders; now the starboard side rowed to give us propulsion. On the foredeck the three Peters and Tim Readman twisted and turned the awning to catch the wind and control the bows of the galley, while the single remaining steering oar hung uselessly. We were coming up to the rocky islet. All being well, we should sidle through the gap. I looked at the chart. With half a gale behind her, *Argo* was on the verge of being shot out into the great sweep of Bafra Bay.

'There's a chance we'll find a patch of shelter just around the point,' I told the labouring crew. 'But the moment we come to the end of the cliffs, we'll have to row like hell to try to duck into it and escape the wind. Get ready, and when I give the word go for it!' I sidled *Argo* gently towards the cliffs, getting as close as I dared to the rocks. As we swirled past the last point, I yelled: 'Pull away! Pull away!' and turned *Argo*'s nose to starboard. We shot round the corner, the crew rowing as desperately as on the worst of the Bosphorus. We had just enough speed to overcome the drag of the wind buffeting off the cliffs.

To my intense relief there was indeed a tiny patch of undisturbed water, no more than 30 yards wide and 20 yards deep; a small fishing boat was already anchored in it, riding out the squalls. *Argo* skittered into the refuge and Cormac threw the anchor overboard. For a moment the anchor refused to hold, and *Argo* began to slide back towards the sheer cliff face, so close that Peter Wheeler stood by with a boat hook to fend off. The oarsmen got the boat underway just in time, and Cormac smeared butter on a lead oar weight, then lowered it to the sea floor to check for sand or rocks. When the lead came up with grains of sand sticking to the butter down went the anchor again, and this time it held.

Peter Wheeler began attending to the broken steering oar. He prised up two of the cook's planks to use as wooden splints, drilled a line of holes in the broken rudder shaft, and began hammering in some wooden pins to hold the splints in place. The whole assembly was then reinforced with lashings of cord. He was still busy on this temporary repair, enough to let us limp into Sinop, when around the headland came a large fishing boat crowded with cheering and clapping Turks. Sinop was celebrating the end of the Ramadan religious festival with a regatta. *Argo* could not have come at a better moment. Please would we row into harbour when the wind eased, they shouted. And then they unfurled a large, slightly misspelled, banner. It read: 'SINOP WELLCOMES THE ARGONAUTS'.

Husnu

8
The Last Lap

If Jason and the Argonauts made their voyage into the Black Sea some time in the thirteenth century BC, as the evidence suggests, what sort of people would they have encountered living along the coast? The curator of Sinop's museum took me to see the remains of the kind of settlement which would have been flourishing on the coast when the Argonauts sailed by. The site was on the crest of a steep hill some 5 kilometres from Sinop, and it commanded a wide sweep of the bay as well as the rolling, hilly country that extended inland towards the mountains that effectively severed the coast from the interior of Anatolia. The late Bronze Age houses had all been built of timber, the natural building material of this heavily wooded area, and the people had made a plain pottery and tools of bronze and bone. The general impression, said the curator, was of a culture that was simple, robust, and had close links with the other tribes living along the coast in both directions. The inhabitants, a people known as the Kaskas, occupied a section of what was in effect a coastal corridor, running from the Bosphorus in the west to the Caucasus in the east, and had contacts with one another along the coast rather than inland to the plateau. Once the Argonauts emerged from the Clashing Rocks and entered on that corridor it would have carried them naturally to Colchis, the land of the Golden Fleece.

The Kaskas are something of a mystery people. They appear about 1600 BC in the Hittite records, and there is reason to suppose that the Hittite rulers established some sort of trade route from their capital at Bogazkoy in north central Anatolia to the Black Sea coast in Kaska territory. The importance of this trade route is only just beginning to be appreciated by historians who traditionally have been much more interested in Hittite contacts southwards to the Mediterranean. But a glance at the map shows that the Hittites' nearest access to the sea was north – to the Black Sea. And this may have some relevance to the Argonaut story. Recently a dozen Mycenaean pottery jars were discovered in the fire-blackened ruins of a small Hittite palace in Bogazkoy. This caused great excitement among the archaeologists, for these jars, humdrum containers for oil, were the first indisputably Mycenaean articles to be found in the Hittite capital. Paradoxically the jars date from a time when the Hittite kingdom was breaking up and the overland routes were in disarray. On the other hand, the jars do coincide with the time ascribed to the Jason legend, and it may well be that they are evidence that contact had at last been established by sea, via the

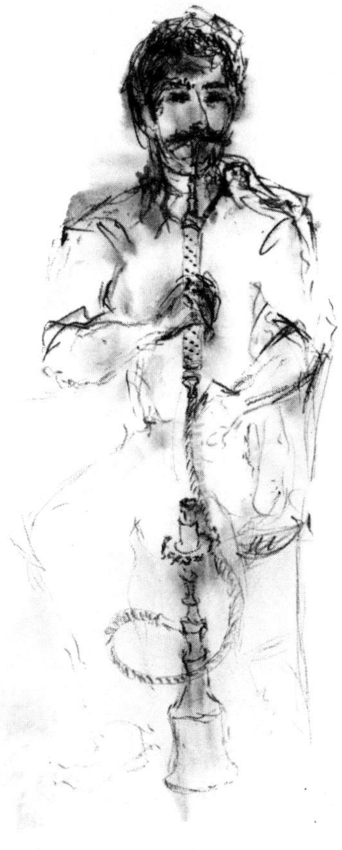

Bosphorus, between the Mycenaeans on the one hand and the Hittites, the Kaskas and the other peoples along the coast on the other. If this is so, then the Jason story would symbolize the first Greek penetration of the Black Sea.

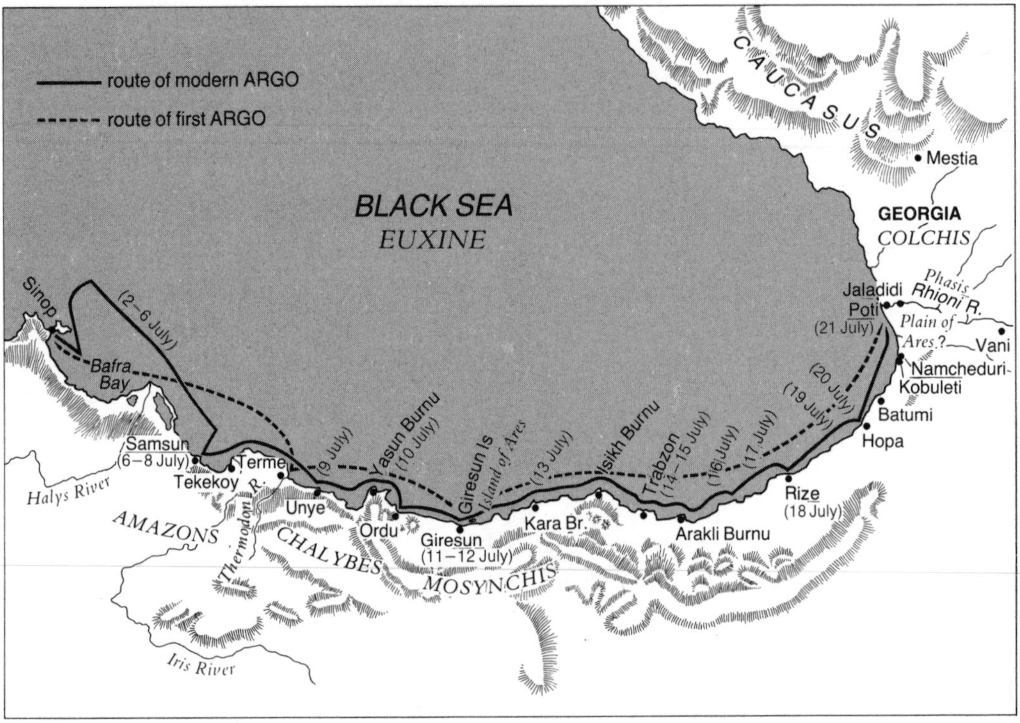

Boom! Boom! Tacca! Tacca! Boom! Every beat of the drum could be heard clearly across the water. The drummer himself was a bizarre figure – naked except for a pair of white undershorts – as he came striding down the harbour pier at Sinop, staring rigidly ahead and pounding on his drum. He did not give a single glance in our direction, even though it was obvious that he had come to see us off. The man was in his sixties, tanned mahogany by months of near-nudity, and at his heels trotted a small terrier, black and white, with a large black patch over one eye like a dog in a newspaper cartoon. The dog, too, glanced neither left nor right, but trotted with its nose a few inches from its master's naked heels. No one else was on the jetty, just this eccentric fakir beating a mad cadence to our oar strokes as we rowed back out into the Black Sea.

For some reason the stiffly marching figure, the insistent thump of the drum and the brisk little terrier trotting along like a warlock's familiar made me uneasy. Peter Wheeler had done a first-class job on mending the steering oar. He had located a woodworking shop and repaired and strengthened the splintered shaft, which now felt solidly comfortable as it rotated in its notch in the crosspiece. The crew had visited Sinop's *hamam,* courtesy of the mayor, and we had tidied up *Argo.* Why, then, should I feel a sense of foreboding? There was a clear sky, a gentle following breeze, and to our left the rearing bulk of Sinop's tabletop headland gave us a placid lee in which to sail. The only slight irritation was that the evening breeze, which was carrying us out into the bay seemed fitful. My plan was to cut across the bay and clear the dangers of Bafra Point by late next evening when we would still have daylight to check our course. I hoped that the wind would hold, so that the crew would not have to begin rowing at dawn to get around the point. If we had known what would happen over the next five days none of us would have raised any objections to rowing, because we were now to have our baptism of heavy weather in a Bronze Age galley.

At midnight the wind shifted into the east, the worst possible direction. To avoid being blown back down onto the cliffs of Sinop in the darkness, I headed *Argo* north towards the open sea to find sea room. The wind began to increase. It was not a dramatic, swift change, but a steady gain in strength as the hours went by. With the stronger wind, the sea began to tumble and break. Now the triple wave described by the fishermen showed itself: occasional groups of three short, steep waves larger than the others came rolling down on *Argo* and sent the galley lurching violently. For a while the crew tried to row as we struggled to claw off the dangerous lee shore, but soon it was completely impossible to handle the oars. The boat was far too unstable. No one could get a grip on the surface of the sea with their blades. Men slipped on the spray-splashed oar benches, cursed, fumbled their strokes and eventually abandoned the attempt. The crew pulled their blades as far inboard as possible and wedged the oar handles under the benches so that the blades angled upward as far as possible clear of the waves. This was not just a question of convenience. There was always the danger that a bank of oars could be caught by a breaking wave, act as levers and trip the boat.

By 2 a.m. the sliver of a new moon illuminated the extent of *Argo*'s distress. She was wallowing from side to side with a sick-making motion. Sometimes the roll was so violent that the oar blades, despite their angle, plunged underwater and emerged again with great gouts of water and an alarming rattle of the oar handles that shook the whole length of the boat. Occasionally a larger wave thrust the boat farther over, and the sea slopped over the gunwale. Then we were obliged to pump out the loose water from the bilge.

It was time to increase our defensive tactics against the sea, and try to ride out the heavy weather as safely as possible. This was the moment of truth for Colin Mudie's design and the seakeeping qualities of a Bronze Age vessel. We did not know how well *Argo* would hold up, or if the weather would deteriorate even further. The early Greek texts were full of tales of galleys which sank in storms, and the greatest losses were always when the fleets were driven on the rocks by gales: that was when men had died by the thousand. I decided that, so long as *Argo* could carry sail, we should

continue to head out to open water. We lowered the mainyard a few feet on the mast, and set the sail loosely so that the wind spilled out most of its strength. After a few experiments we found *Argo*'s natural position, lying aslant to the waves, rising and falling to their advance and giving a lurching sideways heave as each crest passed under her keel which, being only 2 feet in draught, gave very little grip on the water. In essence *Argo* was just a long, slim rowing boat far out to sea in heavy weather, and it was up to her crew to give her the best chance of survival. To try to keep the boat from tipping too much, the crew now lay down on their oar benches and wriggled themselves into position, so that their heads – the heaviest part of the body – were close to the windward rail. It made the cramped conditions even more uncomfortable, because now, whenever the waves lapped aboard, the slop of water drenched the men's heads and trickled down their necks.

Argo *in heavy weather*

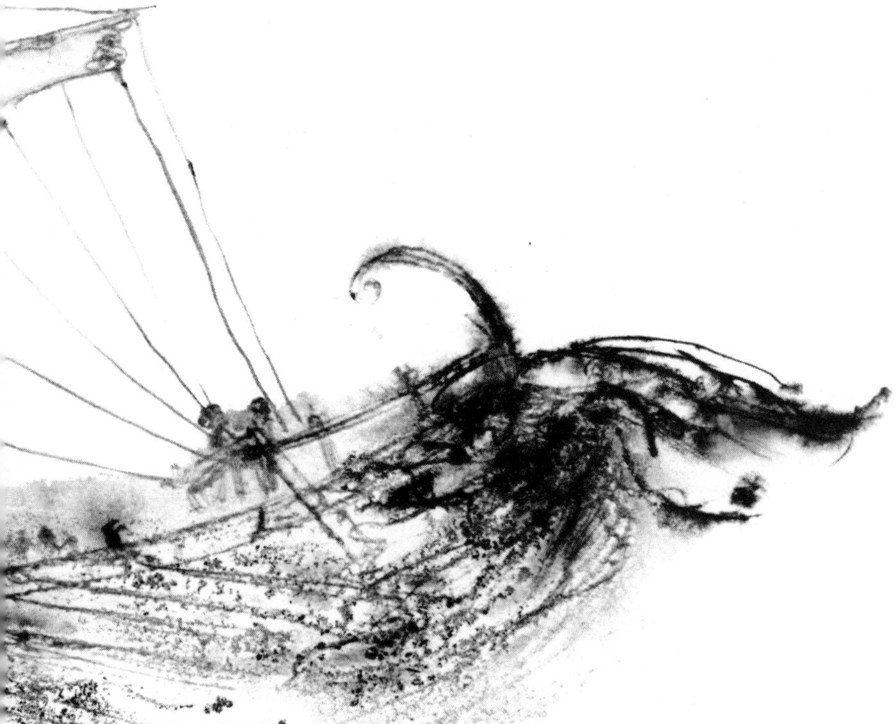

At dawn the faint outline of Sinop headland was only just visible, very low on the horizon, and disappearing from sight as we drifted farther out into the open sea. There was a radio station on the cape, and I tried calling up on the walkie-talkie to ask for a weather forecast and to report our position. But the little handset, no bigger than a camera, was not powerful enough; there was no response. I groped under the central gangplank where the emergency lifeboat-style radio was secured, extended its aerial and tried again; once more there was no reply. In the Black Sea there were few listening watches on ships or shore stations. I folded up the aerial and put the set away. We would just have to look after ourselves.

As the morning dragged by, *Argo* was pushed farther and farther out to sea. The headland disappeared, and we were surrounded by an endless vista of dull, breaking waves under a sullen sky. We saw no ships, for *Argo* was now outside the track used by the handful of coasters that rounded the cape. We were finally on our own, trapped in the classic situation that all galley sailors have feared since the earliest days of navigation: adrift in an open boat, crammed with men who would soon grow tired and dispirited if weather conditions did not improve; too weak and puny in the face of bad weather to dictate our course; and with no chance of getting back to land until the wind blew itself out or changed in the galley's favour. The new Argonauts were as close to the original galley conditions as they had ever been.

The ordeal continued all that day and all that night. 'Another pretty miserable night,' reads my journal, written thirty-six hours later,

> spent with the sea continuing rough, and the boat under reduced sail, flinching over the white-crested waves. We are being steadily driven northward. All the Turks are now down with seasickness, unable to eat and huddled in their blankets on the benches like dead men. Ali tries to eat dried bread to stop his retching, but Umur and Yuksel are totally prostrate and refuse all food. Occasionally a wave comes aboard, or a shorter wave thumps into the side of the boat and shatters into spray which whips across the sleeping men on the oar benches. If it's a larger wave, solid water goes down their necks and into their sleeping bags. . . . The tinned hot dogs we

> ate last night tasted foul, enough to make even Peter Wheeler throw up. I think they must have gone sour in their tins, but it is difficult to cook anything more substantial in these conditions. The only bright spot was when Pete the cook handed out a single slice of water melon to each man – delicious. We are having to be careful about water consumption. I have sixteen men aboard, and our water supplies are limited.

The reactions of the crew varied. A few, like poor Yuksel and Umur, were laid so totally low by their seasickness that they couldn't have cared less what happened. They were dead to the world for almost two days, sodden blankets drawn over their heads as the galley lurched and heaved, and they lay limply amongst the kit. If *Argo* had capsized, they would have had little chance. The majority of the other crew members were phlegmatic. They lay in their sleeping bags or curled up in their oilskins, and occasionally a rogue wave dumped water on them. The only diversion was to wriggle right up to the edge of the gunwale and peer over it to watch the steady succession of waves rushing down on *Argo*, and to wonder just how far each wave, depending on its size and angle, would come up the side of the vessel towards one's nose.

Nine times out of ten *Argo* had a critical point of stability, tipping over on her side as the crest of the wave rushed up the gunwale, closer and closer to the edge of the planking until, just 3 or 4 inches short, she gave a little jerk, levelled out, and the wave top hissed by underneath us. Again and again she wriggled in this manner over the waves, and only occasionally did she take water aboard.

One or two of the crew were beginning to look genuinely distressed. It was the waiting which sapped their morale. As the hours dragged by and *Argo* just went on wallowing and lurching, threatened by wave after wave, it was difficult for newcomers to accept that we should continue to lie so passively to the seas and trust to the design of the boat. In fact, our best plan was to conserve energy and wait for the bad weather to cease. Only then could we try to find our way back to land. In the meantime our safest place was to be as far away from shore as possible, and to help *Argo* ride the seas. We still had the option of turning and running with the waves and wind, relying on the galley's fine upswept stern to rise over the breakers, but there was no way of knowing how much trouble the ram might give in this situation. It might possibly dig into the water, wrench the bow sideways and broach the galley. *Argo*'s heavy-weather behaviour was a venture into the unknown. None of us knew how well the galley would stand up to the conditions, and each member of the crew had his own limits of experience by which to judge. Those witnessing their first heavy weather in an open boat were naturally the first to worry; those with more experience had a higher threshold of concern.

At about 3 a.m. on the second morning the wind at last began to ease, and by sunrise *Argo* was no longer being menaced by the rollers. 'Thirty-six hours of heavy weather in an open boat with a large crew are enough,' my notes go on. 'I hope that it doesn't continue. The best thing about these conditions is that the sun shines even during a Force Seven wind, so that the waves are sparkling and fresh as they bear down on *Argo*. Enthusiastic aggression rather than surly menace. . . .'

One thing the gale did do for us was to put an end to our practice of navigating without a compass. When the wind eased and we could begin sailing again, a small pocket compass mysteriously appeared, placed where the steersman of the watch could see it. We had come 800 miles without the help of a compass, and proved the point that sailing from Greece to the Black Sea was perfectly possible without one. Some members of the crew evidently thought that enough was enough; historical experiment should only be carried so far, and they were more interested in getting back to land as soon as possible. Of course the sun and stars still made it quite clear which direction was south, where the land lay, but the compass was reassuring, though strictly speaking it was more of a psychological prop than a precise navigational aid. Its usefulness was severely curtailed by the fact that we did not know our starting position after a day and a half of heavy weather which had driven us well clear of all land.

My guess was that we were about 30 miles north-northwest of Sinop. Without knowing our starting point or accurately checking our speed through the water, or being aware of the effects of the local currents, we still had no way of calculating when we would come back to land, or where we would strike the coast. Looking up at the night sky as *Argo* turned back for the coast, I found it just as reassuring to see the two stars, Castor and Pollux, shining in the constellation of Gemini in honour of the original Argonauts. By keeping the twins at the end of the starboard yardarm during the first night watch, *Argo* was on course for the Turkish coast.

Food was beginning to run short. There was simply not enough space aboard *Argo* to carry sufficient supplies to feed sixteen men for any length of time, and already we had consumed the normal two days' allowance of bread and vegetables. The reserve supply of food included the tinned hot dogs which were suspected of being tainted, so it was safer to dump them overboard and not risk food poisoning. We were therefore on short rations, and a single egg with a handful of rice was our supper, while breakfast and lunch together consisted of two small biscuits per man and a cup of coffee or tea. But, more important, we did have plenty of fresh water. We could get along without food for several days – and the seasick crew members had no appetite anyhow – but to run short of water would have been disastrous. We had made a point of never leaving harbour without our water containers being at least 80 per cent full, and they had been topped up in Sinop. Now the crew rationed themselves to 2–3 pints per man per day, and even then we had enough fresh water for at least a week.

My main concern now was the wind, which had to stay in our favour for at least two days. If it changed back into an offshore breeze we would be certain to be pushed still farther out into the Black Sea; on the other hand, if it died away we were too far from land to get there by rowing unless we had an absolutely flat calm, and in the Black Sea this was unlikely. There was too much open sea to the north, and the swell built up much more than among the islands of the Aegean. As it was, the troubled sea showed no immediate signs of abating as we swooped and spiralled our way southeast. Then at 8 a.m. on the morning of 5 July, we again heard the unmistakable crack of a steering oar breaking.

This time it was the shaft of the starboard steering oar which had sheered. Exactly as before, *Argo* had been sliding down the face of a wave; the weight of the boat proved too much for the steering oar and the solid timber shaft had snapped in half, leaving the rudder blade flapping. Tim Readman quickly rigged up an emergency auxiliary steering system with an oar stuck over the stern, and for an hour he helped the helmsman keep *Argo* running downwind while Peter Wheeler carried out the repairs with which he was becoming all too familiar. Once again the cook lost his two floorboards, which were snatched up and cannibalized to make splints for the broken steering oar. Then Peter supervised Mark and Cormac in putting a thick lashing around the temporary joint. When the steering oar was lowered back in its notch, it looked far from secure. The blade wobbled from side to side as the emergency joint moved, and the bandage of lashings and wedges stopped it from turning fully so that the steering oar could no longer be rotated in its groove. It now projected down into the water like a very shaky fin keel, but at least it was sound enough to keep *Argo* on course, provided no harsh rudder movements were needed.

The accident did not affect either morale or progress. *Argo* was bowling along merrily at 3–4 knots and in exactly the right direction. The old hands from the Sindbad Voyage had seen similar crises before. On the way to China our Arab ship had suffered chronic problems with her rudder and yet she had brought us all the way to Canton. All that was needed was the ingenuity to make running repairs at sea, coupled with a steady nerve. The fact that this was the second steering oar to break on *Argo* also helped. We had seen it all before, and we knew we could make and mend. It would be much the same if we hit another batch of heavy weather. Now the crew had been through a heavy sea and survived the experience, their confidence would be immeasurably enhanced.

It was just biscuits again for supper, and then during the fourth night at sea we saw the loom of lights on the horizon, which we calculated had to be the major town of Samsun, and began to row towards them. At 8 a.m. we passed the head of the breakwater of Samsun harbour, and soon afterwards tied up to a quay. It was the fifth day since we had set out from Sinop, and the Argonauts were exhausted. What we all wanted now was a good, unbroken sleep and a hot meal. We had been living aboard the galley for far longer than had been the original design. Ali, scouting ashore to find a café for our breakfast, came back with a copy of the morning newspaper. He was grinning. 'Look at the headline on the front page,' he said. 'It's about the Argonauts. It says "Twenty-five British sailors lost in the Black Sea!"'

Samsun is one of the best harbours of Turkey's north coast, and in the late Bronze Age there was already an important settlement at a place now called Tekekoy, 14 miles to the east. Preliminary excavations at Tekekoy have brought to light late Bronze Age graves containing bronze knives, earrings and two ceremonial bronze spearheads. These finds suggest to archaeologists that Tekekoy was one outlet of the land route joining the Black Sea with the major Hittite cities of the interior. The coastline in this area has been drastically altered by the masses of silt, stones and sand brought down by rivers such as the Izilirmak, and deposited as deltas pushing out to seaward. Apollonius had noted how this stretch of coast was a land of changing deltas – the outfalls of the Rivers Halys, Iris and Thermodon, the latter famous as the home of the warrior Amazons, and the Iris renowned for its ninety-six branches and tributaries which meandered back and forth over the Amazonian plain, many of them vanishing underground never to reappear, while the surviving handful joined up to discharge into the Black Sea near Themiscyra. There, said Apollonius, the Argonauts beached *Argo* overnight, intending to challenge the fierce Amazons, but a fine northwest wind sent by Zeus persuaded them to push on again with all speed, heading towards Colchis, so the anticipated battle was avoided.

Something of the same spirit of impatience was starting to take hold of the new Argonauts. We spent two days in Samsun, recuperating from the offshore escapade, while a kindly ex-officer of the Turkish Navy, invalided from active service, expertly repaired the broken steering oar for us. He refused any payment, asking only for a set of *Argo*'s plans so that he could later make a model of the galley. In his repair he used sidepieces of mulberry wood, pins of Turkish oak and fillets of beech. 'We could now award a prize,' Peter Wheeler remarked, 'to anyone who can guess correctly just how many different types of timber have now gone into this boat.'

The moment the steering oar was back in place we set out, skirting the delta of the Yesil Irmak which continues to spew out its gravel and sand northeast of Samsun. 'CAUTION: shoaling having occurred, vessels should not approach within 5 miles of the shore in the vicinity of Iris Point,' warns the Admiralty chart, nervous of the constantly changing depths. We, as befits a galley, were less than 200 metres from the strandline as we approached the large stain of milky-looking water which filters out through the shingle fan marking the outfall of the river.

'We ought to be in sturgeon country now,' said Peter Wheeler, hopefully baiting up an outsize fish hook. 'It would be very pleasant to have caviar for breakfast.'

'Aren't sturgeon caught in nets?' some non-fisherman came back pessimistically.

Conversation was rather subdued as *Argo* plodded forward. Several members of the crew were suffering from monumental hangovers, acquired at a late-night party in Samsun; one or two were too ill to stir. Once again *Argo* was adopting her bad habit of sidling down towards the coast even though we had set the sail as taut as possible, hoping to nudge her upwind.

Then Nick said quietly: 'Why not try moving everyone astern? It might help *Argo*'s sailing.' Two months earlier, soon after leaving Volos in Greece, we had made a similar experiment, moving as much of *Argo*'s stores as possible aft to see if we could make the galley sail closer to the wind. Then it had seemed to produce little difference. Now, however, anything seemed worth trying if it would make *Argo* more of a sailing, and less a rowing, craft. The entire crew, fit or hungover, clambered aft and crowded onto the tiny stern deck. There was not room for everyone to stand. They perched on the stern rail or sat on top of one another in a heap, more than a ton of human flesh abruptly transferred aft. The effect was wonderful. *Argo*'s nose lifted a trifle, and suddenly she was pointing 15 degrees closer to the wind.

'Terrific!' exclaimed Seth. 'No more rowing! We can sail to Georgia!'

In fact Nick's suggestion did more than any other single item to improve the conditions for the rest of the voyage. Obviously our previous experiment near Greece had not been drastic enough. If we were to move ballast, we had to do it massively. Now we altered the stowage of the boat permanently by hauling out the anchors and stowing them under the aft deck, sorting out the heavier barrels and moving all of them aft, then lashing the water containers as far aft as possible, even though it meant carrying water for cooking all the way down the length of *Argo*. And we made a point of being careful were the crew sat, resisting the temptation to drift forward and gather on the tiny foredeck. The temptation was understandable: in the bows there was better shelter from the wind and – above all – this was Peter the cook's domain. The lure of the occasional snack and a cup of tea or coffee was strong.

'At nightfall on the following day,' wrote Apollonius,

> they reached the land of the Chalybes. These people do not use the ploughing ox. They not only grow no corn,

> plant no vines or trees for their delicious fruits, and graze no flocks in dewy pastures. Their task is to dig for iron in the stubborn ground, and they live by selling the metal they produce. To them no morning ever brings a holiday. In a black atmosphere of soot and smoke they live a life of unremitting toil.

Anatolia is, in fact, one of the earliest places on earth where mankind is known to have forged iron, and the reason can be seen on the beaches east of Samsun. The sand is black or a very dark grey where the waves have sorted out the grains of iron-bearing soil washed down by the rivers. This black sand is so rich in iron that the grains can be picked up with a magnet, and the blackest sand can be smelted into crude iron simply by heating it up in the embers of a fire. Iron was so valuable to Bronze Age people that the metal was given as tribute to rulers, as prizes in contests or as the most generous of gifts. The Greeks, as we had seen on Lemnos, believed that the knowledge of metalworking had been brought to them by the god Hephaestos when he came to the island. If, as is likely, the knowledge actually came from the regions along the Black Sea coast of Anatolia, then the most likely route for its transmission was the same sea corridor which Jason and his companions travelled.

Indeed there is evidence in the *Argonautica* that some sort of trade connection existed even before *Argo* passed that way. Jason's great galley may have been the first Greek ship to travel the whole distance along the Anatolian coast, but the Greeks themselves may have penetrated to parts of the area even earlier, either overland or, more probably, by coasting voyages in local craft. Not only had Phrixus with the flying ram gone before the Argonauts to Colchis, but at Sinop, the legend recounts, Jason and the Argonauts found three Greeks, Delieon, Autolycus and Phlogius. These three had been left behind from Hercules' overland expedition against the Amazons, and were glad to be picked up by their countrymen. The possibility that there might have been a well-established coastwise sea route is strengthened by the extraordinarily fortunate encounter which now took place between Jason and four of his cousins, who had been coming by ship in the opposite direction, from Colchis itself. The four young men – Cytissorus, Phrontis, Melas and Argus – were the sons of Phrixus. Their mother was Princess Chalciope, the daughter of fierce King Aeetes of Colchis whom Phrixus had married in the land of the Golden Fleece. After the death of their father, the four young men had decided to visit his country in Greece to claim whatever inheritance was due to them. Setting out from Colchis in a local ship, they got as far as Giresun when a storm blew up in the night. Running for shelter before a howling north gale, and presumably heading for the safe anchorage of Giresun, the Colchian vessel struck a rock and broke in pieces. The young men managed to cling to the wreckage and were cast up on an island sacred to Ares, the God of War. There, very soon afterwards, they were rescued by the arrival of *Argo*.

There is no difficulty in identifying the island of Ares. Only four islands worthy of the name are found along the entire north coast of Anatolia. An exploring vessel which follows the coast would naturally make these islands its stopping places, for the very good reason that the islands provide secure camp sites at a safe distance

Giresun Island

from any hostile natives on the mainland. By the time *Argo* came to the Amazon country she had already passed three of these islands, and the fourth and last island, said Apollonius, was actually used by the Amazons as a place of worship on which they would sacrifice horses, using a sacred black stone as an altar to their war god.

Giresun Island, 1½ miles northwest of the present town, fits the location exactly, while nearby Palamut Rock, an isolated danger, is an excellent candidate for the place where the Colchian ship came to grief. On a coast that is remarkably free from offshore reefs for hundreds of miles, Palamut Rock is an exceptional hazard in just about the worst place. It lies in the northern approach to Giresun harbour and lurks just beneath the surface; only the occasional white break of swell washing over it gives any warning of its presence. The Colchian boat, running for shelter in Giresun during the confused darkness of a northerly gale, would not have had a chance even of seeing the danger before she struck this isolated fang and was split open by the impact. Her crew would have been thrown into the water, and the luckier ones would have swum for Giresun Island half a mile away.

Phineas, the blind seer back at the entrance to the Bosphorus, had warned the Argonauts that they would find the island of Ares infested with hostile birds. 'You must beach your ship on a low-lying island,' he had told them, 'though not before you find some means of driving off the innumerable birds that haunt the lonely shore.' The birds would attack humans. As the Argonauts rowed towards the island, the legend recounts that a bird flew out and shot a feather at them, wounding Oileus in the left shoulder. Eribotes, who sat next to Oileus on the same oar bench, pulled out the feather and bandaged the wound, while Clytus succeeded in shooting down the next bird with an arrow. Half the Argonauts then locked shields over their heads to form a protective canopy over *Argo*, while the others continued to row for the island. As they came ashore they raised a great din, clattering their weapons on their shields and giving a loud shout, so that 'the birds in their thousands rose into the air and, after fluttering about in panic, discharged a heavy shower of feathery darts at the ship as they beat a hasty retreat over the sea towards the mainland hills'. This is clearly an account of the Argonauts landing on an island which was the habitat of large numbers of birds. Giresun Island is exactly that. Rank upon rank of cormorants and gulls could be seen sitting on the rocky flanks of the island as we approached, launching themselves out in squadrons as they took fright at the arrival of the new *Argo*, while others circled ceaselessly in the updraught that was deflected from the humpbacked island.

Landing on Giresun Island still needs caution. There is no harbour, just a rough quay cut into the solid rock on the landward face. No one lives on the island, which is only some 250 metres in breadth, though it was fortified in Byzantine times. Now the island is visited every 20 May by people from the mainland who come to invoke its magic. For here, once again, we found that an Argonaut site has retained a very strong tradition of magical powers. The custom is to go first to a riverbank on the mainland and throw in seven double handfuls of pebbles, followed by a single handful. This symbolizes a release, the act of casting off care and misfortune. Then the supplicant hires a boatman to row him out to Giresun Island and circle it three times, always from east to west. Going ashore, the visitor approaches a solitary black boulder, which stands exposed on the eastern shore of the island. This black rock, some 10 feet in diameter like a huge billiard ball, is made of very much the same conglomerate material as the Clashing Rocks and is pockmarked with small holes. In these holes the believer places tokens of his wish: a pair of small pebbles nestling together comes from sweethearts who hope to marry, a single stone is from a childless couple who want to have a baby. A strip of cloth may be nailed to the rock simply as a token. If he is young and fit, a man can strengthen the magic by climbing around the rock itself, spreadeagled against its rough surface, again three times.

The old boatman who made a living ferrying these visitors out to the island spoke of men who had dug for buried treasure on the island, the centre of which is now covered with thick undergrowth, groves of trees and tumbledown Byzantine ruins. No treasure has ever been found, as far as he knew, but the black rock was famous among all the country folk for its magic. Could the massive black boulder be the same ancient 'black stone' where Apollonius said the Amazons slaughtered sacrificial horses? It is possible. The alternatives would be the low boulders now buried among the ferns and brambles in the centre of the island, where the seabirds constantly wheel overhead as the wind sweeps over Ares Island.

The four sons of Phrixus, half-Greek, half-Colchian, were aghast when they heard that the Argonauts intended to take the Golden Fleece. Did they not know, they asked the Argonauts, that their father King Aeetes was suspicious of all foreigners, and usually put them to death for trespassing in his realm? As for the Fleece, it was held in great reverence by the Colchians, and had been hung in the sacred oak in a sacred precinct. There it was guarded by a huge serpent which never slept. To continue with their mission was an act of madness. Yet, because the sons of Phrixus were blood relations to Jason and owed their rescue to the Argonauts, they agreed to accompany them to Colchis. When the galley got there, they would at least intercede with their father on behalf of the travellers.

From Giresun eastwards the harbours on the Black Sea coast are spaced more closely and a new road wriggles along the shoreline where the mountains run close the sea. In Apollonius' time the forests of this region had been famous as the home of a bizarre people, the Mosynchis, named after the *mossynes* or wooden houses in which they lived. These aborigines had strange, reversed notions of decency. Acts which other races performed in public the Mosynchis coyly did in private, but all normal private acts the Mosynchis did in public, coupling with one another quite unperturbed in the presence of their neighbours. But they were not a cruel people, and when their tribal leader made a mistake they punished him only by imprisoning him in a room for a day with nothing to eat.

Today the slopes of the Mosynchis mountains are remarkable for being covered either with teabushes or with hazelnut groves, acre after acre of them, and everywhere we went we were given hazelnuts to eat – raw, roasted, in sweets or in a paste.

'If we eat any more hazelnuts, we'll all be growing bushy tails, scurrying up trees and hiding them for the winter,' Mark groaned, after yet another shopping trip brought back several kilos of nuts.

Where teabushes grow it rains, heavily and often, and as *Argo* advanced past the terraced hillsides of Turkey's tea-growing country we were constantly saturated with steamy rain showers that watered the tea gardens. By now each member of the crew knew all the others' foibles: John Egan's bursts of ebullience; Seth's cockney bounce and chaotic kitbag, which periodically had to be made to disgorge its extra items; and big Jonathan's habit of wandering up and down the boat at dusk, trying to find space to fit his 6-foot 5-inch frame and tripping over those who had already settled down for the night. 'That's my head you're standing on,' Mark remonstrated quietly one evening from beneath the bench where Jonathan had been standing for two minutes looking around for a sleeping place, blissfully unaware that he was poised on the rowing master's bald cranium. Tim Readman had also taken to sleeping in the bilges as the ideal nest, and in the mornings he would re-emerge, round-faced, blinking his blue eyes, with snub nose and beard and a battered hat pulled down low so that he looked somewhat like Paddington Bear in a good humour.

As the beards of the crew grew thicker and thicker, so their haircuts were growing shorter and shorter. At every harbour we visited someone always seemed to be inclined to have a close crop from the Turkish barber, and came back aboard even more bristle-haired than before. Giresun, Tirebolu and Akcacale all saw the crew's hair grow shorter and shorter. At Trebizond the harbourmaster gave us a splendid meal in the park overlooking the sea, and in the evening a ballad singer, renowned in the region, serenaded us with a newly minted saga about the Argonauts, Turkish, British and Irish, who were so obsessed as to want to row along the Black Sea coast.

Various extra Turkish volunteers came and went: a businessman who ran a car wash and could spare a couple of days; a medical student; a high school pupil. They came, Mustafa told me on the day he signed off the crew to go and get himself a summer job, out of curiosity or on impulse or because of an ideal. Mustafa himself had joined because he sought adventure, wanted to meet new people and to find himself. He had failed his dentistry exams and hoped on *Argo* to win back his self-confidence. He told me that he had learned a great deal more about himself in the twenty-five days he had spent aboard the galley. Now he knew that he could withstand physical hardship, the wet, the hours of rowing, the cramped conditions, the misery of having to stand watch on a damp, cold night or, worse still, having to row in the darkness to hold *Argo* off a lee shore or to pull her head through the eye of the wind. Mustafa went off happily, regretting only the times he had suffered from seasickness and the worst stretches of rowing. As he put it succinctly, 'Sometimes it was really torturing.'

By the time that Mustafa left, the crew were beginning to show increased signs of physical exhaustion. In the final week of rowing along the Turkish coast a lethargy set in. The reason was partly psychological – the oarsmen were husbanding their strength for the last push across the border to the Soviet Union and into Georgia, the modern land of the Golden Fleece. But in part, too, they were genuinely worn out by day after day of cramped living space and physical effort, interspersed with nights that were never comfortable and often broken by sudden demands to row or handle sail. They looked haggard and drawn, and three or four hours of rowing in a morning, which they had once accomplished with such verve, now became a deadening chore which left them tired and lacklustre. After a quarter of a million oar strokes, the thought of even another hundred miles under oars was stupefying. Every man aboard preferred to wait for the wind, however fickle or however late it came. Night or day, rain or shine, *Argo* was on the move just so long as there was wind to fill her sail and rest the oarsmen.

As it turned out, the favourable breezes mostly came after dark, so the crew got even less sleep as *Argo* groped her way forwards, keeping parallel to the string of shore lights and occasionally surrounded in the darkness by the snuffling sounds of schools of small Black Sea dolphins. Our voyage had begun in the lands of the olive, grown everywhere to supply cooking oil. Now we were beyond the zone of the olive, and instead the people of Trebizond had once used dolphin blubber as their only source of oil. When we left Greece in late spring the landscapes had been stark and clear, and on sunny days the air was crisp. Now, in midsummer, the eastern Black Sea was warm and steamy, visibility was poor, and the clouds constantly rolled over the mountains. For ten consecutive days we never glimpsed the sun.

On 18 July the crew went overboard to clean the hull, and we scraped off ten weeks' accumulation of weeds and barnacles, using the sharp edges of our much-abused eating canteens as scrapers. As the muck peeled off the hull, we saw how it drifted in a cloud in the water behind us, a sure sign that even here *Argo* was still nudging a slight adverse current. The scraped-down hull added a quarter of a knot to our speed, and even that fractional gain was deeply welcomed. *Argo* tacked in and out from shore, laboriously clawing up to the wind. When the breeze failed, we heaved out the oars and rowed back towards land until we could anchor, for we hated the thought of being sent backwards by the current or being blown offshore for another bout with the gales. The entire night of 18–19 July we moved in a futile zigzag, going out to sea as far as we dared, then turning back towards the land only to find ourselves at virtually the same place we had left the previous evening.

At first light on 20 July I awoke to find the dawn watch of Peter Warren, Peter Wheeler and Seth, reinforced by Cormac, gallantly rowing the last mile towards a harbour pier. They were bringing *Argo* to Hopa, the last port in Turkey, just 4 kilometres from the Soviet frontier. We had looked forward so much to reaching Hopa that it was a disappointment to land in such a down-at-heel and drab place. It was a shame, I felt, to be leaving from a point that was thoroughly depressing a country that had been so warm and helpful. Hopa's main street was potholed and broken from convoy after convoy of heavy trucks that came to load freight for hauling overland to Iran and Iraq, Hopa being the nearest port on the Black Sea to these countries. The reinforced concrete houses were ugly and neglected and the port, which had been greatly enlarged to meet the Middle East trade, was suffering from a sudden slump in commerce. The vast harbour held only two or three freighters. Hopa had a dead and defeated air; it felt like the end of the world.

Nevertheless the Turks at Hopa were as eager as everywhere else to help us. Previously any boat intending to sail from Turkey to the USSR had been obliged to clear customs and immigration formalities at Trebizond, farther back down the coast. Very few cargo boats made the crossing, and it was unheard of that a boat should sail direct from Hopa to Soviet Georgia. I said I was entirely prepared to take all the crew's passports by road to Trebizond, get them and the ship's papers stamped and come back to Hopa. The officials looked appalled. It was a five-hour journey to Trebizond, they said, and the port police office there might be closed when I arrived. And then I would have a five-hour bus ride to get back. The officials conferred and decided to telephone the governor for help, but he was absent, attending a ceremony. The Argonauts waited on the quayside the whole afternoon, surrounded by our kit barrels which were open for customs inspection. Eventually the governor or his deputy must have returned to his office, because the officials came hurrying down to the quay, beaming with satisfaction.

Argo had clearance to proceed. I did not have to go to Trebizond. The customs man was satisfied. So was the harbourmaster. So was the local policeman. What about our passports? I asked politely. Shouldn't they be regularized? They had been stamped with an inward stamp on our arrival in Turkey – wasn't it necessary to have an outward stamp from Hopa?

'No, no,' I was told, 'that will not be needed. You have very special clearance. And anyhow we cannot stamp your passports because no ship has been cleared from Hopa since the Second World War. In fact no one has given us any stamps! Have a safe journey. *Gule! Gule!*'

So we left Turkey with their farewell ringing in our ears. Translated, it means, 'Go laughing!'

9
Georgia

Two enormous stone pylons mark the sea frontier between Turkey and the Soviet Union. Painted with red and white bands, the two pylons loom starkly on the shoreline, one behind the other, and behind them rise the dramatic slopes of the Little Caucasus mountains. When the two pylons are seen in line from the sea, that is the moment the seafarer straddles the invisible boundary across the surface of the sea which divides the two countries. The two pylons also stand in direct line with a prominent mountain peak, high inland, that the government surveyors must have decided was nature's unmistakable landmark.

Argo, travelling at a sedate 3 knots, crossed that imaginary line in the grey half-gloom of early morning. If, as we had been told, we were the first boat in nearly forty years to have permission to cross that frontier, going direct from the last Turkish port at Hopa to the first Soviet port at Batumi, I did not want to go blundering across the line in the dark, so for most of the previous night we had been experiencing the unusual sensation of trying *not* to make any progress. We had said goodbye to our Turkish Argonauts at Hopa, and then we rowed for half an hour up the coast and anchored in a small, stony cove to eat a late supper, to rest and wait for the night breeze off the land to carry us towards the Soviet Republic of Georgia.

There was a feeling of real excitement and curiosity on board. What would the next day bring? What would Soviet Georgia be like? What sort of reception would we have? Would there be a great difference between the Georgians and the Turks? The frontier was only 80 miles short of our final goal, which was the mouth of the

River Rhioni, called by the Greeks Phasis, on whose bank had stood the sacred oak tree where Phrixus had hung the Golden Fleece. The Georgians lay claim to one of the oldest continuous civilizations in the world; they are the direct descendants of the Colchians who had lived in the Rhioni valley in Jason's time, and some of them still speak much the same language that the first Argonauts would have heard. How would these people view our twentieth-century quest? What would be the final outcome for all our grinding labour – the blistered hands, sore buttocks, uncomfortable nights on hard rowing benches, sweat-stained clothes, putrid bilges, and night watches when, bleary-eyed, one longed to sink back into the warmth of a sleeping bag instead of having to stand at the helm while the minutes dragged by.

One by one, the crew settled down to catch a brief nap before we headed for the frontier. Nothing could diminish their accomplishment in getting so far. They had succeeded in rowing and sailing a vessel of the late Bronze Age for nearly 1500 sea miles, a voyage which Homer and his contemporaries had regarded as a heroic feat by men brought up in a tradition of hard physical toil and sustained effort. In the modern age our only extra advantage was that we knew where we wanted to go. With charts and geographical knowledge, we could avoid the fear of the unknown that the Mycenaean explorers must have experienced. Nevertheless we had suffered from a different sort of ignorance. When we set out from Greece, we had no idea of whether or not our vessel would stand up to the conditions of the voyage. We did not know when to take shelter, what to do when caught by a storm, how to recognize a good galley anchorage or what parts of the vessel were most vulnerable. All this, which the first Argonauts would have known, we had learned the hard way. The new Argonauts, I felt, had reason to be proud of themselves.

As *Argo* nuzzled at her anchor rope in the darkness, I thought of all those who had helped us to get so far, and who would only vaguely know where *Argo* lay at that moment: Uncle John in Athens; Costas, the sixty-one-year-old former airline pilot, and the other Greek voluteers; Erzin, Umur and the Turks; Trondur, back in the Faeroes with his portfolio of sketches to remind him of warmer lands. I regretted very much that they could not be here to see Georgia for themselves, after they had done so much to get us to the final lap of the journey.

Many others were waiting to hear what we had discovered: Colin Mudie, whose design for *Argo* had proved so successful; Tom Vosmer would want to know how the ancient shipwright's techniques had withstood the rigours of three months' voyaging; and there was of course Vasilis. The taciturn Greek shipwright was probably even then sound asleep on Spetses before beginning the new day when like every other day of his working life, he would surely go putt-putting down to his little boatyard on his motor scooter, feed the cats, pick up a *skipani* and go to work on one of his usual wooden fishing boats. Vasilis would never see his masterpiece sail across the Soviet frontier, but at least we still had his favourite *skipani* with us, just as he had asked on the day we left Spetses. The tool was no longer attached to *Argo*'s sternpost, because we had found its razor edge a danger to men climbing over the stern, but Peter Wheeler had it stowed safely in the tool barrel and used it often when carrying out running repairs.

Everything that had gone into creating the Jason Voyage was approaching a climax. Tomorrow we would venture across into new, totally unknown territory. All my planning and scheduling ended on the Turkish frontier; beyond that line the expedition was entirely in the hands of our Soviet hosts. Yet somehow I felt that everything would go smoothly. My confidence had been shared months ago by Sarah Waters, the key member of the team who from the start of the original idea for the expedition had run the project's only 'office'. 'Oh, you'll be well looked after by the Soviets,' she had said. 'There won't be anything for me to do once you cross the border. I think I'll take my holiday then and close the office for a couple of weeks. Just send me a cable when you are on your way back.'

Now *Argo* was poised for those last few miles. The sea grumbled on the beach shingle. The crew slept. At midnight the expected night breeze came, blowing from the land. Cormac hauled up the anchor and the sail was set. *Argo* gathered way, and we headed onwards. Here the coast ran almost north and south, for we were creeping round the farthest limit of the Black Sea, the shore which the Greeks called the 'uttermost bourne', the limit of their seaborne travels. Indeed our longitude was farther east than Mecca. The night breeze was so favourable that *Argo* bustled along too quickly. There was a risk that we would be on the frontier before dawn, so I ordered the sail to be doused, and for three hours *Argo* lay patiently in the water, at right-angles to the wind, and drifting sideways towards the USSR.

Dawn revealed the two pylons, and we unfurled the mildewed sail again. The three red Mycenaean warriors painted on it were worn and faded, but they still marched forwards stiffly towards Colchis, bearing their shields with the ram's head symbol. On the

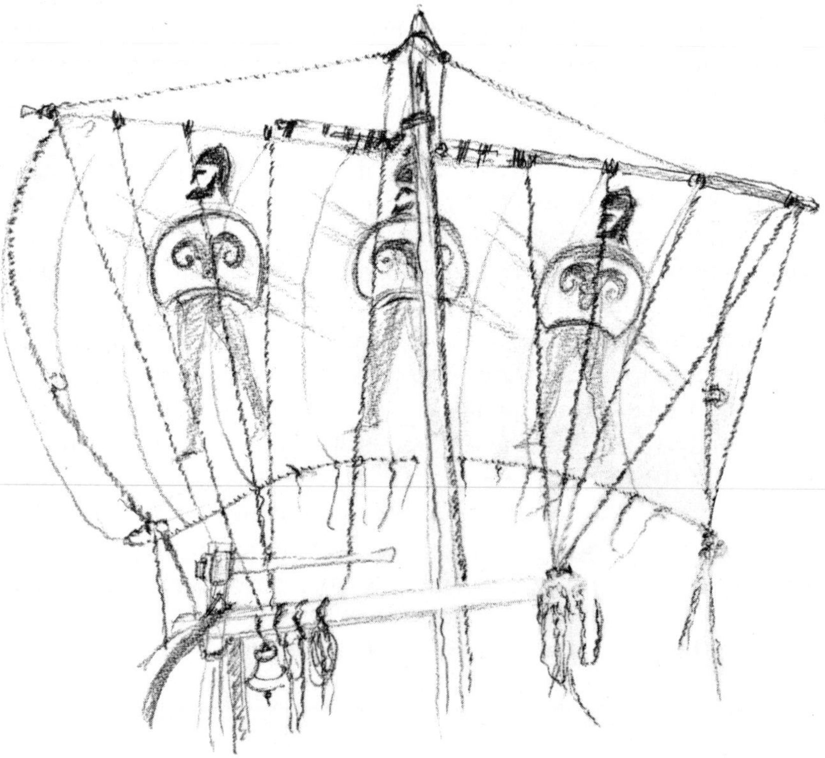

seventy-eighth day since leaving Volos they were about to enter the kingdom of the Golden Fleece. At 0634 hours the two pylons came precisely in line, and we sailed into Soviet waters. There was not a single vessel to be seen; we were quite alone. *Argo* swam stolidly across the surface of the sea, pitching softly to the swell. The early visibility was so poor that one could see scarcely half a mile through the murk. A drizzling rain shower drifted a grey, impenetrable curtain across our path. Something in the dark curtain moved slightly, a darker patch in the general gloom. Squinting forwards, we wondered if there was anyone there to meet us.

For six weeks there had been no contact with the Soviet authorities. Passing through Istanbul I had visited the Soviet consulate and asked a friendly consular officer to inform Moscow that the expedition was going well. He had promised to do this, and had known all about *Argo*, and that was a good sign. But of course it had been impossible to foretell exactly when *Argo* would reach the Soviet frontier; everything depended on wind and weather, and what happened to us on the long haul along the north Turkish coast. It was more than six months since I had written to Yuri Senkevich, the Russian doctor-traveller, and explained to an executive committee of Soviet television my hopes of tracking down the legend of the Golden Fleece in Soviet Georgia. The committee had promised to help, to arrange for me to visit the archaeological sites of Georgia and to discuss my theories with Georgian scholars. There was even talk of bringing a squad of Soviet oarsmen out to *Argo* while she was still at sea, and putting them aboard to help us row up the Georgian coast and into the mouth of the Rhioni River, if that was still navigable. But I knew just how tricky it is to arrange a rendezvous at sea between boats, especially when one vessel is as small and low in the water as *Argo*, and travelling in fits and starts at the mercy of the fickle wind.

The black patch behind the rain curtain took shape. It was a patrol boat, grey ship on a grey background, and it was heading straight towards us. *Argo* was now well within Soviet waters. The patrol boat came down on us, circled us once, and then a second time. The bridge crew stared down at us impassively. We waved. There was no response. The uniformed figures scrutinized us as if we were some dull piece of driftwood. Only a Soviet sailor, hidden from the view of the officers, peeked out of a porthole and waved back surreptitiously. Abruptly the patrol boat engines roared to full thrust. She put over her helm and swung away, heading back into the mist, leaving a white furrow of wake behind her. We saw her resume station, a sentinel lurking against the shoreline. *Argo* sailed forwards, past her. The little galley might no longer have existed.

Suddenly the little walkie-talkie burst into life. '*Argo*! *Argo*! Do you hear me?' a voice said clearly. 'This is *Tovarisch* calling you.'

I grabbed the little radio and answered, '*Tovarisch*, *Tovarisch*. This is *Argo*. Read you loud and clear. Go ahead.' I released the control button, and waited.

There was no reply. The radio hissed gently in my hand, and the voice repeated: '*Argo*! *Argo*! Do you hear me? Please answer.'

I tried again to respond, but without success. It was clear that, while we could hear the mystery ship, *Argo*'s radio was too weak for them to hear us. We could only plod forward in the water, listening to the voice of the unknown radio operator dutifully trying every ten minutes to establish contact. It was like playing a game of blind man's buff.

'Well, at least someone's expecting us,' I commented.

'If that's the *Tovarisch* I'm thinking of,' said Adam, 'then I know her. She's the big Soviet training ship that took part in last year's Tall Ships Race. She's a square-rigger.'

We moved on. The wind was holding fair, and *Argo* was making almost 4 knots through the water. The sun burned off most of the mist and, as the light strengthened, the water around us turned a beautiful opaque pale green, where the shallows and silt altered its texture. It was like sailing through liquid jade. The sunlight gave a pearl-grey tint to the distant cloudbanks, and the rain-washed air had a luminous, limpid quality that one sometimes sees after a thunderstorm has passed. Very faintly, in the far distance, three tiny lines emerged from the horizon. I peered through the binoculars, and the three tiny lines became the topmasts of a ship, advancing in our direction. A quarter of an hour later the masts were visible to the naked eye. They began to blossom with white petals – sails.

Then the hull of the stranger came over the horizon, as she sailed down to intercept us. She was indeed *Tovarisch*, the three-masted square-rigged barquentine of the Soviet training fleet. She was a ship that has appeared on thousands of postcards and calendar pictures, sailed all the world's oceans, and competed in most of the tall ship races. *Tovarisch* is known to every aficionado of the tall sailing ships, and today she was looking her best, the morning sun reflecting off her pyramids of canvas and her white hull set off against the grey clouds and the pale green sea. She looked stunning. And it was quite obvious that she was coming to greet us.

'Now that,' said an appreciative Argonaut from an oar bench, 'is what I call a reception committee.'

Tovarisch adjusted her course to sail by *Argo* no more than 100 yards away. Small figures scurried up the square-rigger's shrouds and spread out along her yards. The upper sails vanished one by one, and were neatly stowed. Then *Tovarisch* turned a half circle and took up station off our port side. The silhouettes of her cadets stayed on the crossyards. A whistle blew – we heard it quite distinctly across the waves – and the Soviet cadets whipped off their white hats and gave three cheers, a neat, orchestrated aerial ballet. The Argonauts, sitting on their grubby oar benches in their ripped and tattered clothes, their motley collection of belongings stuffed in barrels and bags under their feet, the galley scruffy and travel-worn, gazed at the immaculate square-rigger, gleaming with new paint, polish and the meticulous maintenance performed week after week by two hundred or so cadets.

More boats came hastening over the horizon. Yachts were hurrying out of Batumi which had come into sight to the northwest. The lead boat had its name written in 4-foot-high letters along its blue hull – *Kolkhida*, the Georgian version of Colchis. The old legend was obviously well remembered. *Kolkhida* came rushing down at us, tacked smartly and drew level on the opposite side of *Argo* from *Tovarisch*. The yacht's crew were waving. 'Welcome, *Argo*! Welcome to Georgia!' they yelled across to us in English. The helmsman was busily shaking a bottle. It had to be Georgian champagne, for there was a sudden spurt of foam and glasses were being handed along the deck. The yachtsmen raised their glasses in a toast, drained the champagne and tossed the glasses into the sea.

'Hey! How about some for us?' called Tim Readman. There were grins and nods, *Kolkhida* sidled to within 10 yards, and three bottles of champagne were lobbed across to us.

I looked away to port, towards *Tovarisch*. Her rail was lined with spectators, waving and cheering. I could see television camera crews pointing their lenses at *Argo* and in the waist of the ship a block of blue-clad figures all dressed in tracksuits. They looked like a football team posing for a photo. I remembered the promise made to me: they had to be the squad of Soviet oarsmen who were going to help row *Argo* up the Rhioni River. They looked suitably massive.

Our rubber dinghy began a shuttle service to *Tovarisch*. Among the first to scramble over *Argo*'s stern rail was a stocky, fresh-faced man with twinkling eyes. He put out his hand with a grin, and and I recognized him from his photograph.

'You must be Yuri Senkevich,' I said. 'Thank you so much for organizing such a wonderful welcome. It's terrific!'

'I'm glad you like it,' Yuri replied. 'We've been waiting for you for the last couple of days, and everyone is very keen to greet you.'

Suddenly blue tracksuited figures were tumbling aboard from the rubber dinghy – big, powerfully built men in runing shoes. They went down *Argo*'s central gangway, shaking hands with the Argonauts. On each man's tracksuit was sewn the emblem of the Georgian republic. They could not wait to get started on the rowing.

'May we row, please?' asked their leader.

Mark Richards rolled his eyes in mock astonishment at such a request. 'Here! Be my guest! Have my oar!' He scrambled off his oar bench and gave his position to the superfit-looking Georgian athlete, who took a few expert strokes to get the feel of the 14-foot blade. All the newcomers, it turned out, were physical training instructors, trained athletes. Every one was a master of sport of the Soviet Union. Some were specialists in rowing; two were expert kayakists; their team leader had won the Spartakid Championship of the Soviet Union. Even the jovial, slightly less lean figure who ducked under the stern crossbar and offered to take over the steering for me was a competition-class helmsman.

With such a surge of visitors there was scarcely room to stand on *Argo*'s stern deck. Officialdom arrived in the uniformed shape of a senior officer of the Soviet Frontier Guards, with a great deal of braid on his shoulder boards and a galaxy of gold stars on his lapels. He was less interested in checking our documents than in collecting souvenirs of *Argo*'s own rubber stamp – a little outline of the galley – to take back and distribute in his office. Yuri's son, Nikki, arrived to join his father, and I was then introduced to a small, alert man with a very crisp and efficient air about him. By his dark eyes and black hair I guessed him to be a Georgian, and he turned out to be Nugzar Popkhadze, chairman of the Georgian State Committee on Broadcasting and the man responsible for our forthcoming visit. He was a dynamo of activity. How far did I think *Argo* would sail that day, he asked me. Could we get as far as the harbour of Poti at the mouth of the Rhioni River?

No, it was too far, I replied, but if the wind held we should be able to reach Poti the following day. 'Good,' said Nugzar, clapping his hands together briskly. 'We'll be waiting for you.' He did not elaborate any further, but the gleam in his eye should have warned me that I was in for a surprise.

With Nugzar came another visitor whose profession one could have spotted at 50 yards. He looked exactly what he was – a distinguished scholar – but rarely does one see a bespectacled, donnish academic beaming with such obvious pleasure on the heaving stern deck of an open boat. It was Professor Othar Lordkipanidze, whose name had been familiar to me for the past three years, ever since I had first begun to study in depth the archaeological background to the legend of Jason and the Golden Fleece. Othar Lordkipanidze was the name which had signed many of the articles I had read concerning the early Greek contacts with Colchis. He directed a famous excavation at the ancient Greek colonial city of Vani on the bank of the Rhioni, presented highly regarded papers at international conferences and was head of Georgia's prestigious Institute for Archaeological Research.

'We've been looking forward to greeting you to Vani,' he said, 'Everyone is very excited, and all has been prepared. I'll be able to take you around Georgia, and show you the archaeological sites that you want to see.'

What would have happened, I wondered as I absorbed the evidence of all this careful preparation, if *Argo* had failed? It was never certain that we would get as far as Georgia. We might have been defeated by the Bosphorus or sunk in a gale off Sinop. Yet it was obvious that here in Georgia, and at a higher level in Moscow, enormous efforts had been made to prepare for our visit – months and months of planning had been made and checked, resources delegated, schedules dovetailed, oarsmen selected and prepared, *Tovarisch* put on standby, an entire apparatus set in motion. All for a small open boat manned by a handful of volunteers, bobbing along at a snail's pace towards Soviet Georgia. I was glad that I had not even imagined the responsibility while *Argo* was at sea: it made it that much easier to enjoy the welcome.

That night we got as far as Kobuleti, a small coastal settlement some 25 kilometres south of Poti, where the low delta lands of the Rhioni give way to a sandy shoreline covered with pinewoods. The Georgian volunteers were rather disappointed that the breeze was behind us and we could sail onward until the sun went down, until in the darkness the hissing waves warned us that we were running into shallows. *Tovarisch* had earlier stood clear to avoid this shallow zone, and the other yachts went ahead to Poti's harbour for the night. Six Argonauts went with them, whisked away by enthusiastic Georgians. Where they went or whom they were with I had no idea until they showed up next morning, announcing that they had spent the night in Poti being wined and dined. 'There was a woman in the restaurant, at least six and a half feet tall!' announced Tim Readman wonderingly, as he came back like some grizzled mariner too long at sea and full of exaggerated tales for his shipmates.

The enthusiastic masters of sport, who had replaced my missing Argonauts that night, had been introduced to the yoga-like delights of sleeping on hard wooden oar benches and taking turns on anchor watch to see that *Argo* was not driven ashore in the dark. A couple of them had been thoroughly seasick, but that did not dampen their energies. As we began to row the last few miles towards Poti there was a resounding crack and a loud cheer. This time it was not the steering oar breaking, but one of the 1¼-inch diameter wooden thole pins which pivoted the oars. The former Soviet Spartakid champion had pulled so hard that he had snapped his thole pin in half.

Tovarisch now reappeared as our guide and was seen heading into a port which had to be Poti. Dutifully we followed. Half a mile short of the entrance we paused in order to tidy up the boat and make *Argo* half-presentable – sail neatly furled, ropes coiled and our jumbled kit tucked out of sight. Then, with British, Irish and Soviet oarsmen rowing shoulder to shoulder, we made our entry into Poti harbour, past workaday arrays of cranes, gantries, piles of scrap metal and half-built boats on the stocks. As we rowed around a corner and entered the main basin Yuri Senkevich, standing beside me, gave a grunt of surprise. The far side of the harbour was black with people, thousands upon thousands. They crammed the quay wall, overflowed into the public square and clustered on the balconies of the large port office which dominated the harbour. Every window, every ledge, even the high cabins of the dock cranes were packed to capacity. Lying against the quay, already moored, was *Tovarisch* with her three towering masts, together with all the yachts which had greeted us the previous day, even one flying the Bulgarian flag which had crossed the Black Sea to see *Argo*.

'Smartly now! Watch your timing! Keep your eyes in the boat!' As crisply as we could manage, *Argo* rowed the last hundred yards. 'Let go the anchor!' Cormac tossed the anchor down into the harbour mud. 'Starboard side, hold her. Port side, row on.' The Georgian rowers did not need a translation; they all knew what to do. With her oars beating evenly, *Argo* spun end for end. 'Back her down all.' The port side oarsmen reversed their stroke and *Argo* backed into her slot. A stern line was caught by a longshoreman and made fast to the quay. 'Oars inboard!' With a satisfying, thumping clatter the Argonauts slid their oars inboard and rested them across the boat. Then we rose to go ashore, to set foot for the first time in Georgia.

A line of officials was holding back the spectators. As we stepped onto the quay they let through a scampering horde of children, small girls with pigtails flying as they raced one another to reach us first. Each carried a bunch of flowers which was thrust eagerly into the hands of an Argonaut until we were almost submerged in blooms. A resplendent figure loomed up ahead of me, moustachioed and garbed in a long coat like a dragoon, complete with soft leather boots and a silver-mounted dirk at his belt. He seized me by the elbow, and flinging out one arm in a formal gesture he began to declaim sonorously.

'It's a speech of welcome,' said Othar in my ear. 'He's speaking Old Georgian.'

Then I was led forward to meet the mayor of Poti. Wine was poured into two shallow earthenware bowls and fruit was offered. 'These are the traditional welcome gifts for the guest,' explained Othar. Loudspeakers on the balconies boomed out a Georgian anthem, and the jostling crowd began to join in the words in a deep, full-throated chorus. Everyone turned to face one section of the encircling crowd. There, in the front rank, stood perhaps twenty men, most of them in their late fifties or sixties, and posed to great effect in the same sort of dragoon costume – black, long-skirted coats with silver trim, black boots, crossed cartridge bandoliers and white headclothes. They struck a suitably proud stance and their leader stalked forwards. Then he turned towards his attentive men, raised one arm, and the troupe burst into song. The astonishingly complicated, intricate, emotional art of choral song has been brought to its finest pitch with the traditional singers of Georgia. It was a sound which I was hearing live for the first time in my life, a sound which the new Argonauts would hear again and again over the next ten days, and which none of us could ever forget.

Jason and his men did not enjoy anything like such a colourful and heartfelt reception when they came to King Aeetes' realm. They approached the Colchian kingdom with great caution, closing the coast under cover of darkness. The four young Colchian nobles whom they had rescued from the island of Ares had warned them that their grandfather, the cunning and ferocious king, was intensely suspicious of all strangers who came uninvited to his kingdom; he was likely to arrest the adventurers and have them put to death. So the Argonauts made their landfall in Colchis like burglars reconnoitring a well-protected mansion. They rowed quietly into the mouth of the River Phasis during the night, and went a short distance upriver before ducking into the marshes and hiding *Argo* among the reeds. There they held a council to decide how best to tackle the problem of obtaining the Golden Fleece from its owner, the Colchian king.

According to Apollonius, Jason wanted to respect the laws of hospitality. He felt that since Aeetes had offered sanctuary to Phrixus when he had arrived in Colchis years before as a refugee, it was only right that the Argonauts should now openly state the purpose of their mission to the king, and wait for his reaction. They would then learn if he intended to treat them as guests or as enemies. So Jason set out for Aeetes' palace, carrying a herald's wand to show that he came in peace, and accompanied by two Argonauts, Augeais and Telamon, and the four grandsons of King Aeetes who were to explain *Argo*'s mission.

The royal palace, Apollonius said, lay on the right bank, that is the north shore, of the River Phasis. The path there from *Argo*'s hiding place among the reedbeds lay through gloomy thickets of osiers and willows from which dangled the corpses of dead Colchians. By local custom only the bodies of women were buried in the ground. When a Colchian man died, his corpse was wrapped in an untanned oxhide and hung in a tree to decompose in the open air. A thick mist lying over the marshes must have made the approach to the royal palace even more forebidding, but it did successfully conceal the arrival of the strangers until Jason and his companions were at the gates of the royal stronghold.

The king's residence was an imposing structure with several courtyards leading from one to the other, overlooking balconies, side buildings and folding doors opening onto the various offices of the royal household. These included the apartments of the king, his son and heir Prince Apsyrtus, and the building reserved for the palace women, in particular King Aeetes' daughter, the royal princess Medea. When Jason and his companions arrived, the great gates of the royal enclosure stood open, and they walked in to find the king's household engaged in its daily routine: chopping firewood, butchering the carcass of a bull for the royal kitchens and heating water for baths.

The precise details of Aeetes' palace may be something which Apollonius dreamed up: no more than how he thought the palace of the dreaded Colchian king would have looked. Equally, they could have been based on a dimly remembered account of how a traditional Colchian royal stronghold was laid out and organized. Apollonius' claim that King Aeetes, the same man who had ruled Colchis when Phrixus got there, was still alive is a little doubtful, and historians believe that in fact the king's title was a perpetual one, at least as far as the Greek writers were concerned. They seemed to call all the early Colchian kings Aeetes.

Jason's frank approach to the Colchian ruler now led him into great danger. King Aeetes invited the strangers to eat with him and, after the meal, questioned his grandsons as to why they had returned so soon from their voyage, bringing strangers with them. Argus, the oldest of the grandsons, explained how he and his brothers had been shipwrecked on Ares Island, rescued by the Argonauts and brought home to the Phasis. The visitors, he told his royal grandfather, had come to seek the Golden Fleece from Phrixus' sacred ram, and to carry it back to Greece with them. To recompense Aeetes for the Fleece, Jason and the Argonauts were offering to help the Colchian army in their war against their northern neighbours and traditional enemies, the Sauromatae.

King Aeetes exploded in rage. He rounded on Jason, Augeias and Telamon and swore that if they and their companions did not leave his kingdom immediately they would suffer. Their story about the Golden Fleece, he thundered, was a lie. They had really come to attack him and seize the throne of Colchis. They were no better than pirates. But for the fact that they had eaten at his table and were protected by the laws of hospitality he would have torn out their tongues and cut off their hands, sending them back to their companions waiting on *Argo* as a warning not to trespass on his kingdom.

In the face of this outburst, Jason kept his head. He repeated his offer that if they could be given the Fleece, the Argonauts would fight alongside the Colchians against the Sauromatae. And if Aeetes could be generous enough to hand over the Golden Fleece, then Jason and his men would cause the name of Aeetes to ring with praise throughout Greece.

The hapless Jason now tumbled into exactly the same sort of trap that had started the quest for the Fleece in the first place: Pelias' cunning proposition that he would be given the throne of Iolcos if he brought back the Golden Fleece. This time it was King Aeetes who set the snare. He told Jason that he could indeed have the Fleece, if he successfully accomplished a special task: he would have to yoke two fire-breathing bulls that grazed on the sacred plain of Ares, on the opposite bank of the river, where stood the sacred oak bearing the Golden Fleece. Once Jason had succeeded in yoking the two bulls he had to drive them to plough a 4-acre field in a single day. Then he was to plant the furrows with the teeth of a monstrous serpent. From these teeth would spring armed men, and Jason's task was to kill them all before nightfall. The deed, said Aeetes, was not impossible. As king of Colchis, he himself knew how to yoke the bulls, sow the teeth and kill the warriors. If Jason showed himself equally capable, then he could have the Fleece the same day.

Secretly, however, King Aeetes resolved to kill the Argonauts. Even if Jason succeeded in his ordeal, a Colchian war party was to put *Argo* to the torch and burn her crew with her. To punish his four grandsons for their rashness in bringing these dangerous strangers to Colchis, Aeetes proposed to send them into exile.

Princess Medea now enters the story. Apollonius tells how the Princess had already caught sight of Jason as he first entered the palace. That first glimpse of the Mycenaean prince threw her into turmoil, and she fell completely and helplessly in love with the young man. Even as the visitors were parleying with Aeetes Medea was in her rooms, tormented by her burning attraction to the stranger and by a foreboding that something appalling would happen as a result. She already knew that, whatever happened, she could not resist her infatuation. She could not let Jason leave Colchis without helping him, even against her father.

Medea was already known in Colchis as a young woman with magic powers, but she did not have the evil reputation she was to acquire in Greece. In Colchis she was a virgin priestess, and it was said that she knew all the magic herbs, how to prepare them, and how to weave spells and enchantments. The terrible mutation of her role in the Jason story, from love-struck maiden in Colchis to death-dealing queen in Greece, was to become one of the best-known transformations in Greek tragedy. But for the moment the young Colchian princess was a wholly attractive figure. When Jason and his companions returned to *Argo* the young Colchian noble, Argus, told them about Medea's magic powers and exhorted them to enlist her help against King Aeetes. He offered to lead Jason to a place where he was sure to meet Medea, for he knew that the princess would be at the temple sacred to the Underworld Goddess, Hecate.

Jason agreed, and he and Argus set out for the sacred place, accompanied by Mopsus, the seer. Just short of the grove, Mopsus held Argus back, knowing that if the meeting was to succeed, Jason and Medea would have to meet alone. When Medea saw Jason coming through the woods towards her, Apollonius says, 'her heart stood still, a mist descended on her eyes, and a warm flush spread across her cheeks. She could neither move towards him nor retreat; her feet were rooted to the ground.' Jason spoke to her gently, asking her not to be afraid of him. He had come humbly to seek her help. If she could have it in her heart to assist him, he said, then her name would be immortalized for her kindness. He reminded her about the high-born Ariadne who had helped Theseus unravel the maze and locate the Minotaur. She had been rewarded by the gods with her own ring of stars, Ariadne's Crown, set among the heavenly constellations. Medea's beauty, said Jason, was a sign of the warm and tender heart within.

'Jason's homage,' Apollonius wrote, 'melted Medea. . . . At one moment both of them were staring at the ground in deep embarrassment; at the next they were smiling and glancing at one another with the love light in their eyes.' Now Medea revealed to Jason the secret of how he could yoke the fire-breathing bulls, plough the field and defeat the crop of armed warriors. She had already prepared for him a magic salve, an ointment made from a blood-red plant that grew in the Caucasus mountains. If Jason performed a midnight ceremony in honour of Hecate, then smeared his body with the salve, it would render him invulnerable for a day. He could yoke the bulls, plough the field and sow the serpent's teeth. When the armed men rose up from the furrows, he was to throw a boulder among them so that they turned in confusion on one another and fought amongst themselves, until Jason rushed in and finished off the survivors.

Possessed of the secret to succeed with Aeetes' challenge, and swept off his feet by Medea's beauty, Jason asked that when *Argo* left Colchis to return to Greece, she should go aboard with him. Together they would sail to Iolcos, where she would become his wife and they would rule the kingdom. It was his proposal of marriage to Medea that was eventually to lead to the bloody events that came later to be associated with her name.

One of the first questions I put to Professor Othar Lordkipanidze was whether there was any archaeological evidence that such a figure as King Aeetes had existed in Georgia in the late Bronze Age, and whether his capital, known to the Greeks as the city of Aeae, had been located by the archaeologists. Othar replied that the mysterious city of Aeae had been sought by Georgian archaeologists and historians for a very long time, but without definite conclusions. In the next few days he planned to take me to see several places that were possible candidates, though some scholars thought that Aeae was not really the name of a specific place but a general name applied to the whole kingdom ruled by King Aeetes, whose own title meant the 'ruler of Aeae'. But I still needed some exact point on the banks of the River Rhioni to symbolize the end of our own journey in the wake of the Argonauts, so I asked Othar how far up the river lay the first, positively identified, Bronze Age site that had existed in the thirteenth century BC. It was, he told me, at a place called Jaladidi or Great Valley, 15 kilometres inland from the delta mouth of the Rhioni. That spot, I decided, would mark the end of the new *Argo*'s voyage. Othar promised that next day he would go to Jaladidi by car and station himself on the riverbank. *Argo* would row upriver, and Othar would sound his car horn when we reached the crucial spot.

So after the ceremony in Poti harbour we rowed *Argo* to the northern arm of the Rhioni delta where the river runs out through sandbanks and shallows into the Black Sea. The Rhioni delta land stretched out flat under a grey sky. Cattle grazed on the saltings, and the children who had been playing on the beach waded out into the shallows and stood there, with the last of the sea swell surging around their legs, to watch *Argo* come in from the sea. They gazed in wonder, puzzled by the strange newcomer, her painted eyes still staring forwards as she headed eastwards up the great river that the early Greeks had used as their highway into Colchis. As the little galley turned in from the salt water, just ten strokes brought us from the rocking motion of the waves to the calm of the river. And *Argo*, from being a creature of the sea for the past two and a half months, became an animal of the river, quieter and more restrained.

The coastal sand gave way to earth on the riverbank, first pale yellow-grey, and then increasingly dark and silty. Clumps of reeds and low bushes invaded the brackish backwaters. They had provided the hiding place where the first *Argo* had moored, her crew not knowing what kind of reception they would have from King Aeetes and the Colchians. Beyond the reeds grew small, slender trees that our Georgian oarsmen called *tkhelma*, and here and there an isolated willow fluttered its leaves to the breeze which came off the sea. Summer and winter, the Georgians said, the same wind blew in across the land, always from the same direction. Seasonal river floods rose and fell; the channels in the river bed altered and then went back to their former courses, and the central island of the delta inexorably pushed its rim seawards.

A few small houses stood on the bank of the Rhioni. They were little more than fishing shacks or summer cabins. Each had a wooden jetty on pilings, with a couple of punts tied alongside. Their occupants, holidaymakers by the look of them, waved cheerily to us. Then *Argo* came round a bend and we saw ahead of us an old-fashioned railway bridge, carried across the river on girders. The bridge was black with spectators. Hundreds upon hundreds of Georgians had come to this place, knowing that it gave them the best vantage point when *Argo* passed that way. There was a sudden hum of excitement, the buzz of human voices, as they caught their first glimpse of the galley. The sound, and the press of figures, made the bridge look as if it had been settled by a swarm of bees. As *Argo* came closer, more and more people squeezed onto the bridge to get a better view, until finally there was a loud, ominous crack as the pedestrian walkway alongside the rail tracks began to break under the weight of people. Luckily no one was hurt, and the crowd hastily retreated to safety. The bridge, which we had seen sagging under the number of spectators, sprang back to a flatter profile. The extra clearance above water level was useful. *Argo*, with her mast lowered, only just scraped under it. There was no more than 2 inches between her upswept scorpion tail and the rusty steel underdeck of the bridge as the crew manhandled the galley through, reaching up to push on the metal girders. When *Argo* squeezed out the other side, there was a burst of applause from the crowd.

Othar Lordkipanidze had already explained to me in Poti why the Georgians were so enthusiastic about the Jason Voyage. The legend of the Argonauts is embedded deep in the pride and consciousness of the Georgians. The story of the quest for the Golden Fleece is far better known in their country than anywhere else in the world. They learn the tale as young children when it is a fairy story. At school they read it as a basic text. At university they can study it as a source for Georgian history and classical knowledge. Georgia prides itself on an unbroken history that goes back at least 5000 years, and in that history the visit of Jason and the Argonauts is a landmark. It is Georgia's first recorded contact with the ancient civilizations of the Mediterranean. Georgian scholars have produced meticulous translations of the *Argonautica* from ancient Greek into the Georgian language. Art historians have published collections of all the illustrations, classical and more recent, of the events of the Jason story. Georgian girls still bear the name Medea, and a popular brand of Georgian tobacco is called 'Golden Fleece', with a picture of the first *Argo* on the packet. Jason, Medea and the Argonauts are folk heroes within the living culture of the Georgians, and so when a new *Argo* came rowing up the Rhioni the Georgians took her to their hearts. A special popular edition of the *Argonautica* had already been printed and distributed to coincide with our visit; a new brand of Georgian cognac named for the legend; and a large underground cavern, recently discovered by explorers in the Caucasus, was to be called 'The Cave of the Argonauts'.

On the first afternoon of the river journey we travelled 7 kilometres upriver and camped on the bank. Next morning we set out again, rowing up the Rhioni which led like a broad, turbid highway into the interior. The weather was unseasonably wet, and the heavy rain draining off the meadows reinforced the meltwater coming down from the headwaters in the Caucasus, and pushed up the speed of the current so that the oarsmen had to work very hard indeed to make any headway. But with ten Georgian masters of sport aboard, *Argo* had enough muscle power to nose up-current. We churned forward, determined to make every last inch of our quest by our own efforts. One crew man stood in the bows, casting the leadline, for although the Rhioni was in full flood it was spread across mudbanks and shallows, braiding its channels in cutoffs and dead ends.

Lush watermeadows now lined both banks, and the Georgian farmers and their families came down to watch us toiling up-current. Their children tried to keep pace with us, running barefoot through the clinging black mud along the bank and stopping at each little hillock to get a better view. Their excited chatter was like the chirping of sparrows. The day was warm, overcast and humid, and the air so thick that we seemed to be toiling through an endless landscape of brown river water, green fields and a lifeless grey sky. There were no villages, for the meadows were so soggy that the houses were set back out of sight. When we outpaced the children there was only the great river, an occasional heron, a skein of wild duck and the scattered herds of cattle and water buffalo. The only sounds were the plash of the oars, the swirl of water running down the sides of the hull, the panting breath of the oarsmen, and an occasional soft, sucking splash as a section of the loamy riverbank, undermined by the current, toppled into the gnawing flow. Several times *Argo* bumped on the hidden mudbanks; the impacts were harmless – the mud, mingled with river sand, was soft. We reversed stroke, let the current help, and disentangled the boat so that we could grope our way back into the channel and row onwards.

With each kilometre the gentle collisions became more frequent. Every five minutes now we were hitting mudbanks. The effort of extricating ourselves sapped the energy of the crew. By mid-morning I could see that they were tiring. Scanning the surface of the river for the telltale slicks and eddies that warned of more shallows, I began to wonder just how far we could actually get with *Argo* before we finally ran out of water and had to abandon the river journey. Then we came round another meander, and I could see that we had entered a crucial sector. The river spread so wide that a permanent island had formed in midstream. Neither channel on either side of the island looked very promising, so I steered to port and *Argo* plodded past. When we reached the tip of the little island I put the helm over and cut back to starboard, seeking a central channel again. I felt a gentle pluck at the steering oar. In the same moment *Argo* gave a whispering shiver as the whole length of her keel ran softly onto the swell of a submerged sandbar. Not feeling the touch, the crew continued to row for a few strokes. The river current, sliding past the hull, tricked the senses and gave them the impression that *Argo* was still making progress. Then the crew, too, realized that *Argo* was well and truly aground. Gratefully, the tired crew rested on their oars. I was just about to say that it was time to take a rest and break for lunch when a car horn began to blow, steadily and insistently. It was a strange sound in that waterlogged, bucolic landscape. Looking to my left, I saw a mud-spattered car bumping across the meadow; its horn was still blowing a fanfare. In it was Othar Lordkipanidze, and he was signalling to say that we had reached the first Bronze Age settlement on the banks of the Rhioni – Jaladidi. It was exactly the spot where *Argo* had run aground definitively.

I changed what I was going to say. 'Ship your blades!' I called, 'That's it! That's the end of the Jason Voyage! We've made it.'

Pandemonium broke out. Oarsmen jumped up from their benches. There were shouts of: 'No more rowing! Let's celebrate! Where's the wine?' For a few moments we were sufficiently composed to dig out three red rocket flares which we fired into the sky, one after another, to symbolize the end of our journey, and then the celebrations began in earnest. Hastily I put away my notebook, for I knew what traditionally happened next. Two burly Argonauts advanced purposefully down the gangway, ducked under the crossbar, picked up the skipper and hurled me over the rail and into the river. It was shallow enough to stand, and I watched a succession of oarsmen leap, fall or be thrown into the water until not a soul was on board *Argo*. Her entire crew was floundering in the current, cheering themselves hoarse. Most had abandoned ship clutching bottles of Georgian wine, and these were passed from hand to hand. Then we hauled ourselves soggily back on board and there, in midriver, held a victory party that summed up our delight.

A launch caught up with us, bringing a tremendous picnic – chicken, bread, cheeses, grapes, apples, plums, melons, fish – and this feast was spread down the central gangplank. Othar Lordkipanidze, Nugzar Popkhadze and Ilya Peradze, the Georgian boat club official who had been coaching the Georgian oarsmen, came aboard to share the triumph with the drenched but happy oarsmen. Peter the cook vowed he had prepared his last Argonaut meal and would henceforth exist on Georgian bounty, and the visitors watched attentively as one of the Georgian oarsmen demonstrated how to thump the base of a wine bottle with the flat of one's hand until the mounting pressure eventually sends the cork flying out without recourse to a corkscrew. But that was nothing. The most awesome demonstration was when one huge Georgian sportsman extended rigid the little finger of his right hand, placed the tip of the finger against the cork, and with one controlled movement literally forced the cork down through the neck and into the bottle. It was enough to make one's hand flinch in sympathy.

Then the toasts began. Every member of the visiting crew was toasted by name, then every country of every crew member, and those absent Argonauts who had helped row *Argo* on her trip but were not aboard for the final sector of her voyage. The Georgian manner of toasting was boisterously suitable for the occasion: whenever anyone thought of a good subject for a toast he called for the attention of the others, raised his glass and named his theme, and then began the syllables '*Gau . . . ma . . .*' and the rest added with a full-throated roar '. . . *Jous!!*' as they tossed off their wine. In Georgian it translates as 'Good health!' and was to become the watchword for our visit to Colchis. Then the singing began: first with Georgians, with traditional songs, and then the Argonauts with their well-rehearsed rowing choruses which they had sung from Greece to the far end of the Black Sea. As a symbol of the camaraderie it was difficult to improve on the sight of Cormac O'Connor, former curragh racing champion of the west of Ireland, with his arm across the brawny shoulders of Vladimir Beraija, former winner of the Spartakid cup of the USSR, and the two men joining in the chorus of a traditional Georgian song.

Three hours later, when the midriver party came to a close, Ilya announced that the plan was to move *Argo* upriver to a formal ceremony that had been arranged at the town of Vani. Everything, he said, had been organized. A towboat was standing by to assist *Argo*; the boat club had surveyed the river; and the club members had even drawn a river map showing the channels and the depth of water available. Othar and the other dignitaries left to go ahead to Vani, and the joint Georgian-international Argonaut crew leaped into the water, heaved *Argo* off her sandbar and passed a line to the river tug.

10
The Golden Fleece

The plan for the river journey, so immaculately prepared by the Georgians, went splendidly awry. When the volunteers from the boat club had surveyed the river to work out the best channel for *Argo*, no one could have foreseen that mid-July would bring freak rainstorms. The Rhioni's current was now flowing far faster than had been envisaged, and the level of the river was surging up and down by as much as 6 feet in twelve hours. It was impossible to predict the result. Sandbanks would appear and then be submerged; the main river current would switch from one side of a central island to the other; great masses of flotsam came lurching round the bends and menaced the propellors of the tugboat or got entangled in the towline.

We started out with a tow from a river motorboat, but very soon it was obvious that its engines were not powerful enough to breast the current. Someone dashed off for help. Soon afterwards another tug, larger and more powerful, appeared. It hauled *Argo* a few more kilometres upstream before it went aground with a great spewing up of silt from its propellors and a smell of overheated engines as it thrashed around trying to extricate itself from the shallows. We cast off the towline, and a swarm of small skiffs with outboard engines rushed in and took up the tow. Ilya Peradze directed operations with tremendous vigour. He waved his arms furiously and yelled urgent directions to the little squadron of tiny motorboats straining on the towline ahead of us, their engines going full blast like a mosquito fleet as they struggled against the current. The big tug reappeared briefly, helped out for a time, and then finally and noisily ran out of water. It was last seen falling out of sight behind a bend, stuck fast with its crew resignedly poking around the hull with a red and white banded sounding pole to try to find enough deep water for their vessel to escape.

But the Georgians would not give up. By hook or by crook they were absolutely determined to get *Argo* to Vani. Nothing was going to stop them, not even the Rhioni at its most capricious. So what had started as a short aftermath to the main voyage became a complete sub-plot, and one of the most enjoyable episodes in the entire project. There was simply no reining in the enthusiasm of our athletic hosts. When the lead boat of our mosquito fleet ran aground, its coxswain tossed the towline away and the next boat swerved abruptly and tried to find a better channel. Sometimes as many as three or four little boats were ahead of us, scattered across the width of the river, searching for a passage.

Argo needed only 2–3 feet of water to proceed, and yet she ran aground very frequently indeed. Then everyone would leap overboard, push and shove and haul, waist-deep in the river, and by

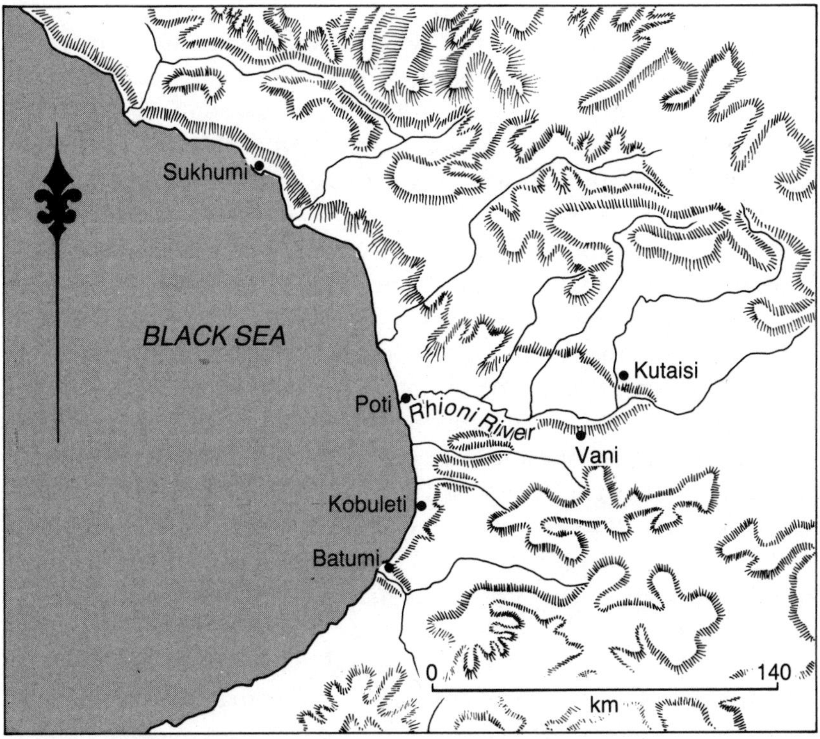

main force heave her back into deeper water. When even the mosquito boats ran out of depth, so that their little outboards could not function, all the Argonauts plunged into the Rhioni and literally manhauled the galley forward, with the water churning past their chests. We knew when we had come back into the main channel, because the lead hauliers disappeared underwater. All this was done with such buoyant excitement and panache that it was impossible not to be swept away with the spirit of the whole exercise. It was quite obvious that our Georgian strong men wanted to feel that they had really helped the expedition to reach its goal, and dragging *Argo* up the river by main force was a splendid demonstration of this. Even a torrential rainstorm that night, the wettest night of the entire voyage, failed to douse their enthusiasm. No one had a moment of sleep. *Argo* lay moored to a muddy bank in the darkness, somewhere in the middle of western Georgia, with the rain sluicing down and the lightning splitting the pitch-blackness. We had lost contact with the towboats; no one on shore knew where we had got to – the conditions were too atrocious to go and find out – and there was no towpath for searchers to find us. Instead, with no food left and the last bottles of Georgian wine to console us, the entire crew sheltered under makeshift plastic sheets and bellowed their full repertoire of songs.

Next day the weather was no better, and with *Argo*'s progress getting slower and slower against the racing current, Othar Lordkipanidze sent for me. The Georgians would look after *Argo*, I was firmly told, and bring her up to Vani. In the meantime Othar wanted to show me his archaeological site there. It would help me understand Georgia's links with ancient Greece and provide some clues as to why the legend of the Golden Fleece had survived.

One clue often lay scattered on the ground. After heavy rain on the hillside above Vani, golden objects are sometimes washed to the surface. A gold decoration from a necklace was picked up from the mud by one of Othar's chief assistants on the same day that *Argo* had sailed into the Rhioni. Over the years the local inhabitants had recovered elegant gold diadems, gold necklaces exquisitely made from thousands of tiny gold balls melded together, gold earrings, gold pendants, gold jewellery of every description. This material dated from the classical Greek period when a Greek city had flourished on the spot, but although this was many centuries after Jason's time, what mattered was that the gold was Colchian gold. It had been obtained in Georgia, and as Othar pointed out, Colchia was so famous in classical times for its gold production that the Greek writers had given it the epithet 'rich in gold', an epithet it shared with Mycenae itself. Thus the golden artefacts of Vani and other classical Greek towns in Colchis kept alive the legend of a gold treasure at the far end of the Black Sea, and the place where the gold was obtained continued to be identified with Georgia.

Another clue for my research was a ceremonial bronze axehead which Othar's team had dug up three weeks earlier. It was a superb piece, the same special axe form which has lasted unchanged in western Georgia from the Stone Age until the present century; in living memory the same shape of axe was still used by Georgian farmers for clearing brushwood. The ceremonial axehead which Othar's people had found dated from the eighth century BC, and on the back of it was the figure of a mounted warrior with a spear and a conical helmet or hat. It was a Colchian war chief, and the earliest known representation of the sort of Colchian tribal lord who may have ruled in the Phasis valley at the time when Jason and his men landed there. This mounted warlord was the closest image that the archaeologists had yet come to discovering what King Aeetes and his descendants might have looked like.

Excavations up and down the Rhioni valley have revealed the nature of Colchian society in the late Bronze Age. The Colchians were farmers who built stockaded settlements and buried their kings surrounded with agricultural tools. This was most unusual, almost unique in early cultures, and Othar suggested that the story of Jason's ploughing ordeal, imposed by the Colchian King Aeetes, might relate to this respect for agricultural prowess. The story of sowing the serpent's teeth could have been copied by Apollonius from the famous tale of Cadmus, who had to face the same ordeal and who defeated the crop of warriors with the same ruse of the thrown boulder. But the fact that Aeetes expected Jason to indulge in an agricultural contest, at which Aeetes said he was expert, may equally have been connected with the early importance of Colchian kings as agricultural leaders.

But what about the fleece? I asked Othar. Granted that Colchis was 'rich in gold' and its kings were associated with crops and agriculture, why did the Argonaut legend stress the sacred nature of the ram's fleece? Othar showed me the clay figure of a ram. It had been found in a Greek grave, and was clearly a cult object. In the next few days, he assured me, he would show me dozens upon dozens of sacred rams, and let me make up my own mind about what they signified.

The following day *Argo* had almost completed her river trek, and we were invited to attend an Argonautic gala which the people of Vani had been preparing for us. On the bank of the Rhioni they had erected a stage in a public park. By late afternoon the sun had broken through the clouds and was bathing the park in a soft, golden evening light, with the trees and bushes washed vivid green after the day's almost continuous rain. The park was thronged with Georgians dressed in their best clothes, and the whole place had a festive air like a small town fête. Othar was smiling broadly as he introduced me to my companion for the evening. It was 'Princess Medea' – a stunningly beautiful Georgian actress who had been hand-picked for her combination of fair skin and jet-black hair, now set in ringlets and held back in classical fashion with a fillet. She was dressed in a pure white Grecian costume with light sandals on her feet, and carried a bouquet of deep red roses. She was grinning mischievously, while her two attendants, equally attractive Georgian girls dressed in the traditional costume of long gold robes of a medieval cut, tried to look suitably demure.

All the Argonauts were asked to sit down in the front row before the stage, and the townsfolk of Vani crowded in behind us. Then the concert unfolded. It began, of course, with another formal speech of welcome by an elder dressed in traditional costume. Then came the choirs, drawn from the local population and singing to perfection. A flautist gave a virtuoso performance, more medieval-garbed Georgian women played gentle melodies on harp-like instruments, and at one point the entire surface of the wooden stage was crammed with forty or fifty boy dancers, about seven or eight years old, who leaped and stamped their way through their number with great gusto and discipline. There were more singers, more musicians, and a touching display when a solo dancer, a vigorous seventy-five-year-old man, was joined by a six-year-old boy who repeated and echoed the older man's steps, a fine symbol of the way in which Georgian traditions are handed down across the generations. Finally a dance troupe from the capital at Tbilisi, the only professional performers in the entire impeccable show, danced a sword dance with their blades clashing and the sparks leaping in the gathing dusk. One was left with an impression of the sheer, ebullient pride of the Georgians in their own traditions, and of the effort that had gone into our welcome. The concert must have lasted between two and three hours, and presented some twelve or fourteen different acts with no more than a twenty-second interval between each. It was a dazzlingly precise display, and kept us spellbound.

The next day the new Argonauts, our Georgian hosts and the squad of Georgian oarsmen all set out to visit the source of Colchian gold. We travelled by road, at first along the Rhioni valley and then into the rolling foothills of the mountains to the north. The valley could have been part of Burgundy. It had the same air of burgeoning fertility and age-old husbandry. There were the same crops, field after field of vines, stands of maize, orchards of plums, apples and pears. There were even tall poplars lining many of the country roads. The houses of the farmers were very distinctive; low structures, often of wood with perhaps a roof of corrugated iron, they were built on short stilts which raised them from the damp, rich earth. At every turn there was evidence of solid agricultural prosperity, good living and bucolic plenty. Vegetables grew in profusion in neatly tilled front gardens. Geese and chickens competed for their pickings with turkeys. Hogs wandered on the roadsides, leading eager clusters of spotted piglets. Even the dogs looked sleek. Fat, wet rain plashed down on the good black soil, and when we crossed the Rhioni by a road bridge the silt-laden river looked fertile enough to plant crops in.

This cornucopia was lavishly presented at table. Our hosts were not going to let their visitors starve, and even at the briefest halt they produced stopgap boxes of cold chicken, bread and fresh fruit. The planned meals could only be described as banquets. When one entered the eating room, whether it was in a private house or public meeting place, the visual impression was daunting. Long tables, seating as many as thirty guests a side, would have been set up and covered with linen, plates, glasses and cutlery, and heaped on them would be every variety and quantity of dish that the hosts could devise. The gastronomic profusion was mind-boggling. Among the selection one could identify sucking pig, sturgeon, caviar, chicken in several guises, roast pork, white fish, shish kebab, roast lamb, meat pâtés, tomatoes, cheese curd, cakes, wheat bread, corn bread, white cheese, yellow cheese and smoked cheese. All this would be washed down with Georgian wines, red or white, brandies, a curious soft drink based on tea, colas, local mineral waters or vodkas, plain or lemon-flavoured. It was like a medieval banquet. As the meal progressed, so more dishes would be carried in proudly and put before the guest until there was no more room to place them, and they would be piled on top of the previous layer of bowls.

That first day we were heading for the country of the Svans, the mountaineers of Georgia. They live mostly in the Great Caucasus range, though previously their territory extended down into the valley foothills. As we climbed upwards we saw the first Svans, immediately recognizable by their grey felt skullcaps, who were working on the road itself, for the route into the mountains was in the process of being improved and properly metalled. The terrain was a road engineer's nightmare. The flanks of the Caucasus reared upwards in great walls, riven by gorges and buttressed by impossibly steep precipices. The road wriggled back and forth, trying to penetrate the massif, following one valley until it could climb no farther, then abandoning that line of attack in order to cross a ridge and make a few more miles up a neighbouring gorge. At times it plunged through raw new tunnels, or clung to artificial ledges notched into the cliff face.

The panoramas were superb. Forests of mountain pine marched across the slopes, and far below in the valley was the river itself, dammed into a long, sinuous lake whose surface was carpeted with thousands and thousands of floating tree tunks, waiting to be collected and sawn into lumber. From the height where we saw them, these floating tree trunks already looked no larger than matchsticks. We stopped for a rest halfway up the tortuous ascent, and Nugzar's staff from the television station could all have doubled as members of a radio choir, for they took the chance to burst into song, using the immense hillsides as an echo chamber for their repertoire of Svan songs. At times it seemed almost as if they were yodelling. The Swiss comparison was even more marked as we emerged into the high plateau. Small, isolated log houses, brown cattle grazing on grass dotted with wild flowers, the distant view of snow-capped peaks, men and women cutting hay in the mountain meadows – all gave an alpine feeling to the Caucasus.

Darkness had fallen before we reached our destination, Mestia, the Svan capital. As we crossed the final pass a figure suddenly loomed up in the headlights, blocking the road. It was a young man mounted on a grey pony. In his hand he held some sort of totem, a pole with a ghostly-looking mask on the top – it was difficult to tell in the jumping shadows – and a fluttering strip of cloth was tied to the shaft. His mount skittered and fidgeted in the glare of the headlights. The car stopped, and Nugzar asked me to walk forward. Behind the rider a phalanx of men was drawn up across the road, with more riders, all dressed in Svan costume and carrying banners. Someone made a speech, and a cow's horn filled with some sort of bitter drink was thrust in my hand. It turned out to be millet beer. The men were a deputation of Svan elders waiting to greet the Argonauts, and there was a clatter and sparking of hooves on the metalled road as the little cavalcade wheeled round and trotted ahead of us to provide our escort into Mestia.

Svanetia, the country of the Svans, is crucial to an understanding of the legend of the Golden Fleece. Historians believe that the mountain culture of the Svans extends back at least 4000 years, perhaps even more, and certainly to the time when the Argonauts are said to have reached Colchis. The language, customs, traditions and beliefs of these mountain people reach into the Heroic Age. The ram appears again and again as a folk symbol, usually with magic or sacred significance. A Svan folk tale, for example, tells that somewhere in their Caucasus mountains is a secret cave in which a ram of gold, tethered with a chain of gold, stands beside a hidden treasure. No one knows how old this story is, but the Svans have been making symbols of the ram since the Bronze Age; and these

Late Bronze Age ram from Kala

symbols are generally taken to be evidence of some sort of ram cult, possibly based on the worship of the ram as a sacred animal.

In the village of Kala, near Mestia, for example, is a small bronze figure of a ram. It was made at about the same time that Jason is said to have sailed to the land of the Golden Fleece, and has a socket in the base, so that it could once have been mounted on a staff. In Kala this ram is still carefully kept in the church. From Raja, in a valley to the east of Mestia, comes an even older bronze ram symbol – a double spiral of ram's horns, found in a grave dating to the mid-second millennium BC. In Larilari, 80 kilometres west of Mestia, an archaeological team led by Schota Tzartolani, another Georgian archaeologist and himself a Svan, was excavating the contents of fifth- and sixth-century BC graves when we arrived in Svanetia. He showed me figure after figure of the sacred ram, cast in bronze and buried with the dead.

Equally important, Svanetia was the prime source of Colchian gold. Next morning we were to witness how the gold was obtained, and that has a crucial bearing on the legend of the Golden Fleece. Four Svan gold miners were awaiting us. They were standing in the shallows of the Enguri River which runs through Mestia, and they were there to show me how the Svans mine their gold. Three of them had once made their living as professional gold gatherers; the fourth, as a young lad, had helped his father in the same trade until the end of the Second World War, when the last government agent to whom these men brought their gold for sale was withdrawn.

Nugzar had arranged the demonstration. The Svans' chief tool was sheepskin. Every spring, when the snows and glaciers in the high valleys began to melt, the Svan miners would climb to the upper valleys, to the feeder streams of the Enguri. Each man went to his favourite place, where he knew by experience that the meltwater was carrying small quantities of gold washed from veins in the rock. Into these streams the Svans placed sheepskins with the fleece side uppermost. The skins were nailed out flat on wooden pallets which were sunk on the stream beds and weighted down so that the stream flowed across them, often in a series of steps from one pallet to the next. As the water ran across the fleeces, the flecks of gold, being heavier than the sand and silt, were trapped in the wool. Each Svan gold gatherer knew when to inspect his gold trap, depending on the richness of the stream and the amount of the water

'*Tovarisch* . . . the three-masted square-rigged barquentine of the Soviet training fleet was looking her best, the morning sun reflecting off her pyramids of canvas, and her white hull set off against the grey clouds and the pale green sea . . . It was quite obvious that she was coming to greet us'

(*Top*) *Tovarisch* escorting *Argo* off the coast of Georgia

(*Above*) 'Officialdom arrived in the uniformed shape of a senior officer of the Soviet Frontier Guards'

(*Right*) 'Suddenly blue track-suited figures were tumbling aboard, big, powerfully built men in running shoes (*top*). All . . . were physical training instructors, trained athletes. Every one was rated a Master of Sport of the Soviet Union. (*Below*) They could not wait to get started on the rowing'

ARRIVAL AT POTI

(*Top*) 'The far side of the harbour was black with people, thousand upon thousand. They crammed the quay wall, overflowed into the public square, clustered on the balconies'

(*Left*) 'We set foot for the first time in Georgia.' The author receives a bouquet from one of the 'horde of children . . . Each carried a bunch of flowers which was thrust eagerly into the hands of an Argonaut'

(*Above*) 'The astonishingly complicated, intricate, emotional art of choral song has been brought to its finest pitch with the traditional singers of Georgia'

After two and half months at sea, *Argo* is rowed up the River Rhioni, on whose banks stood the sacred oak where the Golden Fleece hung. (*Top*) 'Lush watermeadows lined both banks, and the Georgian farmers and their families came down to watch us toiling upcurrent.' (*Foot*) 'We were sufficiently composed to dig out three red rocket flares, and we fired them into the sky to symbolize the end of our journey'

Determined to get to the reception ceremony at Vani, the Georgian volunteers manhaul *Argo* up the river. (*Foot*)
'Everyone would leap overboard, push and shove and haul, waist deep in the river'

Gala at Vani on the banks of the Rhioni, site of a classical Greek colonial town now being excavated. (*Left*) 'The entire surface of the wooden stage was crammed with forty or fifty boy dancers . . . who leapt and stamped their way through their number with great gusto.' (*Below*) 'A flautist gave a virtuoso performance.' (*Foot*) 'My companion for the evening was 'Princess Medea', a stunningly beautiful Georgian actress, dressed in a pure white Grecian costume.' (*Far left*) The author and Yuri Senkevich, the doctor-traveller who had sailed with Thor Heyerdahl, sign a column to commemorate *Argo*'s arrival

Greek writers called Colchis 'rich in gold.' The epithet and the Jason legend are supported at Vani by (*below left*) solid gold bangles with ram's head decoration dating back to the 4th century BC. (*Foot*) 'Into these streams the Svans placed sheepskins, with the fleece side uppermost . . . As the water ran across the fleeces, the flecks of gold were trapped in the wool.' (*Below right*) A Svan gold-gatherer in the Caucasus mountains uses 'a simple wooden trough to pan out the silt in a final search for gold.' This, wrote Strabo, the Greek geographer in the 5th century BC, may be 'the origin of the myth of the golden fleece'

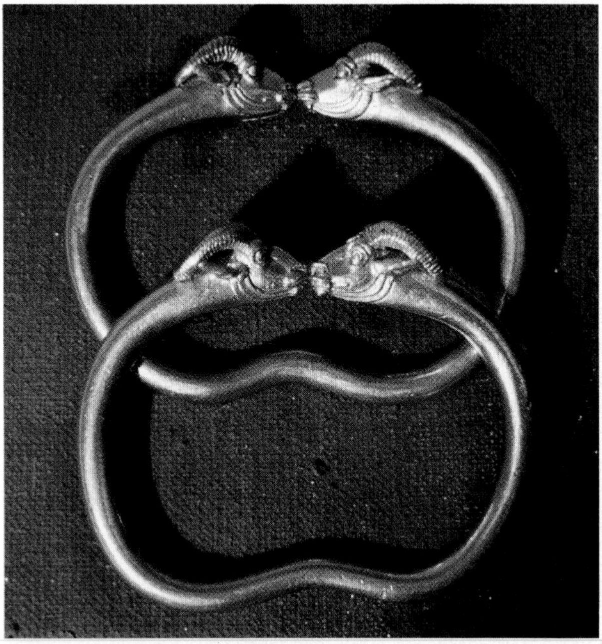

flow according to the season. When the time was ripe, the gold gatherer would remove the sheepskins from the stream, wash out the accumulated silt from the wool, and search through it for gold particles. Exceptionally, in the very richest area, the first fleece, the highest one in the stream bed, would be so impregnated with gold dust that it was virtually a golden fleece.

Strabo, the Greek geographer, had suspected the truth as early as the fifth century BC. 'It is said that in their country [Colchis] gold is carried down by the mountain torrents, and that the barbarians obtain it by means of perforated troughs and fleecy skins, and that this is the origin of the myth of the golden fleece. . . .' Two thousand years later it was astonishing to find men who still knew the ancient technique and had practised it in their own lifetimes. Standing ankle-deep in the icy cold waters of the Enguri, they showed me the tools of their craft: sheepskins pinned to a board, a mattock to spread out the silt on the wool, a scraper to clean the fleece, and a simple wooden trough to pan out the silt in a final search for gold. That afternoon, at a small but moving ceremony, the venerated father of a Svan hero, a mountaineer who had been killed in a climbing accident, presented me with a gold-gathering sheepskin and a Svan costume.

There remained, or so I thought, only one last question to ask. Was there any evidence that the Greeks, or the Mycenaeans as they were then, actually got to the land of the Golden Fleece as early as the time of Jason? No pottery, jewellery or other physical evidence of a Mycenaean presence has yet been found in Georgia, and sceptics could argue that all the tales about the Golden Fleece and the sacred ram could have been invented many centuries later, when Greek colonies were established on the banks of the Phasis; except for one all-important piece of evidence – the linguistic evidence. The Greeks used the word 'Phasis' to describe the great river of Georgia, and to know that name they must have been in touch with Colchis well before the end of the first millennium BC. Rismag Gordesiani, director of the Institute of Mediterranean Studies at Tbilisi, explained the significance of this clue.

Until the latter part of the second millennium BC, he said, the people of Colchis spoke a language known as Kartvelian. The name of the river in this language would have been 'Pati', and the Greeks must have picked up this word when they called the river 'Phasis', following the normal rules of change in pronunciation. Then, some time before 1000 BC, the Kartvelian language of western Georgia broke up. The people of the river valley began to speak a derived language called Mengrelian, and in this language the river was now called 'Poti' (a name which survives as the city of Poti on the delta). But the Greeks still retained the original name, Phasis, which they could only have acquired long before the foundation of their colonies in the Black Sea in classical times. What intrigued Rismag Gordesiani, though he could not yet find a reason for it, was that the antique Greek word for a sheepskin appeared to be related to the Kartvelian word for a fleece.

Was there, I wondered, an even earlier contact between Greece and Georgia than the voyage of *Argo*? How was it that the flying ram came to Greece in the first place to rescue Phrixus when he was threatened with death? How did Jason and the Argonauts know that they should go to Colchis to find the Golden Fleece? These were questions which lay beyond our present search. For the present, the Jason Voyage had done all it had set out to achieve. We had shown that the voyage was physically possible in a ship of late Bronze Age design. Even with only twenty oars, instead of Jason's alleged fifty men, it could row up against the current of the Bosphorus and survive the rigours of the Black Sea. All along the route we had matched the physical evidence with the geography in the ancient tale, and found that it fitted beyond the bounds of mere coincidence. Now, in Georgia, thanks to the help of the Georgian archaeologists, we had seen evidence of a very ancient ram cult, of Colchis 'rich in gold', and witnessed the actual source of a Golden Fleece. There remained, I thought, nothing more to learn about the legend of the quest for the Golden Fleece.

I was wrong. For another week we were swept along on a tumultuous outpouring of Georgian hospitality. We came down from the mountains and were taken to Tbilisi. We were wined and dined, saw monasteries and museums – in the National Museum was a pair of lovely ram's head bangles of solid gold that Othar had found at his site in Vani – and we enjoyed ourselves hugely. Tim Readman, who was to get married as soon as he got home to England, promised to wear a traditional Georgian costume of white at his wedding reception (which he did), and we began to find it difficult to make space for all the presents that were showered upon us: ornamental dirks, drinking bowls and horns, cut glass, trophies and banners and gifts of every kind. Our comrades, the Georgian rowers, accompanied the Argonauts everywhere, and it was with genuine regret that we finally had to get ready to go back down the coast and start back across the Black Sea. It was then that I stumbled, totally unexpectedly, across what I felt was the final proof that the Jason legend had to be based on fact.

Spa choke

On our very last day in Georgia, 2 August, we were taken back to the Black Sea coast towards the oil port of Batumi. On the way Othar asked if I would like to see one last archaeological site. It was near Kobuleti, where *Argo* had spent the first night at anchor off the Georgian coast. I was very keen to take a look because it would have been here on the coastal plain that Jason and the Argonauts would have landed. Here, if anywhere, would be the sort of settlement that he and his men would have discovered when they first landed in the realm of King Aeetes and sought the Golden Fleece.

It was another wet day, and Othar and I squelched up a low mound which rose like a shield boss from the marshy coastal lowland. This was the site, at Namcheduri, that the archaeologists had decided to excavate. Many similar mounds had been identified in the area but not yet dug. When we got to the top of the mound we found that its far side had been cut away, like a cake sliced in half. We looked down at the usual archaeological scene of mud, puddles and what was obviously the remains of an ancient wooden building that the excavators had uncovered in the middle of the mound.

David Khakhutaishvili, the archaeologist in charge, explained that the place had been a sacred site. There had been an outer stockade of timber posts some 10 metres high and 70 metres in diameter, a moat, and here in the centre had stood some sort of wooden structure, very probably a temple, divided into nine small rooms. Casually I asked him whether his team had found any evidence of the ram cult in the temple. By then I had seen so many figures and representations of sacred rams that I was actually shocked when he replied, 'No.' I was puzzled. What sort of cult was practised in the temple, I asked, if not the ram cult? At first his answer was disappointing. The cult here and in the immediate area during the late Bronze Age was related to the bull. The archaeologists had found caches of bull totems in several places, stone or clay tablets about a foot long and ending in a fork, the well-known representation of the horns of a bull.

Then, belatedly, I remembered something that the constant sight of the ram cult figures had driven out of my head over the past few days: Jason's ordeal with the sacred bulls. To gain access to the Fleece he had been obliged to tame the sacred bulls that lived on the plain near the holy tree in which hung the Golden Fleece. And here I was, standing unexpectedly on the edge of a temple devoted to the cult of the sacred bull, a temple located in exactly the right part of Colchis and dating back to the late Bronze Age. The details were astonishingly accurate. Had the Fleece perhaps been kept in a temple or grove sacred to the bull cult?

But there was another element to the legend. From the very first moment that he had been sent on the quest for the Golden Fleece, Jason had been warned that it was guarded by a monstrous serpent which never slept, but patrolled the holy tree on which hung the fleece. Even after Jason succeeded in taming the sacred bulls with Medea's help, he still had to get past the guardian snake. This, according to the legend, he also managed with Medea's assistance. In the night the two of them secretly went to the sacred place, and there Medea charmed the guardian snake so that its eyes closed. Hastily Jason snatched the Golden Fleece from the tree and the two lovers hurried back to *Argo*, which promptly put to sea and made all speed to escape the vengeful Colchians who had been robbed of their holy totem.

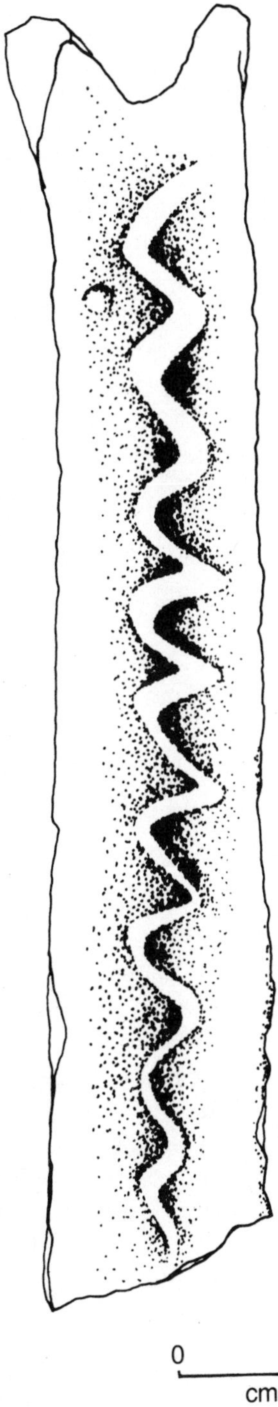

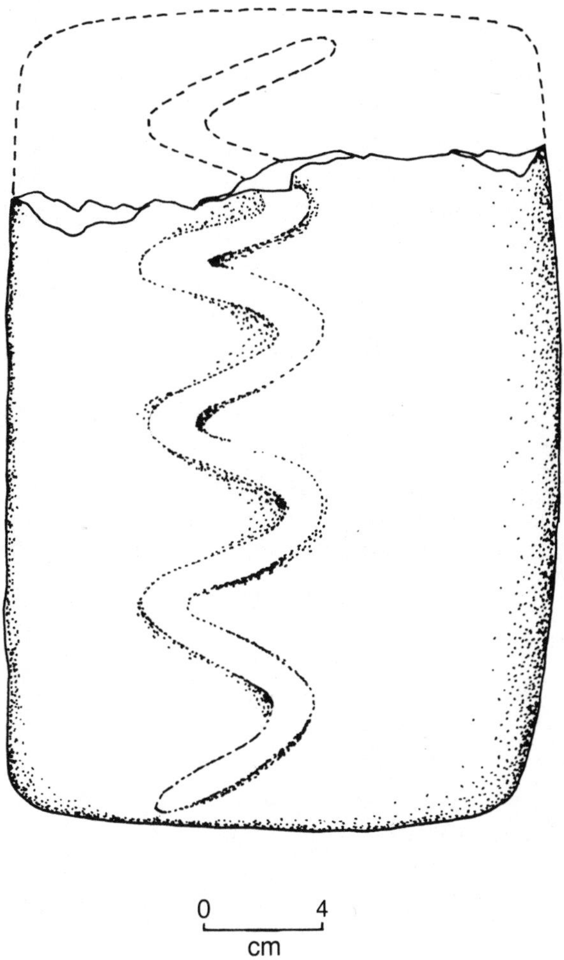

Snake symbols from temple finds at Namcheduri. Left: *bull totem*. Right: *tile*

What about snakes? I put the question to the archaeologist at Kobuleti. Had his team found any references to snakes or serpents?

To my astonishment and delight, he replied, 'Oh yes, let me show you.' He took me to a nearby building where the excavators had stored their finds from the ancient temple and other sites in the area. The archaeologist pulled down from a shelf a distinctive bull's horn cult object, a clay tablet about 15 inches long and ending in the characteristic fork shape, and ran his finger down the front of it. 'Here,' he said. 'Do you see this zigzag groove? It is the symbol of a snake, a protective snake. This is from the eighth or seventh century BC, and we have found tiles, fire nozzles and bull totems even older and marked with this sign of the serpent. We think that the ancient Colchians kept snakes inside their temples as guardians. Even up to recent times it was the custom to keep guardian snakes inside Georgian houses.'

At last everything fell into place. Here, surely, was the final confirmation of the Jason story, the sort of detail which could not have been invented later by Apollonius or the authors who wrote about the Golden Fleece. The archaeological evidence shows that in the late Bronze Age there existed on the coastal plain temples sacred to the bull cult. Inside the temples were kept snakes which guarded the cult objects. The entire story of Jason's ordeal and his theft of the Golden Fleece could be explained in the light of what the archaeologists had found.

The Golden Fleece was precisely that: a fleece from the Caucasus mountains, used in the gold-washing technique, and impregnated with gold dust. It may have been brought to the lowlands, along trade routes that we know existed because pottery made in the lowlands has been found in the mountains, or it could possibly have arrived as tribute, or as a cult gift, from the people of the mountains to the most powerful king on the coast. Naturally the fleece would have been placed in the temple of the coast people, the wooden stockaded temple of their bull worship. To obtain the fleece, Jason first had to circumvent the sacred bulls themselves, and once inside the precinct he would have had to get past the guardian serpent that protected the actual enclosure.

Every single element of the legend matched the archaeology. What had seemed a far-fetched yarn when we began the Jason Voyage had found its solution in Georgia, 1500 miles away from its starting point in Iolcos. Back in Greece the mute stones of Dimini, which the archaeologists thought was perhaps Aesonia, the royal temporary settlement of Jason's family outside Iolcos during their times of trouble, seemed to confirm both the beginning and the end of the ancient quest. Here in Georgia the sacred place of the bull cult protected by its snakes, in the land where the ram was held sacred and the fleece was used to gather gold, was further striking evidence for the truth of the tale. For me that moment on the muddy temple mound near Kobuleti was the end of the search, as it must have been for Jason, close on thirty-three centuries earlier.

Epilogue

What finally happened to Jason and Medea and the wandering Argonauts? How did they come home to Greece, bringing with them the Fleece and the tale of their adventures? Here the original legend becomes very confused. There are as many versions of the return journey as there are poets who wrote about it.

Appollonius says that the Argonauts sailed back first to the Anatolian coast, where at the mouth of the River Halys they put ashore Dascylus, the son of the king of the Mariandyni, so that he could return to his home. Then, with a favourable wind behind *Argo*, they cut across the Black Sea to the mouth of the Danube and turned up into it, following the river until it brought them into the Adriatic by a tributary. Apollonius is confused in his geography, because such a tributary does not exist. Nevertheless, he says that the Argonauts emerged into the Adriatic. There they encountered Medea's brother, Prince Apsyrtus, and the Colchian fleet who were blockading the river mouth. Outnumbered, the Argonauts offered a truce. Apsyrtus was willing to let them go on their way on condition that Medea's fate was referred to the local king, who would decide whether she must return to Colchis, or go on to Iolcos with Jason. Jason agreed to this formula, but Medea was furious and upbraided him for his faint-heartedness. If he really loved her, he would show it by ridding her of Apsyrtus, and she persuaded him into setting a trap for Apsyrtus. She sent word to her brother that she had really been kidnapped by the Argonauts and been forced to go with Jason against her will. If Apsyrtus would come to a secret rendezvous on a deserted island, she would quietly slip away from *Argo* carrying with her the Fleece. Apsyrtus was betrayed. He came to the island alone and unarmed, and while Medea distracted his attention Jason, who had been waiting in hiding, crept up and killed the Colchian, whose blood stained his sister's clothes. This foul deed, the breaking of a truce and the murder of an unarmed man, was to bring down the retribution of the gods. Thenceforth the marriage between Medea and Jason was doomed.

A different version of the tale says that Medea lured her brother aboard *Argo* while still in the Black Sea, killed him and dismembered the body. Then, as *Argo* sailed on, she threw the pieces one by one into *Argo*'s wake, so that the pursuing Colchian ships were delayed as they paused to collect up the morsels and give their dead prince a proper burial on the shores of the Black Sea.

Yet a third version of the return route says that *Argo* continued up the Phasis until the galley reached the World River, which the Greeks at one time believed encircled the habitable world. Sailing south and west, the Argonauts came back into the Mediterranean by portaging *Argo* across the Libyan Desert. There died Mopsus, the seer, who was bitten by a poisonous snake. From the Libyan coast the surviving Argonauts sailed north past Crete where they were menaced by Talus, the great articulated giant of bronze, who patrolled the edge of the island and threw rocks at intruders. He prevented the Argonauts from landing, but Medea cast the evil eye on him and, while he was transfixed, he grazed the weak spot on his ankle so that the fluid ran out of his veins and the giant collapsed and expired. From there the Argonauts sailed home to Iolcos.

Yet other versions of the return route claim that *Argo* left the Black Sea by going northwards up the River Don, sailing around Europe, and came home either by way of the Pillars of Hercules; or down the Rhine and the Rhône; or even the River Po in northern Italy. Of course, all of these routes were fictions. Not one is feasible for a galley. They simply reflect the contemporary geographical notions of their authors who wished to show off their expertise and avoid the rather uninteresting fact that the Argonauts must have gone back the way they had come – across the Black Sea and back down through the Bosphorus, this time with the currents in their favour. No other route is possible.

One Roman author, Apollodorus, was sure that this was the correct route. He noted that in his day sailors were still making sacrifices at the headland on the Asian side of the Bosphorus at its northern end, which they called Jason's Point because it was here that Jason, as he safely left the Black Sea after his expedition, stopped and gave thanks to the gods. Another Bosphorus tradition says that when *Argo* passed southwards down the Bosphorus Princess Medea threw ashore the box containing her stock of magic drugs, which she had gathered in Colchis. Henceforth the place became renowned as a centre for medical cures.

When the Argonauts finally sailed back into the Bay of Iolcos, it was the moment to claim the throne for Jason, now that they had successfully completed the quest. King Pelias still ruled, though he was now an old man. As it was by no means sure that Pelias would honour his agreement, and Iolcos was too strong for the small force of Argonauts to capture by force, Medea, so the story goes, slipped into Iolcos in disguise. Going to the royal palace, she tricked the king's daughters into believing that she could teach them how they could restore King Pelias to his youth. She told them to kill their father and boil his body in a cauldron of a special brew she would prepare. Naturally the daughters of Pelias at first refused to believe Medea's claim, but she hoodwinked them with her witchcraft. Taking an old ram, she slit its throat and tossed it into the cauldron, from which by sleight of hand she then drew forth a young, living lamb. The credulous daughters of Pelias were duped. They went to the king's chamber, killed him as Medea had directed and threw his dismembered body into the cauldron. Even as they realized the enormity of their deed, the Argonauts marched into the city, and the people of Iolcos, without their king, surrendered and accepted Jason's claim to the throne.

That is the most gory version of the homecoming of the Argonauts. A less violent form of the tale says merely that Jason came back with his men, who had long since been given up for dead, and that Pelias peaceably handed over the throne of Iolcos to Jason, whose father and mother had died in his absence. For some unexplained reason, Jason decided not to keep the throne but relinquished it soon afterwards, handing it back to Pelias. Perhaps Jason found life in Iolcos a little dull after his foreign voyaging.

In any event, the romance with Medea cooled. Jason decided to take another wife, the daughter of the king of Corinth, and Medea is said to have exacted a terrible revenge. She sent a poisoned robe to the Corinthian princess as a wedding gift. When the girl put on the robe, it burst into flames and she burned to death in agony, even though she leaped down a well to try to extinguish the deadly flames. This ghastly tale, because it was immortalized by Euripides in his play *Medea*, is much better remembered in modern Greece than the more cheerful events of the quest itself. For that reason, unlike their Georgian counterparts, no Greek girl is likely to be called Medea. In far-off Colchis, by contrast, the daughter of King Aeetes is remembered as a young and beautiful girl who fell so madly in love with the handsome stranger that she abandoned her home and family and followed him to a foreign shore, only to live unhappily. Georgian girls, it follows, should think twice about leaving their land to go abroad with foreigners.

Jason and Medea were not the only ones to suffer a melancholy homecoming. Most Argonauts returned to their homes without incident, but a few met violent deaths. Hercules had never forgotten or forgiven Calais and Zetes for persuading the other Argonauts to sail on instead of putting back to try to find Hylas when he was lost to the water nymph. To avenge that deed, Hercules tracked down the Sons of the North Wind on their return to Greece and killed them on the island of Tenos when they were returning from the funeral games in honour of Pelias. Over their bodies he placed huge, finely balanced boulders which rocked whenever their father, the North Wind, blew across them.

Lynceus, the far-sighted, and Idas, the boaster, fell out with the twins, Castor and Pollux, their former shipmates. They quarrelled, either over two beautiful girls whom both pairs wanted to marry or, more likely, over division of the spoils from a joint plundering raid. Whatever the cause, the rivalry was deadly. The twins pursued Idas and Lynceus, and the latter, using his fabulous eyesight, was able to forestall an ambush, seeing the twins from afar as they lay hidden inside a hollow tree. In a bloody fight Idas speared Castor and killed him; then Pollux managed to revenge his twin brother by cutting down Lynceus, but he himself would have fallen to the mighty Idas if Zeus had not blasted Idas to death with a thunderbolt. This left only Pollux alive. He could not stand the thought of life without his twin, and he beseeched their father, Zeus, to let them exist together. His wish was granted when Castor and Pollux were set among the stars as the constellation identified as Gemini.

Jason himself fared little better. He had moved to Corinth, taking the immortal *Argo* with him. The great ship was dragged ashore, like most vessels approaching the end of their time, and left to decay. One day, feeling lonely and depressed, Jason went to sit in the shadow of *Argo*. The great timber of the prow, rotten with age, finally gave way. The beam fell and crushed him to death.

Nearly all the events which happened on the outward voyage, the time of exploration and hope, have remained positive and optimistic in the telling – the story of the women of Lemnos, the defeat of King Amycus the boxer, the succour given to blind Phineas, the gallant passage of the Clashing Rocks, the rescue of King Aeetes' grandsons from the island of Ares and the successful winning of the Golden Fleece itself. But when the later life of the Heroes became a favourite theme for Greek tragic poets and playwrights the legend lapsed into despondency and gloom, mirroring the events in Greece itself where the Mycenaean way of life was to suffer invasion, war and destruction.

Fortunately no such catastrophe accompanied the modern *Argo*'s return from Georgia. After we had finally succeeded in getting *Argo* upriver to Vani, she was moored beside the concert park so that the local people could have a close look at her. During the hectic adventures of the upriver journey a couple of serious accidents to crewmen had only narrowly been avoided, and I was genuinely fearful that someone would get badly hurt if we attempted the much more dangerous task of running *Argo* back down the flood-swollen Rhioni when the time came to return to the Black Sea. I voiced my fears to Nugzar, who said that he would see what could be done to get the boat down to the coast so that we could depart on our way back to the Bosphorus.

The problem was that transport by road was impracticable. Bridges across the roads were too low to let *Argo* pass underneath when loaded on a road transporter. No problem, Nugzar said with his usual briskness; how about lifting *Argo* out by helicopter? My jaw dropped. *Argo* was an 8-ton load, 54 feet long, and beyond the capacity of all but the largest helicopters. No matter – a team of helicopter pilots actually came to inspect *Argo* to see if they could help. Finally they agreed that a helicopter lift was too dangerous.

Then someone suggested loading *Argo* on a special train. Once again the Georgians were simply not going to be defeated. Engineers came and took measurements and railway officials were consulted. Peter Wheeler went off to a steel fabricating plant and with its chief engineer devised a cradle made of steel girders. *Argo* was a long, delicate load to lift by crane, and if wrongly handled she could snap in half. On the appointed day a mobile crane crawled cautiously over the soggy watermeadow. From its hook dangled the steel cradle. Slowly the cradle was lowered into the racing river, until it rested on the river bed with the tops of the steel uprights poking above the swirling water. All the Argonauts, Georgians and visitors, jockeyed *Argo* downstream with ropes and oars until she nuzzled between the uprights and was lashed in position.

Gently the crane driver wound in his cable, and *Argo* rose dripping from the Phasis. The crane lurched alarmingly as its wheels sank in the boggy ground, and the driver had to leapfrog *Argo* step by step across the meadow until he could place her upon the transporter lorry that would take her to the railhead. That night a special train carried *Argo* across Georgia, and by noon next day she was floating in Batumi harbour, ready to set out for home.

My plan had been to sail back to Turkey, and there hire a fishing boat to tow *Argo* the 800 miles back to Istanbul for winter lay-up. There was no point in rowing and sailing all the way home. The Argonauts were running out of time, people had to get back to their jobs and, frankly, most of them were physically exhausted by the labour of the outward journey. When I mentioned my plan to Yuri Senkevich he agreed.

'But before you decide,' he said, 'let me contact the Soviet Merchant Fleet and see if they can help. The Minister is very helpful. Maybe he can arrange some assistance.'

Two days later a telegram came back from Moscow. Our old friend *Tovarisch* was leaving on a training cruise in the Mediterranean. The Minister's office had arranged for her to be diverted to Batumi where she would take *Argo* in tow for the Bosphorus. The crew could hardly believe their ears: a three-master as our tug! It was a magnificent gesture, and beyond anything we had dreamed.

So from Batumi we travelled behind *Tovarisch* all the way to the Bosphorus, plucked along by the beautiful, square-rigged barquentine, with nothing to do but take turns to keep a towing watch aboard little *Argo*, bobbing along like a child's toy on a string. Finally the mouth of the Bosphorus came in sight. *Tovarisch* was travelling straight through without stopping, so we had already transferred all our kit aboard *Argo* and were just waiting to slip the tow. I thanked Captain Oleg Vandenko of *Tovarisch* and the little rubber dinghy carried me back to *Argo*. The sides of the

Bosphorus closed around us, and *Tovarisch* cut her speed to allow us to cast off the towline. As the Soviet sailing ship passed on down the Bosphorus, we waved our thanks and turned for the European shore.

Poor *Argo* was showing the scars of her travels. Both her steering oars had been snapped a second time, one during the adventures in the Rhioni, the other on the way across the Black Sea. A couple of her other oars were broken; her thole pins were wrecked; and her cotton sail was so rotten from mildew during the damp days in the eastern Black Sea as to be unusable in anything but a light breeze. Like her crew, she was distinctly bedraggled and weary. Rowing with makeshift thole pins, we sidled across the current towards the shore. I scanned the bank for somewhere to tie up, while I went in search of the Turkish customs and port officials to clear *Argo* inward-bound.

Only one person knew that we were returning: I had sent a telegram to Irgun, my loyal friend of twenty-three years standing, to say that we were on our way back. I heard the hooting of a car horn, and there, miraculously, was Irgun himself waving from the end of a jetty. A moment later he was helping us tie the mooring lines. 'Everything's arranged,' he said. 'I've got a friend in the customs office here, and he will do all your paperwork in a few minutes.' I was back with my Turkish family.

The Argonauts stayed four days in Istanbul, winding up the expedition. We unloaded the galley, packed our souvenirs of the extraordinary voyage, and prepared the boat ready for her winter lay-up. I wanted her to be well taken care of, because her voyaging was not yet done. Having unravelled the story of Jason and the Argonauts, I intended the following spring to set sail with *Argo* again, this time to try to trace the voyage of Ulysses as he came home from Troy, the voyage told by Homer in the *Odyssey*.

Dalan Bedrettin, the mayor of Istanbul, declared that *Argo* was to be the guest of the city. With unfailing Turkish hospitality he arranged for *Argo* to be brought ashore and kept for the winter on the banks of the Bosphorus in a boat park opposite Bebek, the same place where we had stood our greatest trial rowing up against the current of the straits. There I said goodbye to *Argo*, her nose peeping out from under her winter cover. One by one the Argonauts had already left or were on their way back to their homes and jobs. Peter Moran and John Egan were going to spend a few more weeks touring in Greece before returning separately to Ireland. Mark Richards and Tim Readman went off dragging a huge wooden chest of souvenirs to take the train by way of Bulgaria to England, where in a few weeks' time Tim was due to get married. The two doctors, Nick and Adam, were on their way back to find medical posts. Jonathan Cloke and Peter Warren had planes to catch. Cormac hoped to be back aboard his Irish trawler for the late summer fishery. The Argonauts were disbanding, but Peter Warren promised to organize a reunion in the New Year when we could get together and reminisce.

Finally, I too had to leave. I promised my Turkish family that I would return in the winter to check on *Argo*. Perhaps Kaan, their son, could help on part of the Ulysses Voyage? Of course, they said, and already Husnu, one of the Turks who had rowed along the Black Sea coast, was asking when I would be setting out again in *Argo*. He and several of the other Turkish Argonauts wanted to help us when *Argo* was relaunched for the Ulysses project.

Next year, I vowed to myself, I would try to bring *Argo* back to Spetses so that Vasilis, the shipwright, could see her. I packed up my belongings and got ready to leave. All my Turkish family were on hand to say goodbye. I was reminded of the day the Argonauts left Vani in Georgia. Then there had been tears in the eyes of the Georgian crew members. Perhaps next year some Georgians too could be involved with *Argo*. Certainly I would invite them. I climbed into the back seat of the car that was taking me to Istanbul airport. As the car began to move away from the kerb, there was a terrific splashing sound. Startled, I glanced back. There, standing in the street, was the maid who worked for the family. She had just thrown an entire pail of water into the road behind the car. It was an old Turkish custom, which meant that the departing guest would return. In my case I knew it to be true.

ARGO
GENERAL LAYOUT

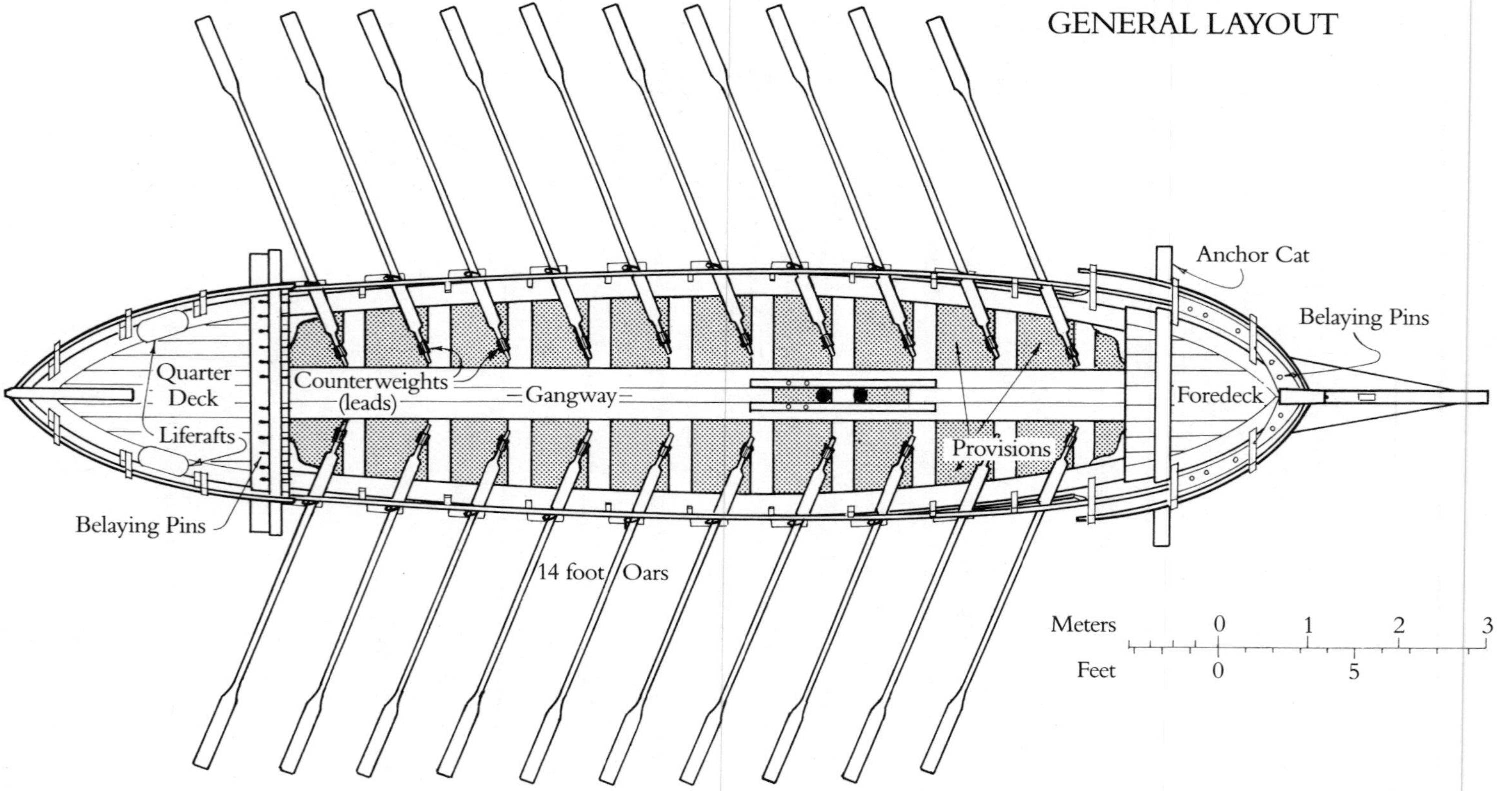

ARGO
SAIL & RIGGING PLAN

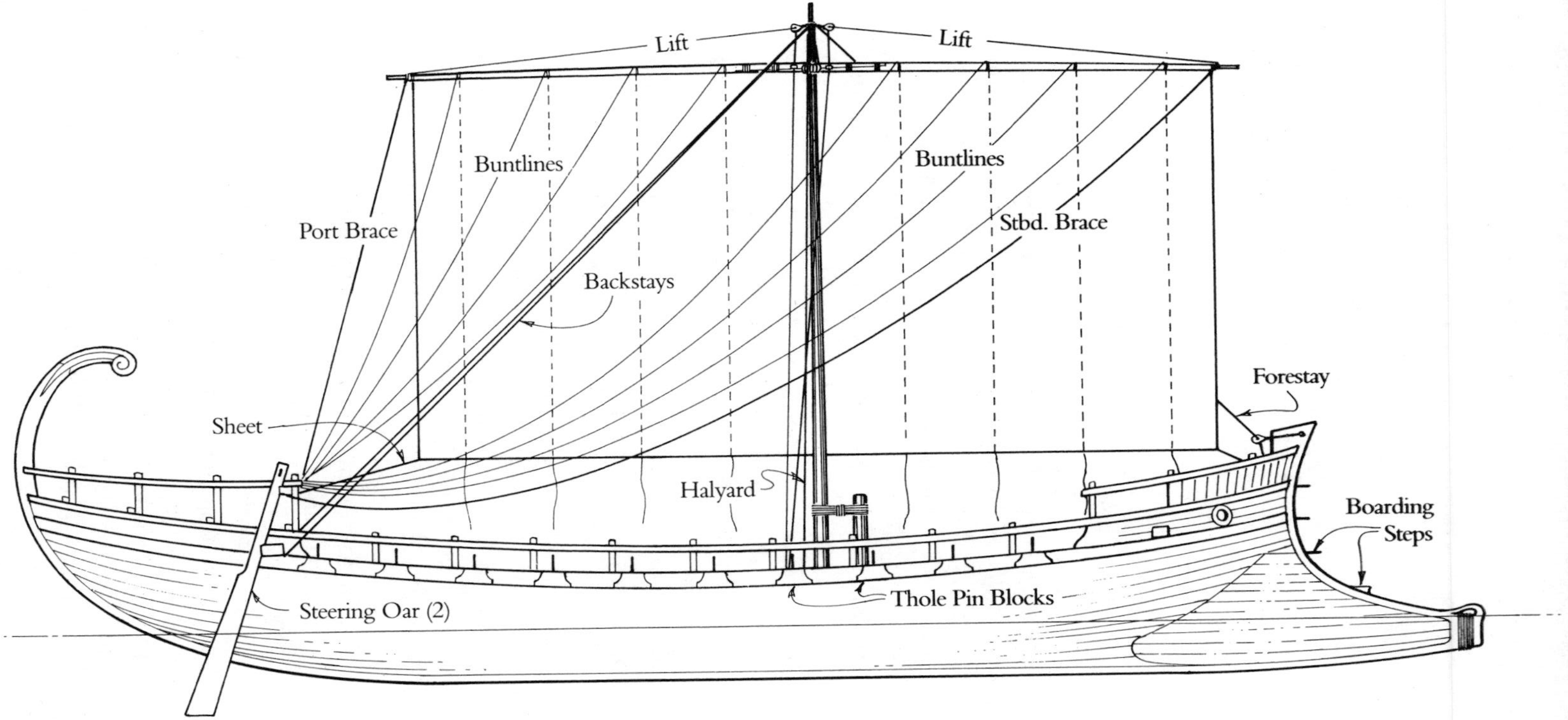

APPENDIX I
Ancestry of the Legend

In the *Odyssey*, Homer refers to 'celebrated *Argo*' which managed to evade the Wandering Rocks when 'homeward bound from Aeetes coast'. And in the *Iliad* he wrote of Euneos, Jason's son by Queen Hypsipyle on Lemnos. As Homer is our oldest surviving source of Greek mythology, this means that the ancestry of the Argonaut story is established as far back as records exist. Quite how far back that ancestry goes, we have no way of knowing, but it is evident from Homer's poetry that he expected his audience to be thoroughly familiar with at least the story of the Lemnian women, the visit to King Aeetes' country, and of course the existence of *Argo* herself.

Homer's near-contemporary, the Boeotian poet Hesiod who lived in the late 8th century BC, must have known the Argonaut story because in his writings he mentions Jason's visit to King Aeetes, his meeting with Princess Medea, and his return to Iolcos with 'the bright-eyed damsel whom he made his loving wife'. In a group of texts known as 'Hesiodic', once attributed to Hesiod himself but now believed to have been written by other authors, there are also references to Phrixus, to Jason's youth, and to the adventure with Phineas and the Harpies.

In the following century, the 7th BC, Minnermus, another Greek poet specifically mentions the Golden Fleece as the object of Jason's voyage, and a Corinthian poet, Eumelos, claims that Jason went to live in Corinth, not Iolcos, after his return from Colchis. As more and more fragments of early Greek writing survive, so the extra details emerge, although not all of them are consistent with one another: Simonides in the 6th century BC confirms the passage of the Clashing Rocks but says that the Fleece was not gold but dyed with sea-purple. In the 5th century BC there was a great flowering of the legend when Jason's story became a favourite theme for poets and dramatists. Aeschylus wrote no less than six plays based on various Argonaut themes, and although most of the plays themselves have been lost, we know that there were a *Phineas*, a *Lemnian Women*, a *Hypsipyle*, and a *Kabeirii*. Sophocles wrote plays on Phrixus' father *Athamas*, on *Phrixus*, the *Colchidians, Phineas*, the fight with King Amycus, and three plays which touched on events during the return voyage of *Argo*. In total, no less than eight tragic poets tackled various Argonautic themes, but the one to survive and most influence modern perception was Euripides' *Medea*. As it was virtually impossible for any early historian or geographer to treat of the Black Sea without some reference to *Argo*, their writings are sprinkled with mentions of peoples and places visited by the Argonauts. The most famous of the early historians, Herodotus, put forward the interesting notion that *Argo* was blown down to the North African coast on the outward leg of her epic journey.

Thus, by the time Apollonius of Rhodes came to compose his epic, the main events of the Argonaut saga were well set. We do not know what sources Apollonius used for his major version of the tale, but his version of the attack on the Argonauts by the monsters of Bear Mountain is very similar to a passage in Homer's Odyssey when Ulysses' squadron is attacked by the Laestrygonians. It is possible that Apollonius also had other – now lost – Homeric material available to him because the geographer Strabo says that Homer wrote about 'the places round Propontis and the Euxine as far as Colchis, the bourne of Jason's expedition'.

The fascination of the legend continued after Apollonius' work. In 40 BC Diodorus Siculus composed a lengthy prose version which is chiefly remarkable for its unwaveringly prosaic approach to the events of the saga. Thus, he believed that the flying ram was the ram figurehead of a warship which carried away Phrixus and Helle, and that the princess fell overboard and drowned in the Dardanelles Strait while being seasick. In the first and second centuries AD there were further versions of the legend by Apollodurus and Valerius Flaccus, and then in the 3rd/4th centuries an Orphic *Argonautica* appeared which gave a major role in the adventures to the musician Orpheus.

From a very early stage, people were intrigued as to whether or not the story was true. Strabo was convinced it was. The saga of the Argonauts, he firmly stated, showed that 'the ancients made longer journeys, both by land and by sea, than have men of later time'. It was Strabo who identified the possibility that the Colchian technique of gold-gathering, using sheepskins, could have some connection with the legend of the Golden Fleece. But the more commentators thought about the tale, the wilder and more far-fetched became their interpretations of the events. The Golden Fleece became a parchment illuminated with golden writing, or even a document which contained the alchemists' secret of how to turn dross into gold. By the nineteenth century folklorists were putting forward theories that the fleece was a symbol of the sun, or it was a raincloud, depending on your choice. If it was a sun symbol, then the sunlight came from King Aeetes who was a child of the sun according to mythology, the ram was the setting sun returning to the east, and Medea was the red glow of dawn and dusk. For those who favoured the raincloud interpretation, the fleece was the purple of a thundercloud, and in Greece the clouds could be seen heading east in summer towards Colchis, and returning in spring and autumn, bearing rain. According to this idea, it was significant that many of the Argonauts were descended from watery spirits such as water nymphs, river gods, and Poseidon himself. Other ideas put forward to explain the Golden Fleece were that it symbolized the ripened corn of the Black Sea coastlands rippling in the wind or that it was a rough sea gilded by sunlight.

It was left to a Cambridge don, Janet Brown, to impose some discipline on all these ideas in her study *The Voyage of the Argonauts* (Methuen, 1925) which remains a standard work. After reviewing the evidence Janet Brown reached the conclusion that 'long before Homer voyages were made to Colchis for gold; a voyage was made by Jason. Jason was a Minyan of Thessaly; by Minyan race he was connected to Phrixus who had been saved by a golden ram and fled eastward'. Jason's voyage, she felt, was 'a real quest for real gold'.

Apollonius' text has been translated in the Loeb Classical Library Series by R.C. Seaton (Heinemann, 1912) and is also available from Oxford Classical Texts (1961). But for ease of access *The Voyage of Argo* (first published in 1959 by Penguin Classics and frequently reissued) cannot be equalled. It was translated by E.V. Rieu in his usual fluent style, and has been used for quotations in this book. Finally, between 1976 and 1981, has appeared the best critical and annotated edition to date: *Argonautiques* – Apollonius de Rhodes,

Vols. I–III, edited by Francis Vian and translated by Emile Delage. This excellent edition is in the Guillaume Bude series, Paris, Societé d'Edition 'Les Belles Lettres', and is the most comprehensive version for text and commentary.

APPENDIX II

Summary of the Text of Apollonius Rhodius

Book I

Crossing the winter-swollen Anaurus on his way to a banquet given by King Pelias, Jason lost a sandal. As soon as King Pelias saw Jason, with one foot bare, he remembered the oracle and decided to send Jason on a mission so dangerous that he hoped the young man would never return.

The ship was built by Argus, supervised by the goddess Athena, but as the tale has been told by other poets, Apollonius will content himself with providing the crew list, as follows:

Orpheus, the musician;
Asterion of Peiresiae;
Polyphemus, an old man but still valiant, from Larissa;
Iphiclus of Phylace, Jason's maternal uncle;
Admetus, King of Pherae;
Erytus of Alope, guileful son of Apollo;
Echion of Alope, his brother;
Aethalides, their kinsman and the expedition's herald;
Coronus of Gyrton, son of Caenus the unconquerable;
Mopsus, who could understand the language of birds;
Eurydamas of Ctimene;
Eurytion, son of Teleon;
Eribotes, son of Irus;
Oileus, the headlong warrior;
Canthus of Euboea;
Clytius, son of Eurthus;
Iphitus, his brother;
Telamon of Salamis;

Peleus of Phthia;
Butes, son of Teleon;
Phalerus 'of the ashen spear', only son of Alcon;
Tiphys of Siphae, an expert mariner;
Phlias of Araethyrea;
Talaus, son of Bias;
Areius, his brother;
Leodocus, his brother;
Hercules, the strongest man who ever lived;
Hylas, squire to Hercules;
Nauplius, son of Clytoneus;
Idmon the soothsayer;
Castor of Sparta, master of horse racing;
Pollux of Sparta, his twin and champion boxer;
Lynceus the sharp-eyed, son of Aphareus;
Idas, the boaster, his brother;
Periclymenus, the many-formed, son of Neleus of Pylos;
Amphidamas, son of Aleus;
Cepheus, his brother;
Ancaeus the strong, son of Lycurgus;
Augeias the wealthy Elean;
Asterius, son of Hyperasius;
Amphion, his brother;
Euphemus of Taenarum, fastest runner in the world;
Erginus of Miletus;
Ancaeus of Samos;
Meleager of Calydon;
Laocoon, his half-uncle;
Iphiclus, a good javelin fighter, uncle to Meleager;
Palaemonius the lame, alleged son of Lernus;
Iphitus, son of Naubolus;
Zetes, winged son of Boreas;
Calais, winged son of Boreas;
Acastus, son of King Pelias of Iolcos;
Argus the master shipwright;
Jason, son of Aeson, rightful heir to Iolcos.

Argo was ready and well found, and her crew made their way to where she lay waiting on the beach at Magnensian Pagasae. At their departure the townsfolk of Iolcos marvelled at such a splendid band of men, and the women prayed for their safe return. In Jason's home, where his father lay bed-ridden, his mother made a long and tearful farewell. Jason calmed her fears and then he too set out to join his companions, waiting on the beach. To their surprise, at the last moment two more volunteers were seen hurrying down from Iolcos – Acastus, son of King Pelias, and Argus the boat builder. Both men were defying King Pelias' express orders not to sail with the expedition.

Now Jason asked the assembled company to elect their leader for the venture. All eyes turned at once towards the incomparable Hercules, but immediately he declined the idea. The man who had brought them together, he said, should lead them. His suggestion was carried with acclaim.

Jason's first command was that the Argonauts should offer a sacrifice to Phoebus, and he sent to his home for oxen to sacrifice. While they were waiting for the cattle to appear, it was time to launch *Argo*.

Stripping for action, the men bound a stout rope around *Argo* to strengthen her, dug a channel down the beach, and laid smooth rollers in it. They tipped *Argo* onto the first roller and then swung the oars inboard and fastened them so their handles projected. Each man took his place, ready to shove, and at a shout from Tiphys the helmsman, the young men pushed *Argo* down into the sea, and checked her with hawsers. Next they fitted the oars to the thole pins, put mast and stores aboard, and made sure that everything was shipshape. Then they cast lots for their positions on the oar benches, by common agreement leaving the centre bench for the two strongest men – Hercules and Ancaeus. They heaped up shingle on the beach to make an altar for Apollo, and when Jason's herdsmen arrived with two oxen, the animals were correctly sacrificed to the God of Departures, with an appeal for a fair passage. Idmon the seer interpreted the flames and smoke, and announced that their mission would be successful. The expedition would undergo many trials, but they would bring back the Fleece. He himself, however, was doomed to die in some remote spot in Asia.

The young men spent the evening camped on the beach, eating, drinking wine and telling stories among themselves. But Jason, assailed by last minute doubts, sat apart from the rest and was chided by Idas. Drunkenly Idas boasted that, because he was a member, the expedition was bound to succeed. He was so skilled with his spear, that he was even ready to challenge the gods. Idas' profanity shocked the others, and he was called to task by Idmon who warned him not to blaspheme. Idas made an angry retort, and there would have been blows if Orpheus had not sprung to his feet, plucked his lyre and begun a soothing song describing the creation of the world. By the time his song was finished, the quarrel was forgotten and the men lay down on the beach to sleep.

At dawn Tiphys the helmsman awoke, and roused the crew to action. Out on the water *Argo*'s speaking beam, cut from the sacred trees of Dodona, cried out, eager to be started on the voyage. The Argonauts went aboard, libations were poured on the sea, and the hawsers hauled in. To the sound of Orpheus' music, the men rowed out, a splendid sight, while the gods looked down in approval, and Cheiron the Centaur came down from the slopes of Mount Pelion to wade out into the surf and wave farewell. As soon as they had left harbour, the Argonauts stepped the mast, tightened the stays, hauled up the sail, and unfurled it. Then, with a favourable breeze behind them, the Argonauts took their ease on the galley's benches as *Argo* ran along the coast, and Orpheus played his music so sweetly that the fishes gambolled in the vessel's wake.

Past Cape Sepcias and Skiathos, *Argo* sailed along the Magnesian coast under a clear sky, until the wind veered against them and they put in to the beach at Aphetae. Here for three days the Argonauts lingered, and on the third day set out again, sailing past Mounts Ossa and Olympus, crossing to Cape Canastra, and by dawn next day were in sight of Mount Athos. As the wind was holding fair, Tiphys decided to press on, and for another twenty-four hours *Argo* ran before a stiff breeze so that by daybreak, when a calm fell, they were able to row the remaining distance to the island of Lemnos.

On Lemnos in the previous year the women had slaughtered all the male inhabitants. Their husbands had spurned them in favour of captured girls taken in raids on the Thracian coast, and the vengeful women of Lemnos had murdered not only their husbands and their Thracian concubines, but every male on the island. The only man to escape was the aged Thoas, father of Hypsipyle. She had set him adrift in a wooden chest, hoping he would be saved. Some fishermen dragged him ashore on the island called Oenoe.

The Lemnian women found that they preferred cattle-herding, ploughing, and wearing armour to the more traditional female tasks, but they lived in constant fear of a raid from the Thracians. So when they saw *Argo* rowing in, they immediately put on their war gear and ran down to the beach.

The Argonauts sent ashore smooth-tongued Aethalidas the herald, who successfully persuaded the Lemnian women at least to allow the travellers to stay the night. Next day, however *Argo* did not cast off and put to sea.

Summoned by Hypsipyle, the Lemnian women held a meeting in the town. Hypsipyle counselled them to treat the Argonauts generously. If they sent wine and food to the ship, then the strangers would have no reason to come into the town. For if they did, they might learn the awful secret of the massacre of the males. Polyxo, Hypsipyle's old nurse, was the next to speak. It was right to welcome the Argonauts, she said. How would the Lemnians survive in the future without men? Who would defend them against foreign attack? And when the present generation grew old, how would there be children to follow them? The solution was to invite the Argonauts ashore and offer them everything – their homes, livestock, and the city itself.

Polyxo's audience was convinced. Hypsipyle sent a messenger to invite the leader of the Argonauts to come to her house, and to inform the other Argonauts that they might come ashore.

Jason, dressed in his finest clothes, made a deep impression on the spectators as he walked from the harbour to Hypsipyle's palace. There she persuaded him that the Lemnian men had only been banished – not killed – for their infidelity, and she demurely offered him the throne of Lemnos. Jason declined the throne, but he and his companions gladly moved into the city, where they were lavishly entertained. Only Hercules and a few picked companions stayed with *Argo*. Day followed day, spent in feasting and merry-making, and still *Argo* did not move. Finally Hercules called a meeting, from which all the women were barred, and rebuked his colleagues. They had forgotten the purpose of their mission, he told them. They would not win the Fleece by enjoying themselves on Lemnos. Rather, they would become the laughing stock of all Greece.

The Argonauts were repentant. They began to get ready to leave, and the women of Lemnos, guessing their intentions, came to say their farewells. Hypsipyle promised Jason that the throne of Lemnos would still be available to him on his return, if he wished; and for his part Jason asked that if Hypsipyle bore his son, then the boy should be sent to his grandparents in Iolcos.

Then *Argo* set out again, going first to Samothrace, where Orpheus instructed them in the secret rites, and afterwards rowing to the mouth of the Hellespont. There they picked up a following wind and under sail negotiated the strait in a single night, arriving at the peninsula of Bear Mountain where they landed at a harbour called Fair Haven. Here, on Tiphys' advice, they left their small anchor stone at the spring called Artacie, and replaced it with a heavier rock.

The Doliones who inhabited the peninsula, greeted the Argonauts kindly, and their king Cyzicus, a man of Jason's age, invited the travellers to join in the feasting to celebrate his recent marriage to Cleite, a princess from the mainland. The Argonauts moved their galley to the town harbour of the Doliones, and a party of them climbed to the top of Mount Dindymun, hoping to see the way they would have to travel. The route they took became known as Jason's Path.

While they were away, a group of savage, six-armed monsters from the mountain suddenly attacked *Argo*, trying to trap her by blocking the harbour mouth with boulders. But Hercules led the boat guard, and fought them off, killing many of them until the other Argonauts arrived, and the monsters were routed with heavy losses.

Putting out to sea, the Argonauts sailed on all day until the wind failed. Then it veered against them and rose to gale force, sending them running for shelter back to the land of the Doliones. At the place where they came ashore, the rock where they hastily cast their hawsers became known as the Sacred Rock.

The Argonauts did not know where they were, and in the darkness the Doliones mistook them for a raiding party, and attacked. There was a bloody fight, and in the struggle Jason killed Cyzicus, while Heracles, Acastus, Peleus, Telamon, Idas, Clytius, Castor and Pollux, and Meleager each killed at least one Doliones warrior. The rest fled back into their city and barred the gates.

Dawn revealed the tragic error, and the Argonauts were stricken with remorse. For three days they and the Doliones grieved for Cyzicus. They held funeral games, marched three times around the corpse in their bronze armour, and then buried him in a barrow – which still stands. The new bride, Cleite, unable to cope with her grief, hanged herself, and the tears which the woodland nymphs shed at her death, caused a spring to arise, called Cleite's Spring by the people of the area, who in their mourning ate only uncooked food and did not grind corn at home, a custom still observed annually in later times.

For the next twelve days the Argonauts were pinned down on the coast of the peninsula by foul weather. Then just before dawn a kingfisher appeared and fluttered over Jason's head as he lay asleep. Mopsus the seer understood the omen, and when the bird flew off and perched on *Argo*'s mascot, he awoke Jason, telling him that he must propitiate Rhea the Mother Goddess who controlled the winds. If he did so, the gales would cease.

After moving *Argo* to a safer anchorage, Jason and his companions climbed Mount Dindymun, from where they could see back to the Hellespont, across to Thrace, and onward to the Bosphorus. There they cut down an ancient vine, and Argus the shipwright skilfully shaped it into an image of the goddess which they set on a rocky eminence and built an altar nearby. Then they crowned themselves with oak leaves, and in full armour performed a high-stepping dance, beating their shields with their swords to drown out the wailing rising from the city of the Doliones. In response the goddess made the trees bring forth abundant fruit, the grass sprouted, and wild animals came out of their lairs wagging their tails. And a spring gushed forth on the mountain where there had never been a water source before. To this day the inhabitants call it Jason's Spring.

By dawn the wind had eased, and in a flat calm they moved on, competing with one another as oarsmen. By afternoon when the offshore wind began to ruffle the sea, only Hercules was left still able to row on with mightly strokes, until at last when *Argo* was in sight of the river Rhyndacus, the oar snapped in his hands, and he was left glaring in helpless fury.

They made landfall that evening on the Cianian coast, and were welcomed by the Mysians. While the rest of the Argonauts set up camp on the beach, Hercules searched the woods for a suitable pine tree to make a new oar. Finding the right tree, he loosened the roots with several blows from his club, then tore it up with his bare hands. Meanwhile his squire Hylas had set out by himself to fetch water. He came to a spring called Pegae, and the water naiad who lived there, seeing Hylas in all his beauty, was filled with desire for him. As Hylas leaned over to fill his bronze ewer with water, the naiad reached up to kiss him. Placing one arm around his neck, with the other she drew him down into the depths.

The Argonaut Polyphemus, going to meet Hercules, was the only one to hear the lad's last cry. Thinking him attacked by wild beasts or brigands, Polyphemus ran towards the sound but could find no one. Drawing his sword, he was searching the woods and calling out Hylas' name when he met Hercules returning with his tree. At once Polyphemus told him of the missing squire, and Hercules, mad with worry, rushed off in search of Hylas. With the morning star a favourable wind arose, and on the beach Tiphys urged the crew to embark without delay. They went aboard at once and put out to sea, and were soon sailing fast before a following breeze. At daybreak they realized that Hylas, Hercules and Polyphemus were missing, and a fierce argument erupted whether or not to turn back. Jason himself was sunk in indecisive gloom, and Telamon accused him of deliberately marooning Hercules, and would have forced Tiphys to turn the boat around, but Zetes and Calais stopped him. Just then the sea god Glaucus arose from the sea and told the Argonauts to sail on. Zeus, he said, had ordained that Hercules should finish his labours, not to go to Colchis, while Polyphemus would settle in Cius, and Hylas was now the husband of the naiad. Telamon apologized to Jason for his outburst, and his apology was accepted with good grace. On shore Hercules obliged the people of Cius to continue the search for Hylas while he went off to continue his labours, and Polyphemus stayed on to found a city.

All that day and the next *Argo* sailed on, until land appeared ahead, and they ran the galley ashore on a wide beach.

Book II

They had landed in the territory of Amycus the arrogant king of the Bebryces, the world's greatest bully. His barbarous habit was to allow no one to leave his kingdom unless they first fought a boxing match against him. Already he had killed several of his neighbours. Coming down to the ship, he issued his usual challenge so rudely that Pollux took it as a personal affront, and immediately accepted the fight. The two men removed their cloaks and prepared to box. Physically they were complete opposites: Amycus like an ogre, Pollux slim and lithe. They donned gloves of hardened rawhide, and immediately set to. Amycus adopted his customary style of rushing at his opponent, attempting to overwhelm him by massive blows, and at first Pollux used his superior technique and ability to avoid the charges, but once he had the measure of his man he stood up to the attack, and the two men traded blow for blow until they drew apart to catch breath. They went at it again, until Amycus tried to batter his opponent with a great downward swing. Pollux turned the blow on his shoulder, and stuck Amycus a deadly blow behind the ear, smashing the bones so that the Bebrycian king collapsed and died.

At this, the watching Bebryces launched an attack on the Argonauts but were beaten off and fled, leaving several dead.

The Argonauts staunched their own wounds and celebrated their victory, and the next morning proceeded up the Bosphorus. Tiphys' skill at the helm saved them from being swamped by a huge wave, and they came ashore at the home of aged Phineas the blind seer. He had been punished with blindness by Zeus because Phineas had been too accurate and comprehensive in his prophecies. As an additional burden Zeus had sent the Harpies to torment him. At every meal the Harpies would sweep down and snatch food from Phineas' table, leaving such a stench as to befoul any food they did not carry away. Phineas knew at once who the Argonauts were, for Zeus had told him that he would be delivered from the Harpies by a band of men seeking the Golden Fleece. Tottering with age, Phineas went to greet the travellers, and inquired if Zetes and Calais were among them, because these two sons of the North Wind were the only men capable of ridding him of the dreadful Harpies. Zetes and Calais took up guard by Phineas as his table was spread for the welcoming banquet. Sure enough, the Harpies immediately swooped in and snatched away the food, leaving an appalling smell. But as the Harpies flew away, Calais and Zetes – using their own power of flight – chased after them with drawn swords. They were overhauling their prey and had even touched them with their fingertips when Iris, messenger of the Gods, intervened. Hastening down from Olympus, she intercepted Calais and Zetes as they flew over the Floating Islands and told them not to harm the Harpies, as they were the hounds of Zeus. She promised that the Harpies would never again torment Phineas. So Calais and Zetes turned back, and from that day the Floating Islands, where they abandoned the chase, were known as the Islands of Return.

Meanwhile Phineas had been entertaining the other Argonauts at his banquet, and explaining the way they now had to go. Their greatest danger was the Clashing Rocks which they would encounter as soon as they set out again on their travels. No ship had ever succeeded in passing between the Rocks which constantly collided together smashing any ship caught between them. But, said Phineas, if the Argonauts were prudent, they would release a dove as they approached the Rocks, and if it flew safely between them, they should take this as a sign and follow the dove's example. Should they succeed in passing the Clashing Rocks, the Argonauts were to turn east and follow the coast for as far as it would lead them. Phineas listed the tribes and places they would pass until finally they reached the mouth of the river Phasis in Colchis. But what would happen there, Phineas refused to say. That, he said, would be to prophesy too much.

For some days the Argonauts were delayed at Phineas' home by adverse winds, but finally they were able to row out, taking with them a dove. Soon they found themselves entering the narrowest part of the straits and heard the clash of the moving Rocks and the thunder of the surf. Rowing on, they rounded a corner and saw the Rocks were beginning to move apart. Euphemus released the dove and it flew at the gap. The Rocks snapped shut with a great crash which sent a massive wave that spun *Argo* right round, but the dove had slipped through between the Rocks, unharmed except for the tips of her tail feathers which were nipped off by the Rocks. Tiphys shouted at the oarsmen to row for the gap as the Rocks drew apart again, and the rowers made a terrific spurt. But even as they entered the gap, they were menaced by a great wave which overhung them. Tiphys' helmsmanship saved them again, and Euphemus ran up and down the galley calling on his companions to row with all their might. But the backwash from a second powerful wave gripped *Argo* and held her back just at the fatal point where the Rocks were due to meet, and it seemed that they were doomed. Just then Athena, who had been watching the terrible ordeal, intervened. With her left hand she held back a Rock, and with her right she thrust *Argo* through the gap like an arrow. The boat sped through, and only the tip of her stern ornament was clipped off by the Clashing Rocks, which from that day forth remained rooted firmly to the ground, as had been foretold would happen when the first ship passed between them successfully.

Now the Argonauts turned eastward, passing the river Rhebus and the Black Cape, and the mouth of the river Phyllis where

Phrixus and the flying ram had halted on their way to Colchis. Sometimes they sailed, often they had to row, labouring like oxen at the plough. At the island of Thynias, they had a vision of Apollo flying through the sky, and so there they built an altar in the God's honour and sacrificed upon it. On the third day a fresh wind brought them to the Acherusian Cape, behind which lies the glen which contains the mouth of Hades. Here an icy breath emerges at dawn and covers everything with rime, and the constant rustling of the leaves of the trees mingles with the rumble of the sea. In this place they were greeted by Lycus, chief of the Mariandyni tribe, and royally entertained. The Mariandyni were enemies of Bebryces, and so paid particular honour to Pollux and his twin for the defeat of the brutal boxer-king Amycus. Lycus promised to erect a monument to them, overlooking the sea where it would be seen by passing sailors.

At dawn, returning from Lycus' feast, the crew were crossing the marshes to reach their ship when a wild boar charged out from the reed beds and gored Idmon savagely. Idmon fell, mortally wounded, and his companions carried him back to *Argo*, where he died, thus fulfilling his own prophesy that he would never return from the expedition. Idmon was buried on a barrow close to the Acherusian height, and soon afterwards Tiphys too died after a short illness, and was buried in a second barrow beside his shipmate. The double loss plunged the Argonauts into deep gloom, and they seemed paralysed by their grief until, at last, Ancaeus chided them into action. Unless the expedition moved on, he said, they would never see their homes again. Electing Ancaeus as their helmsman to replace Tiphys, the Argonauts waited for a favourable breeze, and on the twelfth day took up their voyage once more.

Pausing to pay homage at the tomb of Sthenelus, son of Actor, they sped along the coast under sail guided by Dascylus, son of Lycus. At Sinop they picked up three more recruits – Deileon, Autolycus and Phlogius, stragglers from Hercules' expedition against the Amazons – and at the mouth of the Thermodon went ashore hoping to do battle with the warlike Amazons. But another favourable northwest wind encouraged them to push on, and by the next day they were passing the iron-bearing lands of the Chalybes who never till the soil or pasture flocks but spend their time in endless toil to extract the metal they sell for their living. In turn the Argonauts passed by the lands of the Tibareni, then the mountains of the Mosynechi who live in wooden houses and do openly what other peoples do in private, even coupling together in public. Farther on, they came to Ares island, and as they rowed towards it, saw approaching one of the ferocious birds which infested the place. The bird darted a sharp feather at Oileus, which wounded him in the left shoulder. Eribotes pulled out the feather and bound up the wound, and when another bird was seen flying to the attack, Clytius shot it down with a well-aimed arrow. At Amphidamas' suggestion, the crew put on full armour, and while half of them rowed, the others stood ready to protect the oarsmen with their shields. When *Argo* reached the island, the Argonauts raised such a din by banging on their shields, that all the birds fled in panic, discharging a shower of feathers which rattled off the roof of shields.

On the island of Ares the travellers found four castaways – the sons of Phrixus. These young men had been bound from Colchis, heading for their father's homeland to claim their inheritance – when their Colchian ship foundered in a northerly gale. Clinging to the wreckage they had been washed ashore on Ares Island, and now they approached the Argonauts for succour. When Jason found he was related to the castaways, they resolved to join forces. They went to sacrifice at the temple of Ares where an altar of small stones stood outside a roofless temple. Inside was a black rock fixed to the ground, which was held sacred by the Amazons who came to sacrifice horses there. Jason revealed the purpose of his mission to the four Colchian princes, and they promised they would help the Argonauts reach Colchis and there intercede with their grandfather King Aeetes on Jason's behalf. But even with such help, the princes warned, Jason's quest was perilous. Aeetes was a powerful king, his tribesman were very numerous, and there was no chance of taking the Fleece by force. Moreover it was constantly guarded by a huge serpent which never slept.

Pushing on with a fair breeze, *Argo* next passed the island of Philyra, the lands of the Macrones, Sapeires and Byzeres, and finally came in sight of the Caucasus mountains where Prometheus lay bound while the eagle fed on his liver. At nightfall they reached the mouth of the Phasis river and piloted by Argus, Phrixus' son, turned into the estuary. Lowering the yard and sail, they took down *Argo*'s mast and stowed them all, and then rowed up-river. There Jason poured a thanksgiving libation of sweet wine and, advised by

Argus, ordered his men to row *Argo* into the reedbeds and conceal her for the night.

Book III

The goddesses Hera and Athena, observing that *Argo* had reached her destination, now took counsel together as to how to help Jason obtain the Golden Fleece. They decided to ask Aphrodite for assistance. If Aphrodite could arrange for Medea, Aeetes' daughter, to fall in love with Jason, then a way could be found to obtain the Fleece. Aphrodite agreed to ask Eros, her son, to shoot Medea with an arrow of love, and as Eros was notoriously capricious, bribed him with the promise of a present – a splendid ball made of interlocking hoops of gold – if he would fulfill the mission at once. Eros agreed, and flew off to set his ambush.

Meanwhile the Argonauts, too, had been holding council. They decided that Jason, together with Telamon, Augeias and Phrixus' four sons should go openly to Aeetes' palace and explain their mission. The small group set off through the thickets of willow and osiers near the river where the Colchians hung the corpses of their dead and, shrouded by a convenient mist, reached the gates of Aeetes' palace unobserved. The main courtyard of the palace had soaring columns and was decorated with marble, and there were four fountains wrought by Hephaestus which gushed out wine, milk, oil and water, the latter changed from hot to cold with the alternation of the seasons. For Aeetes, too, Hephaestus had forged a plough of hardened steel and had made bulls with bronze feet and bronze mouths from which spouted blazing fire.

The inner courtyard of the palace was surrounded by rooms and galleries, and the apartments reserved for the queen, for Prince Apsyrtus the son and heir to the throne, and for Aeetes' two daughters – Chalciope and Medea. The latter saw the entry of the travellers and her cry alerted Chalciope who came hurrying out to upbraid her four sons for leaving her in order to go off to seek their father's homeland. By now Eros had flitted in, and was waiting with an arrow notched to his bow. When Medea first laid eyes on Jason, Eros fired the arrow and it struck the mark. Medea was transfixed with love for Jason.

After the visitors had bathed, King Aeetes' servants prepared a banquet for them, and once they had eaten, the king asked his grandsons to explain what had happened. Argus, the eldest, told of their shipwreck and rescue by the Argonauts, and explained how Jason had come to seek the Fleece on the orders of a cruel king. But Aeetes refused to believe the tale. In a rage he accused his grandsons of bringing men to Colchis whose real intention was to seize the throne. But for the laws of hospitality he would have chopped off the hands and torn out the tongues of the impudent visitors. As it was, he commanded them to leave Colchis at once.

Jason replied soothingly that he and his men would earn the Fleece by fighting alongside the Colchian army against the King's enemies. But his offer had little effect. Aeetes, after considering, proposed that Jason could have the Fleece only if he passed a mortal test: he would have to yoke two fire-breathing bulls which grazed on the plain of Ares on the river bank and with them plough a four-acre field. In the furrows he was to sow dragons' teeth from which would spring a host of armed men, all of whom he would have to cut down by nightfall. Only then could he have the Fleece.

Despite this terrible condition, Jason accepted the terms and went back with his companions to *Argo* to inform his crew. There Argus counselled them to enlist the aid of Medea, for she was adept in the magic arts, and her skill might yet save them. This was agreed, and Argus returned to the palace to speak with Chalciope his mother. She, fearing that Aeetes' wrath would now be turned against her sons, also begged Medea for her help. But already Medea was so smitten with love for Jason that she knew she would have to assist him even though it would mean betraying her own father.

After passing a sleepless night Medea, accompanied by her handmaidens, went at dawn to the shrine of Hecate the goddess she served. Alerted by Argus, Jason too set out from *Argo* for the temple precinct, and they met as if by chance. Medea's handmaidens withdrew to leave them alone together, and Jason humbly asked Medea for her help. When he finished, Medea handed him an ointment that she had prepared. Jason, Medea instructed, was to sacrifice to Hecate at midnight, then in the morning smear his body with the salve, and for one day it would render him invulnerable. When he had ploughed the field and the crop of armed men sprang up, he was to throw a boulder among them so that in confusion they fought among themselves. Then he could finish off the survivors. As Jason's and Medea's eyes met, it was Jason who knew he was falling in love. If he survived the ordeal, Jason said, he wanted Medea to return to Greece with him and be his Queen.

The two parted, and that night Jason followed Medea's instructions. He made his sacrifice to Hecate, and in the morning anointed himself with the magic ointment, also sprinkling a few drops on his shield and spear. When his companions tested the effect, they found that even the hardest blow could not damage his equipment. Next the crew rowed *Argo* up river to the plain of Ares where Aeetes and his warriors were waiting to witness the ordeal. Jason leapt ashore, carrying the serpent's teeth he was to plant, and the two fire-breathing bulls rushed out to the attack. Impervious to their fiery breath, Jason seized and yoked them, and with the steel plough drove them to plough the field until by late afternoon all the four acres were planted with the dragon's teeth. Up sprang the crop of earth-born warriors and, as Meda had predicted, a boulder Jason threw among them caused such confusion that they fought among themselves until Jason could hack down the remainder. By nightfall the ordeal was done, and the Argonauts returned to their vessel, while Aeetes withdrew to his city, pondering how he could get rid of the intruders.

Book IV

That night, as Aeetes plotted the destruction of the Argonauts, Medea slipped out of the palace and hurried down to the riverbank where *Argo* lay moored. She urged the crew to row to the sacred grove where hung the Fleece. There, going ashore with Jason, she led him to the sacred spot. The huge serpent heard them coming, and hissed in alarm. But Medea soothed the snake with a gentle song, and as its coils relaxed, sprinkled its eyes with a magic drug so the reptile slept. Jason snatched the Fleece from the oak, and the two lovers fled back down the path to the waiting galley, Jason carrying the shimmering fleece. As soon as they stepped aboard, *Argo* dropped down river in a race to clear the Phasis before Colchians barred their passage.

They were just in time. King Aeetes in his war chariot was already leading a host of Colchian warriors to the river bank, and they arrived only to see *Argo* standing out to sea. In fury Aeetes threatened his people with dire punishment if Medea and the Fleece were not brought back. The very same day the Colchian fleet was equipped and sailed in pursuit of *Argo*.

Hera sent a favourable breeze for the Argonauts, and in just three days she was once again on the Paphlagonian coast where Dascylus, Lycus' son, was set ashore to rejoin his people. At a council the crew of *Argo* decided that their best chance to escape the Colchian pursuit was to return home, not past the Clashing Rocks, but up the Danube and thence down its tributary into the Adriatic Sea. So *Argo* crossed the Euxine to the delta of the Danube and turned into its northern arm. But Prince Apsyrtus, leading the chase, had split his forces, and while one Colchian squadron went by way of the Clashing Rocks, the other had also headed for the Danube. This squadron took the shorter southern arm of the delta, and so emerged into the Adriatic ahead of *Argo*. There they trapped the Argonauts, and in face of overwhelming odds Jason prepared to parlay. But Medea, hearing that his fate was to be decided by the judgement of a local king, upbraided Jason for his faint-heartedness. She proposed a treacherous ambush for her brother Apsyrtus, and pretending to him that she had been taken away on *Argo* against her will, lured him, alone and unarmed, to a secret meeting. There Jason murdered the Colchian prince, a deed so foul that only Circe, the great sorceress and sister to Aeetes, could expiate the crime. But as yet the Argonauts did not know this, until, trying to sail south, they were struck by a gale and *Argo* herself cried out, her speaking beam telling them that they should sail to Circe's island. So, sailing up the Eridanus river and then down the Rhone, they came to the Tyrrhenian Sea and there sought Circe's help. She cleansed the guilt as best she could with her black arts, and *Argo* sailed for home. As they passed the Sirens, Orpheus drowned out their bewitching song with music from his lyre, and Hera arranged a safe passage past the dangers of the Scylla and Charybdis and the raging surf of the Wandering Islands.

But off the island of Phaecia the Argonauts found themselves face to face with the second Colchian squadron which had been lying in wait for them, and they would have been destroyed if King Alcinous of Phaecia had not intervened. He decreed that Medea should stay with Jason if they were truly man and wife. Since Arete, Alcinous' wife, had forewarned Medea of the judgement, she and Jason celebrated their wedding in the sacred cave of Macris. So the Colchians gave up the chase, though *Argo*'s tribulations were not yet at an end. She was blown to Libya by a northerly gale, and stranded in the shallows of the Gulf of Sirte. Searching for water in the desert the Argonauts were guided to a spring by the Hesperides, bewailing the theft of the gold apples by Hercules. Canthus, stealing a flock of sheep to feed his famished companions, was killed by a stone thrown by the shepherd, and Mopsus died from the poisonous bite of a snake. Finally, with the help of a Triton, *Argo* was extricated from the sandbars of the Gulf, and sailed north to Crete. There Talus the bronze giant kept them from landing by breaking off great lumps of rock and hurling them at the strangers, until Medea fixed him with the evil eye and caused him to graze his ankle on a rock. This was Talus' only vulnerable spot, for the vein broke beneath his brazen skin and the icthor flowed out so that Talus collapsed and died.

The Argonauts spent that night on Crete and then sailed on, only to run into a strange pitch-black night. In the darkness they would have been wrecked, if Apollo had not suddenly appeared and lit the danger so that *Argo* found anchorage off Anaphe island. So, by way of Aegina, where the Argonauts took on water, *Argo* finally came back home to the beach at Pagasae.

Acknowledgements

It will be clear from the preceding tale that the Jason Voyage was made possible through the help of a great many people spread across several different countries. The following list of such 'friends of the Argonauts' is by no means complete, but gives some idea of the international spirit of cooperation which helped us reach our goal.

First to be thanked must be Sarah Waters who once again was the all-important project coordinator. With the help of Constance Messenger in Windsor, Sarah ran the expedition's office with her customary finesse. Her role in the Jason Voyage was vital to the final outcome of the expedition, and it was – as always – immensely reassuring to know that Sarah was at the expedition base handling the day-to-day workload faultlessly. On the other side of the Atlantic the staff of the *National Geographic Magazine* once again provided encouragement and the photographic assistance for which they are justly renowned.

In the British Isles help was given by Lord Killanin; Dr John Harvey; Arthur Beale Ltd; E. P. Barrus Ltd (outboard motor for the rubber dinghy); Beaufort Air-Sea Equipment (the very generous loan of liferafts and lifejackets); Henri-Lloyd (oilskins); Munster Simms Engineering (hand pumps); the London office of Olympic Airways; Seafarer Navigation Ltd (emergency radio and other equipment); Telesonic Ltd; and Zodiac UK (rubber dinghy).

In Greece, Wendy Vosmer was splendid in the role which one visitor aptly described as 'house mother' to the building crew, and very many thanks are due to Clem and Jesse Wood for their unfailing hospitality, and also to Andy and Metula. In Greece, too, there were Richard Arnold-Baker; Edward Hekimian; Pandelis Kartapanis, shipwright of Pefkakia; Angelos Kilaidonis; Lance

Rowell; Anastasis Rodopoulos; Harry Tzalas; and Sotiris Zeibekis, harbour master of Limnos. Among official bodies we received help from Olympic Airways and the National Tourist Organisation of Greece, as well as the Mayor and Council of Volos.

In Turkey, I would like to thank the Turkish Navy and in particular four of its admirals: Mustafa Turumcoglu commanding the Turkish Coastguard; Yasar Onkal commanding the Naval College; Sadun Ozturk Commander of the Bosphorus, who very thoughtfully provided a complete set of the Turkish Navy's Black Sea charts, and retired admiral Nejet Serim. At Milliyet newspaper, Sevin Okyay went to great lengths to support the expedition, and it was always wonderful to see her when she came to visit us at various ports during *Argo*'s journey along the Turkish coast. Yelman Emcan at the Ministry of Tourism and Culture thoughtfully directed his staff to assist the Argonauts, and they did so with typical Turkish hospitality and kindness, in particular at Canakkale (Meryem Basli and Lale Sumer), Erdek (Vural Menteseoglu), Istanbul (regional director Cengis Taner) and Samsun (Erdopan Istankoylu). In Istanbul Bill Bauer, manager of the Sheraton Hotel, made our stay far more comfortable than we had ever expected, and Mayor Bedrettin Dalan not only looked after us outward bound but then took care of *Argo* on our return. In Erdek, my thanks also to another hotelier, the proprietor of the Avelok Hotel for his help and hospitality. The Governors and Mayors of regions and towns all along our Turkish route were unstinting in their hospitality, and there are notably happy memories from Akcakoca, Amasra, Cide, Samsun, Sinop and Zonguldak. In Istanbul we were guests of the Fenerbache Yacht Club; in Eregli we were guided round the Caves of Hades by Cengiz Guceri and entertained by Turgut Goray, introduced to me by Alpay Cin the President of the Turkish Yachting Federation whose members maintained the best traditions of comradeship between sailors. When we broke steering oars, Ayhan Demir (Sinop) and Hilmi Gurler (Samsun) came to our assistance during shore-based repairs. Expert archaeological counsel was provided by Necmettin Akgunduz (Sinop) and Nihat Sumer (Samsun). Sevim Berker, working with the BBC-TV team in Turkey, helped us, as did the on-shore film crew, led by John Miller from the Manchester TV Centre, who somehow found time to bring out mail and supplies as well as carry out their filming duties to make a documentary record of the Voyage. The same extra-curricular help was provided by Stephen Phillips, arts correspondent for ITN, during his visits to report the progress of the expedition.

In the USSR, I would like to thank the Ministry of Mercantile Marine for putting *Tovarisch* at our disposal for the return to Istanbul as well as our memorable greeting to Georgia. In advance of our visit to the Soviet Union it was Soviet TV who laid the groundwork. The team at the Foreign Relations department, headed by Lev Korolyev, put me in touch with the producers of Yuri Senkevich's Voyage Club programme (particularly Stas) and the Committee comprising Boris Semyonov, Nina Sevruk, Irina Zhelezova and Zinaida Yevgrafova. Later Sergey Skvortsov and Pavel Korchagin then came from Moscow to Georgia to smooth our paths.

I hope the text has already given some idea of the tremendous welcome given us by the Georgians, and much credit for this must go to Nugzar Popkhadze and Othar Lordkipanidze. Among many helpful scholars Vachtang Licheli and Alexandre Alexidze must stand as representatives for their colleagues. While David Shalikashvili and Tamar Makharoblidze must do the same for our many friends at Georgian TV and Radio. I would also like to make a special mention of the three Svan gold-gatherers who were so kind as to show me the age-old technique of gold-gathering with the use of sheepskins. They were: David Dzaparidze, Walo Gulbani and Alexandre Dzaparidze.

I hope that those 'friends of the Argonauts' whose names have neither been mentioned above nor introduced in the book itself will forgive the omission. By recompense I hope they enjoy the story of the Jason Voyage, and feel that the results have repaid their efforts in our support.

Finally my thanks to Monique Kervran in Greece, Turkey and France where her perceptive analysis of archaeology and her tireless support were deeply appreciated.

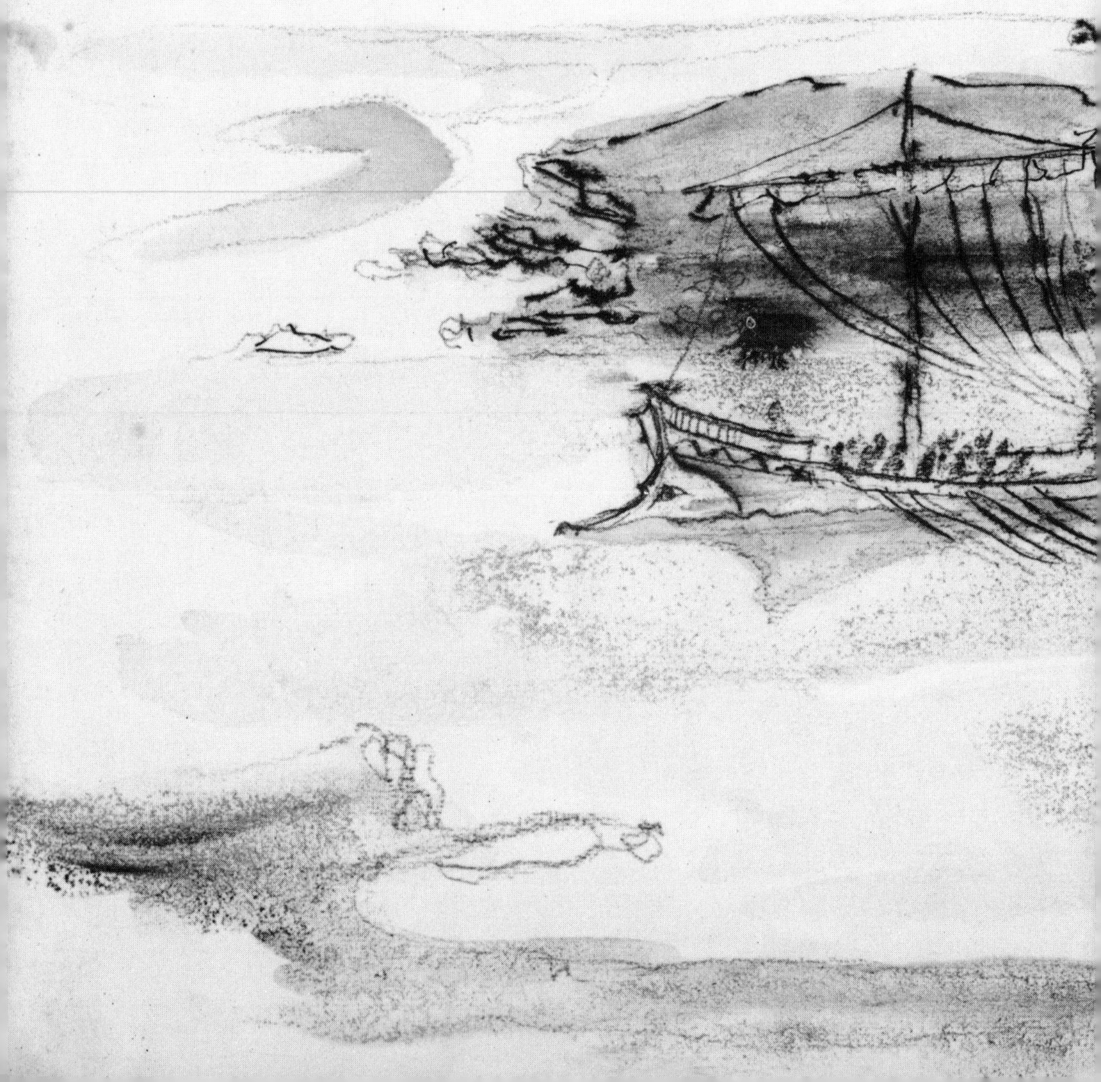

THE MOTION OF THE BODY THROUGH SPACE

Lionel Shriver's novels include *Sunday Times* bestsellers *Big Brother* and *The Mandibles: A Family, 2029–2047*, the *New York Times* bestseller *The Post-Birthday World* and The Orange Prize-winning international bestseller *We Need to Talk About Kevin*. Her journalism has appeared in the *Guardian* and the *New York Times*, the *Wall Street Journal* and many other publications. She lives in London and Brooklyn.

Also by Lionel Shriver

Property

The Standing Chandelier

The Mandibles: A Family, 2029–2047

Big Brother

The New Republic

So Much for That

The Post-Birthday World

We Need to Talk About Kevin

Double Fault

A Perfectly Good Family

Game Control

Ordinary Decent Criminals

Checker and the Derailleurs

The Female of the Species

LIONEL
SHRIVER

THE MOTION OF THE BODY THROUGH SPACE

THE BOROUGH PRESS

The Borough Press
An imprint of HarperCollins*Publishers* Ltd
1 London Bridge Street
London SE1 9GF

www.harpercollins.co.uk

First published in Great Britain by HarperCollins*Publishers* 2020
1

A catalogue record for this book is available from the British Library

HB ISBN: 978-0-00-756078-3
TPB ISBN: 978-0-00-756079-0

Designed by Fritz Metsch

Printed and bound in the UK by CPI Group (UK) Ltd, Croydon CR0 4YY

To Jeff—whose luxurious lassitude
has spared me the plot of this novel.
Added together and divided by two,
we make a perfectly balanced person.

"The glory of suffering might be humankind's biggest, ever-recyclable con trick."

—MELANIE REID, *The World I Fell Out Of*

"Clearly his personal god or *chi* was not made for great things. A man could not rise beyond the destiny of his *chi*. The saying of the elders was not true—that if a man said yea his *chi* also affirmed. Here was a man whose *chi* said nay despite his own affirmation."

—CHINUA ACHEBE, *Things Fall Apart*

ONE

"I've decided to run a marathon."

In a second-rate sitcom, she'd have spewed coffee across her breakfast. Yet Serenata was an understated person, and between sips. "What?" Her tone was a little arch, but polite.

"You heard me." Back to the stove, Remington studied her with a discomfiting level gaze. "I have my eye on the race in Saratoga Springs in April."

She had the sense, rare in her marriage, that she should watch what she said. "This is serious. You're not pulling my leg."

"Do I often make statements of intent, and then pull the rug out: just foolin'? I'm not sure how to take your disbelief as anything but an insult."

"My 'disbelief' might have something to do with the fact that I've never seen you run from here to the living room."

"Why would I run to the living room?"

The literalism had precedent. They called each other out in this nitpicking manner as a matter of course. It was a game. "For the last thirty-two years, you've not once trotted out for a run around the block. And now you tell me with a straight face that you want to run a marathon. You must have assumed I'd be a bit surprised."

"Go ahead, then. Be surprised."

"It doesn't bother you . . ." Serenata continued to feel careful. She didn't care for the carefulness, not one bit. ". . . That your ambition is hopelessly trite?"

"Not in the least," he said affably. "That's the sort of thing that bothers you. Besides, if I decline to run a marathon because so many other people also want to run one, my actions would still be dictated by the multitude."

"What is this, some 'bucket list' notion? You've been listening to your old Beatles records and suddenly realized that *when I'm sixty-four* refers to you? *Bucket list*," she repeated, backing off. "Where did I get that?"

Indeed, incessant citation of the now commonplace idiom was exactly the sort of lemming-like behavior that drove her wild. (That allusion did a grave injustice to lemmings. In the documentary that propagated the mass-suicide myth, the filmmakers had flung the poor creatures over the cliff. Thus the popular but fallacious metaphor for mass conformity was itself an example of mass conformity.) Okay, there was nothing wrong with adopting a new expression. What galled was the way everyone suddenly started referring to their "bucket list" in a breezy, familiar spirit that conveyed they had *always said it.*

Serenata began to push up from her chair, having lost interest in the news from Albany on her tablet. It had only been four months since they'd moved to Hudson, and she wondered how much longer she'd keep up the pretense of a connection with their old hometown by reading the *Times Union* online.

She herself was only sixty, though hers was the first generation to append "only" to such a sobering milestone. Having remained in the same position for half an hour, her knees had stiffened, and extending the right one was tricky. Once it had seized, you had to straighten it *very slowly*. She never knew, either, when one of the knees would do something creepy and unexpected—suddenly go *pong*, seeming to slip slightly out of joint and then pop back in again. This was what old people thought about, and talked about. She wished she could issue a retroactive apology to her late grandparents, whose medical kvetching she'd found so trying as a child. Underestimating the pitiless self-involvement of their nearest and dearest, old folks detailed their ailments because they assumed that anyone who cared about them would necessarily care about their pain. But no one had cared about her grandparents' pain, and now no one would care about the pain of the granddaughter who'd once been so unfeeling. Rough justice.

The segue to a stand was a success. My, what miserable achievements might pass for triumph in a few years' time. Remembering the word *blender.* Taking a sip of water without breaking the glass. "Have you considered the timing of this announcement?" She plugged in the tablet—busywork; the battery was still at 64 percent.

"What about it?"

"It coincides with a certain incapacity. I only stopped running myself in July."

"I knew you'd take this personally. That's why I dreaded telling you. Would you really want me to deny myself something just because it makes you feel wistful?"

"Wistful. You think it makes me feel *wistful.*"

"Resentful," Remington revised. "But if I bind myself to a chair for eternity, that won't help your knees in the slightest."

"Yes, that's all very rational."

"You say that as if it's a criticism."

"So in your view, it's 'irrational' to take your wife's feelings into consideration."

"When making a sacrifice won't make her feel any better—yes."

"You've been thinking about this for a while?"

"A few weeks."

"In your mind, does this uncharacteristic blossoming of an interest in fitness have anything to do with what happened at the DOT?"

"Only in the sense that *what happened* at the DOT has provided me a great deal of unanticipated leisure time." Even this brush against the subject made Remington twitchy. He chewed at his cheek in that way he had, and his tone went icy and sour, with a few drops of bitterness, like a cocktail.

Serenata disdained women who broadcast their emotions by banging about the kitchen, though it took a ridiculous degree of concentration to keep from unloading the dishwasher. "If you're looking to fill your dance card, don't forget the main reason we moved here. It's already been too long since you last visited your father, and his house is a riot of repair jobs."

"I'm not spending the rest of my life under my father's sink. Is this your version of talking me out of a marathon? You can do better."

"No, I want you to do whatever you want. Obviously."

"Not so obviously."

The dishwasher had proved irresistible. Serenata hated herself.

"You ran for such a long time—"

"Forty-seven years." Her tone was clipped. "Running, and a great deal else."

"So—maybe you could give me some pointers." Remington's suggestion was halting. He did not want any pointers.

"Remember to tie your shoes. There's no more to it."

"Look . . . I'm sorry you've had to give up something you loved."

Serenata straightened, and put down a bowl. "I did not *love* running. Here's a pointer for you: no one does. They pretend to, but they're lying. The only good part is *having run*. In the moment, it's dull, and hard as in effortful but not as in difficult to master. It's repetitive. It doesn't open the floodgates of revelation, as I'm sure you've been led to expect. I'm probably grateful for an excuse to quit.

Maybe that's what I can't forgive myself. Though at least I've finally escaped the great mass of morons chugging alongside who all think they're so fucking special."

"Morons like me."

"Morons like you."

"You can't hold me in contempt for doing what you did for, I quote, *forty-seven years*."

"Oh, yeah?" she said with a tight smile before pivoting toward the staircase. "Watch me."

Remington Alabaster was a narrow, vertical man who seemed to have maintained his figure without a struggle. His limbs were born shapely. With slender ankles, firm calves, neat knees, and thighs that didn't jiggle, given a quick shave those legs would have looked smashing on a woman. He had beautiful feet—also narrow, with high arches and elongated toes. Whenever Serenata massaged the insteps, they were dry. His hairless pectorals were delectably subtle, and should they ever bulge grossly from a sustained obsession with bench-pressing, she'd count the transformation a loss. True, in the last couple of years he'd developed a slight swell above the belt, whose mention she avoided. That was the unspoken contract, standard between couples, she would wager: unless he brought it up, such vacillations in his bodily person were his business. Which was why, though tempted, she hadn't asked him squarely this morning whether freaking out about what had to be a weight gain of less than five pounds was what this marathon lark was all about.

The harmless bulge aside, Remington was aging well. His facial features had always been expressive. The mask of impassivity he'd worn the last few years of his employment was protective, a contrivance for which a certain Lucinda Okonkwo was wholly to blame. Once he hit his sixties, the coloration of those features ashed over somewhat; it was this homogenizing of hue that made Caucasian faces look vaguer, flatter, and somehow less extant as their age advanced, like curtains whose once bold print had bleached in the sun. Yet in her mind's eye, Serenata routinely interposed the more decisive lines of his younger visage over the hoarier, more tentative present, sharpening the eyes and flushing the cheeks as if applying mental makeup.

She could see him. She could see him at a range of ages with a single glance, and could even, if unwillingly, glimpse in that still vital face the frail elder he'd grow into. Perceiving this man in full, what he was, had been, and would be, was her job. It was an important job, more so as he aged, because to others he would soon be just some old geezer. He was not just some old geezer. At twenty-seven, she'd fallen in love with a handsome civil engineer, and he was still here. It was the subject of some puzzlement: other people were themselves getting older by the day, themselves watching these mysterious transformations not all of which were their fault, and knew themselves to have once been younger. Yet the young and old alike perceived others in their surround as stationary constants, like parking signs. If you were fifty, then fifty was all you were, all you ever had been, and all you ever would be. Perhaps the exercise of informed imagination was simply too exhausting.

It was also her job to look upon her husband with kindness. To both see and not see. To screw up her eyes and blur the eruptions of uninvited skin conditions into a smooth surface—an *Alabaster* surface. To issue a blanket pardon for every blobbing mole, every deepening crag of erosion. To be the sole person in the entire world who did not regard the slight thickening under his jaw as a character flaw. The sole person who did not construe from the sparseness of the hair at his temples that he didn't matter. In trade, Remington would forgive the crenulations atop her elbows and the sharp line beside her nose when she slept too hard on her right side—a harsh indentation that could last until mid-afternoon and would soon be scored there all the time. Were he to have registered, as he could not help but have done, that his wife's physical form was no longer identical to the one he wed, Remington alone would not regard this as a sign that she had done something wrong, perhaps even morally wrong, and he would not hold her accountable for being a disappointment. That was also part of the contract. It was a good deal.

Yet Remington had no need to draw drastically on the bottomless reserves of his wife's forgiveness for not having been dipped in preservative plastic when they met, like an ID card. He looked pretty damned good for sixty-four. How he'd remained so slim, vigorous, and nicely proportioned without any appreciable exercise was anyone's guess. Oh, he walked places, and didn't complain about taking the stairs if an elevator was out of order. But he'd never even experimented with one of those "seven minutes to a better body" routines, much less joined a gym. During lunch, he ate lunch.

More exercise would improve his circulation, build vascular resilience, and forestall cognitive decline. She should welcome the turned leaf. She should ply him with protein bars and proudly track his increasing mileage on a pad in the foyer.

The whole supportiveness shtick might actually have been doable had he introduced his resolution with suitable chagrin: "I realize I'll never manage to cover *nearly* the distances you have. Still, I wonder if maybe it would be good for my heart to go out for a modest, you know, two-mile jog, say, two or three times a week." But no. He had to run a *marathon*. For the rest of the day, then, Serenata indulged the pretense of intense professionalism the better to avoid her husband. She only went back downstairs to make tea once she heard him go out. It wasn't nice, it wasn't "rational," but this specific subset of human experience belonged to her, and his timing was cruel.

Presumably, she herself began by copying someone else—though that's not how it felt at the time. Both her sedentary parents were on the heavy side, and, in the way of these things, they grew heavier. Their idea of exertion was pushing a manual lawn mower, to be replaced by a power mower as soon as possible. That wasn't to criticize. Americans in the 1960s of her childhood were big on "labor-saving devices." A sign of modernity, the reduction of personal energy output was highly prized.

A marketing analyst for Johnson & Johnson, her father had been relocated every two years or so. Born in Santa Ana, California, Serenata never knew the town before the family shifted to Jacksonville, Florida—and then they were off to West Chester, Pennsylvania; Omaha, Nebraska; Roanoke, Virginia; Monument, Colorado; Cincinnati, Ohio, and finally to the company headquarters in New Brunswick, New Jersey. As a consequence, she had no regional affiliations, and was one of those rare creatures whose sole geographical identifier was the big, baggy country itself. She was "an American," with no qualifier or hyphenation—since calling herself a "Greek-American," having grown up supping nary a bowl of avgolemono soup, would have struck her as desperate.

Being yanked from one school to the next as a girl had made her leery of forming attachments. She'd only inculcated the concept of friendship in adulthood, and then with difficulty—tending to mislay companions out of sheer absentmindedness, like gloves dropped in the street. For Serenata, friendship was a discipline. She was too content by herself, and had sometimes wondered if not getting lonely was a shortcoming.

Her mother had responded to ceaseless transplantation by fastening onto multiple church and volunteer groups the moment the family arrived in a new town, like an octopus on speed. The constant convenings of these memberships left an only child to her own devices, an arrangement that suited Serenata altogether. Once old enough to fix her own Fluffernutter sandwiches, she occupied her unsupervised after-school hours building strength and stamina.

She would lie palms down on the lawn and count the number of seconds—*one one-thousand, two one-thousand*—she could keep her straightened legs raised a foot above the ground (discouragingly few, but only to begin with). She was gripping a low-hanging tree branch and struggling to get her chin above the wood well before she learned that the exercise was called a *pull-up.* She invented her own calisthenics. To complete what she dubbed a "broken leg," you hopped on one foot the circumference of the yard with the opposite leg thrust forward in a goose step, then repeated the circuit hopping backward. "Rolly-pollies" entailed lying on the grass, gripping your knees to the chest, and rocking on your back *one-two-three!* to throw your legs straight behind your head; later she added a shoulder stand at the end. As an adult, she would recall with wan incredulity that when she strung her creations together to stage her own backyard Olympics, it never occurred to her to invite the neighborhood children to join in.

Many of her contortions were silly, but repeated enough times they still wore her out. Pleasantly so, though even these fanciful routines—of which she kept an exacting secret record in crimped printing in a bound blank book stashed under her mattress—were not exactly fun. It was interesting to discover that it was possible to not especially want to do them and to do them anyway.

During the "physical education" of her school days, the meager athletic demands placed on girls were one of the few constants across Jacksonville, West Chester, Omaha, Roanoke, Monument, Cincinnati, and New Brunswick. The half-hour recess in primary school usually sponsored kickball—and if you managed to get up before your teammates lost the inning, you might run an entire *ten yards* to first base. Dodgeball was even more absurd: jumping one foot this way, one foot that. In middle schools' formal gym classes, twenty of the forty-five minutes were consumed with changing in and out of gym clothes. The instructor would direct the girls in unison to do *ten* jumping jacks, do *five* squat thrusts, and run in place for *thirty seconds.* Given this limp gesturing toward strength training, it hadn't really been fair to subject these same girls to a formal fitness assessment in eighth grade—during which, after Serenata sailed past the one hundred mark in the sit-ups test, the gym teacher intervened and insisted in a shrill panic that she stop. For the following decades, of course, she'd be doing sit-ups in sets of five hundred. They weren't really efficient, abdominally, but she had a soft spot for the classics.

To correct any misimpressions: Serenata Terpsichore—which rhymed with *hickory,* though she grew inured to teachers stressing the first syllable and pronouncing the last as a tiresome task—had no designs on professional athletics. She didn't want to earn a place on a national volleyball team. She didn't want to become a ballerina. She didn't aspire to take part in weight-lifting contests, or to attract an Adidas sponsorship. She'd never come near to breaking any records, and hadn't tried. After all, the setting of records was all about placing your achievements in relation to the achievements of other people. She might have engaged in rigorous, self-contrived conniptions on a daily basis from childhood, but that had *nothing to do with anyone else.* Push-ups were private.

She'd never identified in an elaborate way with a particular sport. She ran, she cycled, she swam; she was not *a runner* or *a swimmer* or *a cyclist,* designations that would have allowed these mere forms of locomotion to place a claim on her. She was not, as they say, a *team player,* either. Her ideal running route was deserted. She gloried in the serenity of an empty swimming pool. Throughout her fifty-two years of biking for primary transportation, a single other cyclist in sight despoiled her solitude and ruined her mood.

Given that Serenata would have thrived on a desert island in the company of fish, it was disconcerting to have so frequently been co-opted by, as Remington had said, the *multitude.* Sooner or later, any quirk, any curious habit or obsession, was eventually colonized by a throng.

Impulsively, when she was sixteen, she'd slipped into a shadowy establishment in downtown Cincinnati to have a tiny tattoo inscribed on the tender inside face of her right wrist. The design she requested was snatched, literally, from the air: a bumblebee in flight. With no other customers, the artisan took his time. He captured the diaphanous wings, the inquiring antennae, the delicate legs poised for landing. The image had nothing to do with her. Yet in crafting character from scratch, one reached for what lay to hand; we were all found artworks. Thus the arbitrary soon converted to the signal. The bumblebee became her emblem, doodled endlessly across the canvas covers of her three-ring binders.

Tattoos in the 1970s were largely confined to longshoremen, sailors, prison inmates, and biker gangs. For wayward children of the middle class, what were not yet called "tats" were a defilement. That winter, she concealed the inking from her parents with long sleeves. That spring, she switched her watch to her right wrist, with the face flipped down. She lived in constant fear of exposure, though secrecy also freighted the image with mighty powers. In retrospect, it would have been nobler to have declared the "mutilation" voluntarily and taken the consequences, but that was an adult perspective. Young people, for whom time moved so sedulously that every moment could seem an eternity of reprieve, put a great deal of store in delay.

Inevitably, one morning she overslept her alarm. Come to rouse the sleepyhead, her mother discovered the naked wrist thrown upright on a pillow. Once the teenager confessed that the image wasn't felt-tip, her mother cried.

The point: Serenata would have been the sole student in her high school to brave a tattoo. Nowadays? Over a third of the eighteen-to-thirty-five demographic sported at least one, and the total acreage of American skin aswirl with hobbits, barbed wire, or barcodes, eyes, tigers, or tribals, and scorpions, skulls, or superheroes, was the size of Pennsylvania. Serenata's adventure into the underworld had inverted from intrepid to trite.

In her twenties, frustrated that traditional ponytail ties snagged the strands of her thick black hair, Serenata set about stitching several tubes of colorful fabric, through which she threaded sturdy elastic. After tying the ends of the elastic together, she sewed the cloth tubes into gathered circles. The resultant binders kept the hair from her face without grabbing, while adding a flash of pizzazz to her crown. Some peers found the handicrafts kooky, but more than one coworker asked where to get one. Yet by the 1990s, most of her female compatriots owned a set of twenty-five in a rainbow of hues. She hacked her hair to just under her ears and tossed what were apparently called "scrunchies" in the wastebasket.

It would have been circa 1980, too, that she made one of her effortful bids for friendship, inviting a handful of coworkers at Lord & Taylor's customer service to dinner. For the previous couple of years she had dabbled in Japanese cuisine, an enthusiasm rescued from a dead-end date who'd taken her to a hole-in-the-wall counter that served his countrymen's expats. She had loved the smoothness, the coolness, the subtly. Later back home, she experimented with vinegared rice, green powdered horseradish, and a sharp knife. Eager to share her discoveries, she laid out multiple platters for her guests, aiming for what a later era would call the wow factor.

They were horrified. None of the girls could bear the prospect of raw fish.

Yet nowadays it was not unusual to find three different sushi bars along a single block of a midsize town in Iowa. The dreariest undergrad had a preference for fresh or saltwater eel. It wasn't as if Serenata could take the slightest credit for the centuries-old traditions of a storied island nation in the East. Nevertheless, what was once an idiosyncrasy had been crowd funded.

The watch, which obscured her sin of self-defacement? It had made for an effective disguise because it had once been her father's. Serenata had been wearing oversize men's watches ever since. Lo, come the 2010s, every other woman in the country was wearing massive, masculine-style watches as well. Favorite books that made little or no splash on release—*A Home at the End of the World* or *The City of Your Final Destination*—invariably got turned into movies, and suddenly these private totems belonged to everybody. She'd no sooner revive the nearly lost art of quilting, stitching swatches of worn-out corduroys and old towels while watching *Breaking Bad* before anyone had ever heard of it, than quilting bees would sweep the country as a nationwide fad. If Serenata Terpsichore ever seized upon the music of an obscure band that only played pass-the-hat clubs and wedding gigs, that veritably guaranteed that these same nobodies would hit the top forty by the following year. If she happened to pick up the habit of wearing incredibly warm, soft sheepskin boots hitherto confined to the small Australian and California surfer sets, the better to weather an Albany winter, you could be damned sure that Oprah Winfrey would make the same discovery. Ugg.

The same thing must have happened to plenty of others as well. There were only so many things to wear, to love, to do. And there were too many people. So sooner or later whatever you claimed for yourself would be adopted by several million of your closest friends.

At which point you either abandoned your own enthusiasms or submitted numbly to the appearance of slavish conformity. For the most part, Serenata had opted for the latter. Still, the experience was repeatedly one of being occupied, as if a horde of strangers had camped out on her lawn.

Which, steadily yet at an accelerating pace for the last twenty years, was what had been happening to fitness in any form. She could almost hear them, rumbling the inside of her skull like an oncoming migration of wildebeest, the dust catching in her nostrils, the beat of their hooves pounding from the horizon. This time the multitudes could be spotted not merely aping her tastes in music or fiction in the quiet isolation of their homes, but in aggregate, pounding in droves over the hills and dales of public parks, splashing in phalanxes across all six lanes of her regular pool, clamoring with crazed, head-down pumping in swarms of cyclists, every one of them feverishly desperate to overtake the bike ahead, only to come to a stop at the next light—where the pack would twitch, poised to get a jump on the others like hyenas straining toward a fresh kill. This time the incursion into her territory wasn't metaphorical but could be measured in square feet. Now her beloved husband had joined the mindless look-alikes of the swollen herd.

TWO

Though the right knee rebuked her when it bore the load, Serenata refused to take the stairs one at a time, like a toddler. Hobbling down for tea the following afternoon, she found Remington in the living room. While she was still unaccustomed to his being home weekdays, it wasn't fair to resent the presence of your husband when it was his house, too. Early retirement hadn't been his idea, or, precisely, his fault.

Yet his getup was annoying by any measure: leggings, silky green shorts with undershorts of bright purple, and a shiny green shirt with purple netting for aeration—a set, its price tag dangling at the back of the neck. His wrist gleamed with a new sports watch. On a younger man the red bandanna around his forehead might have seemed rakish, but on Remington at sixty-four it looked like a costuming choice that cinemagoers were to read at a glance: *this guy is a nut.* In case the bandanna wasn't enough, add the air-traffic-control orange shoes, with trim of *more purple.*

He only bent to clutch an ankle with both hands when she walked in. He'd been waiting for her.

So, fine, she watched. He held the ankle, raised his arms overhead, and dived for the opposite leg. As he teetered on one foot while tugging a knee to his chest, she left for her Earl Grey. On her return, he was bracing both hands against a wall and elongating a calf muscle. The whole ritual screamed of the internet.

"My dear," she said. "There's some evidence that stretching does a bit of good, but only *after* you've run. All it accomplishes beforehand is to put off the unpleasant."

"You're going to be a real bitch about this, aren't you?"

"Probably," she said lightly, and swept back upstairs. When the front door slammed, she ventured onto the second-story side porch to peer over the rail. After poking at the complicated watch for minutes, the intrepid began his inaugural run—trudging out the gate and down Union Street. She could have passed him at a stroll.

The impulse was wicked, but she checked the time. The door slammed again twelve minutes later. His shower would last longer. Is this how she'd get through this ordeal? With condescension? It was only October. It was going to be a long winter.

"How was your run?" she forced herself to inquire during a laconic dinner.

"Invigorating!" he declared. "I'm starting to see why you went at it, those forty-seven years."

Uh-huh. Wait till it gets cold, and sleets, and blows a gale in your face. Wait till your intestines start to transit, with seven more miles to go, and you huddle in a cramped scuttle, praying you'll make it before they explode all over your shiny green shorts. See how invigorated you get then. "And where did you get to?"

"I turned around at Highway Nine."

Half a mile from their front door. Yet he was bursting with accomplishment. She looked at him with fascination. He was impossible to embarrass.

And why ever would she wish to embarrass him? Precisely what inflamed her about this stupid joiner impulse of his to *run a marathon* was the way such a mean-spirited desire had already arisen in her head, after her husband's sole athletic achievement constituted running—if you could call it that—again, you see, this contaminating contempt—a single mile. She was not a combative harridan, nor had she been for their thirty-two years together. To the contrary, it was in the nature of wary isolates to give themselves completely and without stint once the formidable barriers they routinely erected before all and sundry had been breached. Most people regarded Serenata as standoffish, and she was fine with that; being seen as a woman who kept others at bay helped keep them at bay. But she was not aloof with Remington Alabaster, as of halfway through their first date. Largely keeping to yourself did not mean you lacked a normal human need for companionship. It did mean you tended to put eggs in one basket. Remington was her basket. She could not afford to resent the basket—to want to embarrass the basket, or to hope that when the basket set his sights on what had become a rather mundane status marker the basket would fail.

She owed him for the fact that what might otherwise have become an arid solitude was instead round, full, and rich. She'd relished being his sole confidante when the situation at the DOT went south; it was too dangerous for him to talk to anyone at work. She missed the camaraderie of shared indignation. Throughout the whole debacle, he'd have been unwavering in his confidence that she was staunchly in his corner. They'd had their differences, especially about the children, who had both, frankly, turned out a little strange. Nevertheless, the measure of a marriage was military: a good one was an *alliance*.

Furthermore, when they met she was floundering. She owed him for her career.

As a child, after a family vacation on Cape Hatteras, she'd declared her reigning ambition to become a lighthouse keeper—thrust on the prow of a spit, raised high with a view of an expanse that could make you feel either very small or very big, depending on your mood, with regal control of a great beacon. She would live in a small round room decorated with driftwood, heating up cans of soup on a hot plate, reading (well, she was only eight) *Pippi Longstocking* under a swinging bare bulb, and watching (ditto) reruns of *I Dream of Jeannie* on one of those miniature black-and-white televisions they had at the hotel on the Outer Banks. Later during the usual equine phase for girls, she imagined growing up to be a national park warden who toured vast public woodlands alone on horseback. Still later, inspired by a newspaper's unusual job listing, she became enthralled by the idea of caretaking an estate on a tropical island owned by a very rich man, who'd only visit with an array of celebrity guests in his private jet once a year. The rest of the time she'd have a mansion to herself—with dinner seatings for a hundred, a chandeliered ballroom, a private menagerie, a golf course, and tennis courts, all without the bother of making a fortune and thus having to build a boring old business first. In the latter fantasy, it never occurred to her that infinite access to a golf course and tennis courts was of limited value with no one else to play with.

By her teens, the backyard frolicking of her childhood having given way to a covert if demanding fitness regime, Serenata entertained jobs that might put exertion to practical employ. She pictured herself as the only woman on a construction crew, pounding spikes, wielding big flats of Sheetrock, and manipulating heavy jackhammers—thus amazing her male coworkers, who would scoff at the upstart girlie at first, but would come to revere her and defend her honor in bars. Or she might become a great asset to a team of moving men (who would scoff, come to revere her, and defend her honor in bars . . .). She contemplated tree surgery. Alas, hard physical labor was apparently low-skilled and low-waged, and her middle-class parents dismissed all these backbreaking prospects as preposterous.

For years, the only child had amused her parents by performing original radio plays. She recorded all the parts on a portable cassette player, punctuating the dramas with sound effects—door slams, floor tromping, crumpling paper for fire. At once, her girlhood's reigning ambition to pursue a solitary occupation seemed to display a gut self-knowledge. What fit the bill, then, was to become a writer.

Oh, her parents didn't regard this aspiration as any more practical than becoming a construction worker. They expected she'd just get married. But at least a literary bent would argue for a college education, which would raise the quality and earning power of her suitors. So with their blessing she enrolled at Hunter, within shouting distance of New Brunswick, emerging like most liberal arts graduates as roundly unemployable.

Serenata's twenties were aimless and hand-to-mouth. She couldn't afford her own apartment, so (anathema) had to share digs with other girls whose twenties were aimless and hand-to-mouth. The menial jobs she procured hardly required a college degree. She tried to make time for "her work" without saying the pretentious expression aloud. Mortifyingly, every other peer she encountered in New York City also described themselves as writers, who were also making time for "their work."

It was manning the phones at Lord & Taylor's Customer Service that turned her tide. A young man called about needing to return a gift of a tasteless tie. He described the gaudy item in comical detail. He enticed her to explain what a customer should do both with and without a receipt, when surely he had the receipt or he didn't. It dawned dimly on the store's representative that he was keeping her on the line. Finally he implored her to repeat after him, "Please watch the closing doors."

"What?"

"Just say it. As a favor. *Please watch the closing doors.*"

Well, it wasn't as if he'd asked her to repeat "Please can I suck your dick." She complied.

"Perfect," he said.

"I'm not sure how one would say that badly."

"Most people would say that badly," he countered—and proceeded to explain that he was a civil servant with the city's Department of Transportation. He'd been tasked with finding a new announcer for recorded public transit advisories, and begged her to try out for the job. She was leery, of course. As a precaution, she looked up the NYC Department of Transportation in the phone book, and the address he'd provided matched.

In the end, it was decided higher up that New Yorkers weren't quite ready for female authority, and she didn't get the job. As Remington shared with her later, one of the other men on the team had declared after replaying her audition tape that no male passenger listening to that sultry voice would ever hear the content of the announcements; he'd be fantasizing about fucking the loudspeaker.

Yet before the disappointing determination was made, she did agree to a dinner date—albeit only after Remington's second invitation. She was obliged to turn down the spontaneous one on the heels of her audition because the bike trip between her East Village apartment and the DOT office downtown was officially too short to "count," and it wouldn't do to dine out when she hadn't yet *exercised.* They agreed to meet at Café Fiorello on Broadway, a high-end Italian trattoria that longtime New York residents would generally consign to tourists. Despite the upscale venue, Serenata, as ever, insisted on cycling.

From a distance in the restaurant's entryway, Remington had apparently watched her standard Cinderella transformation beside an alternate-side parking sign. She toed off a ratty sneaker, balanced on the other foot, and shimmied from one leg of her jeans—ensuring that the skirt fluttering over them continued to cover her person in a seemly fashion. It was still nippy in March, and ivory panty hose had doubled as insulation. From a pannier, she withdrew a pair of killer heels in red patent leather. Steadying herself on one high heel by holding the bike seat, she repeated the striptease with the opposite leg and stuffed her rolled jeans into the pannier. After giving the skirt a straightening tug, she applied a hasty touch-up of lipstick; the ride itself would provide the blush. She removed her helmet, shook out the thick black hair, and bound it with a homemade fabric binder not yet called a *scrunchie*. By then Remington had tucked back into the restaurant, enabling her to check her filthy jacket and the greasy saddlebags, their erstwhile hi-viz yellow now the queasy, sullen color of a spoiled olive.

Over a lobster pasta, her date responded to her hopes to become a writer with a neutrality that must have disguised an inner eye roll. After all, she was rolling her eyes at herself. "I'm afraid the aspiration has started to seem self-indulgent. And everyone I run into in this town wants to be a writer, too."

"If it's what you really want to do, it doesn't matter that it's a cliché."

"But I wonder if it is what I want to do. I do thrive on isolation. But I don't yearn to reveal myself. I want frantically to keep other people out of my business. I prefer to keep my secrets. Whenever I try my hand at fiction, I write about characters who have nothing to do with me."

"Ha! Maybe you do have a future in literature."

"No, there's another problem. This isn't going to sound good."

"Now you've intrigued me." He leaned back, leaving his fork in the fettuccini.

"You know how people on the news are always starving, or dying in an earthquake? I'm starting to realize that I don't care about them."

"Natural disasters are often far away. The victims seem abstract. Maybe it's easier to feel for folks closer to home."

"Suffering people don't seem abstract. On television, they look real as sin. As for the people closer to home—I don't care about them, either."

Remington chuckled. "That's either refreshing or appalling."

"I'd opt for appalling."

"If you don't care about other people, what does that make me?"

"Possibly," she said cautiously, "an exception. I make a few. But my default setting is obliviousness. That's a lousy qualification for a writer, isn't it? Besides. I'm not sure I've got the voice to stand out."

"On the contrary," he said, "you do have the *voice*. I'd gladly listen to you read the entire federal tax code."

She enhanced the silky tone in her throat with a rough edge: "*Really*?" Remington admitted later that the adverb gave him an erection.

They moved on. Merely to be courteous, she asked why he'd ended up at the DOT. His response was unexpectedly impassioned.

"It may sound mechanical, but transport is massively emotional! There's no other aspect of urban life that arouses such strong feelings. On some streets, if you take out a lane of traffic to build a bike lane, you'll start a riot. Miscalibrate a pedestrian light to last a whole two minutes, and you can hear drivers pounding on the steering wheel with their windows shut. Buses that don't come for an hour when it's five below . . . Subways stuck indefinitely under the East River with no explanation on the loudspeaker . . . Terrifyingly designed freeway entrance ramps, where vision of oncoming traffic is occluded by a blind curve . . . Confusing signage that sends you plummeting south on the New Jersey Turnpike for twenty miles with no exit when you want to go north, and you were already running late . . . You may not give a hoot about other people, but transport? Everybody cares about transport."

"Maybe so. I think my bicycle is a horse. A beloved horse."

He confessed to having watched her sidewalk burlesque. "So what if we went somewhere together?"

"I'd meet you there on my bike."

"Even if I offered to pick you up?"

"I'd decline. Politely."

"I question the 'politely,' when refusal would be obstinate and rude."

"Insisting I alter a lifelong practice just to suit you or convention would also be rude."

Like most rigid people, Serenata didn't care whether inflexibility was an especially entrancing quality. You never coaxed the deeply obdurate into a more ingratiating give-and-take. You got with the program.

At the disarming civil engineer's urging, Serenata did indeed audition for a voice-over job at an advertising firm, and was hired on the spot. Similar work came in with sufficient regularity that she was able to quit Lord & Taylor. She gained a reputation. In time, she would extend to audiobooks, and nowadays much of her work was infomercials and video games. If she cared little about other people, she did care about excellence, and was forever delighted to discover new timbres, or to extend her upper and lower registers to convey cranky children and grousing old men. It was one of the pleasures of human speech to be unconstrained by a limited number of notes in a scale, and she relished the infinite incremental tonalities in a glissando of disappointment.

Having moved so often as a kid had left her diction exotically nonspecific and usefully fluid. All variations in the pronunciation of *aunt*, *syrup*, or *pecan* were to her ear equally correct and equally arbitrary. She readily picked up accents because she wasn't attached to her own—and even sly lingual detectives failed to pin the origins of her argot. As she explained to Remington, "I'm from nowhere. Sometimes people mis-hear my first name and write it 'Sarah Nada': Sarah Nothing."

Yet their courtship was curiously chaste. Her guarded quality had tempted earlier suitors to try to overrun the ramparts—with fatal consequences. Perhaps Remington was thus cannily countering her withholding by withholding in return, but she began to worry that he kept his hands to himself because he just didn't find her attractive. "I know you fell for my voice," she noted at last. "But when the voice showed up in the flesh—were the three dimensions a turnoff?"

"You police your borders," he said. "I've been waiting to be issued a visa."

So she kissed him—taking his hand and placing it firmly on an inside thigh, with the formality of stamping his passport. These many years later, the question was: If she'd first been captivated by Remington Alabaster's respect for her fierce sense of territory, why was he now invading it at the age of sixty-four?

"That's it for the upstairs bathroom," the young woman announced, tugging her rubber gloves from the wrist so that they came off disastrously inside out.

Serenata nodded at the gloves lying moist and smelly on the kitchen island. "You did it again."

"Oh, bastard!"

"I'm not paying you by the hour to work those fingers one-by-one back through the other way." Her tone, however, was teasing.

"Okay, off the clock." With a glance at her wrist, Tomasina March—Tommy for short—began the arduous business of poking the inverted forefinger of the first glove and edging it down through the sticky yellow tube by the quarter inch.

Although her parents had hired a cleaner, before the move to Hudson Serenata had spurned domestic help. Oh, she didn't suffer from liberal discomfort with servants. She simply didn't want strangers—*other people*—in her house. Yet reaching sixty had put her over the hill in a panoramic sense. She had crested, and could see from here the decline that spread before her. She could choose to spend a measurable proportion of this surprisingly short and potentially precipitous decay scrubbing the soap buildup around the shower drain, or she could pay someone else to do it. No-brainer.

Besides, though she'd usually have been put off by the proximity of one more exercise fanatic, something about the nineteen-year-old next-door doing hundreds of squat thrusts in her busted-furniture-strewn backyard on the day they moved in had reminded Serenata of her own childhood's "broken legs" and "rolly-pollies." Glad for the pocket money (Serenata paid $10/hour—appallingly, in upstate New York a generous wage), Tommy was a stalky girl, long-limbed and awkward, thin but shapeless. Her honey hair was fine and lank. Her face was open and guileless. Its unwritten quality brought back in a rush how truly awful it was to have this whole stupid life looming before you, a life you never asked for in the first place, and to have not an inkling what to do with it. At Tommy's age, most kids with half a wit would be visited by a sick feeling that by the time they finally cobbled together a plan it would prove too late, because there was something they should have done—*at nineteen*—to put the stratagem into action. It was a wonder that people grew nostalgic for youth. The wistfulness was pure amnesia.

"So where's Remington?" Tommy asked.

"Out for a *run*, believe it or not. Which means we have a whole six more minutes to talk about him behind his back."

"I didn't know he was into running."

"He wasn't. Not until two weeks ago. Now he wants to run a marathon."

"Well, good for him."

"*Is* it good for him?"

"Sure." Tommy was concentrating on the glove. She still hadn't rescued its forefinger. "Everybody wants to run a marathon, so what could be wrong with it?"

"That fact that everybody wants to. I know he's at loose ends, but I wish he'd latched on to something more original."

"There's not that much to do. Whatever you think of, somebody else's done it already. Being original is a lost cause."

"I'm being mean," Serenata said, not referring to Remington—but of course, she was being mean about him, too. "Those gloves—I should just buy you a new pair. Though you'd make quicker work of them if you stopped pacing."

Tommy continued to lunge back and forth across the kitchen while victoriously inverting the forefinger. "Can't. Only at twelve thousand, and it's already four o'clock."

"Twelve thousand what?"

"Steps." She gestured to the plastic band on her left hand. "I got a Fitbit. A knockoff, but same difference. Also, if I stop, this thing won't count your first thirty steps for some dumb reason. In the instructions, it says, 'in case you just shaking hands,' as if anybody shakes hands thirty freaking times. Those instructions are all written by Chinese people who obviously don't know anything about American customs. Not that I mean there's anything wrong with Chinese people," she added anxiously. "Is that what you're supposed to call them? 'Chinese people'? It sounds kind of insulting. Anyway, those lost thirty steps, over and over—they really add up."

"And this matters why? That back-and-forth of yours is putting me into a trance."

"Well, you post your steps. Every day. Online. Just about everybody clocks up, like, twenty K or more, and Marley Wilson, this total cunt from senior year, regularly posts *thirty*."

"How many miles is that?"

"Just under fifteen," Tommy said promptly.

"Unless she's really hoofing it, walking that mileage could take five hours a day. Does she do anything else?"

"Whatever else she does isn't the point."

"Why do you care how many steps other people take?"

"You don't get it. But you should. The main reason it bugs you that Remington's started running is you stopped."

"I didn't say it bugged me."

"Didn't have to. He's beating you. Even if he's only gone six minutes, he's beating you."

"I still exercise by other means."

"Not for long. You went on that whole rant last week about how impossible it is to do anything aerobic that doesn't involve your knees. You can't even swim, when they get too puffy."

It was ridiculous to feel wounded when Tommy was only quoting Serenata back to herself.

"If it makes you feel any better," Tommy added, waving a fully outside-out rubber glove in triumph, "most people who do marathons totally give up running pretty soon afterward. Like those World's Biggest Losers who go right back to being fat. They check that box on the bucket list, and then move on."

"Did you know the term 'bucket list' only goes back about ten years? I looked it up. A screenwriter wrote a list of things he wanted to do before he 'kicked the bucket.' So he called it 'The Bucket List.' Since at the very top was getting a screenplay produced, he wrote a movie with the same title. It must have done okay, because the term went viral."

"Ten years ago, I was nine. Far as I'm concerned, we've said that forever."

"That expression 'going viral' itself *went viral* only a few years earlier. I wonder if there's a name for that—something that is what it describes."

"You care more about the names of stuff than I do."

"It's called being educated. You should try it sometime."

"Why? I told you, I want to be a voice-over artist, too. I can already read pretty good. Now I just have to get better at *once more, with feeling*, like you said."

This peculiarly age-discrepant friendship had first taken off after the girl discovered that Serenata Terpsichore had recorded the audiobook of one of her favorite young adult novels. Tommy had never known anyone whose name had appeared on an Amazon download, so the credit made her next-door neighbor a superstar.

"I think what grates about these abruptly ubiquitous expressions—"

Tommy wasn't going to ask.

"Meaning, suddenly everyone says it," Serenata added. "It's just, people throwing around fashionable lingo think they're so hip and imaginative. But you can't be hip and imaginative. You can be unhip and imaginative, or hip and conformist."

"For a lady who doesn't care about what other people think, and what other people do, you sure talk a lot about what other people think, and what other people do."

"That's because other people are constantly *crowding me*."

"Do I crowd you?" Tommy asked shyly, actually coming to a stop.

Serenata pulled herself up—it was a Bad Knee Day—and put an arm around the girl. "Certainly not! It's you and I against the world. Now that you've paused, the next thirty steps are a write-off. So let's have tea."

Tommy slid gratefully into a chair. "Did you know that within fifteen minutes of sitting down, your whole body, like, changes and everything? Your heart and stuff."

"Yes, I've read that. But I can't stand up twelve hours a day anymore. It hurts."

"Hey, I didn't mean to make you feel bad, before. About the running and stuff. 'Cause anyway, for an old person—you still look pretty hot."

"Thanks—I think. Strawberry-mango okay?" Serenata lit the burner under the kettle. "But being halfway well put together won't last. Exercise has been my secret. A secret that's out, I gather."

"Not that out. Most people look terrible. Like my mother."

"You said she has diabetes." With bad timing, Serenata put out a plate of almond cookies. "Cut her some slack."

Tommy March was not unloved, but under-loved, which was worse—just as full-tilt fasting had a strengthening absolutism, whereas a never-ending diet made you peevish and weak. Her father had cut and run long ago, and her mother rarely left the house. Presumably they were on public assistance. So even in a town with depressed property values—this vast brown clapboard had been a steal at $235K, with two baths, three porches, and six bedrooms, two of which they still hadn't put to any use—naturally Tommy's mother was still renting. She'd never encouraged her daughter to go to college. Which was a shame, because the girl had plenty of drive, but her urge to self-improvement was unmoored. She pinballed from fad to fad with little awareness of the larger social forces that worked the flippers. When she declared herself a vegan (before realizing two weeks in that she couldn't live without pizza), she imagined that the idea just came to her out of the blue.

Typically for the time, then, Tommy was skittish about sugar. As if stealing the confection behind her own back, her hand darted at a cookie like a lizard's tongue and snatched the snack to her lap. "You're still being, like, all grumpy-out-of-it-old-lady about social media, right?"

"I have better things to do. In the real world."

"Social media is the real world. It's way more real than this one. It's only 'cause you shut yourself out of it that you don't know that."

"I prefer to use you as my spy. I used Remington the same way for years. He went out into the American workplace and reported back. As for what he found there . . . A layer of insulation seems prudent."

"I just think you should know . . . Well, on these YA platforms . . ." Tommy had stopped looking Serenata in the eye. "It's got kinda not so great, for white readers of audiobooks to use accents. Especially of POCs."

"People of color!" Serenata said. "Bet you thought I didn't know that. Remington always thought it was hilarious that at work if he'd ever said 'colored people' instead, he'd have been fired. But then, he was fired anyway. So much for hoop jumping, if you're not in pro basketball."

"Look, I don't make the rules."

"But you do make the rules. Remington says that it's everyone slavishly obeying these capriciously concocted taboos that gives them teeth. He says rules that are roundly ignored are 'just suggestions.'"

"You're not listening! The point is, your name came up. And not in a nice way."

"So what's wrong with doing accents again? I'm not following this."

"It's—problematic."

"And what does that mean?"

"It means everything. It's a great big giant word for absolutely everything that's super bad. See, now they're all saying that white readers pretending to talk like marginalized communities is 'mimicry,' and also it's like, cultural appropriation."

"It depresses the hell out of me that you can rattle off 'marginalized communities' and 'cultural appropriation,' whatever that is, when you don't know the word *ubiquitous*."

"I do now! It means everybody does it."

"No. Omnipresent, everywhere. Now, why does my name come up?"

"Honest? Your accents, on the audiobooks. I think it's because you're so good at them. Like, you have a reputation. So when these guys reach for an example, it's your name they think of."

"Let me get this straight," Serenata said. "I'm now supposed to deliver the dialogue of a coke dealer in Crown Heights as if he's a professor of medieval literature at Oxford. 'Yo, bro, dat bitch ain't no better than a ho, true dat.'" She'd given the line an aristocratic English snootery, and Tommy laughed.

"*Please* let's not tell Remington about this," Serenata said. "Promise me. I'm deadly serious. He'd freak."

"Shouldn't tell Remington what?" Himself closed the side door behind him. It was November, and he'd made the usual mistake of bundling up to excess, when the biggest problem of running in cold weather was getting hot. Underneath all that winter sports gear he'd be drenched, and his face was red. The ruddy complexion was further enhanced by a glow of a more interior sort. Good grief, she prayed that she herself had never returned from some dumpy old run exuding this degree of self-congratulation.

THREE

"Right, I've bled and treadmilled and wired up for you, and got the all clear," Remington announced just inside the door. The checkup had not been his idea, and he was humoring her. "Doctor Eden located a minor cardiac irregularity, but he assured me it's common, and nothing to worry about."

"What irregularity?" He'd not have wanted to mention any negative findings at all, but luckily for Serenata her husband was a stickler for the truth.

"I don't remember what it's called." He had chosen not to remember, to prevent her from googling for alarmism. "The point is, I'm fine. Eden sees no reason I can't run a marathon, so long as I up the distance gradually and stick to the program."

"What program?"

"I'm following an online schedule." His tone was officious.

"You couldn't figure out how to run a little bit farther every week by *yourself*?" she said to his back as he returned to the car.

"It's not that simple," he said, lugging two sagging bags from the backseat. "You have to set goals, do longer runs, and shorter ones in between. Vary the pace. There's a science to it. You've never run a marathon yourself—"

"So now we're pulling rank."

"I don't understand this disdain you have for any undertaking that involves anyone else." He clanked the bags beside the dining table. "Why does my consulting the considerable literature on this subject seem to you a sign of weakness? Your declared hostility to the rest of the human race is what's weak. It puts you at an evolutionary disadvantage. Humble yourself, and you can learn from other people's mistakes."

"What's all this?"

"Free weights. I need to work on my core."

Serenata battled a wave of mental nausea. "What's wrong with the word *torso*? And I have free weights. You could have borrowed mine."

"Your attitude from the get-go has hardly been share and share alike. It's better for me to have my own equipment. I thought I'd use one of those empty bedrooms for my home gym."

"You mean you'll commandeer a bedroom," she said.

"Haven't you *commandeered* one for your own gyrations?"

"You also have your study. Though I'm not sure what it's for."

"You can't possibly be goading me for being unemployed. Tell me that's not what you meant."

"No. Or maybe, but that was unkind. I disliked that word *gyrations*. I was getting a dig in back. Sorry."

"A bigger dig. I retract 'gyrations.' Workouts. I'll call them whatever you like."

"Oh, go ahead then, take one of the extra bedrooms. This is a large house, and we're hardly the European powers carving up the Middle East after World War One."

She took Remington's face in her hands and kissed his forehead, to bless their restored truce. It was past six thirty p.m., and in Serenataland, dinner had to be earned.

She slipped upstairs and changed into grubby shorts and a tattered T, anxious whether that "cardiac irregularity" was truly nothing to fret about; doctor-patient confidentiality precluded getting the real lowdown. Although she trusted that her husband wouldn't lie about that "all clear," he was so invested in running this Saratoga Springs event that he could have trivialized an anomaly that was cause for concern.

Of more immediate concern was the snippy tenor of their interchanges since October, which displayed little of the dry, *Thin Man* repartee polished early in their marriage. The past two-plus months had been punctuated by the cheap potshots of empty nesters who without the children underfoot had nothing in common, although years ago their own return to just the two of them had come as a relief. It rankled that she got no credit for restraint. As of earlier this December, after all the training, scores of hours online, and nearly two thousand bucks in gear (she'd kept track), he'd worked up to a respectable five-mile run. But his pace, if anything, had grown even slower! Having completed that landmark distance last Saturday in well over an hour, he had to be clocking a thirteen-minute mile. He didn't faintly appreciate the self-control required to keep from making fun of him.

As ever, this segment of the day inspired nothing like eagerness, and if it weren't getting so late she'd have found herself seized with a sudden determination to fold the laundry. She was always amused by sluggards who explained, you see, they "just didn't enjoy exercise." Granted, some sports were diverting enough to distract from the effort they demanded, but straight-up exercise was odious, and a sane person approached it with dread. This evening was scheduled for a raft of "gyrations" focused solely on her legs, which her orthopedist had stressed *could not be too strong*, a declaration that this patient took as a dare. Of her variety pack of masochisms, the legs routine was streets ahead of the rest in sheer tedium.

She kept the radiator valve closed, so it was freezing in here—leaving exertion as the only route to warming up. As for the TV, it was large, loud, smart, and replete with hundreds of cable channels, as well as Netflix, Hulu, and Amazon Prime. As emergency backup, the hard drive was bursting with recorded films and box sets. With no television, she'd have skipped this whole ninety-minute folderol of holds and lunges and raises and pulls, and shot herself in the head.

Yet the range of optimal on-screen fare was narrow. It shouldn't be too serious, because she couldn't spare the energy to be moved. It shouldn't be too funny, because she couldn't spare the energy to laugh. Subtitles were out. Documentaries were okay, so long as they weren't too arty. What you wanted was *good crap*. Unfortunately, she'd finished the last season of *Crazy Ex-Girlfriend*, which had hit the sweet spot.

Opting lazily for network news, she looped a nylon strap around an ankle and closed the door on its anchor. Tugging through the four stations of the hip-tightening raises—stretching the black rubber TheraBand by pulling the straightened leg (theoretically straightened; suffering "loss of extension," the right one was permanently crooked) forward, to the right, backward, and from the left, twenty times each direction—she considered what proportion of her life so far had been devoted to this sort of monotony. Ninety minutes of a sixteen-hour waking day was . . . It was impossible to make mathematical calculations while tracking repetitions (*one, two, three, four . . .*). Suffice it to say that the percentage was high: a source of pride, or horror? Drawing a last breath, would she echo Jackie Kennedy's apocryphal deathbed keen, "Why on earth did I do all those sit-ups?" Serenata had already spent a massive whack of her discretionary time on this earth deliberately boring herself to death. (Left leg, second set.) *One, two, three, four . . .* She'd also spent a staggering amount of her short finite life *counting*. Like a kindergartner.

In the pharmaceutical ads on-screen, square-faced older men with full heads of salt-and-pepper hair joined comely wives in bright leggings and matching jackets, a colorist's gray streak at the women's hairline a sole gesture toward the geriatric. Despite the debilitations of whatever ailment the actors were aping, in every single advertisement the sufferers were running along a riverside, cycling country roads, or hiking woodsy trails. They were always laughing, which made you wonder what about this ceaseless bustle was so hilarious.

Oldsters in drug commercials used to stare sweetly out the window at the setting sun while pinching china teacups. Something had happened, and Serenata had made a study of it. The transformation had been gradual at first, insidious even, and then, in its perfect universality, abrupt.

The change had been most striking in relation to women, who throughout her girlhood might have yearned to be slender, but regarded discernable muscles on the female form as unsightly, unseemly, and butch. Her own enthusiasm for well-defined biceps was peculiar if not suspect for the time, and in short sleeves she'd more than once been catcalled as a "dyke."

Fast-forward to the present. Models marketing even classically feminine products like fragrances wore running bras. Silhouettes in magazines were still photoshopped to a narrowness that wouldn't allow for kidneys, but the ripples like windblown sand across bare midriffs were new. On the sides of buses, women's blown-up shoulders were cut, their thighs chiseled. On billboards, even lovelies languishing in nightwear slipped calves from the slits of their negligees that were full and taut. With so much money on the line, advertising held a well-researched mirror to the modern ideal, and in the commercial representation of today's daily life, beguiling young ladies were consistently pictured kayaking, mountain climbing, swimming laps, taking spinning classes, overdoing it on rowing machines, and pummeling punching bags. Keen awareness that

Serenata of all people should have found her sex's contemporary aspiration to strength culturally auspicious and altogether marvelous made the frenzied female hard bodies bannered across the marketing landscape only the more grating.

Placing her right foot on the seat of a wooden chair, she pushed the left foot off the floor, stood on the right foot, and brought the left knee chest-high. A hundred on the right, a hundred on the left, exhaling on every rise. The hard part was keeping your balance.

Mind, she regarded this ninety-minute tune-up as no nobler than a tune-up for a car. Conscientious motorists maintained their automobiles, but didn't expect a medal for changing the oil. She, too, was trying to be the responsible custodian of a mechanism. This was a devotion, but not in a sacred sense. She was devoted to the upkeep of the vehicle out of sheer self-interest: it got her from place to place.

Pulling the Velcro taut on the two ten-pound ankle weights, Serenata was reminded by a sharp twinge that were she ever to have considered a daily athletic ordeal as exhibiting moral properties—as raising her high on a ladder of enlightenment or hoisting her to a superior position in the social hierarchy—these ritual efforts at redemption had backfired. She was being punished. Dr. Churchwell's diagnosis had been insultingly prosaic, grandmotherly, and out-to-pasture: osteoarthritis, in both knees, in all three sectors bone-on-bone. Absent a familial history of the disease, he'd pronounced dismissively that the condition had clearly resulted from "overuse." The expectation that, if not virtue, then at least good practice would necessarily be rewarded was naive, but that didn't alter the ferocity of the feeling—that *it wasn't fair.*

At dinner, Remington had an agenda.

"It hasn't escaped me," he began, "that you experience my discovery of endurance sport as something being taken away from you. So

I would like us to examine what I can only call your sense of *ownership* of physical fitness."

"I suppose I do own it," she said coolly.

"You invented it?"

"I invented it for myself."

"So the Greeks who ran the original twenty-six point two miles from the town of Marathon to Athens—they sent a time traveler to steal the idea from you."

"That would be unlikely. Since, as you observed so pointedly earlier this evening, I've never run a marathon, have I? Though I have run sixteen, seventeen miles in one go—that time I got lost in Australia, and had to keep going until I located civilization again—so I could probably have managed another ten, if I were determined to."

"You've always said that if you ever ran a marathon you'd do it by yourself."

"That's right."

"Except that now you never will."

"Well, this isn't exactly Make Serenata Feel Better Day, is it?"

"The only way you'd ever have gotten around to running twenty-six point two miles on any given day is by participating in a group event, the way everyone else does it."

"I find large numbers of people doing the same thing in one place a little repulsive."

"No, you find it a lot repulsive. But for normal people, the company of many others engaged in a common pursuit is uplifting."

"I'm incapable of losing myself in a crowd. I have no desire to melt into some giant pulsating amoeba."

"Does it ever occur to you that maybe you're missing out on something?"

Serenata considered. "No."

"You feel *above* people capable of collective experience."

"Yes, I suppose I do. Church services, football games, and even rock concerts leave me cold. Maybe that seems a pity, but I'd also remain unmoved by swastika-waving rallies for National Socialism."

"As far as I know, you aren't a member of anything. Not a professional organization, not a political party; I can't even remember your joining a private library. So at least you're consistent, though the purity of your lack of communal ties is a little chilling. But I want to get back to this *ownership* business."

"All right," she said tolerantly.

"Think about it: all the sports people play, and have done for generations. You're so proud of doing 'push-ups,' but long ago someone else coined the term. The record books are strewn with achievements beyond your ken: the first woman to swim the English Channel. The bicycle you rode to Café Fiorello, and have insisted on riding to restaurants ever since: you didn't *invent* the bicycle—"

"Ownership is a sensation. I can feel I own something without being given formal title to it."

"But 'owning' physical fitness isn't just irrational. It's mentally ill. Furthermore, for you and me right now, your lunatic patrolling of this territory is highly problematic."

"Oh, don't use that word. According to Tommy, *problematic* is now a label for the trespasses of white people who are unfathomably evil."

"Meaning, white people, period. The unfathomably evil part goes without saying."

For a moment, they were on the same side.

"You understand much better than you're pretending," she said. "Obviously, plenty of people before me have run around, and jumped up and down, and biked places—though nowhere *near* the number who've discovered the bicycle now, nowhere *near.* Obviously, there's such a thing as the professional athlete, too—which isn't what we're talking about. Suddenly you turn on the TV, and all the characters are in the gym. For the last several years, the *one* topic *guaranteed* to shoot to the top of the Most Popular list on the *New York Times* website is anything whatsoever to do with *exercise*. About the only articles capable of nudging a recommendation of interval training out of first place are the ones touting the health-giving properties of red wine. Meanwhile, magazines are crammed with profiles of icons who run fifty miles a day. Or seventy-five, or a hundred. Marathons—sweetie, marathons are old hat. You're supposed to run a plain old marathon before breakfast."

"That's not very helpful."

"I'm not trying to be helpful. I'm trying to explain how I feel. And I'm observing that your turning to exercise for absolution, or a purpose in life, has been imposed on you from the outside. It's a contagion, like herpes. You've always been more suggestible than I am."

"If according to you the whole country is suddenly consumed with fitness, how come Americans keep getting fatter?"

"Because this tsunami of a social tide isn't a matter of results. It has to do with what people aspire to. Nobody cares anymore about getting to Italy before they die, or reading *Moby-Dick*. Goodness, I don't even think they all want to write a novel themselves anymore. It's all about seizing on some extreme athletic event, after which presumably they'll sit on the right hand of God the Father."

"*I* think the rising popularity of endurance sports bothers you because you're being beaten at your own game. A lot more ordinary amateurs are pushing their limits beyond what you ever have, isn't that right?"

"Do I feel like my comparatively minor league *gyrations* are being shown up? Yeah. I probably do."

"In which case, if I complete that marathon in April, a distance you've assumed for years that you could handle—and I tend to agree, though you've never tested yourself, so now we'll never know—your own husband will show you up."

"Is that your intention?"

"No it isn't, and correcting that misimpression is one reason I wanted to have this conversation."

"So far, it's been closer to an interrogation."

"I also think you resent the fact that fitness has become more exalted at the same time that you're growing—somewhat prematurely at sixty—increasingly infirm."

"Well, congratulations, Sherlock."

"I meant that sympathetically."

"It didn't sound sympathetic. But if you are trying to beat me at my own game, even if you claim you're not—triumphing over a cripple seems like cheating."

"To the contrary, if you had the cartilage for it, I might have proposed that we run the race this spring together."

"Liar," she said. "You want credit for that cozy idea, but you can only suggest it because you know it's impossible."

"Who knows what's going to be possible, after you finally bite the bullet and get knee replacements."

"Do you realize what they *do*? I forced myself to look it up. They actually *saw off* the ends of your bones. In videos on YouTube, the doctors and nurses all put on, like, welding masks, to keep off all the blood spatter. One guy who refused general anesthesia described online how his whole body vibrated and he could hear the earsplitting rasp of the blade, as if he weren't in a hospital but on a construction site. They remove the patella and replace your kneecap with a piece of plastic. They'll throw my knees in the wastebasket. And pound metal knobs into my tibias and thighbones, *bam, bam, bam,* the way you sink a wedge in a log to split firewood."

"Knee replacements have become much more commonplace—"

"Just because you do something often doesn't preclude it being a big deal. These operations don't always go according to plan, either, because no major surgery does. I could end up with chronic pain, chronic inflammation, or catastrophic infection."

Remington sighed. "I'm so sorry you may have to go through this."

"Yes. Yes, I know you are." She took his hand. "But if it goes wrong, that operation could ruin my life."

"Isn't that an exaggeration?"

"No," she said readily. "I would have to become someone else. We'd both suffer a bereavement. So if Churchwell is right, you have eighteen months at the outside of being assured the company of the woman you married."

"You'd still be the woman I married with stumps at the end of your thighs."

"Oh, how I wish that were true. Unfortunately, emotions like bitterness and acrimony spread like potato blight. Already when I read about those superheroes running ultramarathons all day long, I think: *just you wait*. You'll end up on a gurney in the shadow of a surgical saw in no time, you fucking idiots. The vision fills me with glee."

"You do have a spiteful side."

"*Side*? I don't think it's just a side." Behind closed doors, one of the joys of their marriage was mutual permission to be horrid.

They rose to collect the dishes, whose remaining tidbits had long before congealed. "You know, this recent fetishizing of fitness has a particular *texture* to it," Serenata said. "You described athleticism as having become 'exalted.' That's an apt word. But I've never seen exercise as exalted. It's biological housework, like vacuuming the living room rug. These days, to wear yourself out is to attain a state of holiness. All these newbies seem to think that they're making the leap from man to god. This . . . sanctimony, this . . . self-importance. It's started to contaminate the flavor of my own workouts, like that metallic taste in my mouth when I was pregnant. So I worry that, well . . . I don't want that anointed, pseudo-Nazi narcissism to infect you, too."

"You're afraid I'm going to become an asshole," Remington surmised. "But, my darling wife, and I say this as affectionately as one can: you're the asshole."

"Well! I'm not sure one can say that affectionately, darling husband."

"Regular, vigorous exercise helps to maintain a healthy weight. It can put type two diabetes into remission, reduces the likelihood of cancer, and may even help diseases like Parkinson's. It improves your sleep. It promotes longevity and mental acuity, and it's often more effective than medication for treating depression—"

"So *you're* one of the readers driving all those articles to the Number One slot."

"Not to mention," he continued, "that you might find a husband's better toned body more attractive. But your reaction to your compatriots becoming more active is despair. You want to hog all the benefits of your lifelong habits to yourself. When you do something, it's a wise, considered discipline, and when everyone else does the same thing, it's a disgusting fad. So: you're the asshole."

Serenata laughed. "Fine, I'm an asshole. Except it doesn't matter how I feel. I can sit there stewing in silent rage that all these other cyclists are suddenly glomming around me at intersections. Not a single one of them will forgo the healthful benefits of cycling and throw the contraption back in the cellar—all because they picked up strange, terrifying waves of hostility emanating from a crazed-looking older woman gripping her handlebars with white knuckles. Emotions, like opinions, are entertainment. If I celebrated this athletic revolution instead, would a single extra American pick up a barbell? No. And I'm not the rah-rah type. So it amuses me to be resentful instead."

"But it does matter," Remington said with sudden seriousness, placing a dishwatery hand on her cheek, "how you feel about me."

In January, Serenata acted on the theory that it was especially after the holidays when old people got lonely. Relatives could be tempted to use having been doting at Christmas as an excuse to skate for a while.

Surveying the streets on the short walk over, she speculated what it was about Hudson that conveyed the impression that the town wasn't exactly flourishing. All the chain-link fences weren't rusted, but some of them were. On a given block, only one building might be boarded, but that created an economic and aesthetic ambiance in considerable contrast to a block on which none of the buildings was boarded. Several businesses along Warren Street were perky and new—often given to wince-inducing wordplay, like Flower Kraut, or Mane Street Hair Styles—but their aura of optimism seemed of the delusional sort. Most instilled a powerful inkling that they weren't going to make it. Church windows were masked with protective sheets of plexiglass, making the stained glass look black, as well as a little hostile, as if ill-behaved local youth with poor prospects might throw rocks. More than one church having been deconsecrated and repurposed planted the suspicion that the congregations of those that remained were on the elderly side and dwindling.

The small town of six thousand people or so was holding up better than most in the region. If you kept abreast of which perky cafés were still open, you could sit down to a decent cappuccino. There were properly up-market restaurants for a passable meal. The train station was on the Hudson Line, which ran directly to the city on a picturesque journey along the river; thus the town benefitted from a range of weekenders and wealthy New Yorkers with summer houses and their visitors, who might linger for a drink or a poke around the antique stores before escaping to scenic verandas in the Berkshires. Nevertheless, as a place to remain rather than pass through, Hudson had a beleaguered feel, as did anywhere whose underlying economy was too dependent on a hospital.

Remington had grown up here. The tendency with small hometowns was to either revile them and flee, or romanticize them—having fled. Her husband had made the mistake of doing both. Confiningly provincial only became charmingly provincial from a distance. Even in his teens, he'd leaped at any excuse to streak south to civilization. When they'd needed to leave Albany if only for its associations, Hudson had beckoned as a safe, comfortingly familiar bolt-hole for the licking of wounds. Perhaps it was predictable in retrospect that Remington was already going stir-crazy. Having sampled the gamut of her country's geography, Serenata never much cared where she was; she was her own location. But anyone ending up precisely where he started couldn't help but fear that in the interim he had gone nowhere. She wished her husband were able to infer that the same experience of stasis and even of doom was bound to issue from running a marathon, once his heart rate settled and his exorbitant sneakers had lost their noxious smell. Lo, there you were, where you'd begun, and nothing had changed.

"Please don't get up!" Serenata shouted through the front door. "You know I've got a key. I only ring the bell to give you fair warning."

The remonstration was wasted. Griff Alabaster had still not relinquished the protocols of hospitality—not that he'd ever been that polite, but he didn't want to be treated like an invalid. By the time she entered from the foyer, he'd struggled to a stand, and was negotiating the obstacle course of his cluttered living room. Refusing the indignity of a walker, her father-in-law planted his cane before him and pulled. Wavering with the instability of the high seas, he traversed the floorboards as if poling a boat.

"Just you today, sugar?"

"Yes, I'm afraid you're stuck with *just me*," she said with a smile, removing the shepherd's pie from her tote. She wondered if he didn't prefer it when she visited alone. He'd long been sweet on her, embarrassingly so. His wife, Margaret, had been industrious but unassuming. She'd only been to secretarial school (she'd picked up her younger son's distinguished-sounding Christian name from the typewriter company); before the industry in Hudson collapsed, she abetted the family's meager income by cleaning fish. When the dowdy, compulsively self-deprecating woman was still alive, her trim, arty daughter-in-law had made Margaret jealous.

"I swear, I saw that boy more often when you folks lived in Albany," Griff said, "'stead of six blocks east."

"Well, you know how seriously he's preparing for that marathon in April!" she said, trying to convey chirpy enthusiasm as she carried the casserole to the kitchen. She'd paid Tommy to clean the place a couple of days before, and the counters were filthy again.

This whole house wasn't exactly messy, but it never changed, except in that steady, inexorable way that you didn't notice when witnessing the decay day by day. The faded floral curtains were often drawn during the daytime to skip the bother of opening and closing them again. Cheap reproductions of Old Masters in homemade wooden frames had light-bleached, until the oils looked like watercolors. It would never have occurred to Griff to buy new throw pillows, much less new furniture, but all the paddings had flattened and exuded cough-inducing dust if you plumped them up. The heavy leather coat he'd worn to work in cold weather was still on its hook in the catchall utility room off the kitchen, but the garment had stiffened into a kind of mounted hunting trophy. The living room walls were darkened by years of an open fire; the kitchen was mottled with stains in corners that Tommy found hard to reach. Though the trinkets littering every available surface weren't likely to Griff's taste—china figurines of milkmaids—they'd been chosen by his late wife, and perhaps more importantly had always occupied a precise location, where they would therefore remain for eternity. Griff gave Tommy no end of grief if while dusting she returned the empty milk-glass candy dish two inches from its appointed perch.

Serenata's father-in-law couldn't bear the notion of *a* home as opposed to his own, but maintaining the viability of his independence was in Remington's and her interest as well. A nursing facility would necessitate selling this house, whose proceeds would evaporate from monthly fees. Her own parents had died in debt, like good Americans. Griff's expiring in situ was their only chance at a modest inheritance—which, what with Remington's punitively reduced pension, the unreliability of her freelance work, a real estate downturn that had shrunk the equity in the Albany house, and a steady drain from two grown children who never seemed to quite get their adult acts together, they might need.

"In my day," her father-in-law called, "you got paid to tucker yourself out!"

"Exhaustion has become an industry," she said, back from the kitchen. "Just think! These days, you could *allow* people to carry all that lumber you lugged around, and hoist your steel beams for you, and you could charge them for the privilege. Just don't call it a 'building site,' but a 'sports center.' Oh, and we'd have to come up with a snappy name—so instead of Pilates, or CrossFit, you could call your regimen . . . *Erection.*"

Griff emitted a wheezy laugh as he sank into his saggy brown recliner. "You have a mind like a cesspit, kiddo."

"I think *Erection* is inspired. You could trademark the term—just change the *C* to a *K*—and start a franchise. Your membership, being gluttons for exercise, could dig foundations, and frame buildings, and hand-plow access roads with miserable little shovels—all the while paying a stiff monthly fee. You'd make a fortune. The income from selling off the actual structures they built would be incidental chump change."

"Folks used to look down on a body for working with his hands," Griff said as she settled in the wing chair once reserved for his wife. "Earning your crust by breaking your back not only landed you in an early grave, but got no respect. Including from my sons, I'm sorry to say."

"You're hardly landing in an early grave, Griff, at eighty-eight. Still, I don't think manual labor gets any more respect now than it ever did. Maybe that's why 'Erektion' would never work: lately you only get credit for running yourself ragged to the point of collapse if by doing so you accomplish absolutely nothing."

"You're one to talk."

"I *am* one to talk. And I have the knees to prove it."

"Never forget your nipping upstairs to put on them skimpy red shorts, first time you crossed this threshold," he reminisced (again). "Rushed out the door without a word, leaving poor Remy to explain—with the chicken steaming on the table. Margaret was livid." His wife hadn't been the only one who was livid—Griff had lit into quite a tirade when the new girlfriend returned from her ten-mile run—but over the years the anecdote had softened.

Much like Griff himself. His forearms broad and scarred, Remington's father had been a burly man prone to rages. A drinker (who still put away more stout than his doctors advised), he'd doled out a fair share of corporal punishment as a father, and by the time they met, the man still wielded a brutal frankness like the retired tool belt with which he'd beaten his sons. She'd found him intimidating. The ease with which they could speak now was hard won.

But then, his figure had grown far less imposing. After forty-some years of physical toil, ill health had forced him to retire; his joints were gravel, and he was suffering from chronic back pain. In the last decade, Griff had shrunk like a parade float with a slow leak—an impression only heightened by his insistence on wearing his old forest-green Hudson Valley Construction work clothes, which dwarfed him now. His default expression of belligerence had over the years been replaced by one of wariness—the same emotion, inverted. It was not in his interest to alienate his caretakers, and to a degree his more amiable latter-day bearing was calculated.

She missed being afraid of him. Griffith Alabaster had been a formidable man, and though he'd never gone to college—the minimal importance of which was only apparent to those who had—he was smart. Even now, he had his lapses, but was nowhere near senile.

"What bee's got under Remy's bonnet? Years of urban planning and mass transit and traffic flow, and suddenly all I hear about is *jogging*. That silly business at the DOT must have something to do with it."

"Oh, it's in the mix. He needs distraction. As hobbies go, running is probably better than taxidermy, or becoming a drunk. Though come to think of it, taxidermy might interest me more. Foxes poised with bared teeth in the basement? I'd be enchanted."

"Only thing worse than working," Griff declared, "is not working."

"But he's not going to get another job at sixty-four. And Remington could be looking at another thirty years. I hate to think of those three decades as time to kill."

"Tell me about it," Griff said.

"He's taken an indignant line. But on some level, he's ashamed. No one wants to leave a job of such long standing with his tail between his legs. I'm sure he feels self-conscious about how it turned out, and worries he's let me down. Let you down, too."

"Truth be told, I was relieved to learn that boy *has* a temper to lose."

"He didn't used to be like this, you know. So imperturbable, so steady-state."

Indeed, Remington's most taxing professional achievement was learning to keep his mouth shut. But self-control was one of those virulent capacities that, ironically, was hard to control. The last few years in Albany, he'd grown laconic even at home, as if to speak his mind would encourage bad habits. When he did talk, he cloaked all his remarks in a disguising mildness, so that listening from the next room you could never tell if he was noting the loss of a sock in the last load of laundry or saying goodbye before blowing his brains out.

"He acted like a man for five seconds, and paid the price," Griff said. "I turn on the TV lately, and there's all these men got their willies chopped off, 'cause they *feel like* girls. I don't doubt it. They act like girls. Real men've got rare as hen's teeth."

"Mm," Serenata said noncommittally. "Possibly some men don't always feel up to being the responsible one, the expert, the authority. The one who has to be strong and confident. Always the protector, never the protected. That's a tall order. Women nowadays get to choose. We squeal and make the men kill the water bug in the kitchen, and then when anyone questions our courage in the face of threat, we can get on our high horse and act insulted. Pretty good deal, when you think about it. We can be world-beaters, and run whole companies, and then claim to be traumatized by a hand on our knee when helplessness is politically useful. Men aren't really given that option. And they're continually set up to look like disappointments. Because masculinity as an ideal is pretty ridiculous.

Then if they do improbably succeed in being fierce, and fearless, and emotionally impassive no matter what horrors befall them—pillars of might and right and agency, slaying the dragons every which way, well—that's only to be expected, isn't it? Lose-lose. Maybe it's no wonder that so many of them want to wear a dress."

"Remy wants to wear a dress?"

"Not last I checked my closet."

"But he finds being a man a terrible cross to bear."

"No, I think he's worn the weight of his sex quite lightly. But he does find the current climate of damned if you do, damned if you don't, unfair. Go soft, and you're a sissy. Keep holding up the side for the team, and you're not only a bully, but a relic."

"I put in a long day's work supporting my family, and I didn't see that as a choice. I didn't feel sorry for myself, either."

"Neither does Remington. Underneath all that calm and placidity, he's homicidal. And he'd like to kill someone in particular."

"But he ain't murdering anybody. He's jogging for twenty miles. What's that prove?"

"Twenty-six *point two* miles," she corrected. "Oh, and you must have noticed that he's dropped a couple of pounds."

"Big whoop." Griff had dropped fifty by accident. "I'd think better of his figure if he slimmed down by bringing me in some firewood. Down to sticks last week, till Tommy stopped by."

"She must've leaped at the job."

"How'd you know?"

"More *steps*," Serenata said enigmatically. "But now that you mention it . . ."

She brought in two wheelbarrow loads from the back, mindful to remember kindling as well. Stacking the logs by the fireplace, she asked diffidently, "Should you still be having open fires? With flying sparks . . . What if you fall asleep?"

"I built more fires than you fixed hot dinners. Only decent thing about winter. I pull that mesh curtain round. I'm old, not a dummy."

"Would you like me to build you one? It's getting dark."

"Wish you wouldn't. Have my own way of laying the logs, and you'd pile 'em different—"

"And you'd bite my head off."

"I don't got that much to do. Nice point in the day, laying the night's fire. Guess I enjoy it."

She focused on her hands as she spanked off the grime. "You know, given that Remington was never very athletic . . . Might you ever consider venturing some appreciative comment, like, I don't know, 'You've really surprised me, my boy!' or 'Good show, kid!' or even—"

"No, and I don't plan to." He'd cut her off with a forcefulness that took her aback. "You're a mother, so you should know this yourself. It's a right pain in the rear to have children always expecting you to pat them on the head for whatever they've a notion you ought to admire. You always got to bear in mind if you say the wrong thing—and ask Remy, I guess I said the wrong thing plenty—they'll end up bawling in the corner and you'll be sorry. So when they're small, you indulge them. You magnet their crummy drawings to the fridge. But once they're grown, they can't expect to be treated like adults, and at the same time expect the empty compliments you chucked them when they were kids. Remy got to live with my real opinions, and suck it up. I was right impressed when that boy drew a line in the sand at the DOT. That respect's freely given. But at my age, I should be past the point where just 'cause I'm his father I got to play pretend in case I hurt his feelings. No grown man over sixty should still be holding out for his daddy's damned approval. Tell me, lamb chop, that you don't also find this whole marathon malarkey tiresome as all get-out."

She took a breath, and chose her words with care. "If it's important to my husband, then I wish him the best. But as an answer to what to do with the next tranche of his life, I do find endurance sport a little . . . *thin.*" She was about to add more, and pulled up short.

"It's *vain,*" Griff announced.

"The race at least gives him a goal." This qualified as a brave stab at sticking up for her husband, surely. "I'll speak for myself, but one's sixties do seem difficult. I guess all ages are difficult. And maybe being your age is even harder. But for Remington and me, there's just not that much to look forward to."

"Anticipation's overrated. For years I was *looking forward* to the days I'd get to sleep in. I been at liberty to sleep till noon since 1994, and still get up at five."

"But our generation is likely to live into our nineties, if not past a hundred. Facing all those decades of decline—well, the future seems sort of horrible. Some days I walk around in a state of apprehension, start to finish—wondering what disease is lurking around the corner, and fretting about what I'm supposed to be doing with the tiny amount of time left before it hits. Remington might be going through a variation on the same thing."

"He reckons he can stop the clock."

"If not turn it backward. But leaving him to his delusions doesn't cost us much."

"A lie always costs something."

"Well, we've only got three more months to go." Serenata rose and fetched her coat. "Oh, I almost forgot." She rustled through her bag. "I brought you a set of CDs. Though you'll need to upgrade your technology soon, because this format is being phased out. It's my most recent audiobook. A thriller, but you never seem too picky."

"Can't follow what's happening most of the time, but you know I'll finish it." Griff had never been much of a reader, but most of his friends were dead. He enjoyed listening to her recordings for company, and to bask in the sound of her voice.

"People make a to-do about how unnatural it is to lose a child," she reflected as he insisted on seeing her to the door. "But it must feel almost as unnatural to watch your own kids *get old*."

"Oh, to me, you and Remy still look like new lovebirds, fresh as peaches."

She raised a forefinger. "You watch that! *A lie always costs something.*"

On the stoop, she leaned down a bit so that he could kiss her goodbye on the cheek. "Um—one last thing," she added. "In April, Valeria and her family are piling into their van, and then we'll drive up and watch the marathon in Saratoga Springs together. If you'd like to come, too . . ."

"Why in God's name would I want to travel all the way upstate to watch a bunch of fools jog past with numbers on their shirts and clutching little bottles of water?"

"Because one of the fools is your son. I'm sure your coming to applaud him at the finish line would mean a lot to him." There. She'd done her duty.

FOUR

She should have been able to predict it. He was a serious, methodical person, and not long ago accustomed to shouldering significant responsibility for the physical functionality of a medium-sized American capital. She couldn't even call the gravity with which he attacked the project disproportionate, when thanks to having responsibility for the physical functionality of a medium-sized American capital yanked out from under him, this ever-loving marathon was the biggest thing in his life.

Still, she'd been surprised by his slavish adherence to an online schedule that some ignorant chump could have just made up. Previous to that sadly seminal evening in July when her knees swelled big as grapefruits, she'd usually slipped off for her regular ten miles with so little ceremony that Remington wouldn't even have noticed she was gone by her return. The trot alongside Normans Kill was a routine to be wedged into her day, after a recording session, scheduled with an eye to the weather, and the solitude it provided was primarily precious for the opportunity to think about other things (like, if she'd been a very different kind of mother, would matters with Valeria have turned out otherwise?). For her husband since October, whatever run or strength-building arose on the chart *was* his day, into which distractions like grocery shopping and visiting his father were required to fit—and strangely enough, so terribly often there wasn't time. To her amazement, when she asked him once what he thought about when hitting the pavement, he'd responded without hesitation, "Well, running, of course."

"But what's there to think about running?" she asked, genuinely baffled.

"Pace, foot strike, breathing," he said impatiently. The condescension now worked both ways.

Naturally, there were smoothies. Self-deservingly large portions of meat. Cases of high-end sparkling water spiked with electrolytes. And the supplements! Rapidly multiplying hard plastic bottles crowded the toaster from the counter to the top of the microwave. Upstairs, he had gathered a collection of liniments. After showering, he smoothed oily concoctions into his muscles to such excess that the sheets on his side of the bed turned a shade darker. He'd taken to wearing five-pound ankle weights around the house, his thudding tread vibrating the worn, uneven floorboards and amplifying the creaks. Extra poundage swung each foot forward in a pendulum lunge, *pa-foom, pa-foom,* imparting an emphatic character even to a trip to the refrigerator.

She could have warned him that running outdoors during a New York State winter was sometimes unpleasant, and at first she'd hoped that he might come to appreciate the array of disagreeable conditions his wife had endured for decades with so little complaint. But Remington's focus on his personal beatification was sufficiently fierce that her own vicissitudes of times past never entered his head. When he returned once that January and closed the door behind him, he pressed his palms to the wood as if to prevent some fiend from following him inside.

"*Wind,*" he announced after a dramatic pause. Apparently the motions of the atmosphere were her husband's personal discovery. If so, the genie would go back in the bottle: he ordered a treadmill.

Not just any treadmill. This was a brushed-steel, state-of-the-art monstrosity with surround sound and a thirty-two-inch touch screen that virtual-realitied your progress over pastured hill and dale, replete with bleating sheep. Or you could choose a display of conifer fronds brushing on either side as you snaked its woodsy mountain trails; she'd not be surprised if it also exuded a resinous scent of pine needles, with a biting singe of forest fires drifting from the distance. With another poke at the menu, you could switch to a watery horizon as you padded the lapping waters of a beach at sunset. During the coastal program, breakers rolled and crashed in the background, while in the audio foreground a bare foot slapped and splashed every time your shoe landed; for all she knew, it smacked your cheeks with a bracing breeze and stung your mouth with salt.

She hated it. The thing was enormous and loud. The thumping sound was far worse than the ankle weights, and vibrated the whole house. When Remington opted for music over sound effects, he tended to prefer either bombastic symphonic selections or dated disco playlists of a trashy sort he'd not even listened to in the 1980s. The acquisition racked up yet another substantial expense, for Remington had fallen prey to the very American impulse to lavish money on what could not be bought.

The worst was the long runs, which at least he executed outside. The night before, he'd go to bed primly at nine, which necessitated dinner at five. Breakfast would be ecclesiastical, a starchy white napkin laid out like altar linen. Lost in priestly reverie, Remington would take each bite of his eggs gravely, chewing for a long time. He drank his orange juice in reverent sips, like communion wine. He spent forty-five minutes in the bathroom. After donning his vestments, he tugged each lace of the orange shoes from the bottom up, tested the tightness with a pensive pace, pulled the bow, and adjusted the tension again. His wife's dismissal of the rite had inspired him to elaborate stretches of half an hour or more. When he finally headed for the door, he departed with such solemnity that you'd have thought they'd never see each other again. "Wish me luck," he'd command mournfully, tucking a strand of hair behind her ear.

"Good luck," she'd say obediently—whatever that meant.

Finally, with two weeks to go, Remington tackled the truly demanding distance of twenty miles. He was gone for *five and a half hours*—during which it crossed his wife's mind that perhaps this whole training regime was a charade, and he was really up the road at their local coffee shop, doing crosswords over refills of decaf. In truth, she was dumbfounded that her husband could run that far, at any pace—since twenty miles was a fair distance even to walk.

When he returned that afternoon, he spread himself on the living room's Oriental carpet, arms extended, long legs straight and crossed at the ankle, head dropped sorrowfully to the side, maintaining this pose of horizontal crucifixion for a solid hour.

Oh, she'd have willingly pampered him on days like this, if he weren't already pampering himself. His glorification of these great feats of locomotion drove her to a blitheness that read as callous. Their contrary perspectives on his grand project were opening up a fissure between them that at their age shouldn't have been possible. This sense of separation hadn't visited since their divisions over what to do about Deacon during his shattering adolescence. (Remington's solutions were ever more authoritarian, while Serenata thought coming down hard on the boy only backfired; Remington would accuse her of proposing to do nothing, and then she'd admit, yeah, probably: impasse.) Long happily married with a complacence that was underrated, she'd forgotten what it was like to not know what was going on in his mind and to be a little paranoid that if she did she wouldn't like it.

There was no disguising it, at least from herself: she couldn't wait for this race to be over.

"I worry there's something wrong with me, to be dreading the arrival of my own daughter." The fact that all the preparations for their guests—making up beds, designing menus, laying in groceries—were now Serenata's problem made her only more cross.

"The sorry truth is," Remington said, "she probably dreads coming to our Godless household, too."

One week of his training remained. Closing on the marathon itself, the program slackened, the better to preserve energy for the big day. Today's distance had been his wife's squalid old standard of ten miles. Thus Remington was actually upright, albeit draped over two chairs at the dining table, hands dripping from his wrists in entitled fatigue. Early in his involuntary retirement he'd offered to take over the cooking. Since October, he'd dropped the kitchen duty cold, and Serenata was back at the stove.

"Valeria claims she doesn't proselytize," she said, stirring a roux. "But she does, and relentlessly. By pushing all that why-don't-you-give-yourself-over-to-Jesus crap, she forces us to reject her. Over and over."

"Which confirms her version of events," he said. "Cold, meanie parents; loving, long-suffering child. But you can't be nostalgic for the days she made herself scarce."

"Not days. Years. And disappearing altogether is a great deal worse than 'making yourself scarce.' She has a lot of gall to refer to our 'abuse.' A child going completely AWOL, from the age of twenty-five to twenty-nine, without so much as a postcard—now, that's abuse."

"Don't get worked up all over again. Not with their arriving tomorrow."

"Oh, I guess I shouldn't stir up old grievances. After all. That's Valeria's department." Actually, Serenata was shamelessly using their difficult daughter to excite a sense of camaraderie. They'd both felt mistreated, they'd both been flummoxed by whatever it was the girl held against them, and they'd both despaired of her membership in the Shining Path Ministry, whose founders were surely ignorant of the fact that they'd named their church after a Peruvian terrorist organization. United in dismay was still united, and she didn't even feel bad about brazenly deploying Valeria's thoughtless history to generate solidarity. Heartache should be good for something.

"She's made such a song and dance about 'forgiving' us—" Remington said.

"Me. It's sweet of you to include yourself, but we both know that her problem is with me."

"It's just, the forgiveness needs to work both ways."

"I have no desire to be forgiven. I didn't do anything. That girl lays forgiveness as a bear trap. Thank her for her clemency? *Gotcha.* Guilty as charged."

"Maybe you've asked for it. All that guff about how you 'don't care about other people'—"

"But I don't."

"It's a pose, and it's a lie. You're often very tender. Look at the way you take care of my father. Look at the way Tommy adores you. You've even been pretty nice to me," he added with a touch too much effort, then qualified, "most of the time. And you were a much more doting mother than you remember. But Valeria, since it dovetails with the story she tells herself—"

"The *narrative* she tells herself," Serenata corrected. *Narrative* had replaced *story*, as *core* had replaced *torso*, as the coyly understated *troubling* in an otherwise febrile political landscape had replaced *cat-*

astrophically fucking horrible. These substitutions were strict. Equally strict, as with the abrupt ubiquity of *bucket list*, was the moratorium on acknowledging that you had ever said anything else.

"Of course—the *narrative*. She gladly takes your description of yourself as a cold, solipsistic misanthrope at face value. So you should stop playing to that silly self-caricature." Despite his theatrical weariness, Remington had roused himself to plant a kiss on her nape at the stove. "Time to face the awful truth: Serenata Terpsichore is a nice person."

She was not a nice person, and had no desire to be one. Her unalloyed hostility to his 26.2-mile holy grail certainly wasn't nice. True, on the surface she'd stopped fighting his vainglorious training. But she was only looking forward to his crossing the finish line as a stepping-stone to the day after that, when they could go back to being a team. She could even brownie-bake that gentle bulge back into his waistline, because they were getting old, and one of the only good things about getting old was mutual permission to be imperfect.

The plan was for Valeria and the two oldest grandchildren to drive over from Rhode Island to visit for a few days, and then on Friday they'd all head up to Saratoga Springs. (Fortunately, Valeria's witless husband, Brian, was staying behind with their younger kids; he was a prim, judgmental man whose reaction to social discomfort was to sit in the corner sanctimoniously paging the New Testament.) The marathon was on Sunday, but Remington wanted to arrive two nights before to "settle" and check out the course. An extra overnight for their whole party would cost hundreds of dollars, another day's worth of eating out hundreds more. But the once-in-a-lifetime occasion would leave many years thereafter to economize. Maybe they could sell the newfangled treadmill. Though if she didn't miss her guess, the American market for secondhand treadmills—and

StairMasters, and elliptical trainers, and rowing machines—was flooded.

Valeria had been a fearful child, somewhat overweight, as she was still, which generated some tension with her rail-thin mother. It was of little importance to Serenata whether her daughter was a bit chubby, though she wasn't about to lay on forty pounds just to make the girl feel better—which it wouldn't. At thirty-one, Valeria had a pretty face, round and dimpled, and regular coloring had revived the golden curls of preschool. Mother and daughter bore some resemblance to each other, but you had to look closely. Perhaps detecting the genetic relationship was visually impaired by their weak resemblance in other respects.

Hauled to yet another city with dreamlike frequency, from an early age Serenata was a self-contained unit, like a portable washing machine on castors whose hoses tuck neatly into the undercarriage. By her teens, she had already become a loner by choice—whereas Valeria's difficulty making friends as a girl had been (or so her mother came to grasp only much later) a source of torment. Serenata had always been a good student, if a particular sort. American public schools simply weren't very demanding, and clearing their preposterously low bars had been effortless; only by college did she develop any idea of what was meant by the expression "studying." Although pedagogical standards for the next generation did nothing but sink further, Valeria had struggled. She was loath to make it known when she didn't understand something, and readily fell behind. But she was quiet, not a troublemaker, thus the kind of educational casualty whom teachers could overlook.

As a girl, Serenata was grateful to her parents for their light touch. If anything, she wished they'd allowed her even longer sessions by herself in her room, where she would experiment with sound effects for her radio plays and try to break her record time for maintaining a headstand. So when raising her own daughter, she tried to be the kind of mother she'd have wanted herself.

Which was a mistake. In the interim, parenting fashion had become hands-on. No one released children into the wild anymore "to play." Parents were expected to get even more upset than their offspring that Marigold Battersby had spurned their kid in Saturday playgroup. So rather than having her mother regard her figure as her own business, perhaps Valeria would have preferred weigh-ins and targets and charts. Treated to a vengeful four-year vanishing act to contemplate her sins, Serenata had finally concluded that what, to her, was freedom, to Valeria was sheer neglect.

It was Valeria's younger brother who grabbed the lion's share of parental attention, for all the wrong reasons. Deacon would have *liked* to be ignored, the better to get up to no good. Contemporary developmental psychology asserted that lying in children was a sign of intelligence, in which case Deacon was a genius. In contrast to his sister's weak sense of self, Deacon knew who he was, all right; he was simply hell-bent on disguising that nature from everyone else. He stole—and once he was caught, it would turn out that he had swiped objects for which he'd have no earthly use: a girl's compact, a CD by a band he disdained, or a teddy bear he was too old for. He preferred the purloining of articles important to people he knew to impersonal shoplifting—which culprits imagined, however errantly, to be victimless—because material covetousness had nothing to do with it. He stole to steal. He liked the sensation. In adolescence he moved on to vandalism, more damage for its own sake. Yet meanwhile he exhibited a glossy politeness that teachers and administrators amazingly bought wholesale. Unable to snow Serenata, he delivered his *and how are* you *today, Mother dear?* with a tongue-in-cheek sneer. And she learned early on that you did not leave *Deacon* unattended in a room or yard, or you'd pay the price; worse, someone else might. Not that it ended up mattering, but she had watched him fiercely. When one of your children was obedient, subdued, and unassuming, while the other was repeatedly sent to the principal's, expelled, and later arrested, the agent of mayhem would suck up all your time. It was said that life wasn't fair; well, neither were families.

Valeria and Deacon had nothing in common, and as children they weren't close. Upending the conventional birth-order dynamic, their daughter had long seemed afraid of her little brother. Whenever she'd plied him with presents as a girl, these gestures came across as appeasement. More peculiarly, Deacon didn't appear to have much in common with either parent. Oh, he inherited Remington's lanky good looks, but none of the contemplativeness or self-control. And she didn't recognize herself in the boy, either. Where she was solitary, Deacon was secretive, and there was a big difference. Where she was uninterested in the abundance of other people, Deacon seemed to wish humanity at large actively ill, and that was an even bigger difference. By and large, it was genetically baffling how these two people had emerged from such seemingly unrelated parents, and Serenata would never have credited such a family as possible before perplexedly waking up in one.

As for their daughter's recent born-again Christianity, she could solve it like a math problem, but not with any gut comprehension. These now-we-gather-at-the-river movements came with ready-made social sets, and their members weren't choosy. You didn't have to be smart, lively, likable, attractive, or funny; you merely had to "accept Jesus as your Savior." Presumably this cheap fealty was a modest price of admission for a girl who'd felt so ostracized in her school days. Left too much to her own devices, or so it turned out, Valeria had always seemed wobbly. She was given to sudden fancies—salsa dancing, Hello Kitty—which she would rapidly drop, and she always caught an enthusiasm from someone else, like the flu. Later she ducked going to college, if only because she had no idea what she might major in, and by nineteen—oh, how lovely it would be if one's children were to come up with truly novel turns of the wheel, which entertained and astonished—got pregnant instead. As a follow-up to the first mistake, she made the same mistake three years later. People were always harping on parental responsibility; too little was made of parental impotence. You could give your children opportunity, but you could not give them form—which meant that you could not give them what most children craved above all else. Were it possible to purchase for a daughter passion, intention, direction, and specificity—or whatever you called being-somebody-in-particular-ness—Serenata would have rushed off to the Identity Store before Valeria turned ten.

Thus the evangelicals offered what a mother could not: a mold for Valeria's Jell-O. Overnight, lo, a shaky young woman had firm guiding principles and practical rules to live by. Best of all for someone who'd underperformed as a student, had never found a career calling, and had always felt more than a little hard done by, the Jesus brigade bestowed on the convert an arch superiority to all the other benighted heathens who hadn't seen the light—like her parents.

That said, Serenata didn't understand the attraction at all, not really. Signing up to be told what to do, what to think, what to say? What a waste of adulthood.

Exactly what triggered the filial absenteeism was never clear. Some six years ago, she and Remington had been parents in good standing, or so they imagined, when it occurred to them that they hadn't heard from Valeria for a couple of months. A call to her cell established that the number had been recycled, connecting to one Lee Fong, who sounded friendly, but did not speak English. Serenata tried the last landline number they had for her in Buffalo, where their daughter had been part-timing at a nail salon. Out of service. Emails bounced back NO SUCH USER. A newsy postal note to Buffalo boomeranged to their mailbox, and the scrawled "Return to Sender" didn't resemble their daughter's loopy handwriting. The assumption that Valeria would contact them in due course at least to apprise them of her new whereabouts proved mistaken. More months went by. They were on the cusp of reporting her missing when Deacon allowed on yet another visit asking for money that he had heard from her, and that she didn't wish to be found, or not by her parents. He said airily that his sister seemed to have "a bone to pick," and declined to elaborate. He enjoyed the power of the go-between a bit too much. They didn't press him unduly for her contact details. At least Valeria was alive.

Cutting off communication without explanation and whisking away their only two grandchildren struck Serenata as cruel and, if she didn't say so herself, unchristian. But as punishment, the stratagem was savvy. Valeria's disappearance exacted a subtle daily toll even when they weren't thinking about her desertion per se, and before she resurfaced the parental boycott had threatened to be indefinite. Savvier still was devising punishment for an unnamed crime, which cast a Kafkaesque suspicion over the whole of the girl's upbringing. No one had branded the child with a hot iron. So what had they done that was so terrible? Aside from that ambiguous impression of having been insufficiently hovering, Serenata still had no idea. Yet she had put together this much: Valeria wanted them to have done something terrible, and powerfully enough that by now she could well have reverse-engineered her entire familial history.

On a seemingly arbitrary date about two years ago, their daughter called her parents in Albany. Serenata picked up the phone, and though she'd every reason to be angry, the feeling was akin to those arcade games when a treasure teetered on the tip of a hook. She remembered moving superstitiously with no sudden jerks. A stiffness hinting at rehearsal, Valeria explained that she had been in therapy and had found Jesus. After consultation with her doctors and extensive prayer for divine guidance, she had decided to forgive her parents for everything they had done to her. She was strong enough now. Adhering to the tenets of her faith, she planned to turn the other cheek, and to embrace a largeness of heart only made possible by direct communion with Our Lord, because moving on from the past was now in the interest of her "recovery." Valeria could have been speaking Urdu for all the sense this made to her mother, but Serenata was patient and let her talk. It must have been twenty minutes before Valeria mentioned in passing that oh, by the way, she had also married and borne two more children.

Serenata hadn't shared the observation about how curious it was that couples with the largest families were so frequently the very people least capable of supporting them, and she continued to keep the thought to herself—even when the girl got pregnant again eight months later. Ever since Valeria restored herself to them, visits had been permeated by the same poisonous caution that had seized Serenata when Remington announced he was running this dratted marathon. She and her husband seemed to be on probation. Given the provisional texture of renewed relations, she hadn't pushed Valeria to spell out what on earth her parents were meant to have done wrong.

Given these fragile circumstances, when their daughter expressed such startling enthusiasm for the trip to Saratoga Springs, Serenata had encouraged her to come and cheer her father on. Yet Valeria's presence was bound to put further pressure on her mother to be unimpeachably well behaved. Artifice, performance, dissociation, a forced gesturing toward the cardboard cutouts of Wife, Mother, and

Grandmother: the whole package was why she'd had reservations about having a family in the first place.

That Monday, Valeria's minivan pulled to the curb at that awkward time of day, about four p.m., which was too late for an excursion or even lunch, but too early to start on dinner. It left only time to *visit*, not a skill at which Serenata excelled with the most companionable of guests, much less with a churchy child who had a chip on her shoulder. Scuttling down the yard to meet them, she had no idea how they'd get through the next few hours, much less the next week's worth of all that *visiting*. These days politics were out. Inquiries about how the eldest was taking to seventh grade were pointless, since Valeria's children were homeschooled. Once they ran through the weather and the second-to-youngest's psoriasis problem, all that would remain were subjects that would get them into trouble.

She stood back and waved as Valeria took her time messing with seat belts, shouting orders to the children, and unbuckling her baby from the booster in back. Serenata hadn't realized that her daughter was bringing the youngest of her brood, too.

But then, why would she leave behind such effective self-protection? Valeria hefted the seven-month-old onto her substantial hip in the spirit of buckling on a holster and six-shooter. You couldn't criticize a mother with a baby, you couldn't say anything disagreeable around a mother with a baby, and you couldn't ask a mother with a baby any uncomfortable, prying, or challenging questions—for the Madonna beside the Dodge Grand Caravan radiated wholesomeness, sanctity, and self-sacrifice, placing the possessor of the baby above reproach.

Everybody should have one.

"Hey, Mama," Valeria said, avoiding eye contact as her mother, confused about the cheek-or-lips protocol, settled for a poorly landed peck near the girl's left ear. Before her four-year game of hide-and-seek, her parents had been "Mom" and "Dad." The reconciliation onward they'd morphed mysteriously into "Mama" and "Papa," like the rock band. Whatever lay behind the rechristening, it felt as if Valeria had forgotten their names.

"Hey, Gramma." The twelve-year-old flicked her grandmother an anxious glance, hands folded piously over her crotch. From either a private ritual or nervous tic, she repeatedly rose onto the balls of her feet, then brought her heels to ground. It was balmy for springtime in upstate New York, but she looked cold.

"Hi, there, Nancee," Serenata said. "Hi, Logan. It's so nice to see you again!" Nancee was a victim of a nomenclatural fad that celebrated an inability to spell as a manifestation of originality. "So, sweetie, did you have a good trip?"

"Oh, sure." Valeria began fussing out diaper bags, totes, and crackling sacks of road food. Three nearly back-to-back pregnancies had taken their toll; she looked closer to forty-five than thirty-one. "We sang the whole way. Show Gramma how we pass the time, Nancee. Sing Gramma 'Jesus Loves Me.' That's one of your favorites!"

Staring straight ahead, Nancee launched into a tuneless, double-quick rendition absent an ounce of fondness. ". . . LittleonestoHimbelong, theyareweakbutHeisstrong . . ."

To her grandmother's horror, Nancee churned through all five verses, including the refrains—rising on her toes in time to a monotonous, pseudo-Soviet Christian ditty whose melodic line had always seemed slightly menacing in its sheer idiocy, and whose lyrics taught children not only to be indoctrinated automatons, but also to have no self-respect. At least the grisly performance gave Serenata a good look at the girl. Even more so than last time, she looked malnourished. Her coloring was ashen. Her shoulders were narrow and sharp. Her arms and legs were sticks, and at the neck of her clinging polyester muscle-T her breastplate striated like the grille of a Cadillac

Coup DeVille. Just like her mother, who hadn't a sporty bone in her body, the girl was clad in below-the-knee nylon leggings logoed with a Nike swoosh, an open zip-up pastel sweatshirt, and souped-up running shoes—in sum, "athleisure wear," which seemed something of an oxymoron. Her body language was fretful—all Valeria's children had developed a darting hypervigilance—but her eyes shone with a steeliness that Serenata recognized.

By contrast, at nine her brother was soft, with his mother's fleshiness. Logan alone didn't look en route to the gym. He wore shapeless jeans and a corduroy jacket—one of the only coats that Serenata had seen on a child in years that didn't look like you'd conquer Everest in it. Given that modern American kids wore nothing but athletic shoes, he must have looked hard for those leather loafers. Buried in his phone, the boy hunched with a truculence of which she could only approve. One of the inscrutable aspects of these born-again families was why the children so rarely told the parents to shove their Jesus Christ Our Lord and Savior right up the ass.

Remington loped down to help with the luggage as Nancee wrapped up her last *the Bible tells me so-o-o*.

"Papa!" Valeria exclaimed with gusto. "My gracious, you look so strong and slim! I'd hardly know you on the street! Saints be praised, you must have trained like the dickens!"

"Oh, just followed an online program," he said modestly.

"I'm so proud of you! I'm just—so impressed! The kind of inner strength you must have to summon, I can't imagine! I hope you don't take this wrong, Papa, but Lord have mercy, I had no idea you had it in you!"

Clearly, Valeria had not always talked like this. Perky evangelical positivism jumped up her speech with implied exclamation marks and lifted the ends of her sentences with wonder. She had to have been aware that programmatic jubilation drove her parents up the wall.

By the time they schlepped the chattel into the house, coats, shoes, plastic bags, and packs of disposable diapers cluttered every surface, and Serenata wondered why she and Tommy had bothered to tidy up. Valeria made a great show of authority in hectoring the kids to take their luggage upstairs and wash their hands and put their empty glasses in the dishwasher and be sure to thank Gramma for the apple juice and Logan, would you please sit up straight with your shoulders back, now that's better. Don't you dare play with that darned phone when you're a guest in someone else's home, it's impolite. The ceaseless instructions established her total dominion over a fiefdom of three, the stay-at-home parent's standard compensation for commanding so little elsewhere.

"So, Mama, how's the knees?" Valeria asked offhandedly, settling at the dining table with the baby.

"Better some days than others."

"Papa said you had to quit running. Isn't that a shame."

"I can still do high-knees running in place on a swatch of carpet."

"But that's not the same. Not real *running*, is it?"

"No, not exactly."

"I guess you're best off being philosophical. Like, you're starting a whole new chapter—the last chapter. And you kind of brought it on yourself, in a way."

"You mean I deserve it?"

"I mean that God gives us what we need."

"I thought that was Mick Jagger."

Valeria glared. "When you get old, you have to draw on the biblical concept of *grace*. You have to bow out and make room for more energetic people to take your place, right?"

"You're quite the expert on the elderly, for thirty-one."

"Maybe you should think of becoming, you know, *impaired* as an opportunity. To become a better person. You might find out that not being all perfect anymore makes you more sympathetic with other people's foibles, too. My pastor says that when we require forgiveness ourselves, we're more inclined to be forgiving of others."

"Sweetie, I think you should save your forgiveness for someone who really needs it. The best treatment for osteoarthritis isn't clemency, but joint replacement."

"You never ran a marathon, did you? Seems like I'd remember that."

"No, but honestly, my darling?" She patted her daughter's hand. "I don't find never having run twenty-six point two miles at one go especially devastating." Serenata excused herself to look up the router password for Logan in the upstairs study, grateful to escape. Wasn't it children who were supposed to squirm at family get-togethers, to beg to be allowed to go play? As she rounded from the ground-floor hall, Nancee was descending the staircase, only to reach the bottom, pivot, and run back up. "Did you forget something?" her grandmother solicited. Nancee froze on the top landing. "Not really."

To her husband's disgruntlement, Serenata had put their grandson in Remington's workout room, which had a foldout futon; Marathon Man was supposed to be taking it easy in the lead-up to Sunday's race anyway. But hunting the boy down to give him the password, she discovered Logan sitting on the floor in the underfurnished spare room she'd given to Nancee.

"You like this room better? Not that I care."

"Nancee wanted the one with the weights and stuff," he said, entering the password. "Of course."

"Your sister doesn't look as if she lifts a lot of weights."

"Well, she does. And whatever. Toe touches. You name it. Her and Cynthia, the girl next-door, they have this contest, with lists and everything. I think it's dopey. I don't even know how she keeps track of who's winning, 'cause she can't add for beans."

"The fitness shtick—it's not your thing."

"It's boring. You do all this stuff, and after—you haven't earned any money, or learned anything you didn't know before. I don't understand what she gets out of it."

"You'd rather read, or watch TV or something?"

"We're not allowed to watch TV," he said glumly.

"You can't watch TV, but your mom will let you go *online*?"

He finally looked up, taking her measure. "She thinks my phone has parental controls."

"Don't worry. I won't tell."

"It's a cinch to crack. Sometimes it's lucky when people think you're stupid."

"Our secret. I won't tell your mom how smart you are, either."

"Thanks."

Heading heavily back to the *visiting*—damn, it was still only five fifteen—she encountered Nancee again, trotting to the bottom of the stairs, pivoting, and powering back up. Spotting her grandmother on the upper landing, she froze again midflight, as if caught at something naughty.

"You're running stairs," Serenata determined. The girl nodded reluctantly. "I used to run stairs. I *invented* running stairs. When I was in college, my dorm was on the twelfth floor. I never took the elevator. Going back and forth to classes, sometimes I'd run those flights ten times a day. Like climbing the Empire State Building. Later in my twenties, I'd use the emergency exit in my apartment building when it was snowing or something. I worked up to two hundred flights at a time."

"Two hundred?" Nancee repeated with a skeptical squint. Perhaps stair running wasn't very grandmotherly. More likely, even an underfed twelve-year-old detested anyone else trumping her personal best.

Downstairs, Remington had joined Valeria at the table—an unfortunate place to convene, because it created an expectation that anytime now they'd be having dinner, which they wouldn't be. There was little enough to look forward to anyway, since Valeria wouldn't *allow* her parents to drink wine in her children's presence—and it was a testament to the delicacy of their relations that her parents let their daughter order them around in their own home. Later everyone would be grateful that they hadn't used up the dither of dinner too early in the evening, thereby leaving a vast desert of *visiting* before bedtime.

"We're a little curious how he makes a living," Remington was saying.

"It floors me, how naive you and Mama can be about Deacon," Valeria said.

"Oh?" Remington said. "I think Deacon has knocked the naivete right out of us."

"Let's put it this way." She checked over her shoulder for kids within earshot, and lowered her voice. "With so many opioid addicts in this country, somebody must be selling them the stuff."

"That's what you presume he does, or what he's told you he does?" Serenata asked, resuming her seat.

"It's obvious," Valeria said. "But I don't expect you to believe me."

"I didn't say I didn't believe you," Serenata said. "It hardly strains credulity, after all."

"No, it doesn't. Because Deacon is damaged. Just like I'm damaged."

Serenata flicked a warning glance at her husband: *don't take the bait.*

"My question is why he's still coming to us for handouts, then," Remington told his wife dryly. "If he has the job Valeria claims—reputedly well remunerated but landing one in a surprisingly low tax bracket."

"I suppose he'd be considered a participant in the 'gig economy,'"

Serenata said. "Unpredictable hours, a notoriously erratic revenue stream, and no health insurance. And we have to consider his high capitalization costs."

"You think what Deacon's up to is *funny*?" Valeria exclaimed. "He's in league with Satan!"

As Valeria drew herself up in offense, shielding the baby, it dawned on Serenata that the urbane back-and-forth that endeared the girl's parents to each other was a prime source of their daughter's antipathy. All this time, she and Remington imagined that their dinner table repartee had charmed their children. Now, *that* was naive.

"I don't find it funny," Serenata said. "But Deacon's default setting is contempt. Selling soul-destroying drugs is just the sort of work that would appeal to someone with disdain for his own customers. I have a horrible feeling he's good at it."

"I've poured out my heart to him on the phone, trying to convince him that God loves all sinners, but only if they repent. He's living in darkness. So are you and Papa. If you'd only humble yourselves before the Lord, and open your hearts, and stop being so smarty-pants, you could know the same boundless joy that I do."

Serenata had learned numbly to ignore the Bible thumping like the dull thud of a drum track leaking through the floorboards from someone else's apartment. If what their daughter was exuding was boundless joy, she'd take despondency, thank you.

"You know, I thought I'd mention," Serenata said, changing course, "though I don't mean to interfere—"

"You just mean to interfere," Valeria said.

"No, but. Don't you worry that Nancee is a little thin?"

"Oh, she's just a picky eater. And she's a real Energizer Bunny. Can't sit still." Valeria bounced the baby on her knee, though the infant didn't seem to be enjoying it. The aggressive nurturing felt pointed: *this* is what good mothering looks like, *Mama*.

"Have you tried protein shakes?" Remington said. "They come in flavors kids would like—strawberry, chocolate, banana."

"Nancee wouldn't come near that. Not if it's marketed for weight gain."

Valeria's responses were inconsistent. But Serenata wasn't going to press the issue. "Jacob is quite a handful, with four other kids to keep track of," she observed politely of the baby. "Do you and Brian imagine that you'll stop at five?"

Valeria examined her mother's face, perhaps for signs of criticism, though Serenata had asked the question as neutrally as she knew how. "If God sees fit to bless us with more precious new lives, the least we can do is welcome His little ones into the world. The size of our family isn't in our hands."

A few packets of contraceptive pills in those hands might do wonders for her daughter's sense of agency, but Serenata held her tongue.

"Isn't it getting a little . . . difficult?" Remington said. "I mean financially."

"Don't you worry, the Lord will provide. He always has."

All five kids were on Medicaid. Brian's parents were "helping," and had bought the Dodge Grand Caravan. Remington had slipped them substantial checks on the previous three visits, claiming jocularly that she'd "missed a lot of Christmases and birthdays" during her *family vacation*. Privately, Serenata had wondered whether what really tipped the scales when their daughter decided to resume contact wasn't so much prayer or therapy as money. So far the Lord had provided precious little.

"You mentioned Brian has been getting some work . . . ?" Remington said.

"He's got a part-time shift at Wal-Mart, but he can't take on any more hours because he needs time for his studies."

"Oh!" Remington said. "I hadn't realized Brian had gone back to school. That's good news! What kind of degree?"

"I mean Bible studies, of course. And then there's our mission. Spreading the gospel. I haven't been able to so much, 'cause of the kids, of course, but also due to my own emotional journey. Which has been super time-consuming and super hard work. Both my therapist and my pastor say I should consider self-healing my full-time job. But that means Brian has to ring twice as many doorbells to pull our weight for the church."

Serenata and Remington locked eyes: our son-in-law is the guy on the porch from whom we hide in the kitchen, careful not to turn on a light or run the coffee grinder.

"So! Papa!" Valeria said, shifting gears. "You've got to tell me about all this training! I'm so excited about Sunday I could bust! You have to explain how you've worked yourself up to the point where you can run a whole *marathon*. You may not realize it, but I bet you're drawing strength from a higher power. Learn to channel that power, like plugging an extension cord into the sky, and it could be like having motors on your shoes! I swear you look ten years younger! Like, how did you start out?"

Remington enthusiastically detailed the progression of distances, the bursts of speed training, the working on his *core*. Serenata sneaked a peak at her watch.

"Sorry," she said quietly, standing. "Lest this conversation wear me out first, I've got to get a little exercise myself."

Valeria's expression curdled. "Typical. Right when we're all getting hungry, and my kids are running on fumes. After a long drive with bad traffic. But never mind, we'll all wait while you hop around. I've already spent enough of my childhood starving and bored to death, waiting for you to finish *exercising*, so what's another two hours."

For once, there was no procrastination, and no dread. Serenata had never been happier to do five hundred sit-ups, and would gladly have done a thousand more.

Getting ready for bed that night, she asked, "So what's on the docket tomorrow?" She'd vowed to act more interested during his last week of training.

Naturally Remington didn't misinterpret the question as regarding what on earth they were going to do with Valeria and the grandkids all day. But his answer—"Forty minutes easy, with four one-minute speed intervals"—was distracted.

"You hail from a pretty prosperous family," he began a minute later as he undressed. "Your father earned the corporate stripes of a successful American man of his generation. Your mother did volunteer work, but that was standard for the 1960s, too. On your own steam, you established yourself, after a mis-start or two, as a recognized voice-over artist, with steady work, producing quality recordings you should be proud of. My father may have hit us, but he was old-school, parents did that back then, and he was always a solid guy who kept up his end of things. Never having taken a dime from the state is a badge of nobility for him, as he must have regaled you more than once; Social Security being his money, he says it doesn't count. Plenty of the buildings he constructed are still standing. My mother typed invoices, and later cleaned fish, coming home reeking every night just to afford clothes for her kids that were clean and new. I was the first in my family to go to college, and bootstrapped myself a full class up, with a career in civil service that should qualify as distinguished, however it ended.

"But our children"—he paused before stepping out of his boxers—"are white trash."

FIVE

They'd planned to drive up to Saratoga Springs late that Friday morning, but the children were fussy eaters. After the preparation and cleanup of multiple breakfasts, Valeria announced it was time for lunch.

Though Serenata had worried how on earth they'd fill the previous three days, this domestic entropy had been the norm every time they committed to an outing—a trip to the Museum of Firefighting (which she imagined Logan would like; he didn't), a boat trip on the Hudson (they missed the last departure), or a tour of the Dr. Oliver Bronson House, with its famous elliptical staircase (restrictive viewing hours required getting out the door at an appointed time: forget it); sadly, the most enjoyable leisure activity in the area, a wine-tasting tour, was out of the question for a devout teetotaler, and even Remington now barely drank. Whenever the baby was changed and fed and bathed, the children were dressed for the weather, and the household's intestines and bladders had been evacuated, it was time to fuel and hydrate once more, the better to shit and pee again. This awful life surely characterized Valeria's days in her own home: frantic with a semblance of activity while running in place—the only kind of running Serenata herself could do now, in intervals, on carpet, bouncing on the balls of her feet, so she was all too familiar with the experience of applying so much onward effort only for the scenery to never change. The one benefit of the visit so far was greater sympathy for her daughter. With still two more of these engines of stasis who sucked the oxygen from their mother like extraction fans, the young woman could hardly be expected to make much progress even on her "super hard" and "super time-consuming" *self-healing*.

Naturally, when Remington had left for the shorter, easier runs prescribed for his final week's training, he attracted nothing but exuberant *Go get 'em, champ!*, while his wife exercised upstairs in secret with the door closed, lest she trigger another burst of Valeria's lifelong resentment. Serenata had foolishly imagined that while the family was here she might also devote a few hours to the Logitech infomercial. Yet folks who didn't work—a cohort, dismayingly, that now included Remington—often found the notion of doing anything other than eat, clean, and shop completely foreign. The one time she'd tried to excuse herself to her studio, she might as well have announced that she was waltzing off for a pedicure. To Valeria, her mother's work was a vanity.

She'd had the same problem writ large when Jacob's birth coincided with recording a tetralogy of fantasy books last August. Typically for the genre, the novels were enormous. The Manhattan studio was booked, the six-week job paid well, and she'd made the commitment before learning that another "precious new life" was on the way. When Serenata explained that she simply could not spend those weeks in Rhode Island relieving the new mother of caring for her *four* other children, Valeria blew up. "Work," whatever that was, didn't count as a viable excuse, especially for the self-employed, who could presumably wedge this frivolous elective activity between loading the dishwasher and brushing their teeth. She accused her mother of being selfish. So on top of recording days long enough that by their end she was losing her voice, Serenata was consigned to feeling like a Bad Grandmother on the dark train rides home—returning, since the Good Grandfather played pinch hitter, to an empty house.

They didn't pile into Valeria's minivan until mid-afternoon, so what should have been a ninety-minute trip was bogged down by Friday commuter and weekender traffic on I-87. A longer drive wouldn't have mattered if it weren't for the consequently more extended torture of Bible songs—"This Little Light of Mine," "He's Got the Whole World in His Hands," and worst of all, "I've Got the Joy, Joy, Joy, Joy Down in My Heart," which the kids sang three times. Touched to have been invited, Tommy was just entering into the spirit of the occasion, but her humming along felt like betrayal. For the relentless *joy, joy, joy, joy*s pounded Serenata's head like a sledgehammer. Surely it was perverse to use the redundancy of your incredible happiness as a bludgeon. Did anyone actually *like* these songs? She'd yet to discern whether Nancee and Logan had been genuinely indoctrinated or were doing a fiendishly well-crafted imitation of having been indoctrinated. She had the same problem parsing vox pops from North Korea.

Saratoga Springs was a wealthy town, lush with mature hardwoods and looming with stately, big-porched nineteenth-century homes, built when the affluent flocked to its spas for the waters. Still heavily dependent on tourism—she and Remington had sometimes celebrated anniversaries here—the town had accrued hefty cultural credentials, with an arts center that housed the New York City Ballet in the summer, theaters, a college prestigious enough that neither of their children would have been admitted had either improbably wanted to apply, and a writers' colony whose implicit pretension made Serenata grateful to have changed careers in her twenties. Broadway, its main drag, was aptly named, with up-market chains housed in sedate red brick. Of course, for most people the place was synonymous with its storied horseracing track. Nancee craned through her open window toward the stables, petulant that the track wouldn't open until July. "Where are the *horses*?"

Lavishing still more limited resources on a normal human activity that in the olden days was free, Serenata had eschewed the budget motels on the edge of town, which might have risked the appearance of an under-ardent attitude, instead booking three rooms at the Saratoga Hilton on Broadway. A private plus: it had a fitness suite.

The lobby was a sea of sportswear. The majority of contestants wouldn't arrive until tomorrow, so this was just the beginning.

As Serenata waited to check in while the others circled for a place to park, the woman behind her in the unexpectedly long line asked, "You do have reservations, right?" Affirmative. "Because they've increased the number of runners admitted this year to five thousand. I think it's cynical—more admission fees, and of course the town is greedy for all the extra tourists. Since so many entrants show up with a whole entourage, the pressure on hotel rooms is intense. Oh, I'm sorry," she apologized. "I'm just assuming—you are one of the marathoners, aren't you?"

"No," Serenata said.

"Well, gosh—I hope you take it as a compliment, then—it's just, you look like one. I mean, like a real runner. Not one of the plodders."

Serenata was both flattered and depressed. "Plodders?" she asked blankly.

The woman lowered her voice. "The dregs at the back. Also known as the run-walk crowd. Emphasis on walk. The charity and novelty acts are bad enough. But nowadays, all these"—she lowered her voice further—"fat, out-of-shape bucket-list box-tickers take seven or eight hours to finish, and still claim afterward they've 'run a marathon.' We're talking, like, a *twenty-minute* mile. Holy crap, in Honolulu, which has no time limit whatsoever, the plodders take a break for lunch. They cheapen what completing this distance means. Sorry, that's just me. I guess my outlook isn't very democratic. Maybe there's a thin line between being in the *elite* and being an *elitist*."

Indeed, the woman had a look that had grown recognizable. Clad in Lycra and an unzipped fleece, she was stringy and weathered with cropped hair. She had a small cave under the center of her rib cage, where even trim postmenopausal women usually gathered flesh. Much like Nancee, she couldn't stand still, lifting one Adidas and then the other, shaking each leg out. At least fifty-five, she doubtless imagined that she didn't look anywhere near that old, though her bony, sinuous frame advertised every year. Alas, you couldn't think such a thing about another woman at Serenata's age without its boomeranging back in your face. Serenata didn't imagine she looked sixty, either.

"I'm surprised this race has grown so big," Serenata said, pushing herself to be sociable. "This is a minor event. Nothing like New York or Boston."

"It used to be if you wanted to pull in tourists you'd found a literary festival. Now every dot on the map sponsors a marathon. Draws much bigger crowds. Whatever limit Saratoga puts on registration, they'll still be turning contestants away. The lesser races are popular with the wannabes, because they don't require a qualifying time."

"You do a lot of these?" The interest was feigned.

"Best thing about marathons popping up everywhere is I can pretty much go from race to race year-round. I hit the Florida, Arizona, and California ones over the winter. I always enter the lottery for London, but no luck so far. The odds are against you. Only forty thousand are allowed in, and two hundred fifty thousand apply."

"Seriously?" Serenata said. "A *quarter of a million people* apply to run the London marathon."

"Goes up every year," the woman said glumly.

Serenata nodded at reception. "Doesn't your circuit get expensive?"

"You sound like my kids. But I'm not about to lie in bed with cats, just so they can get an inheritance. They seem to forget it's still my money. When I was first talking myself into this, I realized that *I'd* forgotten it was my money. What else is early retirement good for? I'm not into bingo."

"But what about injuries?"

Her smile was tight and grim. "How long have you got? Hey, you're up."

Once the others arrived and got settled, Serenata slipped off to the fitness suite before dinner, but the place was mobbed. There were lines for all the machines, with a scrawled waiting list taped to every stationary bicycle. The scene was repulsive. Resigning herself to a few calisthenics in front of CNN, she took the stairs back up to their room, and even on the staircase, commonly deserted in hotels save for the odd cleaner, she had to thread between guests hurtling themselves up and down.

Serenata had outdone herself in the service of appearing to outdo herself. Dinner reservations tomorrow night were considerately early, that Remington might have no trouble hitting the hay by eight thirty, the better to arrive at the race in advance of a seven thirty a.m. starting gun. Their mattress was bigger than some hotel swimming pools, so she shouldn't wake him creeping into bed later that evening. Tomorrow was a rest day, and he planned to drive Valeria's minivan around the course that morning to familiarize himself with any "challenging topography" before the roads were closed to traffic. For the afternoon, she'd booked him into the Roosevelt Spa for a mineral bath and massage.

While Remington was being worked over, she'd also treat Valeria to a Detoxifying Algae Wrap and Arctic Berry Illuminating Facial at the same facility (the anti-cellulite option seemed impolitic). The spa treatments alone would come to over $700, though at least the fact that Serenata secretly considered all these pawings and unguents a load of hooey meant she wouldn't further inflate the bill by steeping in seaweed herself. The real present to Valeria was volunteering to take care of the children while the young woman was being what passed for pampered for three solid hours. Were Valeria anything like her mother, she'd find the hands of strangers prodding all over her body not just a little strange but invasive. But she wouldn't dare to say so. Women were programmed to regard facials, massages, and soaks as the acme of indulgence, and Valeria hadn't the originality to trust her disappointment.

Prudently well in advance, given that apparently up to *five thousand* other parties could be prowling downtown for a festive venue, for the end of the Big Day she'd made reservations for a blowout at 15 Church, where she and Remington had dined for their thirtieth wedding anniversary; should her husband's performance on Sunday prove ignominious, she could always cancel. The restaurant was pricey, and Buttermilk Crispy Oysters with ponzu and foie gras butter was bound to be wasted on the kids. But the trappings of jubilance routinely stood in for jubilance itself. Rare was the bash that better than gestured toward celebration, a sensation so taxing to inhabit in the present that most honorific occasions only truly happened after the fact, when the laureate gazed fondly at photographs. On the other hand, Serenata might be feeling jovial at that. This clubby bunkum would be over, and she and her husband could go home in every sense.

Yet for all her loyal wifery, Remington announced quietly while getting ready for bed on Friday night, "You're not fooling anyone, you know." He declined to explain, because he didn't have to.

While Remington was driving a course that would take an hour even in a car, Serenata had a late, leisurely breakfast in the hotel dining room with Tommy, whom she'd put in a double with Nancee. The two seemed to have something in common—which proved the problem.

"Crunches," Tommy despaired over toast. "Raises, planks, and lifts. Plus a lot of goofy twirling and leaping things I think she made up. It's like sharing a room with Hurricane Sandy. I said I was heading out after dinner last night to rack up some steps, but I really hit the halls just to get away from her."

"Isn't 'racking up some steps' on the same continuum? What's the difference?"

"You know how it works. Anyone who does less exercise than you is pathetic, and anyone who does more than you is a nut."

"So Nancee's a nut."

"She's an exercise bulimic."

"Have you caught her throwing up?" Serenata asked sharply.

"I mean she pukes energy."

"She looks ill to me."

"She doesn't eat enough to build any muscle. So all the jumping up and down doesn't accomplish anything."

"And what does all your Fitbitting accomplish?"

"Watch it. You're the one who claims everyone's *copying* you. What did being a fitness fanatic for fifty years 'accomplish'?"

Serenata added a contemplative smear of butter to a miniature cranberry muffin. "When I was younger, I was testing myself. Setting goals and exceeding them. The trouble is, you can't keep beating yourself indefinitely."

"Like Fitbit," Tommy said. "Once you've ever done thirty thousand steps in a day, any less steps—"

"*Fewer,*" Serenata said.

Tommy glared. "Any *fewer* seems kind of sad."

"Personal bests are a tyranny. Run ten miles, and tomorrow you have to run eleven, or the ten even faster. The problem may apply to more than just athletics."

"Obviously the answer is to stay really shit at everything."

Serenata laughed. "Maybe. But trying to surpass yourself, you'll always approach a limit. Of what your body is capable of, but also of how much you care."

"Yeah, I'm running into that with the Fitbit, too," Tommy said. "I mean, it's just a game, in case you thought I actually take it seriously. I want to beat Marley Wilson. But I'm starting to, like, slightly not give a shit, 'cause of what you said. The limit thing. And once you start coming up against the limit, it stops being interesting."

"And that's assuming it ever was."

"You know, I still don't totally understand why you don't want Remington to run. It seems kind of mean."

"I don't really care if he runs by himself. It's this mass goat fuck I can't stand."

"Shut *up*," Tommy whispered, gesturing at the other diners. "You're being *inappropriate*. Pissing on marathons, and not being 'supportive' of anyone who wants to run one—I can't hardly think of anything more uncool. It's like, almost worse than being a racist or something."

"Thanks for the tip."

"You've no idea what it's like online right now. People post how much weight they're pressing, how many squats they do, how low their heart rate is. There's all these Instagram glam shots of girls with six-packs all greased up and tensed in running bras. The standards keep going up, too, what counts as really 'fit.' What seemed awesome last year now gets dissed as totally lame. It's one thing to get so you can't beat yourself anymore, like you said. But it's way worse to get beaten by everyone else."

"A lot of those online posts must be exaggerated."

"Maybe. But some of these guys really do spend all day, every day, in the gym. All I've got is our backyard. You and Griff will have to get a whole lot filthier if I'm going to spring for a hundred twenty-five dollars a month at BruteBody year-round."

"Is that really the best use of your savings?"

"Without those machines, I can't keep up. Last year, my friend Anastasia celebrated her eighteenth birthday at BruteBody. The 'party' was a bunch of unbelievably hard and complicated boot-camp routines to techno-rap. They all kept an eye out for anyone who couldn't keep up so they could razz you later. There wasn't even any cake. The main event was a contest: who could skip rope the longest without messing up. I did okay, but I didn't win. *You*, though," Tommy charged. "*You* feel superior to everybody."

"I do not! I want to have nothing to do with most people. That doesn't mean I feel superior to them."

"Liar. It's obvious, just in the way you stand. All tall and straight and a little pulled back, and then when people are around you don't like, you don't talk very much, and I can tell what you're thinking."

"Do you think I feel superior to you?"

"Well . . . I don't like it when you correct my grammar and stuff."

"I'm only trying to help you. Do you want me to stop?"

Tommy folded her arms and thought about it. "Nah. I mean, it's irritating, but at least you care. Nobody else listens to me. When you go all schoolteacher, I know you're paying attention."

Pious yogurts on all sides drove Serenata to fetch a second muffin.

"You know, over time," she said on return, examining the baked good critically, "the reasons I exercise have changed. At your age, sure, I wanted to be attractive—and strong, not just thin. But for years now . . . That daily routine has been mostly about maintaining a sense of *order*. Order and control. I do it because I've always done it. I'm completely convinced that if I ever stop exercising, everything else in my life will fall apart. Instantaneously. And disastrously."

"What, like you'd become an alcoholic heroin addict—on welfare, who smokes?"

"And shoplifts. And steals from charity piggybanks at checkout."

"Maybe you should try quitting, then," Tommy said with a grin. "Sounds like you'd finally have some fun."

They dined that evening at the barbaric hour of five thirty. Valeria made such a fuss over her father's order for his "last supper"—"carb loading" being out of fashion—that her mother finally interrupted, "Sweetie—he's not about to be executed."

When she returned to the room after a mutinous nightcap—at the teetotal dinner, the confining rectitudes of Jesus and fitness freakery had overlapped—Remington was abed but restive. She recognized his frequent glances at the clock from the latter days at the DOT, when he worried about getting to work on time, but also about what would happen when he got there. Only when she smoothed against his back, kissed his neck, and wrapped an arm around his chest did he quiet. They'd always been a good fit. Although the cleaner lines of his leaner frame the last few months were pleasing to the eye, he'd been wiry to begin with, and his naked body at rest felt comfortingly unchanged. An alarm set for five a.m. seemed extreme, but this one time, she thought, dropping off, she wouldn't mind getting up with him out of solidarity.

Wrong.

With psychic violence, the alarm rang during her deepest slumber. Until this moment, the weekend had exhibited the indolence of a getaway, so why was she stumbling for the bathroom light switch when it was pitch-dark? What shocked her fully awake was a burst of rage. This whole undertaking was stupid. She'd been pretending for months that it wasn't stupid, and now that she had to keep pretending just one more day she wasn't going to make it. Her pose of taking this circus seriously, or at least of tolerating it until her husband's groupster infatuation went the way of the Hula-Hoop, had fatally, as they said in the marathon biz, hit a wall.

While Remington stuck moleskin to the parts of his feet that chafed, she found Tommy already stalking the hallway, dressed and ready to roll. Not to be outdone, Nancee was close on her heels, hopping behind her on one foot.

"Twenty-two hundred steps!" Tommy said, raising the hand with the aqua strap. "Now, that's what I call getting a jump on the day." Bright-eyed and bushy-tailed, the young woman seemed not the least irked by the savagery of the hour.

Yet despite all their daughter's previous gung ho go-Papa, in the room down the hall Valeria responded neither to a decorous tap-tap nor, at first, to full-tilt pounding on the door. Slit-eyed and tousled, she finally appeared in a waffled hotel robe. "Jesus, Mom, it's the fucking middle of the night!" She forgot that she never took the Lord's name in vain. She forgot that she now said "Mama." She forgot that she didn't curse. If Valeria got up at the crack of dawn more often, they might get on.

Serenata borrowed the minivan keys and promised to drive back later to pick up the slugabeds. Given Remington's pace, his daughter and grandkids wouldn't miss his crossing the finish line if they slept in till eleven and ordered the eggs Benedict.

Other parties were gnawing energy bars in the lobby; the hotel dining room was closed. Kitted out in the green and purple nylon in which he had initiated this six-month fool's errand, Remington was swinging his personalized goodie bag: bananas, energy gels the colors of plastic toys, Red Bull, and something called "chews." But Serenata wanted *coffee*, thank you, and all the cafés down Broadway would be closed, too.

"You could be a *little* more cheerful," Remington said on their way to the van.

"At this time of day? I'd settle for civil if I were you."

The grounds of the Performing Arts Center in Spa Park were humming when they arrived at six. Peppy staff wore hot-pink T-shirts proclaiming SARATOGA SPRINGS GIVES YOU A RUN FOR YOUR MONEY! Remington reverently pinned his black-and-white race number, 3,788, to his shirt, and snapped on the chipped ankle bracelet that would record his time to the hundredth of a second when (and if) he finished. The spectators and contestants rapidly thickened.

Serenata reviled crowds. Furthermore, the world record for this distance was about two hours, and this event had a cutoff of eight hours. There was no earthly reason to begin the race at seven thirty a.m. They could have released the first group of men, eighteen to twenty-four, at noon, in which case she'd be well rested and fortified by cranberry muffins.

The up-and-at-'em start time was all for show. For humanity divided into mutually hostile camps: bounders out of bed and burners of the midnight oil. The distinction went way beyond schedule. The late nighter was synonymous with mischief, imagination, rebellion, transgression, anarchy, and excess, not to mention drugs, alcohol, and sex. The early riser evoked traditional Protestant values like obedience, industry, discipline, and thrift, but also, in this gladness to greet the day, a militant, even fascistic determination to look on the bright side. In short, rise-and-shiners were revolting, and being flapped by so many birds getting the worm felt like getting trapped in an Alfred Hitchcock remake. These bouncy, boisterous, bubbly people loved their seven thirty start, which shouted earnestness and asceticism, and any attempt to move the time to noon for next year would trigger a riot.

Mercifully, as the sky lightened refreshment stands were opening, so Serenata bought the two girls doughnuts and herself coffee. It was weak and tasted like dirt, but coffee in the morning was as much idea as beverage—an idea of normalcy and entitlement—so the cardboard cup settled her mood from fuming to surly. When a younger booster jostled the coffee onto Serenata's shirt, instead of apologizing the woman shot her a smile of manic benevolence. "Isn't this *exciting*?"

"Why," Serenata said flatly. "Why is this exciting."

"Wow, you've really got to work on your attitude," she huffed, and flounced off.

As Serenata threaded with Remington toward the flag under which his age group was gathering, a distinctive subsection of the over-the-hill contestants began to exert a queasy fascination. All men in their seventies and eighties, they were lean to the point of desiccation, with limbs like beef jerky. They went shirtless, despite the morning's chill. In April, they were tanned. Their eyes burned with mission. They did stretches with the self-conscious air of feeling observed. Their watches were flashy: erstwhile professionals or CEOs, then, climbing yet another ladder in retirement. She caught snippets of their conversation, which were all of a piece: "Under five, if there's a God"; "Break the nine-minute mile, I'll sleep sound tonight"; "Finished four twenty-two eighteen in New York, but that race has become such a free-for-all . . ." The wizened immortals cut only side-glances at each other, in that reluctance to quite take in the full person that marks the highly competitive. Should he really catch the bug, was this a snapshot of Remington's future? Because the geriatric elite had one more trait in common: as company, they'd be unbearable.

Several hundred young men had now assembled behind the starting line. After a welcome speech from a town functionary, the gun went off at seven thirty precisely. The spectators roared, screaming and waving placards (WE BELIEVE IN LEONARD!). The men surged forward in a mass, filling the roadway from the Arts Center to its edges like corpuscles in a vein. If she didn't find the spectacle uplifting, she had to concede, however sullenly, that at least these eager-beaver entrants weren't hurting anybody.

More to the point, Remington wasn't hurting anybody, including her. He'd worked hard for this, and in the context of a rough couple of years. This event mattered to him, and it wasn't her business to decide for him what should and shouldn't matter. Although he sure knew how to pick his spots, it wasn't his fault that she'd ruined her knees. So when at 8:40 men sixty to sixty-four were summoned on the loudspeaker, she placed a hand on each cheek and looked him in the eye. The little wryness in her delivery would certify the sentiment was sincere: "Go get 'em, champ!"

This wasn't mere going through the motions of "supportiveness," and to show he knew the difference he embraced her for longer than he could afford, because the age-group starting times were strict. Good grief. When had she last been tender? He must have been starving.

Scanning for her charges, Serenata spotted Tommy dragging Nancee harshly by the wrist. "She keeps trying to join the pack," Tommy said when they met up. "Then the other spectators think it's so *cute*. I've told her and told her, she's only here to watch."

"Look at all those moldy oldies!" Nancee whined. "If they can make it, I could, too, no problem!"

"You have to pay an entry fee," Serenata said. "And be over eighteen."

"That's not fair! I'm way faster than them fuddy-duddies. Let me go, and I'll show you!"

"Nancee, sweetheart. I'm sure you're one of the fastest in your neighborhood—"

"Not only fast! I can run a really, really long time! A lot longer than *you*."

At this point, the girl's claim was horribly true.

When Serenata drove the girls back to the hotel just after ten, Valeria, Logan, and the baby were breakfasting in the dining room.

"See, Mama," Valeria said, "you can download this app, enter Papa's registration number, and follow exactly where he is in the race!"

The course on the app cut a long straight diagonal on Ballston Avenue, whose scenery over eleven miles Remington had described as "abusively monotonous." The return journey described two peaks—up Goode Street, right on Charlton, left onto Middleline, and right on Geyser for the final four miles back to Spa Park: a shocking length of public roadway to close to traffic for a self-regarding middle-class pastime.

"Oh, wow!" Valeria said. "They've just declared the winner!"

"Who gives a crap," Logan muttered.

"Golly," Valeria said. "Our number three-seven-eight-eight has twenty miles to go. Good news, actually. We've plenty of time to visit the house of the Lord, kiddoes."

The reaction of the two older children was impassive. They didn't squirm, or kick the table in frustration, or even glower. Fascinating.

"Papa is running for the glory of God, whether he realizes it or not," she regaled her mother. "This is the perfect day for you to raise your face to the light. Why don't you join us? You never know what might happen."

"I have a pretty good idea," Serenata said. "But after the service, you could use the app to find intersections where you can cheer your father on. He'd like that."

"Won't you want to cheer by the roadside, too?"

"I think I'll save my enthusiasm for the finish line."

"What enthusiasm?" Valeria said sourly.

"What about you?" Serenata asked Tommy, once the family had bustled off to some happy-clappy revivalist hootenanny. "Want to plant yourself along the course and yell 'Go, Remy, baby!'?"

"Honest?" Tommy said. "Standing around watching other people exercise. Not my idea of a good time."

"Let's see . . ." Serenata tapped the calculator. "Even if he keeps averaging a twelve-minute mile, Remington won't finish for another four hours. Since my husband is sacrificing himself for our sins, I don't see why we shouldn't enjoy ourselves."

Surely she was intent on a rigorous workout, too, to prove she was still a contender? Au contraire. From a funny little belligerence arose an ease, a lightness, a liberation. She'd fit in calisthenics in front of *Frasier* the two days previous, and couldn't remember the last time she'd taken an exercise day off. Today? She'd take a day off.

For her very awareness that Remington was at that moment thudding down Ballston—straining to slow his breathing, using the runner in front to maintain a pace with which he wasn't quite comfortable, and panicking that the first right turn was still nowhere in sight—inspired his wife to extend across her chair, arms draped languidly to either side. She'd rarely so inhabited a state of repose. Why, she felt like a movie star. Everything seemed so terribly pleasant.

On Sundays, brunch lasted till one p.m. So many hotel guests were running or watching the race that the bountiful buffet was barely touched. Serenata floated to the long white table and assembled an alluring plate: brioche with a loll of smoked salmon. A wedge of honeydew topped with three fresh raspberries. A perfectly fried piece of bacon—not flabby, but with a droop to it. A miniature lemon tart with a garnish of fresh mint. She and Tommy ordered more coffee, which was fresh and strong and hot and didn't taste like dirt. Every tidbit was delectable. They went back for seconds.

In the main, Serenata hewed to a sartorial formula: dark leggings or black jeans, scoop-necked tops in muted solids, black ankle boots, and a timeless leather jacket; Remington said she dressed like one of those thriller heroines who were experts at kickboxing. So she seldom shopped for clothes. Yet today the quotidian diversion presented itself as positively heady. Leading Tommy down Broadway, she assumed a long idle saunter that made simply walking feel as sumptuous and silky as that smoked salmon. The air on her cheeks was bracing, yet not so cold that she tightened against the chill. At the hoary old age of sixty-one, she passed a fellow arranging a sidewalk table of horseracing souvenirs and turned his head. The knees were taking one of their capricious timeouts from torture. Fingertips resting lightly on the navy leggings, she followed the undulation of her thigh muscles. Funny, she'd spent so much of her life working her body, pushing it, punishing it, but far too little just hanging out in it.

Tommy looked at her companion askance. "Why do you look so happy? I thought the marathon would put you in a bad mood. But you seem almost drunk."

"Turn it off."

"What?"

"The Fitbit. Turn it off."

Consternated, Tommy came to a halt. "Why?"

"Do as I say. Then we're headed for that boutique, and we'll find you some killer gear." She wouldn't proceed until the aqua wristband went *bee-beep.*

At first anxious about accepting her neighbor's largesse, Tommy soon plunged into the spirit of their spree. Together they found her a lined, sleeveless dress in white cotton; the draping at the dropped waist smoothed over the gawkiness of the girl's frame. Serenata located a soft, flannelly floor-length garment in light blue denim with long sleeves and pearled snaps—the ideal weight for the midday breeze, and a stunning accompaniment for the dress. Short, blond leather boots completed the look. For herself, she found a long black rayon wrap with trench-coat styling and the same slither she looked for in shirts. "Lord," she declared to the mirror. "All I need is a revolver."

Instead, she bought a cocky black fedora. Tommy was more suited to a sun hat in straw with a thin ribbon that uncannily matched the denim. Blues, Serenata informed her charge with authority, were prone to clash.

There was lunch. Suffice it to say that the arugula salad with shaved Parmesan and a side of tomato bruschetta improved on Remington's *chews.*

"What I want to know is . . ." The new outfit imparting a fresh sophistication, Tommy wielded her slender breadstick like a cigarette holder. "Are you faking?"

"Faking not being jealous and miserable? What do you think?"

Tommy poked the breadstick in the olive caponata as if extinguishing an ash. "If it's an act, it's darned well done."

"I don't see why I'd be jealous of my husband huffing the streets of Saratoga when we're having such a charming time. How's the intrepid doing, anyway?"

"Huh," Tommy said, checking her phone. "He's slowed down. He still has ten, eleven more miles to go. Don't take this wrong, but his time kind of sucks."

Serenata stretched. "Why don't we go back to the hotel for a swim?"

"That seems like backsliding. More exercise. You're taking the day off."

"I don't want to exercise. I just want to be in water."

Once they met back up at the deserted indoor pool, Serenata descended its steps slowly, taking time to acclimatize. Ordinarily, she'd immediately start swimming laps. Why, in her adulthood, she couldn't recall *ever* gliding serenely into water for the sake of the sensation alone. Floating on her back with her eyes closed. Slipping below the surface, touching the drain, and dolphining to air. Parting the water with a few expansive breaststrokes not to meet a stringent private requirement, but to feel the pressure against her cupped hands, the ripple across her neck.

Yet Tommy lingered at the shallow end. For pity's sake, no one had ever taught her to swim. For their last twenty minutes, Serenata supported the girl's torso in place so she could practice breathing for the crawl. Should the usual edict to complete a mile or two have prevailed, she'd never have made time for the lesson.

After a long hot shower upstairs, she hastily toweled her hair, slid into the flowing rayon trench coat, and bunched the damp hair under the fedora. She and Tommy would be the only spectators at the finish line who weren't clad in sympathetic athletic apparel. At 3:20 p.m., she reconnoitered with Tommy in the lobby and called Valeria.

"You're cutting it awful close," her daughter snarled.

"Not especially. According to Tommy's app, Remington won't approach the finish line until after four. I thought you might pick us up, and we can watch together. Have you been able to cheer him on at various points?"

"It's been a little trying, to be honest. Constantly finding a place to park. Changing and feeding Jacob in the backseat. And then Nancee keeps *walking* alongside Papa at the same speed, and I'm afraid she's been demoralizing. Also, at our last vantage point, there was some woman . . ." Valeria trailed off.

"We'll be at the back entrance, by the parking lot."

When the harried young woman pulled up in the minivan, she shot a malignant glance at her mother, who looked svelte, stylish, and refreshed: the very picture of what three hours of spa treatments the day before had failed to do for Valeria. Logan announced grumpily from the back, "This is the boring-est day ever. When I grow up, I'm never gonna stand around clapping just 'cause a bunch a people went *jogging*. My hands hurt. When anybody claps for *me*, it's gonna be 'cause I actually did something."

"Grampa is totally slow," Nancee said. "I coulda run that course three times by now. It's embarrassing. Tons of the other oldies finished hours ago."

"Now, honey," Valeria said. "Remember 'The Tortoise and the Hare.'"

"But 'slow and steady' *doesn't* win the race," Nancee said. "Some other guy won it, and Grampa's practically last. Besides, that story is dumb. Everybody knows the rabbit is way faster, and no one really wants to be the crummy turtle."

They'd no trouble parking at the Arts Center. Most runners and their retinues had cleared off by early afternoon. The crowd was so sparse that their party could stand right by the finish line. The grounds were littered with confetti, burst balloons, and discarded noisemakers. Committed to every finisher's enjoying a salute, a small, dedicated group of staff in pink T-shirts was positioned beside the banner. Whenever a laggard approached, this volunteer cheering section punched the air screaming, "Way to go!" or "Only a few more feet, man!" or "Earned your brewskie tonight, bro!" The limited selection of encouragements was regularly recycled. Each time another marathoner crossed the line, running 26.2 miles seemed a little less amazing.

At this tail end of the field, many participants were running for charity in costumes. Amid the commercial Batman and Underdog outfits tottered homemade creations: a papier-mâché Eiffel Tower, a possum, a human calculator, and a giant slice of cheese. Between them wove the power walkers, chins high, elbows out.

At 4:10 p.m. Remington was advancing on the home stretch. A time of about 7:25 translated into an average mile of 19:30—which was appalling. Serenata mulled over what to say to buck him up, and to ensure he'd accept his role as guest of honor tonight at 15 Church. She'd hate to cancel the reservation. After six months of training, he deserved better than a room-service ham sandwich.

If she wished for his sake that his time were a little better, she was genuinely astonished that he was completing the course at any speed. Nevertheless, she relished the prospect of the months ahead, during which he'd grow gradually less touchy about the whole fandango, until they could laugh and roll around on the bed and remember this weird period of their marriage, and at last he'd ruefully admit that, as for endurance sport, well, okay, right—he wasn't very good at it.

"There he is!" Valeria cried, spotting the wilted purple and green kit. "Go, Papa! You can do it! Jesus loves you, whether you know it or not! Glory be! You show 'em! Go for it! You're almost home! Go, go, go! Yay! Yay, Papa! Rah, rah, rah!"

Her daughter carried the gene that Serenata lacked. Perhaps it skipped a generation: this mystifying capacity for getting swept up in the fervor of crowds. For once resisting the urge to disparage the girl as "a joiner," instead she found Valeria's rare display of filial loyalty rather sweet.

Not wishing to be ungracious, Serenata brought her hands together *pat-pat-pat* whenever another "plodder" completed the course. Yet as Remington began his last hundred yards, her bellowing of bolstering slogans would have seemed fake. So she dropped her hands and settled on a smile. It was a warm smile, a private smile—a smile of truce, of quiet apology for having been a bit of a dick, and women could be dicks; a smile of welcome and congratulation and restoration of whatever in the last six months had been put out of whack. It was the smile of a wife.

Yet Remington's expression was neither haggard nor infused with desperate gratitude that the ordeal was almost over. He looked *rapt*. Rather than scan the straggle of spectators for his spouse, he gazed to the left, nodded, spoke quietly, and chuckled. Even when she shouted, "Remington!" he didn't turn toward her voice.

Stung, Serenata dropped the smile. That competitor alongside was not overtaking as she'd first imagined, but conversing in conspiratorial tones with her husband. The fact that Remington's running mate was matching his tortoise-like pace was odd, because this woman was a hare. Perhaps in her late thirties, she had the kind of figure used to sell gym memberships—the kind of figure that no one had really, that would have appeared in advertisements for CrossFit only after having been doctored. Banded with fine intersecting lines, her body recalled the diagrams of human musculature in anatomy textbooks. She looked flayed.

The shoulders were broad and cut. Her forearms were veined. Bandaged by a lavender sports bra, her breasts were tight and high. Her stomach was flat, and shadowed by the telltale ripple of a crunch fanatic. The shorts were skimpy enough that if she didn't shave her bikini line everyone would have noticed. Narrow knees and ankles punctuated dense thighs and full calves. Dancing at Remington's side on the balls of her feet, she made running three miles per hour appear balletic. Her cropped sandy hair gleamed with fashionable gray highlights, and its smart styling looked salon-fresh. Maybe her neck was a tad thick, and on the short side. Still, face it: she was *pretty*.

Serenata returned to pallid clapping. As Remington and his new little friend crossed the finish line, the two high-fived. Clutching him in a bear hug, the anatomy illustration rocked from shoe to shoe. Here Serenata had worried he'd be gutted by his poor showing. Instead he acted elated. He embraced Valeria, then Tommy. He accepted his grandson's lackluster handshake. He lifted Nancee overhead. He kissed the baby. It was humiliating to have to stand in a receiving line at all, much less last.

"Congratulations," she said formally, and pecked his cheek.

"Thanks," he said airily. "Serenata, this is Bambi Buffer. I don't think I'd have made the last five miles without her."

"Bambi" biffed his shoulder. "Oh, sure you would have." Her voice was throaty, deep with a rough edge, and Remington's weakness was aural; Serenata should know. "I keep telling you, man, you got the stuff!" If she spared the wife so much as a nod, it was the sort you gave to ancillary characters who simply weren't going to feature.

There was no question about keeping the restaurant reservation. They all piled into Valeria's minivan—including "Bambi," who was staying in the same hotel, and whom Remington had invited to join them for dinner.

With little ado upstairs, Remington showered and set an alarm.

"You're not saying much," Serenata noted. All her earlier grace and élan had fled.

"It's not a day for talk," he said on the bed with his eyes closed.

It was sure a "day for talk" with that "Bambi" woman.

He slept like a corpse until seven fifteen, awaking invigorated. He dressed in a dark suit and crisp white shirt with an open collar. She couldn't remember ever before having rued the fact that her husband was still, at nearly sixty-five, an attractive man.

When a large party is getting seated for a meal, one enjoys a brief window in which to position one's self next to the people one actually wishes to talk to, and Serenata missed it. She landed without design on a corner, a chair removed from Remington. The chair had Bambi in it.

In a clinging cherry-red sheath whose high neck disguised her only aesthetic shortcoming, the gate-crasher knew how to wear her body. Because that's what she was wearing, her body. The dress was an afterthought. If anything, it was wearing her.

"I'm surprised you were pulling up the rear today," Serenata said, trying furiously to avoid overt reference to the woman's physique.

"Oh, that was my second time around," Bambi said, perusing the appetizers. "I often do an extra lap, to spur on any newbies who seem to be struggling."

Now a marathon was a "lap." "That's altruistic."

"Mm, not totally. Hey, Rem. You been here before. How do you rate the oysters?"

Their guest ordered heavily—more than one first course and multiple sides. The contemporary female being famously fearful of food, hunger was seductive in a woman; if nothing else, the appetite hinted at other kinds. Bambi's eyes proved the equal of her stomach, too. She inhaled every dish set before her, and single-handedly ravaged the breadbasket. Table manners weren't her forte. She ate like a fucking animal.

"Tried to tell you, dude," she held forth to Remington while stripping frogs' legs. "Your big mistake was training for that race by yourself. I've seen it a million-bazillion times: harness the energy of other athletes believing in you, and rooting for you, and helping to bring out your best self, your true self, your *über* self—the God inside every damn one of us—and performance improves by, I ain't kidding, a hundred percent." Bambi's folksy pronunciation—"*hunerd* percent"— didn't seem to hail from a regional dialect, for which Serenata had an ear. Rootlessly eclectic, the vernacular conveyed a generically down-home, tell-it-like-it-is toughness.

"I really respond to that idea of everybody having a little kernel of God in them somewhere," Valeria said. "That speck of the divine is what links us up with God Himself—like a sim card connecting with a satellite."

"If people thrive athletically in social contexts," Serenata said, "don't you just mean they respond to competition?"

"That's a poisonously negative way of putting it," Bambi said. "I'm talking about the giganto power of the many over the pissy power of the one. Rem, you gotta try one a these. I'll trade you for a scallop."

"I didn't think about it at the time, that I was training on my own." Remington piled pancetta and truffle shavings onto the gifted sea scallop. "I may have been unwittingly influenced by Serenata. My wife doesn't believe in group participation, do you, my dear? Marathons, for example," he cited mischievously, "disgust her."

"Your loss, honey." Bambi forked the plump scallop in one bite. "See, Rem, you've shut yourself off from the *community* of other athletes, and that's put you at a disadvantage. Place yourself in the middle of the whole movement, and you can feed off an awesome force, like, a whole collective consciousness. 'Sides which, like I told you after we eased you past that wall you hit, in the end this isn't about the body. Has nothing to do with the body. I could take any guy's body on earth and turn it into Michelangelo's *David*, long as inside he has the *stuff*, man."

"What about people in wheelchairs?" Logan said.

"Watch the Paralympics someday, kid, and you'll see it's all about heart. It's about truth. About becoming what you were fated to be, about being reborn in a state of perfection. About the will to greatness."

"The will to power?" Serenata said. "I think Nietzsche got there already."

Bambi ignored her. "Hey, figure we can nab another couple bottles of this cab-sav?" she proposed, nodding at the empty that listed for seventy-six dollars. "I'm running dry."

"I didn't think fitness freaks were drinkers," Serenata commented to Tommy at her right.

"Work hard, play hard!" Bambi said. "You guys who hung out on the sidelines can pick-pick and sippy-sippy, but us athletes got us some serious refueling to do."

Serenata had ordered the first bottle at the risk of Valeria's disapproval. Should the evening turn into a booze-up, the grandparents were bound to be chastised as immoral influences. But Bambi was such a force of nature that when a replacement bottle arrived, Valeria poured herself half a glass.

Meanwhile, Tommy looked miserable. The outfit from the afternoon's shopping had subtly rearranged itself—the denim wrap had dropped down one shoulder; the dress was wrenched askew—so as to look like everything else she wore, in which she looked drowned and forlorn. The source of Tommy's dejection was surely Bambi, who personified all those online paragons eternally upping their games whenever Tommy was close to catching up. By contrast, swooning from across the table and uncharacteristically shy, Nancee was in love.

"I should never have turned off my Fitbit," Tommy mumbled, fiddling with the band. "Now I'll never make my steps today."

"So, *Bambi*, what do you do?" Serenata inquired.

"Personal trainer," the woman said through her food.

Serenata said, deadpan, "What a shock."

"You?" she asked tersely.

"I'm a voice-over artist. Audio—"

"Whoa, too passive for me. All that sitting."

"Actually, recording video games is surprisingly physical—"

"It's unorthodox"—she'd turned back to Remington—"but I don't recommend much resting up after a marathon. Sure, take tomorrow off. But then get right back in the saddle. You gotta master the body, teach it who's boss."

Holding her emotional breath, Serenata had succeeded in making it through Remington's infernal marathon. In kind, to enter the glorious rest of her life in which she'd never again lay eyes on this insufferable cunt, she only had to make it through this meal. Merely being conversational, she inquired, "So where do you live?"

"Well, that's what made Rem and me decide we were destined to come in as a team. Since whadda ya know—we both live in Hudson!"

Officially, the point at which the couple returned to their hotel room marked the beginning of restored normal life that Serenata had been anticipating since October.

"So!" she said, closing the door on a great deal more than the hallway. "The marathon. After all that training. Was it worth it?"

"Sure," Remington said coolly, removing his jacket. "It was interesting."

"Funny. *Interesting* was exactly what I thought it wasn't."

"You were just watching. Only at the end, I might add. You make a lousy spectator."

She tossed the fedora on a chair in disgust. "I can't believe her name is actually *Bambi Buffer*."

"It's obviously a work handle." Remington had been on a high all night. Only alone with his wife did he seem exhausted. "Like a stage name."

"Which is worse. She can't even blame her parents."

"Her encouragement was a great help to me at the end of that race. So I was sure you wouldn't mind that I asked her to join us."

"Why should I mind? Just because she's a fucking idiot?"

"That's unworthy of you. I can't recall her saying anything especially dumb."

"All that *find the God in yourself*? I call that dumb."

"Know what she told me on the way back to the van? 'Your wife is pretty dark.'"

"And getting darker. You used to like it." Serenata attempted to control herself. This wasn't the night for a spat.

"Anyway, you're going to have to get used to Bambi. I'm hiring her."

Serenata turned sharply from her toiletry kit. "To do what? The race is over."

"Because on one point, you were right."

"This I have to hear."

"You said from the start that finishing a marathon isn't a claim to fame anymore, but a cliché. Even Bambi agrees that completing that distance has become old hat."

"Well, it's still an achievement—"

"*Triathlons,*" he said. "*Triathlons* are where it's at."

SIX

"Have you noticed, in these arts programs," Remington noted in midsummer as they were tidying the lunch dishes with NPR in the background, "how often you hear, 'You wouldn't be able to say that now'? And they're usually talking about a film or a stand-up routine that's only three or four years old. *You wouldn't be able to say that now.* Soon you won't even be able to say what it is that you're not allowed to say. We'll become convinced that to express anything at all is extremely risky, and the species will go mute."

"Don't forget, there's a certain contingent that doesn't seem to feel stifled in the slightest."

"Yes, and they're not helping. The implication is that to say anything is to speak abominations."

"Why are you limping?"

"It's nothing. A hamstring."

"A hamstring is a great deal of something, in my experience. It can take months to heal."

"Bambi says you have to power through injuries. You can't allow them to defeat you."

Serenata could never get used to her husband's saying that woman's loopy handle with a straight face. "In a battle with the body, the body wins every time."

"Only if you let it. Bambi recommends imagining yourself back on the veldt, pursued by a lion. Would you stop, and elevate your leg on the limb of an acacia, and rub hippo grease into your poor sore little hamstring, and tell the lion to come hunting you in three months' time when you can really give chase, if not three thousand years later, after the invention of ibuprofen?"

"I should 'power through' two knees without cartilage, then. I should go back to distance running, despite the crepitus, and the bone bulging out of the right one, and the pains shooting up my thighs, because giving into the agony is a display of weakness?"

"You're picking a fight. I might add, another one."

True, but he hadn't answered her question.

"You know, I'm a little tired of being told how 'privileged' I am," he said a minute later, alluding to the NPR interview with an activist playwright. "How as a member of the 'straight white patriarchy' I have all the power. I'm supposedly so omnipotent, but I live in fear, less like a man than a mouse. I check everything I plan to say three times before I allow it out. At least when I'm training I keep my mouth shut. I might fall on my face, but I won't be arrested."

"That sounds a little paranoid."

"It is not. I was informed in no uncertain terms that she might have pressed charges. *Criminal* charges. For threats of bodily harm."

"My dear," Serenata said with foreboding. "Let's not get into that again."

"We already criminalize emotions. 'Hate crime.' You get an additionally long sentence for how you *feel*. I'm confident that most Americans now believe that *being* a racist is against the law. Not doing racist things, or saying racist things, but the state of being racist should get you thrown in jail."

"In that case, the whole population belongs behind bars."

"We're well on our way to criminalizing anger, too. If you express so much as impatience at airport security, you will literally be arrested. Or all those students. If you shout at them, they don't feel 'safe.' Anger is too frightening. It has to be managed away, in special courses that teach you how to get in touch with your inner pussy. Anger is now regarded as a form of assault. It's too masculine an emotion for Wuss World, where masculinity is also a form of assault. So we contain all male fury, within lead walls like toxic waste. It doesn't surprise me in the slightest that a man my age would suddenly with no warning smash the window of his hotel room and strafe a country music festival."

It started a few years ago: Remington's adoption of a robotic monotone, especially when delivering what might otherwise qualify as a rant. The absence of inflection was more chilling than rage. He made no eye contact. He spoke to the sink.

"You know, when you're running, swimming, and cycling, I don't believe you think about running, swimming, and cycling," Serenata said. "I think you think about Lucinda Okonkwo."

"I think about *not* thinking about Lucinda Okonkwo. It takes vigilance. But you seem to imply that concentrating on going from one place to another is empty in some way. If that's the case, then life is empty. Life comes down to nothing more than the motion of the body through space."

The assertion seemed a mantra of sorts. "So if I remain perfectly still, I'm dead."

"It's impossible to remain perfectly still, which should tell you something about the nature of being alive. Why do you think I chose to work for the Department of *Transportation*? Traversing distance. That's all there is to do. It's no different for us than for a fly, buzzing around the room, jiggering across a windowpane, and then it dies."

"For you, then, a triathlon is just jiggering across a windowpane."

"Yes."

"Your friend *Bambi* seems to promote a more exalted version of the project."

"It's to her professional advantage to frame the endeavor in more attractive terms."

Determining the precise nature of the "project" was Serenata's project. She was privately compiling a list of her husband's objectives. (1) To kill time—to systematically massacre the barren months that lay before him, like a modern-day great white hunter. (2) To embrace silence, and so to embrace a passive defiance. Breathless on a track, plunged into the pool at the Y, head to the wind in a velodrome, he couldn't talk, which afforded a narrow refuge. If not impossible, it was harder to burn heretics for what they didn't say. (3) Not to repress anger so much as to become chronically too exhausted to give rise to it. (4) To become a man again, but with a frenzied futility that contained the noxious qualities of his sex within the safe circumference of the hamster wheel.

The appointment of Lucinda Okonkwo as his immediate superior had obviously come as a blow. At fifty-nine, Remington Alabaster had blithely assumed that he'd rise to head of the department, as he might have much earlier if his colleague Gary Neusbaum hadn't run out the clock on retirement. Salary was at issue, of course, but more, pride. Lucinda Okonkwo was twenty-seven.

Remington described her as insecure, and she may have felt that way for good reason. At college, she hadn't majored in transportation, civil engineering, or even urban planning, but gender studies, and she had no graduate degree. Naturally the City Council never said so per se, but Lucinda's exhibiting the "intersectionality" of a seven-exit traffic circle must have made the new hire irresistible.

"She's black," Remington told his wife the night after he'd learned the news. "I mean, African-American—"

"Drop it," Serenata said. "You're among friends. Besides, I don't think that term earns you a gold star anymore."

"No, but Lucinda is *African* African-American, which confers extra points. She's second-generation Nigerian, which means she nominally gets credit for being an immigrant, too. She's a she—"

"Careful, even pronouns can get you into trouble. Try, 'She's a *they.*'"

"Or a *zee,*" he said. "But on the diversity section of her application, she apparently answered all the questions about gender and sexuality 'Prefer not to say.' Which terrified the HR people at City Hall. You can't protect yourself against discrimination suits when you don't even know what you're discriminating against."

"What's left? Don't tell me. She's in a wheelchair. Can you say wheelchair? Do you have to say 'wheelchariot'? I have a hard time keeping up."

"She's not *differently abled,* no. The problem is otherwise, and please don't take this wrong. She's extremely attractive. Meaning, she's a sexual harassment case waiting to happen. If it's ever her word against mine? With one look at that figure in an era when we're supposed to 'believe women' no matter what kind of crackpots they might be, anyone will assume that I couldn't control myself."

"But from your description, she has no qualifications for the job. You said her only previous position was working at a shelter for victims of domestic violence."

"You mentioned gold stars? That's a gold star. When I applied for my first post in the Albany DOT, I'd been working for the New York City DOT: boring and obvious. I'd never have snagged the job today."

Indeed, to describe Lucinda Okonkwo as having been promoted to her level of incompetence, via the "Peter Principle" popular in Serenata's adolescence, wouldn't have been strictly accurate. Skipping altogether the multiple stair steps of proficiency that classically preceded the final stage of ineptitude at which, according to the theory, managers indefinitely stagnated, Lucinda had been *airlifted* to her level of incompetence. Thus to be fair, the fact that she had no idea what she was doing was not her fault.

A rational man, Remington didn't hold Lucinda accountable for a Council mistake. Cultivating a demurral that couldn't have come easily in relation to a woman less than half his age, he claimed to have approached his new superior in a spirit of collegiality. But youth and inexperience made Lucinda understandably defensive, and defense often expressed itself as aggression. So intent on proving who was boss, she mustn't have entirely believed that she was already the boss.

Serenata met Lucinda more than once. She had full breasts, powerful hips, and high cheekbones. Her bearing was statuesque. In middle age she might possibly run to fat, but in the full bloom of young adulthood her mass was magnificently distributed and made her only the more formidable. She'd a habit of looking unwaveringly straight at you, as if sighting through crosshairs; even Serenata had broken eye contact first. Born and privately educated in the States, Lucinda spoke with an American accent whose degree of Black English inflection fluctuated (with whites, she went street; with black employees, she could sound aristocratic). Everyone in the department was afraid of her.

Remington had also met her parents, when they drove up from the city to see where their daughter worked. He described them as lavishly courteous and warm. They both spoke English with a musical African lilt. The mother was slender and also quite beautiful, in a colorful blouse with echoes of her homeland, but a slim Western skirt. The handsome father's charcoal suit was classily tailored. Yet despite a junior professional standing in relation to their daughter, Remington was several years older than Lucinda's parents, so the couple accorded him the deference their culture demanded toward elders. Unusually for their nationality, Lucinda was an only child, and perhaps they'd spoiled her. But in any event, Remington's problem with Lucinda was not that she was Nigerian. The problem was that Lucinda was American. All too.

Lucinda Okonkwo was well educated, in a particular vein. In due course, Remington had altogether too much cause to research her campus activism in back editions of the *Columbia Spectator.* Serenata had sometimes wondered what happened to university firebrands—who spent their undergraduate years brandishing placards, campaigning to de-colonize the curriculum, and getting professors sacked for screening ostensibly "alt-right" YouTube videos—once these tempest-in-a-teacup hotheads graduated into the larger world of actual bad weather. Well. Now she knew.

At first, Remington was unfazed by his new superior's initiatives—the gender-neutral restrooms, or the requirement to introduce yourself including your "preferred pronoun." Announcing "I'm Remington Alabaster, and I'm a he" was no skin off his nose; he was able to find it comical; and public employees were accustomed to statements of the obvious. Sexual harassment and racial awareness workshops were opportunities to catch up on his expenses. Oddly, as second-in-command of the Department of Transportation, he reserved his zeal for issues of transportation. So long as Lucinda kept to social justice, Remington could get on with his job.

He and Gary Neusbaum had already transferred ownership of Albany's streetlights from a private utility to the city, with the aim of lowering both carbon emissions and metropolitan lighting bills by switching to more contemporary illumination. Increasingly popular with urban bureaucrats across the country, light-emitting diodes consumed a fraction of the energy that yellow-tinted sodium lamps drew, and lasted up to three times longer. Yet a range of subsidiary matters remained to be resolved: whether the new LED streetlights would be shielded on top, thus preventing upward glare that disturbed wildlife; whether the units would be shielded on the sides, to prevent light invasion from piercing residential windows; whether the city would invest in a decorative, retro post and housing to suit Albany's original architecture, or purchase a starker yet more economical product; and most of all, what Kelvin rating to opt for.

Much of Remington's work was arithmetic: obtaining accurate cars-per-day figures on a side street that residents had petitioned to have closed to through traffic or quantifying the low ridership on a bus route with an eye to reducing scheduling frequency. But the research on LED streetlights that Remington had just begun when Lucinda took over soon became the source of a passion one associates not with math but with art.

Inflamed by revelation, he had dragged Serenata from the door on her return home from a late recording session, intent on showing her a series of photographs on the family tablet. All the shots captured the same roadside scene, but each was illuminated by LED streetlights with different Kelvin ratings: 2.3, 2.7, 3, 3.5, 4, or 5.

"Look, I admit the two point three is a little dingy," he'd said. "But the two point seven is perfectly pleasant. You could picnic under that light. You could kiss your girlfriend under that light, or even propose marriage. It's an LED, but it's human light. It still has warmth, a hint of the golden. It still shines with benevolence, with kindness. If you were one of those people in that photograph, and someone emailed you the pic, you wouldn't be likely to anguish, 'Oh, no, where did all those mottles on my face come from?' You might think instead, 'Hey, I look pretty good in that red shirt, don't I?'

"But now . . . Look at Kelvin ratings four and five. You could slit your wrists under that light. Better yet, murder somebody else. Why not, when that figure on the left already looks like a cadaver? That's the kind of light in which people confess to being terrorists under torture. It's the gruesome glare in which you'd shoot those movies, you know, about kidnapped women kept starving and pregnant and chained in the basement. When I first read about the hoopla in some communities over *streetlights*, for pity's sake, I thought, come on, people, get a life. But now I get it. High-Kelvin LEDs are mercilessly destroying the touch and feel of urban nightlife all over the country. Honestly, blue-spectrum LEDs are a form of emotional vandalism. They're not only about how things look. They're about how people feel. Like—terrible."

"I have to agree," Serenata said, swiping between the shots. "The atmospheric difference between these lightings is extraordinary."

"Lower Kelvin diodes are *slightly* more expensive, and *slightly* less energy efficient. But the massive trade-off in ambience more than compensates for the sacrifice."

The methodical Remington Alabaster commonly thought in terms of interlocking systems. He'd always enjoyed the puzzle-solving of controlling traffic flow, but the pleasure was quiet, like a watchmaker's—a private satisfaction that a mechanism ticked along. But his devotion to the gentle, enfolding glow of low-Kelvin diodes, and his ferocious opposition to the brutal, ghoulish blue spectrum to which too many municipalities were subjecting their residents—often in the face of virulent local opposition—was the first instance in which he'd taken on a professional cause with crusading fervor. For once, his central concern wasn't functionality or finance but aesthetics. He believed vehemently that blue light was ugly, and was therefore profoundly damaging to the daily lives of millions of Americans, a discrete subsection of whom he could personally rescue from its suicidal blare. He further believed that the aesthetic bled not only to the psychological but to the existential. Under the cold, prying, pseudo-Soviet beam of high-Kelvin interrogation, all of life itself seemed bleak.

The months of Remington's streetlamp research saw a late blossoming of their marriage. The distance narrowed between their work worlds. Serenata dwelt in a universe of tones—nuance, mood, suggestion, pauses that said more than words—and her husband's new dedication to color in a visual sense ineffably connected with her own dedication to color in a vocal one. He had hitherto left most decisions about household decor to his wife, so she was pleased to discover that he had an appreciation for beauty after all, one that also translated into a revived appreciation for his wife. They had more sex. When he finally delivered his thick report, they were both a little bereft.

Lucinda Okonkwo responded with stonewalling silence. When after months of no uptake on his recommendations he asked whether she'd found time to survey his findings, she said something like, "You wouldn't be telling me how to do my job, would you?" No, no, certainly not; it's just that he was *terribly interested* in her opinion. "I got stacks of way more pressing problems to deal with. You wouldn't be asking me to *privilege* your report, would you—which took you a weirdly long time to compile, truth be told—just because a white department lifer got a bug up about freaking streetlights?" Obviously, Remington backed off.

Alas, it was around this time that Lucinda ran short of ideas for how to upend the awful inequities of modern-day Albany, right the grotesque historical wrongs of her shameful country, and save the planet. She'd already commissioned a report on the department's gender pay gap. She'd already declared the office a no-go zone for single-use plastic—which meant that employees shoveled in their lunches out of doors before chucking their deli containers in the public trash can on the corner. She'd already introduced a climate-change points system, which rewarded employees for biking or walking to work and staying home on vacations; winners would earn a bottle of no-alcohol chardonnay. In a highway meridian park, she'd already ordered the exhumation of a plaque that celebrated a local nineteenth-century philanthropist, now that archived letters documented his belief that homosexuality was depraved. Because the city's byways were cluttered with the names of "too many dead white male presidents," she'd already changed Buchanan Street to Robert Mugabe Terrace and Roosevelt Street to Jacob Zuma Way. Alas, little territory remained over which to exercise her decision-making powers other than Albany's actual transportation system.

Making a costly gesture toward a low-carbon future, she commanded the construction of elaborate bike lanes on both sides of Highway 20/Madison Avenue, which might have been all very well and good—except that she did no study in advance of the modest demand. Designed with wide concrete barriers between bicycles and traffic, the lanes took nine months to construct, backing up traffic for half a mile during rush hours. Once opened, the bike lanes continued to create a crippling pinch point for cars. Yet the paths extended a mere two hundred yards, after which cyclists rejoined the main roadway at a perilous juncture. In practice, then, savvy two-wheelers shunned the lanes altogether. Remington believed that intrusive, merely symbolic projects of this nature made motorists revile cyclists even more than they had already, and neither party needed any encouragement to despise the other.

In the interest of traffic calming, Lucinda commissioned raised platforms for dozens of downtown intersections. Each ramped elevation comprised thousands of small, fiddly cubes of granite. Yet the slopes proved far too gentle to slow drivers in the slightest. Worse, she spent most of the project's budget on classy materials, and cut corners on labor. Carelessly grouted, the cobbles began to rattle when vehicles traversed them after only a few days. Within three months of the project's completion, the stones were sinking, lying at cockeyed angles, and fracturing into shards.

Lucinda's messing with one-way systems was a catastrophe for the Dunn Memorial Bridge. The untried, innovative material she selected for repaving began to decay the first time a UPS van drove down a resurfaced road, picking up gooey chunks of gravelly terra-cotta tarmac with its tires. Her free bus passes for recent immigrants, the underprivileged, and other "vulnerable" groups was widely abused, and left a massive hole in the budget.

Three years after Remington delivered his streetlight findings, Lucinda announced in a departmental meeting, casually, amid a range of other business, that the conversion was going ahead. Afterward, Remington stopped by her office. That evening, he recounted their conversation to Serenata as best as he could:

"So—you got around to looking at my report, then?" Not invited to sit down, Remington remained standing.

"Skimmed it," Lucinda said. "Thing was thick enough to use for some toddler's booster chair. Too many trees, Alabaster. Time's short. I need forest."

"I thought it was important to be thorough. This is a long-term investment—"

"*Too* thorough amount to a kind of sloppy. I can't spend all day reading booster chairs."

"It's just, that report raised a number of issues that need to be resolved before the conversion goes ahead. For example, R&M makes a faux-gaslight, nineteenth-century-style post and fixture that, while a little pricey, might be worth the historical touch around the capitol—"

"Albany taxpayers don't want fancy-pants street furniture. This is a modern American city, not a Sherlock Holmes movie set. If you and your wife are partial to antiques, I could steer you toward a shop on Learned Street. But not on the department's dime."

She'd not been nearly as concerned with taxpayer value for money when commissioning those crumbling raised platforms.

"More substantively," Remington said, "there's the shielding question. The nonprofit Dark-Sky has documented disturbance to nocturnal wildlife from vertical light escape; I included their report in my appendix. As for lateral escape, other municipalities have met widespread popular uproar over the invasive penetration of powerful LED streetlights into people's homes—"

"Let 'em get curtains. There's your 'shielding.' Streetlights supposed to be bright. That's what they're for. So you can see. Is that all, Alabaster? Seem to me you're making this way more complicated than it need to be."

"No, that's not all. The biggest issue is obviously Kelvin rating. I concede there's room for debate over the middle range—"

"Mister, I'm a busy woman."

"But I'd lobby for as low a rating as possible. Considerable data substantiates that blue-spectrum light interferes with the production of melatonin, and disrupts sleep rhythms—"

"This isn't more of you worrying about the raccoons, is it?"

"Human sleep rhythms. It's the same sleep disruption caused by looking at smart phones and computer screens before bed. As a woman, I'd think you'd especially respond to the gathering evidence that prolonged exposure to blue-spectrum illumination may significantly increase the incidence of breast cancer—"

"You buttering up to me, figuring I'll go weak at the knees and do whatever you say so long as you go on about *breast cancer*? That's some manipulative shit. It's a kind of misogyny, wanna know the truth. Sexist condescension."

"I apologize. I shouldn't have made assumptions."

"No, you should not." The response was typical. Whenever you gave ground, she took it.

"You see, blue light exposure also substantially raises the incidence of prostate cancer."

"Oh, so now it's a *man*'s problem, it matters."

Remington confessed that at this point he'd been stymied. "Then there's the intangible but," he resumed unsteadily, "I would argue, not incidental matter of the appearance of this city at night—when we want residents to feel enthusiastic about eating out and going to clubs, which stimulates the economy. And we want our citizens to be happy, don't we? To feel good."

"Now you're losing me for true, Alabaster. Happy citizens aren't in the DOT's remit, or I'd of ordered fifty crates of diazepam 'stead of a full container load of LED streetlights from Guangzhou."

"What?"

"I been trying to tell you, friend, but you just had to go on about all your hokey gaslights and breast cancer and *shielding*. I already place the order. It's warehoused and ready to be installed. And I didn't get the goods from Amazon. It's not like I can print out a return label and carry a box to the post office. We're talking done deal."

"Well, what kind did you order?"

"Standard, off-the-shelf, cheap as I could get. That's my job. The department's in overspend. The savings is a double-whammy, too. The electric bill for streetlights about to go through the floor."

"And what Kelvin rating did you choose?"

Lucinda met her subordinate's eyes defiantly. "*Five.*"

Serenata wasn't obliged to fill in the blanks of her husband's employment tribunal. Owing to a mistrust that proved justified, he turned on the recording function on his phone.

As described secondhand by the Albany city employee Remington Alabaster, hauled up on disciplinary charges for threatening behavior and racially and sexually aggravated assault, the other principals were:

CURTIS PEPPER: White male, somewhat shy of forty years old. Suit with interesting blue sheen, jacket short in the sleeves; untucked V-neck green T-shirt. Dark leather shoes, *no socks.* Ostensibly the chairman of the Human Resources Diversity and Equality Committee, but tends to lose control in the wake of his more forceful female associate.

BRANDON ABRAHAM: Black male, over fifty. Loosely fitting, unassuming gray suit with carelessly wound tie—but still, a tie. A few unimportant pounds overweight. Amenable expression, with difficulty meeting the defendant's eyes. Looks tired. Often steals glances at his watch.

TRINITY CHASE: White female, mid-thirties. Short, jagged hair, bleached white, which makes her look older. Not bad looking but squarely built; defies her sex's reputation for softness. Wearing disconcerting mismatch of clothing that seems to pass for trendy: long-sleeved velour turtleneck in bright cornflower blue, plaid track bottoms whose turquoise clashes with velour top, and untied platform tennis shoes. Tasteful nose piercing. Fiercely upright posture compromised by slight predatory lean toward the accused. Fiery but officious. Takes copious notes.

CURTIS: Now, before we get going, I'd just like to acknowledge to this committee that I'm a little embarrassed to have been designated the chairman—*chair,* sorry—because I'm painfully aware of representing the white patriarchy. At least I identify as bi, so I have some sensitivity to the issues confronted by marginalized communities, by dint of my sharing the LGBTQIA space. Still, as far as I'm concerned we're all three on the same level here. If anything, as a privileged white male I have way less right to speak, and I'm humbled by your comparatively more extreme encounters with imbalances of social power. Now. Remington—I can call you Remington?

REMINGTON: Given the indignity of this whole tribunal, being called by my first name is the least of my problems.

TRINITY: It's not a "tribunal," Mr. Alabaster. It's an informal hearing in which we'd like to hear your side of the story. I'm troubled that your attitude seems so adversarial. We're only interested in the truth.

CURTIS: You're aware that, uh . . . [*flapping of paper*] replacing high-pressure sodium street lighting with light-emitting diode technology could significantly reduce Albany's carbon footprint, thus mitigating climate change. You're also aware that, you know . . . despite high initial capital costs, conversion is also in the city's long-term economic interest.

REMINGTON: In that you're reading from the preface of *my own report*, I am obviously aware of these matters.

CURTIS: But according to Lucinda Okonkwo, who testified to this committee last week, you became resistant to the very project that she'd entrusted you with.

REMINGTON: Gary Neusbaum entrusted me with it, actually. But my so-called "resistance" to LEDs in general is a mischaracterization.

TRINITY: According to Ms. Okonkwo, your approach to the conversion was "obstructionist," your dealings with your superior on this issue were "oppositional," and your concern with the minutiae of implementation grew "unhealthily obsessive."

BRANDON: Like, Lucinda seems to think you saw a bunch of problems where she couldn't see how there were any. So you like, got on the wrong side of each other. I've seen how that can happen. It almost always gets worse and worse. Instead of talking out differences of opinion rationally, everything gets all personal. So nobody wants to back down, because any compromise would seem like surrender. That's how cases like this end up before this committee.

REMINGTON: But I didn't initially approach this conversion as a contest of wills, Mr. Abraham. I simply identified a range of issues that had given rise to protest, sometimes highly organized and vociferous protest, in other cities. I realized that all these objections could be headed off by choosing the right housing and fixture.

CURTIS: But according to Ms. Okonkwo, the products you recommended were too pricey. And much less energy efficient. Which would defeat the purpose of the conversion in the first place: to save both money and the environment.

REMINGTON: They were *slightly* more expensive, and *slightly* less efficient, which I documented in detail in my appendix. Amortized over the lifetime of the units, the *incrementally* higher cost and *minor* reduction in energy savings would be more than offset by a range of beneficial trade-offs.

TRINITY: According to Ms. Okonkwo, all you cared about was that the new lights were "pretty."

REMINGTON: That's a trivializing way of putting it. But yes, I did think the city should take into consideration the powerful aesthetic impact of public illumination. Blue-spectrum light has been strongly associated with depression—

TRINITY: Don't you think that *mood lighting* is an awfully middle-class, even elitist concern? Do the poor and marginalized communities of this city care first and foremost about appearances?

BRANDON: Hey, just because you're broke doesn't mean you have no feelings about what shit looks like.

TRINITY: Still, I said *first and foremost*—aren't the poor and marginalized more likely to care about the cost-effective use of their tax dollars?

REMINGTON: "The poor and marginalized" contribute very few tax dollars. Since for the lower income we're largely spending other people's money, I don't imagine they care about our economizing in the slightest.

"You shouldn't have said that," Serenata pointed out, pausing the recording at the horrified silence.

"But it's true," Remington said.

"That's why you shouldn't have said it."

CURTIS: You're not exactly doing yourself any favors here, Remington.

BRANDON: Come on, Curtis. Statistically, the guy's got a point.

TRINITY: We're not talking about statistics, Brandon. We're talking about attitude. Furthermore, the vulnerable communities for which you exhibit such contempt, Mr. Alabaster, are especially concerned with safety. So the street lighting Ms. Okonkwo preferred—

REMINGTON: Purchased. Flat out, with no consultation.

TRINITY: The lighting that she *purchased* is rated as extremely popular in high-crime neighborhoods, because their brightness makes residents feel safe.

REMINGTON: They *feel* safer—

TRINITY: You don't care about how vulnerable people feel?

REMINGTON: They are not, in fact, any safer—or any less *vulnerable*. As I documented in Appendix D, high-Kelvin-rated diodes have no correlation with a reduction of the real crime rate.

BRANDON: Can we just say you two disagreed, and get on with it?

CURTIS: So Remington—when you learned that Ms. Okonkwo—your superior, who after all was only obliged to consider your findings, but didn't necessarily have to take your advice—

REMINGTON: I believe Ms. Okonkwo only consulted the document that I delivered to her *three years ago* in order to do the exact opposite of what I recommended. At every point during her tenure, her decisions have been purely reactive. I may even have performed a useful service. Only her strict adherence to an oppositional formula—doing whatever I thought she shouldn't, and refusing to do whatever I thought she should—has rescued her management of our department from perfect chaos.

TRINITY: You seem to have a hostility problem, Mr. Alabaster.

REMINGTON: I do indeed, Ms. Chase. Ably observed.

BRANDON: [*muttering*] That Lucinda can be prickly.

Serenata stopped the recording again. "I'm just curious. That Curtis guy made a big deal about calling you 'Remington' and even asked your permission, and then this Trinity person keeps calling you 'Mr. Alabaster.' What's with that?"

"Huh. I didn't notice that at the time," Remington said. "But listening to it now? I think, conveniently, either choice is an insult. 'Remington' is presumptuously chummy, as if we're all friends here, which under the circumstances impugns my intelligence. 'Mr. Alabaster' is depersonalizing and artificially formal, now that in practice pretty much nobody in work situations uses titles and surnames. 'Mr. Alabaster' makes me sound older and fustier, but also accords the proceedings a judicially exalted texture at odds with the obvious:

the whole hearing is absurd. Interestingly, all those citations of 'Ms. Okonkwo,' by contrast, accord my so-called superior a reverence and respect that confers righteousness on the white members of the committee."

"Nicely parsed." Serenata tapped PLAY.

REMINGTON: If you want another example of this *reactive* principle of hers, take the restaging of traffic lights all over town—which I vehemently opposed. The entire network is now deliberately out of phase. You stop at one red light, only to stop at the next. And the next. Taxi drivers are livid.

BRANDON: Son of a bitch. Are you telling me that's on purpose? I swear, sitting at every intersection on Clinton Avenue adds ten minutes to my commute.

REMINGTON: All to "discourage car use."

CURTIS: Well, doesn't it?

REMINGTON: What it does is send idling through the roof, and all this stop-start driving exacerbates air pollution.

TRINITY: Unless the cars aren't there at all.

REMINGTON: Excuse me?

TRINITY: Unless Ms. Okonkwo is right, and motorists get so frustrated that they use other forms of transport.

REMINGTON: I've been in this department for over thirty years, and take it from me: frustrated drivers lean on their horns in the short term. In the long term, they vote out whole City Council administrations and replace them with elected officials who put the traffic-light phasing back the way it was.

CURTIS: Look, Remington, can we return to our central agenda, please? When Ms. Okonkwo told you about this LED purchasing order, what did you do?

REMINGTON: I slammed my hand on her desk.

CURTIS: And why did you do that?

REMINGTON: Because I lost my temper.

CURTIS: And would you say that you "slammed" the desk very hard?

REMINGTON: That is what the word *slammed* was meant to convey, yes.

CURTIS: And would you say that the sound your hand made was extremely loud?

REMINGTON: It was fairly loud.

CURTIS: And how did Ms. Okonkwo react?

REMINGTON: I think she was startled. *I* was startled. I very rarely lose my temper.

TRINITY: If you had it to do over again, Mr. Alabaster, would you have kept yourself under control?

REMINGTON: [*pause*] I'm not sure.

TRINITY: The consequences of this inappropriate behavior could be grave, Mr. Alabaster. And you're *not sure* that you wish you could take it back?

REMINGTON: It was a relief. I wouldn't make a habit of it. But expressing my feelings from the gut . . . As I said, it was a relief. And the gesture made my opinion of her capricious decision far clearer to Ms. Okonkwo than anything I might have said.

BRANDON: Any chance we could resolve this with a simple apology? Because it seems like this incident is getting blown up all out of proportion. So Alabaster here lost his rag. Would you be okay with telling Lucinda you're sorry, man?

REMINGTON: I'm not apologetic about my strenuous opposition to nearly all her policies. But on reflection, I suppose I am sorry that I gave into my anger, however briefly. Because in doing so I gave that young woman exactly what she wanted.

TRINITY: Due process-wise, I'm afraid we're well beyond making this all go away with a mere apology. Especially an insultingly insincere apology like that one.

CURTIS: According to Ms. Okonkwo, your dealings with her from the very beginning of her employment were "weirdly careful." Your exchanges were, she said, conspicuously "by the book." She says you were "pulled back, all inside himself, like he's looking at me from way far away." You seemed "more like some guy from England than a regular American." Does that description ring true to you?

REMINGTON: I have been careful. I wouldn't say "weirdly" so.

TRINITY: But why would you need to be careful?

REMINGTON: [*pause*] I sensed Ms. Okonkwo was on the lookout.

TRINITY: On the lookout for what?

REMINGTON: Just . . . on the lookout. I felt that whatever I did and said was being scrutinized. I sensed I should watch my step.

"You shouldn't have gone there," Serenata said.

"They took me there. And it didn't matter where we *went*," Remington said impatiently. "In a kangaroo court, the kangaroo can hop all around the edges of the cage, or even play dead. It doesn't matter. The kangaroo's fate is sealed."

CURTIS: So that would explain why Ms. Okonkwo described you as "wary" and "guarded" and "reticent" and tending to "speak only when spoken to."

REMINGTON: I tried to be cordial. I did sometimes make small talk about her family..But can you explain the purpose of this line of questioning, please?

CURTIS: Well, when people seem to be putting a whole lot of effort into controlling themselves, you can't help but wonder what all they're controlling.

TRINITY: Right. We can't help but wonder what exactly it was that you were so determined to keep from getting out. What disturbing things you might have done and said if you hadn't felt "scrutinized."

REMINGTON: Let me get this straight. You've hauled me before this committee because I *lost* control for two seconds. And now I am being raked over the coals because the rest of the time I *exercised* control?

CURTIS: Do you consider yourself a racist, Remington?

REMINGTON: No. Although I have yet to witness anyone declaiming about how they're not a racist without sounding like one.

CURTIS: And do you consider yourself a misogynist?

REMINGTON: I can't imagine how I could possibly be a "misogynist" and still have married a woman who's far smarter and more talented than I am.

"Flatterer," Serenata said. "You knew I'd be listening to this."

BRANDON: You should meet *my* wife, man. That woman makes me look like a genius. Folks think, if he's married to a lady that sharp, that guy must really have something going on.

CURTIS: And, Remington, do you have a problem with immigrants?

REMINGTON: Ms. Okonkwo was born in this country, and last I read that makes her an American and not an "immigrant." You can't have it both ways.

TRINITY: But is there any chance that some of the thoughts you've been so determined to stifle because you've felt "scrutinized" . . . Given all the post-9/11 anxieties about terrorism, well . . . When you look deep into yourself, might some of these dangerous thoughts you've suppressed qualify as Islamophobic?

REMINGTON: I fail to see the pertinence of your question.

TRINITY: I'm afraid it's all too pertinent. Since 2001, anti-Muslim hate crimes in this country have multiplied by several times. In this climate, you honestly believe your own attitudes haven't been influenced by the abuse, and the tarring with a single jihadist brush, that's all over social media and the internet—

REMINGTON: Ms. Chase, Lucinda Okonkwo and her whole family are Christians.

"Ha!" Serenata paused the recording at the discomfited silence. "They just assumed she was Muslim."

"It was another box their diversity hire was supposed to check," Remington said. "I'm sure they were grievously disappointed. About half of Nigeria is Christian, so their assumptions about Lucinda were supremely ignorant—although every time I flustered them, the worse I knew it would go for me."

REMINGTON: Listen, may I please speak freely?

CURTIS: I hope you *have* been speaking freely, Remington.

REMINGTON: Lucinda Okonkwo is belligerent, high-handed, and unqualified. She's also lazy. I don't think she's unintelligent, which makes her especially culpable.

TRINITY: And you don't think you're a racist.

REMINGTON: Her autocratic ordering of new streetlights for this entire city was typical—after no small-scale trial, no consultation with either the public or her own colleagues, and no consideration of my report, aside from the flip-through that would guarantee she selected the perfect opposite of the products that I recommended. I would submit that she resents my long tenure in this department, my consequent experience in matters about which she is poorly informed, and my academic credentials in this field—

TRINITY: Isn't the truth of the matter that *you* resent Ms. Okonkwo being given the job of department head four years ago, and not yourself?

BRANDON: She's got you there, bud. You had the seniority big-time. I'd have been resentful, in your position.

REMINGTON: Of course I resented it. But I'd never have held on to a sense of grievance if the new department head was skillful and dealt with his—or her—employees in a spirit of cooperation. I got on brilliantly with Gary Neusbaum for decades.

TRINITY: How surprising. Another aging straight white male.

REMINGTON: My point is, I dislike my immediate superior, I concede that, I do—but not because I'm racist, or sexist, or anti-immigrant. Not because I'm a whatever-ophobe. I dislike her *personally*. As an individual. Is that possible anymore? Is it legal to harbor animosity toward a specific person who just *happens* to belong to a "marginalized community"?

TRINITY: Prejudice often runs very deep, and thrives on an unconscious level. I don't know how you could possibly tell the difference between this so-called personal dislike and your own bigotry.

REMINGTON: So the answer is no. No, you cannot personally dislike anyone anymore.

TRINITY: The answer is that your so-called personal dislike is going to look suspicious to this committee.

CURTIS: I'm afraid we're going to have to focus here on the central charge of violent assault by a subordinate in the workplace.

REMINGTON: But I didn't touch her. How can you call that "violence"?

CURTIS: Your actions, as described, were violent.

REMINGTON: [*crackling, from disruption of mic*] According to the internet dictionary at the top of my Google search, *violence* means "behavior involving physical force intended to hurt, damage, or kill someone or something." I didn't even hurt her desk.

CURTIS: Well, that's the dictionary definition.

REMINGTON: I think I *said* it was the dictionary definition. And what other definition is there? I don't want to go all *Alice in Wonderland* on you, but words have to mean something in particular or there's no point in using language to communicate.

TRINITY: Your superior felt threatened. She feared for her physical well-being, and even feared for her life—

REMINGTON: You cannot be serious.

TRINITY: Threatening members of staff is grounds for dismissal.

REMINGTON: Just because she *felt* threatened doesn't mean she *was* threatened.

TRINITY: I'm afraid it means exactly that. You can't argue with what people feel.

REMINGTON: But just because she *told* you she felt threatened doesn't mean that she actually felt that way.

TRINITY: How else are we to learn how she felt other than by having her tell us? We can't do a Vulcan mind-meld. Feeling threatened was her lived experience.

REMINGTON: Excuse me, but what exactly is the difference between "lived experience" and "experience"?

BRANDON: Can we stay on the subject? This thing is running kind of late.

REMINGTON: Sorry, Mr. Abraham, but I think that is on the subject. That is, you people are following a script whose terms you didn't originate. Lockstep identikit vocabulary suggests a subscription to a rigid orthodoxy that is distorting the nature of this case.

TRINITY: Our frame of reference is progressive contemporary mores, and you seem to be clinging to the past, when you and other people like you always retained the upper hand. Well, times have changed.

REMINGTON: What has not changed—what has always been the case with human beings—is that "feelings" are no more factually sacrosanct than any other form of testimony. So you *can* "argue with what people feel." Because people lie about what they feel. They exaggerate what they feel. They describe what they feel poorly, sometimes out of sheer verbal inadequacy. They mistake one feeling for another. They often have *no idea* what they feel. They will sometimes mischaracterize their emotions with an eye to an ulterior motive—such as to slander a man who does indeed "threaten" them, but only with his comparative professional competence.

TRINITY: Are you saying that Ms. Okonkwo lied to us?

REMINGTON: I imagine she's been accurate about what happened. I doubt her veracity in regard to the texture of our encounter. I don't believe I frightened her. To the contrary, after having been trying to goad me to anger for years, I think she felt supremely satisfied.

TRINITY: She tells us she was frightened. How else are we to know how she felt?

REMINGTON: [*weakly*] But people lie about what they feel . . .

"Tell me this doesn't go round and round all day," Serenata said.

BRANDON: You know how I feel? I feel worn-out. I feel like we're getting nowhere, and we're going to be here till midnight.

REMINGTON: My apologies, Mr. Abraham, but what about how I feel? For example, I *feel* persecuted. Doesn't that mean, ipso facto, that I *am* being persecuted?

TRINITY: Mr. Alabaster, you're privileged. You hold all the cards in a stacked deck. You're an older straight white male who has attacked a young female-identifying person of color—

REMINGTON: Just as a point of information, whatever happened to "African-American"?

TRINITY: *Person of color* is HR's preferred term of art. *POC* is also acceptable.

REMINGTON: Don't you find this eternal merry-go-round of racial terminology a little humiliating? Surely there's an element here of making whitey dance.

[guffaw]

"Who laughed?" Serenata asked.

"Brandon," Remington said. "In fact, Brandon was the only one who *ever* laughed."

TRINITY: There's no need to be offensive, thank you.

REMINGTON: Honestly, Mr. Abraham. When you're around other *persons of color*, just you and the brothers, do you call each other *persons of color*? Or for that matter, even *African-American*?

BRANDON: What we say, just us, well—I can't repeat it here.

REMINGTON: See? This churn of euphemisms is solely for the crackers, and for interfacing with crackers. But do you notice how the word for *white* never changes? Even though it's broad-brush and genetically kitchen-sink. My whole life, *white* has simply sat there. Short, unhyphenated, inglorious, lowercase.

TRINITY: What of it? You're feeling neglected? You want some special new word? A capital letter? Why don't we uppercase White Nationalism, then? It's certainly on the rise. Would that make you happy?

REMINGTON: I simply meant—if we keep having to re-launder labels in order to rinse off the stigma that immediately re-attaches to the latest "term of art," the linguistic redress of racial prejudice obviously doesn't work.

BRANDON: I'm totally cool with "black" myself, if that helps. Can we get back on track here? My wife's waiting dinner.

REMINGTON: Fine, I agree, and I'm really sorry about the digressions, Mr. Abraham. But because this label appears to entirely invalidate *my* feelings, and also seems to translate into my having no rights whatsoever, can we look at this "privileged" business—?

TRINITY: Straight white men have had nothing *but* rights, so if it swings slightly the other way—

REMINGTON: [*plowing on*] Lucinda Okonkwo was privately educated at Horace Mann prep school. She went to Columbia and would have had to pay full tuition, because—well, I've asked her about her background, and she's quite proud of the fact that her father made a killing in the oil industry back home. In Lagos, the Okonkwos are upper crust—which she went out of her way to emphasize to me, in a spirit I can only characterize as one of *entitlement*. Her family now lives in an area of Manhattan that I could never afford, much less could my parents have afforded. I grew up in a cramped, grungy house off the beaten track in dumpy Hudson, New York. I was the first in my family to go to college. My father was a construction worker, and my mother cleaned fish. Who's really "privileged"?

TRINITY: Ms. Okonkwo has been subject to racial and gender-based discrimination of a sort you couldn't possibly imagine.

REMINGTON: But *you* can.

TRINITY: I've made it my life's work to try to imagine it, though I always defer to lived experience. Whatever her family's economic position, Ms. Okonkwo would have grown up subject to the discrimination—

REMINGTON: You don't call this show trial discrimination? We wouldn't be here if Lucinda had slammed a hand on *my* desk.

TRINITY: *Please.* She was subject to discrimination born of America's greatest crime against humanity, the mass enslavement of her people. In comparison to which your mother cleaning a few fish, Mr. Alabaster, is neither here nor there.

REMINGTON: Sorry to be niggling—can we use that word anymore, *niggling*? But Ms. Okonkwo's parentage is Nigerian. A full twelve percent of the slaves—

TRINITY: We prefer "enslaved people." They were not, in their essence—

REMINGTON: Twelve percent of the *enslaved people* exported to the United States were captured and sold *by Nigerians*. It was a joint effort. Now that we visit the sins of the fathers upon the sons—and daughters—that makes Lucinda one of the oppressors.

BRANDON: [*quietly*] You know they think they're better than us, don't you?

TRINITY: That was a breathtaking example of blaming the victim, Mr. Alabaster.

REMINGTON: You're aware that Ms. Okonkwo sued her last employer—I should say her last and *only* other employer—for racial bias?

TRINITY: That merely supports my point. Ms. Okonkwo would have been systematically—

REMINGTON: It demonstrates a pattern.

TRINITY: Two examples don't make a pattern.

REMINGTON: They do if you've hired such a young, inexperienced employee that two examples are all you've got. She sued a nonprofit, too, with meager resources, which settled out of court, and was subsequently obliged to fold.

CURTIS: I'd like to get back to the charges under consideration: threatening a member of staff, violent, potentially criminal assault, insubordination, intimidation—

REMINGTON: *Intimidation?* That's a stretch. In wrestling, that woman would get three-to-one odds against a weed like me.

TRINITY: So: not only are you a white supremacist—

REMINGTON: [*laughs*] Now it's *white supremacist*? Hyperbole is the red flag of a weak argument.

TRINITY: —And not only are you a misogynist, but you're a xenophobe who blames POCs for their own enslavement.

REMINGTON: While we're throwing around trendy pejoratives? I don't much like the word, but let's talk about *ageism*, then. This whole proceeding is designed to oust a dinosaur whose management seniority makes his salary burdensomely high for the city, isn't that right? Even better, if you fire me before I retire, you reduce my pension to peanuts. I should remind you that unfair dismissal of inconveniently older employees is illegal. The next hearing at which we meet, you folks could be the ones in the hot seat.

TRINITY: So being accused of a hate crime isn't enough for you? You're threatening this committee, too.

REMINGTON: [*raising his voice*] *Hate crime*? Is this the point at which Number One promises to send me to a Siberian re-education camp instead of having me executed, if only I confess—?

CURTIS: [*loud rap*] We really have to return to the core allegations, here!

[elongated pause]

REMINGTON: [*dryly*] I'd like it lodged in the record that Mr. Curtis Pepper just slammed his hand on the table.

[pause]

REMINGTON: I'm *terrified.*

[paper shuffling]

TRINITY: [*quietly*] Curtis, I think we've heard all we need to, don't you? Mr. Alabaster, you're excused.

[stacking of files on table, scraping of chair legs, fading rap of shoes]

BRANDON: [*under breath*] Hey, man. Sorry about all that. It seems like this whole thing got out of control. But they got their ducks in a row before I came on board. Don't think I don't know it, too: I'm just here to make the committee look good.

REMINGTON: [*also under breath*] Don't worry, I knew my goose was cooked before I walked in here.

BRANDON: That woman—she's a piece of work, she is.

REMINGTON: Trinity?

BRANDON: Her, too. But I mean *Lucinda.*

"That closing irony," Serenata said. "Will it help you?"

"It'll make things worse," Remington said. "I made them feel embarrassed, no one likes to feel embarrassed, so the level of hostility will only ramp up."

"If they do end up firing you—"

"I expect the letter to hit the franking machine by noon tomorrow."

"When it will be dark, presumably." Remington looked blank. "Arthur Koestler. You are in a funk. You don't even get your own allusions."

"I should never have alluded to Stalinism. The comparison was historically obscene. Fighting hyperbole with more hyperbole just lands you in the mud with the idiots."

"I thought you kept a grip pretty well, until the end. But by way of perfect payback, you could post this recording on YouTube. There's a constituency—if not necessarily the constituency you want—that would spread this like wildfire. And not to your HR department's advantage. Especially with the table thumping, you could make them a laughingstock."

Remington was old-school, and considered the ploy déclassé. Nevertheless, replaying choice segments became a dinner-party staple in the proceeding weeks, and the few close friends who rallied around found the inquisition hilarious. But the loss of Remington's salary wasn't funny, the drastic reduction of his pension wasn't funny, and the ignominy that attached to the range of prejudices of which he was accused wasn't funny, either—for in the febrile climate of the time, the only evidence required to certify you as a racist was that someone had called you one. More than one secondary friend and colleague withdrew from their acquaintance.

The couple stayed in Albany just long enough for the first tranche of Lucinda's top-Kelvin-rated streetlights to be installed. Her decision to convert the sodium lamps to LEDs first in her former subordinate's neighborhood of Pine Hills may have been no coincidence. The new fixture screamed through their bay windows, insinuating through every crack to score the carpet like a *Star Wars* light saber even after Serenata hung blackout curtains. It pierced the window over the front door, slapping a blaring square of blue-white on the opposing wall like an eviction notice. It seared through their bedroom's narrow wooden blinds and left parallel streaks on the bedspread, as if some predator had raked it with claws. Once the streetlights blazed into a whole second daytime after sunset, their leafy street looked like a prison yard, and skulking in and out of the house they felt watched. The area's inquisitional nocturnal character naturally recalled the HR grilling, and they put the house on the market after a few months. The brave march of technological advancement may have knocked a few thousand off the closing price, because nighttime viewings were so depressing. Return to Remington's hometown of Hudson was financially sensible and considerate of his failing father, but it wasn't where they'd imagined they'd retire—if they'd ever imagined retiring at all, which, like most permanently young people, they hadn't.

Thus in the wake of his dismissal, Serenata's husband felt insulted, humiliated, and unmanned. He felt punished all out of proportion to his "crime," and unappreciated for over thirty years of dedicated service to the city of Albany. He was footloose. Having expected to spend up to ten more years applying a lifetime's expertise to his calling, he was disappointed. He felt ashamed of himself, and doubly ashamed of himself for feeling ashamed of himself. He craved self-respect, but was now ousted from the very arena in which he had always earned it. Early retirement made him feel old. As Serenata had tried to explain to his father, he had too little to look forward to, and had no idea how to navigate the decades that might or might not lie before him in the absence of tangible goals. Walking it back, his indoctrination was inevitable. He couldn't have made a more perfect target for MettleMan.

SEVEN

"You do realize that organized endurance sport is an industry," Serenata idly observed while making dinner later that summer.

"Soft drinks are an industry," Remington said. "We still buy Poland Spring soda water."

"Your spiritual aspirations are being taken advantage of."

"Poland Spring takes advantage of our thirst. Why shouldn't MettleMan capitalize on my other thirsts? Someone might as well."

"Because the money they make off your psychic dehydration is money we can't easily spare."

"Our children are grave disappointments, which relieves us of any obligation to provide them an inheritance. We're old. There is no future. That makes me feel free."

"It makes you feel panicked. Besides. We could live thirty more years."

"Look at my father," he said. "I don't want to."

"That's easy to say."

"That's right," he agreed. "It's very, very easy to say."

"Am I to infer that you intend this undertaking to be a form of suicide?" she asked lightly. "Because I'd count that as abandonment."

The better to one-up a competing franchise, MettleMan boosted the distances of its epic triathlon an increment over previously established standards: not a 2.4- but a 2.6-mile swim; not a 112- but a 116-mile cycle; not a 26.2- but a 26.4-mile run—one feat after the other, with nothing but a frantic change into suitable clothing between events. (Even the original distances seemed perversely specific. What was wrong with swimming *two* miles or cycling *one hundred*?) Making the ordeal closer to a quadrathlon, the cherry on this sundae of insanity was a single chin-up on the finish line—a modest enough exploit you would think, yet a final exertion rumored as the great bridge too far for any number of contestants, especially women, who would sometimes collapse under the bar in tears now that no MC would call out on the loudspeakers, "You are . . . MettleMan!", and they'd not get their fluorescent-orange trophy mug.

Serenata had never been wowed by marathoners, even if confidence that she could have conquered that distance in her heyday was undermined by never having conquered it in practice. For years, a two-mile swim had been routine. Ditto cycling a century, which she'd exceeded countless times in her twenties, when to visit a friend in Woodstock she'd saddle up and hit the George Washington Bridge pedestrian walkway, if only to save money on bus fare.

Yet after a two-mile swim, she always lay flat on the deck for twenty minutes, perfectly inert, every muscle spent. Even after a plain old ten-mile run, she'd often faded off with Remington that evening, eyelids heavy over the main course. As for cycling over a hundred miles, it had always filled her with an hysterical obsession with dinner. Once when she'd clocked the requisite distance after a late start toward Amherst, only to find herself in a rare commercial desert in Connecticut—no restaurants, fast-food outlets, or mini-marts—she'd sullenly set up camp in a roadside wood, gnawing the stale half onion roll and the remains of her peanut butter from lunch with a fury that would have driven a sizable generator.

One by one, then, each feat seemed achievable. All three without pause seemed both flagrantly impossible and mentally ill. Tommy was right: people who exercised less than you were pathetic; people who exercised more than you were nuts. Doubtful that even at her strongest she'd have been up to a MettleMan, she couldn't trust her contempt for it. In the face of her husband's deranged aspiration, she was horrified, intimidated, and completely outclassed. Ergo, she had to keep her mouth shut.

According to Bambi—and Remington's whole catechism was now *according to Bambi*—one trained for a "full Mettle" a minimum of nine months. The client for whom the trainer successfully trawled in Saratoga Springs in April would never have gotten up to speed in time for the annual northeastern MettleMan in Lake Placid two months later. So Remington had set his sights on June of the following year.

That was a long time to keep your mouth shut.

Little matter, since the clamor that descended on their household when Remington returned from training with the rest of his tri club—that's right, there was such a thing as a *tri club*, and enough fitness fanatics even in tiny Hudson, New York, to fill out the membership—she rarely got a word in edgewise.

Remington was the more gregarious spouse, long accustomed to the society of the workplace, without which he felt cut off. Joining the Hudson Tri Club restored that sense of shared mission. As the oldest by twenty-five years, he gave the younger athletes hope for their futures while never threatening to overtake them on a bike. Paying his dues with casual self-deprecation, he took gladly to his role as token geezer, and in short order became something of a mascot. Like the rest of the club, he joined BruteBody, to which Remington often repaired for hours, presumably clanking through strength-building sets, but also shooting the breeze and chugging energy drinks with his newfound soul mates.

Serenata did not, strictly speaking, hate them, or she didn't hate them all. But she did hate them as an aggregate, and as an invading army. They'd taken to calling her "Sera," which however you spelled it sounded like "Sarah," and that was not her name. Even the cheerful, improbably overweight Cherry DeVries, who really *was* a housewife, treated her like The Wife. Whenever the crew descended, histrionically tired, Serenata was expected to hang jackets, fetch drinks, and knock up impromptu suppers. True, she might have retreated upstairs. But Remington was living more and more of his life away from her. Mutely distributing rounds of G&Ts like some barmaid was worth the abasement to spy.

For who led this ragtag band of second-string superheroes? Who set the distance and sport for the day and charted the course? Who was their inspiration, their savior, and their taskmaster, both feared and revered, if not idolized?

"Are you sure she knows what she's doing?" Serenata finally asked her husband, when his pounding onward on that sore hamstring had not—surprise—allowed it to heal.

"Obviously. Look at her."

"Yes, I've noticed you doing that rather a lot. Just checking her qualifications?"

"You and I are physically faithful, but we're allowed to window-shop. And these days, it's a relief to find one woman who enjoys being looked at—"

"And how," Serenata muttered.

"The 'male gaze' is supposedly an insult. But Bambi would only be insulted if men looked away. Her body's her calling card. It's also her creation, her artwork."

"I don't see *art*. I see maniacal self-involvement. I see spending hours and hours in the gym, every day, and rarely doing much else."

"That's her job."

"It's a dopy job."

"Nothing stops you from joining BruteBody and developing your forearm flexors, if hers make you that jealous."

"I have a real career. I've put some effort into not falling completely apart, but it's a sideline. I try to maintain a sense of proportion."

Or so she claimed. Yet Serenata had grown convinced that this cultivation of the body to the exclusion of all else had somehow sprouted from her own original sin. Was she not always asserting, however tongue-in-cheek, that the rest of the world was "copying her"? So her ten-mile teeming along the river had tracked the seeds of fitness fundamentalism into the house. She couldn't discourage her husband without sounding like a hypocrite. She'd created a monster.

"My trainer believes in me."

"You buy her belief in you. Stop paying that $1,200 monthly retainer, and just see how long her faith in your prowess lasts."

Although Serenata was pretty good at divining what made people tick, Bambi Buffer's motives remained elusive. Obviously the woman wanted the money. Few amateurs in this mildly depressed small town would be able to afford a retainer that size. Why, their household couldn't afford it, either. But even a well-paid trainer wasn't obliged to drop by a client's house five times a week, to prop her feet on an opposite chair and smooth a palm along the hard hillocks of her quadriceps, or to reward his occasional quip with a deep-throated laugh incommensurate with the modest joke. In her doting there seemed, if not an element of the maternal, at least one of possession. Remington had become *her creature.*

Crushingly, too: ever since the spontaneous lesson on marathon day, Serenata had been teaching Tommy March to swim at the Y. Like most adults who never mastered this crucial survival skill as kids, Tommy had freaked out the moment she couldn't touch the bottom of the pool. Easing the girl past that primitive terror had been psychologically interesting, since giving into panic invited exactly what you were afraid of, and the experience of near drowning reinforced the fear. The key turned out to be the soothing lower tones of Serenata's voice, which could induce a state close to hypnosis. Thus by July, the stalky girl had blossomed into an aquatic natural. Her instructor's reward? In August, Tommy joined the tri club.

Remington's long absences allowed Serenata plenty of solitude for catching up on voice-over work. But it was one thing to be left alone, another to feel left out. Rather than get lost in a script, she'd check the computer clock too often. Unsettled, she'd stop the recording to drift downstairs and fail to remember what she'd come down for.

When it was time to exercise, the ritual dread had grown more intense. It was bad enough that running no longer got her out of the house. It was bad enough that biking was blighted by bevies of zealous "fellow" cyclists. It was bad enough, too, that the pool at the Y was forever churning with members of the tri club, whose self-importance could put her off her laps the way a waft from a restaurant toilet could put you off your meal. But now the home calisthenics she'd substituted for all that *motion of the body through space* would not only be tedious; they also felt measly. Compared to the *tri club*'s, her workouts were a joke. This dwarfing was so disagreeable that she was sometimes tempted to skip exercise altogether. But she refused to let these maniacs control her.

Thus on a bright late Saturday afternoon in early September, Serenata duly undertook her high-intensity interval training, trying to put out of mind that at the same time Remington's tri club was feverishly cycling seventy miles cross-country. She took care to stay on the cushioning double layer of fluffy bath mats, to raise her knees all the way to her waist, to maintain a ramped-up pace whose rhythm clashed with the recurring intro soundtrack of back-to-back *Big Bang Theory*, to quell her irritation when the bath mats constantly separated, and to determinedly ignore the building inflammation in her right knee. With fifteen repetitions of a thousand steps, and one hundred cool-down paces between each set, her high-knees running in place lasted one hour and fifty-eight minutes—and still felt paltry.

When she had four sets to go, voices sounded at the side door. As the rabble downstairs grew louder, she upped the tempo, rushing to join the party. Funny how a crowd you wanted no part of could still make you feel excluded.

Entering the roomy, rustic kitchen at last, Serenata found the tri club all in Lycra—which did Cherry DeVries no favors. She wasn't obese, but looser fitting sportswear would have been kinder, and she'd bought aspirational shorts a size too small. By contrast, Tommy's secondhand gear was overlarge and fatigued, and she kept pulling her waistband up and tugging gathered fabric down her thighs. Universally unbecoming, cycling shorts having ever come into fashion was inscrutable.

Mind, the style was *almost* universally unbecoming. On Bambi Buffer, the sleek shorts in sunny yellow conformed to her sharp hip bones, across which a yardstick could have balanced without touching flesh in between. They showed off her ass as hard and high. Each buttock shadowed when she took a step and the glutes contracted. A sleeveless V-neck, her tight powder-blue vest zipped up the front, pressing breasts the better part pectoral muscle into a semblance of cleavage. She'd burnished a smashing summer tan. Sun had lightened her tawny hair, its close boyish cut recently trimmed.

"I can't tell you what a relief it is to no longer be the only woman in this club," Cherry confided to Tommy. "That ride has set my you-know-where just raging. Yeast infection. The guys wouldn't understand."

"Hey, whadda ya mean, you've been the 'only woman'?" Bambi said, pulling a bottle of red wine from the rack. Another sat empty on the counter.

"You don't count, Bam-Bam. Whatever you are, plain old 'woman' ain't it." Lanky, about forty, and the club's sole MettleMan veteran other than their Dear Leader, Sloan Wallace had two identical double-*M* tattoos on his right bicep: four peaks of adjacent orange, like a child's drawing of a mountain range. If you didn't recognize the signage, you weren't an initiate but a slob.

"Think about getting a wider seat, Cherry," Bambi said, popping the cork.

"Or let me take a look at the height and tilt." Chet Mason was the club's technocrat. "The bones of your ass should hit the back of the seat. You may be sitting too far forward on the tongue—"

"Whoa, baby!" cried Hank Timmerman, the sleazebag. "Sounds like some happy ride!"

Remington pecked his wife's cheek distractedly. "Hey, we have any snacks? Everybody's starving."

These convocations now frequent, Serenata had begrudgingly laid in crackling bags of solidified palm oil. The crunchy crap would be just the beginning.

Bambi nodded at Serenata's ratty cotton shorts. "Had your own little home workout?" She was prone to address The Wife at a perpendicular, throwing the odd lazy looping side-glance, as if underhanding a softball.

"Yeah, you know, one of those Jane Fonda videos," Serenata said. "I know she's pushing eighty, but I still can't keep up with her. And I find getting sweaty kind of icky."

"Sweat's the Chanel of tri, honey," Bambi said coolly, taking an inattentive gulp from a juice glass. She'd managed to locate their last bottle of pricey Napa syrah.

"Bam-Bam gets extra Kettle chips," Sloan said, "after all that doubling back to check on Rem. Rest of us did seventy; add the babysitting, I bet Bam put in one-forty."

"You do realize I'm riding the brake," Remington said genially. "Just so Bambi gets a proper workout."

"You really shouldn't feed the beast," Sloan said. "Bam's being a glutton for punishment is still greed of a kind."

"You should consider replacing that clunker, Rem," Chet recommended. "Titanium tri bikes are so fucking frictionless that the biggest problem is falling asleep."

In contrast to Serenata's battered warhorse, circa 1991, Remington's $1,300 "clunker" was only five months old.

"Rem says you've biked a bit yourself?" Bambi asked as their hostess fetched Sloan another beer.

"Here and there." Vulgar submission of an athletic CV was out of the question.

"At your age, Sera, you might consider an e-bike," Bambi suggested. "I recommend plug-in models to older clients all the time. Keeps them on the road, even with, you know—bum joints."

"Yes, I've considered one of those," Serenata said brightly. "But it seems more cost efficient to go straight to the mobility scooter."

She retreated to the women by the stove.

"You don't have to make supper for this crowd every time," Cherry said. "We could always order takeout."

"Oh, pasta's no big deal," Serenata said, pulling out their largest pot. Having tried the takeout option, she knew the drill: getting everyone's orders straight was exhausting, and she and Remington would get stuck with the bill.

"What do you want me to chop?" Tommy offered, jumping up.

"Aren't you tired?"

"Some," she allowed, then lowered her voice. "Fucking Sloan is always showing off in the lead, and I just . . . Twenty-five *m-p-h*, steady? And twenty uphill? I can't keep it up. Then I fall back, and feel like a girl."

"Don't tell anyone, but you are a girl," Serenata whispered. "If you're going to participate in a mixed athletic club, cut yourself some slack."

"But aren't *you* tired?" Tommy solicited as Serenata filled the pot with water. "I heard you upstairs when we got here. HIT is a killer."

"Yes, but unlike some people I think that's my business. Here. Parsley."

As the three women did what women almost always ended up doing, the men defaulted to a stock sport: razzing their absent member Ethan Crick for having begged off the afternoon's cycle training at the last minute.

"So what was Crick's excuse this time?" Hank said.

"Stubbed his toe," Sloan supposed. "Swelled up something awful, and wouldn't fit in his bike shoe."

"He's been shaving his legs to decrease his wind resistance," Remington said, "and now he has ingrown hairs."

"He did fwee cwunches wivout AC," Hank lisped, "and cowapsed fwum heat stwoke."

"Oh, it was a ton more creative than that. You know Ethan," Bambi said. "Something about how this particular back muscle knots, so that whenever he turns his head a paralyzing pain shoots up his neck. That bozo never just has a headache."

"But I know what he means," Serenata said, stemming cherry tomatoes. "From hunching for hours over the handlebars, a shoulder muscle cramps and pinches a nerve. The pain goes straight up the back of your neck, and it feels like a bee sting."

"Funny," Bambi said reluctantly. "That's what Ethan said. 'Like a bee sting.'"

Serenata should have stayed out of it, but this hacking on Ethan Crick had become an ugly club dependency, because it made them feel hardier by comparison. She was relieved that Remington had escaped being the club's punching bag. Nevertheless, this mild-mannered ophthalmologist was the only member of the tri club who resisted Bambi's defiant approach to injury. He'd no desire to wreck his body in the process of perfecting it. Yet Ethan's proclivity for moderation might indeed have ill-suited him to MettleMan, whose website claimed that moderation was for chumps.

"Weekend after weekend," Sloan said, "Crick is getting just the practice he needs. He's a DNF in training."

"What's a DNF?" Serenata asked.

They recited in unison with melodramatic horror, "*Did Not Finish.*"

"I've heard more than one MettleMan DNF has actually offed himself," Sloan said. "Talk about double loser."

Bambi clapped Remington's shoulder. "Mind you, now! Not one of my clients has ever DNF'ed. You finish, or I don't let you start. Sloan's right. I seen folks' spirits crushed for life—*for life*—by staggering to that chin-up bar after midnight."

"That's when the race always cuts off?" Serenata asked.

"Like Cinderella," Bambi said. "*Bong-bong-bong*, riches to rags."

"I think quitters should be branded," Chet said. "Sizzle it right on the ass with a hot iron: '*D-N-F.*' Which also stands for 'Disgraced Numb-nuts Fuck-up.' "

In his mid-twenties and perpetually gung-ho, with puppy-dog eyes and floppy brown hair, Chet was a local kid who'd gone to some community college, studying one of those broad, bland subjects like media studies that left you in much the same place as before you enrolled. He was now a barista at a Hudson internet café, and still living at home. A gym junkie, he'd developed a bunchy, constricted physique that wasn't altogether fetching. Lately he'd latched on to the idea of becoming a triathlon pro. He certainly seemed to have the chops. Still, with these events now attracting participants in the tens if not hundreds of thousands, no big commercial sports company was likely to shell out gear, expenses, and a stipend for a male triathlete who was barely five-foot-eight.

Sloan Wallace was the one who looked the part. Leggy, lean, and languorous, he must have been at least six-three. But Serenata couldn't imagine Sloan going up against an intimidating elite for Nike sponsorship. He was a small-pond competitor, who after ditching the scramble of Wall Street had moved up to Hudson to start a second life renovating classic cars. He appeared to be good at it and eked out a living preying on the adolescent ambitions of retirees with capital. In a one-horse town like this, he attracted the awe of younger provincials, who all thought re-chroming the grille of a 1957 Pontiac Bonneville was the coolest job ever. Sloan had cachet in these parts, and his suave, syrupy bearing made him a magnet for women. Naturally he was divorced—he was the sort of man always looking to trade up—and in the world of endurance sport, his brazen braggadocio was an asset.

"So are your kids really into your tri thing?" Tommy asked Cherry over broccoli. "Or are they all like, 'Where's my dinner?'"

"Oh, the kids are super supportive," Cherry said. "When I come back from training, they bring me pillows and herbal tea."

"What about your husband?"

Cherry paused the paring knife over a floret. "I guess Sarge is another story."

"Why's he down on the idea?"

"He thinks it's ridiculous, to be honest. Not triathlons, but the idea of my doing one. He thinks I'm only trying to lose weight. He thinks I don't have a chance in heck of finishing, so I'm only setting myself up for a fall. Then I'll comfort eat and only get fatter."

"*Are* you trying to lose weight?"

"Well, sure. But that's not the only reason I'm doing this. We got married pretty young—even if we didn't think we were young, you know how that is, or you will in a few years. I tended a grocery store till after high school, but I've never had a real job, because I got pregnant right away—which is fine, of course, I love Deedee to bits. But I want something, you know, to be proud of. I'm proud of all three of my children, but they're not my personal accomplishments. They're people, and they're their own accomplishments. Sarge has the antiques shop, and though it's been through some tough times, he can still say he's made a go of a business. I want to be able to say I've done something, too."

"Are you hoping to, like—show Sarge?" Tommy asked. "That he's underestimated you?"

"Better believe it! Though I'm worried that if I ever do become a triathlete, well—that it'll just make him mad."

"Is he mad already?"

"Yeah. He's pretty mad. He thinks I'm out-guying him—if that's a word."

"If it isn't, it should be," Remington chimed in, while searching out another bottle of red. "The women are *manning up*, and the boys all want to wear dresses."

"They can have 'em!" Cherry said. "I'd rather have breathable spandex."

Serenata had once supposed that during training surely Cherry DeVries kept Remington company at the back. He said no—Cherry maintained a position solidly in the middle of the pack. The assumption that a heavy woman would lag exhibited a certain prejudice, but mass had to have been a disadvantage—exaggerating her drag in water, increasing the pull of gravity on a bike, and forcing her to propel more weight on a run. If she kept up with Tommy, Cherry was the more impressive athlete.

Serenata threw herself into parboiling the broccoli and dissolving anchovies in hot olive oil, all the while telling herself that no one had forced her to make this meal, and nothing was more unbearable than people who freely elected to do something and then turned around and resented the imposition. But after the interval training, the right knee was yowling. The worst possible activity for these joints wasn't walking or running but *standing*—also known as *cooking*. Fetching snacks, refilling drinks, and initiating supper for eight, she'd been on her feet for three hours. Slicing olives, she rested all her weight on the left leg. Unused, the right knee stiffened, and crossing the room to salt the pasta water she had to haul the bum leg straight. As Bambi stretched out at the dining table and crossed her legs prettily at her slender ankles—she'd had the presence to bring flattering ballet flats to change into—Serenata noted that her own knees had puffed up again. The swelling had spread to her lower thighs, creating an unpleasantly tubular effect. Since childhood, her legs had been her finest feature. In the end, she lurched to a drawer for a longer apron, not to protect her shabby sports clothes from anchovy grease but to conceal her *finest feature* from the tri club's critical gaze, including the appraising eye of her husband.

"You're limping," Tommy whispered.

"In that I'm the one doing the limping," Serenata snapped, "why do you think I need to be *informed* of that?"

Tommy looked as if she might cry. She was only twenty years old. Surrounded by prospective antagonists, you didn't take out your frustrations on your only ally.

Serenata quickly laid a hand on Tommy's arm. "I'm sorry. Thank you for noticing. You're the only one who does."

"Have you scheduled the surgery yet?" Tommy asked sternly.

"No." Serenata turned back to the olives. She should never have bought the kind with pits.

"Why not?"

"I'm managing."

"You're not managing. They're only getting worse. You keep exercising on them every day, and then afterward you can hardly walk."

"I don't want to get knee replacements. People say online you'd better get both done at once, because when you find out how awful it is, you'll never do the other one."

"It's not like you can wait till you're in the mood. You'll never be in the mood. At some point you won't be able to exercise at all, and then you'll be sorry."

"I'm already sorry. I've seen pictures of the scars. They're hideous."

"Scars? Who cares. You're getting old. You're being a little princess."

"I won't be lectured by a whippersnapper."

"The *whippersnapper*'s riding you 'cause nobody else is, far as I can see. Why doesn't Remington notice you limping? Why doesn't Remington mash a phone in your hand and make you fix a date?"

"Because Remington doesn't care about anything to do with *me* anymore." The words were out before Serenata could stop them. She'd barely rescued herself from announcing more starkly still, *Because Remington doesn't care about me anymore.*

"But he's your husband." Tommy sounded bewildered.

Serenata smiled tightly. "We are specializing in statements of the obvious tonight. I just meant, he's not thinking about my problems right now. If you're ever in a long-term marriage, you'll find out: spouses drift. It doesn't mean they're cheating or anything. Their attention wanders. And then it comes back."

Tommy looked skeptical. Serenata didn't find this version of events persuasive herself. Rattled, she dumped three pounds of rotelli in the pot, though the water hadn't quite come to a rolling boil—much like the unease in her marriage.

This time when they settled down to dinner, Serenata placed her wineglass firmly next to Remington's usual chair at the end of the long, planked table. That didn't prevent you-know-who from taking the chair at his other elbow, but at least she'd not be exiled at the opposite end with Hank, who'd been hitting the G&Ts and was getting wasted.

"Check out the commuters chugging around town," Bambi said after the pasta had been demolished, touching Remington's slender wrist. "They most always go *choom-choom-choom*—pressing heavy on the downstroke, then letting up on the upstroke. But what you want is a smooth, steady application of force. Remember to pull up on the cleat. You don't want variable surges of power."

It was a wonder that the average schoolchild mastered riding a bike at six, given that operating the mechanism was so terribly complicated.

Serenata had remained quiet throughout the meal, while Chet got excited about brands of wet suits, Cherry confided her embarrassing incontinence on long runs, and Bambi chided Hank to stop teeming ahead and then blowing out too early. Passivity was as enervating as the conversation, so at last Serenata put a hand in.

"I wonder," she said carefully, "if a lot of older people are able to take part in endurance sports because they weren't especially active when they were young."

Bambi looked up sharply. "How do you figure that? Sitting on your butt being the best preparation for getting off it."

"I talked to some elderly marathoners in Saratoga Springs," Serenata said. "Every single one discovered exercise in their fifties or even sixties, like Remington."

"That's not surprising," Bambi said. "It's an era thing. This is a movement, sweeping across the country, and pretty soon we're gonna see a whole super race—"

"Social trends are part of it. But maybe what makes it possible to demand so much from an aging body is that you haven't already worn it out."

"Exercise don't wear you out, honey. It builds you up."

"Only up to a point," Serenata said. "The body is a mechanism, with moving parts that degrade from use. Some of those parts break down, like the parts of a car if you drive it too far."

"The body's an organism, not a machine," Bambi said. "It thrives from being stressed. The more you ask, the more you get. Maybe you never asked enough."

"Oh, Serenata's asked plenty," Remington intervened. His defense was touching, but Bambi ignored it.

"There are limits," Serenata said.

"That has to be the most suck-dick motto I ever heard. How about, *Fuck limits.* Limits are all in your head. See, this is what I was warning you about, Rem."

"Negative thinking," Remington said.

"All this, *oh, he's gonna wear out like a car.* It's fear-based. But I guess that's the kind of mind-set you get when you make a living from talk."

"That's me," Serenata said. "Blah-blah-blah."

"My wife is an accomplished voice-over artist." Remington pressed his trainer's arm with a forefinger. "I told you to watch that."

"Bambi's right about limits, though," Cherry said. "At first, I didn't think I could run to the end of the block. But I've been plumb dumbfounded what it turns out I can do! You have to keep telling yourself not to be a little baby."

"But sometimes that 'little baby,'" Serenata said, "might be aware that you're damaging yourself, that you're overdoing it."

Tommy grinned. "Bambi doesn't believe there's such a thing as overdoing it."

"But the vogue for extreme sports is pretty recent," Serenata said. "Is there any research on what happens to people who keep at it year after year? For decades?"

"Planning to find out!" Chet said down the table. "By Rem's age, I'll be tri-ing to the moon!"

"Either that or you'll be wheeled around on a gurney with a tube down your throat," Serenata said sweetly. "That's the question."

"I learned a hip word from Rem the other day," Bambi said. "You know your hub's pretty smart?"

"After thirty-three years, I might have noticed that."

"*Catastrophizing*," Bambi pronounced with relish. "That's what you're doing, and it's corrupting my client. *Catastrophize*, and you can wreck all my hard work."

"I thought it was Remington's hard work."

"Joint effort, hon. This crew builds muscle as a team. And know what the most important muscle is? Not the glutes, not the quads, but the mind. Familiar with that expression 'muscle-head'? Supposed to be an insult. It ain't. Your mind *is* a muscle, and your hub's brain, with a little help from his friends, is getting big and hard."

"With a certain ass in the saddle out front," Hank said, "it's not only his brain getting big and hard."

"When I was in high school," Serenata said, turning a blind eye to the juvenile trash talk, "the jocks were considered the morons. Now that the educated class has discovered athletics, suddenly sport requires vast cognitive powers."

"You can overthink tri, no question," Bambi said. "But smarts is still an advantage. Rem here has met his distance, every single time. He's a little slower than the rest of us—"

"You're overgenerous," Remington said. "I'm a lot slower."

"But this guy, he's never once set out to finish a certain number of miles and stopped short. You *are* aware of that?"

"Sure," Serenata said casually. In truth, she was not aware of this.

Bambi clapped Remington's shoulder again; it was a habit. "You got the determination. I can coach technique, I can design you a sked, but the *ferocity* got to be there from the start."

"Some forms of determination are dangerous," Serenata said.

With a guffaw, Bambi poured herself another glass of red, then topped up Remington's to the rim. Should Serenata want a refresher, too, she'd have to open another bottle. "You are a trip and a half, sunshine. I got half a mind to print that on our club T-shirts: SOME FORMS OF DETERMINATION ARE DANGEROUS."

Serenata clarified, "I'm not happy about that hamstring."

"You and Crick," Bambi said. "Worrywarts in a pod."

At the other end of the table, Chet was talking up his future as a tri pro to Sloan. "Once you start pulling in the sponsors, they give you all this free stuff! Running shoes, bike shorts, swimming goggles, you name it! And especially if you land a title or two, some of these deals include a serious whack of cash. So I've got my eye on one of your muscle cars. Kind of appropriate, right? Like that 1964 GTO."

"I shouldn't be telling you this," Sloan said tolerantly; no way did that man believe Chet would ever make pro. "But mechanically, that GTO is shit. You'd be way better off with the '67."

"Chet," Serenata said, "do you have any backup ambition? A plan B? Because even if you do go pro, it must be hard to maintain peak performance at such a grueling sport for more than a few years."

Bambi slammed the table hard enough that at the DOT she'd have been fired. "Sweetie pie, you generate more clouds of doom than a fog machine in the movies. It must be so dismal in your head, I don't know how you get out of bed."

"Plan Bs are for suckers," Chet said. "A backup would be planning for failure."

"Yeah, you're not supposed to let those thoughts into your mind,"

Tommy agreed. "Like that MettleMan bumper sticker I put on my bedstead: DOUBT NOT."

"Has a biblical ring to it," Serenata said. "Like Moses."

"If that's your idea of ridicule," Bambi said, "you're gonna have to make more of an effort. Tri is a belief system, all right. But the belief is in yourself."

"But if *all* you believe in is yourself," Serenata said, "isn't that on the slight side? It sounds awfully like egotism. If nothing else, it sounds lonely."

"Look around you," Bambi said. "We're among plenty of friends. You're the one sounds lonely."

Serenata pulled up short. She did feel lonely.

"Tri's been my salvation, man." Hank had passed through the raucous phase of inebriation, and had progressed to the maudlin one. Cherry having extricated herself from his arm around her by at least pretending to need the bathroom, he'd now draped himself over Chet.

If Cherry was unfeasibly heavy for endurance sport, Hank was unfeasibly gaunt. His jagged black locks always looked unwashed. His stick-thin limbs were covered in straggles of disagreeable dark hair. He was still pale in early September. His expressions ranged from leering to desperate. Perhaps twenty-eight, he'd been imprisoned for possession at least once.

"When I was inside, the only thing kept me sane was the weights room," Hank went on. "I promised myself this time when I got out I'd keep it up, right? I wouldn't make bad decisions. I'd realize I had an illness, right? And the illness is inside me, but I'm not actually the illness, right? So first thing on release I joined BruteBody on one of them one-month free trials. They kept telling me in the joint that I had to believe it was possible to change, or I could be a danger to myself. Sure enough, it wasn't much more than a week of going to the gym every day when I start to spot the warning signs. Racing thoughts. Intrusive thoughts. Basically, I just couldn't stop thinking about scag. I knew I was right on the edge of scoring. And that's when Bambi rescued me, man. Instead of copping a bag, I find myself out on this run with her, man. And I look back now and think it's funny, since I bet it wasn't longer than five miles or even less, but it seemed like *forever,* man. Like it just about killed me. But now I can go twelve, even fifteen, no problem, right? I got something to live for. I'm not addicted to scag, I'm addicted to going out there and fucking killing myself, man, on the road and in the pool. It's a totally different high, a clean high. So I got to thank you guys, right? I'm gonna tri, tri, tri, tri, over and over again, man."

Serenata had heard this testimonial before. The tuneful *tri, tri, tri, tri* recalled Nancee's "*joy, joy, joy, joy* down in my heart!" on the trip to Saratoga Springs.

Tommy joined Cherry in volunteering to help clean up.

"For ten bucks an hour?" Serenata's wisecrack came out doleful.

"Nah," Tommy said. "For you? Seven-fifty."

The removal of dishes cleared space for Bambi and Remington to arm wrestle. Even after all that red wine, Bambi would have little trouble winning the day, though she kept her opponent's arm straight up for long enough to ensure that the older man saved face. Besides, the pressure he applied brought out the dazzling definition of her bicep.

Serenata watched unresponsively with her chair pulled back from the table, though she felt a great deal farther away than that. On the occasions she and Remington had asked people to dinner in times past, the biggest problem had been entering into a rapid, playful back-and-forth that excluded their guests, because the couple never managed to invite anyone they wanted to talk to more than to each other. Equally alienating for visitors who just wanted to move on to the cheese course, they would wrestle for too long over a point neither would concede, just as these two were going at it now—albeit with a literalism that Remington of old would have considered crass.

The rest of the club was cheering and hooting, and the other three men lined up to be next. When Bambi lowered Remington's arm, she didn't bang it, but arced it gracefully to the wood with a hint of sorrow. You'd think that a husband would be glad of being well matched, for rhetorically their marriage was a draw. But maybe he was one of those curious men who found it more erotic to be beaten.

Hank was up next, and didn't have a prayer. "I let you win," he said, slackening in the hot seat. "More—sivulrish."

"I'd be more *chivalrous*," Bambi said, "not to mention more professional, if I kept you from taking on any athletic challenge when you're slammed."

"One to talk," Hank said darkly.

"My veins run with red wine," she said. "And I can hold my liquor."

Although appearing to find it harder than he expected, after a brief grapple Chet flattened his coach's arm. Bambi's eyes flashed before she covered the fury with bluster: "Well, if you couldn't drop a girl after all those curls, I'd say you need a new personal trainer!" She curved even defeat into her own success. She really didn't like losing.

When Sloan took his turn, the antagonists were a matched set. They both had the naturally well-formed limbs of born athletes, and the elongated figures of avatars in video games. Meeting each other's gaze, each seemed to apply gradually more force, but nothing moved; the sides of their palms grew whiter. Only after a full minute did it become apparent that Sloan was merely holding her there.

"So how long do you want to do this?" His voice was relaxed.

"You're a condescending son of a bitch, aren't you?"

"I'm a man," he said.

"Same thing."

Wham. Bambi's forearm hit the table.

"Pretty impressive force, considering," Sloan allowed.

Bambi massaged her wrestling hand. "Yeah, right. That felt a little like arm wrestling with, like, the *wall.*"

Sloan laughed. "From you, I guess being compared to a mindless slab of Sheetrock is a compliment."

Bambi raised a forefinger. "Planks! More of a gender-level playing field."

Then they were off to the living room, audience trailing. Serenata watched limply from the doorway. Side by side, the two paragons extended over the Oriental carpet, propped on their toes and elbows, forearms forward and flat on the floor. Chet started his stopwatch. Obviously this parlor game was tacky. So their hostess wasn't about to mention that she could maintain that plank herself for a solid five minutes. Besides, among the super race, a mere five minutes was sure to draw derision.

A contest over who could hold a stationary pose the longer was dull. Restless, Chet and Hank began to perform feats of strength with the furniture. Serenata tried to catch Remington's eye to get him to discourage them, but her husband was lifting an armchair overhead. Finally, Sloan sank to the carpet and rolled onto his back.

"Nine minutes, twenty-four seconds!" Chet declared.

"Uncle, bitch," Sloan said. "Happy now?"

But Bambi maintained the position. "Tell me when it's ten!" Her voice was strangled. Only once Chet announced the ten-minute mark did she also collapse, flopping onto her back and gasping.

"Should have known better, Wallace." Still catching her breath, Bambi rose to a stand. "Sheetrock abs."

"How long did it take you to work up to *ten minutes*?" Remington asked.

"Oh, these puppies are a life's work, pal," Bambi said. "You know how pregnant women always have folks wanting to touch their stomach? Well, that's what happens to me in gyms, only without the kid."

"Seriously?" Remington said. "And you let them?"

"Sometimes," Bambi said coyly. Lifting the baby-blue vest, she tensed her abdominal muscles. "Have a feel."

Tentatively, Remington laid a hand on his trainer's midsection.

"Stop."

They all turned to the doorway. Remington took his hand back.

"I think that's quite enough," Serenata said soberly, and turned to the kitchen to help the two other women finish cleaning up. The humorless admonishment put the kibosh on the evening's antics, and within a few minutes their guests had left. She was sorry to see Tommy go. Being left alone with her husband was less of a relief than usual.

Serenata sat on the edge of the bed, facing away. Spouses don't feel close all the time. She and Remington plunged separately into other aspects of their lives, and then reported back. The very obliviousness of these periods of engrossment in other matters, their very ability to put their spouse's entire existence out of mind for hours or even days, sprang from a sensation of safety—a happy complacency. This felt different.

Remington was toweling his hair after his midnight shower. He allowed his terrycloth robe to drape open. He'd become more at ease with nakedness in the last year. Serenata had grown less so. Having undressed, she was aware that the knots of the chenille bedspread would be dimpling her ass, just as the sock-lines scored her ankles and marred what remained of the tibias' once-beguiling slope. The peach-tinted polish on her toenails had partially chipped off, perhaps a point of inattentive grooming that was an early sign of letting herself go. Where the polish was missing, the ugly vertical striations of aging keratin showed through. Crushed in bedraggled running shoes for decades, the toes had contorted, mashing together and overlapping, as if made of wet clay and someone had stepped on them. From a seated vantage point, that inside bulge of a right knee bone was at its most apparent. The distortion was subtle enough—schoolboys weren't likely to point and laugh on the street—but call it what it was: a deformity. Her breasts had long ago dropped; when she experimented with clenching her pectorals, they effectively mounded a second set of mini-mammaries above the first, as if she were a freak, or had tumors. Because her shoulders were drooping as badly as her breasts—precisely this evening, a lifetime commitment to good posture seemed to have run its course—a slight sag of flesh creped over her abdomen, destroying any impression that their muscles were made of Sheetrock. She watched what she ate, but she'd had babies, for which women were reliably punished twice.

Commonly, they had no problem with silence. It only meant they had nothing to say. This silence called for filling, for if it went on much longer something would get worse, or perhaps something awful would happen. Perhaps something awful would happen anyway.

"You didn't seem to have a very good time tonight," he said.

"I wonder why that would be."

"They're not bad people."

"I never said they were bad people."

"You can be very judgmental."

"I exercise judgment. Unlike some people."

"We were horsing around. It was harmless."

"It was embarrassing."

"You're the only one who was embarrassed."

Serenata forced herself to sit more upright. "My dear, I'm sorry to say this, but your obsession with endurance sport has made your conversation a little trying. You used to talk about politics, or urban planning, or even about the television programs we watched as kids—and I'm highly entertained remembering those insufferable child actors in *Flipper.* I've enjoyed analyzing why we both watched so many programs we hated, and why children so often despise other children on TV. But now it's all techniques for getting your wet suit off fast enough during 'T1.' If I didn't have a good time tonight, that was mostly because I was bored."

"The subject of physical fitness has never bored you when it was your fitness."

"You're quite wrong. It bores me to death. Which is why I rarely talk about it, in case you haven't noticed."

"You talk about it more than you realize."

"Well, then, I'm sorry for boring you, too. You know, you say I didn't have a good time tonight like an accusation. As if I refused to have a good time."

"You didn't exactly dive into the spirit of the occasion."

"What spirit would that be?"

"Letting our hair down after a hard ride. Good-natured rivalry. Comparing notes on a challenging long-term project."

"It's not my project."

"You put yourself outside the project and pronounce upon it."

"You hardly spoke to me all night."

"We had guests."

"Yes. And I made a considerable effort to engage with your trainer."

"Everything you said was critical."

"What about what she said?"

"You put her on the defensive."

"Do you find it interesting that the whole club is white?"

"Not really. Hudson is a majority white town."

"It's barely over half white, actually," she said. "A quarter black, coming up on ten percent Latino. I looked it up."

"It wouldn't be surprising to form a small all-white club, even if the town were majority nonwhite." His delivery steady and uninflected, Remington had returned to the punishing neutrality he preferred when subjects of this sensitivity arose. "It might be politically awkward, but most people are more comfortable around people like themselves. They self-sort, often unconsciously. Blacks, Hispanics, and Asians do the same thing. It isn't precisely racism. More a natural desire to recognize one another, and to be able to relax. Those perfectly 'diverse' cliques of friends, like a Coca-Cola ad teaching the world to sing—they're a television fiction."

"But I've glanced at your triathlon videos. The people drawn to this pastime are overwhelmingly white. I think that means something."

"Are you insinuating that endurance sport is only for the well-off?"

"Not at all. Ethan may make a passable living as an ophthalmologist, but he wouldn't get wealthy off a town this size. Sloan had money once, but restoring cars is time intensive, and I bet he barely breaks even. The others are struggling, even Bambi if it weren't for you, and Hank bounces between drug addict and career criminal."

"So what are you getting at?"

Serenata hadn't formulated what she was getting at before she went down this road. As her destination came into focus, she wanted to turn around. "There's a . . . regression, a . . . narrowing, a . . . retreat. A withdrawal. A lowering of horizons. A gross reduction of expectations. A new materialism, which doesn't even extend to patio furniture. The material is the body. It's a shrinking down to the very least you can be without being dead. A battening down of the hatches, a crawling into a hole."

"It doesn't feel like any of that. Getting physically stronger translates directly into strength of other kinds."

"It's a particular brand of flourishing, at the sacrifice of other flourishings. For all that mental resilience your trainer touts, it's anti-intellectual. Which is weird, for you. Have you noticed you've stopped reading? Sports magazines, training manuals, yes. But I can't remember the last time you tackled one of those state-of-the-nation tomes you used to furiously underline in red felt-tip."

"Apparently you're spending your time keeping track of how I spend mine, and I don't see how that's any better."

"Also—have you noticed that we hardly ever have sex anymore?"

"I'm sixty-five. And after training, I'm often tired. Are you proposing we do something about it—like, tonight?"

Serenata's laugh was involuntary. Getting from where they were now to sexual intercourse would have entailed running an emotional marathon before lights-out. "I was wondering whether you miss it."

"Of course. But my powers—we may have to accept that they're on the wane."

"At present, you're focused exclusively on your physical *powers*, which I'm led to believe are only on the increase."

"Listen." He walked around the corner of the bed and touched her shoulder. "I'm not having an affair with my personal trainer."

A year ago, she'd never have imagined this B-movie cliché arising in their bedroom. "Since I didn't think you were, I'm a little perplexed why you feel the need to clarify that."

"You focus on Bambi Buffer to give your jealousy a face. But the jealousy is bigger than one woman. You're jealous of the whole package—the club, the training schedule, my gains, my goals, the project. On that score, I can't help you."

"This 'project' is unworthy of you, and I can't pretend to think something nicer."

"Why do you always have to diminish it?"

"I don't need to diminish it. It's already small."

"The experience of pushing past a mental barrier, and still completing another ten laps when you're at the end of your rope—it isn't small."

"The achievement is small. Ordinary and not an achievement at all."

"Most things are ordinary and not major achievements. I've been fired. I'm retired. Just how do you want me to be spending my time instead?"

"I don't even know," she said honestly. "Just not like this."

"Your taking against this from the start has been a terrible mistake."

"That's the question, then. Who's making the mistake."

"You're trying to come between me and the fulfillment of my potential—"

"Please. The language of vainglorious positivism is worse than *intersectionality* and *micro-aggressions*."

"If anything, our household has suffered from an excess of irony. It's a common disease of the over-educated. All that superior drollery is a cover for effeteness and passivity. It's a fear of putting ourselves on the line."

"You've put yourself on the line plenty. That's why you were fired."

"Ask any other American who's in the wrong in this situation, and they'd say you."

"I'm aware of that. But we're not asking them. I'm asking you. Which would win out if you had to choose? Triathlon"—none of them said *a* triathlon, or *the* triathlon, just *triathlon*, which made it sound more majestic, like an awesome force of nature that simply is, gravity or magnetism, not a series of separate sporting events but something big and indivisible, just as faithful adherents to other religions didn't reference *a* God or *the* God, but simply *God*—"or your marriage?"

"That's a false choice and beneath you. It seems to me that not putting our marriage on the table is one of the rules. An unwritten rule, which makes it only more sacrosanct. Besides which, it's been thirty-three years, and we're old."

"Old enough to stay together out of laziness. From lack of imagination."

"Are you threatening me?"

He was shouting. That made her quiet. "I'm trying to talk to you."

"Because if anyone should threaten anyone here, shouldn't it be the other way around? Aren't you the one who, implicitly or explicitly, has been pissing on my entire purpose for the last year? Aren't I the one who should be reaching my limit?"

"There's no such thing as a limit, according to your guru."

"I'd prefer not to think of our marriage as an endurance sport."

"Maybe you should," she said. "Maybe then you'd take an interest in it."

EIGHT

"I'm not saying we're about to split up," she blurted to her father-in-law in March, after yet another painful pause. When at a total loss for conversation, she ended up unburdening what she probably shouldn't, because the only unexhausted material she could lay hands on was her inmost thoughts. "But we've always enjoyed each other's company. And now I—don't. Enjoy his company. Or not as much."

"It's this triathlaton business," Griff said warily. At ninety, he'd not want to hear that his son was in danger of divorce. Leaving aside his practical and emotional dependence on Serenata, a divorce would mean change, and to Griff even a rearrangement of his late wife's porcelain figurines was anathema.

"Even when he's not training, he reads sports autobiographies, or listens to inspirational podcasts by 'tri' record-setters. I can't tell you how sick I am of the soundtrack to *Chariots of Fire*. He used to read bios of Robert Moses, or the latest Thomas Friedman. I miss the blues, and films with tragic endings. But he won't subject himself to anything sad or dark."

"Remy's always been single-minded. Time was, he was single-minded about *you*. From that first tryout for those subway announcements, I could tell he'd fixed on roping this lady in—the one with the sultry voice. He never confided in his parents much, so when he couldn't stop mentioning you, I knew you were it." Griff's strategy was hardly subtle. Recollection of their courtship was meant to revive romantic coals.

"I'm sorry that he's also been making so little time to come see you—"

Griff snorted. "Try *no* time. That boy hasn't been by here in months."

"He thinks you're hostile to his endeavor. You contaminate his pure heart."

"He's making a damned fool of himself. Tell him to take up cribbage. He can have my board. It's a respectable hobby for a man in his sixties."

"I'm afraid we had a fight," Serenata said, twisting her hands. "Or rather, I got so angry, we *didn't* have a fight. I didn't think we could afford one."

"Not that *woman*, was it?"

"Not this time. But you're right, that trainer he's hired . . . She's younger and physically perfect. She makes me feel haggard, flabby, and hideous."

"Now, sugar, that's one terrible waste. You're the prettiest filly in Hudson."

"I'm a mare, not a filly, and of an age no one rides anymore." Serenata blushed; the off-color insinuation had been inadvertent.

"Remy showed up with that hussy sometime last fall—"

"You never told me you met *Bambi Buffer*!"

"Didn't want to cause trouble. Wasn't sure how aware you were that he was swelling around town with that gal."

"I'm painfully aware. She drops by our house at all hours."

"I wasn't impressed," Griff said. "Mannish."

"To most people, she's a feminine icon. Strong is in."

"Flat-chested," he said. "And *bossy*."

"Don't tell me," Serenata said. "She went straight to the kitchen and helped herself to a six-pack of your best stout."

"Worse. Barely in the door, the lady starts hectoring me about how 'seniors' shouldn't give into being 'sedentary.' Messes with the furniture, to demonstrate how I'm to practice popping up and down in a chair—like I'm getting up and can't remember what I wanted and sit down again. Practice for senility is what I call it. And then she helicoptors her arms in the air to get me to whirlybird along with her, and shows me how to stand on one leg for an eternity, like a goddamned stork. Impertinent. Didn't put the chair back. No appreciation for how much effort it takes at ninety just to fix a sandwich. They weren't here five minutes, and that pushy pain in the backside still wore me out."

"She's paid to be pushy."

"I'd pay that tyrant just to stay out of my house."

"Well, while you're at it, pay her to stay out of mine."

"This *arrangement*, with Remy. Which I can't say I understand, and I'm not sure I want to. Ever ask yourself what she gets out of it?"

Citing a retainer the size of Griff's monthly Social Security check seemed impolitic. "She collects people. She has an insatiable appetite for admiration, so she surrounds herself with acolytes who depend on her to shore up their own self-esteem. She convinces her disciples that they're superior to all the peons who are fat and lazy and sleep late. It's not that different from Scientology."

But Griff wanted nitty-gritty. "Is my son carrying on with that woman? When those two showed up here, I didn't care for it. Like they were a couple. If he's cheating on you, say the word, and I'll read him the riot act. I raised him better than that."

"He's going through a weird period, but he still has too much class to visit his father with a mistress in tow. Still, he is besotted with her. Not in love exactly, but bewitched. I'm the naysayer; she tells him what he wants to hear. You've heard of horse whisperers? Well, she's a sports whisperer. Maybe she's good at it. Remington has sure run, swum, and biked farther and faster than ever before with Bambi egging him on."

"You say that like I'm supposed to care."

"No, but Remington cares. Either *he* believes she can summon a whole new self out of him—a man who's fierce and indestructible and glass-half-full—or she really can. I guess I'm afraid she can. I don't want a brand-new husband who's idiotically self-important. I liked Remington the way he was. Modest, for example."

"Don't know about that. Always thought of that kid as right full of himself. Couldn't wait to get out of Hudson, and earned all those degrees."

"He was a good student, and a confident professional. But he never used to be an inconsiderate cretin. Right, he won't visit his father when it's only a ten-minute walk, and he no longer prunes your hedges—but you think it's only you? I have to do everything now. Shopping, picking up, cooking, finding an electrician to replace the broken shaving socket in the bathroom. Remembering our grandchildren's birthdays, wrapping the presents, and posting them on time—not that I give a shit about birthdays, but we can't provide Valeria any excuse to disappear off the face of the earth for another four years. I know Margaret would have done most of that in your day, but I work, too, and my carrying the whole household isn't part of the contract. He's the one who's retired, for Pete's sake, and he did more domestic heavy lifting with a full-time job."

"You said you had a fight, or near to. You fell out over the housework?"

"It was even more hackneyed than that. We fell out over money. But money in three dimensions. Money that would have taken up space in the garage, except that it's too *damp* in there, so he keeps his precious ward propped beside the dining table, like a newly adopted child we're plying with chocolate pudding."

"Lost me there, pumpkin."

"Sorry, I'm being opaque. He bought a bicycle."

"I thought he had a bicycle."

"He did. But this one . . . is pricier."

"When he was a boy, I got Remy a bike for forty bucks—and he hardly rode the thing. Eventually I got it: bicycles were for sissies. The tough kids all rode mopeds."

"This titanium marvel was more than forty bucks," she said, with dizzying understatement. "But for years Remington brought in the bigger income. Strictly speaking, it's his money. So I'm not supposed to say anything. These days, I'm never supposed to say anything about anything. Like, I can't say that trying to buy athletic excellence is pathetic."

Regarding the probing of deep emotion, Griffith Alabaster had always been awkward at best. Yet he may finally have registered that you'd never address what really mattered in life if you were still giving the crux wide berth at ninety. "You do still—care for my son, don't you, sugar?"

In return for her father-in-law's courage, she answered as honestly as she could. "I love the man I married. But I'm not sure he is the man I married. Here's the thing." Elbows on her knees, she faced the old man—who'd not be here much longer, and she didn't want to kick herself once it was too late for never having spoken to him plainly.

"My parents were Methodists," she said, "but I think their faith was skin-deep. It was mostly social, and because we moved so often, churches were a useful shortcut, especially for my mother. But once I hit my teens, I told them that to me the whole Christ story seemed far-fetched. I didn't want to keep claiming to believe something I didn't. They acted disappointed, but didn't force me to keep going. It wasn't that I lost my faith; I never had it. I'm sorry, because I know Margaret was a devout Catholic, but I've always found religious belief not only foreign, but mindless and—well, a little repellent. The stories you're meant to buy into are absurd. To me, religion is a form of mass hypnosis, or collective psychosis."

"Something to be said for churches," Griff said. "They get folks to gather round each other in times of need. I'm not sure you lapsed youngsters have come up with anything better."

"No, we haven't—which is sort of my point. See, Remington has always been a rationalist. We've enjoyed sparring over a host of issues, but neither of us has ever subscribed to a dogma. On the electoral rolls, Remington is registered as an independent. That's always been important to me about your son: he's a freethinker. His refusal to ape the version of virtue imposed by the political fashions of the time is one of the reasons he lost his job. If he'd abased himself, he might have kept it."

"Remy's got backbone."

"He used to. But I'm not sure loyalty to somebody else's principles qualifies as backbone. Because if you'd asked me years ago what was the one thing that might cripple my marriage, I'd have said the one thing that could never happen: religious conversion. That's why Valeria's having gone born-again has been so alienating. Technically, we've restored relations, but in truth I have no idea who she is anymore. All her Jesus guff has an element of spitefulness about it, and that much I understand. But willingly giving over to a crowd, and signing up wholesale to some kooky creed of other people's contrivance—I don't understand that at all.

"Griff, MettleMan isn't just an exercise regime. MettleMan is a cult. That's why I can't give you a one-word answer to whether I still love your son." She sat back in the chair. "The man I fell in love with has been kidnapped."

"And what about Remy's promises as a husband? *You* haven't been 'kidnapped.' And you're the best thing ever happened to that boy."

She threw up her hands. "I am—irrelevant! For Remington, anything or anyone that doesn't have to do with *triathlon* isn't in the picture. Unless I'm stocking up for another binge with his tri club, I'm just a nuisance. After all, according to the Book of MettleMan, the height of spiritual achievement is perfect self-absorption."

Serenata couldn't sit still, and returned to pacing. "So in Syracuse next month? He and his club are doing a 'half Mettle'—meaning not completely insane, but only sort-of-but-still-basically insane—and I'm expected to go and wave pom-poms. But I don't want to! It's not only that I hate all this *tri* shit, but I especially hate the idea of reinforcing my role in his life as the one on the sidelines! Besides which, because he *is* getting older, and he's *not* a natural athlete, and his body *isn't* used to this degree of strain, I'm really worried he's going to hurt himself. But to Remington, that's just me being 'dark,' and trying to stop him from achieving nirvana, so any concern I express he interprets as raging antagonism. On the other hand, it's more than possible that I did this to myself, and I did this to our marriage, because I'm rigid, and insensitive, and territorial, and bitter about my knees, and maybe if I'd done nothing but hooray and Hail Mary and holler hallelujah from the start, we'd still be happy as clams."

She'd been ranging the living room with her hands flailing. The outburst was intemperate. But she couldn't confide to Tommy anymore, now that the girl had drunk the Kool-Aid, too; she'd left her few plausible friends back in Albany; least of all could she pour out her heart to Remington.

Her father-in-law frowned. "Not thinking of doing anything rash, are you?"

"Oh, I'm not the first person to be stymied by what's worse: no marriage, or a bad one." She bombed back to the wing chair. "So should

I go to this 'half Mettle,' or not? Staying home seems traitorous, and I leave him at the mercy of *Bambi*."

"You trust a man, or you don't. If you don't, following him around won't do a lick of good. Once this 'Mister Metal' folderol is over—not the littler thing next month, but the big hoo-ha in June—you reckon Remy'll have had enough?"

"I'd like to think so, but that's what I assumed about the marathon last year. Boy, was I wrong. For all I know, he's decided to enter triathlons for the rest of his life. He's not making plans to do anything else."

"Won't that boy get *tired*?"

"The real danger is that I get tired first, Griff."

"Please don't leave me." His voice was shaking.

"Never," she said. Rising to take his face in her hands and kiss his forehead, she whispered in his ear, "But that's what I could stand to hear from Remington."

She put her mac and cheese in the oven, and set the timer so he wouldn't forget. She fished the melting zucchini and crusting cauliflower from the fridge; she always threw a few into the weekly order from AmazonFresh, but Griff didn't have much time for vegetables. Her Swiffer of the kitchen floor was hasty, since Tommy would be in on Friday. In the bathroom, she stacked some extra toilet paper within easy reach, and swabbed the area in front of the bowl, where old men tended to dribble. She laid out his pills, and freshened a glass of water with a slice of lemon.

"Thanks for letting me complain," she said, gathering her things. "And don't lose any sleep over this, because it's out of both our hands. Remington will escape from the clutches of his sect. Or he won't."

When she got home, Remington was still at the gym. The redundant free weights and bells-and-whistles treadmill upstairs were gathering dust. He preferred to worship with his congregation.

She shot a glare at the tri bike propped against the wall. It was constructed of elliptical tubing at peculiar angles, and the handlebars were built so you laid your forearms flat and held on to upturned grips. For the inanimate, it had an aggressively snobbish ambiance. In contrast to the gaudy colors of Remington's running gear, the contraption was ostentatiously sophisticated: a slick slate-gray with a sandy matte finish and slim, tasteful accents of branding in bloodred. A bicycle should appear storied, well traveled; this mechanism was immaculate. It didn't look like something that you'd ride in a park, but more like an art object you'd display in a design museum, where you'd slap the hands of little boys who tried to touch it. Before this haughty intruder slid into their house, she'd never have believed that a bicycle could cost ten grand.

"Gosh, I take it all back," she said aloud over her phone. "Maybe there is a God." For the email that had just pinged in was an offer of work: an extensive recording session in lower Manhattan for a new video game, and the terms were generous. If Remington was going to drop ten big ones on a bike, she had to accept the job. Better yet, the dates would perfectly preclude tagging along to watch the half Mettle in Syracuse. Brilliant.

The phone stirred again: Valeria.

"Thanks a lot, *Mama*," the young woman exploded once her mother had barely said hello. "You'll be glad to hear that Nancee's in the hospital."

"What's happened? And why on earth would I be glad?"

"She's been admitted for exhaustion. And they seem to think she's anorexic."

"Well, you know, back in April I did try to call your attention—"

"She's a picky eater, but she doesn't starve herself," Valeria snapped. "I'm her mother, and I should know."

Valeria was in a vengeful mood, and contributing Tommy's

diagnosis that Nancee was an "exercise bulimic" might not be perceived as helpful. "Did something happen, or is she just run-down?"

"Better believe something *happened*. There's a water tower near our house, and somehow those kids managed to pull down the ladder to the stairway on the outside. The silly girl started running up and down it. Thankfully Logan was keeping watch, not to mention Our Lord and Savior—"

Serenata gasped. "She didn't fall, did she?"

"No, but she could have. Because at some point, she collapsed. Logan was a good boy, and called 911. And me, of course. I had to find someone from the church to watch the other kids, so by the time I got there the medics had already climbed up three flights to carry her down. She may have fainted from dehydration."

"Has she done this sort of thing before?"

"Logan isn't saying. Deacon did nothing but torture me—not that you ever noticed—but Logan is very loyal."

"How is she doing now?"

"Nice of you to get around to asking," Valeria said. "She's on a drip to restore fluids, and they're feeding her intravenously. She's alert, and I'm afraid she's not what you'd call an ideal patient. The nurses are convinced she's freaking out because of the nutrition. I guess they've seen skinny girls ripping out the needles before. But that's not it. I know my girl. She just doesn't like lying in bed. She's promised to keep the IV in, so long as they'll let her march up and down the halls with the thing on wheels. But the doctor is insisting on complete rest, and it's turned into something of a battle."

"I'd hate to go up against Nancee over anything. She's wiry but ferocious."

"You can't imagine how awful it is to see your own child in restraints, like a crazy person. But I got her to admit what she was up to. Apparently in running up and down all those stairs, she was trying to beat some sort of record. And guess *whose*?"

Serenata allowed the question to dangle.

"Did you or did you not," Valeria went on, "tell my daughter that you run *two hundred flights* at a time?"

"I may have mentioned that I did that in my twenties—"

"What kind of grandmother are you? Throwing down a gauntlet like that to a little girl?"

"I wasn't throwing down a gauntlet. I noticed she was running up and down the stairs here, and I was only trying to establish a sense of camaraderie."

"You were indoctrinating my daughter into the same lunacy I grew up with!"

"Sweetie, you're one to talk about indoctrination."

"Children are very suggestible!" Valeria shouted. "You can't go planting ideas in their heads without taking responsibility for the consequences!"

"I'd remind you that thanks to your impromptu pause for station identification, your father and I missed out on four highly formative years of your two oldest children. By the time you deigned to get in touch with your parents again, Nancee was already, as you put it yourself, an 'Energizer Bunny.' I didn't invent this thrall to exertion, either. It's in the ether. It's on TV and in the movies and in advertising and all over the internet. For pity's sake, look at what's happened to your father! You flatter me, my dear, but Nancee didn't get the idea of distinguishing herself through sheer fatigue from *me*."

But Valeria had already hung up.

Nancee was just the beginning.

Something was off about Tommy from the moment she arrived. True, her eagerness to busy-bee about the house had lessened somewhat, now that she'd discarded her Fitbit knockoff. (Failing to track a single mile of cycling and insufficiently waterproof for the pool, the mechanism no longer performed its prime function of giving its user *credit.*) But it was still not her habit to begin a stint of cleaning with an immediate plop in a chair.

"Sure you're up for this?" Serenata scrutinized her neighbor while preparing the girl tea. "You look beat. We could always reschedule."

"I'm still trying to get out of paying for a full membership at BruteBody . . . So the other guys in the tri club trade off having me as a . . . as a . . . guest. I don't like to ask too often. Have to take advantage . . . when I'm in." Tommy slumped. It was not entirely clear how she would scrub the upstairs porcelain when she could barely talk.

"Meaning?" Serenata put out shortbread. Maybe the girl had low blood sugar.

"Yesterday. Stationary bike. Really . . . shoulder to the wheel. Sloan got me into the gym this time, and he never . . . never notices me at all."

"Mm-hmm." Serenata had harbored some suspicions along these lines. "Why do you care whether Sloan notices you?"

Tommy glared up through the wisps of her fine honey hair. "Duh. He's, like, the hottest guy in the club—if not in Hudson . . ."

"Or in the world," she finished for the girl with a smile. Goodness, having recently turned sixty-two had many a downside, but thank heavens she was no longer twenty.

"He's like a . . . like a fucking god."

"Take it from me, friend, you never want to have a relationship with a god. They always turn out to be mere mortals in Groucho glasses."

"You're old," Tommy slurred. "You don't remember anything."

"There's plenty from my early twenties I wish I *didn't* remember.

Sorry to be such a downer, but he's twice your age. He's a divorcé whose kids are almost as old as you are. But I know, I know: the heart wants what the heart wants."

"Yesterday—I guess I was trying to impress him," Tommy confessed. Her consonants had thickened. "Full hour, cranked . . . up. Sweat like a . . ." A metaphor seemed beyond her. "Got totally soaked. Wiped me . . . out."

Delivering the tea, Serenata pushed the plate forward. "Energy."

"No cookies," Tommy said. "Feel fat. Pants . . . don't fit."

Serenata drew the hair from her neighbor's face and tucked it behind an ear. "You don't look fat. You look puffy. That's different." Tommy's color was peculiar, too, but remark on its yellowish cast would only make the girl feel more self-conscious.

"Thighs are killing me. Tight. Might just . . . take the day off."

Serenata peered. "Cleaning, or working out?"

". . . Both."

In the lead-up to this half-Mettle malarkey, Tommy's proposing to take a day off from exercise was unheard of. Had Tommy been out in the woods? Serenata asked. Picked off any ticks? No. Had she eaten anything unusual? No. Had she eaten anything at all, since yesterday? No. "You're not well. I think you should see a doctor."

"Uh-uh. No big deal. Just need . . . rest." In Tri World, "rest" was commonly consigned to the same trash heap as "limits" and "overdoing it." Tommy struggled to a stand. Her thighs had bulged overnight from adolescent to menopausal.

Serenata let the girl go—she wasn't Tommy's mother—but the encounter was disturbing. Later that evening, she tried Tommy's cell, but the call went to voice-mail, and a text went unanswered.

Sleep that night was not improved by Remington's being up and down more than once, pacing and stretching at the bedpost, trying to get the clenched skein of fine muscles on the tops of his feet to relax. The seizures had grown chronic since he'd upped his laps in the pool. The spasms spread to the toes, which straightened and separated unnaturally with raised tendons. It was her helplessness in the face of his agony that kept her up. He was clearly trying to be quiet but couldn't keep his breath from rasping. The moonlight through the curtains chiaroscuroed his face into a Kabuki mask of anguish: forehead curdled, eyes squeezed shut, as if not being able to see his feet would make them go away. She loved his feet—his long, dry, shapely feet—and hated to see them convert to instruments of torture. In this light, too, his ever-stringier frame looked less muscular than withered.

Over the tablet at breakfast, she recounted the news from India. "So a teenage girl was gang-raped, and her parents objected—as one might. The village elders levied a punishment on the men of a small monetary fine and one hundred sit-ups. The rapists were enraged, beat the shit out of the parents, doused the girl with kerosene, and burned her alive."

"The lengths to which some people will go to get out of sit-ups," Remington said.

"Gosh, I wonder what penalty that village levies for first-degree murder. Jumping jacks?"

"Only diagonal toe-touches," Remington said. "You don't want them to get too tuckered out for their next rampage."

The interchange was of a sort that once routinely characterized their breakfast-table banter, and she was grateful for it—too grateful.

With still no word from Tommy, she nosed around the web in accelerating agitation, and finally walked around to the Marchs' front door. She had to marshal courage to knock. The few pleasantries she'd lobbed in the mother's direction had been received with suspicion. What did that hoity-toity older lady next-door get out of a relationship with a twenty-year-old kid aside from a clean sink?

"Yeah?" the mother said, opening the door partway. Heavy, bad complexion, prematurely haggard—no wonder her daughter was an exercise nut. "Tommy's not feeling too good."

"I know. That's why I stopped by. I need to ask her a question."

"All right. I can ask her for you."

"Fine, then—ask her about her urine. What color is it?"

"Seems kind of personal, don't it? Why's that matter to you?"

"Please. This is important."

With a glare, the neighbor turned without asking Serenata inside. At length, Tommy shuffled to the door, keeping upright by hanging on the jamb. So advanced had the puffiness grown that for the first time her resemblance to her mother was apparent.

"What's this about wee? It's the least of my problems. I'm turning into a whale, and everything hurts."

"The color. In the toilet bowl, when you pee."

Tommy frowned. "Well, come to think of it, sort of brown. But I thought it was rust in the pipes again."

"Your session at BruteBody, with the stationary bike. Up to a point, you want muscle to break down, so it builds back stronger. But if you take it too far, the fibers get into your bloodstream, and your kidneys shut down. If I'm right, this is nothing to mess with, Tommy. It could kill you. I'm taking you to Columbia Memorial *right now.*"

Tommy didn't have the energy to put up a fight. While Serenata offered to take her mother as well, the woman mumbled something about hospital bills, and begged off. But Tommy was covered by Medicaid. Her mother was a shut-in. Besides, to Mrs. March, Serenata's having arrived at a diagnosis made Tommy's ailment her fault.

"Aren't you being alarmist?" Remington asked when she rushed in for the key fob. "That condition is very rare."

"Not as rare as it used to be."

"And convenient. For your side."

"My *side*?"

"You heard me. And you're kidnapping one of my club members."

It was the same verb she'd used about him. "Not to sound grand, but I prefer to think I'm rescuing her."

"This isn't good timing, for the half Mettle. She should be hitting the road."

"You haven't seen her. She's more like hitting the floor. And medical calamity is notoriously difficult to schedule at one's athletic convenience."

The wait at the ER was extensive, and neither the nurse at reception nor the doctor they saw at last had heard of the diagnosis, either.

"Oh, man, rhabdo!" Bambi exclaimed familiarly, after Serenata updated the club on Tommy's condition around the dining table two days later.

"She'll be hospitalized for about a week," Serenata said. "I'm sure she'd appreciate you guys going by to say hello. Just don't mention how bloated she looks. She feels unattractive enough already."

"Bet she didn't hydrate enough," Bambi said confidently.

"Maybe," Serenata said. "But she also pushed herself too far, and that's why she went into full-blown kidney failure. Her creatinine count was off the charts. They're pumping her with fluids and may do dialysis. There's no way she can enter the half Mettle."

"That's according to you."

"That's according to Columbia Memorial. Recuperation from rhabdomyolysis can take weeks or even months. Frankly, though I haven't pressed the matter with her yet, a full MettleMan is off the table, too."

"Ever notice how happy you sound when delivering bad news?" Bambi said.

"Tommy's my friend, and her circumstances certainly don't make me happy."

"But she's right, my dear," Remington said. "You do sound satisfied. You've won the girl back to your team."

"In this club, the two 'teams' are the supermen and the slobs," Serenata said. "That makes me the queen of the slobs. Is that what you think?"

"That's your formulation, not mine," Remington said.

"It's just, this whole thing is a lot easier when your spouse believes in you," Cherry said. "Take it from me. And that's all Rem means, honey. We all know you're not big on tri. But nobody here thinks you're glad poor Tommy's in the hospital."

Meanwhile, Ethan Crick was diffidently sliding off a running shoe. He peeled off the sock, and then hobbled to their hostess to ask quietly for a Band-Aid. Ethan must have been set on living down his reputation as a whiner, since he was trying valiantly to be nonchalant about the massive blister on his big toe. It appeared to have ripped open and healed over more than once, only to be abraded again on the club's fourteen-mile run that afternoon. The surface was gluey, and its edges were bleeding.

She led him to the bathroom and scrounged the medicine cabinet for a large enough bandage. With an air of benevolence and an innocent moon face, the ophthalmologist wasn't at all pudgy, but his body had blunted contours that no amount of running or weight lifting would sharpen. He'd never attain the sleek build and rippling definition of a Sloan Wallace. She prayed he didn't care. Fat chance.

"Let the sweat dry off, or this won't stick," she said. "And we have to trim the rumpled skin. It hardens when it's dead, and then it tears." Having located the nail scissors, she had him prop the foot on the tub, recoiling slightly from the smell. The wound was the gooey yellow of frothed egg yolks. Worse, the foot had taken his body's blunted quality to an extreme. "This blister's badly infected, Ethan. Doesn't it hurt?"

"Well, sure, some, I guess."

"How in God's name did you run fourteen miles on this? And why?"

They both knew why. "It was a little tricky."

"I thought you were the sensible one."

"Being sensible doesn't get you much respect, in this crowd."

"I'm applying some Bacitracin. But for your whole foot to swell up like this, the infection could be getting into your bloodstream."

He shrugged. "I have a healthy immune system."

"Please. You're a doctor."

"Eye doctor."

"You need antibiotics. Did you know that Calvin Coolidge's son *died* from an infected blister on his foot?"

"Here we go, more *catastrophizing*!" Proprietary about her seven dwarfs, Bambi had stuck her head in.

Nevertheless, Serenata wouldn't let up until Ethan agreed to go directly to the walk-in clinic downtown; he just had time to make it before the doors closed.

"Did you check out how he played up that limp?" Chet said the moment Ethan left. "Like Quasimodo or something."

"His foot is a mess." Serenata wasn't having a reprise of Crick bashing so that they could all feel invincible in comparison. "And sepsis is not a character failing."

Hank Timmerman's offer to refresh everyone's unfinished drinks covered for getting another G&T for himself. He was always at a loss for words around Serenata, whose chronic aloofness made their un-relationship worse. Having gathered that she sometimes read books aloud for a living, he asked as she handed him the tonic, "So—have you ever read Lorrie Moore's *Birds of America*? I thought it was really good."

A perfectly passable effort at small talk, were it not for the fact that Hank had asked her this exact same question five times now. Heaven knew in what rehab joint a copy of those short stories was kicking around, but she was obliged to infer that *Birds of America* was the only book he'd ever read. The first time he'd asked about Lorrie Moore, she'd been touched by his effort to connect, and responded with enthusiasm. But binge drinking obliterated all memory of having already used this icebreaker more than once, and her replies had grown terse.

"*Yesss,*" she hissed icily.

He looked stung. Being a little nicer wouldn't have cost her much, but Tommy's situation was preying on her mind and made her cross. It was all so unnecessary.

"That kid's gonna be crushed if she has to quit," Chet said as Hank delivered more beers. "She's into tri super heavy."

"Well, maybe she could get into something else 'super heavy,' then," Serenata said. "She's only got a high school education, and aside from a vague aspiration to become a voice-over artist, she has no plan for her life. So maybe I am glad she's in the hospital, Cherry. As long as she fully recovers, rhabdomyolysis could be a blessing in disguise. For Tommy, MettleMan is a distraction."

"Distraction from *what*?" Bambi said. "Rising to a challenge is what we're put on earth to do."

"I read about an event somewhere in England," Serenata said, "where dozens of people run around a four-hundred-meter track for twenty-four hours straight. The last winner ran a hundred and sixty miles. That's six hundred and forty times around the track. The contestants start to hallucinate. They literally make themselves demented. One runner said the object of the exercise was 'to feel dead.' This kind of event is proliferating all over the Western world. We invented the computer and put a man on the moon. Now we're running in manic circles, like tigers churning ourselves to butter. A once-great civilization, disappearing up its ass."

"It's *hard* to run an ellipse over six hundred times," Bambi said. "You try it."

"It's hard to thread six hundred and forty tiny beads on a limp string."

"Look, we all know about your knees, Sera," Sloan said. "Isn't this sour grapes?"

"I think you can survive one skeptic," Serenata said. "The whole of American culture is cheering you guys on."

"That's not totally true," Bambi said. "There's an element—a pretty fucking big element—that hates our guts. They can be pretty vocal about it, too."

"No joke," Sloan said. "You should hear my ex. 'Oh, you're just into this big ego trip, and you only want to ogle yourself in the mirror.' Before we split, every time I left to train, I'd get it in the neck about how I should be taking the kids to the park. But for Mettles, you have to throw your family under the bus. Otherwise they'll drag you down with them, slumming around on Sunday mornings in bathrobes, with croissants, and travel supplements, and plastic toys."

"I got into it pretty deep with a customer at the café last week," Chet said. "I'd been talking about tri with a regular, and this guy at the next table gets all on his high horse about what a waste of time it is. Like, if we're going to expend all that energy, we should really be working at a homeless shelter—"

"That old saw!" Bambi said. "The why-don't-you-volunteer-for-a-food-bank thing—"

"Or dig wells for starving Africans," Chet said.

"No, no, I always get told I should be visiting the elderly," Cherry said. "Calling bingo in nursing homes."

"But why is the logical alternative to strenuous exercise a posturing altruism?" Remington said. "Really, who stands at the door and decides, 'Well, I could go for a run, or I could go teach immigrants English at my local community center'?"

"I don't know, but I hear this stuff every time I grab a stool at a bar," Bambi said. "What kills me? These same cunts whose dainty ethical sensibilities are so offended by your spending your life the way you fucking well want to—you can bet your last dollar *they* don't volunteer at any damned homeless shelter."

"And MettleMan events raise tons of money for charity!" Cherry said.

"Ever notice how all the guys who take a poke at tri are fat? I mean"—Hank shot a nervous glance at Cherry—"not hard fat, but, you know, blobby fat."

"That's what really bugged my ex," Sloan said. "She started to look her age, and I didn't."

"The slugs just feel inferior—" Bambi said.

Hank punched the air. "'Cause they *are* inferior!"

"—And they're jealous."

As ever, Serenata had retreated behind the butcher-block slab of the kitchen island, like their bartender. This conversation was stock. Any questioning of their purpose read as your own personal inadequacy. Presumably the only way to acquire the standing to cast convincing doubt on the merits of MettleMan was to complete one first. So she could only prove to these people that she didn't want to do what they were doing by doing what they were doing.

"I've never understood what it is about *envy*," Remington speculated, "that makes people disguise it to themselves as a different emotion altogether—sometimes as plain dislike, but more often as *moral disapproval*."

So, Serenata would have rejoined gamely, had it been just the two of them at dinner. *I can never deny feeling envious, because the sensation would appear to me in another guise. It's what you've always said about being called a racist, isn't it? That your very refutation makes it true? And now the same goes for anyone who says a discouraging word about MettleMan: you're just gutless, indolent, and weak. Voilà, your dubious enterprise is forever above reproach.* But she and Remington were anything but alone.

"*I* don't envy anybody." Bambi looked straight at Serenata. "Not a fucking soul."

She glared right back. "According to Remington, if you did, you'd *disapprove* of them instead. Maybe you secretly envy us benchwarmers, then—sleeping in, popping Pringles, and enjoying our lives while you suffer." Her punctuating smile was mirthless.

"So, Rem," Hank said, "seems like you recovered pretty good from last weekend. Any problems since? You must've took in a shitload of water."

"Yeah, and dirty water," Cherry said. "I meant to ask, did it make you sick?"

Remington's rigid shake of the head was perhaps misinterpreted.

"The main thing is," Chet said, "did you make sure to hit the pool this week? You know, jump back on the horse. You don't want to get all phobic or anything."

"What's this about?" Serenata asked.

The club went quiet. Sloan mumbled to Remington, "You didn't tell her?"

"Didn't tell me what?"

"Comes with the territory," Sloan said. "It wasn't a big deal."

"Remington. What wasn't a big deal?"

"He's here, ain't he?" Bambi said. "He ran fourteen miles today, and he's fine."

"Until a minute ago, I took it for granted that my husband was fine. So what happened that should make me grateful that he's even 'here'?"

"I didn't want you to worry about it," Remington said. "Because, obviously, there's nothing to worry about."

"You're talking about last Saturday, aren't you? When you got home weirdly late and you couldn't get warm. It was seventy-four degrees in here, and you wanted me to build a fire. You were shaking. You barely ate a thing, and went straight to bed. Why?"

"We did a swim in open water, in the Hudson," Remington said. "I told you that. I just didn't mention that I—got into difficulties. I may have gotten a chill—"

"My bad," Bambi said. "The water temperature was borderline, so it was a judgment call. Had it to do over again, I'd have gone with wet suits."

"How long a swim was this?" Serenata asked.

"About a mile and a half, give or take," Remington said.

"Have you ever swum that far before?"

"Yes, but in a pool. Open water's a little different."

"Quite," she said. "Your 'difficulties.' Are you trying to tell me that last weekend you nearly drowned?"

"I'm not trying to tell you that. I am telling you that."

"And why didn't you drown?"

"I pulled him out, Sera, of course I did," Bambi said. "I always loop back to check on stragglers, and I hit the pedal to the metal the moment I noticed Rem was in trouble. It's part of my job. My lifeguard skills are top-notch. Got Rem onshore in no time. Called the rest of the club in, too. I don't often cut a training session short, but I do make exceptions when necessary, since whatever you think I'm not totally out of my fucking mind."

"And were you obliged to give mouth-to-mouth?"

"Well, yeah. But don't worry, it was hardly what you'd call romantic."

"I think it is what I'd call romantic. I guess I owe you thanks. For saving my husband's life."

"Well, no, like I said, I was just doing my job. All in a day's work."

"Except you also put him in the circumstances where he required saving."

"I put myself in those circumstances," Remington said. "If I overestimated my present abilities, that's my fault."

"According to your trainer, these 'difficulties'—that is, I assume, coming within a whisker of floundering to the bottom of the river until you become another trashy castoff along with the spare tires and shopping carts . . . If she says the incident was so pro forma, 'all in a day's work,' why didn't you tell me about it?"

"You know exactly why I didn't tell you about it."

When she was about eight and still learning to swim, Serenata had paddled accidentally into the deep end of a public pool, tried to stand up, and panicked. A lifeguard noticed right away, so she couldn't have been thrashing and taking in chlorinated water salted with gallons of primary-school pee for more than about thirty seconds before a young man threw an arm around her from behind and pulled her to the shallows. But it was a long thirty seconds—a small lifetime of blind animal terror, burned so vividly into her memory that these many years later she could replay those "difficulties" as if they'd occurred yesterday. She refused to believe that the experience of drowning was any less profound at the age of sixty-five than it was at eight. Particularly since by sixty-five you're better equipped to understand just what you may be in the process of losing. Yet her husband came back and failed to mention having inhaled death itself, all because he didn't want to give her ammunition in a difference of opinion over his participation in a sporting event. If the reason for his reticence was absurd, it was also sad. He had all these new friends, but when they went home, she wasn't the only one who felt lonely.

NINE

"You didn't tell me that Remington almost drowned." Serenata said this gently, lest it seem an accusation of betrayal. Already punished beyond reason, Tommy hardly needed to be dumped on for the deficiencies of a marriage older by half than she was.

"So he told you." Tommy flopped her cheek phlegmatically on the flat hospital pillow. "I didn't want to rat him out."

If the girl had converted overnight from superwoman to slug, it was the kind someone had poured salt on. She looked as if she were melting. Even constrained by compression stockings, all four limbs had expanded, and her fingers were sausages—so tight and plump that they'd split in a frying pan. In losing its angles, her newly broad, bland face had lost its intelligence, too.

"You're very loyal," Serenata said. "It's okay to be loyal to someone besides me."

"For a while, we thought he was actually going to snuff it. Even when he started breathing again, seemed like he'd cough, and cough, till his lungs came out." Her mouth might have been full of pudding. The sloppy enunciation wasn't from a physical inability to form the words. Her whole person was bathed in apathy, reflected in the colorlessness of the hospital room. She didn't speak clearly because she didn't care—about what she was saying, or anything else.

"I've watched him swim. He's a sinker. I didn't want to mention this when I was teaching you the crawl, but there are such people. It's body density more than technique. But don't worry. You're not a sinker." She hoped the designation carried metaphorically to Tommy's larger life, which the young woman seemed to believe was over.

"Not now!" Tommy said, with no gaiety. "I'd float like a beach ball now."

"The fluid's started to drain, hasn't it?"

"Not so's you'd notice," she said glumly. "Feels like it's only gotten worse. This IV keeps pumping me full of more water—"

"They have to flush out the myoglobin. They did warn you that getting back to normal size could take a while."

"They said it could take *weeks*. And my whole body hurts. I just lie here all day while every muscle turns to mush. I can practically hear it."

"What does it sound like?"

"Like when there's an air pocket in our kitchen drain. The dirty water backs up, and then a big, fat, greasy bubble burps up through the scum: *blu-blub*."

"I've read that you can go two whole weeks without exercise before the muscles weaken."

"That's bullshit."

Serenata didn't believe it, either. "All that matters is you get well. Your kidneys are finally kicking in. You can always get fit again when this is over."

"Uh-huh." Tommy's eyes were squeezed from the edema, and her glare was slitty. "Would that 'just get well' crap make *you* feel any better?"

"Of course not. Hey, what's that?" Serenata asked. "I never noticed it before."

Tommy flipped her wrist over, but her friend had already spotted the bumblebee. Its workmanship wasn't quite up to the same standard—

Serenata's had been inked by a master—but the newer image was more vivid.

"I was gonna show you," Tommy said, "but then I worried you'd think I was copying you."

"Let's not think of it as imitation, but as *homage*. I take it as a compliment."

"Really? You're not mad?"

"Really. I'm touched."

Tommy pulled herself up on the pillow. "So the half Mettle is in three weeks, and if I can only get back on the road—"

"Forget it," Serenata said. "In three weeks, you'll count yourself lucky if you can walk to the bathroom by yourself. Forget MettleMan, and that includes June, too. Because in your shoes, here's what *would* make me feel better: MettleMan is a franchise. It can trademark the name, but it can't trademark running, swimming, and cycling—any more than I can, which is why you're always ridiculing me, and rightly so. You don't need the organization, or its imprimatur—"

"Imprimatur?" Tommy said with disdain.

"Its seal of approval."

"I want the tattoo."

"You don't need the tattoo. You have our bumblebee."

"I'm gonna lose all my friends."

"Not me," Serenata said. "And if the other members of the tri club care about you, too, they're not going to drop you because you got sick."

"Don't pretend to be an idiot. If you're not doing tri, you don't count. You've been around those guys enough to know the drill. You're in or you're out. Now I'll be one more slacker they make fun of."

"But that's creepy, isn't it? If it's true? And that includes me, too. In their terms, I'm a slacker."

"I know."

Confirmation of what she knew already still smarted. "Have any other club members been to visit?"

"Only Cherry," Tommy said. "And even she couldn't wait to leave. It's like they're afraid they're gonna catch something."

"They're afraid of what they've got already: the capacity to join the rest of us jerk offs with one trip on a curb."

"I feel disgusting. I can't stand looking in the mirror—"

"Then don't."

"I've got nothing to live for," Tommy slurred. "I wish I was dead."

"Oh, you do not."

"This rhabdo-whatever is all my fault. I've never been good enough, and I'm still not. If my thighs had been stronger to begin with, this would never have happened. It's all because I wasn't in good enough shape. That's what they'll say behind my back, too. They'll say the problem was I was never in their league."

"If your thighs had been any stronger, then you'd have pushed yourself to cycle even faster and longer, all to impress Sloan Wallace—and you'd still have nuked your quadriceps into toxic waste. Your only weakness was for a pretty face. Though that's a big weakness, in my experience. Fatal."

"But Remington was hot-looking. You said."

"Yes. Not especially to his credit of course, but he's nicely formed. Also, from the start, I was drawn to how contained he was—how steady he was, how focused. Concentrated, held within himself. Though this same distilled quality seems to have morphed slightly. There's something in his face right now that I don't like."

"What's that?"

"Fanaticism." The word lingered.

"Well, you have to be a little crackers to go for a full Mettle, right?" Tommy said. "It's like going on, you know, *jihad*. But unless you slob out, the only other choice is to be all medium and plain. To say grandma things like 'Everything in moderation.' To not go for a real run, but go *jogging*. To have a personality like the temperature of a baby's bottle."

"No, the alternative is to get a grip, my dear," Serenata said briskly. "You got caught up in a fad, and you may not be through with the fad, but the fad is through with you. We can go back to reading scripts together. You've got a strong voice, and you only need to learn how to use it. You don't need a degree for my kind of work; you just need to be good at it. MettleMan was costing you time and money. Let's learn to make money, and at something more satisfying than swabbing floors. Then if you happen to have the spare time to do a few push-ups, fine. You think completing a MettleMan would make you special, but lots of people have completed one by now, and it's not special. Let's work on making you something special for real."

Alas, it was too early for a pep talk, and it fell on deaf ears.

After Tommy had been home for a week, she was able to join her next-door neighbor in slow, shuffling walks that gradually lengthened to reach downtown. Getting her out of the house at least meant she put on real clothes, even if much of her wardrobe still wouldn't fit; frumping around in shapeless nightgowns made her only more depressed. She'd managed to progress from truly desolate, to dejected, to merely forlorn. Now the resilient young woman was well on her way to a healthy disgruntlement. Preparing for the five-day video-game gig in Manhattan, Serenata felt more regretful about abandoning Tommy to potential emotional backsliding than she did about leaving Remington to fend for himself in Syracuse—which he detected.

"Did you go shopping for a job that would give you a schedule conflict for just the right day?" he inquired, packing.

"You know I didn't, and we've been through this. We need the money."

"Still—you're glad that now you don't have to go."

She discounted a range of more equivocal responses before answering, "Yes."

Putting a load of laundry away, Serenata stored three boxer shorts in his top drawer. Remington removed the three boxer shorts and placed them in his luggage.

"On the swimming segment," she said. "Will there be lifeguards?"

His glance was flinty. "Onondaga Lake will be buoyed, with fully crewed boats at regular intervals."

"I was expressing concern, not condescension."

"Naturally." Ah, the Remington dryness.

"Tommy said you almost died."

"At many points in our lives we almost die, and pull back from the brink. I had a close call yesterday crossing the street. I wouldn't expect you to hold that against me."

"I would if you got run over by tempting fate."

"Can I infer that you'll skip the full Mettle in June as well?" His tone was pleasant.

"I told you, I'll be there. I promised."

"But what if something comes up? And we still 'need the money'?"

"I *said* I'd be there. But as for Syracuse, Valeria is coming, so you'll have your cheering section. I might remind you that over the years I have run, cycled, and swum many thousands of miles. Not once can I remember insisting that you go out and watch."

Tomorrow, planning on an extra day to prepare for his penultimate feat of stamina, Remington would drive to Syracuse for three nights at the Courtyard. The hotel's room charges would ravage the earnings of her first day's recording, which so tragically coincided with the half Mettle. They'd sacrifice the proceeds of her second day's work to cover the hefty entry fee for the race. Were she ever on the lookout for an investment opportunity, MettleMan would be a growth stock.

But she didn't want to waste the evening before they were parted stewing in fiscal resentment, so when Remington raised a theoretical scenario over dinner, out of the blue, she was eager to seem game.

"Thought experiment," he proposed. "Let's say you're walking alone at night in a largely deserted urban area that's a little sketchy. A figure following behind you is making you anxious. You glance over your shoulder. It's a man, all right, but it turns out he's white. How do you feel?"

"Relieved."

"Why is that?"

"I could be unlucky, but my default assumption is that he's harmless."

"Is that because you feel a sense of solidarity with 'your people'? Because white folks will stick together, and would never hurt one another?"

"Hardly. I feel no sense of solidarity with white people. But blacks have higher rates of incarceration . . . Which is partly because of a rigged justice system, but still . . . I've heard blacks admit their fellow *brothers* on the street can make them edgy, too."

"What else do you assume about our nameless white guy, absent any additional information?"

"How old is he?"

"Say, twenties."

"And we're talking middle class or above?"

"Sure. You're not in South Boston. Say he's wearing a Yale sweatshirt."

"Which doesn't mean he went there."

"Which means he at least wants you to think he did. Not a big ghetto pretension."

"Unless he's conspicuously buff, I'd assume he's weak." Serenata surprised herself, but it was true. "In every sense, come to think of it."

"And if you were to imaginatively project yourself into the mind of a *person of color*—another young man who regards this street as his turf—what does a representative of a *marginalized community* think when he spots our white guy?"

Serenata was starting to get the feel of the exercise. "That the interloper is naive. That he shouldn't be here, and doesn't know where he's going. That he's credulous and doesn't watch his back. He might be capable of braggadocio if flanked by flunkies—"

"All men are more daunting when running in packs."

"But on his own? He's probably a coward. I don't like to stereotype, but in the *hypothetical* instance that this *POC* is inclined to be the tiniest bit predatory? Open season. A white guy won't stick up for himself. He's easy to steal from, and easy to push around."

"Good. Anything else?"

"White guy is risk averse. Any trouble, and all he'll care about is scraping through it in one piece. He won't make a stand to preserve his pride; he'll accept any humiliation to save his skin. He may really have gone to Yale, but he's under-confident in a street sense. He's extremely frightened of other men who are black or Latino—though maybe not of Asians, but that just makes him ignorant. So, yeah, he might be technically well educated, but as for being up to speed in a self-preservational sense, he's illiterate. He's timid and desperate to avoid conflict. Careless of his valuables—which he regards as replaceable. Gullible. Probably lives with his parents."

"I submit," Remington said, raising his fork, "that men in their teens and twenties are the most dangerous creatures on earth. They're competing for mates, and trying to establish dominance in the male pecking order. The world over, these are the terrorists, the gang members, the perpetrators of most nonstate murders. But the backstop presumption runs that young white men of any means have effectively been taking testosterone blockers. They may be brilliant at coding or semiotics; as animals, they've been disabled. They can't take care of themselves in unfamiliar situations. They can't think on their feet. They've been raised around their own kind, and by women, and by men who are controlled by women. As a group, they're perceived as incompetent even as social animals. They're bad at badinage; they suck at quick comebacks; they aren't witty. They're helpless without money."

Serenata drummed the table. "I've met a few exceptions. I like to think I married one. But broadly—your witness statement sounds about right."

"But here's another question," Remington said. "If we were in company, and you and I repeated all these slanderous generalizations about young 'privileged' white men, would our set piece be considered inflammatory, or provocative? Even if the gathering were *diverse,* would anyone call us racists? At a dinner party, would anyone of any color or persuasion flounce from the table in consternation?"

"If anything, we'd get a round of applause." She sat back. "What does all this mean to you?"

"I'm not sure."

The peculiar conversation was strangely bonding.

As they lay reading in bed—Remington a book called *Endure: Mind, Body, and the Curiously Elastic Limits of Human Performance,* she a recent *New Yorker*—Serenata took advantage of the genial mood. "You know, the concept of this short story might interest you."

"Okay." Perhaps also grateful for the rare softening of the domestic atmosphere, he laid his book politely on the spread right away.

"In the future, you can hook yourself up to a machine called the Morphatron. It works out every muscle in your body while you sleep—like plugging in an electric car and letting it charge. So everyone's in perfect condition. You can set it to burn any extra calories, so nobody is fat, either. In fact, after going through a phase of gorging, people get bored with eating and have to force themselves to finish meals. This Morphatron has custom settings: some guys go for the Schwarzenegger look or prefer a swimmer build; women will choose to look like ballerinas, or Michelle Obama. It has an aerobic program, so heart disease has gone way down, and so has cancer. There are still heritable diseases, but otherwise the whole global population is in impeccable health. Except—you saw this coming—there's one guy who insists on working out the old-fashioned way. There aren't any gyms anymore, and they don't manufacture weights or Nautiluses, so he jury-rigs his gear with cans of food and backpacks. He runs until he's shattered, and he has the paths to himself, because all the other pre-fit people have more interesting things to do. Everyone thinks he's crazy. If he'd only plug his body in, he'd be in way better shape than he can ever get grunting and 'feeling the burn.'"

"*Brave New World*, with one noble savage."

"Agreed, the premise is straight-up *Twilight Zone*. But here's my question: If you could skip all the torment, and all the expenditure of time, and still get the same or even better results, would you plug in?"

"Of course not. I assume that's the moral of the story. Fitness without effort would be empty. Tri is all mind over matter, force of will. It's about reaching—but, ironically, never quite attaining—total self-domination . . . Excuse me, am I boring you?"

Serenata had grabbed her phone and was punching figures into its calculator app. "No, no—sorry. It's just, I've wanted to add this up for ages. Say I've exercised for an hour and a half, every day, since I was about eight . . . That's just over 29,000 hours . . . Divided by 24 is . . . 1,209 days, or . . . Three and a third years. Since when you subtract eating, sleeping, cooking, shopping, and shitting, at *most* you have maybe twelve hours out of any twenty-four that's discretionary, *exercise* has occupied six or seven years of my life. And that's not including biking, which in my book counts only as transport."

"I've always gotten the impression you consider that time well spent."

"I'm sick up to my eyeballs of doing burpees. I'd hit the Morphatron in a heartbeat."

To catch the 6:17 a.m. train to Penn Station, Serenata arose about the same time as Remington in Syracuse, where the race started at the typically barbaric hour of seven sharp. Taking her bicycle to Manhattan was more trouble than it was worth, but having commuted by bike for years in the city before they moved to Albany, she couldn't bear the prospect of squeezing onto the subway like all the other suckers.

Trusty steed stashed in the baggage car, she assumed her window seat with a view of the Hudson. Nagging awareness that Remington was at this moment climbing into his wet suit interfered with her ability to read. Staring out the window as the sun rose, she gave over to an underrated entertainment: thinking.

She'd characterized MettleMan to Griff as a cult, so maybe it was worth considering what about this vogue for extreme endurance sport slaked a religious thirst, even for secular types like her husband. Repudiation of the flesh was a near constant across the faiths, whose fundamentalist strains encouraged fasting, flagellation, celibacy, and self-denial; during Lent, you renounced something you especially liked. Religion had always been hostile to pleasure. Like many more formal theologies, MettleMan elevated suffering, sacrifice, and the conquest of the spirit over the petty, demeaning desires and complaints of the mortal coil. It was replete with saints (the pros) and ecclesiastical raiments (finisher T-shirts). It offered rites of initiation—today's half Mettle was one—and christenings, like the baptismal inking of mountainous orange double-*M* tattoos on Sloan Wallace's arm. MettleMan invited the faithful into a fellowship of like-minded souls, and so fostered a sense of belonging. More importantly, it also offered un-belonging—the exclusion on which religions often relied even more than on community. So just as traditional creeds shunned the unbeliever, the heretic, the *kaffir*, the cult of tri elevated a select elite over the flabby, the flaccid, the inactive. It dangled the prospect of redemption, resurrection, and rebirth, even to serial sinners like Hank Timmerman—since Bambi may have cast her disciples as uniquely sanctified, her chosen people, but she also hocked the commercially convenient notion that any sluggard could gestate into a champion within nine months.

MettleMan erected a ladder of ascending enlightenment—from layman to penitent to aspirant to the full beatification that Remington had his eye on in June—though the ladder foreshortened skyward and vanished into the firmament. For throughout this infinite process of purification, you could always go on another pilgrimage, and always better your time. As Remington noted, you forever approached yet never attained the athletic ideal, so there was always something to do. Better still, unlike most sacred journeys, these increments of greater sanctity were quantifiable: four minutes and eleven seconds, say, off the 2.6-mile swim.

For the church of exercise delivered clarity. That is, it laid out an unambiguous set of virtues—exertion, exhaustion, the neglect of pain, the defiance of perceived limits, any distance that was longer than the one before, any speed that was swifter—which cleared up all confusion about what qualified as a productive use of your day. Likewise, it defined evil: sloth. Most of all, apropos of Remington's testimonial about the ameliorative powers of a raised heart rate on Parkinson's, insomnia, diabetes, dementia, and depression: only through exercise could you forestall disease, degeneration, and mental decline. Taken to the *n*th, then, the church of exercise promised not only the end if not reversal of all aging and infirmity, but eternal life.

It was the oldest scam in the world.

At eight fifteen, she retrieved the bike (whose name, unbeknownst to anyone but his master, was Carlisle), hooked on her pannier, wheeled through the concourse, and hoisted the crossbar onto her shoulder to climb the station stairs—a practiced maneuver to which an ominous twang in her right knee was an unwelcome addition. Outside, the sun was shockingly hot, after air-conditioning on the train had driven her to a sweatshirt. This was shaping up to be another of those weird springs in the Northeast, with sudden heat waves worthy of August; weather.com predicted a high in Central Park of 91°F. Damn. She should also have checked the weather in Syracuse.

After walking Carlisle north on Seventh Avenue, she saddled up and sailed down West Thirty-Fourth Street toward the West Side bikeway, only to be immediately engulfed by two dozen other cyclists. It was rush hour, and they were rude, of course, churning feverishly past the older woman and her antiquated men's road bike. But the crazed pedal pushers were also foolhardy, cutting it much too close on the light at the bottom of the hill and streaking across the West Side Highway on a dead red. Serenata had a job to do, whose execution being flattened by a quick-off-the-mark Uber driver wasn't likely to improve, and she alone stopped to wait for the next green.

Running the length of the island alongside the Hudson was the busiest bike lane in the United States. Once a sumptuously capacious two-lane cycling superhighway, the Manhattan Waterfront Greenway now suffered from an invasion of electric scooters, Segways, in-line skates, illegal mopeds, battery-powered skateboards, runners with an infernal affection for the meridian, and baby strollers the size of a double-decker tour bus. And that was in addition to the explosion of actual bicycles, whose number, by Serenata's seat-of-the-pants calculation, had multiplied in the last two decades by ten to twenty times.

Swarmed by converts to a form of transportation for most of her life widely derided as geeky, as ever she resolved to rise above. She would remain calm. She would cultivate a Zen obliviousness to passing slights such as being brazenly cut off or overtaken dangerously on the inside. She would employ the maturity of her advancing years to serenely accommodate the rising popularity of pedal power—which was, after all, in the larger public interest, leading to improved air quality, lower carbon emissions, less obesity, reduced health-care costs, and a happier, more energetic population.

As ever? She failed.

She despised them. Every single one. Hot-shit skinnies in Lycra covered in loud branding on fixed-gear track bikes with no brakes that were conspicuously infelicitous for urban stop-and-start. Wall Streeters with laptop panniers and prissy Velcro straps around the ankles of their suit pants. Whole tourist families on matching rentals riding five abreast and weaving mindlessly out of lane. Underpaid Central American food app deliverymen doing thirty-five whose English was at least good enough to understand NO E-BIKES in foot-high illuminated red letters on park service notice boards. Teenagers texting on smart phones juddering blindly onto adjacent bark cover. Haughty twenty-somethings in designer gymwear who never registered that they didn't need to pass you because you were going the same pace they were, if not a little faster. Gangs of kids on BMXs popping wheelies in the wrong direction. She hated them all. They had invaded her turf, and they were in her way.

Worst of all were the Citibikes, heavy, municipally provided dray horses that could be rented for a pittance. Half the traffic on this path comprised these navy-blue clunkers. Negotiating the free-for-all entailed ceaselessly overtaking this semistationary flotsam—in addition to squeezing around the hulking cement barriers plunked every fifty yards squarely in the middle of the path, the would-be preventive fruits of a vehicular terrorist attack whose obstruction amounted to yet more terrorism.

Perhaps a particular vanity was to be found in making wicked tracks on a piece of junk. In that case, before overtaking a particular Citibiker along the straightaway approach to Canal Street, she should have noted the cyclist's frantic RPM—the signature of the sort who regards being overtaken by anyone at all as a personal affront, and being overtaken by a woman as tantamount to open-air castration. Within seconds of her slipping past the young man—a nondescript white guy in his twenties—he had poured it on furiously, knees jutting at cockamamie angles, and pulled back out in front.

She should let it go. She was a grown-up. She'd cycled the equivalent of the circumference of the Earth multiple times, and had nothing to prove. If anything, she'd arrive at the studio before the building was open, and would have to get coffee. She could ease up, and savor the glint of the sun in the skyscrapers across the river in New Jersey. Yet like most people's, her inner twelve-year-old was forever battling to get out. It got out.

When she geared down and then back up, Carlisle responded like the stallion she had always privately imagined him to be. Nearly clipping an oncoming commuter in the opposite lane—this encounter was turning her into an idiot—she surged past the impertinent Citibiker, with every intention of maxing out all the way to Vesey Street, since a lunatic like this loser wasn't likely to give up.

Pop.

The blaze of agony in her right knee immediately installed the sense of perspective that she was always pushing on Remington.

Barely able to breathe or even see, she coasted to the side. The milquetoast shot past.

People who felt fine were rarely mindful of the fact that their whole state of being—their ostensible personality, what mattered to them, what they thought about, and especially what they didn't think about—was predicated on this feeling-fineness. In an instant, Serenata became a different person. She didn't care about the Citibiker, she didn't care about which point Remington had reached in his stupid half Mettle, and horribly, at this very moment, she didn't care about the fate of her marriage. Least of all did she mind about the accelerating popularity of cycling, as the other bikes whizzed by like meteors in a shower. She was no longer a fit, well-kept woman powering to a lucrative job at a Gold Street studio, but an object of pity—although the piteous in big cities often failed to extract the emotion specified and simply vanished. Professionalism died hard, so she couldn't put altogether from her mind the necessity of arriving at the studio on time, but the means by which she would achieve this punctuality was profoundly in doubt. The faithful Carlisle had converted from steed to yoke; he complicated hailing a taxi.

The pain was disconcertingly private. It seemed inconceivable that she was experiencing something so enormous yet invisible to the hundreds of recreationists coursing this artery. Pain put you in a lonely place, for if you weren't feeling it you didn't believe in it, and if you were feeling it you couldn't really believe in anything else. The state was so separating that it amounted to a form of solitary confinement. No one else cared what she was going through, and she was sympathetic with this obliviousness, too, because she had become a useless person, an even greater burden than Carlisle.

She slipped off the seat enough to verify that the putting of any appreciable weight on her right leg was simply not going to happen. That was the other interesting thing, or it would have been interesting had it been possible to become interested in anything, which it wasn't: Remington and his tri friends were always talking up "pushing through the pain," but in that case the pain was of a penultimate sort that perhaps deserved a different word. This pain-pain, if you will, was not a barrier through which one pushed. One could as well "push through" the Grand Coulee Dam.

Whiffling as Remington did when his foot muscles seized in the middle of the night—had she been compassionate enough? Oh, probably not—Serenata mounted the seat again while tilted to the left. Treating Carlisle like a Razor scooter, she could feebly propel the machine—which no longer felt like a horse—by pushing off with her left foot. Keeping humbly to the very edge of the bike path to stay out of the way of all that hectic feeling-fineness, she eked her way down to Vesey Street.

By the time she propelled herself in this shuffling manner across Vesey and then Ann Street to Gold, preferring the sidewalk and suffering glares, coffee was out of the question. She was late. Locking up was the usual nightmare; these days it was as hard to park a bike in New York as a car. The full-on blast of agony seemed to have subsided somewhat, so that it was just possible to limp, if still at great cost, to the buzzer. Serenata Terpsichore Totally Different Person didn't take the stairs.

Greeting Jon and Coca, a director and engineer she'd worked with before, she worried that her grimace made her appear averse to the workday ahead. She negotiated the outer studio by leaning on the top of a soft chair and then on the desk of the digital soundboard as inconspicuously as possible.

Jon was stringy and undernourished, with the complexion of a man who hadn't been out of doors for ten years. "You okay?" he asked.

Her lurching between furniture had been conspicuous, all right. "Oh, sure," she said. "I mean, I had a little *incident* on the West Side bike path on the way here is all." Even the director was half her age. The word *arthritis* would not pass her lips.

"Ever since they dumped all those concrete girders everywhere," Coca said, "I won't take it. It's not just the pinch points. It's the reminder—that some douchebag plowed his truck through all those people just trying to have a nice time on a nice day. I'd rather take Tenth Avenue and think about something else."

Maybe twenty-five, Coca was distractingly attractive. He appeared mixed race, like Brazilian but with a hint of Filipino or Thai and possibly some Italian. The combination had worked out stunningly, like those casual recipes you invented on the fly, and by accident or instinct the unmeasured ingredients struck a perfect balance that you'd never replicate no matter how many times you tried.

The morning's recording was straight dubbing in the sound booth, which Serenata would traditionally perform standing up. Suddenly preferring to sit would call only more attention to her infirmity, so she kept her weight on her left leg and steadied herself with a hand on the desk. *Kill Joy* had the rather perverse premise that the player was aiming to murder the very character whom the script built up as sympathetically intrepid. Though the graphic of her character looked about sixteen, she'd been cast to read Joy because the protagonist was a fashionably "strong woman" who'd seem more formidable with an older voice. Besides, Serenata could dial up any age they liked.

"Fierce, but vulnerable," Jon instructed in her earphones, after his young female assistant arrived to read the opposing character's dialogue on the other side of the glass.

Her computer screen displayed the dialogue spreadsheet. It never helped to allow into her head that most of the lines were dumb. The assistant's lifeless delivery of the yet-to-be-recorded male lead made them sound even dumber.

"More frightened," Jon said after the read-through. "How long was that, Coca?"

"Forty-two seconds."

"Tighten it up. A little faster." To keep the video modifications to a minimum, the timings of the audio and animation had to roughly match up.

She gave them what they wanted: "more sparkle of life," "a few years younger," "horrified—a little improv, just sounds, maybe a little, you know, 'Wha . . . ?' or 'What the . . . !'" She repeated the same line three or four times with different modulations, so that the producer, who was listening on Skype from Chicago, could choose his preferred coloration. Still, the morning's output lacked her distinctive flair. They did unusually numerous retakes for an old pro. The knee pain was sullen, glowering, like a disruptive activist who'd been asked to leave a lecture and had instead retreated resentfully to a back row. When she tried too hard to move around the booth as if nothing were the matter, the knee rebuked her with flashes of the original anguish on the bike path. She couldn't seem to rest in the pocket of the lines, but was forever focused a trace ahead of the words in her mouth.

Assuming a nonchalant slump in the exterior studio on a break, Serenata lengthened both legs and crossed her ankles, covering for the fact that she couldn't bend the right knee. "I was glad this gig came in," she said, after the assistant left to fetch coffees. "For some reason, the audiobook work has dried up."

"Well, that's hardly surprising," Jon said.

"How's that? I thought audio was a growth market. Going up more than print."

"You have something of a reputation."

"After thirty-five years of this stuff, I'd think so. And this morning may have been a little pro forma, but I hope my reputation is for doing pretty good work."

"Yeah," the director said. "Kind of too good."

"You'll have to explain to me how one can ever be 'too good.'"

"The accents," he announced, as if no more needed to be said.

"What about them?"

"You're known for them, aren't you? And that whole thing's gone toxic."

Serenata frowned, scrounging for what Tommy had told her a year or two ago. "Is it this 'mimicry' issue?"

"That's the buzzword," Coca said. "Touché."

The director said, "The audio companies have gotten so much grief on social media for using white performers to read, you know, black, Chinese, whatever dialogue that it's not worth the hassle. A few producers have brought in special, you know, people of color to read those lines, but that makes the project way more expensive. So if there's racial or ethnic stuff in the book, it's easier to hire a POC to read the whole thing."

"Hold it," Serenata said. "Including the white parts."

"May be hard on veterans like you," Coca said. "Still, the reasoning goes that the privileged have had their day."

"It's not my day?" Who was she kidding. Today was definitely not her day.

"Anybody's ever had a day," Jon said airily, "I guess that makes them lucky."

"These minority readers," Serenata said. "Do they do white accents? Like, some drawling cracker from the Deep South? Or the flat nasality of Nebraska?"

"Mm . . ." Jon hummed. "Some do, some don't."

"So why isn't that 'mimicry'?"

"Turn about," Coca said. "Guess you find out what it feels like, on the other foot."

The right leg stiffening, Serenata slipped her own other foot atop the opposite ankle. "Is that the way we're going to fix things?" she wondered aloud. "By swapping who treats whom like shit?"

"Got a better idea?" Coca said.

This whole area was Remington's bailiwick, and she felt at sea. She'd no desire to offend the engineer. "Maybe. Like, we all quit bruising for a fight. An authentically rendered accent pays tribute to the fact that there are lots of ways to speak English, right? And some vernaculars are especially affecting or expressive."

"Yeah, but those 'vernaculars' don't belong to you," Coca said.

"Does my own vernacular belong to me?"

"Far as I can tell, you don't have one."

"Of course I do. There's no such thing as neutral English."

"If that's what you call an accent, then yeah, you can have it." The two seemed to find the whole idea of Serenata speaking in an "accent" hilarious.

"All these new rules . . ." Serenata said wistfully.

"There's always been rules," Coca said. "Now there's just different ones."

Fortunately, Jon ordered sandwiches, so she didn't have to be seen lurching off to lunch.

The afternoon's recording was motion capture. High-powered pure action scenes would be recorded using gaming stuntmen, who could do rolls, down-and-dirty fights, and leaps from a height. But the less demanding physical stuff integrated with dialogue used the actor playing the part, and today's ructions would have been easily within her gift—on most days. Yet even getting into the mo-cap suit in the changing room was painful. Working the form-fitting black neoprene over her right leg entailed bending it, and even the suit failed to disguise that the joint had blown up. As Jon's assistant affixed some sixty shiny round sensors on Velcro pads across her limbs, over her torso, down her back, and on the cap on the top of her head, simply standing squarely with her arms out required the gritty resolve on which she commonly drew for interval training.

The mo-cap studio was large, open-air, and dotted along its perimeter with cameras to record the motions of her figure, later translated to Joy, her avatar. The set was typically primitive: two lashed-together straight-back chairs and a round wooden disk mounted on a pole, meant to approximate the front seat of a car and a steering wheel. Mo-cap sets recalled the minimalist modernism often employed to stage Samuel Beckett; all the lushness and detail would be left to the animators. In this scene, Joy was to have a ferocious argument with the male lead on her cell phone. As the difference of opinion heated up, she'd grow inattentive, and lose control of the car. Serenata would be obliged to roll violently around the two chairs and end up on the floor, as the car tumbled down a ravine and she was thrown out the door. All in a day's work—ordinarily.

Her first version was destined to be her best—and it was a pity they weren't using facial capture as well, since her expressions of fear, alarm, and agony were oh, so very true to life. The problem came when she had to get up and do it again.

"Serenata," Jon said in her earphones after calling a halt to the second take. "You're not supposed to sound like you're dying *before* the car runs off the road." Frustrated, he cut the session short at four.

Back out on the baking sidewalk, she requested a large capacity Uber, whose driver loaded Carlisle into his minivan for the ride to Penn Station. The disgrace of resorting to a car dovetailed with disappointment in herself over the day's performance. She was always persnickety about her work, critical, convinced particular lines had come out dead, or she'd curse herself for letting a subtle fluff on a consonant go by when she should have insisted on reading the line again, but this more encompassing shame was new. It was a brown feeling.

Unfamiliar with whatever route the *disabled* were meant to take, she wheeled Carlisle to the top of the station stairs and leaned on the frame, looking helpless, until a strapping young man volunteered to hoist the bike to the concourse. Unaccustomed to the kindness of strangers, she wasn't 100 percent sure that Carlisle hadn't been stolen until the boy waited for her to hop the stairs one at a time while groping the railing. "I'm not meaning any insult or anything," he said, "but it seems like you might do better with a cane than a bike."

"It's a cane on wheels," she said (Carlisle would be offended). Though she'd have been mistaken for younger than sixty-two not long ago—like, early this morning—her rescuer clearly regarded her as an old lady. A glance in the studio's restroom mirror that afternoon had confirmed that her pain-makeover personality came replete with a new face: gray, drawn, lined, and asymmetric.

Scootering along as she had down Vesey Street would still qualify as riding in the station, which was banned, so she supported her right side by clutching the handlebars with her left hand while leaning the right one heavily on the crossbar.

Now feeling responsible for her, the Samaritan seemed reluctant to walk off. "You going to be okay?"

Since a truthful answer was *probably not*, she volunteered instead, "My husband is doing a half triathlon today, while I can barely walk."

"You mean, one of the Mettles?" When she nodded, he lifted his T-shirt sleeve. A jag of orange tattoos disappeared around his bicep. The smile glinted with a gold front tooth as he punched the air in farewell. "Hell, yeah, good for him! I done five."

Good grief, was this what it was like in Berlin in the 1930s? First you'd see one, and then a bit later you'd see two, until before you knew it these men in dun shirts were everywhere.

After handing off Carlisle at the baggage car, she accepted an engineer's offer of a helping hand into the carriage and lunged to her seat by holding onto headrests. Once the train got underway, she checked her messages again. Even at his slowest, Remington had to have completed the course by now. His nose was out of joint about her absence in Syracuse, but his not even sending a text seemed churlish. She shouldn't expect him to telepathically intuit while larking about Onondaga Lake that something dreadful had happened to his wife. Yet they both dwelled in bodies, notoriously hazardous housing that couldn't possibly have met modern health-and-safety standards. An occasional solicitation of how *she* was doing didn't seem too much to ask.

DID YOU FINISH? she texted. ARE YOU OKAY? BUY YOURSELF A NEW YORK STRIP AT DELMONICO'S! I BET YOU'VE EARNED IT. PLEASE CALL WHEN YOU'VE SETTLED. No reply. Maybe, as after the marathon, he was sleeping at his hotel. Finally by six o'clock, she texted Valeria, HOW'S DAD? Immediately, the phone rang.

"I'll tell you *how's Dad,*" Valeria said in a shouty voice. "He's in Saint Joseph's Hospital."

"*What?*" Whatever had gone down, Valeria had a remarkable ability to imply in few words that it was all her mother's fault.

"You might have noticed that it's hot!" Perhaps the temperature was Serenata's fault as well. "Way too hot, and Papa's not used to it."

"No, he doesn't do well when it's warm." He didn't do well when it was not warm, either. "Did he stop, then? Bow out?"

"No, he was totally amazing! Like, he finally found the God in himself, the way Bambi said—"

"Valeria, would you please can all that praise-the-Lord guff for now and tell me what happened to your father."

"I'm *trying* if you'd be a little *patient.* I managed to be right there at the finish line, because, you know, there were sort of hardly any runners left—"

"You mean he was last."

"I guess so. Maybe. Yeah. But there's a heroism in that, isn't there?" Valeria said defiantly. "I mean, sure, he was going slow. I could probably have walked faster, if you want to know the truth. But it was hot! When the people still watching saw him coming around the final bend, they all went crazy! Cheering, and clapping, and banging these inflatable bat things against the barriers! As he trudged closer I noticed his face was a funny color, and his gait was unsteady, like he was having trouble keeping his balance. His eyes were all glassy, like he wasn't actually seeing anything. Still, he didn't stop. I've never seen anything so brave in all my life. I've never been so proud. I've never felt so strongly that the Lord was on Papa's side—"

"Enough," her mother said. "Why is your father in the hospital?" (A better question might have been, Why is *everyone* in the hospital?)

"When *you* tell a story, you expect everyone to be riveted by every detail. When anyone else tells a story, you're all, shut up and get to the point."

This was utter torture. "Go on. *Detail* away."

"At the end—if you care, and I have to wonder, since you weren't there—he was all, like, floppy, and staggering, and not running quite in a straight line. So the staff and medical people were all, like, hovering, but I guess they're not supposed to help you or you might not get your medal or whatever . . . So he's weaving, and we're all rooting for him, but also starting to get nervous that he's so close but even now he might not make it . . . And you wouldn't believe this, because, you know, right over the finish line there's this bar overhead, and I guess if you don't do that last chin-up then technically you don't finish. And you know what a stickler Papa is, like, you did it or you didn't do it. So he slaps at the air, and has trouble even finding the bar, but then he grabs it, and man oh man, he was so shaky, and we're all like, oh Lordy, is this astonishing man going to get this far and still stumble at the very last hurdle . . . And then he barely,

barely, like, both arms trembling, gets his chin *just* on top of the bar, and the little crowd of us went completely bananas and I burst into tears. I've never been so moved . . . so touched . . . so overwhelmed in all my born days."

"That's nice," Serenata said tightly. *"And?"*

"Well. Then he collapsed. Down in the dirt, passed clean out. The medical team went *whoosh,* and draped him with cold wet towels, and someone got ice and someone else brought orange juice while they took his pulse—I was trying to get over to him, so I heard a medic say his heart rate was uneven and way too fast. And I know you've got some weird problem with her, but Bambi was right in there, and you should be glad she was. She laid Papa out with his feet elevated, and fanned him with newspapers, and sprayed him with mist, while one of the medics on call stuck a thermometer under his arm. Before the ambulance got there, he started coming to, but it was sort of creepy because, though he seemed to recognize Bambi, he didn't seem to know who I was, or even where he was, or that he'd just finished a whole half MettleMan."

"Valeria, do I need to get up there tonight? I'm on the train to Hudson, but I could stay on to Albany, where I could pick up a train to Syracuse—"

"There's no need for all the dramatics," Valeria said. "He's going to be okay. His temperature's already come way down. They're keeping him in overnight just to be extra careful, but they seem to think he'll be totally fine to drive home tomorrow."

"This sounds like heatstroke."

"Heat-something. Yeah."

"If you're absolutely certain he doesn't want me to meet him there . . ."

"Depending on the train schedule, you'd get here at eleven, maybe even after midnight. Papa would be asleep; you'd see him in the morning, only to drive back to Hudson. It would be a big Florence Nightingale song and dance serving no earthly purpose but to make you look good."

Valeria was right for once. Given that Syracuse was hardly en route to her second day of recording tomorrow, the fact that Serenata was still drawn toward the empty gesture was a bad sign. In times past, neither she nor her husband would have entertained grand flights to one another's side of no practical utility, and "looking good" in the other's eyes would have been a foreign consideration for two people who looked good to each other already.

"Fair enough," she said. "But—I'm sorry if this sounds trivial—could you make sure to pick up his finisher coffee mug? You know he's going to want it. Also"—it was embarrassing to have to ask her daughter this—"would you ask him to call me? If he's feeling up to it."

"Oh, sure, I guess. But at the moment to be on the safe side they're running some tests. Besides, you're not exactly Papa's favorite person in the world right now."

Serenata neglected to point out that your "favorite person in the world" should have been the very definition of the person you were married to.

"No, technically it was heat *exhaustion*. It's only heatstroke when your temperature rises above a hundred and four."

Remington was just a few minutes in the door, but beyond a ritual embrace she didn't see the point of pussyfooting. "And yours rose to . . . ?"

"Only a hundred and three." Aside from a pinkening from strong sun the previous afternoon, his color looked normal, though she detected a new precariousness. He wouldn't ordinarily have sunk into a chair at the dining table immediately after a three-hour drive.

"*Only a hundred and three,*" she repeated. "If I recall correctly, a hundred and four is right around the point you're in danger of brain damage."

"With ice packs and rehydration, my core temperature came right back down."

"Have you ever considered that you might not be cut out for this stuff?"

"Triathlon isn't something you are or aren't 'cut out for.' It's a challenge you decide to rise to."

Fetching him seltzer from the fridge, she managed the short distance by leaning on the kitchen island. He didn't notice.

"Yesterday hit a historic high for New York State on that date," Remington said at her back. "I don't see hyperthermia as something to be ashamed of."

"Did I say it was?"

"You have a *chiding* quality."

She couldn't imagine marshaling the wherewithal to chide. When she'd awoken early that morning, inflammation in the right knee had spread, and was at this moment traveling wildly up and down the leg—the length of her shin, through the ankle to the top of her foot, up the back of her thigh, and deep into the muscles of the buttock. Over-the-counter anti-inflammatories hadn't touched it. When the fluctuations of fire hit peaks like the one right now, she could feel the pain in her eyes, where the pupils were constricting to pinpricks.

"You're projecting," she said, pouring the water while storking on her left leg. "You imagine I'm *chiding*, when really you're chiding yourself."

"Excuse me, I inferred from your remarks that you think my getting overheated should teach me a lesson: I'm 'not cut out for this stuff.' But this nay-saying of yours is all in my head? You're not trying to get me to quit. No, you're bolstering my confidence: 'Go, team! So you got a little flushed, now hit the trail!' "

"You already have a cheerleader who's utterly oblivious to the risks you're taking, and who's now saved your life twice that I know of. Isn't that supposed to create some special lifelong bond?"

"As my beloved wife and helpmate, you might easily have been the one to fan and mist me, feed me sips of orange juice, and cover me in cold wet towels. But you'd have had to be present. You can't object to my intimacy with someone else and at the same time boycott any opportunities to boost ours."

Sliding on her right hand around the island, she delivered the seltzer.

"For example, don't you think you're forgetting something?" he asked.

"Lemon?"

"Congratulations. If with some difficulty, I finished the course."

"You mean, 'Congratulations for almost killing yourself again.' I didn't realize that was standard social etiquette."

"It's certainly standard etiquette after your husband has completed a feat as demanding as even a half Mettle, or anything close. Lots of people get hugs, flowers, and slaps on the back for finishing a five-K fun run."

"Congratulations," she said stonily.

"Well, that was quite the empty exercise."

"You asked for it."

"No, I asked for something else."

"All these years when I've gone out for a run, or a swim, or a long bike ride, have I ever come back demanding that you *congratulate* me?"

"I'm sorry if I sound insulting, but the scale of your sporting achievements has never been in a realm that would deserve exceptional recognition."

"Got it right there: you do sound insulting." It wasn't in the interest of putting her case forcefully, but she'd soon have to sit down. One of the many unsolicited revelations of the last day and a half: pain was tiring. It even seemed to entail a form of athleticism.

"You're doing your very best to deprive me of any sense of accomplishment, after I've exerted myself to the very limits of my ability—in fact, beyond those limits—"

"If you get this fucked-up finishing a *half* Mettle, what makes you think you can get through a whole one? In only two months' time? In June, when it could be even hotter."

"It's true, I did face—*and overcame*—a medical crisis. I get home, and my only reward is seltzer. Try as I might, I can't remember ever having snidely dismissed something you set your sights on, strived for, and finally succeeded at. I can't remember ever having pissed all over anything that was so important to you."

"What you want from me is patently unavailable," she said, finally plopping into a chair. "It's never been available, from the start of this thing, and you knew it wouldn't be. So if you wanted my admiration, you should have set about achieving something else. It's not fair to say, 'I'm doing this dumb thing. But you're never, ever allowed to observe how dumb it is. I won't accept your merely pretending it's not dumb, either. You have to *believe* it's not dumb, in your very soul.' In demanding some passionate, prostrate *congratulations*, you're asking me to completely relinquish my independent judgment—to relinquish *myself*. Suddenly just because you're my husband, I'm expected to wholeheartedly get on board whatever goofball notion takes your fancy."

"You're expected," he said quietly, "to be a little less selfish."

"Check this out for being selfless," she said. "How's your hamstring?"

It was dreadful to watch his face and actually see in it the indecision about whether to lie to her. "It aches." He'd settled on farcical understatement.

"It's been, what, nine months?"

"Something like that."

"And it's never healed."

She should have been asking about that damned hamstring nonstop, but only her short course in the astonishing existence of agony the day before had brought out the suffering of others in relief. She might have been looking at the world through infrared glasses—and when she turned the viewfinder on her husband, his entire figure lit up crimson.

"That means," she went on, "each time you go for a run, every second step hurts. So you're not leaping hill and dale in a state of transcendent bliss. You're gritting your teeth through an ordeal you can't wait to be over. This whole venture—it's so joyless! What's the point?"

"The point is obviously not *joy*." He pronounced the word with the disdain that Tommy had lent to *imprimatur*.

"Then I repeat: What *is* the point?"

"If you don't understand by now—and I think you do; I think your incomprehension is disingenuous—then we're not going to improve your grasp of my purpose with more talk. So let's wrap this conversation up, shall we?"

As a gesture of conclusion, he took his bag upstairs.

"Hey, I'm surprised to find you home," he said on return. "I'd have thought you'd still be recording in Manhattan."

Old Remington would have remarked on her unanticipated presence first thing. It took some nerve to ride her for being selfish, because New Remington's world stopped at his skin, and the exigencies of other people's lives dawned dimly if at all, and on delay. The note-in-a-bottle message "Your wife isn't supposed to be here" might have just dropped in their backyard from an Amazon drone.

"I was fired," she said.

"Whose desk did *you* slam?"

"For once, I was sent packing for good reason. I did take the train down, but my concentration was poor, and my delivery was subpar. And there's a physical aspect to gaming VO that I don't appear to be up to. They're recasting my character. They'll have to rerecord the work I did yesterday, but the director didn't have any choice. I agreed with him, actually. So I took the train right back up."

Remington's eyes narrowed. "What's wrong?" He seemed to be seeing her for the first time this afternoon, though from far away.

"My right knee exploded. There's a hard knot at the back the size of an egg, and now the whole leg is inflamed, ass to toe. I am no longer functional. And yes, of course I've made an appointment, though I know what he'll say. Churchwell told me that at the outside I had a year and a half. That was a year and a half ago."

"Knee replacement."

"I can't put it off anymore. I can't exercise."

"I'm sorry."

"I am, too."

TEN

Knee replacements had become ordinary—even if a certain ordinary orthopedist had breezily informed a certain ordinary patient that the generation behind her was sure to get injections of stem cells to regenerate connective tissues instead. Thus right around the corner, though not in time for her to benefit, sheering off the ends of the leg bones with a hacksaw and pounding big foreign chunks of metal into their amputated stumps with a polo mallet—that is, attacking the dysfunctions of the human body as a crude carpentry project, as one might repair a garden shed or porch railing—would be regarded the height of barbarism. *Thanks, doc. That makes me feel so much better.*

Thus there was no call for alarm or complaint. Scads of other people had submitted to this same brutal surgery, gone through the same excruciating recovery (or failure to recover), and rolled the same medical dice that, should they come up snake eyes, would preclude not only completing one hour and fifty-eight minutes of high-intensity interval training, but also walking to the mailbox. For that matter, the yawn-inducing nonchalance now expected of candidates for joint replacement surely pertained to the likes of aging and death: They happened to everybody, so what was the big deal?

The big deal was that personally Serenata Terpsichore had never before inhabited a body tenderly preserved for decades—*curated* for decades, since the fashionable verb was now applied to everything from thrift stores to salad—that, despite best efforts, was falling apart. However predictable the monotonous cycle of renewal and decay in the big picture, on a granular level the tragic structure of the human life was forever startling. As she'd understood from childhood that the body wasn't built to last, she should hardly have been surprised when her own body didn't last, either. Nevertheless, she *was* surprised. Even the surprise was surprising.

To her further chagrin, the steady corruptions of the flesh were especially astonishing for her *type*. Much as she'd questioned Bambi's claim that the more extreme the demands placed on a body, the more it thrives—and much as she'd paid lip service to the sensible notion that biological moving parts wear out—she herself had bought wholesale into her generation's popular myth that the body solely flourishes with use. Throughout her life, she had exercised, hard, for a duration, virtually every day. According to legend, she had therefore earned reprieve from the tawdry ailments of sedentary mortals—many of whom were in fact physically better prepared to go the distance into old age than Serenata was now. The cult of MettleMan got up her nose to the degree it did because as a larger umbrella faith it was her church, too. The spouses simply differed on fine points of catechism, like a Methodist and a Pentecostal.

Whether the self was apiece with the body or rode around in a body like a passenger in an open-topped jalopy was one of those irresolvable questions, but it did seem to Serenata that you couldn't have it both ways. You couldn't walk around in a beautiful body and feel, yourself, beautiful when you were seventeen in hot pants, and then conveniently draw a sharp distinction between the *it* of you and the *you* of you when your vacuum cleaner was snarled by fistfuls of fallen-out hair from postmenopausal alopecia. You couldn't identify with the body's powers without also identifying with its deficiencies and even ugliness when those powers failed.

She was under no illusion about other people; that is, lazily, she saw man and manifestation as roughly one and the same, which meant that others also conflated Serenata the remote, obstinate, spitefully private character with a five-seven brunette whose nose was a touch Roman and on the sharp side. After all, it took mental effort to separate body and soul; it took affection, and attention, and the long view. Even with Remington, she had to concentrate in order to see him as an enduring presence—who hadn't changed much and who if anything, the last two years notwithstanding, had improved—rather than as, increasingly, an older man, if not an old man, who by dint of equal parts sweat and lunacy had grown emaciated, with mean little muscles that wouldn't last a month when his own arthritis struck. But with herself, of course, and this was surely universal, body and self were distinct; they would have to be, in order to be *in relationship*.

Plenty of people hated their bodies, and sadly, this antagonism could grow into the central battle of their lives, like bad marriages in a country that forbade divorce. In this respect, Serenata had been fortunate. Until recently, she and the body had for the most part been a team. The relationship was congenial, though there was an eternal tussle over which party was really in control. By conceit, the self was boss, and this was a myth; only at the body's behest was Serenata here at all. Still, she felt responsible for an organism that was at once robust and fragile. Despite its high mileage, it was readily undone by a moment of clumsiness on the stairs or a bad oyster. The dumb ward had to be serviced, fueled but not too much, rested, and, in the absence of the miraculous Morphatron, manually put through its paces; sometimes these animal-husbandry routines wore thin. But overwhelmingly the relationship on the overlord's side had been one of tenderness.

Somehow, the sorrow of watching a sturdy, long-serving charge falter and degrade was not the same sorrow of knowing that she herself, too, would soon perish. Though it would seem so, the claim that she dwelt in a well-crafted creature was not a boast. This body had come to her. The creature was not of her making. She had been *entrusted* with it. If she had broadly done right by it, you would not call that a boast, either. Yes, there was a small pride involved, in having made the body do things it didn't want to that were for its own good, in having fed it something a little better than a steady diet of Velveeta nachos, but this was the pride of a caretaker, not so different from the satisfaction that a faithful janitor takes in the shine of swabbed floors.

Some parts of the body stirred her tenderness more than others. Small bits, in fact, came in for the same hostility that she sensed Valeria, for example, felt toward her whole package. Serenata hated her cuticles. She did not understand the purpose of a transitional scum that did nothing but split, dry, and tear. Left to their own devices, these epidermal predators would clearly have spread to the very tips of her nails, smothering the keratin the way malign algae blooms suffocated whole Great Lakes. In her disgust, she had been wont to strip the things in ragged shreds from fingers and toes, whereupon the bloody remains would stain the pillowcase and ruin her socks. The wounds hurt and took weeks to heal, but she thought of the amateur surgery as reprisal. While she might have felt sheepish about the miniature "self-harm," she felt nothing of the kind. The cuticles had been disciplined into submission, and the conquest was gratifying.

Her legs were another matter. The primary drivers of Remington's *motion of the body through space*, they were the strongest aspect of the organism, and qualified as shapely in the terms that her culture prescribed. Proportionately, they were long. The thighs at tension were solid. In profile, the tibias swooped gently from the knees like ski slopes. The calf muscles cut shadowed commas when she wore heels. The ankles were suitably slender. Wolf whistles when she wore short skirts had never offended her. The stems on which she perched were the lines where self and flesh converged. If in any sense soul was synonymous with body, Serenata was at one with her legs. And now she was offering them up in a grotesque act of human sacrifice.

Naturally her accelerating dysfunctions didn't stop at the knees. A recurrent pang in her right wrist put her on notice that her push-ups were numbered. Or an ankle would freakishly sprain from stepping off a low curb at the wrong angle. Muscle spasms in her back were frequent, arbitrary, paralyzing, and occasioned by nothing she did or refrained from doing. For the last six months, her spine went *pong* every time she rose during her usual five hundred sit-ups—a creepy out-of-kilter slippage that doubtless portended traction. The creaks, the pops, the straining of guy ropes, the groaning of her hull together fostered the suspense of *Titanic* right before the ship sinks.

Worse, abruptly, it was as Tommy March foretold: the right knee had pretty much stopped working altogether. While still characterizing its implosion as an arthritic "flare-up," Dr. Churchwell conceded that at a certain point a flare-up failed to subside and installed unremitting torment as the new normal. Athletically, she was grounded.

Regarding double replacements as tantamount to putting his patients through a six-car pileup, this orthopedist recommended getting the second knee done in three to six months' time—which presented the happy prospect of barely recuperating from one ordeal only to go through the whole horror show all over again. With the right knee in such critical condition, the surgeon fit her into his schedule at Columbia Memorial at the end of May, claiming to have moved heaven and earth on her account. Yet from Serenata's perspective, that meant six long weeks of melting like a bar of soap in a flooded dish.

Meanwhile, Remington had hit the home stretch of training for his full Mettle. He now hewed to a regime of running, cycling, and swimming, all three sports, every other day, with strength training at BruteBody on the odd ones. Rarely laying eyes on each other during daylight hours, she and her husband shared a postal address. In every other respect, their parallel universes barely intersected. Until this cliff-edge ejection from the world of expending energy, she hadn't realized how heavily their marriage of late had depended on the slender Venn diagram of overlapping habits. The excess of the convert might have dwarfed her daily ministrations upstairs into the merely gestural, but heretofore continuing to clear what she'd once considered a fairly high athletic bar had kept her seething sense of inferiority in check. But now the bar was on the floor. She had joined the loamy, misshapen tubers on the living-room sofa.

This impression of total physiological collapse was ridiculous. Even a waterlogged bar of soap didn't dissolve into a gelatinous puddle overnight, and a relatively slim female figure nicely toned for its age would progress toward liquefaction still more gradually. Yet her emotional disintegration was instantaneous.

Disrobing at bedtime, she kept her back to her husband, stripping off her jeans in haste and pulling her shirt overhead in a single desperate motion that snagged the care label on her hair clip. Though she'd formerly have draped the shirt on a hanger for wear a second day, now she didn't even tug it right-side-out before flinging it atop her jeans on the rug, the better to wrench off her running bra and dive into the bedding. Though late spring was warm enough that she'd have commonly sprawled the mattress uncovered, legs extended, arms outstretched, basking in the breeze of the fan on low, now she kept the sheet tucked to her chin. Previously, it wasn't that she'd been conceited about her figure, or put it on parade, but she'd never felt impelled to cover it up. Now she hid from both her husband and herself, averting her gaze from the full-length mirror if she needed to scuttle from the room, limping, to pee. She hadn't realized how comfortable she'd been with her naked body until she was ashamed of it.

By contrast, if also with a limp that he tried to disguise, Remington strolled naked from bedroom to bath with unself-conscious ease. Indeed, before sliding into bed he could happily roam the house bare-assed for an hour or more. He'd already acquired a dark tan, which stopped so starkly a few inches above the knee that he appeared still to be wearing cycling shorts. The endearing swell at his midsection having long ago melted, he sported not an ounce of fat, so that when he walked, sinews rippled in his legs and buttocks in a continuous light show, like the old pixilated billboards in Times Square. Yet he'd just turned sixty-six. Though she'd never tell him so, he looked every year and then some. His figure had grown cadaverous. Creased the more from all that sun, his face looked hunted, wide-eyed, almost crazed.

Often wondering if she'd any real appetite for the rest of her life (and did that mean, in the absence of natural causes, she was threatening suicide?), Serenata was acutely aware that all her melodrama was uncalled for, even if the rending of garments took place mostly in her mind. Equating the end of squats with the end of the world was humiliating; hovering overhead, a more adult intelligence looked down on herself in every sense. Through no fault of her own—or she didn't think it was her fault—her functionality had been compromised. Yet no levelheadedness she summoned could change the fact that imposed idleness had thrown her into a tailspin. What had been offended was deeper than vanity. As mechanically as she portrayed her daily fidelities to Remington, exercise, of all things, had grown nonsensically bound up with who she was, and without it she felt reduced and not a little lost. After the surgery, which would turn her into an invalid proper, the disassociation would only get worse.

She criticized Remington for his disordered priorities, but she was just as neurotic as he was. As May advanced, the signs became unmistakable: excessive sleep; trouble completing even minor voice-over jobs of a few lines; tendency to sit for bizarrely long periods doing nothing; avoidance of mundane chores like laundry, now insurmountable; reluctance to see Tommy or Griff—reluctance, really, to leave the house at all. Clearly, she had sunk into a profound depression. All because she couldn't commence the five hundred burpees that most sane people would do almost anything to avoid.

Deacon couldn't have picked a worse time to visit, which must have pleased him.

When he phoned, their son claimed to be between digs and in need of a bed to bridge the gap, though he was typically vague about the date his apocryphal new apartment would become available. When she asked about his things, he said he "didn't have much stuff." Perhaps it was materialistic to regard someone with negligible possessions as untrustworthy, but if you couldn't take care of a few dishes and a desk lamp by twenty-nine, what else could you not take care of?

With grave misgivings, she and Remington agreed to take him in for a *very short while*. Despite Valeria's suspicions about the nature of her brother's livelihood, they hadn't any proof, and he was still their son.

Deacon's evasiveness about when he'd show up had apparently been code for "tomorrow." That night, Remington had barely worked up his resentful declaration that the boy was not going to interfere with his training regime by *five minutes* or *five feet*, with an air of just getting started. Yet the very next afternoon, Deacon was at the door. Or through the door, since during the young man's last extended period of freeloading their first summer in Hudson they'd provided him a key, which he hadn't returned.

"You could have knocked," Serenata said, tailing lines of green beans for what would *not*, it seemed, be a candlelit tête-à-tête with her husband. Chopping anything in a chair at the dining table still felt awkward. Her knife skills were tailored to standing up.

"Family," Deacon said with a shrug. Kinship was a concept of which he availed himself when it suited him. "You never knocked when barging into my room."

"I did at first. But that only gave you fair warning to hide all the swag you'd stolen."

"Nice to see you, too." He unshouldered a bag that would have fit in a budget airline's overhead bin. As ever, the young man was a measure underweight, so the oversize rayon T-shirt and smartly cut slacks draped his frame with the chic flutter of garments on a manikin. He'd doubtless worn the same outfit for days. Preferring the subtle spectrum of laurel, teal, artichoke, and sage in which the affluent now painted their houses, he always bought expensive clothes, but he was lazy.

"That's all you own in the world?"

"Easy come, easy go." The expression might have been coined specifically for Deacon Alabaster. He picked up jobs readily enough but just as readily quit. With slim low-slung hips and a gaze both challenging and opaque, he had the effortless good looks and distant bearing that made him a magnet for the pretty but insecure girls he went through like Kleenex. She'd not have been surprised if he'd also sired more than one *easy come* child along the way, whom he'd have unthinkingly left behind in the careless spirit of genetic littering.

"So where's Dad?"

"Where do you think? Trooping the trails with his floozy."

"What? Like, *jogging*?" Since they only heard from Deacon when he wanted something, he wasn't up to speed. One of them must have mentioned the enterprise, since *tri* was all Remington talked about, but if so their son hadn't listened. He'd never seemed interested in either parent, especially not in his father. Deacon had the style of Remington as a young man, but none of the substance. As a consequence, Deacon had only to walk into the room for his father to feel mocked.

"He's entering a triathlon in two weeks."

"Why?"

The simple question left Serenata stymied. "I've asked him before. His answer has never been satisfactory. He seems to think his motivation is self-evident."

"Yeah, those masochists are all over Windham." Never having suffered from the ambition that might have driven him to the city, throughout his twenties Deacon had drifted from one struggling upper New York State town to another—Dormansville, Medusa, Preston-Potter Hollow—where the rents were low and life was neither hard nor pleasant. He seemed to relish the arbitrariness of living just anywhere.

Fetching a beer, Deacon elucidated. "Always in the way, traipsing in the road, since there's no sidewalks. Fists clenched, faces purple and blotchy, like spoiled eggplants. Any day now they'll be dead, and what did the motherfuckers do when they had the chance but make themselves as miserable as possible."

Their son was chronically contemptuous. Yet he'd accomplished little enough—nothing, in most people's terms, aside from hand-to-mouth survival—so it was a puzzle where this superiority was sourced. It was, his mother had concluded, the scorn of the nonparticipant. He hadn't sullied himself with wanting something and trying to get it, which protected him from any sense of failure or disappointment. Remaining apart from the silly toiling, the overcoming of petty obstacles, the fruitless striving, and the sad little comings-up-short that punctuated the pointless churn of all the other suckers in his surround gave him an above-it-all quality that his peers found mesmeric.

"Also, I should warn you that tomorrow I'm getting my right knee replaced."

"Why would you bother to do that?"

"Thanks for your concern," Serenata said. "I'm in pain, and I can barely walk."

"Then don't walk."

"Doc, it hurts when I do this?"

Deacon looked blank.

"It's an old Henny Youngman joke. The doc says, 'Then don't do that.'"

"Pretty lame."

"I am lame. That's the point."

It passed for enjoying each other's company. Why, so far she *was* enjoying her son's company. In some curious fashion she couldn't put her finger on, at this precise moment of dread and desolation, Mr. Who Gives a Shit was the ideal houseguest.

"So both your parents are, as they say, *stressed*," she continued. "I should put you on notice before he gets here, too, that your father doesn't have a sense of humor about this triathlon business. I don't recommend even gentle ribbing. He's very nervous about his ability to complete the course. As he should be. A two-and-a-half-mile swim; well over a hundred miles on a bike; a marathon; and a final chin-up, just in case you improbably get through the rest of that crap without keeling over. I don't think I'd have been able to do it, even in my heyday." She paused; she may never before have said that aloud. "*And* if anything does go wrong in Lake Placid, don't ever say anything. Just promise me. Say absolutely nothing."

"You mean, 'Hey, Dad, I heard you entered this dopy race and fell flat on your face!' Like that?"

She laughed. "Like that. He's got way too much riding on this thing. If the gamble doesn't pay off, he'll be busted."

Rolling a cigarette, Deacon eyed her theatrically, swaying back and forth to examine her face. "You think it's retarded."

Another short laugh escaped, despite herself. Mother and son had always enjoyed a collusion, which she tried to resist. He had no moral compass. Yet she appreciated his anarchic streak. (Well—it was more than a streak.) He treated other people atrociously, but he went his own way. He wasn't a joiner. "You can't smoke that in here. And what I happen to think of your father's endeavor doesn't matter."

Again, the keen appraisal, his head askance. It was fortunate that Deacon was so indolent. When he troubled himself, he was too canny. "I bet it does matter. I bet what you think of all his huffing and puffing is all that matters."

A touch flustered, she nodded at the unlit rollup. "While we're on house rules, I have to ask you something."

"*House rules?* Honest, Mom, I don't remember your being such a downer."

"I want you to tell me how you make a living."

It was always difficult to ask Deacon direct questions. He had a sidling nature; he was good at dodging bullets. To pin him straight on was to invite him to lie. Deacon lied breezily enough, but she found being lied to sufficiently disagreeable that to avoid the falsified answers she usually avoided the questions, too.

"I'm an entrepreneur," he said with a smile.

"Who sells or makes what?"

"People need things, I get them."

"Like what?"

"Whatever. Depends on the market."

"Your sister thinks you're dealing drugs."

"Valeria thinks a lot of things. She thinks Jesus cares personally about her and her drooling, farting, Wal-Marty family. She thinks she's a 'survivor' of child abuse. Valeria's the last person I'd go to for intel about anything."

"So you're not dealing drugs? I don't mind weed. I mean opioids, or heroin."

"I'm sort of curious why you care. Theoretically. Like, I do know plenty of addicts. Supply and demand: they're going to get their fix from somewhere. Plenty of scaggy losers right here in Hudson. Does it make you feel all pure, just so long as they don't get their buzz from me?"

"If we catch you dealing from this house, you're out on your ear."

He chuckled. "Look. If I was into contraband, I wouldn't be lugging around a suitcase of twist-tied baggies. I'd be higher up the food chain than that."

"Because you're such a self-starter. Such a go-getter."

"No, because I aim to get by, and not put myself in the way of any grief. Turns out that doesn't require much. You don't call attention to yourself. You only take advantage of opportunities that land in your lap. You keep your head just high enough above a sea of shit so you can breathe, like dog-paddling in the toilet."

She wasn't going to get past Deacon's stonewalling. At least, as she'd promised Remington, she had delivered their ultimatum. "Also," she added. "No drug taking on the premises, either."

"Do I have to clean my room and set the table?"

"Come to think of it, that would be nice." She wasn't sure about her sudden impulse. Honesty was an experiment. "Deacon, I'm very frightened of this surgery. The physical therapy afterward is horrendous. Surgeons talk an optimistic game, but the people I've met who've had it done are still limping a year later. They can hardly do any exercise, and they gain weight."

"So? Haven't you done enough? Christ, all through my childhood, for hours on end—pounding around Albany, or retiring to your secret torture chamber with its special instruments for waterboarding yourself or something. Put your feet up!" Deacon propped his own heels on a chair. "I'd think you'd be relieved to have an excuse to throw it all over."

"I am, a little," she admitted. He could be her confessor. "The day is so much longer. And there's not this punishment sitting at the end of it. Maybe in declining to sample the pleasures of lethargy, I've been missing out. You don't do anything, do you? I mean, exercise."

"Get out of bed. Slog to the john. Roll a ciggie to recuperate from my terrible exertions. Speaking of which?" He dangled his handiwork.

"Oh, go ahead. Get a saucer. I don't really care." She wasn't sure what impishness had gotten into her, but Deacon was a bad influence, and she was in the mood for a bad influence. She felt feckless, and fuck-it, and flippant.

"Honest." Deacon lit up with a savor that made her envious. "Why not *give up*? You're in your sixties, right? That whole physical plant of yours is going to hell in a handbasket—or a casket—whatever you do. Stop trying to compete with twenty-year-old nymphets who can beat you hands down just by walking down the street in a potato sack. Relax, and throw yourself into the arms of the inevitable. Got to be some advantage to becoming a doddering old bag."

"Thanks."

"Look, you've rated, right? My friends always thought you were smokin'. So hang it up while you're ahead! You're still not a bad-looking broad for a grandmother of . . . Sorry, I've lost count. Is it four or five kids now? In any case, add another notch to your belt. Valeria says she's preggers again."

"Good God, tell me you're pulling my leg."

"When I tell jokes, I don't use the same punch line over and over."

"Would you fetch the chenin blanc in the fridge? You're driving me to drink."

Deacon glugged half the bottle into a balloon glass. "Now seriously," he said, bringing himself another beer. "I don't understand women like you. I see it all the time, too, these rung-out dishrags gasping on treadmills. They're ruining a perfectly decent afternoon, they still look like shit, and they also look pathetic. They're kidding themselves in this totally public and embarrassing way, when plenty of these bitches are rich as fuck, and could be whooping it up and ordering the prime rib. Mom, you've done your bit. You were hot stuff for what, forty-five years? So stop starving yourself. Stop counting alcoholic *units*. Let go. And fuck the knee replacements. Get a walker that has wheels and a little basket for your shopping. Or don't go anywhere. Catch up on *The Simpsons*."

"You are a serpent," she said with a toast. "But this woman—with whom your father now spends most of his time—do you have any idea what his trainer looks like?"

A key rattled in the side door. Given the clamor of voices, to her incredulity on this of all evenings, her husband had invited the tri club. It being still nominally his house, Remington was first in the door, at which point he froze. "Put that out right now."

Deacon would have stirred a milder reaction by meeting his father with a shotgun. "I'm fine, thanks so much for asking." He took another deep drag before reluctantly crushing his rollup in a dish. "And how are *you*, sir?"

Remington turned to his wife. "Since when? What's wrong with you?"

"Where do you want me to start?"

"And please put your feet on the floor," Remington told their son. "We're going to need all these chairs."

"Gosh." Again, Deacon complied in slow motion. "Another lovey-dovey family reunion."

"We may not be gushy, but we can at least keep it civil." With effort, Remington stuck out his hand, which Deacon shook with a limp clasp. "Welcome home."

The club filtered in. They'd done another swim/bike/run day, which the members with jobs could only manage on weekends. As the full Mettle approached, the group had grown jittery and prone to conflict. Cherry DeVries was sometimes weepy. Hank Timmerman had more than once absconded. Chet Mason gave long, uninvited lowdowns on gear, when they'd already bought their gear. Ethan Crick had lost what little sense of humor he'd ever had about his reputation as a hypochondriac. Even Remington had shed his easy self-deprecation, and this evening reacted testily to Chet's grousing that the rest of the club had to wait repeatedly, hours even, for him to finish each leg of the course—"Well, I got there in the end, didn't I?"—whereas in times past he'd have made a joke at his own expense. Having completed Mettles before, only Bambi and Sloan retained their insouciance, though they were watchful of their brood. Earlier in the year, the group had returned tired and cocky; now they returned tired and cross.

Remington introduced the club members to Deacon, whose placid expression conveyed that he was not trying to remember their names. With one exception: "*Bambi?* Seriously? I guess you can call me Thumper then."

"All right, *Thumper.*" Unlacing a running shoe on the chair

Deacon's feet had vacated, Bambi put on a pedestal for display what Remington called her artwork.

"You're one of those lumpy chicks," Deacon said.

"You could say that." Unlacing the other shoe, Bambi shot him a once-over glance. "But you're not one of those lumpy dicks."

"Nah," Deacon said with a smile. "I'm just a dick."

The teasing spirit in which the club had once vied over who was faster had given way to a more acrimonious rivalry with higher stakes. "I only struggled on that hill because the derailleur was jumping gears, so sit on this," Chet told Hank blackly with a raised middle finger. As Bambi ramped up to exceed her own personal best in Lake Placid, it seemed that she no longer looped back to check on stragglers, but churned neck and neck with Sloan, who eventually pulled well ahead in all three sports. For Bambi, their competition was now tainted with a drop of acid. She played her sex to her advantage off-road. But at the end of the day, Bambi didn't really like being a girl.

This evening, it was the presence of Deacon Alabaster that really rattled them. The stranger in their midst evinced not the slightest interest in their times. When they cited extraordinary distances with the feigned casualness of name-dropping at parties, he didn't bat an eye. On reflection, when Serenata spelled out the exploits that his dad would tackle in two weeks, Deacon had acted perfectly unfazed. She might as well have said his father was entering a limerick-writing contest. The club was smugly inured to the raging, transparently insecure "why aren't you working in a homeless shelter?" type. But the company of the dismissive and blithely unimpressed was kryptonite.

Worse, here was a guy who hadn't done a calf raise, a deltoid dip, or a bicep curl in his life—a guy whose idea of exercise was carrying a six-pack and bag of corn chips from the 7-Eleven to his car.

Yet owing to the aesthetic multiplier effect of two attractive parents, he was handsome—meaning, rivetingly handsome, *who-the-fuck-is-that?* handsome. In times past, his mother had found this disjunction perplexing or even a touch maddening. Right now, she thought it was great.

Worse still for this crowd, Deacon was hip, a mysterious attribute that her son had embodied since he was eleven or twelve, when he was as popular in the schoolyard as his sister was ignored. During his juvenile delinquent days (assuming they were over) his smooth, aloof, unruffled affect had been infuriating. What exactly hipness comprised was difficult to identify. Suffice it to say that if you needed the texture explained to you then you didn't have it. If you didn't have it, you couldn't go get it, either. Cool was not available for purchase, and it could not be learned.

Thus Deacon drove the tri club to distraction. They were all self-actualizers, and here was this slick customer who epitomized the one characteristic that they could not earn. The only one of their number who evidenced an iota of hipness was Deacon's father—though Remington's was an old-fashioned William Powell version, well spoken and well mannered. Sloan passed for hip in Hudson, but he needed the props of those classic cars. Even Bambi was too needy to be hip—and she'd never win the esteem she craved from Deacon, whose unadulterated indifference to everything she valued was not, to all appearances, a pose. Moreover, Bambi reviled defeat, and no gambit better assured victory in any game than refusing to play it in the first place.

For his parents, Deacon's visits were mostly expensive headaches; by custom, they paid him to leave. But tonight he lent his mother's skeptics' corner a welcome clout. To capitalize on this rare plurality of apostates, she texted Tommy to join them. That first summer, Tommy had mooned day after day at their son as he dozed in the backyard hammock. After learning that Deacon was here, she showed up in five minutes flat. Together, the three of them occupied one end of the table, the rowdies at the back of the class.

"Hey, Bambi." Serenata raised the hardback that Remington was halfway through. "Have you read the new bio of this renowned ultra-runner? Though he's dead, you know."

"Donald Ritchie? Yeah, somebody at BruteBody mentioned he left the building last year."

"I thought it was interesting that he kicked it at only seventy-three."

"Why interesting?" Bambi said warily. "That's old enough."

"Not these days. And he was in pretty bad shape. Diabetes. Lung problems. Actually, he had to stop running altogether at sixty-six. Remington's age." Serenata had only scanned the end of the book: the good part.

"So? Is this another Jim Fixx sneer? Ha-ha, the author of *The Complete Book of Running* keeled over while jogging at fifty-two? So getting off your ass can't possibly be good for you. *Running kills.*"

"To establish any correlation between endurance sports and premature morbidity," Remington instructed his cynical spouse, "one *somewhat* early death is about as statistically significant as, 'There was this guy I knew.'" He turned to his trainer. "It's like my wife here claiming that 'all the people she's met' who've had knee replacements can barely walk and get fat. She'd tell you herself that she's an antisocial misanthrope. So how many strangers are we talking? Two maybe. Three max. I don't call that scientific."

"Lots of distance runners die early," Serenata said. "Heart attacks, mostly."

"Not at a higher incidence than the general population," Remington said. "Besides, who says the purpose of elite athletics is to increase longevity? Even if a less taxing existence did mean living longer—to *do what*? Really, what good is living to a hundred and ten? I'm not that keen getting past seventy."

"That's in four years," she said softly.

"I can add," he snapped.

Were she to be generous, Serenata could attribute her husband's irritability to the likelihood that, if she was distraught about the next day's operation, he was also anxious on her account. But she wasn't feeling generous.

"Hey, check this out." Tommy had grabbed the biography and was reading the summary on the back. "This Scotch guy ran a hundred miles at a time, in under twelve hours! That's like . . ."

"A steady eight-minute mile," Bambi said. "Mediocre for a marathon, but not bad for four of the fuckers back-to-back."

"That's nothing," Remington said. "Ritchie ran the entire length of Great Britain—eight hundred and forty miles—in eleven days."

"What was the problem?" Deacon said. "There was a rail strike?"

"You have no respect," his father said.

Deacon licked the paper of another rollup. "Got that right."

"During that long UK run," Serenata read over Tommy's arm, "he developed 'a feverish cold' and then faced 'vicious head winds and sleet.' The cold turned into bronchitis . . . He had 'stomach pains, intestinal blood loss, a sore mouth, regular nose bleeds, chest pains, and torrential rains.' Some people really know how to vacation."

"You can't tell me that you don't admire that," Remington charged her.

"So"—Deacon raised the knife with which his mother had tailed the beans—"if I flay myself alive, I'll finally earn Daddy's approval."

"And why would *that* be admirable?" his father said.

"Suffering for suffering's sake—what's the difference?" Deacon said.

"Donald Ritchie set records!" Historically, only restraint borne of his own beatings in childhood had kept Remington from coming to blows with the boy.

"But records for what?" Deacon's tone remained detached, his slouch languid, but he wasn't backing down. Twiddling the unlit rollup in one hand, he was still holding the knife in the other. "I could set a record for how long I took to bleed to death."

Serenata rose as briskly as her knee allowed. "Deacon simply raised the legitimate question of what running the length of any large island in bad weather and poor health actually accomplishes." She held out her hand for the knife. "Discussion closed."

Her phone rang: Valeria. She took the call to the back porch. "Mama, I made sure to put it in my diary that you're getting that operation tomorrow."

"That's very nice of you to remember."

"I asked around at the church, and everybody says it's terrible! Like, you're in awful pain for months and months, or even years! Online it says that up to one in five patients will be in pain kind of like, all the time, for the rest of their lives!"

"Thanks, Valeria. That's very helpful."

"Well, I think it is helpful! An older gentleman in our congregation said the one thing he wishes somebody had told him ahead of time is what a torment it was going to be. He said it actually tested his faith. He didn't know why Jesus would put him through such a thing. He still uses a cane, and he got his knee ten years ago."

"Well, then. It's kind of you to prepare me."

"And that's not all," Valeria went on.

"Oh, great," her mother said.

"All that running in place and jumping around you do—that's well and truly over. I guess you can do an itty-bitty bit of biking. And go on short walks. That's about it."

"Actually, with the newer joints, you can play tennis, golf, and even ski."

"That's what doctors say up front to get the money, Mama. Then there's all these exceptions—like, just about everybody—along with the blood clots and faulty hardware they also don't tell you about. Did you know if you get a 'deep infection' they'll yank the whole thing out again, and they may even cut off your leg?"

"I'm touched that you've been googling so vigorously on my account."

"I'll be praying for you, Mama."

"That's sure to make all the difference, isn't it? And Deacon tells me you're due congratulations again."

"That's right," Valeria said, her voice tightening. "Due right around Christmas, like Jesus himself. We're real happy about it." But for once she didn't *sound* happy. Why, for a moment it seemed she might cry.

"And how's Nancee doing?"

"*I* think she's in the pink. But those pesky therapists have her on what they call an 'exercise diet.' It's the silliest thing! I'm supposed to keep an eye on her, and if she heads upstairs, I have to follow her and make sure she only goes up once."

After Serenata wrapped up her reassuring family call, Ethan said when she came back inside, "Hey, Sera! Rem just told us your surgery's tomorrow. We all wanted to wish you good luck."

"Yeah," Chet said. "But I heard if you're in half-okay shape to start with, you get through it a ton easier." It was the closest anyone in the club had come to acknowledging that Remington's wife was not, altogether, a slug.

"I was gonna say break a leg," Bambi said. "But I guess they're doing that for you, huh?" Cherry chimed in with the compulsive false confidence of the well-meaning. "You'll be right as rain before you know it!" After Sloan and Hank also expressed greeting-card-grade support, the group moved on to other subjects with palpable relief. The simple scaled-up meal Serenata had halfheartedly entertained suddenly seemed insuperable, and she put the beans in the fridge. Girding for mutilation, she had nothing to spare for these people.

Fielding one more phone call briefly cheered her up. It was Griff, whose very awkwardness about what to say was strangely moving. He promised that when she was up and about he'd teach her to play cribbage. She said it's a deal. Getting him off the phone was excruciating—neither was a master of social graces—since when you'd already said goodbye and then remained on the phone (he'd add "I'll be thinking of you, sugar!" and she'd rejoin, "Thanks, I'm so glad you called!"), you'd already used up your arsenal of conclusion. At her wit's end, she finally cried, "Well, bye, Griff!" and hit the red button as fast as humanly possible.

"Have you gotten back to training, honey?" Cherry was asking Tommy. "Because you look so much better!"

Tommy glowered. "I still look like a jellyfish. I've done a little running, but it's slow and doesn't feel good. The weird thing is, the dinky distances are harder. They don't wow anybody, including me. I'm supposed to 'take it easy,' but I hate taking it easy. So half the time I really do take it easy, and watch TV instead. Turns out the sky doesn't fall. While she's been laid up, too, Serenata and I have been reading her commercial scripts aloud. I'm getting better at sight-reading. I used to need to rehearse, but with VO, especially in the gaming scene, you got to be able to read cold."

Cherry's attention wandered as soon as Tommy stopped talking about running. "I'm ashamed to say this, sweetie, but a couple of times now, Sarge has—he's hit me. He's never done that before. Last time, he knocked me down. I've even wondered if he's hoping he'll hurt me bad enough that I can't compete in Lake Placid."

"God, that sucks, Cherry," Tommy said. "But is it really worth it?"

"Of course it's 'worth it.' What do you mean?"

"Well, Sarge is obviously being a jerk, and I guess you could always walk out. Maybe you should. But if you don't want to do that . . . Is a Mettle worth risking your marriage? I mean, you've got those three kids."

Cherry drew herself up. "I know you're disappointed, Tommy, but I didn't think you'd gotten bitter. I can't believe you're trying to talk me out of my MettleMan."

"I was only thinking, you know, in the long run . . ." Tommy said, beating a feeble retreat. "Like, afterward, what have you got, if you don't have your family?"

"I have my finisher coffee mug, my finisher T-shirt, and my finisher self-respect." She huffed back to the A-students.

Meanwhile, Hank had discovered the remains of the chenin blanc. Bambi put a hand over his glass. "I thought we all agreed: no booze from now till it's over."

"Whatever happened to 'work hard, play hard'?" Hank said.

"In the home stretch," she said, "it's all 'work hard.' Now you get high on tri."

Serenata uncorked a cabernet. Deacon switched to whiskey, and Tommy joined him. Drawn to open bottles, Hank shuffled closer to the punks at the table's far end.

"I'm thinking about hitting the ultras next year," Sloan said. "I'm up for Lake Placid, but doing one Mettle and then putting your feet up starts to feel too easy."

"You mean, the two or three Mettles in a row, or the five?" Chet asked.

"The question," Sloan posed philosophically, "is whether to do a double or triple first, or go straight to the quintuple. You want to really challenge yourself, right?"

"I can't hardly imagine getting through one whole triathlon," Cherry said. "I'm flabbergasted anybody can get up the next morning and do a full Mettle all over again."

"Hell, Cherry," Chet said, "I'm not sure what the record is now, but last I checked there's been at least one guy who's done thirty—thirty Mettles in thirty days."

"Seems like an awful lot of bother and expense," Deacon said. "With one bullet, you can accomplish the same thing in three seconds for fifty cents."

The go-getters ignored him. "We should aim for thirty-one, then!" Hank declared, flushed from the cabernet he'd chugged from a camouflaging coffee mug.

"Sloan, isn't talking up the 'ultras' demoralizing for your friends?" Serenata asked. "It makes doing only one MettleMan seem like no big deal." It didn't occur to anyone that waxing eloquent about outermost feats of strength and stamina in front of a woman on the eve of incapacitating surgery might also be in poor taste.

"Always good to keep your eye on the next mountain," Sloan said. "Otherwise, you've got this flatness problem. You get a huge rush after you cross the finish line, and even the next day—after sleeping fifteen hours—you're still fired up. But then it's like, what's next? You need a longer-term game plan. Without a new goal, you can get kind of low, you know? Like, everything is over, and the best part of your life is behind you."

"Unbelievable," Deacon said, pouring another shot. "This shit for you guys is the 'best part of your life.' I gotta feel sorry for you fuckers."

"And what passes for the best part of your life, *Thumper*?" Bambi asked.

"Banging a sweet kid just past the age of consent, and topping up her tight little box in the morning. Grabbing a pastrami on rye with extra mustard. Boosting my mood with a cost-effective shortcut that doesn't involve gasping around a reservoir fifty times. Hitting the road to Hudson, and basking in a mother's love." Throwing a credibly appreciative glance at Serenata, Deacon just pulled the remark back from sarcasm.

"Sounds great to me!" Tommy clinked her shot glass against Deacon's and downed it. "But I want some melted Swiss on that pastrami."

"To each his own, losers," Bambi said.

"I'm starting to think you're right," Chet told Sloan. "The ultras have to be where the money's at. Like, your routine Mettle is already seeming almost sad, right? To pull in the big-league sponsors, I bet you've got to do at least the quintuple. And in good time, too. Not cranking that final chin-up just before the stroke of midnight—"

"Chet, could you put a lid on the big talk?" Ethan interrupted. Seated equidistant between the troublemakers and the teacher's pets, the ophthalmologist had barely said a word all evening. "You haven't finished one MettleMan yet."

"I *know,*" Chet said. "But Sloan's right. You gotta keep expecting more of yourself. Like he said, find the next mountain—"

Deacon started crooning "Climb Every Mountain" from *The Sound of Music.*

"I don't need another *mountain,*" Ethan said, once Deacon had forded every stream but before he could follow any rainbows. "Christ, we're not even through with this Lake Placid nightmare, and you're already talking about doing three in a row after that, or five, or *thirty.* Why not sixty, or a hundred? Why not swim, and run, and bike all day, every day, until . . . until what? As for the obvious end point, I hate to say it, but Deacon's right."

"Fuck me," Deacon said. "I've never heard that in this house before."

"I got into tri to begin with to get into better shape," Ethan said. "To feel better, and to feel better about myself. But I'm not feeling better. I get sick, I'm supposed to keep training through it, so I just get sicker. Basically, all the time, I feel sort of terrible. It's always something: a strain, a sprain, an inflamed tendon—"

"Wait till your sixties," Serenata said. "It's like that without getting out of bed."

"Well, yeah—half the time, I do, I feel *old*. Creaky. Achy. Sore. Technically, I guess I'm stronger, but most of the time I feel wiped out. You guys are always ragging on me for being a pussy, but I have a full-time practice. To keep to Bambi's training schedule, I've had to get up at five, and lately four-thirty, or even four. So I'm chronically under-slept. And I'm starting to wonder if this Mettle thing is safe. The distances are unreasonable—"

"They're supposed to be unreasonable," Bambi said.

"Yes, Ethan," Remington said. "The whole idea is intentionally a little crazy."

"There's *crazy* as in *wild and crazy,* and then there's *crazy* as in dangerously fucked-up," Ethan said, backing his chair out and standing up. "Because I admit it, I'm losing the plot. I thought I did, but lately I don't understand why we're doing this anymore. Chet's right on one point: we're none of us setting any records. And Deacon's right, too: even if we were, so what? This thing has ended up taking up a lot of time, and a huge amount of psychic energy, and meanwhile, with all these injuries, I'm actually in worse health. And now I listen to you guys get jacked about the idea of going up yet another level even if we do get through a full Mettle. So I just realized tonight—this stuff is too out for me. I like the idea of that pastrami and Swiss. I like the idea of going for a five-mile run, at a moderate pace, to work up an appetite for dinner. I like the idea of taking a shower, and talking to my wife about something else. In sum, guys: I quit."

No one said anything as Ethan gathered his things and left.

"Wow," Cherry said.

"Wow," Tommy said.

"Face it, he never had the stuff for tri," Bambi said. "With all those doubts, he had DNF written all over him. Let this be a lesson to all of you. It's like I've warned you before: the one thing you *never* allow yourself to question is why you're doing this in the first place. It's total death. You disappear up your own ass in two minutes. You open the floodgates to the laziness of the body, and you drown in the body's complaints. It's like listening to that little dude with horns and a fork on your shoulder. So we're better off without that softie. All along, he's just been a drag on our resolve. Ethan Crick is weak."

Curiously, however, the morale of the remaining stalwarts seemed unaccountably shaken, and they all drifted home.

"They'll never be the same again," Serenata said while still abed early the next morning. She'd been wide-eyed for hours. "They won't look the same, they won't feel the same—even if the operations go technically well. I'll always set off metal detectors. I'll have become part machine. I'm en route to becoming inanimate."

"You'll still be a ways from Robocop," Remington said. "Besides, you don't want your knees to be the same. They hurt like hell."

"On the other side of these two carve-ups, they'll hurt far worse."

"Why are you so apocalyptic? The whole point is to *improve* your mobility. Which is why lots of people approach joint replacement with optimism and good cheer."

"So I have an *attitude problem.*" She got up and jerked on a robe, but there was no purpose to heading downstairs; she wasn't allowed to eat or drink as of the previous midnight. Not even being able to make coffee deprived the morning of structure. She wouldn't be able to concentrate on the paper. There was nothing to do but wait.

"You've actually said this means your life is over," he said, "and you might rather be dead. How do you think that makes me feel?"

"The way I did when you told your club that you don't want to live past seventy."

He raised a hand in concession. "Fair enough. Let's make that seventy-two."

"Ever since your marathon jag, you've focused *entirely* on physical competence. So for you to act mystified why I might regard becoming a hopeless cripple as something of the end of the party is hypocritical beyond belief."

"Might your *attitude problem* negatively affect your surgery's outcome?"

"That's New Age hooey." She tied the belt of her robe into a furious knot. "Do you think you can talk me into 'optimism and good cheer'? Why does the fact that this surgery cuts me to the quick, and undermines who I am to myself, and threatens me with having to become someone I don't want to be—why is that such an affront to you? Why do I have to feel the way you tell me to? Because all I'm hearing here is that this isn't happening to *you*."

"We're in different places right now."

"You knew this surgery was on my docket. You *chose* to put yourself in a different place. You've removed yourself from me, and run off to Tri World, like Peter Pan to the Island of Lost Boys. I think you were afraid of really staying with me through this. As if I might suck you into my creepy old-age problems. Just like last night—you dragged that whole club back here with you, so you wouldn't have to be alone with your wife, who'd be crawling the walls. If you picture our marriage as a room, you've marched to a far corner. You've left me all by myself. This tri thing, I thought at first it was your angry overreaction to Lucinda Okonkwo, but now I cotton: it's marital desertion, pure and simple. Except you don't need to find your own apartment."

"I appreciate that you're anxious, but you're being irrational—"

"Deacon saw it in a heartbeat. This perverse pursuit of yours is all about me. About becoming me, or replacing me, or besting me—"

"It's only 'about you' insofar as I'd have thought, at the outset, that I'd earn your regard!"

"I already held you in high regard!"

"But I need to hold *myself* in high regard. And at my age, I have only so much time left. If I'm going to do triathlon, it's now or never."

"So what's wrong with never?"

To her astonishment, he had literally walked to a far corner of the bedroom, where he stood naked, hands on hips. "I've sometimes fantasized about what it would be like to have a wife through my own valley of the shadow of death who would make me fear no evil, because *thou art with me.* Who wished me the best and would be waiting on the finish line with a kiss and champagne."

"True, I was thinking more like cava."

"The close proximity of your knee replacement and my MettleMan isn't ideal."

"Huh. Yuh think?"

"But the date for Lake Placid has been set for over a year."

"So this near-synchronicity is my fault."

"No one's fault. It's merely unfortunate."

"For whom?"

"For us both. I won't be as helpful during your recovery as I'd have liked to be."

"I think that pretty much makes it unfortunate for *me.* As for the coincidence, it isn't one, is it? It was foreseeable, more or less. You practically planned it."

"I did no such thing. And the last thing I planned is Deacon's showing up now of all times, too. I'm sorry. It's an extra logistical burden, and he's no ocean of sympathy."

"I've found him a surprising comfort. And if I have trouble with pain management, at least I know where to get opioids."

"That's not funny."

"Not long ago, you would have thought so. You've fallen fatally under the spell of the over-earnest . . . What are you doing?"

"Getting into my cycling clothes, obviously."

"I thought you were going to take me to the hospital."

"I'm planning on it. But I'm meeting Bambi in half an hour. We're working on my gearing technique, going for lower resistance and a higher RPM. Since you don't have to go to Columbia Memorial until noon, I can fit in a thirty miler."

They had always been a talky couple, but the danger of all those words was talking around feelings, or over feelings, or about feelings by way of avoiding actually feeling feelings, and the real moments between them took place in the interstices between the words. This interstice was more than a crack; it was widening to a maw.

"Look," he said, noticing the absence of a sprightly reply. "We're hardly in the Garden of Gethsemane, are we?"

ELEVEN

"Where *is* he? It's ten to twelve!"

Deacon picked toast crumbs from his plate with a forefinger and tsked. "I always remember Dr. DOT as on the *dot*."

"He's not answering his phone, and I refuse to leave another humiliating voice-mail. I cannot believe that this of all mornings he decided to spend with that woman."

Deacon was clearly enjoying this visit's reconfigured family architecture. However divided they'd been in his adolescence over how to contend with a hooligan, his parents' differences back then were merely methodological. In the main, they'd presented a united front—worse, formed a glib, self-reinforcing if not self-congratulatory unit of two, who corroborated that they were right, about everything, by agreeing with each other. As Serenata had only recently appreciated, the couple's show-off Noël-Coward banter had been infuriating. The children saw their parents as sealed in an unassailable bubble, though she thought of the problem otherwise: she and Remington were too happily married. They didn't need other people enough—not friends, not relatives, and not, alas, their own kids. They'd been too satisfied with each other's company, which read to outsiders as self-satisfaction, and their contentment came across as exclusionary. At last the bubble had burst. If she were honest with herself, she was more at ease with Deacon now, because she'd hitherto held back from her son out of loyalty to her husband. The boy made Remington so angry.

"That Bambi chick is a piece of work," Deacon said. "You shouldn't let her get to you. She's yanking your chain on purpose."

"I don't mean to be insulting, but I still don't understand what she sees in your father. I think I've put it together, and then I look at the two of them, so incongruous, and my theories fall apart."

"You said she has a thing about winning," he said. "People like that, doesn't matter what the prize is. She'd compete to her last dying breath for a plastic whistle."

"I know they rarely start surgeries on time, but they're very strict about showing up at admissions by your appointment. If I'm late, I risk losing the slot."

"Isn't that what you'd secretly like anyway?"

"All my life I've prided myself on making myself do things I didn't want to. But I did, sort of, want to do my push-ups. I don't want to do this. It turns out I'm as terrible at making myself do what I really don't want to do as anybody else. We have to go."

Chivalrously, Deacon carried her overnight bag—a small gesture he'd never have made when the bubble was intact—and held open the door of his dented Mercedes.

"Not bothering to get back on time . . ." Ducking in, she supported her right leg by holding on to the door. "I don't know, maybe it's a good sign that he can still hurt my feelings."

"Your honeybunch may not be able to make you feel all warm and gooey inside anymore," Deacon said. "But the ability to fuck you up, well—it's the last magic power to go."

"I'm not sure how consoling that is. Still, thank you for being here."

"De nada," he said at the wheel, reversing.

"If this morning's absenteeism is anything to go by, I'm going to need your help. Obviously, I won't be able to bike. But according to the pre-op seminar they made me take—and it was full of fat people; I wasn't flattered by the company—I also won't be able to drive. You can't move your leg fast enough to shift from the accelerator to the brake. As for incapacities, that's only for starters."

"You can still back out of this if you want to."

"I'm loath to give your father's trainer any credit, but last night she was right on one point: you can't allow yourself to question the premise. Never ask why."

"Seems like that's the first thing you'd do."

"I know it sounds counterintuitive. And it's especially disconcerting for someone like your father, who's so contemplative by nature. But once you make a commitment, it's a big mistake to force yourself to keep remaking it. My knee is killing me. It's going to keep killing me unless I let them saw me to pieces like a bookshelf."

It was a short drive, during which she kept looking out for Remington—pedaling feverishly toward their house, admonishing himself for allowing his trainer to goad him into ten extra miles. When they turned into the Columbia Memorial parking lot, she pictured him skidding into their drive, throwing his precious tri bike carelessly on the lawn, and banging through the side door, praying that they hadn't left without him. All through the admissions paperwork, too, she kept shooting glances at the entrance, through which at any moment her husband might burst at a run. When she returned the clipboard, the receptionist directed her to the surgical waiting room, where, she was advised, she'd be welcome to bring a friend or family member.

"I could be waiting a few minutes, or a few hours," Serenata told her son. "You've done your bit. It's okay if you want to go."

In times past, Deacon would have left. He was anything but an altruist. "Nah," he said. "I brought your portable Scrabble."

She asked the receptionist to direct her husband to the waiting room should he deign to make an appearance, changed into a formless gown and sock slippers with nonskid feet, and stored her clothing and valuables in a locker. Every medical functionary she dealt with, even the one who provided a blanket for her assigned gurney, asked for name, birth date, and body part. She kept her monotonous responses pleasant; they were simply being careful. She and Deacon were given a flimsy privacy with a wraparound curtain. When Dr. Churchwell showed up with a Magic Marker and wrote TKR on the joint soon to be tossed into a medical waste bin, she was a little nonplussed that after all their dealings with one another he was still afraid he'd forget and take out her spleen instead.

The travel Scrabble set turned out to be a godsend. It gave her something to concentrate on. It reprieved them from making conversation. Most of all, it distracted her from supposing that while she'd accused Remington of "marital desertion," she'd never really believed that he didn't want to see her through this tribulation, never really believed that he spent more time with Bambi Buffer than with his own wife because he was infatuated with his trainer, and never really believed what she'd told her father-in-law: that her marriage was in any sense in peril, or diminished, or unhappy like everyone else's. Maybe she told other people things as a substitute for telling herself. She'd made all these dire assertions, and then when nothing dire came of airing them, that seemed to prove they weren't dire after all, or even true. As time ticked on, she played *E-X-U-D-E* with a triple-letter score on the *X*, not bad under the circumstances, until finally the anesthetist appeared, wanting to know if she ever took drugs.

"I think you're asking the wrong party," she said, with a dry glance at Deacon—not bad under the circumstances, either.

After the blood pressure, heart rate, and O2 sat readings, she and Deacon managed three more turns. When they brought the syringe for setting the IV, she objected that she couldn't go under now, because the game wasn't over and she was winning. Neither the anesthetist nor his assistant smiled, for she could feel herself transitioning in their eyes from a *who* to a *what*. It wasn't that they were callous, but that for their professional purposes the fact that someone lived in this artifact had become incidental, or downright inconvenient.

According to Deacon's watch, it had been over two hours. Remington was still a no-show. The tiles restored to their bag, Serenata could no longer obsess over how to squeeze any appreciable points from a rack with six vowels, four of which were *A*'s. Instead she was pelted with all the thoughts she'd been batting away, and not only today but for months, perhaps the whole last year.

For the first time, she wondered who would get the house. For the first time, she weighed up whether either of them would want the place once it became a repository of such jarring late-life desolation, or whether limited resources alone would demand that they sell the property and split the proceeds. For the first time, she questioned whether she'd stay in Hudson, and worried about how devastated Griff would be if she left town. And for the first time, she recognized how much she lied to herself about cherishing solitude, which was only sumptuous when contrasting with something else; solitude without respite went by another name. It was an unwelcome reverie that might have seemed poor preparation for major surgery, but the surgery itself made the reflections apt. If you could offer up your own leg to be cut into pieces, any severance was possible.

As a nurse was about to slip a mask for gas over her face, Serenata started to cry. The wave caught her unawares, as if she were facing the shore and a swell had smacked her crown. It wasn't altogether clear what overwhelmed her, Remington's astonishing abandonment, or the fact that she didn't want to do this and she wanted to go home. When the nurse asked, "Is there something wrong?" the question was, again, not cold exactly, but mechanical. They didn't care what she felt, but only what the body felt.

"I'm sorry," she said in a lull when she could get words out. "I don't think I was this childish when I was a child." Deacon held her hand, and while it might have been better had her husband held her hand, her son was acting more decent than at any time since she could remember, and she had a rare inkling on the waft into oblivion that maybe she hadn't always been an atrocious mother.

Emerging from general anesthesia wasn't so much an awakening as a resurrection. The distinction revealed just how rich and eventful the experience of sleeping was, and how aware one was, throughout a night's slumber, of the passage of time. Sleep was in no way an absence, so it was foolish to imagine dying as in any sense like drifting off in bed. Coming to, Serenata could groggily infer that after holding Deacon's hand something had happened. But the time was missing. It had been hacked from her life, sawed out.

When a nurse arrived to administer an anti-emetic, she wondered if sloshing to nonexistence and back again induced a spiritual seasickness. The nurse's face was ravishing, shades of purple mixing with burnt sienna, and her expression radiated warmth and acumen; so deep was the brown of her eyes that the pupils seemed to drill to the back of her head. Serenata was overwhelmed that a total stranger would worry about whether her stomach was unsettled. She was filled with the same burgeoning gratitude when her vital signs were taken by a second nurse, whom she kept thanking, and reassuring that, yes, she felt comfortable, that's good of you to ask. They all seemed to care so about how she was, though they'd no reason to, and it was all so touching and human and true.

The walls sectioned into soft, gradated grays, like a painting—a subtle painting, at which you could gaze for hours and always find something new. From a far window shafted a single luminous bar, its supersaturated yellow distinct to the midyear's early evening sun; it was the light that photographers lived for, in which every subject appeared golden and chosen by God. As Serenata lay being, so recently returned from not-being, she was newly alert to the luxuriousness of breathing—how marvelous, that you could draw in the very atmosphere, extract from it what you needed, and give most of it gratefully back. How amazing it was to be present. She reproached herself—gently, tenderly—for ever questioning the toil and trouble of remaining in this astounding and unfathomable place, with its colors and shapes, its smells and tastes, for many more years. Simply bearing witness to the physical world was worth the price of admission.

She thought of Remington, claiming that he didn't want to live beyond seventy or was it seventy-two, and of course that made her think of Remington more broadly. She had a trace memory of his disappointing her, but that was swallowed by a larger impression that she had disappointed him, too. She'd been unkind to him, repeatedly unkind, and she had withheld herself. He wanted something, it wasn't entirely clear what, any more than it was clear to Remington either, and he was probably not going to get it, or at least not the way he was going about the quest. But she had to allow him to make his own mistakes and then come back to her, because if she did not he would not. He was doing something that was not a part of their lives together but it didn't hurt her. He was doing something that lots of people were also doing, and just then it did seem curious that she'd ever had a problem with activities in which lots of people took part. Like all those other people on bicycles. She'd loved her long life on a bicycle, so there was no reason she shouldn't want everyone else to enjoy the liberation, the rush of air, the giddy lean into a curve of a bicycle, too.

And that was when she realized she was on drugs.

Dr. Churchwell swung by, airy and brisk as usual. Around sixty-five, he kept his dyed-blond hair in a boyish tousle. It was immediately clear from his closer proximity to the door than to her bed, and from the bland, offhand quality of his pronouncement upon her surgery's success, that by the time she formulated any questions that she badly needed answered, he'd be long gone. In truth, she'd never especially liked Dr. Churchwell, although he was reputedly the best knee surgeon at Columbia Memorial, a moderately sized institution in a small town, so she couldn't be too choosy. Chronically supercilious, he'd spent a goodly portion of their appointments extolling his achievements as a squash champion. With the hucksterism of a television evangelist, he likewise bragged about the NFL players and Olympic team members on whom he'd operated who still sent thankful Christmas cards—and he left Serenata under no illusion that a sorry amateur's piddling ten-mile runs would ever qualify her own cards for his living-room mantel.

Yet under the influence, Serenata could discern behind the arch expression and battered complexion the dashing med student so many mothers would have hoped their daughters would marry. The physician's preening was cover for a garden-variety anxiety about getting old. The more closely he skirted the infirmity of his patients, the more fiercely he worked to maintain a distinction between them, and to carve out a place for himself as an exception—an exception to laws that doctors knew better than anyone allowed for no exceptions. Inexorably, in another five years or so, he'd have to retire, and no one would care about his squash trophies. He'd just be some old guy, like the rest of us, but with more money. As for the boasting, his work was respected but mechanical. He needed to christen certain patients as special to make himself seem special, and maybe it was a good sign that some of them were people to him and not just hunks of furniture. Besides, everyone treated surgeons with such exaggerated deference that in a way their clichéd narcissism was not their fault.

"The operation was perfectly routine," he said, after she'd tried to solicit a little more detail.

"I'm sorry I bored you."

"I do five of these in a day," the surgeon said. "Though I must say, your patella and the articular surface of your lateral condyle looked like someone had taken a pile driver to them. You really should have had this done earlier—*as I advised*. You came to me at the very outside of the window I gave you. I'm skeptical we'll achieve anything close to full extension when you recover."

"In case something went wrong, I've wanted to take advantage of my real knees as long as I could."

"Yes, yes, I hear that all the time. You're all fraidy cats, terrified that you won't be able to play a full round of croquet. Fair enough, but if this aversive delay of yours translates into a limp, you've only yourself to blame. Now, I'm keeping you on Oxycontin for another three days, but then we're moving to NSAIDs. Just don't slacken on the PT, or you don't have a prayer of attaining that extension."

She was a little injured that her orthopedist displayed so little understanding of his patient after seeing her for two years. "I'm not a slacker. I'm more the type to overdo it."

"Well, don't overdo it, either," he said with annoyance. "You could damage the scar tissue and invite inflammation the size of last year's wildfire in California. Worse, you might even loosen the cement, and we'd have to do the whole thing all over again. Now, *that* would be boring." With no goodbye, he was gone.

"You have a visitor, Mrs. Terpsichore," a nurse said a few minutes later, poking his head in the door. He'd mangled her surname, and Serenata didn't care. Absent pharmaceutical intervention, she'd have been crushed that the visitor was not her husband. Instead, when Tommy filtered shyly to the side of the bed, she was enchanted.

"Hey," Tommy said. "How are you feeling?"

"High as a kite," Serenata said. "I suspect I feel dreadful and I have no idea."

"It went okay?"

"Yes, though I'm afraid Dr. Churchwell found my case a little dreary."

"With this medicine stuff?" Tommy said. "I don't think you ever want to be interesting. Have you looked at it?"

"No."

Together, they peered under the blanket. "Oh, wow."

Covered in a thick white rectangle, the bulbous tubular object attached to Serenata's torso did not appear to belong to her body. "It reminds me," Serenata said, "of those big pork roasts in the supermarket, covered with a giant slab of scored fell, tied up with butcher's twine, and bulging in cellophane on an oozy Styrofoam platter. Even the bandage—it's like that little diaper they put under the meat, just upside down."

"Baby, I've been there," Tommy said. "You're like, 'I don't recognize this humongo blob! How'd I get inside a Macy's parade float?'"

"You were so upset. You kept saying, 'I didn't even get to eat any pizza!'"

"You were the only one who was nice to me."

"I'm relieved to hear I've been nice to someone. I don't think I've been very nice to Remington." Her throat was dry. "For the life of me, I don't remember why, either."

"It'll come back to you," Tommy said. "You just have to get off the opioids."

"In that case, I'm not sure I want to get off them."

"Pretty standard reaction. Why do you think they're so addictive?"

"I had no idea . . ." Serenata struggled to formulate what she was thinking. "I'm surprised what this feels like. I'm comforted to discover that these drugs make you so warmly disposed toward people. I mean, I'm glad it turns out that so many young people like you are mostly desperate to feel *benevolent.* Apparently this country is full of people who crave the experience of generosity and optimism. It's strangely moving—that they'll put themselves and their health at risk—they'll go broke or even steal—just to keep thinking of other people as wonderful, and as on their side. That's not a bad thing to find addictive. Maybe Deacon's not as depraved as I've worried he is."

Tommy laughed. "It's almost creepy, but for a change of pace, I kind of like you this way. All philosophical and sappy. So I hate to break it to you: I think you only get that 'Joy to the World' buzz at the beginning. Later you keep taking the stuff just to keep from killing yourself."

"I like my version of opioid addiction better."

"Listen . . ." Tommy paused. "We talked about it. That is, Bambi—sorry—well, she called me. We decided it'd be better to tell you afterward. We didn't think you should get all worked up right before surgery."

"Tell me what?" Pain meds didn't preclude a capacity for alarm.

Tommy raised her hands. "Now, don't freak out! He didn't die or anything. But Remington had a bike accident."

"How bad was it, then?"

"Actually, for your purposes?" Tommy cocked her head. "Probably not quite bad enough."

The assertion didn't register. "Where is he?"

"Here. So he officially gets credit for coming to the hospital when you had your knee done. Except for the first four hours he was in the ER waiting room. He's finally been able to see somebody, and I think they're checking him for concussion. And they must be doing X-rays. He was hurting pretty bad while we hung out with him in the waiting room, and he was super shaken up. But I doubt they're going to admit him overnight. He's cut up, and bruised, and he has these long bloody scrapes on an arm and a leg from sliding along the ground. Still, Bambi doesn't think he broke any bones."

"Did she save his life again? That would make three times. My, a charm." From behind the cotton candy of narcotic goodwill, a glint of sardonicism.

"Now, that's the old Serenata! There wasn't any mouth-to-mouth this time, though I guess she did call the ambulance."

"Not that this matters, really, but . . . It's what I'd worry about: Carlisle."

"Who's that?"

"I'm just asking, what happened to his bike? That Little Lord Fauntleroy may be pretty full of itself, but it's Remington's beloved."

"Totaled. He bent the frame. Kiss of death."

Serenata sighed. It wouldn't do to find the death of this rival too satisfying. "What's ten grand down the drain—so long as I keep taking these meds."

"He does still have the old bike," Tommy reminded her.

After a rap on the door, a female PT came in with a wheeled walker. "Gab fest's over, girls! Time to get to work."

Getting out of bed was slow, confusing, and awkward. Therapist at the ready, Serenata leaned heavily on the frame. The right knee wouldn't bend, but she was cheered when the mandatory shuffle around the room didn't hurt at all, and she wondered whether everyone made far too much of this wretched recovery business, until she clocked: the elephantine leg was still numb. *Oh.* Thereafter, Deacon stopped by, complaining that now both his parents were train wrecks, and they hadn't warned him that a stint living at their house in Hudson would entail "turning into some full-time nursing-home orderly." The objection couldn't have been called good-humored.

At last, the door yawned open to reveal Himself. He was wearing a mismatched shorts and T-shirt combo that one of the women must have grabbed from home—clothes from a few years ago that drooped off him now. Presumably the Lycra cycling gear had been totaled, too. A square of gauze was affixed to his forehead; one cheek was grazed and pointillated with bloody pits. His limbs were covered in so many bandages that he looked like a cartoon.

"So," she said, "we're both back from the wars."

"It's not as bad as it looks," Remington said. "But I'm hugely sorry about this morning—"

"Don't. I understand now. But it was important to me that you went with me. It's important that it was still important."

"That should go without saying."

"Nothing goes without saying. Not right now." She flipped the blanket back to expose the pork roast and nodded at the bandage on his thigh. "Look at you. You're copying me."

"Isn't that what you think I've been doing this whole time? Copying you?"

"I've never been quite sure which proposition is more distressing, that your late-life athletic renaissance has everything to do with me, or nothing to do with me. Would you please sit down? Just looking at you standing there makes me tired."

When he sat, he winced. "Tommy assured me the surgery went fine?"

"As far as I know. And you?" she asked. "Nothing broken?"

"Bruising, swelling, some laceration. Mild concussion—those helmets . . ."

"They're TinkerToy," Serenata said. "And no one tightens the straps enough, because if you do you get a headache. When a helmet is even halfway comfortable, it rides back on your forehead. Then, pitch over the handlebars, you might as well be wearing a Mets cap. With the explosion of cycling in this country, I don't understand why bike helmets are still so hard to adjust, still look so geeky, and still don't work." Powered by the garrulousness taking over now that the general anesthesia had lifted, such convivial commiseration had been signally lacking in their dealings with one another from "I've decided to run a marathon" onward.

"I was told I was lucky," Remington said.

"You sure don't look lucky. What happened?"

"It was a new route, to mix things up. If she, you know—"

"If we couldn't avoid her stupid name for over a year, we can't avoid it now."

"All right, *Bambi* would have warned me, but she hadn't been on this stretch of B-road before, either. She was well behind me, because she wanted me to work on pacing myself, or she might have wiped out, too. We were headed down a hill, and the tarmac was that washed-out gray, with imbedded gravel. So it was impossible to tell that at the very bottom of the descent the surface suddenly turned to gravel-gravel. Loose gravel. In a car, the change of surface wouldn't have mattered much. On a bike . . . No traction. I skidded, then got thrown clear of the bike, which hurtled into a tree."

"People our age should never take down-hills at speed," Serenata said. "People Tommy's age shouldn't, either, but only we ancients know the stakes."

"If you considered the stakes, you'd never do anything."

"Then maybe we should never do anything."

Just then, something gave way in him. His head dropped; he slumped. Serenata had had bike accidents herself, and like any other trauma there was a delayed reaction. She edged carefully to the far side of the single mattress and folded back the bedding. He could just fit alongside her, nestling his temple into the hollow of her shoulder as she wrapped an arm around his back. He slipped a hand under her hospital gown and cupped a breast, always a neat fit in his palm.

If the end of the day had once been steeped in dread, now it was the whole day. When she returned home after two nights in Columbia Memorial, recovery became her full-time job, since any economically productive activity was inconceivable. Demotion from Oxycontin to Tylenol was like a CEO's plummet to the mailroom. Every time the PT showed up for an hour of home therapy, every time she repeated the exercises with a gun to her head later in the day, and every time she lurched from a living-room recliner to the kitchen (only after contemplating for fifteen minutes whether a cup of tea was worth the trip), it was *whoosh* up the same giddy learning curve that she'd climbed on the West Side bikeway—the same fast-forward short course in pain, the same *surprise!-this-is-what-agony-feels-like-and-this-is-why-no-one-likes-it*. She soon grew to regard going upstairs as on the same scale of commitment as moving to Cleveland.

From the start, too, Serenata was obliged to relinquish her precious conceit about having a "high pain threshold," because it turned out her threshold was as low as anyone's, as low as low could be; it was on the floor. All that vaunted "discipline" of hers turned out to be of no use in executing exercises that before her bones were sawed off wouldn't have counted as exercise at all. Besides, reasonably fit people experienced little appreciable pain when they worked out; it was out-of-shape people who really suffered. Thus the presumption that had helped propel her to schedule the surgery in the first place—that she was accustomed to "pushing herself," so she'd "bounce back" in no time—was revealed over the course of three minutes on Day One to be a self-serving, bald-faced lie. As for her image of herself as stoic, that was out the window, too. Wrapping an elastic band around the ankle and forcing the right leg to bend from a 110-degree angle to a 109-degree one, she wept. In front of the therapist, in front of Remington, and the tears didn't even fill her with shame, because shame, like the tears themselves, didn't help.

The whole business was so humbling that she rapidly lost every last shred of self-respect. She was a tired, beaten-down, aging woman whose utility to humanity was zero, whose idea of bliss was sitting still, and whose few ruminations on her circumstances she had thought before: how lonely pain was, and how unreal to people who weren't feeling it, too; how quickly people got bored with other people's pain after an initial display of cheap pity; how the peculiar inability to quite remember the sensation must have served as a primitive survival mechanism, since if you could truly remember agony you'd never forgo the security of the lair even to forage for food. In their repetitiveness, the recurrent reflections were one more torture.

The fact that Remington was also beaten up was a complication. The long scrapes on his arms, in which imbedded chunks of gravel had left deep pits, needed the dressings changed regularly and had to be slicked painfully with antibiotic ointment. On the side of his body that had taken the hit, his shoulder was puffy and sore. Given its restricted range of motion, he might have damaged his rotary cuff. He had a sizable hematoma on his elbow, and the interior bleeding had spread in branching violet all the way down and around his forearm. He also had swelling, bruising, and pitting from the gravel along the one whole leg, and once the thigh scrape barely started to heal, the scab cracked and bled when he walked. The ankle having been yanked in a direction Nature never intended, his Achilles was pulled, paining him with every step. Hard falls occasioned not only a delayed emotional reaction, but also a delayed physical one. After a day or two, a bodywide ache set in, as if you were a house after an earthquake, and now your framing was askew, your two-by-fours were straining at their nails, and your windows and doors were out of plumb.

They found some camaraderie. Yet they inevitably suffered from a low-key competition over which spouse deserved more sympathy, even if the contest made no sense. Sympathy was not zero-sum. Deacon didn't feel especially sorry for either parent, so the only sympathy to fight over was each other's, and they could have agreed simply to swap. Besides, like a cut-rate cologne whose flowery scent instantly evaporated, sympathy didn't do either of them any good.

One irksome problem was getting blood and various paler discharges on the sheets. Neither had the energy to scrub the percale every morning, and if Deacon was ill-tempered about runs to the supermarket, he wasn't going to toil over a sink with his parents' gory bedclothes as if trying to destroy evidence. So the stains would set. They went through fresh sheets nightly, until Serenata resolved that until they both stopped oozing they'd have to sleep on sheets they'd already ruined. The bed soon resembled a Red Cross cot during World War One.

Perhaps oddly, they didn't discuss it. Remington's mute, downcast lumber around the house read, yes, as an understandably sober demeanor after a close call with mortality, but also as the inevitable funk into which anyone would sink after training over a year for an event he could no longer enter. (Unfortunately, it was too late to get back his whacking MettleMan deposit.) He'd take a while to resign himself to the disappointment, so it seemed strategic to give the sensitive subject wide berth. Presumably he would address the letdown when he was good and ready. Maybe in time he'd take a positive view of the experience, even if it hadn't culminated in the expected triumph. He must have gotten something out of all those training sessions in and of themselves. Underneath the bandages, he was in better shape. More adept than his wife at getting along with people from different walks of life, he'd flourished in the company of the tri club. In due course, he might look back on this period as introspectively informative and socially rich. If he had also escaped the potential ignominy of failing to complete the course, she was hardly going to mention *that*. Any intimation that withdrawal was reprieve would sound like an accusation of cowardice. He was pulling out because he'd had a terrible accident. In Tri World, that was a far more respectable excuse than Ethan Crick's sudden attack of sanity.

With the benefit of hindsight, Serenata might even come to soften on his infuriating weakness for that trollop (the archaic pejorative was perfect). He was sixty-six. Younger attentions had been flattering. Once the wounds healed and he regained his energy, maybe they could go back to having sex again, and with a renewed enthusiasm to which residual fantasies about his erstwhile trainer might contribute—just so long as Remington didn't propose a three-way with the detestable woman in real life.

Most of all for Serenata, now that a full Mettle was summarily off the table, the challenge was to disguise her relief.

"What are you doing?" It was the one-week anniversary of her surgery and Remington's crash. She was at the dining table, doing extension and flexion exercises to the eye so farcical that they might have been mistaken for restless leg syndrome.

"What does it look like?" Remington tugged his laces. "I'm going for a run."

Serenata's heart fell. Apparently she'd been hoping he'd throw in the towel on exercise altogether. But keeping active would be good for him, and this sour reaction to Remington's finally getting out of the house was mean-spirited. It was the knee replacement talking. Her own current version of a marathon was hunching down the four steps from the side door and hobbling to the end of the block with a walker. And even there, she had to ask Deacon to lift the walker to the drive; she couldn't carry it and hold on to her cane and the rail as well. She'd have to be mindful of this if-I-can't-then-you-can't-either spitefulness. Recovery was awful enough without also becoming a shrew.

"Isn't it a little soon?"

"It's a little late. The Mettle is in six days."

The screen door banged behind him. "Hey, champ!" a familiar female voice shouted from the end of the drive. "Ready to roll?"

Serenata continued to sit in the chair. Deacon came back from whatever mysterious activities occupied him for most of the day. With unusual alertness to mother-as-domestic-statuary, he asked, "What's up? Your face—you look like someone just hacked the other leg in half."

"Your father is still planning to do that triathlon." Her voice was flat.

"No big surprise. You don't want him to. QED."

"Spouses in their sixties aren't supposed to make decisions like teenagers."

"Take it from me. Let it go. What's the worst that could happen?"

"Funny, that's exactly what I've been thinking about."

"If you're right and he can't do it, then he won't do it," Deacon said. "Simple."

"Deacon, I hate to ask this, since you just got home. But would you mind going out again for a while? I have to talk to your father when he gets back, and in private."

"Okay—but you know you're not going to talk him out of it."

"All right, I'll take that as a dare."

By the time Remington returned, she was ready for them.

"Well, that tumble you took has slowed you down a mite," Bambi was saying behind him when the duo came back in. Though it was in the eighties, her pink running bra was pristine; she hadn't broken a sweat. "Hey, Sera! Haven't seen you since the big carve-up. How's the prosthesis?"

"The *prosthesis* is thriving. It's the rest of me it's attached to that's having a hard time." Serenata tried to keep her tone matter-of-fact when she observed, "Sweetheart, you're bleeding."

Perspiration had loosened the tape on Remington's bandages, which had blossomed in red speckle. The wounds were to be kept dry, so in lieu of a shower he was moistening a dish towel at the sink. "The abrasions crack," he said, rubbing his face and neck. "That's inevitable. Can you excuse me, ladies? I'm going upstairs to change."

The two women were rarely alone with one another. It was awkward.

"Give it a year or two, and you'll be tooling the aisles of Price Chopper without a cane," Bambi said. "I could give you some exercises that would help."

"Thanks," Serenata said. "But I'm in the care of a PT, and more exercises are the last thing I need. Listen, do you mind my asking—is it your idea that Remington still enter the full Mettle, even after that bike accident? Have you in any way enticed him—I mean, challenged him, or flung down a gauntlet? Made him feel embarrassed about the idea of bowing out?"

"Honey, you just don't get tri. For Rem to do it at all, it has to be his idea. Do tri to make somebody else happy, you won't make it ten feet."

trade in New York State. I'll go on your website and leave a scathing one-star review. I'll also go on every other pertinent website I can find—every sports magazine, every workout blog, every commercial gym within hundreds of miles, including BruteBody—and I'll trash your reputation in the comments. To make sure you don't endanger the well-being of anyone else, I might even overcome my loathing for social media."

Bambi stood up. "I don't take kindly to threats. And you're hardly in the shape to make any. So how's this for a threat: I can tell Rem what you just said. He won't take kindly to that, either."

"'Take kindly' to what?" came from the hallway.

"Blackmail," Bambi said as Remington entered the kitchen. "Rem, I'll see you at the pool tomorrow at three, after I've had a chance to find those waterproof dressings. Just now, thanks for the offer, but I think I'm gonna skip that iced tea."

"What was that about?" Remington asked once she'd slammed the screen door.

"A difference of opinion."

"Over?"

"Take a guess."

Remington fixed himself a sandwich; he may have been hungry, or simply eager to busy himself. He couldn't imagine he was getting out of this conversation.

"Your swelling is still not down," she began as he separated slices of smoked turkey. "You can't raise your arm above your shoulder. Just like your hamstring, your Achilles is strained or inflamed, and on the same leg. Your bruises do nothing but darken as the blood rises to the surface, which means the injuries are deep. Every time the scabs crack you open a new route to infection. Didn't that run you just went on hurt?"

"That's irrelevant." He liked it. He liked that it hurt.

Hectoring would be deadly. Likewise ridicule, and trying to win. She'd gone at this all wrong from the beginning.

"Darling. My beloved." Modulating the voice by occupation should be good for something. Better still, to speak tenderly was to feel tender. "Sit down?"

Reluctantly, he brought his plate over. He didn't touch the sandwich.

"I can see why you can't trust me," she said. "I know I've seemed competitive. Defensive of what always used to be my territory. Resentful that you've exceeded my own feats of stamina. Angry about suddenly becoming such a shipwreck—though if I take some small comfort from your being in the same boat, there's nothing wrong with wanting to feel close to you, is there?"

"Not unless the closeness is smothering."

"And I'm sorry I called this enterprise of yours 'dumb.' It's true I can't help what I think. But the merits of a triathlon are beside the point now. Even according to Bambi, you almost drowned. You were a hair away from heatstroke—"

"Not this again."

"I'm not bringing up your trio of near-death experiences as a bludgeon. But of the three, it's Syracuse that bothers me the most. You can die from heatstroke. Your internal organs shut down. And you didn't stop. You wanted me to be impressed that you still finished that race, and I was, but not the way you hoped. Your continuing to run when you were delirious means *I* can't trust *you*. It's official: you don't know when to quit. Are you trying to kill yourself?"

"Of course not. Though there would be worse ways to make an exit."

She leaned forward. "I am your wife. You made promises when you married me. I am supposed to be able to have and to hold you. I'm only sixty-two. I may not look the part right now, but it's not impossible that I live to ninety. I know neither of us is especially thrilled by old age. Nobody is. But there's only one thing worse than our getting decrepit together. You've been given fair warning—three times. Entering that race would be dubious enough if you were in peak condition, but look at you! Covered in bandages, and bruises, and contusions! I can tell by the way you move around the house that your whole body aches—every muscle, every joint, down to the bones. That was a horrible accident. I realize you weren't to blame. Without any road signs about the change of surface, anyone could have wiped out in that gravel. But being oblivious to what that accident has done to you seems ungrateful for the miracle that you survived at all."

"What would be ungrateful is not taking full advantage of coming out relatively unscathed. Using a few scrapes and bruises as an excuse to give up would be gutless, and would make me feel gutless. I can't understand why you'd want to live with me in a state of emasculation."

"I want to live with you, period, and in what state is secondary! So please. *Please* don't do that triathlon. I'll tell everyone that it was my fault you quit, that I forced you. I know you're suspicious, and I've given you reason to be, but this time I'm not trying to stop you because I'm jealous, or because we've been in some stupid contest over this for months on end and I want to have my way, or even to get you away from Bambi Buffer. It's because I love you, and this race is dangerous. Please, I'm begging you." And now she did the worst possible thing that she could do at this time: she got down on her knees.

"Get up!" he cried, springing to a stand. "Get off that fucking knee!"

"I'm begging you." If she was being manipulative, she couldn't have come up with a better guarantee of generating real tears than her current posture. "Don't do this MettleMan. I know it's a sacrifice, but I don't ask you for that much. So make the sacrifice for me. I despair of getting old anyway; I can't bear the idea of doing it alone."

Remington dragged her upright by the armpits and dumped her back into the chair. "You're always separate, so unto yourself, so needless. You disdain the comforts of other people's company. You're contemptuous of their support. You scorn shared enthusiasms as mindless conformity. I suppose that means I'm special, that it matters to you that I'm here, an actual other person you can stand. All right. I'm glad of that. And it's true. I agree. You don't ask me for much. So it is *wicked, wicked,* that when you finally do, it's for the only thing in the whole wide world that you *know* I can't agree to."

TWELVE

"If you slander my trainer on the internet," Remington said at the wheel, sounding ominously calm, "I will track down every site on which you've mentioned her name with a Google search. I'll append the comment that my aging, sedentary wife is stuck at home and physically fearful after a recent knee replacement. I'll say she's resentful of my discovery of new goals and new associates, and intimidated by my trainer's physique. I'll portray my wife as having tried to keep me from fulfilling my athletic destiny for years. I'll quote you, accurately, as having derogated the whole tri movement as 'goofball,' 'small,' 'unworthy of me,' and oh, my favorite: 'all-white.' I know that community better than you do, since you've no idea what *community* means. So I can assure you whose story will sound more convincing. If anything, you'll raise Bambi's profile, rally allies to her side, and generate more clients for her business."

That was all he said on the whole three-hour drive to Lake Placid on Friday morning. For months Serenata had struggled against her attendance at this preposterous exercise in mass hysteria. For the last few days, she'd pleaded to be allowed to go.

By the outskirts of their destination, the streets were bunted with banners: LAKE PLACID WELCOMES METTLEMAN CHAMPIONS! The four-peaked orange logo fluttered in jagged flags on every lamppost. Big red digital advisories warned motorists to expect delays on Sunday, when cyclists enjoyed the right of way on the fifty-eight-mile double loop. As their car crawled bumper to bumper through the tourist town's main drag, adjacent vehicles sported multiple bicycles on roof racks. Bumper stickers read SOLID METTLE and SUCCEED OR DIE TRI-ING. Special offers on passing sandwich boards offered discounts to diners with official orange entrant badges. The quaint, comely municipality's local businesses—shops for popcorn, flavored olive oils, unguents—were sure to benefit from an uptick in trade.

Their motel proved more of a motor lodge than the palatial quarters befitting a brave-heart. But between health insurance deductibles, reduced household income owing to the new "mimicry" taboo, Bambi's ridiculous retainer, and two whopping entry fees for this franchise, economizing was no longer a choice. Besides, all Serenata really cared about was that accessing their room on the forecourt didn't involve any stairs.

At check-in, the genial proprietor asked Remington if he was entering Sunday's race. In contrast to Saratoga Springs, no one else in line at reception mistook Serenata—leaning on her aluminum cane, the knee bandaged below baggy shorts, the right calf fat, tight, and discolored—for a fellow contestant.

Her presence was an inconvenience. For his wife to come along to the athletes' briefing that afternoon, Remington had to battle traffic back into town to drop her off at the MettleMan site, a large square covered in white tents. Without an invalid in tow, he might have wended to the briefing on his bike. But she'd lobbied to attend even the event's ancillary froufrou because ostensibly she yearned to participate in "the whole experience."

Propped on a bleacher for forty-five minutes while Remington found a place to park, Serenata considered: she did want to keep an eye on him. She was loath to conduct the weekend in a spirit of unrelenting antagonism. And if he insisted on going through with this farce, she was under some obligation to provide moral support.

All those other cars had been bursting with friends and family. But while she'd gone through the motions of inviting Griff, his opposition to his son's display of geriatric vanity was implacable. When she asked Deacon to come, he *laughed*. Tommy couldn't stand the prospect of applauding behind a barrier at an event she'd been slated to enter. Valeria's dour husband, Brian, had come to interpret Nancee's ceaseless physical agitation as demonic possession. Because worship of athletic perfection was a form of "idolatry," he'd even made Valeria drop her spinning class at the Y. As for triathlons, they were an "arrogant confusion of man with the divine." His pregnant wife was flat out forbidden from repeating her frenzy at the finish line in Syracuse. Hank Timmerman had intrigued a small local production company into filming a documentary of his inspiring journey from ruin to rebirth, and was hopping a ride with the crew. The other remaining members of the tri club were driving up separately with their own carloads of supporters.

Thus Remington had arrived in Lake Placid with a cheering section of one, and a dismal excuse for a well-wisher at that. As the stands filled with "lumpy chicks" and "lumpy dicks," as their son would say, his only backer's aversion bordered on nausea.

Remington located her on a bottom bleacher right before the instructional talk for first-timers was to get underway. The temperature was in the mid-eighties, so he'd changed from his slacks and button-down into running shorts and a muscle T. One of the biggest transformations of aging was the way that healing grew horribly slow, as if your cells were reluctant to waste the energy of replacement on an organism en route to the scrap heap; Serenata's tiniest cooking burn now took three weeks to peel to pink skin, and it would scar. Consequently, Remington still looked like an escapee from Intensive Care. Heads turned.

The twenty-something kid on his other side raised an eyebrow at the bandages and bruises just beginning to jaundice. Remington muttered, "Bike wipeout—at speed."

"Wow," the boy said. "And you're doing the race anyway. That's fantastic!" Had she indeed tried to vilify Bambi Buffer online for not forcing a client to concede his infirmity, Serenata never would have gotten anywhere with these people.

"My coach says the main thing in a Mettle is to 'stay within yourself,'" the boy went on, staring straight ahead. Oddly pale and puny, he seemed to be talking mostly to himself. "The biggest mistake he says first-timers make is getting swept up in other people's pace. Then later you blow out. 'Never race faster than you train,' Jason says." The compulsive jittering of his leg was shaking the whole bleacher. The event still two days off, the poor kid was already petrified.

All the information a buoyant young instructor proceeded to provide was clearly explained in his handout. But just as Serenata's joint replacement class merely replicated its handbook, no one trusted you to read anything anymore. Online, text was ceding to the podcast. Civilizationally, we were regressing to oral history around a campfire.

Most of the instructions regarded a plethora of bags—for transitions or one's private "special needs," like peanut butter cups or dry socks. The instructor emphasized the importance of attaching your race number to each and delivering the right-colored bag to the right deposit point. It was vital to arrive here at this time, there at another time, and to report for getting body markings (age, race number) within a set window. During the race, littering earned a "red card," and so did pissing in a residential front yard instead of using a Porta-John; two red cards and you'd "DQ." Water stations with nutritional gels, Gatorade, and bananas would be located every ten miles on the cycle route and every mile on the run—though chicken broth would only be served after dark. Bikes could be collected until one a.m. on Sunday night, and starting at six a.m. on Monday. Getting thousands of people to exhaust themselves all at the same time seemed a considerable organizational undertaking.

"Now, unlike our competitors," the young man said, wrapping up, "Mettles don't have time cutoffs for the first two segments, so you're not going to DNF if you cramp up and take longer than usual on the swim. Some folks are, you know, shit-hot runners but a little slower on the bike, and we don't think you should be penalized for mixed levels of proficiency. *However.* There is an overall event cutoff, and it's *very strict.* If your chin doesn't hit the bar on the finish line by the stroke of midnight, *poof,* your carriage turns into a pumpkin. Got that? Furthermore, midnight is when the Mettle is *over.* So if you're still out on the trail, our people are gonna pick you up. Our volunteers will have put in a lot of hard work on your behalf. It'll be late, they have families, and they deserve to go home. If you didn't make it by the gong, you can always try again next year. Besides, think of it this way: we need that strict cutoff to make sure your becoming a MettleMan means something. If we let you take three weeks to complete the course, that orange-and-gold finisher mug wouldn't be good for anything but coffee. Now, go out there, and show 'em what you're made of!"

With time to kill before the opening ceremony, Remington and Serenata dawdled through the commercial booths, which sold not only high-end sports clothing, but also veino-muscular compression socks; shots of cayenne, ginger, and honey to ward off muscle cramps; protein supplements of beef gelatin or bone broth; muscle rollers; and exotically contorted tri bikes, with inbuilt hydration systems connected to vinyl feeding tubes.

Close relatives of the high-strung steed he'd hurled into a tree, the bikes made Remington doleful, so they hit the franchise tent. Under the sign BOAST OF A LIFETIME! were piles of T-shirts: TRI NOW. WINE LATER; METTLE DETECTOR; I'M BETTER THAN YOU ARE (AND I CAN PROVE IT); SELF IS THE FINAL FRONTIER; LIMITS ARE FOR LOSERS; YOU ARE YOUR TIME. There were MettleMan logoed tea towels, shot glasses, bath plugs, beer mugs, handbags, knapsacks, lunch boxes, ankle bracelets, aprons, watches, wastebaskets, sports diaries, vape pens, paperweights, picture frames, pencil boxes, flip-flops, smart-phone cases, and toothbrushes, as well as MettleBaby teddy bears and bibs. On a popular rack, orange windbreakers were emblazoned in gold across the back, FULL METTLE JACKET.

"What did I tell you?" Serenata quoted *Goodfellas*. *"Don't buy anything."*

Impatient with his wife's pace on the way back up the hill, Remington remarked, "We should have brought the walker." It was a line she'd never have expected her husband to mutter when she was still in her early sixties.

In the lakeside public park, a stage sat beside an outsize video screen playing advertisements for more gear, as hip-hop pounded from the sound system. Children were showing off toward the front, doing handstands and cartwheels. On the hillside, groups were gathered on blankets, sipping electrolyte drinks and nibbling whole wheat burritos. The scene would have been bucolic, save for an edginess that was palpable. Snippets of discernable conversation were largely about the weather, and it wasn't small talk. The chances of rain on Sunday had risen to 50 percent, and a portion of this gathering wouldn't have the option of staying indoors with the crossword.

Serenata waved, glad to see that Cherry DeVries had brought her whole family—not only the three kids, but also a burly man overdressed for the heat, seated at the edge of their bedspread, and vengefully gnawing a hero.

"Sera, I don't think you've met my husband, Sarge," Cherry said. So at odds with the lithe, gangly stunners strewn on every side, her plus-size figure made her conspicuously more likable.

"It's so nice of you to come and support your wife," Serenata said.

"Cherry's a weaver on interstates," he said. "I wasn't about to entrust my kids to three hours on I-87 with my wife at the wheel."

"So how's the knee?" Cherry asked.

It was never clear what this frequent solicitation was meant to elicit. "Just standing here is making me suicidal"?

"Fine," Serenata said instead. That's what the solicitation was meant to elicit.

Remington located Chet, Sloan, and Hank with much backslapping and high-fiving. After all the attrition and accelerating rivalry, the tiny club seemed to have knit back together with a sense of all-for-one. Flitting among her chicks, their mother hen leaned down to each member in turn to impart last-minute advice: "Now, I know you're pumped, Hank, but remember this isn't a party. And don't let that film crew get in the way of the staff." "Hey, don't get casual, Sloan. It's never easy, I don't care if we've done them before." "Chet, early to bed tonight, too. Ten p.m. max. And tomorrow, I want you guys *asleep*, not just brushing your teeth, by eight thirty." As for whatever she told Remington, she was too down into his ear for Serenata to hear it.

Bambi was in her element. Even in this company, her physique stood out. Ranging palsy-walsy among former clients, she took her time, bestowing blessings ("Lookin' tight, Rex!") or teasing admonishments ("How many times I tell you, Paul? Lay off that calzone!"). The cameraman with the documentary crew couldn't get enough of her. "Hey, I thought this show was about me," Hank carped. "You were gonna interview me about my *bad decisions*—"

"Filler footage," the cameraman said, still panning.

The *filler footage* had chosen her opening ceremony outfit with care: a soft salmon leotard with spaghetti straps and a nap to the fabric that made you want to pet it, filmy cream-colored shorts that fluttered in the breeze to expose the cut of her hip flexors, and killer heels that for some reason didn't sink into the lawn. That body must have saved her business a bundle on advertising.

To spare herself tottering onto the grass with a knee that wouldn't bend beyond ninety degrees, Serenata perched on a rock by the lake. Onstage, testimonials got underway: by charities raising funds for obscure diseases; by the eldest of this year's intake, who at eighty-five was on his sixth full Mettle; and by the previous year's winner, a pro with a guileless, generically handsome face who praised his patient "tri widow" and "tri orphans" for never complaining that he wasn't around for waffles on weekends, and who looked about eight feet tall. Indeed, as she gave the hillside a once-over, the pros were easy to spot. The men were all so towering that they might have been a different species. Their shoulders were broad, but everything else was narrow: the tiny dropped waists, the slight hips, the taut little buns. They tended to have long feet and big hands. But the most mysterious aspect of this breed apart was that they weren't sexy. One simply didn't hanker to fuck a man who desired himself.

Although the MC extolled the multiple nationalities, the range of ages, and the numerous first responders and ex-military among this year's entrants, Serenata's private canvas of the crowd didn't produce big surprises. She located two black athletes, whose insouciant bearing conveyed a prosperous upbringing. One Chinese, check; one Indian, check. Although women were reputably represented, the vast preponderance of the participants were white men.

As for the ages, once you discounted supporters (heavier, more sunburned, more covered up), the cohorts seemed to clump. Like Tommy March, the legion of under-thirties hailed from a generation whose concept of "self-improvement" was integrally bound up with diet and exercise, whereas for Griff's contemporaries the term had meant broadening your vocabulary and learning French. Then there were the second-lifers over fifty—tan, spare, and gray, with close-cropped hair to disguise the balding. They had the same look in their eyes that she'd come to recognize in Remington: enflamed, the focus a gauzy middle-distance. Perhaps they'd built companies or fortunes, but the results had been unsatisfying. The youngsters wanted status. The oldsters wanted meaning.

At last, MettleMan's founder took the mic—a bear of a man named Doug Rausing whose potbelly suggested a latter-day preference for administration. He thanked sponsors and invited the top one hundred finishers to apply for the twentieth anniversary Mettle-of-Mettles in Alaska.

"Believe it or not," Rausing boomed, "when this organization started out eighteen years ago, our first race had only seventy-seven scrappy, never-say-die athletes. Since then, we've grown to a worldwide movement. If you've never been through this test of your very essence before, you may find nearly fifteen hundred contestants a little overwhelming. So I want to say a special word to all you first-timers. It may seem like you're in a crowd, and you can sure count on your brothers and sisters in this fellowship of torment to watch your back. But in the end, you're on your own, because that's what MettleMan is all about: facing down what you're made of, facing down if you've got the goods. No matter how many other athletes you see around you when you plunge into that cold lake early on Sunday morning, you are profoundly and, we all have to admit, sometimes disturbingly—*by yourself.*

"I'm betting that more than a few of you are anxious. Hell, maybe even scared to death. But one of the reasons you're battling inner demons is all the *outer* demons you've been combating ever since you first got up the nerve to go public with a commitment that's on the face of it pretty far-fetched. At every step of the way, you've been undermined. Maybe they even laughed at you. Didn't they? Didn't they laugh at you?"

The crowd chuckled in recognition.

"Because *they* say it's impossible," Rausing continued. "*They* say it's insane. *They* say that humans aren't meant to conquer such distances, in the water, on a bike, on foot, one after the other, without rest. *They* say you'll collapse. *They* say you'll do irreversible damage to your body, and end your life beaten down and ailing and drowning in regrets. But whatever happens on Sunday, there's only one regret you want to avoid: never tri-ing—that's *T-R-I*—in the first place. You'd regret listening to the spoilsports, the scaredy-cats, and the sissies. You'd regret listening to the whimpering, sniveling little voice that your tormentors—the naysayers, the excuse-makers, the nervous Nellies, the armchair cynics, the gloomy Guses—have actually *succeeded* in installing *inside your very head*!

"So you tell that little voice to scram. That voice is the sound of failure, inadequacy, and resignation. It's the voice of the Little Engine That Couldn't. It's the voice of the third-grade teacher who gave you a C-minus, the parent who sent you to your room, the counselor who said you'd never get into Princeton. The therapist who wanted to put you on Prozac, the professor who said you'd never graduate, the employer who deleted your job application, the editor who rejected your Great American Novel without reading past page three. It's the same voice that tells you that your country is in decline, your compatriots are all drug addicts, and the future belongs—with apologies to Bao Feng over there, who's a fine citizen of these United States—to the Chinese. It's the voice of the devil, friends. It's the voice of the devil.

"Listen only to your deep self. Concentrate only on getting to that next buoy, and then to the buoy after that. On getting to the top of that next hill, and then to the top of the hill after that. On getting to that next mile marker, and then to the mile marker after that. Pain? Pain is the fire in which we are smelted, and out the other side of that furnace we are tempered like steel. We are the human race, Mach Two. We are the stronger, leaner, meaner, fiercer, more powerful members of mankind who will prove there are *no* limits, and there is *nothing* we can't achieve, because WE—ARE—METTLEMEN!"

The crowd erupted with cheers loud enough to cover Serenata's murmur, "Leni Riefenstahl, where are you?"

"Tell me one more time that I don't have to do this," Remington said, peering through their motel room curtains at the wet parking lot, "and I worry I'm going to hit you."

It was three thirty a.m. The night before, allergic to observing the bedtime of an eight-year-old, Serenata had holed up in the bathroom with a towel under the door to block the light and read on the toilet with the cover down. As she'd only drifted off beside him an hour and a half ago, Remington wasn't the only one who wanted to hit someone. But outwardly, she resolved to seem chipper. Ever since Bambi had ratted her out, she never complained, never criticized, never made snarky remarks. This was her husband's show. She had put up a brave fight, and she had lost.

She ventured out the door. It was pitch-dark. The air was cool and dank. "Right now it's just a mizzle," she reported.

"Now it's sixty percent at seven," he said, poking his phone, "and it goes up from there."

"Well, there's rain and there's rain, right? Sometimes a light mist is refreshing."

Fortunately, she'd brought along a camp stove and espresso pot. Screw the power bars and gels; she'd also brought a box of miniature powdered-sugar doughnuts.

"You didn't have to get up with me, you know." Somehow it was a relief that he couldn't resist a doughnut. "I have to check in by five. You won't have anything to do. And how will you get down there to watch?"

"Uber. Or you could drive me down with you. I could help you get into your wet suit. It's tricky, with the bandages, and your shoulder."

"The volunteers assist in transitions, and they're good at it." He seemed to feel badly about rebuffing her. "But I'll need dry clothes when it's all over. Taking this bag to the finish line would be a big help. Also . . . Sorry, never mind."

"Never mind what?"

"I was going to suggest you could pick up the bike for me while I'm on the marathon segment, from that big sea of racks, which would give us a jump on the traffic Monday morning. But with your knee—"

"A bike makes a nifty walker. I could get it back here in another Uber. I'm supposed to use the knee anyway, and I missed a PT session on Friday."

He gave her the bike pickup slip. "But if it's too challenging, we'll retrieve it on Monday morning; we'll just have to wait in a long line. Don't hurt yourself."

As he shouldered the tote with his sharkskin-style wet suit, she tried to formulate a parting thought—but all she could think to say was that he didn't have to do this. Judiciously, she hugged him hard on the forecourt and kept her mouth shut.

With nothing to do at the motel but eat more doughnuts, Serenata arrived at the spectators' knoll early enough to get a front-row view of the swimmers' entry-point beach around the bend. The sky dim and grainy, she needed the light on her phone to pitch her folding stool on stable ground. She used to stand twelve hours a day. But she was getting a feel for how effortlessly you could switch camps. Once you immigrated to the land of lassitude, all those whirling dervishes leaping and spinning and flailing around grew incomprehensible.

Thus when a staffer onshore pounded the franchise's signature brass gong with a fluffy orange mallet and the first tranche of swimmers, all pros, tumbled into the water, Serenata didn't wish she could have joined them. Especially not when the morning's drizzle gave way to a deluge. Slanted sheets swept the surface of the lake, which bounded upward in reply, as if it were raining upside-down. Droplets drummed the plastic orange buoys like tympanis. She'd borrowed an umbrella from the motel reception, and even the splashes spanking off the nylon onto her legs were irksome. Much was to be said for physical comfort—for rest, for ease; for being dry, sheltered, neither too cold nor too hot, and well fed. Fine, many of her compatriots were overdosing on their own well-being. Nevertheless, for most of human existence the driving aim of the species was not to toil, but to stop toiling; not to suffer, but to stop suffering. It would seem unappreciative of all the forebears instrumental in the evolution of sturdy umbrellas and convenient little folding chairs not to relish the fact that rather than swim a ferocious 2.6 miles in driving rain she could simply sit here.

Doing the crawl in heavy rain could induce a sensation of drowning; the distinction between air and water blurred. Thus the pros' knifing from buoy to buoy was frankly astonishing. Pretty much anyone could ride a bike, and anyone could run. But swimming was a skill, and those strokes were a marvel.

Which didn't prevent her fellow spectators from being blithe and inattentive. The pros didn't seem to arrive with entourages; however oddly, this was a job, and leaving the family at home would keep expenses down. No one on the knoll was rooting for these athletes. To the contrary, a woman nearby complained to her companion,

"George says the pros are ruining this sport for everybody. Not only do they show everyone else up, but when they retire, they enter the age groups as amateurs. Then they win—like, *duh*. It's not exactly cheating, but it's close."

Self-classified by their time, groups of swimmers were staggered every five minutes. Expecting to take over two hours to complete the swim, the final cohort hit the water at 6:35, just after the pros began their second lap—presumably to keep the slowpokes from being run over.

There: Remington was last. His stroke was unmistakable. Each forward arm hit the water with a hard plop. A heaviness had always characterized his crawl, and the shoulder injury would make the right-hand reaches only more labored. His having failed to mention the pain all week was a bad sign. The rain settled into an unrelenting steadiness. This wasn't a passing shower, but a rainy *day*.

Serenata was vigilant. Boats were stationed at regular intervals, but entrant #1,083 was nothing to those lifeguards but a number, and she didn't trust them.

Around seven a.m., the male pros slogged to shore and hit the sand at a run. All the female pros were out of the water ten minutes after the lead. Serenata focused her portable binoculars. Remington still hadn't cleared the far bend that marked his first half-lap.

By the time her husband did reach that bend, a clump of amateurs was overtaking him on their second lap. It was already seven fifteen. One difficulty he'd have to contend with would be all these other swimmers, who weren't necessarily in a considerate frame of mind, who had their own problems with cramps or freak-outs, and whose goggles may have clouded or been knocked sideways, so that even if they were polite, in this torrent they could barely see. Collisions looked common. Splashes from adjacent competitors would add to the rain; being jostled on every side would be discombobulating;

being constantly overtaken by swimmers who'd already completed three-quarters of the course would be demoralizing.

When at last Remington curved around the raft by the shore and began his second lap, it was 7:55. He'd taken an hour and twenty minutes to complete 1.3 miles, a time that most people could beat with a breaststroke. The majority of contestants had left the water, though about three dozen racers were still going at it, all ahead of him. As time went on, the distance between Remington and the next-to-last swimmer lengthened. By 8:50, that penultimate contestant—a woman—sloshed to shore and stumbled through the orange-carnation archway. With nearly half a lap to go, Remington was alone in the lake.

He'd slowed down. That previous half-lap had taken him not forty but fifty minutes, the pace of a dog paddle. The rhythm of his plopping arms had decelerated. One of the motorized dinghies plowed to his side. A lifeguard leaned down, doubtless to ensure he was not in distress, but maybe also to ask if he'd like to climb into the boat and call it a day. She prayed he'd take them up on the offer. *Just tell them, "Sorry, but I had a serious accident right before this race, and I didn't realize the toll it took on me." That's the truth, and it confers no dishonor. Just please get out of the water and out of the rain. We can go back to the motel, where you can take a long, scalding shower. I'll fix you hot cocoa from the in-room amenities, adding coffee creamer and sugar to make it more fortifying. When you're feeling warmer and stronger and get back in dry clothes, we'll find a cozy place for a big breakfast, with sausage and pancakes. You won't even have to talk. And I'll never, ever say I told you so.*

The inflatable retreated—though it followed him watchfully from a few yards back.

All the other bystanders on the knoll had cleared off. Inattentive to the positioning of her umbrella, Serenata was getting soaked, but she was beside herself. She tried waving, and semaphoring by opening and closing the umbrella, but Remington didn't appear to notice, and the distraction might have been less than helpful anyway.

At long last, he reached the shallows and Lazarethed to shore. It was 9:41 a.m.: three hours and six minutes, which must have set a record, if not the kind he would covet. She should have felt proud of him, and maybe she did. But this pride felt more like dread.

She folded up the stool, slipped it in her tote, and looped the bag around her shoulder. As she ventured carefully with the cane in one hand and the umbrella in the other, her purchase in the mud was precarious. She shuffled over to the chute through which all the other contestants had already run toward "T1," while behind the barrier onlookers had cheered and waved placards for friends and relatives. Now Serenata was the only spectator. Staff in matching orange T-shirts and cheap translucent ponchos loitered impatiently in the wings, eager to start rolling up the sopping carpet of artificial grass and wrap this wretched segment up. Heading to the tent where a volunteer would peel off the wet suit and help him into his cycling gear, Remington loped leadenly toward his wife, bare feet splashing the AstroTurf.

When they locked eyes as he passed, his expression was hollow. He didn't seem to recognize her. Aside from a distant growl of thunder and the splat of his feet, the silence was sepulchral. Cheering this spectacle of self-destruction would have been perverse. She made a feeble effort at an encouraging smile, and looked away.

Having hobbled to a road that overlooked the MettleMan site, she'd a view of the ocean of bike racks. There must have been slots for 1,500, though Remington's would be easy to find; it was the only one left. When her husband emerged from the T1 tent and a volunteer in a poncho delivered the handlebars, Serenata waved, but he had more on his mind than looking for his wife. From this distance, she couldn't be sure if the wobble as he mounted and pedaled off was all in her head.

Maybe it was the rain, or maybe after eighteen years of hosting this event the locals had grown blasé, but the supporters on the sidelines were sparse. Grim conditions endowed the occasion with an air of can-we-just-get-this-over-with. Yet suddenly cheers, whistles, and clackers created a simulacrum of excitement. Sweeping down the hill and banking on the turn with spray sheeting off their tires, the pros were completing their first fifty-eight-mile cycling lap.

Serenata didn't care. She'd never understood cycling as a spectator sport, which made paint drying seem like a nail-biter. However unseemly self-pity under the circumstances, she was still wet and cold, and the knee was yowling. She shambled up the hill on the commercial side of the cycle route and found a restaurant with outdoor tables and big umbrellas. There she was surprised to find the documentary film crew, surrounded by eggs and hash browns.

"Why aren't you guys out collecting footage of miraculous rebirth?" she asked.

"Contrary to what they told you in science class," the hipster cameraman said, "butterflies sometimes revert to caterpillars."

"Did Hank punk out?"

"We were out kind of late last night, considering," the lantern-jawed producer said. "But he assured us that he'd trained to do this shit on not much sleep."

"If you were all 'out' last night," she said, "do you mean he got plastered?"

"I didn't keep track," the director in an old OBAMA '08 cap said diplomatically.

"Did he by any chance start asking you about Lorrie Moore's short stories?"

"Now that you mention it," the director said, "yeah."

"He was plastered," Serenata said.

"When we pounded on his motel room this morning," the cameraman said, "he wouldn't open the door. Fucking hell. Up at four thirty for nothing. Once he missed the swim check-in, we all went back to bed."

"It's not only getting up in pitch-dark that was for nothing," the producer said. "The doc's kaput, and what are we doing in fucking Lake Placid in a downpour? Motel, meals, gas—we're seriously out of pocket."

"I doubt it's any comfort, but however bad you feel," Serenata said, "Hank's going to feel worse. He's been training for this race for months."

"Maybe the Hankster couldn't face the weather forecast," the director supposed. "I mean, look at these guys." He gestured to the flooded cycling course, of which the eatery enjoyed an excellent view, as the last of the pros came through. "They're mental."

"At least, for reasons I don't entirely understand," Serenata said, "the pros make money off this stuff. But for everyone else"—she leaned confidentially across the cameraman's eggs—"*there's absolutely no reason to do this.*"

"But isn't your husband in this race?" the director asked.

"Uh-huh. I'm afraid so."

"Ha!" the director said. "That's the first discouraging word I've heard since we got here. Pull up a chair."

Serenata ordered pancakes and sausage.

The cameraman nodded approvingly. "Not sure why, but ever since we landed in this throng of demigods, all I want to do is eat, sleep, drink, and watch TV. Anything that doesn't involve making an effort or getting wet."

"While my husband ran the Saratoga Springs marathon last year," she said, "I spent loads of money on clothes I didn't need, ate an enormous lunch, and hit the hotel pool, where I refused to do anything more tiring than float."

"I can't wait for the pendulum to swing back to hedonism and hell-raising," the cameraman said. "I think I was born into the wrong generation. This one, it's all about *redemption*, have you noticed? Earning, and striving, and getting holy. All the guys I went to film school with at NYU are in love with purification—forswearing meat, dairy, carbs, out-of-season produce, and plastic. They don't have an indulgent or mutinous bone in their bodies. Oh, and they're not just into redemption, either. Add *rectitude*. They all want to be hallway monitors."

"When I was young, we broke the rules. Far as I can tell, your peers love nothing more than making up more of them." She flicked her hand. "And enforcing them with a whip."

He touched her wrist. "Nice work. Though I'm surprised. Everyone gets tats."

Outliers recognized each other. "Cincinnati, 1973. *They're* copying *me*."

They were flirting, a little. It was nice. The pancakes arrived. The stack was enormous.

"Couldn't you salvage what you've shot," she supposed, "by doing a more general documentary on the rising popularity of the triathlon?"

"Yesterday's news," the cameraman said. "These gonzo endurance races are all over the country. And now the heavies are into ultra-hyper-maxed-out-shitting-yourself stuff, on the tundra in January, or in Death Valley in July. Which makes this one seem pissant in comparison. So we needed the addict-finds-enlightenment angle. About all I've got worth saving is a few clips of that Bambi broad to provide inspiration in moments of, ah, *self-reflection*."

"Speak of the devil." Serenata was gratified to note as the woman streaked past that Bambi's favorite baby-blue and canary-yellow cycling outfit was so spattered with black mud that the ensemble was probably ruined.

"That Rausing shyster," the director said, looking up from his phone, "says they've already had three wipeouts on the bikes, including one multiple-cyclist pileup. Crap traction. One accident was pretty serious. Busted the guy's head open."

Worried, Serenata broke out her own phone. For the cycling and running segments, contestants wore the same electronically tagged ankle bracelets Remington had worn in Saratoga Springs, so she could track his progress with the MettleMan app she'd downloaded at the motel. In the whole field, #1,083 remained last, but the blue dot was still moving faster than a man with a busted head.

When they finished eating, the camera crew decided to check out and head back to Hudson—punitively, without Hank. They gave Serenata a lift back to her motel, where she took what should have been her husband's scalding shower and changed into the dry clothes he needed so much more than she did. By noon, #1,083 had crossed the halfway point in the first lap. Restless, she Ubered back to town and bought a heavy sweatshirt; it was chillier than she'd been prepared for. She sampled wild-mushroom olive oil and strawberry balsamic vinegar with scraps of French bread. She dropped into the popcorn store and picked up a novelty seasoning that was supposed to taste like beer-can chicken.

As the blue dot approached the end of its first lap, she returned to the same restaurant with its superlative view of the course, ordering a basket of fried calamari to justify her occupancy of the table. She missed the camera crew. It had been a relief to share solidarity with her fellow "spoilsports, scaredy-cats, and sissies."

Immediately below Serenata's table, an agonizingly thin woman in athletic gear too summery for the chill had stationed herself behind the spectator barrier with a gratingly loud cowbell clacker. The faster amateurs were already finishing their second lap. *Every—single—fucking* time another cyclist passed, the self-appointed cheerleader went into a frenzy of hooting and clacking, as well as shouting the usual inanities: "Go, baby! You show 'em! Never say die, baby! Keep it up! We're all behind you! Kill—it! Kill that lap!" The constant clacking was a torture.

At last the app showed the blue dot curving around the bend. Serenata abandoned her calamari and leaned over the wooden rail around the restaurant's deck. There he was, head down, in the timelessly dopy helmet, and like the rest of the riders, covered in mud. His bandages were diarrheal. In a rare two seconds during which the emaciated fan let up on her ceaseless clacking, Serenata projected with the deep purr that had captivated the man returning his tie to Lord & Taylor, "REM-ING-TON." He turned his head and treated her to a private nod.

Which would have to keep her going for another how many hours? She checked her watch. He'd done that lap in 4:09. He was therefore averaging . . . 14 mph, which considering how shattered he'd looked after the swim was downright okay. So: he hadn't drowned. He hadn't had another bike accident. And if he kept this up, he'd begin the marathon+.2m at about six p.m., which actually gave him half a chance of finishing before midnight. Taking her own temperature, she appeared to be impressed and disgusted in equal measure. Only one sentiment was unambivalent: she'd no desire to spend what remained of their lives in passable health going to events like this one. How she felt about his finishing the full Mettle before the gong was entirely predicated on whether its completion satisfied him, or gave him a taste for more.

That cameraman was onto something about the heathen's natural reaction to all this repudiation of the flesh. She finished the calamari.

According to the app, the winner would come in around 3:40 p.m. Though hardly on the edge of her chair about which total stranger took first place, she wasn't up for another round-trip to the motel. So she lurched back down the hill toward the finish line, where the last few hundred feet of the running track curved around the rows of bike racks, now filling back up. A fair crowd had accumulated behind the spectator barrier. Making shameless use of her disability to receive special treatment, she managed to establish her portable canvas stool as a front-row seat. She arranged the right leg at partial extension while enjoying a good view of the finish line's archway, its orange carnations grown bedraggled in the steady downpour. Between the vertical supports stretched a horizontal pole: the chin-up bar.

For diversion, she looked up the race numbers of the Hudson Tri Club. Hank Timmerman had been disappeared. Right now, ambitious amateurs were already throwing their bikes to volunteers and rushing into the T2 tent, but Cherry DeVries had many miles to go. Serenata found herself rooting for the woman; should she come up short, Sarge would never let her live it down. Sloan Wallace wasn't in the same league as the pros, but he was already three-quarters through the run; he occupied the level of excellence that might have given him a crack at placing if it weren't for the current and recently retired professionals about whom the woman on the knoll had complained. It took resolve to look up *Bam Bam*, whose blue dot, she was gratified to note, was significantly behind Sloan's. That would bug the trainer no end.

"Good Lord!" Serenata exclaimed aloud. Chet Mason was listed "DNF." Her heart was strangely broken on the young man's account.

Volunteers passed around long orange strips, one of which Serenata accepted with perplexity. It looked like a condom for a horse. Around her, more experienced spectators blew them up into batons, as if to make balloon animals. Only when a roar went up on the other side of the bend did she get the drill: spectators leaned over to pound these inflated orange sausages on the hollow plexiglass barrier in rhythmic unison, the while shouting "Go! Go! Go! Go!" as the leading pro hove into view. It was a primitive tribal drumming session in plastic.

Although having flagellated himself for nine hours and forty minutes, the paragon in front, streaming with rain and spatter, was running all out. He leaped at the bar, rose in the same single fluid motion to bring his chin above it, then lifted his long legs overhead and arced back to ground with a gymnast's dismount. A practiced maneuver, and flashy.

"YOU . . . ARE . . . METTLEMAN!" boomed over the loudspeaker.

Volunteers rushed to the winner with towels and a space blanket, as another looped a garish medal around his neck. He was ushered to photographers on the sidelines.

Thirty seconds later, the number two finisher came in—impressively, a woman, lanky, gristled, flat-chested, and so insanely light that the cherry-on-top chin-up looked effortless. Yet once her feet hit the track accompanied by another "YOU . . . ARE . . . METTLEMAN!"—the coronations were unisex—her legs gave way, and she crumpled into the mud. This time the volunteers gathered her into a wheelchair, and hurried the racer through the flaps of a tent marked with a white cross.

Medical attention before the photo op was more the form than not. After the triumphant pounding of the home stretch, most pros were shaking and could barely stand, if at all. One was rarely witness to the expenditure of every last iota of energy, strength, and will, and to what it looked like the moment those quantities were perfectly spent.

But the *poom-pooming* of the batons was giving Serenata a headache. Being incapacitated, and feeling a little threatened by the press of the crowd, she relinquished her prime position, using the cane to part the waters. She pulled herself up on the bleachers where the athletes' briefing had been held, the more distanced view of the finish line wholly adequate, given how little she cared. Each time another contestant came in, the announcer bestowed the same booming baptism of "YOU . . . ARE" etc. with improbably fresh enthusiasm. Checking the app again, she was perturbed that Remington hadn't made more headway on his second bike lap.

She ripped off the price tags and drew on her new sweatshirt, over which she donned the hooded rain poncho from the same shop; the arm holding the umbrella was getting tired. Tugging the nylon tightly around her as drips pattered off the visor, she huddled down for the long haul: the loyal helpmate, the faithful wife, the poor excuse for a fan. They said time passed more quickly when you got older. Well, not always.

By about five p.m., a familiar face penetrated her catatonia: Sloan Wallace had just come in. Assuming he'd entered the water at about 6:10 a.m., he'd finished the course in under eleven hours. Since these people talked ceaselessly about their times, she was painfully aware that "cracking eleven" was not only Sloan's driving ambition, but Bambi's, too. Serenata checked the trainer's blue dot with an evil smile: the bitch would never make it.

But she had nothing against Sloan, so she limped down toward the shelter marked FINISHERS' TENT. Inside, the pros sat by themselves at separate folding tables, not talking to one another, with dull, vacant expressions, like robots that had been switched off. They left nearby baskets of Pop-Tarts and granola bars untouched. The dozen amateurs who'd come in were distinguishable by their clusters of excited friends and family. Yet when she waved to Sloan, just finishing off a liter of Gatorade, he was surrounded by no such retinue, and looked glad to see her.

"I came to congratulate you," she said. "I'm so sorry about the weather. It must have been grueling."

"Yeah, and to think we were mostly worried about the heat!"

"So—where's your family?"

"My ex wouldn't let the kids come," he said. "I have custody every other weekend. This is her weekend."

"Pretty mean-spirited, not being willing to switch."

"Tell me about it."

After they chatted about the course's travails and Serenata affirmed that Remington was still going doggedly at it, she asked, "Any idea what happened to Chet? The app says he's DNF."

Sloan's face clouded. Chet was more or less his protégé. "Damn, that's a shame. I can't believe he'd just quit. Hey, Patti!" he shouted to a volunteer. "Any idea what happened to Chet Mason? Short, compact, about thirty, and had to pull out?"

"Oh, him," Patti said. Gossip about contestant misfortune must have spread quickly. "Muscle spasm in his calf. That's spasm, not cramp, and I guess there's a big difference. They say he tried to keep running, too, and it was totally awful to watch. You know . . ." The girl illustrated with a humping galumph. "I saw him when they brought him to the med tent. Some guys fake injury when really they just can't hack it. But that calf muscle, well, you could *see* it in this gross bunchy knot. He could hardly put any weight on the leg. Not the kind of problem you go to a hospital for—it just has to work itself out—but they wouldn't let him back on the course. Man, I've never seen a grown man cry like that. I mean, he was bawling like a baby."

"From the pain?" Serenata asked.

"I don't think so," Patti said.

"Look what the cat dragged in!" Sloan exclaimed. "What took you so long?"

"What do you think, I stopped for *muffins*," Bambi snarled, approaching their table as she toweled off the mud. "Didn't even beat my PB, much less crack eleven. Though I assume from that smarmy expression that you did?"

"Ten fifty-six fourteen," Sloan said with a smile. "Not bad for a sloppy course."

"I don't appreciate going through this much shit only to feel like a fucking jackass," Bambi groused. Misery had eaten a layer off her character like paint stripper. Gone was the sunny veneer. She exuded malice and resentment, like a normal person.

She turned to the volunteer. "Hey, kid, what'd you say about Chet?"

Patti enjoyed some attention for once (question: Why did anyone *volunteer* for this thankless go-fetch? It wasn't for the glory) and repeated her performance.

"Fuck, my first DNF," Bambi said. "And that camera guy told me at the swim check-in that Hank went AWOL. What a bunch of douches. Hey, gimme that." Having never even said hello, she grabbed Serenata's phone, which would obviously be tracking her husband. "Rem's way too far behind. He's one punk runner, you know. Fucker doesn't have a prayer of finishing. Gotta love this year's stats: one quitter, one casualty, two DNFs, and a no-show."

So much for positive thinking.

Serenata returned to the bleachers. As the light faded a shade at six p.m., she granted that Bambi had a point. Had Remington kept up his original pace, he'd have transitioned to the run by now. The cyclists rolling into T2 reduced to a trickle. By seven p.m., #1,083 was the only bike on the course.

The tracking app eliminated any suspense, so when at 7:40 he banked around the curve, she was ready for him. The wait had provided opportunity to brush up her math skills. His average speed had sunk from fourteen miles per hour to ten. Including getting changed, he now had to run a distance in under 4:20 that the winner might have dispatched in 3:14, but which in the previous year's race the whole field ran at an average 4:57. Why, for today's run even the beatified Bambi Buffer had clocked 4:10. What were the chances that Remington could run 26.4 miles in only ten minutes longer than his Amazonian trainer, when in Saratoga Springs he'd taken almost seven and a half hours to run 26.2? ZEEEEEE-RO!

There was nothing like sitting around for hours cold and damp with zip to do for working up an explosive disgust. Balancing on the cane on an upper bleacher—from which, not only could she see him tool down the last hundred yards of the course, but he could see her—she belted at a volume any voice coach would have warned could damage her instrument, "Remington Alabaster, that's enough! Give it up, and let's have dinner! You'll never make the cutoff!"

Three minutes later the fucking idiot was out the other side of the T2 tent in his running togs.

After a third meal in the same restaurant—it was the closest to the site—she limped back down to the finish line. The distances were short, but this was cumulatively way too much mileage for her knee in one day. She'd been popping NSAIDs like Good & Plentys.

Of course, no need to hurry. It was nearly eleven p.m. when she paid the bill, and Remington's blue dot wasn't halfway through the run. He'd been averaging 3.5 mph: a brisk walk. Were he to run the remaining fifteen miles in an hour—while enjoying a festival of abrasions, a pulled Achilles, a strained hamstring, a damaged rotator cuff, and contusions that had probably done muscle damage—he'd have to rival Hicham El Guerrouj's 3:43 record for the mile fifteen times in a row.

Even unimpaired, Remington had a curious running style. His step high, all his energy seemed to plow into the vertical. From any distance, he appeared to be running in place. Though he was slight for his height, his feet hit the trail with the same dead plop with which his arms hit the water on a swim. Indeed, he managed to haul that sinker quality from the pool to dry land.

Physically, he was a wreck when he started. Emotionally, she couldn't predict how exactly he'd take failing to finish—aside from *not well.*

The curve of the home stretch was now lit up with multicolored lights. The rain having finally stopped improved attendance. This crowd was noticeably more feverish than the audience for the pros. The runners coming in during the final hour were likely to be what the rest of the world regarded as "ordinary people" who were attempting the extraordinary, which they'd imported large groups of rabid supporters to witness. Thus Serenata no sooner established her special disability stool than a battle-ax brunette shoved her hard enough that she almost fell off. "I got three people comin' in, honey. Gotta be in front." With the emergence of every subsequent contestant from around the bend—all of whom couldn't have been "her people"—the pushy spectator screamed at a volume that most women would not have been able to muster during natural childbirth.

Admittedly, the racers at the tail end of the field made for a moving spectacle. These were the housewives, the gas station attendants, the schoolteachers, and the cable guys who were unaccustomed to the spotlight. Sometimes on the short side, or maybe a little plump, they weren't the perfectly proportioned paragons who sold $200 running shoes for Madison Avenue. Most of the eleventh-hour participants would have possessed neither the cash nor the pomposity to spring for personal trainers, and would have relied on websites or a book. The determination that powered them to this finish line must have been relentless. Like Ethan Crick, for months on end many would have been arising at four or five in the morning to swim, bike, or run before heading to a full day's work. Some of the women must have risked substantial familial ridicule during the painfully gradual muscle building required to raise their chins above that consummate bar. It wasn't up to Serenata to decide that this crowning moment—"YOU—ARE—METTLEMAN!"—couldn't be the highlight of their lives.

A subset of the folks barely beating the cutoff would probably have expected to finish many hours earlier. Lean, tall, buff, and male, this conspicuously fit contingent must have found the difficulty of the course a shock. Even with the enticing orange archway within sight, some of these guys were having a murderous time forcing one foot in front of the other, while moving about as fast as Serenata post-surgery with a cane. They doubtless felt a little embarrassed to be finishing in the same time as the likes of . . . Cherry DeVries!

Serenata had yet to hoot, whistle, or pound an inflatable orange wiener against the barrier, much less screech like this lunatic to her left. Yet when the familiar mother-of-three hoofed into view, she broke into a grin and yelled, "Good for you, Cherry!"

"CHER-*REE*! CHER-*REE*! That a girl! You did it! Pumpkin, we love you to death! CHER-*REE*! CHER-*REE*!" It was Sarge.

Shoulders back, head high, Cherry marshaled a final surge of speed. Lunging onto the plastic stool provided, she sacrificed three seconds off her time to bask in the roar before grabbing the bar to do one slow, flawless chin-up with her eyes closed. When she dropped to the ground as the MC deputized her an official MettleMan, it was impossible to tell if she was laughing or crying.

Serenata ceded what little space the screamer had allowed her and threaded to the area outside the finisher tent. By the time she found Cherry, Sarge had an arm around his wife and was posing while the kids took photos on their phones. The man was beaming. Go figure. Maybe triathlons weren't entirely evil.

Serenata cut in and gave the muddy woman a hug; that was it for the new sweatshirt. "You're a great example to your daughters," she whispered in Cherry's ear.

"So what's up with Remington?" Cherry asked.

"He's running a little behind."

Cherry checked her watch. "Oh, no! Is he not going to make it?"

"It looks unlikely. But he'll be touched that in the state you must be in you still asked after him."

"Gimme some sugar, champ! Didn't I *tell* ya you could do it?" Now changed into skinny jeans and a clinging pink sweater, Bambi grabbed Cherry around the neck in a possessive clutch. "Realize you're my only first-timer success story this year? Your pic's going on my website, kid. I expect a written testimonial by end of week."

As Sloan embraced the unlikely finisher ("Welcome to the *real* club, Cherry! Drop by the shop, we'll go get that tat together"), Serenata stepped back to check Remington's dot on MMInc. "That's weird," she said aloud.

"What's that, hon?" Cherry asked.

"His dot hasn't moved for twenty minutes."

"Maybe he's stoking up at a water station. Lemme see." Cherry was clearly nonplussed when she saw how many miles the dot had still to go. "Or maybe, you know . . . He's seen the writing on the wall. It's ten to twelve, sweetie."

But Remington would only quit if forced to. He may have left his phone behind, but he had a watch. He'd known perfectly well when he started that run that he didn't have time to complete it before midnight. As the bronze gong crashed at the stroke of twelve, Serenata felt the vibration in her gut.

Multiple runners came in thereafter, and though they all went through the formality of the chin-up, the MC had gone insultingly silent. They were tired, they were wet, they were far fitter than the average bear, but they were not MettleMen. Medical staff and the volunteer issuing space blankets remained, but all the tension of the occasion went slack. Staff began picking up litter.

As several rugged buggies were revving up, Serenata approached a driver. "I'm concerned about my husband, number 1,083?" She pointed at the dot on the app. "He's about thirteen miles back, and he's been in the same place for half an hour."

"Don't you worry, we're off to pick up all the stragglers."

"Could I come with you?"

"Sorry, we have to save the empty seats for the folks we're picking up. They might not have quite made it, but they'll be tired and—understatement—not in the happiest frame of mind."

"Well, could you at least call me when you find him, so I know he's all right?"

"No prob."

She lodged her number on the staffer's phone. Yet when the helpful young man called half an hour later, he said, "Ma'am? We found the number 1,083 ankle bracelet, but not the guy it was attached to. He took it off."

"He's still out there. You have to find him."

"Sorry to get all legalistic on you, but I sorta like, *don't* have to find him. Check out the fine print on the release he signed. This outfit takes no responsibility for mishaps. Now he's removed his tag, which is way against the rules, we really wash our hands."

"But we're talking about an older man, an elderly man, with some serious injuries, who's never done this before, out all by himself—"

"Ma'am, we've all had a long day. Your husband, or at least his bracelet, was our last straggler, and we're heading back to base. Want my advice? If he doesn't show, check the bars. You wouldn't believe how hard some of these guys take not making the cutoff. There's actually a dive out on 86 called 'The DNF.' Popular with the locals."

"The only bar my husband is headed toward is that chin-up bar. He wouldn't want you to pick him up. I bet he hid from the lights of your buggy—"

The call had already terminated.

Dismayed, she wandered the area behind the finish line, where the atmosphere resembled the all-business party's-over of striking a rock concert set. She ducked into the finisher's tent, which had turned into something of a hang. Cherry and her family were gone. The only person she recognized was Bambi, with her back to Serenata, pink-and-black cowboy boots propped on a table. She was knocking back red wine brimming in a large plastic beer cup with another taut, tough-looking young woman.

"You're a trainer, so you know what a bummer it is," Bambi was saying. "And this one, it was like a clinical experiment, right? Your basic silk purse–sow's ear science fair project. Like, he started out, bar none, absolutely the sorriest athlete I ever coached. Know what he clocked in the Saratoga marathon? *Seven twenty-six.*" The other woman hooted. "So you know me: I rise to a challenge. It's fucking compulsive, actually. I spotted this plodder in Saratoga, I couldn't control myself. I figured if I could shove this Clark Kent into a phone booth—well, the bragging rights would have a shelf life longer than Cheez Whiz. A born-again story on that scale could bring in loads more biz. I even had some money riding on it with Sloan—*another* contest the bastard won today. If that guy wasn't such a good fuck, he'd be unbearable."

"As it is . . ." the other woman allowed, wiggling her eyebrows.

"Only thing harder than that boy's deltoids is his dick. Worth buckets of I-told-you-he-couldn't-do-it. Anyway, good thing I made a fair whack of change on the old guy's retainer. Compensation for the wife, wanna know the truth. The geez's biggest handicap. Bitch wrapped around his ankles like a human ball and chain. What a tight, dismal cunt. One of those 'I do ten jumping jacks a day, so I'm one of you!' types. And *whoooo-ee*! Was she jealous."

"I know that drill," the colleague said, taking a swig straight from the bottle. "All you gotta do is walk into the room."

"And they feel all weak and fat and sad."

"'Cause they are." The two toasted.

"And this geez," Bambi said. "He was following me around like a puppy dog. I let him do me once. Just a hand job. No harm done. You know, all this training, you get a little *tense*."

"Those old guys, they're always so grateful. Like you've let them handle a museum piece. That eighty-five-year-old, doing his sixth? He's one of mine. I let him put his hand down my shirt, I swear he almost *cried*."

Serenata had heard enough. "Bambi, Remington is missing. He's taken off his bracelet, and can't be tracked."

Bambi turned, and didn't look in the least caught out. "What am I supposed to do about it?"

"Most of the running course is off-road. I can't take a taxi. Someone has to head back up the trail and find him."

"Lady. First you threaten me, and now you want a favor?"

"Yes," Serenata said.

"Sipping lemonade on the sidelines, maybe you think this event is a walk in the park. It ain't. I'm tired. I'm pretty drunk. I owe you jack. I'm not going anywhere but back to my motel to get laid."

This wasn't the time to mull over what little Bambi had said that was surprising.

In Serenata's PT sessions, the therapist had just started her on the stationary bicycle. Which meant she was barely capable of riding the kind that went somewhere. It was still twenty minutes to one.

Double-checking the race number against the pickup slip, a volunteer handed her Remington's bike with a glance at her cane. "You gonna be all right?"

"That remains to be seen."

Leaning on the handlebar and frame as she had on Carlisle in Manhattan, she wheeled the bike to the finish line. She located an Allen wrench in its onboard tool kit to lower the seat. She found the handout from the athletes' briefing and studied the topographical map of the running course, memorizing the details as best she could. Leaving the collapsible stool, poncho, and umbrella behind, she tucked the hooked end of the cane snugly beside Remington's change of clothes in the tote, looped its long handles diagonally around her shoulder, and arranged the bag on her back. Standing on her left leg, she angled the bike toward the ground, and eased her right leg over the seat. The extension required was excruciating. When she got the bike unsteadily underway, she was reminded that the sole session she'd done on the stationary one at the therapist's had been painful and short.

She began the deserted running course in reverse. After that harridan screeching in her ear loudly enough to trigger temporary hearing loss, the quiet was glorious.

Beyond silence, there was little to savor. At the top and bottom of every orbit of the right pedal—maximum flexion and extension—her pupils flared in dumb shock. Applying torque on the right was a torture, too, so she relied disproportionately on the left leg. Not easy, because the pedals were clip-on, and she didn't have cleated shoes. The frame was too big, and the brakes were touchy. Given the mud alone, she took it slow. At least the course was well lit and well marked, with jagged orange flags flapping in the breeze every ten feet.

She'd be well within her rights to be angry, and somewhere in there she probably was. He was clearly determined to finish unofficially even after missing the cutoff; he'd be picturing himself doing that final chin-up under the moon, with everyone else gone home. He'd unquestionably hidden from the retrieval buggy. But at the rate he was "running" he wouldn't get to that chin-up bar, assuming they left it up, until four a.m. Never mind the fact that he should never have entered today's event in the first place. This whole triathlon debacle had mangled their marriage at the very point in their lives when they most needed to rely on each other. What, she was going to flounce off and find another husband at sixty-two? Not to mention that he should have kept his fucking hands off Bambi's pussy. The trainer was the type to laser away every last hair. Maybe he liked the novelty, all that creepy prepubescent smoothness.

But in times of crisis, anger was usually a phase, and she seemed to have skipped it. Remington was injured, and he was old. He'd never lost the *sound* of a reasonable man, but the presentation of reasonableness was a lifetime habit; lately, his rationality was all tone and no content. He'd grown a little crazy. His still being out in the woods at this time of night when the race was actually over: that was more than a little crazy. Fury would have been beside the point. She was worried, and she was frightened.

One of the distinguishing features of the Mettle was the off-road run. Competing franchises conducted their marathons on tarmac. A narrower dirt trail added challenge. With roots and rocks, footing was trickier. Overtaking was more difficult. If you didn't take advantage of wider sections, you got stuck behind clumps of slower runners, who would—the horror—ruin your time. Yet what Doug Rausing may not have intended was that an off-road running course would also be more challenging for a bicycle. She was glad so many runners had flattened the path and kept the mud down by splattering it all over their clothes, and grateful that the organizers had strung such powerful lights along a route bound to be run by the end of the field in the dark (for once, she was a big fan of the LED). Still, a dirt track was harder to negotiate than a road, and the hills were murder.

At multiple points the trail was intersected by paved roads, where volunteers would have stopped traffic with flags for the runners to cross. The Plan, then: find Remington. Given the awful price she was paying with her knee, convince him—and this was the part of the plan in which she had little faith—to stop. Go together to the nearest intersection and summon an Uber.

Since they were meant to occur every mile, counting deserted water stations gave her a sense of how far she'd advanced; the bike had an odometer, but she couldn't discern the numbers without her reading glasses. Once she'd passed five stations, she shouted, "REMINGTON!" every minute or two.

The route crossed another two-lane highway. Looking both ways, she coasted to the flags and lights opposite and climbed the small hill through the woods in low gear. "REMINGTON!" Growing impatient after she crested the rise, she allowed herself to gather a little more speed on the descent.

Everything went black. The front tire hit something. The back tire slid sideways and out from under her. As she hit the ground, something rattled and skittered.

She took stock as her eyes adjusted. They'd turned off the lights. Of course. Why keep them blazing when the event was over? Mercifully, she'd landed on her left side. Her shoulder and hip had taken the impact. She hadn't been going fast. Carefully, she sat up. Everything, so far, seemed to work.

The cursed weather system having finally moved on, the sky had cleared. But the moon wasn't much help in a section like this, with trees overhead. The lights being shut off would slow her down, and in woodsy stretches like this one she might have to walk the bike by the light of her phone. She pulled the tote around and grubbed blindly through the bag of Remington's clothes, the cane, restaurant receipts, ibuprofen, the athletes' briefing handout. By feel, she located the granola bar she'd filched from the finishers' tent. Her wallet. Reading glasses. The ubiquitous bottle of water.

No phone.

That distinctive skittering.

Groping in the pitch-dark, she patted the ground all around her, trying to scan systematically in widening concentric circles. Mud. Rocks. Leaves. Bicycle. She needed the light on the phone to find the fucking phone.

It was an obligatory turn in the contemporary thriller, right? To keep the audience from jeering, "Why didn't she just use *Google Maps*?" you had to get rid of the phone.

Serenata spent a good ten minutes groping the vicinity. But the one thing she couldn't do with this knee was crawl. In fact, the joint replacement handbook said that you might never kneel comfortably again for the rest of your life. In the immediate area where she'd fallen off the bike, it was dark enough that the phone could have been glaringly obvious in daylight and not far away after all and she still wouldn't see it.

Resigned, she wiped her muddy hands on the canvas tote before shoving it to her back. Righting the bike—she wasn't used to one that didn't have a name—she used the machine as a rolling walker to eke her way toward the patch of moonlight at the bottom of the hill. "REMINGTON!"

This was turning into an even bigger fiasco than it had started out. In brighter sections she could still ride, but through the forested ones she could only half-walk, or use the bike as a giant skateboard, as she had on the West Side. "REMINGTON!" The flickering orange flags were mockingly jolly.

At last she emerged into a clearing, where the path striking across a meadow was wide, smooth, and flat. She was in the process of awkwardly mounting the bike for the straightaway when a rumple in the vista snagged her eye. A rumple like a person.

In the middle of the path, he was laid out in the cruciform pose he'd assumed on the floor after his first twenty-mile run—a posture she'd then found comic. Scootering like fury, she cast the bike aside and stooped. In the light of the moon, his complexion was blue. He looked dead.

She found a pulse. But it was weak and erratic. When she patted his cheeks and kissed his forehead, he was unresponsive. She lifted his eyelids, but had no idea what she was supposed to look for.

She should never have gone on this fool's errand. She wasn't accustomed to her new great big uselessness, the pure burden of her postsurgical self. She should have called 911 from the MettleMan site and left rescue to professionals. But regrets were no help now.

One of those intersections with a B-road was less than a mile back. She covered him with the fleece from his change of clothing and balled up her sweatshirt to cushion his head. She left him the granola bar and the bottle of water. On the way back to the intersection, in her haste in one of the dark sections, she had another spill. Now the front wheel had bent, and wouldn't spin past the brakes. She grabbed the cane from the tote and hightailed the last few hundred yards in a lurching sprint. Lo, there was such a thing as pushing beyond a barrier of pain that would seem impassable; when the stakes were high enough, you could indeed streak straight through the stony edifice of the Grand Coulee Dam. In retrospect, it was astonishing that the oncoming car stopped, rather than swerving around the wild woman on the meridian—who was waving a hospital-issue cane, of all things—and stepping on the gas. She must have looked demented.

AFTERWORD

The "generation" was a conceptual artifice. The word hammered hard brackets within a flowing, borderless continuum, as if trying to contain discrete sections of river. A cohort as large as Serenata's, too, would encompass such a range of people that any perceived homogeneity would have to be imposed: a further artifice. Nevertheless, boomers, as they were known, had secured the dubious reputation for denial in the face of aging. In their clinging to fugitive youth, they had made themselves the butt of many a younger stand-up—though chances were that Tommy March, or Chet Mason, wouldn't relish decrepitude any more than boomers did. What was to like?

This idea that in historical terms boomers were unusually deluded about the inexorability of their decay now struck Serenata as unfair. For the abundance of human existence, no one got old. They died. Mass aging was a recent phenomenon, and in joining the "old-old" on any scale she and her peers would be pioneers. Besides, Serenata Terpsichore had never herself grown old before, so it made a certain sense that she wouldn't be very good at it.

What would seem to be required was humility. But this brand of humility wasn't the sort you graciously embraced. It was foisted on you. You grew humble because you had *been humbled.* Aging was an experience to which you succumbed, and you adapted to new circumstances not because you were shrewd, but because you hadn't any choice. *So go ahead,* she beamed to her younger brethren. *Make fun. Of our self-deceit, of our vanity that survives anything to be vain about. Your time will come.*

She and her husband had been humbled. Though Remington had recovered from his heart attack, his cardiologist discouraged any jogging whatsoever. Swimming the doctor restricted to the breast- or backstroke. *Mild* biking was okay (although since Lake Placid Remington had developed an odd aversion to his nameless bicycle, which Sloan had kindly retrieved from the trail; its master only repaired that warped front wheel in order to put it on eBay). Yet Remington engaged in none of these muted activities. Tommy was right: once you'd sampled the extremes, the notion of going back to "grandma" moderation was less attractive than quitting.

His wife's recuperation from her knee-replacement replacement was even more arduous than recovery from the original surgery, and rendered less satisfactory results. Extension and flexion were further reduced. Flaming pain on stairs was apparently permanent. But after a couple of years they could go for walks. Sometimes lingering and contemplative walks, though her gait evidenced a slight hitch until the left knee was also replaced, at which point both legs were a tad shorter. Serenata lost the ripple in her arms, and Remington restored the swell at his waist, but worse things happened at sea, and their frailty as it advanced stirred a compensatory spousal compassion. The scenery during these local perambulations was repetitive, but they could talk, and the boats and wildlife along the river still displayed more variety than high-knees interval training ever had.

They lived modestly—again, of necessity. Health insurance copays and the expenses of Remington's bygone obsession had eaten up a goodly proportion of the equity left over from the sale of the house in Albany. As the ban on "mimicry" spread, lucrative audiobook jobs grew rare. For a while, before her Social Security kicked in, Serenata was reduced to writing online college admission essays for students to plagiarize. Ignominious work in its way, but in the process she learned a great deal more about bee keeping, *King Lear,* and invasive plants. More fodder for walks.

With time on his hands again, Remington spearheaded the campaign in Hudson to convert the town's streetlamps to LEDs with a low Kelvin rating, heavy shielding, and a housing in keeping with downtown's nineteenth-century architecture. Substituting socially for the tri club, the small committee of refreshingly mixed-race volunteers included the civic-minded Ethan Crick and, more surprisingly, Brandon Abraham, who took early retirement from Albany's DOT and along with his dazzling wife bought a place in Hudson; Brandon and Remington soon became drinking buddies. Learning from his mistakes, Remington urged the committee to approach the town council in a spirit of camaraderie and shared self-interest.

Once the new energy-saving public illumination was installed, it noticeably increased tourism and vitalized Hudson's fledgling nightlife. Other towns sent emissaries to study the comely designs, returning to their municipalities with enthusiasm for the faux gaslights' warm nocturnal ambience. When the Hudson town council subsequently resolved to make artists' studios out of the dilapidated shoreline fishing shacks in which Margaret Alabaster had cleaned sturgeon, they went straight to Remington for the vetting of blueprints. In one meeting about a less historically respectful proposal, he forgot himself and slammed a hand on the table. When he fell about apologizing, the council was befuddled. After he told them his old DOT story, slamming the table to bring the boisterous group to order became a tireless running joke.

Fully recovered from rhabdomyolysis, Tommy developed a cool disdain for contemporaries who took their fitness regimes too seriously, this scornful phase marked by knocking her fake Fitbit behind the bedstead (still plastered with DOUBT NOT—a flexible motto) and not bothering to grub down amid the dust bunnies to retrieve it. For working up a sweat, a tango class proved genuinely enjoyable. Under Serenata's tutelage, the girl became a popular choice for gaming VO; she had an ideally lithe, lanky figure for roles grown ever more physical. Since the knees made this work, too, out of the question, any jobs that came Serenata's way from old contacts she threw to her neighbor. Tommy soon moved to Brooklyn, which was a loss, but she returned to her ailing mother often enough that the two neighbors stayed friends.

When Serenata ran into Cherry DeVries at Price Chopper, the woman's cart was mounded with brownies and chips, as well as diet soda and Weight Watchers chicken pot pies—the American yin and yang. Cherry's proportions had redistributed along the lines of her Before picture. But she waxed so eloquent about the year she'd devoted to triathlon that its transient effect on her figure seemed immaterial. "Honestly," she enthused, after thanking Serenata for being so generous with her hospitality back in the day, "that whole thing—not just the race itself, but all the training—I swear, it was the most wonderful experience of my life. Ever since, my kids treat me different, and even Sarge does. He *respects* me. He's never laid a hand on me again."

"He may be afraid of you," Serenata said. "Ever consider entering another one?"

"Oh, heaven's no." She raised the double-*M* orange tattoo on her left forearm. "I proved what I needed to, to my family, and to myself. I can't tell you how much happier I've been ever since. Now, you take care of yourself, sweetie."

Score one for MettleMan.

Remington resumed visits with his father, who tactfully refrained from rubbing his son's nose in the calamity of Lake Placid. They played a lot of cribbage. The couple's investment of time and tenderness amounted to the purchase of an insurance policy, which when Griff dropped cleanly dead at ninety-four paid off. They would miss him, but they wouldn't berate themselves for having neglected the cantankerous but secretly soft-touch old man while he was alive.

Remington's well-off brother in Seattle was happy for his sibling to inherit their father's house. The property proved a godsend when Valeria finally left her party-pooper husband and needed an affordable bolt-hole in which to raise six kids. Grandparental babysitting came with the territory, something of a trial, though exposure to sane, secular relatives could help keep the children from growing up into brainwashed nut jobs.

Yet after giving up on homeschooling out of sheer exhaustion, Valeria grew disenchanted with the church, whose born-again branch in Hudson was more cliquish than Rhode Island's Shining Path, and thus too reminiscent of the playgrounds of yore where she'd been cold-shouldered. After her brief but diligent period of heavy drinking, the local chapter of Alcoholics Anonymous proved sufficiently evangelical to fill the void, while also providing just the right combination of self-pity, superiority, and chiding parental proselytizing (her mother, so went the theory, drank too much wine). Why, the second cult substituted so neatly for the first that Serenata wondered if her daughter had forced herself to become a drunk for six months purely to get in. At least the tales Valeria brought back from meetings, lurid with the depths to which dipsos can sink, beat all that insipid *joy, joy, joy, joy down in my heart* by a mile.

Alas, her older children had been indoctrinated a bit too well, and routinely threatened their lapsed parent that if she didn't once again embrace Christ the Lord as her Savior she was going to hell. There was rough justice in Valeria herself being eternally Jesused at.

Nancee remained wary, inward, and weird about food, but she did get into SUNY at New Paltz on a track scholarship, even if a remarkable gift for running in circles would lead to something of an occupational dead end. By contrast, her brother Logan got early admission to Rensselaer; as a chemical engineer, he'd have his pick of jobs. Nonetheless, it was a mystery how such a whip-smart-kid could still believe that the human race shared the Earth with dinosaurs.

Having lost too many customers to the ER, Deacon wasn't prone to moral soul-searching, but he did question the viability of an entrepreneurial venture whose consumer base was self-eliminating. When Chet Mason became Sloan's right-hand man for refurbishing classic cars, Deacon assumed Chet's vacated barista position. The work was suitably low-exertion, and allowed Deacon to languidly hold court. But between beginning to lose his hair early and the downshift of metabolism many men experience in their thirties, Deacon put on a little weight and was in danger of losing his looks. Astonishingly, after dating Bambi Buffer for a few months, if only to goad his father, Deacon, of all people, caught the fitness bug.

Deacon and Bambi didn't last, of course. But when the trainer stopped into his café after their listless breakup, he gleaned news that for his mother should have been nastily satisfying. Rather young for skeletal decay, which must have been hastened by the pounding she'd given her body for decades, Bambi had been diagnosed with "degenerative spondy-somethingorother": a vertebra had edged out of alignment, and the consequent impingement of her sciatic nerves put her in a disabling pain that precluded running, swimming, biking, and weights—anything, in fact, other than sitting or lying abed. The condition would only get worse. Were she eventually to submit to back surgery, spinal fusion would still place marathons, triathlons, and probably her business to boot firmly in the past. Behold, a short course in *limits*.

But Serenata didn't find this turn of the wheel satisfying in the slightest. However ephemeral Bambi's living sculpture proved, the trainer had created a thing of beauty, and the passing of any beauty from this world was nothing to celebrate. The woman was bound to be miserable, doubly so, from both the pain and the melting of her artwork. Any increase in the quantity of misery in this world was nothing to celebrate, either.

Having mourned a similar loss, Serenata was inclined to identify rather than crow. To the casual eye she hadn't changed all that drastically now that she no longer devoted ninety tiresome minutes of every evening to keeping in shape. But she knew the difference. She was an increment thicker. When she stood and rested the tips of her fingers on a thigh, it was no longer firm. She missed the rippling play of light across her shoulders, but arthritis in her wrists now ruled out push-ups. Her legs were marred with vertical scars. Her calves failed to form commas at tension. She remembered her body of a few years before with the wistful, faintly puzzled fondness of a good friend with whom, through no fault on either party's part, she'd lost touch.

She sometimes remembered that exchange in the Gold Street studio, when the engineer referred to "in your day," and she'd responded with playful injury, "It's not my day?" No. It was not her day. She had been fortunate to have been strong, energetic, even fetching, and for decades; as the director had observed, she was fortunate to have ever had a day. But that part of her life, which entailed being looked at, if largely looking at herself, was over. It was fair. Now other people got to have their day. For your day to be over might have been disappointing, but it wasn't tragic.

For the key to the "bucket list" wasn't to systematically check off its to-do items, but to bring yourself to throw the list away. There was a thrill to letting go of the whole shebang—reluctantly, then gleefully.

There was a thrill to dying by degrees. She advanced toward apathy with open arms. She wasn't about to advertise the fact—the argument wasn't worth having—but Serenata was not obliged to give a flying fig about climate change, species extinction, or nuclear proliferation. She had her eye on the door, and had every hope of escaping a great human reckoning almost certainly in the offing. It had been too long since the last one, and a correction of sorts was overdue. All civilizations contained the seeds of their own collapse, and dodging the homicidal havoc lurking right around the corner, merely by dint of having been born a bit earlier than the fresh-faced unfortunates, would qualify as sly. She no longer fought a misanthropy that was increasingly blithe, even whimsical, and which as she approached her own oblivion was shedding its hypocrisy. The very best thing about getting old was basking in this great big not-giving-a-shit. Younger folks like Tommy would decry her happy boredom with all the looming threats that exercised them as criminally irresponsible and unforgivably callous. But Serenata had earned her ennui. Marvelously, nothing she did exerted any appreciable influence on the rest of the world. Nothing she'd ever recorded professionally had changed anything or anyone a jot. Her inconsequence made the planet safer for everyone. She didn't like other people much, nor they her. She didn't plan on worrying about the fate of her fellows as she met her own. Aging was proving one long holiday. She was harmless—although she'd be the first to agree that she and her heedless ilk should probably be denied the vote. The future didn't need her, and she didn't need it. Others behind her would discover it soon enough: the bliss of sublime indifference.

Their lives were almost over, and the finality had a sweet side. A burden had been lifted. The decisions still to be made were few. If the main story was over, all that remained was wrap-up—the luxurious and largely gratuitous tying up of loose ends, like looping satin ribbon around a Tiffany box. Wastefully, Remington had grown convinced that he had something to prove at the very age at which he should have been discarding the whole silly idea of proving anything to anyone. Because, really: Who cared? In due course, no one would remember that they'd lived at all, much less would anyone remember whatever they'd accomplished or failed to accomplish. (Owing to plague, an asteroid, or the sun frying into a red giant, the same amnesia would inexorably obliterate Madonna, Abraham Lincoln, Stephen Hawking, Leonardo da Vinci, Aristotle, the most recent winner of *Dancing with the Stars*, and—sorry, Logan—Jesus Christ. So there was no reason to take being forgotten about personally.) Acceptance that their lives had now mostly been lived didn't have to be depressing, either. The recognition could involve a reflective aspect, a wonderment, a cherishing of all that had gone before.

Although Serenata found growing old astonishing, she knew the surprise to be ordinary; what was exceptional were those rare codgers who accepted their disintegration as only to be expected. Besides, having been nonexistent before one's conception was also astonishing; being here, when before one had not been, was astonishing; then to be here no longer: fine, yes, altogether astonishing. But perhaps nothingness was the easiest state to conceive, the most natural state—the state that required no imagination. In which case, not having been here before was *not* astonishing, while being here was; and thereafter, to once again not be here was not astonishing, either. The hard part, then, was the in-between: the long slow exhale from being to void. How much kinder it would have been, to turn off, like an appliance. The gradual, drawn-out corruption of the body while its host was still trapped inside was a torture of a sort they would have contrived at Guantanamo, or Bergen-Belsen. Every old age was an Edgar Allan Poe story.

So she balanced her grief with a rudimentary gratitude. The

organism in which she sheltered continued to serve its primary animal purposes. With the help of new prescription glasses, it could see: the birds taking wing as the Hudson shimmered in the setting sun; the face of her husband, in which she could still discern the young civil engineer who'd extolled feverishly, "Transport is massively emotional!" It could hear: Miles Davis's *Kind of Blue*, or Remington's views on the merits of the traffic circle, which were ever so much more engaging than his opining about *tri*. If not as quickly as before, it got her from place to place: to one more truly atrocious production at the Hudson Playhouse; through a wine-tasting tour; home. It could feel: the breeze tickling the hairs of her arms at that temperature just before you reached for a sweater; her husband's body, which had worn in perfect tandem with hers so that the parts still faultlessly grooved together in bed, like the chain and cluster on a bike, which eroded in such concert that to replace either, you had to replace them both.

Although no one should have taken for granted even such crude functionality beyond the age of fifty, the culture of the time continued to apply far higher performance standards. More than ever, social status was determined by fat-to-muscle ratio, definition, and belt-notching feats of stamina, so that endurance events of every description did nothing but multiply. According to Deacon, triathlons—even the ultras—had grown passé. Obstacle-course races, or OCRs, were "way cooler," he said. "Crawling under live wires. Lugging hundred-pound sandbags up thirty-degree gradients. Rope climbing, spear chucking. Mud up to the eyeballs. Finish one of those courses, you're so wiped you literally can't think. I'm serious. After that Spartan? I tried to log into my bank account, and I couldn't answer the security questions. I spent five minutes trying to remember the name of my high school."

"Sounds great," she said. The irony went right past him.

Meanwhile, the use of artificial intelligence accelerated, just as Silicon Valley had foretold. Robots that could learn, create, and make informed decisions had eliminated the few remaining manufacturing jobs in New England, and had reduced agricultural employment to a handful of supervisors on local farms. The latest wave of AI was duplicating the work of the professional class: medicine, accountancy, law. Any number of paintings, popular songs, and even novels generated by sophisticated algorithms had become commercial hits.

"I was a little embarrassed about it," Serenata said on a ritual riverside stroll one early summer evening, "so I don't think I told you that I ordered a copy of that computer-generated best seller, *Amygdala*. I was just curious."

"Understandably," Remington said. "What did you make of it?"

"I don't know whether to find this exciting or mortifying, but in all honesty I got pretty hooked. I was obviously aware that underneath it all was just a formula, but the formula works. I wanted to know what happened."

"Here's the test: Did the resolution of the plot surprise you?"

She turned to him with a defeated expression. "*Yes.*"

He laughed. With its deepening crags, his face increasingly resembled Samuel Beckett's. "What about the prose?"

"It was fine!" she said in dismay. "I wouldn't call it great poetry, but there weren't any gaffes. No *oh, God, that's such a terrible metaphor,* no dialogue where it's like, *no one would ever say that in real life.* They've taught it to write prose you just don't especially notice. Actually, I gather that they've fed AI the classics, and computers have also learned to generate distinctive styles. Now, that's real 'mimicry.' Pretty soon we'll have new Hemingway, new Graham Greene, new Dickens. We won't be able to tell the difference."

"I have no doubt that AI could design a more efficient system of traffic flow than I ever did. If it hasn't already, AI could competently replace the entire Albany DOT."

"One employee in particular," Serenata said. "Anyway, I was thinking. About Deacon and his OCRs. Not to bring up a touchy subject, but you and MettleMan. All the hard-body advertisements, Main Streets taken over by gyms. Well, it makes a certain dumb sense, doesn't it? It's as if we're swapping places. Machines have become better people. What's left to do? People become better machines."

He squeezed her shoulder. "You may be onto something there. You know, I'm getting hungry, and the light's failing. What say we turn around?" When she agreed, he peered into her face and said apropos of nothing, "You're still a very, very handsome woman."

"To you," she said.

"What else matters?"

They kissed. Two runners rushed around them, looking annoyed; the elderly couple in the way would be ruining their *time*.

"We're grossing them out," Serenata said.

"Young people don't have sex anymore. They're too tired."

"You're one to talk. For two fucking years you barely touched me, you jerk."

"Well, then. I have some catching up to do."

Hand in hand, they made their way back toward the house. There was a heron, and there were turtles. There would be flank steak, already marinating in the fridge, and a pricier than usual Burgundy that she'd been saving: everything to look forward to, and nothing to dread. Dusk was the very time of day that she'd often squandered upstairs, grunting and panting with *The Big Bang Theory* in the background. When Serenata crossed into menopause, she'd been delighted to see the back of periods. What the hell, aging out of burpees had its upside, too.